Eleventh Edition

PRINCIPLES AND METHODS OF ADAPTED PHYSICAL EDUCATION AND RECREATION

David Auxter, Ed.D., CAPE
Senior Scientist
Research Institute for Independent Living

Jean Pyfer, P.E.D., CAPE
Professor Emerita
Texas Woman's University

Lauriece Zittel, Ph.D., CAPE
Associate Professor
Northern Illinois University

Kristi Roth, Ph.D., CAPE
Assistant Professor
University of Wisconsin–Stevens Point

Mc Graw Hill

Boston   ...dison, WI   New York   San Francisco   St. Louis
Bangk...   ...pur Lisbon London Madrid Mexico City
Milan   ...   Seoul Singapore Sydney Taipei Toronto

The McGraw·Hill Companies

PRINCIPLES AND METHODS OF ADAPTED PHYSICAL EDUCATION AND RECREATION
International Edition 2010

Exclusive rights by McGraw-Hill Education (Asia), for manufacture and export. This book cannot be
re-exported from the country to which it is sold by McGraw-Hill. This International Edition is not to
be sold or purchased in North America and contains content that is different from its North American
version.

10 09 08 07 06 05 04 03 02 01
20 09
CTP BJE

Cover photo is provided courtesy of the National Center on Physical Activity and Disability (NCPAD)
at www.ncpad.org.

The Internet addresses listed in the text were accurate at the time of publication. The inclusion of a
Web site does not indicate an endorsement by the authors or McGraw-Hill, and McGraw-Hill does not
guarantee the accuracy of the information presented at these sites.

When ordering this title, use ISBN 978-007-126741-0 or MHID 007-126741-7

Printed in Singapore

www.mhhe.com

BRIEF CONTENTS

CONTENTS

CHAPTER 3

**Determining Educational Needs through
Assessment 56**

CHAPTER 4

**Developing the Individual Education
Program 91**

CHAPTER 5

Teaching to Meet Learners' Needs 140

CHAPTER 6

**Delivering Services in the Most Inclusive
Environment 177**

CHAPTER **7**

Enhancing Student Behavior 225

PART

III

Children and Youth at Risk 249

CHAPTER **8**

Physical Fitness and Sport Conditioning 250

CHAPTER **9**

Children at Risk: Psychosocial Issues 276

CHAPTER 18
_____

Other Health Impairments 572

Glossary G-1

Index I-1

PREFACE

For this edition we have invited two knowledgeable professionals to join our writing team. Each of them has practical teaching experience and provides outreach programs to individuals with disabilities in their communities.

Dr. Kristi Roth is an assistant professor and the adapted physical education program coordinator at the University of Wisconsin in Stevens Point. She completed her doctoral degree studying with Dr. Carol Huettig at Texas Woman's University, specializing in adapted physical education and pedagogy. She spent 10 years teaching and consulting adapted physical education in the public schools before beginning her university teaching career. In addition to teaching and conducting research, she directs a campus-based community service program for children and youth with disabilities. Because of Dr. Roth's advanced knowledge of the use of technology in teaching and monitoring physical education progress, she was invited to write the teacher's manual that accompanies this text. Users will find her PowerPoint presentations, technology use, and student activities very practical and helpful.

Dr. Lauriece Zittel is an associate professor and director of graduate studies in kinesiology at Northern Illinois University. Her master's degree is in early childhood special education. She completed her doctoral degree in adapted physical education at Oregon State University, where she studied with Dr. Jeff McCubbin. Dr. Zittel taught K–12 general physical education and coordinated the adapted physical education program for 7 years in the public schools prior to beginning her university career. In addition to teaching and conducting research at the university, she is director of the Moving Exploring Experiencing Together (MEET) program, which is a university-based community service program for preschoolers with and without disabilities. She also directs the Training in Recreation Experiences (TREC) program, which provides assistance to adults 18 years and older who have difficulty gaining access to community recreation programs. She has demonstrated her professional leadership by serving as president of the National Consortium for Physical Education and Recreation for Individuals with Disabilities. Dr. Zittel's broad range of experience brings practical information to users of this edition of the textbook, a gap that was created by Dr. Huettig's untimely death.

CONTENT FEATURES

Content throughout the new edition has, once again, been thoroughly researched, referenced, and updated. In addition, many new photographs have been added to enhance the text.

Part I: The Scope

In the first part, we provide an overview of adapted physical education—its definition, its historical development, and the significant forces that have had an impact on the development of quality play, leisure, recreation, sport, fitness, and wellness programs for individuals with disabilities and their families.

Part II: Key Techniques

The comprehensive process required to determine the educational needs of an individual with disabilities and the development of the individual education program are highlighted next. Strategies for effective instruction and behavior management are described in detail. A model for delivering instructional services in the most inclusive, least restrictive environment is shared, as are specific strategies for the delivery of services in the public schools.

Part III: Children and Youth at Risk

Our children are at significant risk in two ways. More than ever, our children are obese and physically unfit; this significantly compromises the quality of their lives and jeopardizes their health. In addition, more than at any other time in our history, more children are entering our schools with significant physical, social, and psychological disadvantages. The challenges these learners represent to themselves, to the schools, and to society are addressed in Part III. In addition, strategies the physical educator can use to help all children grow and reach their full potential are shared.

Part IV: Needs of Specific Populations

In Part IV, specific types of disabilities and suggestions for intervention strategies are described. While we recognize that each person has unique qualities and needs, for ease of communication we have grouped similar conditions together. Each condition is defined, characteristics are given, assessment strategies are suggested, and specific programming and teaching techniques are detailed.

COVERAGE OF CONTEMPORARY ISSUES

We have addressed specific issues of critical importance to the general physical educator, adapted physical educator, therapeutic recreation specialist, and sport, fitness, and wellness professional, including the following:

- Regulations incorporated in the Reauthorization of IDEA, Individuals with Disabilities Education Improvement Act (IDEIA)
- Legislation that has a significant impact on the education of learners with disabilities, including the No Child Left Behind Act

- Issues involving the health and wellness of all children and adults, including those with disabilities, and the legislation and regulations that address those issues
- The increased emphasis on the provision of all educational services for learners with disabilities in the "general" program using the "general" curriculum
- Strategies for teaching effectively within a learning community composed of students and professionals representing diverse cultures, abilities and disabilities, linguistic backgrounds, socioeconomic status, ethnicity, gender, and gender preferences
- Techniques for interacting effectively with the families of learners within a diverse learning community
- Specific strategies for the adapted physical education consultant to enhance the physical education experience for children with disabilities
- Specific techniques for the general physical educator to effectively use the services of the adapted physical education consultant.
- Methods for effective collaboration with other professionals

NEW TO THE 11TH EDITION

- Chapter 1—"Adapted Physical Education." Information about the disabling process, the built environment, and evidence-based practices has been added. In addition, legislation impacting physical activity that has been passed since the last edition and current legislative initiatives that address the growing problem of obesity are included.
- Chapter 2—"Adapted Physical Education in the Public Schools." At the suggestion of the reviewers of the 10th edition, this chapter was moved from later in the text to become the second chapter to provide for a stronger introduction to our profession. Updated resources and technologies available to enable the adapted physical educator to perform more efficiently have been added.

- Chapter 3—"Determining Educational Needs through Assessment." Information about goals and objectives has been modified to parallel changes that resulted from the 2004 Reauthorization of IDEA (IDEIA). The discussion of the assessment tools available to determine the motor and physical development of children and youth has been updated.
- Chapter 4—"Developing the Individual Education Program." The information presented in this chapter has been modified to parallel changes that occur in IDEIA, and the chapter has been rearranged to flow more smoothly.
- Chapter 5—"Teaching to Meet Learners' Needs." Information about evidence-based practice and response to intervention (RTI) has been added, as well as ways the Reauthorization of IDEA and the enactment of the No Child Left Behind Act (NCLB) impact physical education services.
- Chapter 6—"Delivering Services in the Most Inclusive Environment." All of the material has been updated to parallel changes in the 2004 Reauthorization of IDEA, and resources related to sports and recreational activities for children with disabilities have been added.
- Chapter 7—"Enhancing Student Behavior." The importance of the use of assertive, effective discipline has been emphasized and other content has been modified in accordance with reviewers' suggestions.
- Chapter 8—"Physical Fitness and Sport Conditioning." In this chapter we have placed greater emphasis on the increasing problem of obesity in this country and have added a discussion about the relationship among food insecurity, proper diet, exercise, and obesity.
- Chapter 9—"Children at Risk: Psychosocial Issues." This chapter addresses the newly coined condition fetal alcohol spectrum disorders and includes information about the impact of experiencing abuse or neglect as a child, as well as the impact of watching violence on television on the attitude and behavior of the individual as a teen or an adult.
- Chapter 10—"Infants, Toddlers, and Preschoolers." The information about assessment instruments appropriate for use with this population has been updated.
- Chapter 11—"Intellectual Disability." In accordance with a nationwide initiative, we have retitled the chapter and the terminology used throughout the chapter to move away from the term "mental retardation" toward a term that more accurately reflects the intellectual functioning of a large percentage of people.
- Chapter 12—"Pervasive Developmental Disorders." This chapter emphasizes that autism spectrum disorder is the fastest growing developmental disability in this country, with 1 in every 150 American children diagnosed with the disorder. We have added information about intervention strategies that have proven to be successful with individuals with autism.
- Chapter 13—"Specific Learning Disabilities." We have updated the requirements regarding how states determine whether a child has a learning disability to comply with IDEIA and have added information about summer camps designed specifically for individuals with learning disabilities.
- Chapter 14—"Mental Health Disorders." The new classification system for mental disorders (internalized and externalized disorders) is introduced and explained. A section on illicit drug use and abuse has been added.
- Chapter 15—"Physically Disabling Conditions." All of the information about the conditions covered in the chapter, including terminology, has been updated.
- Chapter 16—"Communicative Disorders." Information about Deaflympics competition and terminology has been updated.
- Chapter 17—"Visual Impairments." Strategies to improve perceived competence of children with visual impairments and new assessment instruments have been added.
- Chapter 18—"Other Health Impairments." This chapter includes updated information about the inattentive behavior of children with ADHD and added information about pre-diabetic conditions.

PEDAGOGICAL AIDS

- "Objectives" are shown at the start of each chapter to identify and reinforce the goals to be accomplished.
- Case Studies and accompanying "Application Tasks" and "Critical Thinking Tasks" help students gain an understanding of learners who are taught in the public schools and guide students to a real-world application of the content.
- Key terms are defined in the Glossary at the back of the text.
- Chapter content is summarized at the end of each chapter to reinforce key concepts and aid students with the process of preparing for examinations.
- Review Questions end each chapter to foster classroom discussion, review, and application of the concepts learned.
- Student Activities help students apply the content learned and introduce topics for further exploration.
- References and Suggested Readings have been thoroughly revised to provide the most current documentation.
- Updated lists of recommended Web sites and videos in all chapters encourage further exploration of topics.

ANCILLARIES

The 11th edition of *Principles of Adapted Physical Education and Recreation* features an instructor's Web site, www.mhhe.com/auxter11e, that offers the following resources for instructors. To gain access to the Web site, instructors should contact their McGraw-Hill sales representative.

- **Instructor's manual.** The instructor's manual has been completely reworked to make it more instructor-friendly. Also, ways to use technology in adapted physical education have been added.
- **Test bank.** The test bank has been updated in accordance with changes in the content of the text.

- **PowerPoint presentations.** There are PowerPoint presentations to support instruction for each of the 18 chapters. These PowerPoint presentations can be downloaded and easily modified to meet the specific and unique needs of the instructor and his or her students.
- **Instructional Incentives.** Instructional incentives are available to make the learning environment more interesting. There are games, classroom-modified versions of "Who Wants to Be a Millionaire" and "Jeopardy." In addition, there are crossword puzzles and other activities to engage students in the learning process.
- *Gross Motor Activities for Young Children with Special Needs.* This handy guide includes over 250 developmentally appropriate activities and games designed to promote equilibrium, sensory stimulation and discrimination, body image, motor planning, locomotor skills, cross-lateral integration, physical fitness, relaxation, "animal games," and cooperative play activities. Instructors can download the guide and make it available to their students.

ACKNOWLEDGMENTS

The authors would gratefully like to acknowledge the many contributions of individuals who provided their wisdom, effort, and support in the preparation of the 11th edition of this text.

We would particularly like to acknowledge the following individuals, not just for sharing their "vision" regarding the future of adapted physical education and adapted physical activity, but because they are brilliant, ethical, and principled leaders in our field:

Dr. Greg Reid
Past President of the International Federation of Adapted Physical Activity
Professor, Physical Education, McGill University

Dr. James Rimmer
Executive Director, National Center on Physical Activity for Individuals with

Disabilities Professor, Department of Disability and Human Development, University of Illinois at Chicago

We would also like to thank the following professionals for their exceptional commitment to quality play, leisure, recreation, sports, fitness, and wellness for individuals with disabilities and, specifically, for their willingness to share photographs and program information:

Ms. Nicole Eagan, Special Olympics, Alaska

Dr. Linda Hilgenbrinck, Director of Adapted Physical Education, Denton, Texas, Public Schools

Ms. Donna Lovetro, Adapted Physical Educator, Mesa, Arizona, Public Schools

Tom Songster, Senior Vice President, Special Olympics

Dr. Bob Arnold, Director, Adapted Physical Activity Program and Center on Disability and Health

We would also like to acknowledge the following programs, first for their members' incredible commitment to enhancing the lives of individuals with disabilities and their families, and second for their willingness to share photographs illustrating their programs in the 11th edition:

Achilles Kids
Adventures Without Limits
Calgary Power Hockey League
Disabled Sports USA
Disabled Sports USA Far West
Island Dolphin Care
National Ability Center
National Multiple Sclerosis Society
National Sport Center for the Disabled
Special Olympics, Alaska
Spokes N' Motion
USA Water Ski
Wilderness Inquiry

And we would like to particularly thank and honor the parents and participants in the Texas Woman's University Aquatics Program for Learners with Disabilities. They are part of our extended family.

In addition, we would like to acknowledge the efforts of

Jimmie Lynn Harris, Reference Librarian, Texas Woman's University, with special thanks for her comprehensive, creative, computer-assisted library searches; she saved us hours in the library

Dr. Trish Hughes, for developing the Bruininks-Oseretsky Test of Motor Proficiency summary data graph in Chapter 3.

Comments and criticisms from users of the 10th edition were carefully considered and addressed in this new edition. A panel of reviewers was selected to assist with the revision of the manuscript to meet the needs of instructors and their students. To these colleagues, we would like to express our sincere appreciation:

Robbi Beyer
University of Texas, San Antonio

Ronald Davis
Ball State University

Linda Dye
William Patterson University

Lori A. Gravish
Penn State University

Wanda Hargroder
Louisiana State University

Melanie A. Hart
Texas Tech University

Mel L. Horton
Winthrop University

Marcia R. Karwas
California State University Monterey Bay

Christine Stopka
University of Florida

Finally, we would like to thank our editors at McGraw-Hill. Chris Johnson, executive editor, has responded to our every request in a timely and professional manner. His ongoing support during the illness and loss of Dr. Huettig was inspirational. In addition, we thank Sarah Hill, our developmental editor. Her gentle way of encouraging us to produce a manuscript that met the highest standards helped us to raise the bar for this edition. The same compliment is extended to Jill Eccher who assisted with production of this edition. She has an incredible professional eye. We very much appreciate the assistance Julia Akpan, technology developmental editor, gave to Kristi as she wrote the teacher's manual.

David Auxter
Jean Pyfer
Lauriece Zittel
Kristi Roth

This edition is dedicated to the memory of Dr. Carol Huettig, a consummate adapted physical educator who contributed generously to past editions of this textbook.

I

The Scope

In Part I we provide an overview of adapted physical education—what the term means, its historical development, the benefits strong programs have to offer persons with disabilities, and the barriers we must overcome if we are to provide quality, outcome-based services in the future. Distinguished individuals who have contributed significantly to our field have shared their visions of the directions in which we must continue to move if we are to fully realize the dream we all share—accessible, quality leisure, recreation, sport, physical fitness, and wellness opportunities for *every* individual, throughout the life span.

1

Adapted Physical Education

■ OBJECTIVES

Define adapted physical education.

Explain physical education as a mandated, direct special education service.

List several of the benefits of physical education for learners with disabilities.

Briefly describe the many, varied roles of the adapted physical educator.

Briefly explain the major events in the history of physical education for individuals with disabilities.

Briefly explain the physical education initiatives in Healthy People 2010.

Share strategies for transforming physical education for learners with and without disabilities in the twenty-first century.

Describe how adapted physical educators can ameliorate and/or reverse disability.

A dapted physical education is the art and science of developing, implementing, and monitoring a carefully designed physical education instructional program for a learner with a disability, based on a comprehensive assessment, to give the learner the skills necessary for a lifetime of rich leisure, recreation, and sport experiences to enhance physical fitness and wellness.

Adapted physical education and recreation are critical components for the well-being of children with disabilities. The Centers for Disease Control and Prevention, the federal agency responsible for promotion of the health of the nation, has stated that one of its highest health priorities is participation in leisure physical activity. The contributions of adapted physical education to the U.S. public health goal are clear. The old notion of the "inoculation theory" that a dose of physical activity during the years of school will provide a health benefit for the rest of one's life has been discredited. Rather, to establish and maintain health, ongoing participation in physical activity is necessary. The role of adapted physical education, in addition to keeping children with disability physically fit during the school years, must provide skills that involve physical activity that can be generalized into home and community for a lifetime. Brief discussions on who is disabled, the process of becoming disabled, and the contributions that adapted physical educators and recreation specialists can make follow.

WHO IS DISABLED

There are persistently recurring myths and misconceptions among the public that disabilities are rare and refer only to highly observable physical handicaps. The data on prevalence of disability reveal a different picture:

- There are 53.4 million people with disabilities in the United States.[45]
- Eighty percent of Medicare beneficiaries acquired their disability after age 18 years.[24]
- Forty-five percent of persons age 75 and older are disabled.[45]
- Nearly 30 percent of persons over the age of 20 years will become disabled.[15]
- There are 6 million school-age children with disabilities.[36]
- There are 30 million persons in a given year with diagnosed mental health conditions.[34]

Thus, nearly every extended family across three generations will most likely have a member with a disability.

Myth of Disability

There is a perception by many persons in the public that *disability* refers to persons who are in wheelchairs; however, in reality, the number of persons in wheelchairs is small. Most disabilities are invisible from the public because they are neuromuscular, cardiovascular, chronic respiratory, and/or mental disorders.

Impact of Disability

Disability is an issue that affects every individual, community, neighborhood, and family in the United States.[23] It is a costly social, public health, and moral issue. What determines a disability is the extent to which a person's physical and mental conditions limit his or her ability to meet the demands of his or her physical and/or social environments. Once a disability is identified, interventions should be implemented to lessen the impact of the disability. Adapted physical education strategies can help individuals improve functional capacity and avert further deterioration in physical and mental functioning.

Disability Clarification

There are many federal definitions of disability. For instance, the Individuals with Disabilities Education Act definition of disability refers to medical conditions associated with *adverse educational progress.* The Social Security definition of disability is associated with *ability to work,* not educational progress. Each of these definitions is limited. Because how one defines disability impacts the approach taken to address the disability, attempts have been made to clarify the causes and results of disabilities.

The Institute of Medicine (IOM) developed a model in collaboration with the Centers for Disease Control and Prevention and the National Council on Disability that builds on the World Health Organization (WHO) definition of disability.[22] The IOM model places disability within the context of health and social issues. It depicts the interactive effects of biological, environmental (physical and social), lifestyle, and behavioral risk factors that influence each stage of the disability process. Adapted physical educators and recreation specialists should use this model and become more active players at each stage of the disability process because they have the skills needed to intervene at several different stages in the process.

Depending on the circumstance, progressively greater loss of function may not need to occur and the progression toward disability could be halted or reversed. Adapted physical education strategies can be applied at any of the stages that precede disability as well as in the disability stage itself. Intervention can focus on facilitating development, restoration of lost function, or prevention of complications (secondary disabling conditions) that can exacerbate existing conditions or lead to new ones.

THE DISABLING PROCESS

The disabling process involves disability risk factors, pathology, impairment, and functional limitation. Examples of stages of the disability process are depicted in Table 1-1. Quality of life or well-being can be affected at each stage of the disability process. An example of diminished health that could lead to a disability follows:

Disability risk factor: inadequate physical activity and nutrition

Symptoms: defects in insulin secretion and/or action (diabetes, see Chapter 18)

Physical impairment: affects vision and the lower extremities

Functional limitations: blindness or lower limb amputations

A variety of personal and social environmental factors can influence the progression of disability and secondary disabling conditions. Some of these factors are health status, psychological state, socioeconomic status, educational attainment, and the presence of multiple conditions of disability. However, regardless of which of the factors is contributing to the condition, adapted physical educators and recreation specialists can moderate the situation by addressing the risk factors, utilizing evidence-based practices, employing assistive devices and technologies, and/or addressing the built environment.

CONTRIBUTIONS BY ADAPTED PHYSICAL EDUCATORS AND RECREATION SPECIALISTS

Risk factors are biological, environmental (social, physical), and lifestyle or behavioral characteristics that are causally associated with health-related conditions. Several specific examples are given in Figure 1-1. Identifying such factors can be a first step toward streamlining a plan of action to combat the disabling process and develop appropriate interventions.

Table 1-1	Disabling Process Stages
Disability Risk Factors	Physical inactivity, poor nutrition, substance abuse, smoking, improper eating habits, risky behavior that places a person's health in danger, child abuse, risky sexual activity, domestic violence, lack of access to medical care, hypertension, arthritis, back pain, depression, postural disorders, and others
Symptoms	Joint pain, defects in insulin secretion and/or action, depression, low vision, hypertension, chronic cough, underachievement, and tiredness
Physical or Mental Impairment	Impaired organs of the body, such as the cardiovascular system, including the heart; musculoskeletal organs; mental health; vision; mental retardation; hearing; and the immune system
Functional Limitations	Inability to meet the demands of tasks in social and/or physical environments

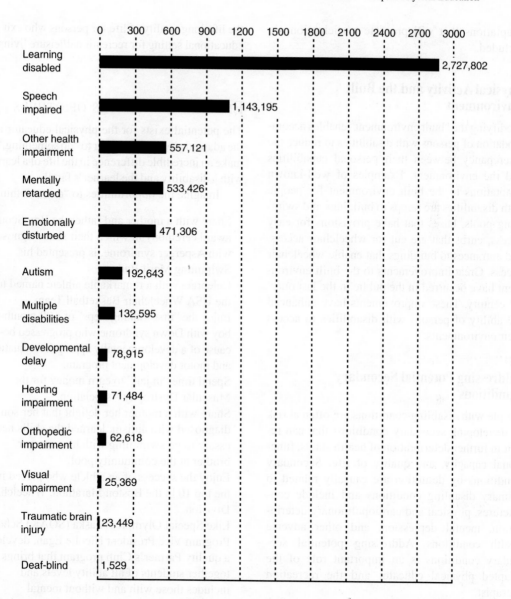

Figure 1-1   Number of School-Aged Children (6 to 21) with Disabilities Who Received Special Education Services in the 2005–2006 School Year
From IDEA Part B trend data, 2006

Utilizing Evidence-Based Practices and Assistive Devices and Technologies

Evidence-based practices and adaptations to help persons with disabilities benefit from an active lifestyle are addressed in Chapters 13 through 18. Types of disabling conditions, characteristics of the disabilities, teaching strategies, and specific suggestions of activities, modifications, and adaptations that will promote participation are included.

Physical Activity and the Built Environment

Modifying the "built environment" enables accommodation of persons with disabilities to reduce the discrepancy between their personal capabilities and the environment. Examples of well-known adaptations to the built environment for people with disabilities are ramps to buildings and swimming pools, buses that have provisions for easy access, curbs that are cut for wheelchair access, and entrances to buildings that enable wheelchair access. Great improvements to the built environment have occurred in the public in the last quarter century. These improvements have enhanced the ability of persons with disabilities to access their environments.

Addressing Potential Secondary Conditions

People with disabling conditions are often at risk of developing secondary conditions that can result in further deterioration of health status, functional capacity, and quality of life. Secondary conditions by definition are causally related to primary disabling conditions and include contractures, physical and cardiopulmonary deterioration, mental depression, and other adverse health conditions. Addressing potential secondary conditions is an important role of the adapted physical educator and the recreation therapist.

Applying evidence-based practices, utilizing assistive technology, and addressing modifications needed in the built environment are ways these professionals can contribute to the active lifestyle of persons with disabilities and provide them with the tools for avoiding development of secondary conditions tied to lack of physical activity. Adapted physical educators and recreation personnel can, through development of skills and attitudes that generalize into recreational environments, impact the life-long quality of life for persons who exit the educational setting for recreational/leisure living in the community.

ENRICHING THE LIVES OF OTHERS

The potential exists for the physical educator and the adapted physical educator to "do something," to make an incredible difference in the life of a learner with a disability and the learner's family.

Imagine the opportunities to "do something":

- Share with a mother and father the Boy Scout award ceremony in which their son, diagnosed with Asperger syndrome, is presented his Swimming Merit Badge.
- Celebrate with a remarkable athlete named to the USA Wheelchair Basketball Team.
- Enjoy the "first walking steps" of a 20-month-old boy with Down syndrome who progressed because of a developmentally appropriate aquatics and motor development program.
- Spend time "in jail" to earn money for the Muscular Dystrophy Association.
- Share with a mother her delight that her son, diagnosed with autism, learned the skills necessary to go swimming with his younger brother at the community pool.
- Enjoy the success of an athlete who placed in the top 10 in the Boston Marathon, Wheelchair Division.
- Like Special Olympics Alaska (SOAK) School Program Vice President Nicolle Egan, develop a quality Partner's Club program that brings together students of all ability levels and includes those with and without mental disabilities, through physical fitness, sports training, and competition.[3]
- Teach a child with a visual impairment to play Frisbee with a friend.
- Help a teenager with severe, multiple disabilities develop her own wheelchair aerobics routine to her favorite country-western music.
- Be a personal trainer for an athlete such as Jason Pipoly, of San Antonio, Texas, the first paraplegic swimmer to cross the English

Channel; he completed the swim in 13 hours and 48 minutes on August 18, 2002.

- Coach a Special Olympics team and be part of a worldwide program that currently (2007) serves over 1.2 million athletes worldwide.
- Help a student using a wheelchair learn to navigate an obstacle course and do a "wheelie."
- Teach a young boy with Duchenne muscular dystrophy skills to swim using an elementary backstroke, a skill he will be able to use throughout his life span.
- Coach a teenager with a hearing impairment who wrestles on his high school wrestling team.
- Teach a little one the play skills necessary to engage in parallel play.
- Play tennis with (now retired from competition) Randy Snow, the first wheelchair athlete inducted into the Texas Sports Hall of Fame.
- Develop an inclusive, after-school leisure, recreation, sport, fitness, and wellness program.
- Race downhill alongside a young woman using a sit-ski.
- Raise money for the Canadian Electric Wheelchair Hockey Association.
- Design a behavior enhancement program for a little girl with a conduct disorder to help her monitor/improve her behavior in physical education.
- Like visionary adapted physical educator Donna Lovetro and her colleagues in Mesa, Arizona, develop an in-school fitness center that duplicates community-based fitness centers to prepare students for seamless transition into those centers as adults.
- Develop a swimming program, emphasizing the freestyle and back crawl, for learners with dyslexia, to help them develop cross-lateral integration.
- Reassure the young mother of a 13-month-old boy with Down syndrome that his atlantoaxial instability simply requires wise choices of leisure, recreation, sport, and fitness activities and need not significantly limit his opportunities.
- Eat pizza with your athletes and their family members after a victory in the United States Association of Blind Athletes regional meet.

- Develop a strength training program for an athlete like Zoe Koplowitz, a 55-year-old woman with multiple sclerosis, who completed her 16th New York Marathon in a time of 29 hours and 45 minutes on November 3, 2003.
- Lead an aqua aerobics session daily to meet the needs of older adults with osteoarthritis and osteoporosis.
- Develop sign language skills in order to communicate with your deaf students.
- Coach judo for the United States Association of Blind Athletes.
- Share skills, in the home, with a young mother of a significantly low birthweight baby, so she can encourage and foster developmentally appropriate play.
- Help a young girl with spina bifida learn to ride a tricycle to encourage/foster her walking.
- Contact local leisure, recreation, and sport facilities and help them accommodate individuals with disabilities who would like to use the facilities.

DEFINITION OF SPECIAL EDUCATION

The term *special education* means specially designed instruction, at no cost to parents, to meet the unique needs of an individual with a disability, including

1. Instruction conducted in the classroom, in the home, in hospitals and institutions, and in other settings
2. Instruction in physical education

DEFINITION OF PHYSICAL EDUCATION

Physical education for individuals with disabilities was specifically defined in P.L. 108-446, and that definition was retained in the Improved Educational Results for Children with Disabilities (IERCD).[52,54] The term means the development of

1. Physical and motor fitness
2. Fundamental motor skills and patterns
3. Skills in aquatics, dance, and individual and group games and sports (including intramural and lifetime sports)

The term includes special physical education, adapted physical education, movement education, and motor development. The three essential components of physical education for persons with disabilities are developing and implementing an individual education program (IEP), assessing child performance, and teaching the defined curricula of physical education. When specially designed physical education is prescribed on the child's IEP, educators will provide physical education to ensure children and youth with disabilities an equal opportunity to participate in those services and activities. Each child with a disability is to participate in physical education with children without disabilities to the maximum extent appropriate.[52,53,54]

DEFINITION OF ADAPTED PHYSICAL EDUCATION

Adapted physical education is the art and science of developing, implementing, and monitoring a carefully designed physical education *instructional* program for a learner with a disability, based on a comprehensive assessment, to give the learner the skills necessary for a lifetime of rich leisure, recreation, and sport experiences to enhance physical fitness and wellness.

BENEFITS OF PHYSICAL EDUCATION FOR LEARNERS WITH DISABILITIES

Qualified and dedicated physical educators and adapted physical educators can "do something" because there are significant and long-term benefits of a quality physical education program for learners with disabilities. Programs can enrich their well-being by providing the prerequisites to healthy leisure physical activity. More specifically, quality programs can promote:

- The development of equilibrium, sensory discrimination and integration, and sensory-motor function
- The development of locomotor and nonlocomotor skills

- The development of object-control skills
- The development of play, leisure, recreation, sport, and physical fitness skills
- The development of physical fitness for maintenance of daily living skills and health/wellness.
- The development of a repertoire of movement skills necessary for independent and functional living
- The development of physical and motor prerequisites to vocational skills required for independent living
- Prevent and manage chronic health conditions
- Prevent the development of secondary disabling conditions

The benefits of a quality physical education program for learners with disabilities cannot be minimized. The major obstacle, however, is that the benefits are not clearly understood by the local, state, and federal educational administrators who make program decisions and allocate budgets. (See Table 1-2 for visions of the future.)

ROLES OF THE ADAPTED PHYSICAL EDUCATOR

The adapted physical education (APE) teacher is the person responsible for developing an appropriate individual physical education program for individuals with disabilities. The APE teacher is a physical educator with highly specialized training in the assessment and evaluation of motor competency and the implementation of programs in physical fitness, play, leisure, recreation, sport, and wellness. The APE teacher is a direct service provider, not a related service provider, because special physical education is a federally mandated component of special education services.[52,53,54] There has been confusion that adapted physical education is a related service due to circulation of misinformation and state education departments' misinterpretation of the federal law.

Depending on the size of the school district, the numbers of students with disabilities who require adapted physical education, the caseload, and the unique skills of physical education and

Table 1-2	Visions for the Future

Dr. David Auxter (shared at the specific request of his co-authors)
Director of the Research Institute for Independent Living
Washington, D.C.

Public health officials and policy makers have realized the need for effective Adapted Physical Education programs. Childhood obesity, which is the precursor to many chronic health conditions due in part to inadequate physical activity, has tripled during the past decade. Federal congressional estimates are that the consequences of inadequate nutrition and physical activity associated with obesity result in health care costs that approximate $100 billion a year. New coalitions composed of public health organizations and educators have recently been developed to move public policies to engage children and adults into physically active lifestyles. Their efforts have results in both federal administrative and legislative initiatives to address sedentary lifestyles to ameliorate chronic health conditions. Sedentary lifestyles disproportionately affect persons with disabilities.

Public policy initiatives to address problems associated with insufficient physical activity require a new paradigm for Adapted Physical Education personnel. It is now well accepted that the "inoculation theory" of shots of physical activity **only** in physical education classes is inadequate to produce positive and lasting health results. Rather, new initiatives supported by public policy makers require an integrated approach that generalizes recreational skills that involve physical activity learned in Adapted Physical Education classes to community settings. This requires an integrated approach where Adapted Physical Education personnel collaborate with community recreation planners, businesses, public health and medical practitioners, community information outlets, and local public policy makers to change sedentary patterns that sustain community-based leisure physical activity in postschool years.

Dr. James Rimmer
Executive Director, National Center on Physical Activity for Individuals with Disabilities
Professor, Department of Disability and Human Development
University of Illinois at Chicago

Future Role of the Adapted Physical Activity Professional
The therapist's role in getting the individual with a disability to transition from rehabilitation back into community life has diminished. An acute injury, such as a spinal cord or head injury, hip or knee replacement, stroke, or amputation, etc., leaves the newly injured with a formidable list of things that must be achieved before reentering the home setting. With hardly enough time to teach vital skills essential for survival, the therapist is left with little or no time to discuss the importance of wellness and living a healthy lifestyle through proper nutrition, exercise, and general health maintenance. The future role of the Adapted Physical Activity professional will involve working closely with rehabilitation providers in assisting people with disabilities to have a safe and effective way to become physically active when they return to their community. The APA professional will be involved in informing people where and how to exercise in their community; will assist them in using an exercise facility or local park, swimming pool, or other recreation facility; will teach clients how to access various parts of an exercise facility, such as a fitness center, including use of the locker room, pool, weight room, etc.; will provide personal training/coaching for exercising at home or participating in lifetime or competitive sports; and will train fitness and recreation professionals who have no background in disability on proper procedures for working with new members with disabilities. While the therapist's role will focus on vital skills necessary for compensating with a new injury, secondary condition, or disability, the APA professional will work with the client *after rehab* and throughout the life span.

The APA professional will be the link between rehabilitation and lifetime physical activity. HMOs, Medicare, and Medicaid will provide subsidized fitness memberships to people with disabilities and chronic health conditions, so that there is a seamless transition from rehab to wellness. Subsidized fitness memberships are already starting to be offered by some HMOs and will some day be covered by the federal government in a manner similar to subsidized medications for the elderly. When this happens, the APA professional will have to be certified, which makes our current APENS certification an important component to our profession.

(Continued)

Table 1-2	*(Continued)*

Dr. Greg Reid
Past President of the International Federation of Adapted Physical Activity
Professor, Physical Education, McGill University

We are moving from an expert model where instructors/coaches and other professionals make all the important decisions in the lives of individuals with a disability, to a collaborative model where those with a disability receive support when needed, but otherwise assume major responsibility for activity and life choices. As such, adapted physical activity (APA) will increasingly foster models of self-determination and self-regulation. APA will emphasize physical *activity* and therefore become more concerned with strategies that promote sustained physical activity. North American APA specialists will become influenced by ideas and research from the wider international community. Long-term intervention projects will emerge from our researchers who will seek rigorous empirical support for their interventions. Finally, kinesiology researchers, not usually linked with APA, will increasingly contribute to our knowledge base as they become intrigued with a particular disability from their unique theoretical perspective.

special education professionals, the APE teacher may assume any or all of the following roles:

- Direct service provider (hands-on teaching)
- Assessment specialist, completing comprehensive motor assessments of individuals with disabilities and making specific program recommendations
- Consultant for physical education and special education professionals and paraprofessionals providing physical education instruction for individuals with disabilities
- IEP/multidisciplinary team committee member who helps develop and monitor the IEP
- In-service educator, providing training for those who will provide physical education instruction for individuals with disabilities
- Student and parent advocate
- Facilitator of a "circle of friends" for a learner with a disability
- Program coordinator who develops curricular materials and develops intra- and interagency collaborations to meet the needs of individuals with disabilities
- Transition facilitator who helps the IEP/multidisciplinary team develop an appropriate individual transition plan for those students preparing to leave school and move into the community

- Facilitator to coordinate efforts with existing health programs to ensure learners with disabilities have access to quality health care
- Coordinator to ensure individuals with disabilities have access to quality wellness and health promotion programs to reduce complications associated with secondary disabling conditions, like hypertension, obesity, diabetes, and cardiovascular disorders
- Collaborator with local recreation planners[8]
- Collaborator with community information outlets and local public policy makers[8]
- Collaborator with public health and medical practitioners[8]
- Personal trainer/coach for individuals with disabilities exercising at home or participating in lifetime or competitive sports[38]
- Educator for fitness and recreation professionals who have no background in disability on proper procedures for working with individuals with disabilities[38]
- Facilitator in encouraging/supporting the self-determination and self-regulation of individuals with disabilities[37]
- Disseminator of research/information regarding effective intervention in adapted physical education[74]

PREVALENCE

Child Find efforts to identify and serve children and youth with disabilities in the public schools have been successful. In the 2005–2006 academic year, over 6 million learners with disabilities received special education services.[21] Information regarding the number of children with specific disabilities served by special education is included in Figure 1-1.

Each year, the U.S. Department of Education, Office of Special Education and Rehabilitation Services (OSERS), reports to Congress pertinent facts about the education of learners with disabilities. Recent data indicate

- Children with disabilities in special education represent approximately 9 percent of the entire school-age population
- Approximately twice as many males as females receive special education services
- Approximately 85 percent of school-age children who receive special education have mild disabilities[21]

In addition, the Office of Special Education Programs reports serving 698,938 preschool children with disabilities during the 2005–2006 school year, or 5 percent of all preschoolers who lived in the United States.[21] This represents a 50 percent increase in the number of children needing service since 1990–1991. The overwhelming number of infants, toddlers, and preschoolers requiring special education intervention is related to, but not limited to, the following:

- Growing numbers of infants affected by drug and alcohol use in utero
- Inadequate prenatal care during pregnancy
- Drastically increased numbers of children being raised in poverty
- Inadequate nutrition
- Inadequate health care
- Housing and schools in toxic environments
- Increased numbers of children who are victims of abuse and neglect
- Parents with limited or no appropriate, nurturing parenting skills

- Medical technology that allows more premature and medically fragile infants to survive

There is also a reason for concern regarding the number of students who have been identified as needing special education services because of conduct, behavior, and emotional disorders. Less than 1 percent of school-age children in the United States are identified as having conduct, behavior, and emotional disorders for special education purposes.[21] This figure appears to be a significant underestimation of the actual number of students who are in desperate need of quality intervention.

It is important to note, however, that it appears that IERCD will significantly limit the rights of students with conduct, behavior, and emotional disorders and, subsequently, eliminate their right to be educated in a least restrictive environment. At present, the Senate bill associated with IERCD allows schools to suspend any student, including those unable to control his or her behavior because of a conduct, behavior, or emotional disorder, who does not follow school conduct rules.

HISTORY OF ADAPTED PHYSICAL EDUCATION

The history of adapted physical education is rich and reflects significant growth. The actual history of adapted physical education began with the implementation of P.L. 94-142 in 1975. The traditions associated with the profession, however, are tied to the advancements in the medical professions and in rehabilitation services. Advancements in medicine, rehabilitation, and the education of individuals with disabilities have been tied, ironically, to war. World War I and World War II, in particular, found veterans returning to civilian life in need of significant medical and rehabilitation services. Many services previously considered hospital services became separate, recognized medical fields; these included physical therapy, occupational therapy, and corrective therapy. However, the main impetus for educating individuals with disabilities did not occur until early in the twentieth century and as late as the early 1960s for persons with mental retardation or emotional disturbance. President Franklin D. Roosevelt made it infinitely clear, by his remarkable example, that a disability need not interfere with greatness. The incredible efforts of the Kennedy family, devoted to improving the lives of individuals with mental retardation, and the International Special Olympics program need to be acknowledged.

In 1952, the Committee on Adapted Physical Education of the American Association of Health, Physical Education, Recreation and Dance adopted a resolution to accommodate children with disabilities in physical education programs of diversified developmental activities designed specifically to meet their individual needs.[5] The commitment to individuals with disabilities was strengthened in the early 1970s when a group of adapted physical educators dedicated to providing appropriate programs for students with disabilities met in Washington, D.C. The purposes of their meeting were to define what constituted appropriate physical education for persons with disabilities and to develop a strategy for ensuring that physical education was identified in P.L. 94-142. Some of the professionals who championed physical education, as a mandated educational service, at that important meeting included Dr. David Auxter, Dr. Lane Goodwin, Dr. Jean Pyfer, and Dr. Julian Stein. They were successful in their lobbying efforts. That led to a national thrust to prepare physical educators with specialized training in providing programs for persons with disabilities.

In the spring of 1991, the National Consortium for Physical Education and Recreation for Individuals with Disabilities (NCPERID) in conjunction with the National Association of State Directors of Special Education (NASDSE) and Special Olympics International conducted an "Action Seminar" on adapted physical education for state directors of special education and leaders of advocacy groups for individuals with disabilities. This conference had two goals:

Hand Propelled Bikes
Courtesy Northeast Passage, Chapter of Disabled Sports, USA, Durham, NH.

- Identify the barriers that were preventing full provision of appropriate physical education services to individuals with disabilities
- Establish an action agenda for addressing and resolving these problems

To counter the trend of providing less than appropriate physical education experiences to students with disabilities, in 1994 the National Consortium for Physical Education and Recreation for Individuals with Disabilities published national standards for adapted physical education.[25] The purpose of the Adapted Physical Education National Standards (APENS) project was to ensure that physical education instruction for students with disabilities was provided by qualified physical education instructors.[2] To achieve this end, the project has developed national standards (please refer to Table 1-3) for the profession and a national certification examination to

Table 1-3	APENS Standard Categories

1. Human development
2. Motor behavior
3. Exercise science
4. Measurement and evaluation
5. History and philosophy
6. Unique attributes of learners
7. Curriculum theory and development
8. Assessment
9. Instructional design and planning
10. Teaching
11. Consultation and staff development
12. Student and program evaluation
13. Continuing education
14. Ethics
15. Communication

For more information regarding APENS standards, please go to the APENS Web site at www.cortland.edu/apens.

measure knowledge of these standards. This major movement in the field of adapted physical education was led by visionary educator Dr. Luke Kelly. Under Dr. Kelly's careful supervision, the APENS standards and examination were developed maintaining a complete commitment to the process of ensuring validity and reliability.

This project was/is critically important to the field because, unlike other special education areas (mental retardation, learning disabilities, early childhood, etc.), most states did not/do not have defined certifications or endorsements for teachers of adapted physical education. In addition, the quality of physical education was compromised because the definition of who was "qualified" to provide physical education services to individuals with disabilities was left to the individual states and their respective certification requirements.

On May 10, 1997, the first national administration of the APENS certification exam was given at 46 sites around the country. A total of 219 teachers completed the exam, and 175 passed. In January 2007, Dr. Tim Davis, APENS chair, from SUNY Cortland reported, "As for data on CAPES, we are close to reaching our 1,300 mark, and have strong interest. Finally, great persons like Pam

Skogstad have been great change agents and gotten state legislation passed so that APENS is accepted as the 'national board certification' for APE teachers in Alaska. Several other states are pursuing this—Alabama, Louisiana, and New Jersey."[17]

In the past several decades, the emerging discipline of adapted physical education has witnessed amazing growth. The *Adapted Physical Activity Quarterly* (APAQ), the official journal of the International Federation of Adapted Physical Activity, was first published in 1983. APAQ is the journal in which professionals share their research regarding adapted physical activity. *Palaestra: Forum of Sport, Physical Education, and Recreation for Those with Disabilities,* edited by Dr. David Beaver and Phyllis Beaver, is a quarterly publication released in cooperation with the United States Olympic Committee's Committee on Sports for the Disabled and the Adapted Physical Activity Council of the American Alliance for Health, Physical Education, Recreation and Dance, dealing with adapted physical activity for individuals with disabilities, their families, and professionals in the field. *Sports 'n Spokes,* for the past two decades, has been a magazine dedicated to the active wheeler. *Sports 'n Spokes* covers competitive wheelchair sports and recreational opportunities for individuals who use wheelchairs.

The National Consortium for Physical Education and Recreation for Individuals with Disabilities (NCPERID) was formed in 1973 to promote, stimulate, and encourage significant service delivery, quality professional preparation, and meaningful research in physical education and recreation for individuals with disabilities. NCPERID has played a major role in shaping the direction of the adapted physical education profession. Its members, primarily adapted physical education and therapeutic recreation professionals involved in teacher preparation, actively serve as advocates for favorable legislation and funding at the national, state, and local levels; disseminate information about new legislation; and stimulate and conduct research.[32]

The Adapted Physical Activity Council (APAC) is affiliated with the American Association of Physical Activity and Recreation of the American Alliance of Health, Physical Education, Recreation and Dance. APAC's mission is to promote quality movement experiences for individuals with disabilities through research, advocacy, publications, programs at conventions and workshops, position statements, standards of practice, and cooperation with other organizations committed to people with disabilities.[4]

In the spring of 1999, Dr. Jim Rimmer, director of the Center on Health Promotion Research for Persons with Disabilities, Department of Disability and Human Development, University of Illinois at Chicago, received a $7 million grant from the Centers for Disease Control and Prevention to establish the National Center on Physical Activity and Disability (NCPAD).[1,39] The NCPAD is a clearinghouse for research and practice information to promote healthy lifestyles for persons with disabilities. This commitment to the health and wellness of individuals with disabilities is cause for celebration. In the new millennium, the field of adapted physical education has the potential to affect significant change in the health and wellness of individuals with disabilities. The NCPAD was developed through a cooperative venture of the University of Illinois at Chicago and the Secondary Conditions Branch of the Centers for Disease Control and Prevention. The NCPAD is designed to gather, synthesize, and disseminate information related to fitness, physical activity, and disability. The goals of the center are to help reduce the incidence of secondary conditions and to improve the overall quality of life for persons with disabilities through promotion of higher levels of fitness and healthy lifestyles. The NCPAD reflects a national priority to address the public health benefits of physical activity and physical fitness for individuals with disabilities. This is particularly critical because individuals with disabilities are more likely than the general population to be at risk of developing secondary health conditions (obesity, high blood pressure, diabetes) due to sedentary lifestyles.

The American Association for Physical Activity and Recreation (AAPAR), an association of the American Alliance of Health, Physical Education, Recreation and Dance, has become a vital force, particularly as a powerful advocate for the underrepresented. Its mission is

> Enhancing quality of life by promoting creative lifestyles through meaningful physical activity, recreation, and fitness experiences across the lifespan with particular focus on community-based programs.

A significant impetus of AAPAR is the monumental work of Dr. Monica Lepore, who has spearheaded the development of teacher programs designed to improve the quality of instruction in adapted aquatics. The Adapted Aquatics section of AAPAR now offers certification as a Master Teacher of Adapted Aquatics, Adapted Aquatics Instructor, Adapted Aquatics Adjunct and Adapted Aquatics Assistant.

Perhaps one of the most exciting events in the history of adapted physical education is that John Passarini, an adapted physical education teacher from the Wayland Schools in Boston, was not only recognized by the Council for Exceptional Children as its "Outstanding Teacher" but also recognized as a Walt Disney Outstanding Educator. Dedicated, passionate teachers like John Passarini, given the title "Giver of Wings," give credence to our profession.

The need for quality adapted physical education and adapted physical activity programs is very clear. Unfortunately, many state education agency personnel, school board members, school district administrators, and parents have yet to understand the importance of physical education in the lives of all students, including those with disabilities. The value of physically active leisure for the health of Americans is well understood by some federal and state policy makers. There are initiatives in some states that address the issue of obesity of children of their state. The state of Arkansas has taken the lead in implementing projects to reduce overweight and obesity in the state. There are measures to track progress, and more than 90 percent of school-age children's weight is tracked using the body mass index (see Chapter 8). Other states are making plans for similar initiatives. Unfortunately, many state education agencies, school district administrators, and parents have yet to back efforts that upgrade adapted physical education and recreation programs for students with disabilities in addressing obesity issues.

FEDERAL LEGISLATION AND THE RIGHTS OF INDIVIDUALS WITH DISABILITIES

There is a long history of federal legislation that supports the education of learners with disabilities. Perhaps the most significant civil rights litigation tied to the education of learners with disabilities was *Brown v. Board of Education, Topeka, Kansas,* in 1954.[10] Though the litigants, parents, sued in protest over "tracking" their African American children into noncollege preparatory classes, the affirmation of the courts regarding the significance of education in the lives of ALL children was a landmark case. The court wrote

> [Education] is required in the performance of our most basic responsibilities. . . . It is the very foundation of good citizenship. In these days, it is doubtful that any child may reasonably be expected to succeed in life if he [or she] is denied the opportunity of an education. Such an opportunity, where the state has undertaken to provide it, is a right which must be made available to all on equal terms.[10]

The rights of persons with disabilities became a central concern during the 1970s, when landmark court cases ruled that children with disabilities had a right to a free and appropriate education and training and persons in institutions had a right to rehabilitation. These court decisions paralleled and created the initiative for federal legislation such as the Rehabilitation Act of 1973[51] and the Education for All Handicapped Children Act of 1975 (P.L. 94-142).[52] Before the enactment of the Education for

A Javelin Thrower with an Above-the-Knee Amputation
Courtesy Orthotic & Prosthetic Athletic Assistance Fund, Inc., Alexandria, VA.

All Handicapped Children Act of 1975, the special education needs of children with disabilities were not being fully met. More than one-half of children with disabilities did not receive appropriate educational services that would enable them to have full equality of opportunity. One million children with disabilities in the United States were excluded entirely from the public school system and did not go through the educational process with their peers.

At the beginning of the 1990s, the passage of the Americans with Disabilities Act (ADA) and, in the early 2000s, the Improved Education Results for Children with Disabilities (the Reauthorization of IDEA) further addressed the rights of persons with disabilities. The ADA act had a significant impact on the civil rights of individuals with disabilities in the public and private sectors.

DISABILITY CIVIL RIGHTS LEGISLATION

The rights of individuals with disabilities have been enhanced, primarily, through four major pieces of federal legislation. This legislation includes the Rehabilitation Act of 1973, the Education of All Handicapped Children Act of 1975, the Americans with Disabilities Act (ADA) of 1990, and the Improved Education Results for Children with Disabilities.[51,54] These four pieces of legislation were created to provide equal opportunity for individuals with disabilities. The similarities are

- Equity of services for individuals with disabilities when compared with those without disabilities
- Accessibility to environments and programs, so that there is equal opportunity to derive benefits from services in the public and private sectors
- Encouragement of integration of individuals with and without disabilities

All of the acts apply these basic principles but focus on different contexts.

Current Federal Legislative Initiatives

There were several federal initiatives of the 109th Congress designed to address obesity of American children, including children with disabilities. A brief description of this legislation appears in Table 1-4. Table 1-4 is a brief summary of major legislation that has had an impact on the education of learners with disabilities. Court decisions that have had an impact on the education of individuals with disabilities are summarized, briefly, in Table 1-5.

While the laws are designed to provide significant protection of individual education rights and to ensure access to programs and services, including leisure, recreation, sport, fitness, and wellness programs, there remain significant obstacles to the provision of quality services.

One of the significant problems that has emerged, in that the rights/assurances for individuals with disabilities are tied to the law, is that there is increasing litigation that "tests" the law. In particular, lawsuits against the public schools have proved incredibly costly in terms of both financial cost and human work hours. And, unfortunately, it has created a situation in which the

Table 1-4	Federal Initiatives to Prevent Obesity: Implications for APE and Recreation

H.R. 161 1H Healthy People Healthy Choices Act of 2005. Provides for an outreach campaign by the Centers for Disease Control and Prevention to increase participation in healthy lifestyles by minority populations who are disproportionately impacted by higher rates of obesity.[58]

H.R. 2844 National Health, Nutrition, and Physical Activity Monitoring Act of 2005.
Is designed to foster greater understanding of human dietary eating patterns and physical activity levels and to provide timely information to the public.[59]

H.R. 4860 and S. 1324 Childhood Obesity Reduction Act. Reduces and prevents childhood obesity by encouraging schools and school districts to develop and implement local school-based programs designed to reduce and prevent childhood obesity, increase physical activity, and improve nutritional choices.[61,68]

H.R. 5698 and S. 1325 Improved Nutrition and Physical Activity Act (IMPACT Act). Provides funding for research support, training of health care providers, and services for all ages to increase physical activity and improve nutrition through school and community-based intervention.[62,69]

S. 732 Safe Routes to School. Facilitates walking and bicycling to school.[64]

S. 799 Prevention of Childhood Obesity Act. Designed to coordinate federal departments and agencies to develop evidence-based measures to address the problem of obesity.[65]

S. 1074 Healthier Lifestyles and Prevention America Act (HeLP America Act). A comprehensive approach designed to encourage healthy lifestyles that include physical activity in schools and communities.[66]

Table 1-5	**Federal Legislation That Has an Impact on Physical Education for Individuals with Disabilities**
2004	Individuals with Disabilities Education Improvement Act (IDEIA) (P.L. 108-446) This act aligns the educational services provided to students with disabilities with NCLB and reinforces inclusion and evidence-based education.
2003	Reauthorization of the Child Abuse and Protection Act (P.L.108-83) The reauthorization of P.L. 93-247 retained the mandate that a person who suspects child abuse must report it or commit a felony.
2003	Reauthorization of the Amateur Sports Act The reauthorization reinforces the rightful place of "elite athletes" with disabilities in the community of "elite athletes" who participate in amateur athletics, particularly the Olympics and the Paralympics.
2003	Improved Nutrition and Physical Activity Act of 2003 The act is designed to encourage collaboration of public schools with community resources; the intent is to include persons with disabilities. The act provides training for personnel to improve participation in physical activity, particularly to prevent and ameliorate obesity.
2003	Workforce Reinvestment and Adult Education Act The act is designed to provide significant education opportunities for vocational training, including individuals with disabilities. The recreation portion of the Rehabilitation Act of 1973 was reauthorized in this act.
2001	Physical Education for Progress Act The act is designed to improve physical education for ALL children, including children with disabilities in the public schools, by providing competitive grants.
2001	No Child Left Behind Act This act puts significant federal support behind the improvement of reading and mathematics scores and compromises other critical curricular areas, including physical education, health, history, art, computer science, and music.
1997	Reauthorization of IDEA (P.L. 105-17) The reauthorization emphasized education for learners with disabilities in the general education program and increased the emphasis on parental participation in the assessment and IEP process.
1990	Americans with Disabilities Act (P.L. 101-336) The act expanded civil rights protections for individuals with disabilities in the public and private sectors.
1990	Individuals with Disabilities Education Act (IDEA) IDEA continued the emphasis on FAPE, IEP, LRE, and **physical education as a direct, educational service.**
1988	Assistive Technology Act (P.L. 103-218) This act made technology (basic and sophisticated) available to learners with disabilities in order to function within the public school system.
1975	Education for All Handicapped Children Act (P.L. 94-142) The act mandated (a) free, appropriate public education for all children with disabilities between the ages of 3 and 21 years; (b) Individual Education Plan; (c) education in the least restrictive environment; and (d) **physical education as a direct, educational service.**
1973	The Rehabilitation Act (P.L. 93-112, Section 504) The act mandated that individuals with disabilities cannot be excluded from any program or activity receiving federal funds solely on the basis of the disability.

Table 1-6	Court Decisions (Litigation) That Have Had an Impact on the Education of Learners with Disabilities

2006   *Arlington Central School District Board of Education v. Pearl and Theodore Murphy*
Parents are not entitled to recover fees for services rendered by experts in IDEA actions.

2005   *Schaffer v. Weast*
The burden of proof in a due process hearing regarding the IEP is on the parent if the state is silent on the matter. It limits parents' rights to acquire services they deem important from school districts.

2003   *Neosho School District v. Clark*
School districts must develop and implement appropriate behavioral management plans (BMPs).

2002   *Girly by Girly v. School District of Valley Grove*
The court required the school district to "prove" that a child with special needs cannot be accommodated in the general classroom with supplementary aids and services prior to placement in a special education program.

1999   *Cedar Rapids, Iowa, Community School District v. Garret*
The court ruled that school districts must provide necessary nursing services to ensure a student is educated in the least restrictive environment.[12]

1994   *Clyde K. and Sheila K. v. Puyallup School District*
The court ruled that, if children with emotional and behavior disorders adversely affect the learning of other children and the educational environment, they may be removed and placed in a more restrictive environment.

1994   *Sacramento City Unified School District v. Rachel*
The court developed a four-factor standard for educational placement in the general program: (1) the educational benefits; (2) the nonacademic benefits; (3) the effects the student with a disability has on the classroom learning environment; and (4) the cost of placement in a general classroom.

1991   *Greer v. Rome City*
The court mandated (1) the IEP must include supplementary aids and services in the general program; (2) if necessary, the general curriculum must be modified to accommodate a child with a disability; and (3) the parents must be advised of all LRE options, not just the option that requires the least effort on the part of the school district.

1984   *Irving Independent School District v. Tatro*
Services needed to enable a child to reach, enter, exit, and/or remain in school are required.

1972   *Larry B. v. Riles (California)*
IQ tests cannot be used as the sole basis for placing a child in a special education class.

1972   *Mills v. Board of Education of the District of Columbia*
Every child has a right to equal opportunity for an education. Children with emotional disorders cannot be excluded from school. Lack of funds is not an acceptable excuse for failure to provide services.

1970   *Diana v. State Board of Education (California)*
Children cannot be placed in special education on the basis of culturally biased/language biased tests.

parents with the most resources (money or power) can demand and receive for their children educational services that are not accessible to the children of the poor and disenfranchised, the children who inevitably need our services the most (see Table 1-6).

EDUCATIONAL REFORM AND SPECIAL EDUCATION

There are two major pieces of federal legislation that interface with one another. One is the Reauthorization of IDEA (P.L. 108-466), and the other is the No Child Left Behind Act of 2001 (NCLB), which is being reauthorized at this writing. There are provisions in NCLB that require schools to accommodate more children with disabilities in regular class instruction. NBLD is not without its critics. Some of the criticisms involve (1) moving children from failing schools to other schools, rather than correcting the school issues; (2) teaching tests; and (3) high-stakes testing, where focus is on academic achievement, rather than physical education, art, and music.

However, the most significant problems in the public schools have little to do with education per se. Parents list the following as the top five problems:

- Fighting and violence
- Lack of discipline
- Lack of financial support
- Use of drugs
- Overcrowding[40]

One of the major problems with America's schools, however, is that opportunities are not equal. As a result, the achievements of students in schools that cater to the rich and to the poor in our country are also far from equal.[6] These inequities in public education are reflected in employment outcomes for persons with disabilities. These inequities simply continue a tragic cycle in which there is an increasing disparity between the "haves" and the "have nots."

It is important for physical educators, adapted physical educators and recreation personnel to realize, however, that physical education has widespread support from parents. There is evidence that, if the majority of parents support physical education, there is hope that physical education can retain or regain its important place in the school curriculum.

There is an initiative that may actually make a difference in the education of an ethnically, culturally, linguistically, gender, gender preference, and ability/disability diverse student population.

Aquatics can be a wonderful lifetime and family activity.
Photo by Kristi Roth, University of Wisconsin Stevens Point.

It is an increased emphasis on the family as the critical unit in the education of students with and without disabilities. It is suggested there is a need to switch from "child-centered" schools to "family-centered" schools[16] and "full service schools". This would require significant interagency collaboration among education, social services, human services, and health services, so that the needs of families can be met. The focus is on a return to the days when the school was the focus of the community and all community members worked together for the sake of the children.

SERVICE LEARNING AND ADAPTED PHYSICAL EDUCATION

An exciting trend in special education is the involvement of students with disabilities in service learning opportunities.[42] Historically, professionals, paraeducators, volunteers, and students without disabilities have provided service to meet the needs of learners with disabilities. However, it is very clear that the learner with disabilities has much to offer as part of the community involved in improving our collective life. An article in *Today,* a publication of the Council for Exceptional Children, states,

> In service learning, students engage in community service and while doing so meet IEP, academic, and/or curricular goals. Special

education teachers who have used service learning report many positive gains for their students. Not only do students with disabilities learn content, they also improve social skills, gain a sense of belonging in the school and community, and see a real-world relationship to what they are learning.[42]

PHYSICAL FITNESS, HEALTH, AND WELLNESS

The critical relationship between a physically active leisure life and health and wellness has been well established. Siedentop wrote,

> During this century we have witnessed what is now commonly referred to as the epidemiological transition, the shift in the main cause of death from infectious diseases to degenerative cardiovascular diseases and cancers. . . . To substantially increase the percentage of citizens who value physical activity enough to voluntarily make decisions to be regularly active despite attractive alternatives, we need to move from a traditional focus on remediation to a focus on prevention; and we need to view prevention not only as altering the risk-status of individuals but also as developing and sustaining attractive, inclusive, physical activity infrastructures for children, youth, and adults; that is, we need to focus on the social determinants of physical activity.[43]

The surgeon general's report on disability and health has two essential recommendations related to the health of persons with disabilities. One is healthy lifestyles that include physical activity and the other is public education of the benefits of exercise. Persons with disabilities can promote their own good health by developing and maintaining healthy lifestyles. Prevalence of risk in persons of inadequate physical activity is nearly twice as great when compared with persons without disability.[48]

Recommendations from the Centers for Disease Control and Prevention and the American College of Sports Medicine make it clear that every adult should accumulate 30 minutes or more of moderate-intensity activity on most, preferably all, days of the week.[48] The surgeon general released

the following recommendations regarding physical activity and health:

- People of all ages can benefit from regular physical activity.
- Significant health benefits can be obtained by including a moderate amount of physical activity (e.g., 30 minutes of walking briskly or raking leaves, 15 minutes of running, or 45 minutes of playing volleyball) on most, if not all, days of the week.
- A modest increase in activity can improve the health and quality of life for most Americans.
- Longer and more vigorous activities can provide additional health benefits.
- Some of the prominent health benefits of appropriate activity include reduced risk for premature mortality, heart disease, colon cancer, hypertension, and diabetes mellitus.
- Other benefits include improved mental health and improved fitness of the muscles, bones, and joints.[48]
- Physical activity has the potential to prevent secondary disability.

Increasingly, the complex problems associated with the poor health of our citizens with and without disabilities require coalitions of those with a commitment to the provision of quality physical education, health, and wellness services. The National Coalition for Promoting Physical Activity includes (a) American College of Sports Medicine, (b) AAHPERD, (c) American Heart Association, (d) Association for Worksite Health Promotion, (e) International Health, Racquet and Sportsclub Association, and (f) National Association of Governor's Councils on Physical Fitness.[33] In addition, the National Association for Nutrition and Activity, with over 200 member associations, provides public policy initiatives to confront obesity through physical activity and nutrition.

FEDERAL LEADERSHIP FOR HEALTH AND WELLNESS

The Centers for Disease Control and Prevention has awarded significant grants to the American Association for Physical Activity and Recreation (AAPAR) and the National Association for Sport and Physical Education (NASPE) to promote physical activity among youth and older adults. Another significant partnership has been established between the American Alliance of Health, Physical Education, Recreation and Dance (AAHPERD) and the American Heart Association; their collaboration will enhance Physical Best, a comprehensive health and physical fitness assessment and curriculum.

While there has been an increased focus on the physical activity needs of adults, there has also been an increased focus on the physical activity needs of children. The Council for Physical Education for Children (COPEC) of the National Association for Sport and Physical Education (NASPE) of the American Alliance for Health, Physical Education, Recreation and Dance developed the following guidelines for children:

• Elementary-school-age children should accumulate at least 30 to 60 minutes of age-and developmentally appropriate physical activity from a variety of physical activities on all, or most, days of the week.
• An accumulation of more than 60 minutes, and up to several hours, per day of age- and developmentally appropriate activity is encouraged for elementary-school-age children.
• Some of the child's activity each day should be in a period of time lasting 10 to 15 minutes or more and should include moderate to vigorous activity. This activity will typically be intermittent, involving alternating moderate to vigorous activity, with brief periods of rest and recovery.
• Extended periods of inactivity are inappropriate for children.
• A variety of physical activities selected from the Physical Activity Pyramid is recommended for elementary school children.[32]

However, the National Coalition for the Promotion of Physical Activity reports that less than 50 percent of the schools offer physical education programs.[33]

Clearly, the schools can and should meet the physical activity needs of children. McKenzie wrote,

Schools have the potential to be the primary source of physical activity. . . . An established part of the community infrastructure, schools serve nearly all children and adolescents, have a staff of physical activity experts, require almost all children to take some form of physical education, and house facilities and equipment specifically designed to promote physical activity.[29]

However, it remains clear that many students do not have daily access to a quality physical education program that gives them the opportunity to engage in 30 minutes of moderately intense activity.[33] The percentage of schools that require physical education declines throughout the academic program, from 1st grade to grade 12. Approximately 50 percent of the schools require physical education in 1st–5th grade, but this reduces to approximately 25 percent in 8th grade. It is further reduced to only 5 percent in 12th grade.[11] While this is discouraging, at best, it is more discouraging to learn that only 8 percent of elementary schools and 6 percent of middle/junior/senior high schools provide *daily* physical education.[11]

The increasing demand for improved academic performance, heightened by the passage of the No Child Left Behind Act of 2001, has caused administrators to reduce and/or eliminate physical education from the curriculum.

Part of the failure to emphasize and honor the physical education needs of learners with disabilities is tied to the budget crisis in education. Educational priorities of local school districts must be recognized. In times of state and local budget constraints significant decisions regarding priorities need to be made and, unfortunately, these decisions often involve program cuts.[13] In the early 2000s, many physical education programs were cut throughout the United States, including adapted physical education programs. Adapted physical education teachers and other personnel involved in adapted physical education programs must explain the health and quality of life values of adapted physical education programs to administrators, community leaders, and parents in hopes that an increased understanding of the potential benefits will forestall subsequent program cuts.

HEALTHY PEOPLE 2010

There is an increasing interest in and understanding of the profound personal, community, and national impact of contemporary health practices in this country. Murray wrote,

> At the same time we are cutting back on physical education, our society is spending more than ever on health care. Last September, the U.S. Department of Health and Human Services (HHS) predicted that health care expenditures from 1997 to 2007 would increase from $1 trillion to more than $2.1 trillion. During that time, hospital growth is expected to lag behind growth in drug companies, number of physicians, and other professional health care services. Although the most optimistic projections suggest health care costs will double over the next decade, ironically, the public continues to treat the need for health-related education with benign neglect.[31]

The critical importance of physical education in the health and wellness of young people is supported by the following Healthy People 2010 objectives:

22.8   Increase the proportion of the nation's public and private schools that require physical education for all students.

22.9   Increase the proportion of adolescents who participate in daily school physical education.

22.10 Increase the proportion of adolescents who spend at least 50 percent of school physical education class time being physically active.

22.12 Increase the proportion of the nation's public and private schools that provide access to their physical activity spaces and facilities for all persons outside of normal school hours (that is, before and after the school day, on weekends, and during summer and other vacations).[11]

EDUCATIONAL STANDARDS

School reform initiatives that focus on the improvement of educational standards increased dramatically after the passage of NCLB. NCLB escalated and intensified academic standards. Of concern to the physical educator and the adapted physical educator is the fact that this focus does not include, and may seriously jeopardize, physical education, health, and recreation outcomes for learners with and without disabilities. The core activities do not include health and physical education; there is undue attention to the so-called academic curriculum at the expense of physical education, health, and recreation curricula. It must be noted that other curricular areas absolutely critical to the development of students are compromised as well—art, computer science, history, music, and government, for example.

However, there are federal legislative initiatives to amend NCLB to establish content standards for physical education, including measurement of proficiency of all students in physical education. Tests will be administered not less than one time during grades 3 through 5, 6 through 9, and 10 through 12.[60,67]

THE TEACHER'S REALITY

Teachers continue to play a critical role in the lives of children and youth. Good physical education

Photo by Laurie Zittel

teachers and adapted physical education teachers continue to be the "pied pipers" of the professionals who work with children and youth. Children are drawn, of course, to teachers who love to do what children love to do—play and move. And those who truly love children and love to teach continue to be the backbone of this society. Certainly, the profession becomes even more important as children have more and more needs that must be met.

LEISURE AND RECREATION OPPORTUNITIES FOR INDIVIDUALS WITH DISABILITIES

If, indeed, the adapted physical educator and the physical educator have the opportunity to provide quality instruction to learners with disabilities, a world of opportunity opens for the learners and their families. There have been several federal initiatives that have supported programs of physical activity to confront issues of prevention of chronic health conditions especially:

> House Resolution 204: Describes the role played by national and community organizations in promoting awareness of the importance of early diagnosis and assessment of obesity by the federal government.[56]

> House Resolution 557: Proclaims a Winter Outdoors Month and calls attention to the need for all people to exercise and get outdoors in the winter.[57]

> Joint Senate and House Resolution 66: Advocates for high-quality after-school programs that provide safe, challenging, and fun learning experiences that include physical activity to develop physical, social, and emotional aspects of life.[55]

> Senate Resolution 257: Recognizes the health risks associated with childhood obesity and encourages parent, school, and civic organizations and students to support the goals of National Take a Kid Mountain Biking Day.[63]

There are community-based recreational programs whose primary purpose is to engage in self-fulfilling leisure activity with a concomitant health benefit. There are recreational programs that are generic and those that are specifically tailored for disabled-only populations. Examples of each type of community-based programs follows.

Generic Community-Based Recreation Programs

Generic community-based recreation programs are designed for all Americans, including children, youth, and adults who are disabled. It is the intent of the Americans with Disabilities Act that persons with disabilities have access to public accommodations, including community-based recreation programs with reasonable accommodations. Generic community-based recreational activities that include physical activity may be (1) boys' and girls' clubs, (2) YMCAs and YWCAs, (3) community-sponsored recreation programs, (4) public golf courses, (5) parks and recreational areas, (6) hiking and other recreational clubs, (7) camping programs and facilities, (8) physical fitness centers, (9) bowling centers, (10) ballroom dancing instructional programs, (11) programs that teach and enable participation in the martial arts, (12) programs that teach yoga, and (13) community-based recreational activities that involve physical activity.

Special Community-Based Programs for Persons with Disabilities

There are public and private initiatives to provide specially designed recreational opportunities for persons with disabilities. One federal initiative is the program entitled "I Can Do It You Can Do It."[50] This program, which is sponsored by the Department of Health and Human Services through the National Institutes of Health, provides funding opportunities for programs that enable children and youth with disabilities to participate in physical activity. The foundation of the program is mentoring. Community-based organizations, sometimes in collaboration with public schools and institutions of higher education, may compete for funding. There are also private initiatives of specially designed recreational opportunities.

Wonderful programs, such as Wilderness Inquiry, give individuals with disabilities and their families the opportunity to participate in quality outdoor recreation experiences together. Northeast Passage works to create an environment where individuals with disabilities can recreate with the same freedom of choice and independence as their able-bodied peers. The National Ability Center is dedicated to the development of lifetime skills for persons with disabilities and their families by providing affordable, quality sports and recreation experiences. The benefits of these experiences build self-esteem and confidence, enhancing active participation in the fabric of community life. Since 1976, the Breckenridge Outdoor Education Center has offered quality outdoor learning experiences

Include All Children in the Least Restrictive Environment
Photo by Carol Huettig.

for people of all abilities, including people with disabilities, those with serious illnesses and injuries, and "at-risk" populations. As a nonprofit organization, the Breckenridge Outdoor Education Center is dedicated to helping people reach their full potential through custom programs for groups and opportunities for individuals. With adventure trips, internships, and volunteer positions, people of all abilities can get involved.

There have been few projects in the Department of Education that have addressed the issue of the transition of special education students into recreation programs that involve physical activity. Few are actually helping learners with disabilities and their families learn to access and enjoy leisure and recreation opportunities available in their communities.

Sport for Individuals with Disabilities

Sport opportunities continue to grow and improve for individuals with disabilities. The United States Congress has indicated support for the concept that there are benefits from sports competition. It has offered resolutions to provide positive testimony to the benefits of Olympic competition— specifically, paralympics.[70,71] "Competitive sports bring together athletes from different cultural backgrounds in friendly competition. The competition forges new relationships, bound by friendship, solidarity, and fair play. It encourages physical fitness and leisure activity. It takes pride in the commitment to excellence."[65] The reauthorization of the Amateur Athletic Act specifically references the inclusion of persons with disabilities in amateur athletics.

Dr. Karen Depauw wrote,

> The U.S. Congress recently approved a change to the definition of elite athlete (as defined by the United States Olympic Committee) to include athletes with disabilities; a very positive end to a struggle that began more than a decade ago. The significance of this action lies in the official recognition and acknowledgement that athletes with disabilities, both male and female, are indeed athletes.[18]

A Young Athlete Competes in His Chair

Courtesy of Jefferson Parish Public Schools, Special Education Dept. Harvey, LA.

Dr. David Beaver wrote,

On Wednesday, October 21, 1998, Senator Ted Stevens' (R-Alaska) much awaited amendments to the original Amateur Athletic Act, PL 95-606 (1978), were passed by Congress as part of the Omnibus Appropriations Bill. . . . Hailed by many as historic landmark legislation for athletes with disabilities, the new bill amends the original with provisions reflecting the growth of competition by athletes with disabilities within Olympic and amateur athletic programs, and ensures the continued development of sport opportunities for individuals with disabilities. However, for those interested in the mission of PALAESTRA, the most important aspect of the amendments of 1998 lies in those sections recognizing sport for athletes with disabilities; on their parity with other athletes, and programs provided

under the aegis of the USOC; in the recognition of the International Paralympic Committee, the Paralympic Games, as well as the acknowledgment of the USOC as the National Paralympic Committee for the United States.[9]

There are literally hundreds of organizations devoted to quality athletic competition for individuals with disabilities. You can gain easy access to information about many of those organizations at the Texas Woman's University Project INSPIRE Web site.[44]

It is also very exciting to note that the business sector has started to realize there is definitely a market for carefully designed equipment necessary for the athlete with a disability to be more successful in his or her sport. Companies such as Radventure, Flex-Foot, Orthomerica, Endolite, Deming Designs, Disability Options, and Orthotic and Prosthetic Athletic Fund are deeply committed to providing quality sport equipment for individuals with disabilities. And major equipment and supplies companies, such as Sportime and Flaghouse, have been innovative in the development of equipment for individuals with disabilities to use in leisure, recreation, fitness, and sports activities. Unfortunately, athletes with disabilities, particularly in the rural parts of the country, may find it difficult to access sports programs and competitions designed to meet their unique needs. It appears that virtual competition, using the Internet, may prove to be one avenue to allow individuals all over the world to compete in individual sports with athletes with similar disabilities. Although there are critical limitations to this type of competition—just as there are critical limitations in e-mail versus personal communication—it may provide one vehicle for competition.

There are generic community-based sport programs and specially designed programs for specific sports for persons with disabilities. Persons with disabilities have accessed generic high school sport programs, community-based sport activity, and even world-class Olympic competition. Persons with disabilities usually self-select the most appropriate athletic forums for themselves. In general, they avoid the segregated sports activities if there are appropriate options for sports participation in generic programs.

THE TRANSFORMATION OF PHYSICAL EDUCATION FOR ALL CHILDREN

The National Association for Sport and Physical Education of the American Alliance of Health, Physical Education, Recreation and Dance has taken the lead in establishing national standards for physical education. The NASPE National Standards for Physical Education suggest that a student should

- Demonstrate competency in motor skills and movement patterns needed to perform a variety of physical activities
- Demonstrate an understanding of movement concepts, principles, strategies, and tactics as they apply to the learning and performance of physical activities
- Participate regularly in physical activity
- Achieve and maintain a health-enhancing level of physical fitness
- Exhibit responsible personal and social behavior that respects self and others
- Value physical activity for health, enjoyment, challenge, self-expression, and/or social interaction

Learning Colors through Active Play
Photo by Carol Huettig.

Unfortunately, children who hate gym class grow into adults who associate physical activity with ridicule and humiliation. And dread of physical activity is taking its toll on our health.[72]

Dr. Judith Young, vice president for programs of AAHPERD said, "We've shifted focus from performance-related activities to reaching a level of fitness that supports good health."[73] Physical education programs that are more sensitive to the developmental needs of children and youth and that focus on their fitness and health include activities in which they can participate actively as adults. These activities include, but are not limited to, aerobic dance, weight training, fitness walking, mountain biking, hiking, inline skating, aqua aerobics, cross-country skiing, snowshoeing, swimming, yoga, rock climbing, kayaking, and canoeing.

Action steps that could be taken to improve adapted physical education follow:

- Research the physical education needs of poor, vulnerable, and minority children and youth
- Focus research on the child's family and community
- Refocus the curriculum to ensure children are prepared for community-based leisure, recreation, fitness, and sport activities
- Refocus energies into supportive extra-school activities
- Refocus the curriculum based on student interest
- Reestablish physical education as a critical part of the neighborhood and community[27]

Dr. Rainer Martens has written eloquently of the need to transform physical education. Essentially, Martens has noted that adults (teachers and parents) forget that children and youth like to play and move because it is fun. It is critical that physical educators and adapted physical educators avoid the following:

- Adult goals for organizing activities for children are often not the same goals the children have. Adults are often performance-oriented, and children often are seeking only to have fun. This discrepancy in goals often leads to conflict between teacher/coach and children.

- As part of adults' performance orientation, they routinize learning of physical activity skills to the point of making them exceptionally boring. It may be the best way to teach these skills in the short term, but it is not the best way to encourage children to participate in the activity for a lifetime.

- Adults may replace games and unstructured play with calisthenics, a pernicious way of exercising thought up surely by a sadistic military sergeant. Calisthenics are boring to most people, and people must be highly motivated to do them for extended periods of time. There are many more enjoyable ways than calisthenics to have children be physically active from which they will derive the health benefits we deem desirable.

- We squelch fun also by using physical activity as punishment for misbehaving. It's obvious to everyone (except all those who continue to prescribe to this practice) that doing so turns kids off to physical activity.[28]

Certainly, as physical educators and adapted physical educators, the very future of students with disabilities lies in the palms of our hands. And that future has not been placed in our hands gently; it has been thrust on us because of an incredible need for good teachers—physical education teachers who are committed to learners with disabilities—to step forward and make a difference. With imagination, we can transform our profession and refocus our energies.[20] At the beginning of the chapter, we described a number of specific ways that adapted physical educators can "do something" to make a difference. Now that you have read the chapter, we again ask you to imagine how to make a difference. Here are some possibilities:

- Help a family get involved with a Wilderness Inquiry trip into the boundary waters in Minnesota.
- Volunteer with Island Dolphin Care, Inc., a nonprofit agency in Key Largo, Florida, where

A Child with Cerebral Palsy Shakes Hands with a Dolphin
Courtesy Island Dolphin Care, Inc., Key Largo, Fla.

dolphins and their human counterparts provide quality intervention for children with disabilities.

- Go virtual reality mountain climbing with an adolescent with Duchenne muscular dystrophy.
- Teach a 10-month-old child with Down syndrome to swim.
- Coach a streetwise adolescent to use her remarkable basketball talent to score over 30 points in a Special Olympics game.
- Clap to acknowledge the remarkable dance of a troupe of boys with Duchenne muscular dystrophy using their electric wheelchairs to express their feelings.
- Serve as a guide runner for a marathoner who just happens to be blind.
- Take a little boy with nemaline rod myopathy to see his first-ever sledge hockey tournament.
- Encourage older adults with secondary disabilities to participate in an aqua aerobics program.
- Use your experience as a coach to volunteer with the National Wheelchair Basketball Association.

- Help two little girls with spina bifida communicate via e-mail (modern-day pen pals), even though they live thousands of miles apart.
- Share a pizza with a bocce team after a victory.
- Develop a "Partners" Special Olympics program in your school district.
- Help an aerobics dance teacher modify the dance steps, so that an individual in a wheelchair can participate in her class.
- Hug a parent grieving the loss of her envisioned child.
- Coach young athletes with cerebral palsy in the USCPPA.
- Watch a father's joy as his little girl with a below-the-knee amputation executes a perfect balance beam dismount.
- Play virtual reality golf with a young man with a traumatic brain injury.

- Lose a tennis game to your opponent who used a wheelchair.
- Help a teenager with spina bifida climb a rock wall.
- Ride a tandem bicycle in a 25-mile road race with a partner with a vision impairment.
- Walk three days a week for 30 minutes with a friend with an above-the-knee amputation and prosthesis.
- Develop a play group for young mothers of children with and without disabilities so that the children can learn to play together.
- Share a sign language joke with a teammate.
- Ocean kayak to watch the whales with athletes with spinal cord injury.
- Create a Web page designed to foster the growth of quality physical education for learners with disabilities.

SUMMARY

The twentieth century saw drastic and remarkable growth in physical education for individuals with disabilities. Certainly, the law has provided the impetus for this growth. There have been major changes in the public schools in the past several decades. These changes have at once challenged and frustrated the physical educator with a commitment to serving children and youth with and without disabilities. Certainly, the physical educator in the twenty-first century must demonstrate increased skills in facilitating cooperative play and in developing critical thinking skills and must demonstrate cultural competence. Best practice in adapted physical education involves knowing who is disabled and providing evidence-based programs for all children with disabilities through generalizing skills acquired in physical education to long-term, lifestyle patterns in the home and community. This includes the prevention of obesity. There are increased opportunities for individuals with disabilities to lead full and healthy lives, enjoying leisure, recreation, fitness, sport, and wellness opportunities because of a quality physical education program. This is possible only if physical educators reenvision the future of the discipline.

REVIEW QUESTIONS

1. What is adapted physical education? How does it differ, if it does, from general physical education?
2. What are the similarities among the major pieces of legislation affecting physical education for individuals with disabilities?
3. What are the benefits of a quality physical education program for individuals with disabilities?
4. What is APENS? Briefly describe its impact on the field.
5. What is NCPAD? Describe the mission.
6. Briefly describe the basic physical activity guidelines for adults and children.

STUDENT ACTIVITIES

1. Join ADAPT-TALK at sportime.com/adapt-talk/.
2. Join your state Association of Health, Physical Education, Recreation and Dance. Attend its state convention; particularly, focus on those sessions devoted to teaching learners with disabilities.
3. Visit the recommended Web sites and travel through their links into the world of cyberspace.

REFERENCES

1. AAHPERD's National Associations Land CDC Grants: *UPDATE* November/December: 1, 5, 2001.
2. Adapted Physical Education National Standards (APENS) at www.cortland.edu/apens. 2003
3. Alaska Special Olympics at www.specialolympicsalaska.org. 2003
4. American Association for Physical Activity and Recreation (AAPAR) at www.aahperd.org/aapar.html.
5. American Association of Health, Physical Education, and Recreation: Guiding principles for adapted physical education, JOPHERD 28(4):15, 1952.
6. Andreas B: *Still mostly true.* Decorah, IA, Storey People, 1994.
7. *Arlington Central School District Board of Education v. Pearl and Theodore Murphy,* No. 03-785-cv, July 28, 2006. (2nd Cir. 2005).
8. Auxter D: Personal communication, December 2003.
9. Beaver D (Editor's Corner): A coming of age: Sports for athletes with disabilities and the Amateur Sports Act, *Palaestra* 14(4):5, 1998.
10. *Brown v. The Board of Education,* 347 US, 483, 1954.
11. Burgeson C, Wechsler H, Brener N, Young J, Spain C: Physical education and activity: Results from the School Health Policies and Programs Study 2000, *JOPERD* 74(1):20–36, 2003.
12. *Cedar Rapids, Iowa, Community School District v. Garrett,* U.S. Supreme Court, No. 96-1793, March 3, 1999.
13. Center on Budget and Policy Priorities: The state fiscal crisis, www.cbpp.org, 2003.
14. *Clyde K, Sheila K v. Puyallup School District,* 21 IDELR 664 (9th Cir, 1994).
15. Consortium for Citizens with Disabilities, www.c-c-d.org, 2005.
16. Corrigan D: Keynote address. Challenges for personnel preparation in special education conference, Washington, DC, Office of Special Education Programs, September 1999.
17. Davis T: Personal communication, January 2007.
18. DePauw KP: Girls and women with disabilities in sport, *JOPERD* 70(4):50–52, 1999.
19. *Greer v. Rome City School District,* 950 F 2d 688 (11th Cir, 1991).
20. Harrington WM: Our collective future: A triumph of imagination, *Quest* 51:272–284, 1999.
21. IDEA Part B Trend Data, www.ideadata.org. Part BTrendDataFiles.asp. 2007
22. Institute of Medicine of the National Academies: *Disability in America: A new look.* Washington, DC, www.iom.edu, 2006.
23. Institute of Medicine of the National Academies: *Disability in America: Toward a national agenda for prevention.* Washington, DC, www.iom.edu, 1991.
24. Kaiser Commission on Medicaid and the Uninsured, www.kff.org/medicaid, 2005.
25. Kelly LE: *National standards for adapted physical education.* Washington, DC, U.S. Department of Education, Office of Special Education Programs, 1994.
26. Land, KC: The Foundation for Child Development Child and Youth Well-Being Index (CWI), presentation at the Brooking Institute, Washington, DC, March 15, 2006.
27. Lawson HA: Rejuvenating, reconstituting, and transforming physical education to meet the needs of vulnerable children, youth, and families, *J Teaching in Phys Educ* 18:2–25, 1998.
28. Martens R: Turning kids on to physical activity for a lifetime, *Quest* 48:303–310, 1996.

29. McKenzie TL: School health-related physical activity programs: What do the data say? *JOPERD* 70(1):16–19, 1999.

30. McKenzie TL et al.: Student activity levels and lesson context during third grade physical education, *Research Q Exercise and Sport* 66:184–193, 1995.

31. Murray BA, Murray KT: A nation out of shape, *Am School Bd J* August:29–33, 1999.

32. National Consortium of Physical Education and Recreation for Individuals with Disabilities at http://ncperid.usf.edu. 2003

33. National Coalition for Promotion of Physical Activity: *Physical activity for youth: Policy initiatives.* Washington, DC, www.americanheart.org, 2002.

34. National Mental Health Association, http://nmha.org, 2005.

35. National Standards for Physical Education, National Association for Sport and Physical Education an association of the American Alliance for Health, Physical Education, Recreation and Dance, Reston, VA, www.aahperd.org/naspe, 2007.

36. Office of Special Education and Rehabilitative Services, www.ed.gov/about/offices/list/osers/osep/index/html, 2005.

37. Reid G: Personal communication, December 2003.

38. Rimmer J: Personal communication, December 2003.

39. Rimmer J, Schiller WJ: New center announced, *International Fed Adapted Phys Act Newsletter* 7(4):3, 1999.

40. Rose L, Gallup A: The 30th annual Phi Delta Kappa/Gallup poll of the public's attitudes toward the public schools, *Phi Delta Kappan,* September:41–56, 1998.

41. *Schaffer v. Weast,* 41, IDELR, 76 (4th Cir, 2004).

42. Service learning—Students with disabilities give to others, *Today* (Council for Exceptional Children) 10(4):1, 7, 2003.

43. Siedentop D: Valuing the physically active life: Contemporary and future directions, *Quest* 48:266–274, 1996.

44. Texas Woman's University, Project INSPIRE, www.twu.edu/INSPIRE, 2005.

45. U.S. Census, www.census.gov, 2000.

46. U.S. Department of Children and Families, www.acf.gov, 2005.

47. U.S. Department of Health and Human Services, *Goals 2010.* Centers for Disease Control and Prevention: Atlanta, GA, 2006.

48. U.S. Department of Health and Human Services: *Physical activity and health: A report of the surgeon general.* Atlanta, GA, Centers for Disease Control and Prevention, National Center for Chronic Disease Prevention and Health Promotion, 1996.

49. U.S. Department of Health and Human Services: *Disability and health: A call to action.* www.surgeongeneral.gov/library/disabilities, Washington, DC, August 15, 2005.

50. U.S. Department of Health and Human Services, Office of Disability: *I can do it, you can do it.* www.hhs.gov/topico/healthandhumanservices/physicalfitness.html, Washington, DC, 2006.

51. U.S. Department of Health, Education, and Welfare: 504 regulations for the Rehabilitation Act of 1973, Rehabilitation Act amendments of 1974, and Education of the Handicapped Act, *Fed Reg* 45:339–395, 1990.

52. U.S. 94th Congress: Public Law 94-142, November 29, 1975.

53. U.S. 103rd Congress: Individuals with Disabilities Education Act, 1995.

54. U.S. 108th Congress: Public Law 108-446, Improved Educational Results for Children with Disabilities Act, Congressional Record 150:S11653-11660, Washington, DC, 2004.

55. U.S. 109th Congress, House and Senate joint resolution HCon 66, Lights On After School, Washington, DC, September, 2005.

56. U.S. 109th Congress, House and Senate joint concurrent resolution HCon 204 expressing the sense of the Congress with respect to obesity in the United States, Washington, DC, July, 2005.

57. U.S. 109th Congress, House of Representatives resolution HR 557, Winter Outdoors Month, Washington, DC, November 2005.

58. U.S. 109th Congress, House of Representatives, HR 161, Healthy People Healthy Choices Act of 2005, Washington, DC, January 2005.

59. U.S. 109th Congress, House of Representatives, HR 2844, The National Health, Nutrition and Physical Activity Monitoring Act of 2005, Washington, DC, June 2005.

60. U.S. 109th Congress, House of Representatives, HR 4359, amend section 1111 of the Elementary and Secondary Education Assistance Act to include physical education as a required subject, Washington, DC, November 2005.

61. U.S. 109th Congress, House of Representatives, HR 4860, Childhood Obesity Reduction Act, Washington, DC, March 2006.

62. U.S. 109th Congress, House of Representatives, HR 5698, Improved Nutrition and Physical Activity Act (IMPACT Act), June 2006.

63. U.S. 109th Congress, Senate resolution S. 257, National Take a Kid Mountain Biking Day, Washington, DC, September 2005.

64. U.S. 109th Congress, Senate, S. 732, Safe Routes to School, Washington, DC, March 2005.

65. U.S. 109th Congress, Senate, S. 799, Prevention of Childhood Obesity Act, Washington, DC, April 2005.

66. U.S. 109th Congress, Senate, S. 1074, Healthier Lifestyles and Prevention America Act (HeLP), Washington, DC, May 2005.

67. U.S. 109th Congress, Senate, S. 1276, amend section 1111 of the Elementary and Secondary Education Assistance Act regarding challenging academic content standards for physical education, Washington, DC, June 2005.

68. U.S. 109th Congress, Senate, S. 1324, Childhood Obesity Reduction Act, Washington, DC, June 2005.

69. U.S. 109th Congress, Senate, S. 1325, Improved Nutrition and Physical Activity Act (IMPACT Act), Washington, DC, June 2005.

70. U.S. Senate: Senate Concurrent Resolution 47, Recognizing the International Olympic Committee, Washington, DC, 2001.

71. U.S. Senate: Senate Resolution 99, Resolution supporting the goals and ideals of the Olympics, Washington, DC, 2001.

72. Vail K: Fit for life: Trading in old-fashioned gym class for the "new PE," *Am School Bd J* August:31–32, 1999.

73. Young J: PEP 2003 Appropriations; COPEC Corner, *Teaching Elementary Physical Education* 14(3):40, 2003.

74. Zittel L: Personal communication, December 2003.

SUGGESTED READINGS

Davis T, Stopka C: P.E.—smart sports education, *Sports 'n Spokes,* 32(1):19–33, 2006.

Sayers L, Shapiro D, Webster G: Community-based physical activities for elementary students, *JOPERD,* 74(4):49–54, 2003.

RECOMMENDED WEB SITES

Please keep in mind that these Web sites are being recommended in the winter of 2007. As Web sites often change, they may have been moved, reconfigured, or eliminated.

American Association for Physical Activity and Recreation
   http://aahperd.org/aapar

(Note: Of particular interest is its new position statement on physical education for students with disabilities.)

Adapted Physical Education National Standards
   http://www.apens.org

National Center on Physical Ability and Disability
   http://ncpad.com

Texas Woman's University Project INSPIRE
   www.twu.edu/INSPIRE

PE Central
   www.pecentral.org

PE Links 4U
   www.pelinks4u.com

RECOMMENDED VIDEOS

Insight Media
2162 Broadway
New York, NY 10024-0621
1-800-233-9910
www.insight-media.com

Physical Activity for All
YAN2632/DVD-ROM/200/30 min/$129.00

Special People, Special Needs
YAN2642/VHS tape/2000/51 min/$149.00

II

Key Techniques

The types of services needed by learners are common; however, each individual has a unique profile that must be addressed in the most appropriate fashion. For learners to benefit fully from physical education, their specific needs must be identified, a program to address those needs must be designed, a teaching approach to facilitate each learner's needs should be provided in the most positive and inclusive environment, and school systems must provide the necessary resources to ensure programmatic success. We address each of these critical components in this part.

Adapted Physical Education in the Public Schools

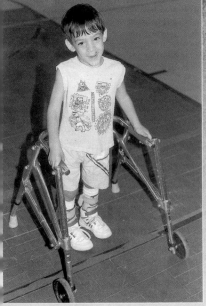

All Children Need to Participate in Physical Activities

Picture by Carol Huettig.

■ **O B J E C T I V E S**

Briefly explain the adapted physical education program within the public schools. Give examples of a philosophy and definition.

Briefly explain the mandates of three federal laws that have an impact on the education of learners with disabilities.

Describe the personnel involved and function of the members of a quality motor development team.

Describe the six levels of involvement in a parent/school/community partnership and give examples of each.

List inexpensive equipment that can be used in the physical education program for children with and without disabilities.

ADAPTED PHYSICAL EDUCATION

Adapted physical education is usually, but not always, aligned administratively with special education, rather than the physical education department. This creates a huge problem for the adapted physical educator and, more important, for the child, because 83.4 percent of our children with disabilities receive their physical education instruction within the general physical education program.[4] While general physical educators are responsible for the education of children with and without disabilities, the special education department controls the finances. Hence, decisions regarding personnel, particularly paraprofessionals, are made by the special education department.

In a large school district or large special education cooperative, one member of the adapted physical education staff may be designated the lead teacher or department chair. This person will make decisions regarding the roles and assignments of the other adapted physical education staff members. This person is also directly accountable for the activities of the staff and reports to his or her immediate supervisor.

In small school districts, the principal determines what will occur in the school, and those decisions depend on the understanding that person has, as well as the resources that are available. If the principal is knowledgeable about the special education laws, an adapted physical educator may be sought to come to the district once or twice a month to test students and suggest modifications to the general physical educator. If the school district has access to a special service cooperative, the center may have an adapted physical educator on staff to provide testing, consulting, and workshops throughout the districts served by the center.

One of the major responsibilities of the adapted physical educator is to communicate regularly and effectively with his or her direct supervisor. Frequently, neither the director of special education nor the building principal understands the potential and importance of a quality adapted physical education program in the education of learners with disabilities. The adapted physical educator must be a vocal and tenacious advocate for the learner with a disability and for the field. The teacher should inform these persons about the requirements of the law and share legal updates and current articles describing state-of-the-art practices in adapted physical education.

The single most effective way to communicate the worth of the program is through demonstrated student results, based on measurable, observable outcomes and through student and parent testimony regarding the effectiveness of the program.

Timely information that clarifies the goals and objectives of the program and describes the "before and after" status of students served in adapted physical education may help the administrator understand the value of the program. If possible, the administrator should be invited to attend a class or an activity that demonstrates quality programming to meet individual student needs and highlights the accomplishments of the students. It is vital that the adapted physical educator secure the support of district administrators and building principals if the program is to receive its share of district and school resources and if the adapted physical educator is to be considered a vital and integral part of the instructional team within the district.[10] The director of the adapted physical education program and its teachers are responsible for meeting federal, state, and local mandates regarding the provision of a quality physical education program for all children with disabilities who need a specially designed program in order to learn and grow. The components of a quality adapted physical education program manual include the following:

Philosophy

Definition of adapted physical education

Goals and objectives

Criteria for eligibility

Referral process

Assessment procedures

IEP

Continuum of services, placement, and personnel

Service delivery models

Accountability

Philosophy

Under the expert direction of April Tripp, Ph.D., the Baltimore County public schools developed a model adapted physical education program. Following is their philosophy:

The philosophy of Baltimore County Public Schools (BCPS) is to provide all students, including those with disabilities, with a quality physical education program. BCPS must ensure that students with disabilities have access to a program that includes the learning goals stated in the Essential Curriculum for physical education based on the Maryland State Department of Education Framework and Learning Goals. If special services are required to assist students with disabilities to master the Essential Curriculum or to meet individualized physical education goals, these services should be provided under the guidance of an adapted physical education consultant. Instructional methods, settings, materials and time should be modified to create as optimal a learning environment as is provided for students without disabilities. Students with disabilities should be provided with fitness assessment and the opportunity to benefit from a community-based, health-related physical education program.[2]

This philosophical statement is in keeping with that of the National Association of State Directors of Special Education, which described the aim of physical education curriculum/programs as being to develop physical fitness and sport skills that can be used to maintain one's health and allow one to participate in recreational activities.[15]

Definition of Adapted Physical Education

Adapted physical education is the art and science of developing, implementing, and monitoring a carefully designed physical education *instructional* program for a learner with a disability, based on a comprehensive assessment, to give the learner the skills necessary for a lifetime of rich leisure, recreation, and sport experiences to enhance physical fitness and wellness.

Goals and Objectives

The goals of the adapted physical education program should be consistent with those established by the state education agency for every learner who participates in physical education. This is critical, given the current emphasis on the inclusion of learners with disabilities in the general physical education program. (See Table 2-1.) The Baltimore

Table 2-1	Responsibilities of the Adapted Physical Educator

- Assessment and comprehensive evaluation within physical and motor development
- Development of the individual physical education plan (IPEP)
- Implementation of the IPEP
- Representation of adapted physical education at individual education program (IEP) or multidisciplinary team meetings
- Provision of direct instructional services to children with disabilities, when appropriate
- Consultation with general physical education and general special education personnel
- Consultation with community-based leisure, recreation, and sport facilities managers regarding program and facility accessibility
- Curriculum development and/or revision
- Communication with parents
- Management of budget
- Purchase and maintenance of equipment

County public schools have developed objectives for their program that can be used as a model by others:

1. To create a partnership between physical educators and APE consultants for providing quality physical education instruction to students with disabilities
2. To value and address diversity in psychomotor skills for students with disabilities in physical education
3. To accept students with disabilities as individuals with unique psychomotor needs
4. To develop maximum psychomotor potential for students with disabilities
5. To expand positive learning opportunities and results in physical education for students with disabilities
6. To provide ongoing skill development and support to students with disabilities in physical education
7. To explore and provide adaptations that will allow students with disabilities to be full participants in physical education[2]

Criteria for Eligibility

The specific criteria for eligibility for adapted physical education remain confusing and inconsistent from school district to school district and state to state. The local education agency must determine the eligibility criteria based on the interpretation of federal law by the state education agency. Eligibility criteria may be established based on the extent of the learner's gross motor delay, age-related performance, or score on a given standardized instrument. A few states have identified specific criteria for eligibility in adapted physical education. These "stars" include California, Louisiana, Minnesota, and Wisconsin.

The lack of criteria in other states makes it virtually impossible for itinerant adapted physical education consultants to serve learners with disabilities in the public schools consistently and fairly. Individuals hired to conduct comprehensive adapted physical education analyses are asked to determine if the student assessed "qualifies" for adapted physical education; without specific criteria, this decision is based solely on the experience and judgment of the individual consultant.[10]

However, in the event federal legislation (S1276) is enacted, states would be required to test for physical education performance. This initiative would require states to have statewide physical education standards and administer tests that are consistent with the standards. Louisiana has physical education standards that are based on the National Physical Education standards developed by NASPE. (See Chapter 1.)

Referral Process

Referral, assessment, and placement procedures are the very foundation of the adapted physical education program and are vital to ensure that each eligible student receives the appropriate intervention, an individualized education program. The instructional model for adapted physical education follows these steps:

1. Accumulation of information about the student
2. Screening and, with parental consent, a comprehensive assessment
3. Development of a program to meet the student's individual needs as part of the IEP/multidisciplinary team
4. Determination of the instructional modifications necessary to meet the learner's educational needs
5. Consideration of placement
6. Implementation of the program
7. Monitoring of progress

See Chapter 3, Table 3-4, for the Denton Independent School District prereferral and referral form.

Assessment Procedures

It is vital that the adapted physical education assessment be completed by a trained professional who has extensive experience in assessment in physical and motor development (see Table 2-2). Because it is unusual for a general physical educator to have specific training in the comprehensive assessment that identifies gross motor delays and their causes, many school districts hire adapted physical education specialists specifically for assessing and recommending an appropriate instructional program. For more information regarding assessment procedures, refer to Chapter 3.

Table 2-2	Assessment Skills of the Adapted Physical Educator

The carefully trained adapted physical educator has unique skills to assess and evaluate gross motor performance within the following areas:
- Reflex and equilibrium development
- Sensory stimulation and discrimination skills
- Sensorimotor integration
- Locomotor and nonlocomotor competency
- Play, game, leisure, recreation, and sport-specific motor patterns
- Physical and motor fitness

IEP

The IEP is the cornerstone of the educational process that ties together the parent and data from the comprehensive assessment and information from the child's classroom and physical education teacher, with a specific program to intervene to meet goals and objectives specially designed for the student. Chapter 4 is devoted to the IEP.

Continuum of Services, Placement, and Personnel

A continuum of instructional options is the basis of a district's ability to provide physical education services within the least restrictive environment. Information regarding the continuum of instructional and placement options is included in Chapter 6. The ways in which a multidisciplinary motor team can contribute to program development and delivery are discussed later in this chapter. Related service personnel roles are described in Chapter 4.

Service Delivery Models

The San Francisco Unified School District has developed a continuum of service delivery models, according to which adapted physical education can be any of the following:

1. *Direct services:* Designates direct physical education services provided by an adapted physical education specialist to students who have special needs, as indicated by an assessment and evaluation of motor skills performance and other areas of need

2. *Collaboration:* Designates services provided and/or implemented jointly with other school staff members to assist students in meeting individualized goals and objectives through all of the physical education options described. Services may be provided in a way intended to lead students progressively through various types of physical education options or in a way that combines elements of various options to meet the students' individual needs

3. *Consultation:* Designates assistance given to parents, general and special education teachers, or general physical education teachers who conduct the general, modified, or specially designed physical education program options. Assistance may include suggestions for individualizing instruction by making modifications or adaptations, and identification of supplementary devices or teaching aids to facilitate skill development by individuals with exceptional needs.[19]

Accountability

The adapted physical educator must be accountable for the delivery of appropriate education services. Taxpayer scrutiny regarding the use of funds in education has, particularly, highlighted the need for accountability. In some states, federal and state funding of the local special education program is based on the number of documented contact hours between the professional and the student. Contact hours are usually documented with a service log. Service logs are used to record daily involvement in the adapted physical education program. Those logs are routinely checked by the adapted physical educator's supervisor. A sample of such a log is provided in Table 2-3. In addition to a daily log that accounts for time and student contact, the adapted physical educator, like other teachers in the district, may be responsible for lesson plans that may have to be submitted to a building principal or to the lead teacher. Adapted physical education teachers with large caseloads (more than 50 students) will find it impossible to manage the paperwork, including daily lesson plans, without the use of computer technology. The teacher who can generate daily lesson plans using a basic word-processing system and a prepared template will save hours daily. The procedure greatly simplifies the process of writing plans because basic information required on every plan does not have to be written by hand. In addition, generating the plans on the computer allows the teacher to readily trace the progress of each student within each class. A sample lesson plan is included in Table 2-4.

Table 2-3	**Sample Daily Service Log**		
Date	**Service**	**Student(s) Served/School**	**Time**
2/10	Direct service—teaching[*]	EC Class/Adams	8:00–9:00
	Direct service—teaching[*]	S/Ph Class/Adams	9:00–10:00
	Travel to Cabell		10:00–10:15
	Motor/fitness assessment	J. Flores/Cabell	10:15–12:00
	Lunch/travel to White		12:00–12:45
	Consultation—PE teacher	K. Black/White	12:45–1:30
	Travel to office		1:30–1:45
	Written report	J. Flores/Cabell	1:45–3:15
	Prepare for IEP meeting		3:15–3:45
2/11	Direct service—teaching[*]	EC Class/Foster	8:00–8:45
	Direct service—teaching[*]	HI Class/Foster	9:00–9:45
	Travel to Cabell		9:50–10:00
	IEP meeting	J. Flores/Cabell	10:30–12:00
	Travel/lunch		12:00–12:45
	Direct service—teaching	S/Ph Class/Grant	1:00–1:45
	Travel to community pool		1:45–2:00
	Direct service	MD students/district	2:15–3:30
	Swimming instruction		

*See attached lesson plans.

Table 2-4	**Daily Lesson Plan**
Teacher:	Buddy Nelson
Class:	Preschool Program for Children with Disabilities
School:	Walnut Hill Elementary School
Date:	December 7, 2008
Warm-up:	"If You're Happy and You Know it"
Rhythms:	"What a Miracle," "Swing, Shake, Twist, Stretch," "Flick a Fly"
Equilibrium activities:	Magic Carpet Ride, Crazy Sidewalk, Freeze
Relaxation:	Pretend to be a rag doll and a sleepy kitten

The Office of Special Education Programs has developed a system for monitoring states for accountability. "Indicators" that will be measured are performance outcomes for children, family involvement, effective transition, and enhanced social development through positive behavioral support methods.[22]

SERVICE DELIVERY IN ADAPTED PHYSICAL EDUCATION

The basic criteria for an adapted physical education program have been discussed previously. The strategies used to ensure that a student receives the instructional services he or she deserves vary greatly, depending on a number of variables:

• The number of students served by the school district
• The location and geographical size of the school district
• The administrative hierarchy
• The administrative commitment to adapted physical education
• Parental interest in and commitment to adapted physical education

- The number of trained/certified adapted physical educators hired to teach within the district
- The caseload

Few school districts have actually embraced the intent of P.L. 94-142 and the Individuals with Disabilities Education Act to address the physical education needs of learners with disabilities. One example, however, is the Jefferson County Parish outside New Orleans, Louisiana, which boasts a staff of more than 35 adapted physical educators, 5 hired solely to do comprehensive adapted physical education assessments. These adapted physical educators are able to address the physical education needs of their students with disabilities to prepare them for quality leisure, recreation, physical fitness, and sport experiences throughout the lifetime. Unfortunately, this is the exception, not the norm. Because few school districts have actually made a commitment to adapted physical education within the curriculum, the strategy for delivering services varies dramatically. See Table 2-5 for a continuum of service delivery strategies in adapted physical education.

Increasingly, the well-trained adapted physical educator (CAPE or state-certified professional) finds himself or herself thrust into the role of consultant, even though his or her preservice training focused on the provision of instructional services to learners with disabilities.[3] See Table 2-6 to consider the roles and responsibilities of the adapted physical education consultant. It also becomes increasingly important that the general physical educator be able to take advantage of the services of the APE consultant. Few teachers have received adequate training to prepare them for their collaborative roles. See Table 2-7 for specific suggestions for the general physical educator to maximize time spent with the adapted physical education consultant.

INTERACTION WITH OTHER SPECIAL EDUCATION PERSONNEL

Within the larger structure of the school district and local campus, the effective adapted physical educator

Table 2-5	**Service Delivery Options**

Required educational service by a CAPE or state-certified adapted physical educator

Assessment and IEP development by a CAPE or state-certified adapted physical educator who serves as a regular consultant to the general physical educator; instruction by general physical educator

Assessment and IEP development by a CAPE or state-certified adapted physical educator who serves as an occasional consultant to the general physical educator; instruction by general physical educator

Assessment and IEP development by a general physical educator or special educator with occasional review by a CAPE or state-certified adapted physical educator; instruction by general physical educator

Table 2-6	**Roles and Responsibilities of the APE Consultant[3,10]**

- Complete a comprehensive adapted physical education assessment.
- Make specific program recommendations.
- Work with the IEP/multidisciplinary team to develop an individual physical education program.
- Consider accommodations/modifications of the following instructional variables (refer to Chapter 6).
  - Curriculum
  - Assessment
  - Extent and nature of program participation
  - Instructional (personnel) support
  - Teaching style
  - Grading
  - Equipment
  - Management of behavior
- Work with the general physical educator.
  - Identify needs.
  - Develop a plan for addressing the needs.
  - Develop a system for accountability for both the consultant and the general physical educator/special educator.
  - Monitor progress.

Table 2-7	Strategies for the General Physical Educator to Maximize Use of the APE Consultant[10]

- Make sure the APE consultant feels as if your gymnasium/school is his or her second home.
- Give the APE consultant a place to work (if possible, a phone) in your office or gymnasium.
- Put the APE consultant's scheduled visit on the bulletin board.
- Communicate with the APE consultant regularly via e-mail or campus mail.
- If the APE consultant deserves a "thanks," do so regularly with cards, notes, or letters, with copies to the consultant's supervisor.
- Advise the APE consultant of upcoming IEP meetings (if the special education staff has advised you of the upcoming IEP meetings).
- Invite the APE consultant to PTA presentations, schoolwide play days, holiday celebrations, etc.
- Be sure to introduce the APE consultant to key building personnel.
- Be prepared for the consultant's visit with specific questions.
- When necessary, loan the APE consultant equipment needed for assessment/intervention.
- Regularly complete service logs or portfolio notes for the APE consultant.
- Videotape student performance or behavior, so that the consultant has all the information needed to intervene.

works in close cooperation with other direct service providers and with related service personnel. The most crucial interactions are with the learner's general physical educator, special education teacher(s), and related service personnel. The relationship between the adapted physical educator and the physical therapist, occupational therapist, and recreation therapist, and in some districts the musical therapist, is particularly crucial, given the direct concern of each professional regarding the child's motor efficiency. Related service personnel play an important role in physical education programs for children with disabilities. In addition to providing services that will help the children benefit from the program, they may also enhance the program by

- Communicating directly with medical personnel
- Identifying students with special motor needs
- Making APE referrals of students with special motor problems
- Recommending specific exercises and activities
- Providing computer or assistive technology necessary for the student to learn auxiliary skills in physical education—for example, playing computer golf; indeed, there are virtual reality computer programs that allow students with limited movement potential to rock climb, whitewater raft, sky dive, and participate in other leisure, recreation, sport, and fitness activities

Professionals involved in the education of a learner with a disability must share their knowledge, expertise, and technical skill not only with the learner but also with each other. The most efficient way to ensure cooperation among the adapted physical educator and related service personnel is to formalize the relationship by forming a multidisciplinary motor team.[20] The use of a multidisciplinary team to provide services is an excellent way to ensure communication among service providers. The members of the interdisciplinary motor development team should include the adapted physical educator, the general physical educator, the physical therapist, the occupational therapist, and the recreation therapist. The speech therapist may also function as part of the motor development team. The multidisciplinary process is, however, complex and there are many barriers:[9]

- Philosophical differences
- Lack of time for collaborative meetings
- Lack of training regarding collaborative skills, including communication and listening skills; this appears to be a critical obstacle in the collaborative process; increasingly, undergraduate programs in adapted physical education are trying to ensure their students are trained to collaborate with other professionals[13]

Common functions of members of motor development teams made up of adapted physical educators, physical therapists, occupational therapists, and recreation therapists can include the following:

1. *To screen and evaluate students with functional and/or educational problems to determine needs for special services.* See Table 2-8, a motor team screening form developed in District 19, Oregon. This screening instrument gives direction to physical educators, special educators, and general educators who may need to refer children to the motor development team. Once the members of the motor development team receive the information, they decide which specialist should serve as the lead member of the evaluation process. That lead person initiates and organizes a subsequent full-scale gross motor evaluation, which reduces the amount of duplicated effort. For example, both the occupational therapist and the adapted physical educator routinely use the Bruininks-Oseretsky Test of Motor Proficiency. As a member of the motor development team, either the adapted physical educator or the occupational therapist may administer the test and share the results with other professionals on the team.

2. *To develop an IEP or ITP, as part of the total multidisciplinary team, to specifically address the child's motor needs.* Members of the motor development team develop an IEP or ITP that addresses the needs of the child.

3. *To implement an intervention program that facilitates learning.* Once the IEP or ITP is approved by the entire IEP/multidisciplinary team, the members of the motor development team implement the intervention program. Like the assessment, the intervention program is cooperative. Each member of the team addresses the child's motor needs. Instead of limiting focus to one component of motor development, all professionals

on the team share responsibility for implementing the program or designate one service provider to represent the team.

4. *To manage and supervise motor programs.* Each member of the motor development team assumes a specific responsibility for the management and supervision of the program. If a team leader has been designated, each member of the motor development team will communicate directly with that person regarding the student's progress.[11,12]

5. *To document service delivery.* Careful documentation of services delivered is a vital part of the process. Each member of the team must be accountable not only to the child served but also to each other. If it is to function effectively, the motor development team demands professional accountability. This is often done by using a service provider log. (See Table 2-9, a sample of a motor development team service provider log.) If the IEP/multidisciplinary team agrees to collaboratively address one or more objectives on the learner's IEP or ITP, this type of log is vital for communication among professional members of the motor development team. The log may also serve as crucial documentation of the services provided during the annual review of the child's progress.

6. *To cooperatively provide or create resources that help other professionals meet the motor needs of students with disabilities.* Members of the motor development team have specialized knowledge that should be shared with educators who are in daily contact with the learners. In some school districts or special service cooperatives, the members of the motor development team have created motor development handbooks for use by teachers in early childhood classrooms, self-contained special education classrooms, or the general physical education. In others, the members of the motor development team have developed curricula for use by special educators in prevocational preparation programs.

Table 2-8	District 19 Motor Team Screening Form

Name: _____ DOB _____

Date of referral: _____ Grade: _____ Teacher: _____

School: _____

Specialist: _____ Physician _____

Was student retained? _____ Yes _____ No

PE time: _____ Recess time _____

Current disabling conditions: _____
_____

Does the student use adaptive equipment (braces, crutches, etc.)? _____
_____

Please check those items that have been observed.

Gross Motor

___Lacks age-appropriate strength and endurance
___Difficulty with run, jump, hop, or skip compared with others his or her age
___Stiff and awkward in his or her movements
___Clumsy, seems not to know how to move body, bumps into things, falls out of chair
___Demonstrates mixed dominance
___Reluctant to participate in playground activities

___Play pattern is inappropriate for age group (does not play, plays by self, plays beside but not with, stereotypical) (circle one)
___Has postural deviations
___Complains of pain during physical activities
___Demonstrates unusual wear patterns on shoes and/or clothing

Fine Motor

___Poor desk posture (slumps, leans on arm, head too close to work) (circle)
___Difficulty drawing, coloring, copying, cutting
___Poor pencil grasp and/or drops pencil frequently
___Lines drawn are light, wobbly, too faint, or too dark

___Breaks pencil often
___Lack of well-established dominance after six years of age
___Student has difficulty using both hands together (stabilization of paper during cutting and paper activities)

Self-Care Skills

___Difficulty with fasteners (buttons, zippers, snaps, shoe tying, lacing) (circle)
___Wears clothes backwards or inside out; appears messy
___Difficulty putting clothes on or taking them off

___Difficulty with the eating process (opening packages, feeding self, spilling, using utensils) (circle)
___Oral-motor problems (drools, difficulty chewing, swallowing, difficulty drinking from straws) (circle)
___Needs assistance with toileting (wiping, flushing, replacing underwear/clothes) (circle)

Academic (Check Those Areas Presenting Problems)

___Distractibility
___Following directions
___Hyperactivity
___Memory deficit
___Difficulty naming body parts

___Slow work
___Restlessness
___Organizing work
___Finishing tasks
___Attention deficit

(Continued)

Table 2-8	(Continued)

Tactile Sensation

___Seems to withdraw from touch
___Craves touch
___Tends to wear coat when not needed; will not allow shirtsleeves pulled up
___Has trouble keeping hands to self, will poke or push other children
___Apt to touch everything he or she sees ("learns through fingers")

___Dislikes being hugged or cuddled
___Avoids certain textures of foods
___Dislikes arts-and-crafts activities involving different textures (clay, finger paints)
___Complains of numbness, tingling, and other abnormal sensations

Auditory Perception

___Appears overly sensitive to sounds
___Talks excessively
___Likes to make loud noises
___Has difficulty making self understood

___Appears to have difficulty understanding teacher/paraprofessional/peers
___Tends to repeat directions to self

Visual Perception

___Difficulty discriminating colors and shapes doing puzzles
___Letter and/or number reversals after first grade
___Difficulty with eye-tracking (following objects with eyes, eyes and head move together)
___Difficulty copying designs, numbers, or letters

___Has and wears/doesn't wear glasses
___Difficulty transcribing from blackboard or book to paper
___Difficulty with eye-hand or eye-foot coordination (catching, striking, kicking)

Emotional

___Does not accept changes in routine easily
___Becomes easily frustrated
___Acts out behaviorally; difficulty getting along with others
___Tends to be impulsive, heedless, accident prone
___Easier to handle in large group, small group, or individually (circle)

___Marked mood variations, outbursts or tantrums
___Marked out-of-seat behavior
___Noncompliant
___Unstable home situation
___Notable self-stimulatory behaviors

Additional Concerns

Assigned to: _____

Date received: _____   Evaluation date: _____

7. *To conduct cooperative in-service motor development training for other school personnel, parents, and volunteers.* Professionals on the motor development team share functions yet retain professional integrity and responsibility for the motor development and motor proficiency of the child served.[20] Each has a unique contribution to students and professionals who provide direct or related instructional services to students with disabilities. The traditional emphasis by each professional who may function as a member of a motor development team is illustrated in Figure 2-1. It is important to note that this model is not restrictive. The intent of the motor development team is to share professional competency, judgment, and expertise.

Table 2-9	Motor Team Service Provider Log for Adam

One of the program recommendations, based on Adam's comprehensive adapted physical education assessment, was an exercise program to strengthen abdominal muscles and extensor, adductor, and abductor hip muscles.

Date	Service Provider	Child's Performance
11/12	C. Candler, OTR	Performed 15 abdominal curls while seated on a physiotherapy ball, feet flat on floor
11/14	H. Unger, PT	Performed 10 long-sitting, hip abduction exercises, using a medium theraband for resistance
11/15	B. Huettig, CAPE	Swam 100 yards using a "lifeguard" front crawl with his head out of the water
11/19	C. Candler, OTR	Performed 17 abdominal curls while seated on a physiotherapy ball, feet flat on floor
11/20	B. Huettig, CAPE	Swam 125 yards using a "lifeguard" front crawl with his head out of the water

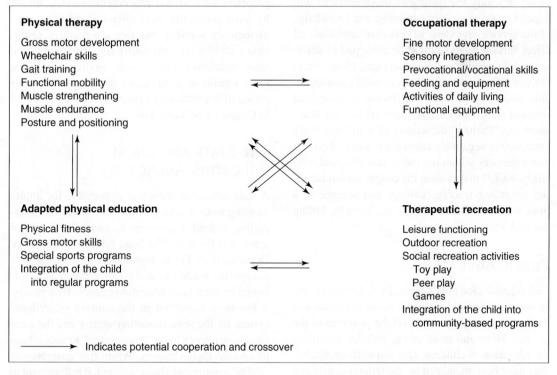

Figure 2-1   Motor Development Team

From Sugars A: *The adapted physical educator as a member of the motor development team*, TAHPERD State Convention, Lubbock, TX, 1990.

This type of model for the delivery of services to children with motor deficits is particularly important in school districts and cooperatives unable to locate sufficient numbers of certified, trained professional staff. For example, if a school district is unable to hire and retain a licensed physical therapist as part of the staff, it may be necessary for other professionals to implement the program designed by a contracted therapist. In school districts with limited adapted physical education teachers, it is vital that the general physical educator who provides direct service be provided information necessary to deliver appropriate educational services. Physical education services must be provided to students with disabilities enrolled in public education.

Though federal law makes it infinitely clear that "lack of money" or "lack of personnel" is not an adequate reason for failure to provide the services, in reality the quality of those services will depend on the availability, training, and knowledge of the service providers. In best-case scenarios, all direct service providers will be equipped to determine and provide the needed services. However, in the vast majority of schools, personnel knowledgeable about the physical and motor development needs of students with disabilities are limited. It appears the "Puritan" dichotomy of mind and body continues to negatively affect the priority of educational services within the public schools. And, certainly, NCLB makes clear the congressional priorities regarding reading, writing, and science at a time when childhood obesity is, literally, killing our children.

PUBLIC EDUCATION

Federal education policy typically reflects congressional priorities and interests; those priorities and interests may or may not reflect the priorities of the people. More and more often, policies regarding the education of children with and without disabilities have been mandated by the federal courts and challenged within the state and federal judicial system. The U.S. Department of Education is challenged with the responsibility of interpreting

federal legislation and helping the states implement such policies. Within the Department of Education are several subagencies responsible for setting the agenda and providing direction for each state. The Office of Special Education and Rehabilitative Services (OSERS) has the primary responsibility for setting the agenda and providing direction regarding the delivery of educational services for students with disabilities.

THE ROLE OF LITIGATION IN DETERMINING PRACTICE

After laws are enacted, court cases frequently determine the intention of the law. Court cases have determined what is meant by a free, appropriate public education, what is meant by an appropriate educational setting, what constitutes an appropriate educational setting, what constitutes an appropriate educational placement, what is meant by *least restrictive environment,* and what supplementary services and aids are required to enable a child with a disability to participate in the least restrictive educational environment. The more significant court cases that impact the education of learners with disabilities were presented in Chapter 1 in Table 1-6.

THE STATE AND LOCAL EDUCATION AGENCY

A state education agency is responsible for implementing federal policy at the state level and interpreting federal legislation to meet the needs of learners in the state. The State Education Agency or Department of Public Instruction within each state has specific guidelines and policies that must be followed by each local education agency. Historically, it has been important in the nation's educational system for the state education agency and the local education agency to be "empowered" to decide how to educate their children. While this guarantee of "rights" continues to be significant, it is important to note that there are states and local education agencies that do not honor or recognize the rights and the needs of children with disabilities and their families or hold them as priorities. When this is the case, it is the responsibility of the courts to interpret laws.

Typically, the state education agency is responsible for decisions regarding the instructional standards and the strategies that will be used to evaluate whether students served within the local education agency are meeting those standards. A local education agency or education cooperative, a cluster of small school districts without sufficient resources to provide education for their children independently, is responsible for implementing state policy and interpreting that policy to meet the needs of learners within the district or cooperative. It is the responsibility of the school to contribute to the fullest possible development of each student entrusted to its care. This is a basic tenet of our democratic structure. The state of Arkansas is an example of a state government initiating programs to address the growing problem of obesity. Legislation was passed to ensure that all school children were measured for obesity and then provided follow up programs of physical activity and good nutritional programs to confront the obesity.[1] Similar state initiatives are underway in Georgia, Connecticut, Delaware, and Maryland.[16] The notion of "home rule" is critical in the education of children within the United States. Since the founding of this country, citizens in individual communities have long held the belief that it is their responsibility and their right to educate their children. In most school districts, the responsibility for educating the district's children is placed in the hands of the members of a school board. In most communities, individuals who serve on this school board are elected officials, responsible to the voters for their performance. The school board is responsible for implementing state policy and interpreting that policy to meet the needs of learners within the particular school district. There are efforts to address the issue of childhood obesity at local levels. For instance, prior to seeking public funding for programs to combat obesity, the San Francisco Unified School District assessed public opinions about (1) student and parental concern about obesity, (2) staff willingness to participate in change, (3) community interest in participation, (4) program implementation

capacity, and (5) community and business concerns. This resulted in city funding of a proposition that was passed to promote healthy lifestyle practices and programs.[23]

The primary administrator within the school district is usually called the Superintendent of Schools or the Chief Executive Officer. The responsibilities of the superintendent or chief executive officer include the assurance of a quality education for all children. This individual, particularly in a large district, often has associate superintendents, who help with quality control and assist with decisions regarding student services, budget, personnel, and facilities and equipment. Within that structure, historically, an individual has been designated as the Director of Special Education. That person is responsible for implementing school board policy as it relates to students who are in need of special education services in order to be successful learners and, ultimately, productive and capable citizens.

Site-Based Management

Site-based management is a strategy to increase school effectiveness by allowing the major players (e.g., the principal, teachers, parents, students, and community members) more control over policies and procedures that affect their school. The potential beauty of site-based management is that the very people responsible for the quality of learning are held directly accountable for that learning and are given greater decision-making authority in that process. However, the site-based management process is only as good as the building leader(s).

If the school has a visionary principal, virtually any management style will be effective in bringing about significant learning outcomes for children with and without disabilities.

The physical educator and the adapted physical educator can and must ask to be a part of the school-based team. Far too often, excellent physical educators do their jobs quietly and without fanfare in the gymnasium without recognition. In this day of limited budgets and increased emphasis on the "academic

Table 2-10	Unique Contributions of the Physical Educator in a Site-Based System

The physical educator, adapted or general physical educator, is uniquely trained to do the following:
- Lead site-based committees or teams in cooperative learning activities based on the "New Games" philosophy
- Develop campus-based wellness programs for teachers, staff, students, and their parents
- Help develop a before- or after-school program to keep children in a safe and nurturing environment while parents work
- Assume leadership of a committee designed to develop positive relationships between community members and the school

subjects," the physical educator/ adapted physical educator must be vocal, visible, and strident regarding the needs of children with and without disabilities. (See Table 2-10.)

School-Family Partnerships

Epstein[8] has developed a model for the development of school/family/community partnerships to best serve the children within any given community. She has identified the following six types of involvement of families and community members within the schools:

Type 1: Parenting. Help all families establish home environments to support children as students.

Type 2: Communicating. Design effective forms of school-to-home communications about school programs and children's progress.

Type 3: Volunteering. Recruit and organize parent help and support.

Type 4: Learning at home. Provide information and ideas to families about how to help students at home with homework and other curriculum-related activities, decisions, and planning.

Type 5: Decision making. Include parents in school decisions, developing parent leaders and representatives.

Type 6: Collaborating with the community. Identify and integrate resources and services from the community to strengthen school programs, family practices, and student learning and development.

The following are suggestions for the regular physical educator and adapted physical educator for increasing involvement in each of the six types of involvement:

Type 1: Parenting
- Provide parents and members of the learner's extended family with information that will help them develop reasonable expectations regarding the motor development of a student with a developmental delay or disability.
- Provide parents and members of the learner's extended family with information regarding developmentally appropriate play (e.g., the child needs to learn to engage in cooperative play before he or she can engage in competitive experiences with success).
- Model appropriate play and motor intervention strategies for parents (e.g., toss a ball in a horizontal path when a student is learning to catch, so that the child is not overwhelmed by trying to track an object moving through horizontal and vertical planes).
- Share information with parents about strategies for making inexpensive equipment for the student to play with in the home (e.g., an old mattress or an old tire covered with a secured piece of carpeting makes a wonderful trampoline).
- Share information about community resources and opportunities for students with disabilities to participate in play; games; and leisure, recreation, and sport activities.
- Provide family support and information regarding securing health services for the student.
- Serve as an advocate for the parent and family.

Type 2: Communicating

- Use your computer to generate a physical education and/or adapted physical education newsletter or ask for a column or space in the school newspaper.
- Develop an adapted physical education Web site for the school and/or district to communicate with parents and community members.
- Send home brief notes to communicate with the student's family, such as the computer-generated certificate shown in Figure 2-2.
- Call a parent to praise the student's progress. Far too often, teachers communicate with parents only when there is a problem.
- Be an active participant in regularly scheduled parent-teacher conferences. Communicate to parents a willingness to meet at other times as well.
- Write positive comments on student report cards.

Type 3: Volunteering

Encourage parents to serve as the following:

- An assistant in classes
- A director or an assistant in before- and after school recreation, intramural, or sports programs

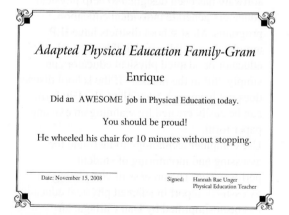

Adapted Physical Education Family-Gram

Enrique

Did an AWESOME job in Physical Education today.

You should be proud!

He wheeled his chair for 10 minutes without stopping.

Date: November 15, 2008   Signed: Hannah Rae Unger
                                            Physical Education Teacher

Figure 2-2 A Customized Certificate Is an Excellent Way to Communicate with a Student's Family

- An assistant coach
- A director or an assistant on school play day
- The editor or publisher of the newsletter
- A parent-to-parent trainer
- A raffle organizer to raise money for equipment
- An assistant playground supervisor
- A clerical assistant to generate certificates, progress charts, etc.

Type 4: Learning at Home

- Provide information to parents regarding curriculum and activities required at each grade level.
- Provide information to parents with strategies for helping the learner develop the motor skills necessary to participate in play; games; and leisure, recreation, and sport activities; include information regarding the development and maintenance of physical fitness.
- Demonstrate age-appropriate activities that parents can use with groups of children at a park or in an open area within their apartment or project complex.
- Provide a calendar for parents that helps them follow unit themes and special activities.

Type 5: Decision Making

- Invite parent participation as a member of the site-based school committee.
- Invite parent participation in a subcommittee of the Parent-Teacher Association/Organization (PTA/PTO) that addresses the physical education/adapted physical education program.
- In districts where there is a special education advisory committee, ensure that a parent with a commitment to physical education/adapted physical education is on that committee.

Type 6: Collaborating with the Community

- As the physical educator or adapted physical educator, ask to serve on boards or committees of community recreation and/or sports organizations.

- Develop a collaborative physical education or recreation program to meet the needs of learners within the community, using shared facilities, shared equipment, and, if possible, shared personnel.
- Recruit community personnel to help develop and build playgrounds for the schools. Particularly in large, urban districts, playgrounds are often nonexistent or antiquated.
- Encourage older learners to provide service within the community as coaches and recreation leaders.
- Invite the parents and other relatives of children into the school to teach games, sports, and dances of their country of origin. (See Table 2-11.)

The role of the physical educator and adapted physical educator in the provision of adapted physical education services to children with disabilities whose parents choose to educate them in the home has yet to be examined in depth. Clearly, there are significant interpersonal skills that an educator must develop and use when interacting with family members in their home.[18]

Table 2-11	The School as Part of the Extended Family

Following are strategies for enhancing the family-school partnership:

- Find out what the parents really want from the school. What "outcomes" do they expect after their children receive educational services?
- Encourage many different types of parental involvement in the school, based on the comfort level of the parents.[8]
- Make communications with parents positive. Unfortunately, all too often, parents are contacted by the school only when their child is in trouble.
- Create parent-involvement opportunities that are sensitive to parents' work schedules, time constraints, needs for child care, etc.[8]
- Find and develop a small room, designated for the parents, that has child development information, computer/Internet access, access to a printer, etc.

COMPUTER TECHNOLOGY AND THE PHYSICAL EDUCATOR/ADAPTED PHYSICAL EDUCATOR

There are a number of ways physical educators and adapted physical educators can use the computer and the Internet to enhance the performance of learners with and without disabilities in their classes:

- Promote physical education classes and activities via a Web page.[14]
- Post student achievements, accomplishments, and awards on the Web.
- Conduct sporting events with learners from all over the world.[7] Have a track and field competition, with specified metric events, between physical education classes in Rosholt, Wisconsin, USA, and Perth, Australia.
- Assign students to gain information via the Web, rather than using more traditional learning strategies. For example, they can gain information regarding the history of sport (Negro Baseball Leagues, www.blackbaseball.com), rules, equipment, sport organizations, techniques, etc.
- Use computer technology to generate and maintain IEPs, IFSPs, or ITPs. Computer software has been designed to help physical educators generate individual education programs. Most school districts have IEP templates available, so that the physical educator or adapted physical educator can simply "fill in the blanks." If the school district does not have such a template, the IEP form can be easily created by scanning an existing paper form.
- Use computer technology to facilitate the assessing and monitoring of student performance. The process of completing an assessment report in adapted physical education has been simplified by Dan Cariaga, an accomplished adapted physical educator with the San Luis Obispo County, California, Student Services Division. He has developed a

computer-based system that converts raw data on several assessment tools, provided by the physical educator or adapted physical educator, into standardized scores and assessment reports appropriate for presentation to the IEP/multidisciplinary committee.[5] He also has developed software that includes a series of goals and objectives that can be used to develop the physical education IEP. Both can be accessed at http://a-ape.com.

- Organize, monitor, and analyze fitness test data using computer technology. Specific software, such as Fit-N-Dex, is designed to organize, monitor, and analyze fitness test results quickly and efficiently. It allows the physical educator to enter the data and get results on individual student performance, class performance, or grade performance and compare the data year to year, and so on. It allows the physical educator to create reports for students, parents, and administrators that are professional and easy to read. This is available from Cramer Software Group (www.cramersportsmed.com). It is, of course, possible to use a database to develop an individually designed system.
- Use Special Education Management Software to manage data, prepare IEPs and reports, report APE data, and share APE data. This information can be accessed at www.rediker.com/SEMSnet.html.
- Participate in programs such as the President's Physical Fitness Challenge by accessing its home page at www.presidentschallenge.org.
- Use interactive computer programs available on the World Wide Web to study subjects such as human anatomy (www.innerbody.com).
- Use computer software to enhance instruction. Michigan State University has developed an American Sign Language browser that can be used for learning to sign a multitude of words. This information can be accessed at http://commtechlab.mse.edu/sites/aslweb/browser.htm.

- Use computer software to facilitate inclusion. Dr. Peter Downs and Active Australia[6] have created an interactive software program called "Willing and Able: Count Me In," designed to foster inclusion in physical education and sport.
- Encourage learners and their parents to use interactive CD-ROM computer technology to participate in games that encourage the learning of rules, strategy, and technique. These computer games—golf, tennis, football, baseball, and so on—allow even a child with limited movement potential to play with a peer. Programs such as Maniac Sports allow a student who is confined to bed the opportunity to experience hang gliding, mountain climbing, and downhill skiing vicariously. For example, a learner in the last stages of Duchenne muscular dystrophy may have only limited control of one hand. With that hand, the learner can manipulate the joystick.
- Teachers and paraeducators can use physical education and adapted physical education Web sites to improve instruction of learners with disabilities.[17,21]

EQUIPMENT

The physical educator or adapted physical educator is responsible for a great deal within the school community. The physical education teacher who serves children with disabilities in the regular elementary physical education program may wish to supplement basic equipment needed for quality elementary physical education instruction with additional equipment. The following is a list of the basic equipment needed for such a program. This list also represents the basic requirements for an adapted physical education program in a more restricted environment:

a. Wide balance beams or balance boards (6, 8, 10, and 12 inches wide)
b. Oversize scooter boards

c. Shoe polish/washable paint for marking floors
d. Plastic hoops
e. Jump ropes
f. Balloons (for children over five years of age who don't mouth equipment)
g. Punch balls and beach balls
h. Balls (assorted sizes, types, textures)
i. Velcro paddles and Velcro balls for catching
j. Wands with ribbons attached
k. Beanbags (including large and heavy beanbags)
l. Huge group parachutes
m. Cage balls
n. Tug of war rope
o. Oversize tennis and badminton racquets
p. Oversize, soft and short, bats
q. Nerf-type soccer balls, footballs, and volleyballs
r. Junior-size balls
s. Height-adjustable equipment
t. Floor and incline mats
u. Carpeted barrels
v. Bells, drums, maracas, etc.

With some ingenuity, the teacher can provide an excellent adapted physical education program for students at the elementary school level with minimum equipment. Play equipment can be made inexpensively. Following are suggestions for inexpensive equipment for use in the physical education program:

a. Rope for skipping, making shapes, jumping over, and climbing under
b. Cardboard boxes to climb in and through, to catch with, and to use as targets (particularly empty refrigerator, television, and washer/dryer boxes)
c. Tape/chalk to make shapes on the floor for moving on, around, and in
d. Half-gallon or gallon plastic jugs for catching, throwing, and knocking over
e. Scrap lumber for balance beams

f. Yarn for yarn balls
g. Carpet squares to skate on, slide on, sit on, and use as targets
h. Old garden hoses to make hula hoops
i. Old ladders to walk on and through
j. Traffic cones for obstacle courses

Equipment for middle and secondary physical education for learners with disabilities is very similar to that used in general physical education. A few special pieces of equipment that may facilitate the performance of learners with disabilities in fitness, leisure, recreation, and sports activities include (a) beepers to attach to targets for the visually impaired/beeper balls; (b) oversize racquets, bats, golf clubs (large heads); (c) basketball standards with return nets; (d) junior size/lightweight balls; (e) portable bowling ramps and balls with retractable handles; (f) goals balls; (g) fluorescent balls; (h) sit/pulk skis; (i) adjustable net standards; and (j) guide ropes with moveable, plastic handles.

The modification of equipment frequently enables individuals with disabilities to participate in leisure, recreation, sport, and physical fitness activities from which they would otherwise be excluded. Entrepreneurs have come to understand that individuals with disabilities are as serious about quality leisure, recreation, sport, and physical fitness activities as individuals without disabilities. Within the past few years, there has been a remarkable growth in the manufacturing of equipment that enhances athletic performance for individuals with and without disabilities. Hundreds of types of shoes can be selected specifically to improve performance in a given activity. There is also a wide variety of sport wheelchairs and modified equipment designed to improve performance in a given activity. There are, for example, specific wheelchairs designed for sprint racing, distance road racing, basketball, tennis, rugby, football, and wilderness trekking.

SUMMARY

The provision of quality adapted physical education services for learners with disabilities requires a carefully designed referral, assessment, and instructional program. These programs reflect "quality services" when there is a cooperative effort between professionals and parents in order to meet the unique needs of the learner.

The physical education teacher and adapted physical education teacher must work together as advocates for a quality program for children with and without disabilities. Clearly, that communication is the most critical in the provision of services.

The quality adapted physical education program requires excellent communication among all involved. Adapted physical educators and general physical educators serving learners with disabilities may have a vital role as a member of a motor development team made up of professionals with a particular commitment to developing skills that involve physical activity for lifelong recreational pursuits.

REVIEW QUESTIONS

1. Explain the relationship between litigation and legislation that has an impact on the education of learners with disabilities.

2. Briefly explain how computer technology can be used to enhance physical education for learners with disabilities.

3. Explain the responsibilities of the motor development team in the provision of educational and related services for learners with disabilities.

STUDENT ACTIVITIES

1. Do a Web search to examine the philosophy, goals/objectives, and service delivery models in adapted physical education in a variety of schools.

2. Ask a parent of a child with a disability to describe how/if the parent was involved in school-based activities.

3. Do a Web search to explore the sophisticated equipment now available for learners with disabilities who want to participate in leisure, recreation, sports, and fitness activities. In particular, examine the variety of sports wheelchairs, prosthetics, and modified equipment.

REFERENCES

1. Arkansas Center for Health Improvement, Fayetteville, Arkansas, 2006.

2. Baltimore County Public Schools APE Philosophy, www.bcps.org/offices/physed/curriculum/adapted_philosophy.html. 2003

3. Block ME, Conatser P: Consulting in adapted physical education, APAQ 16:9–26, 1999.

4. Burgeson CR, Wechsler H, Brener ND, Young J, Spain, CG: Physical education and activity: Results from the school health policies and programs study, 2000, *J School Health* 71(7):279–283, 2001.

5. Cariaga, D: *Adapted physical education,* San Luis Obispo County, CA, Student Services Division, dcariaga@tcsn.net. 2007

6. Downs P, Active Australia: *Willing and able: Count me in,* Disability Education Program, Participation Division, Australian Sports Commission, PO Box 176, Belconnen, ACT 2616, www.ausport.gov.au/partic/dishome.html.

7. Ellery PJ: Embracing computer technology in physical education instruction, *Chronicle Physical Education in Higher Education* 7(3):3, 18, 1996.

8. Epstein J: Theory to practice: School and family partnerships lead to school improvement and student success. In Fagnano C, Werber B, editors: *School, family, and community interactions: A view from the firing lines,* Boulder, CO, Westview Press, 1994.

9. Horton M, Wilson S, Gagnon D: Collaboration: A key component for successful inclusion in general physical education. *Teaching Elementary Physical Education* 14(3):13–17, 2003.

10. Huettig C, Roth K: Maximizing the use of APE consultants: What the general physical educator has the right to expect, *JOPERD* 73(1):32–35, 2002.

11. Kasser S, Lieberman L: Maximizing learning opportunities through activity modification, *Teaching Elementary Physical Education* 14(3):19–22, 2003.

12. LaMaster K, Gall K, Kinchin G, Siedentop D: Inclusion practices of effective elementary specialisits, APAQ 15:64–81, 2003.

13. Lytle R, Lavay B, Robinson N, Huettig C: Teaching collaboration and consultation skills to preservice and inservice APE teachers, *JOPERD* 74(55):13–16, 2003.

14. Mills B: Opening the gymnasium to the World Wide Web, *JOPERD* 68(8):17–19, 1997.

15. National Association of State Directors of Special Education: *Physical education for children with disabilities,* Document Reproduction Service No. ED349777, Education Resource Information Clearinghouse, 1991.

16. National Coalition for Promoting Physical Activity: State Advocacy, Washington, DC, April 2006.

17. PE Central, http://pe.central/vt.edu. 2003

18. Rudner LM: *Scholastic achievement and demographic characteristics of home school students in 1998,* ERIC Clearinghouse on Assessment and Evaluation, College of Library and Information Services, University of Maryland, College Park, 1998, http://olam.ed.asu.edu/epaa/v7n8.

19. San Francisco Unified School District, www.sfusd.k12.ca.us/dept/sped/services/adaptedPhysicalEducation.html. 2003

20. Sugars A: *The adapted physical educator as a member of the motor development team.* TAHPERD State Convention, Lubbock, TX, 1990.

21. Texas Woman's University Project INSPIRE, www.twu.edu/INSPIRE. 2003

22. U.S. Department of Education: *Focused monitoring: A model for the present.* Washington, DC, Office of Special Education Programs, 2002.

23. Wynns J: *Healthy food and physical activity in the San Francisco Unified School District.* Washington, DC, Bookings Institution, March 14, 2006.

SUGGESTED READINGS

Huettig C, Roth K: Maximizing the use of APE consultants: What the general physical educator has a right to expect, JOPERD 73(1):32–35, 2002.

RECOMMENDED WEB SITES

Please keep in mind that these Web sites are being recommended in the winter of 2007. As Web sites often change, they may have moved, reconfigured, or eliminated.

Dan Cariaga's adapted physical education assessment information and goals and objectives
http://a-ape.com

San Francisco Unified School District.
www.sfusd.k12.ca.us/dept/sped/services/adaptedPhysicalEducation.html

RECOMMENDED VIDEOS

Insight Media
2162 Broadway
New York, NY 10024
1-800-233-9910
www.insight-media.com

Assistive Technology: A Way to Differentiate
Instruction for Students with Disabilities
UAN3742/DVD/2005/45 min/$159.00

Keys to Compliance: A General Educator's Practical
Guide to Meeting Special Ed Requirements
UAN3188/VHS tape/2003/20 min/$139.00

Physical Activity for All
TAN4610/WIN DVD-ROM/2000/$129.00

Determining Educational Needs through Assessment

■ **OBJECTIVES**

Explain the purposes of assessment.

List the different types of assessment.

Identify four factors that must be considered when selecting an assessment instrument.

Explain what is meant by administrative feasibility.

Provide examples of techniques that can be used to organize test results.

Courtesy of Orthotic & Prosthetic Athlete
Assistance Fund, Inc. Photo by Julie Gaydos.

It is becoming increasingly clear that traditional educational practices that have served our society well in the past must be modified to keep pace with changing societal demands, as well as the growing diversity of students being educated in our schools. It is apparent that, for our society to survive and grow, all students, regardless of gender, ethnicity, and functional capacity, must be adequately prepared to participate successfully in a multicultural society that is increasingly dependent on advanced technology.[9] School curricula must be designed to provide students with information, skills, and problem-solving capabilities that will enable them to function fully in the career and community of their choice. A critical component of an effective curriculum is a means for determining at what levels students are functioning, the types of interventions needed to gain full benefits from their school experiences, their progress toward mastery of the school curriculum, and validation

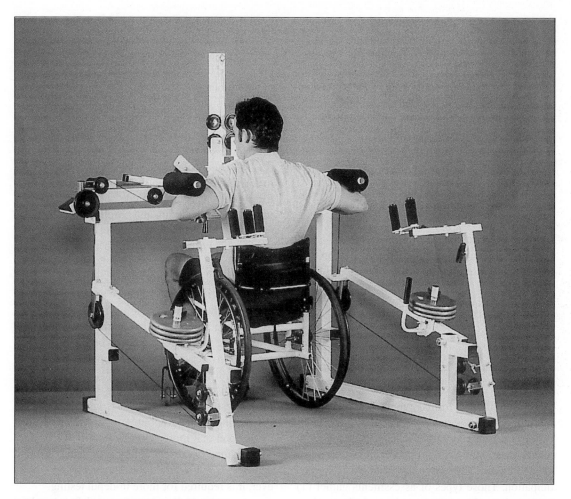

A Person with Tetraplegia Strengthens His Deltoids
Courtesy of GPK, Inc. El Cajon, CA.

that what has been learned has application in the society. Appropriate assessment techniques can provide this information.

In this chapter a broad range of assessment information will be presented. The purposes of assessment, the types of instruments available to meet those purposes, ways to evaluate specific instruments to determine their appropriateness, and tips on administering tests have been included. Ways to arrange test results to facilitate interpretation will also be covered. Recommendations for instruments that can be used with students who have specific types of disabilities, and ways to

modify the testing situation to meet their needs, will be included in each of the chapters that address those populations.

PURPOSES OF ASSESSMENT

Assessment is a problem-solving process that involves a variety of ways of gathering information. Testing is the administration of specific instruments that are used to gather assessment data.[11] Motor assessment instruments provide different types of information. It is important to match the selection of the instrument with the purpose of the assessment. Assessment instruments should provide the teacher information about what activities should be included in the curriculum. Too frequently, the teacher selects assessment instruments that reflect what is currently being taught. Assessment is an inseparable part of the student's ongoing educational program, and it is particularly critical for students with disabilities.

Assessment of students in educational settings has at least seven purposes.

1. To identify those who might be experiencing developmental delays
2. To diagnose the nature of the student's problem or delay
3. To provide information to use to develop the IEP and determine appropriate placement
4. To develop instruction specific to the student's special needs
5. To evaluate student progress[11]
6. To determine support services needed[5]
7. To determine which skills need to be developed to enable the individual to access programs available in the community[5]

In addition to formal types of physical and motor assessments, quality adapted physical education programs usually include needs assessments to determine what supports and services are needed by each student to fully benefit from participation. Those types of assessments gather (1) student data, (2) support needs, and (3) services needed to generalize skills learned in the physical education program to the community.[5] Other types of information the adapted physical education teacher may want to gather are (1) student participation in extracurricular activities, (2) play and leisure-time preferences, (3) the extent to which the program is meeting the students' goals, and (4) student satisfaction with the program.

MATCHING TYPE OF ASSESSMENT TO PURPOSE

Both formal and informal tests serve important functions in the educational process. Formal tests are those that have been developed for a specific

purpose and have been standardized. Informal tests are those that have been developed for a general purpose and have not been standardized. The purpose of the assessment should dictate the type of instrument selected and the standards the instrument must meet. The more critical the decisions that are made from the assessment, the more rigorous the requirements for the instrument the evaluator will use.

Informal techniques used for screening groups to determine whether any individuals are experiencing significant delays include checklists, activities used in the curriculum, and observation of students during their regular physical education class or during recess. Formal tests used to pinpoint specific areas of delays include physical fitness tests, gross motor development tests, and skill tests and/or motor proficiency tests that have been standardized. Whatever the method used, it is recommended that the information be recorded, so that documentation is available for the permanent record file. An example of an observational checklist that was developed for use in the Denton, Texas, Independent School District appears in Table 3-1. Using an informal test, once a teacher observes a student not performing to the level of his or her classmates, it is understood that more rigorous testing is necessary to determine the extent and type of delay. Parental approval is not required for informal testing; however, it is required for more in-depth testing.

Assessment information used for developing a student's IEP and for selecting appropriate activities can be gathered from a variety of sources, including parental reports, informal test procedures, and formal testing. Those areas found to be below expectations for the student's age become the present levels of performance that are required to be recorded on the IEP. Measurable annual goals written for the student are directly related to the present level of performance areas found to be lacking. Periodic reports to document the progress a child is making on the annual goals are shared with parents/guardians. The effectiveness of a physical education program can be continuously monitored by determining the extent to which the students are mastering short-term

Table 3-1	Denton Independent School District
	Adapted Physical Education Prereferral/Referral Form

Regular Educator   Educational Diagnostician   APE Teacher

_____ _____   _____ _____   _____ _____
Initial   Date   Initial   Date   Initial   Date

Student _____ ID# _____ DOB _____
School _____ Type of Class (Unit) Teacher _____
Evaluation Requested by _____ Medical Concerns _____
Major concerns about student in Physical Education _____
_____

School Contact for APE Teacher _____
Method of Ambulation _____ Form of Communication _____

Below are some behaviors that indicate a student's ability to move efficiently and interact effectively with others. Please check the appropriate response in the Regular Education (RE) column. If these tasks do not apply, list your concerns in the comment section on the back of this page.

PSYCHOMOTOR DEVELOPMENT	YES		SOMETIMES		NO	
	RE	APE	RE	APE	RE	APE
Demonstrates capability for voluntary movement						
Reacts to noise/activity/touch						
Rolls from front to back						
Sits assisted/unassisted						
Stands assisted/unassisted						
Walks in cross pattern						
Runs in cross pattern						
Ascends/descends stairs						
Jumps with mature pattern						
Hops (one foot) with mature pattern						
Leaps with mature pattern						
Gallops with mature pattern						
Skips with mature pattern						
Slides with mature pattern						
Walks a straight line/heel-to-toe						
Stands on one foot for five seconds						
Catches an 8.5-inch ball with mature pattern						
Bounces and catches a playground ball to self						
Kicks a stationary ball with mature pattern						
Kicks a rolled ball with mature pattern						
Throws a ball with mature pattern						
Turns own jump rope using rhythmic form while jumping						
COGNITIVE DEVELOPMENT						
Can remember visual and/or auditory information						
Can understand cause and effect						
Exhibits appropriate on-task behavior						
Can follow directions						

(Continued)

Table 3-1 (Continued)						
PSYCHOMOTOR DEVELOPMENT	**YES**		**SOMETIMES**		**NO**	
	RE	**APE**	**RE**	**APE**	**RE**	**APE**
AFFECTIVE DEVELOPMENT						
Indicates a dislike for physical activity						
Prefers to play solo						
Has a low frustration tolerance, cries easily						
Tends to be impulsive						
Is physically/verbally aggressive toward others/self						
Has a short attention span						
Distracts others						
Respects authority, rules, and others						

Student _____

Adapted Physical Education Prereferral/Referral Form—Page 2

BODY MECHANICS/POSTURE: (Check all that apply)	**YES**		**SOMETIMES**		**NO**	
	RE	**APE**	**RE**	**APE**	**RE**	**APE**
❏ Posture—head/trunk/feet misalignment						
❏ Muscular/skeletal/neurological impairment						
❏ Underweight/overweight						
MOBILITY SKILLS (NONAMBULATORY): (Check all that the student demonstrates.)						
❏ Transfers in and out of chair						
❏ Has acceptable range of motion						
❏ Can open doors						
❏ Can push up ramps						
❏ Can reverse direction						
❏ Can use brake						
❏ Can pivot in chair						
❏ Can perform a wheelie						

Teachers' Comments

_____
_____
_____
_____
_____

Thank you for your time. Please return this completed form to the Special Education Diagnostician in your school.

(Continued)

Table 3-1	*(Continued)*

To Be Filled Out by the Adapted Physical Educator

Date of Classroom Visit(s): _____   _____   _____   _____   _____

Recommendations:

❏ The student is functioning within acceptable limits in regular Physical Education and does not need any further evaluation at this time.

❏ The student is able to be included in regular Physical Education class with appropriate modifications by either the regular Physical Educator or consultation services by the Adapted Physical Educator.

❏ The student appears to be experiencing difficulty in the area(s) indicated above and will need further screening/evaluation by the Adapted Physical Education Teacher for appropriate placement with some type of special services.

❏ The student can benefit from activities provided by the Classroom Teacher.

_____	_____	_____
Signed	Date	Position

Courtesy Denton, Texas, Independent School District.

objectives and long-range goals that have been included on their IEPs.

A standardized test that has been used to assess persons with intellectual disabilities for over 50 years is the Vineland Adaptive Motor Scales. This test, which has just been revised, measures adaptive functioning and was influential in the defining and classification system of mental retardation.[2] The Vineland is an interview for teachers, parents, and service providers that is designed to measure the level of adaptive functioning of persons from birth to 90 years of age in five domains: (1) communication, (2) daily living skills, (3) socialization, (4) motor skills, and (5) maladaptive behaviors. There is a teacher's edition for use with 3- to 22-year-olds.

LEGAL MANDATES FOR DETERMINING PRESENT LEVEL OF PERFORMANCE

The type of testing used for students with disabilities must conform to federal and state laws and district practices. Physical education appropriate for students with disabilities is broadly defined

in the federal laws (see Chapter 1). Those laws do not dictate the type of testing that should be done but do set the conditions surrounding the testing process. The IDEIA (2004) revisions generally restate longstanding policy set out in the prior regulations.[10] Those requirements are located in Table 3-2.

In most school districts, the question of whether testing is done and the type utilized are left to the discretion of individual teachers. Because appropriate testing is basic to designing a physical education program that will meet the needs of the student with a disability, it is critical to the effectiveness of a teacher.

The reauthorized IDEA (P.L. 108-446) revisions generally restate longstanding policy set out in the prior regulations and align IDEA with NCLB. In general, the IEP must be linked to each child's education in the general curriculum, and children with disabilities are to be assessed according to their state's content standards. Although, at this writing, the provisions for testing special education students in the regular curriculum apply only

Table 3-2	1997 IDEA Evaluation Requirements

May not discriminate on a cultural or racial basis

Are provided and administered in the child's native language

A variety of assessment tools and strategies are used to gather functional and development information, including information provided by the parent, and information related to enabling the child to be involved in and progress in the general curriculum.

The standardized tests used in the process must have been validated for the specific purpose for which they are used and must be administered by trained and knowledgeable personnel in accordance with the provided instructions.

All variations from standard conditions must be described.

Child is assessed in all areas related to the suspected disability, including, if appropriate, health, vision . . . and motor abilities.

Assessment tools and strategies are used that provide relevant information that directly assists persons in determining the [physical] education needs of the child.

Assessment tools, required in the general [physical] education program, must be administered to students with disabilities with modifications, if needed.

to the academic areas, there are federal initiatives to tie physical education testing to NCLB. There is no national test for physical education; however, there are content standards in physical education in some states.

NCLB requires that states provide one or more alternative assessments and have a statewide accountability system based on adequate yearly progress (AYP) in reading and math. To address the growing problem of obesity, some states are planning to incorporate physical education testing and standards into the prescribed curriculum. These state initiatives are aimed at facilitating (1) children and youth with disabilities to participate in after-school programs that involve physical activity, (2) participation in school health programs, and (3) utilization of school personnel who demonstrate healthy lifestyles. All of these initiatives could be incorporated into the adapted physical education program.

The ultimate goal of the adapted physical education program is to enable children, youth, and adults with disabilities to participate in leisure physical activity in community environments. Quality physical education programs will facilitate

that transition. For young children, play is the mode for physically active leisure. In later years the type of leisure physical activity will be selected by the individual and balanced among other needs.

Because play is the primary occupation of young children, the school playground provides a naturalistic setting in which to assess students' leisure characteristics and interests[7]. Leff[8] has studied tools to use to assess children's playground leisure behavior. Two instruments the physical educator might use are the Children's Assessment Participation of Enjoyment Test[6], and the Developmental Play Assessment.[8]

Play eventually evolves into more leisure options and more leisure environments as children grow older. As that occurs, assessment should include a match between leisure skills acquired by children and youth with disabilities and opportunities in the community. The Social Interaction in Leisure Assessment is a useful instrument for persons with disabilities. It is a computerized assessment instrument used to determine the recreational knowledge and social skill of persons who are intellectually impaired.[1]

AUTHENTIC ASSESSMENT

Authentic assessment is testing that provides the teacher with information needed to develop a meaningful physical education program for each student. What is meaningful depends a great deal on the knowledge and skill of the teacher as well as the time available to him or her. Teachers who are committed to a predetermined curriculum will measure students' ability to demonstrate competence of the components of the curriculum (curriculum-based). The teacher who is preparing a transitional program for a student who is 14 years or older will conduct task analyses of activities available in the community (ecological inventory) and then will design a program to teach the missing skills to the student. The teacher who believes all activity should primarily contribute to physical fitness will measure fitness levels. The teacher of the young student will focus on the basic locomotor, object-control, and perceptual motor skills needed to be successful later with sport-specific activities. The teacher with advanced training in basic neurological building blocks will probe down through physical fitness tasks and sport, functional, and perceptual motor skills to determine if all the underlying sensory-motor components are functioning fully. The types of tests available to address each of these kinds of assessments are presented in Table 3-3.

The scoring method used for any given test depends on what the test is designed to measure. Tests are designed to measure a person's performance against established criteria, key elements in the task, or key elements in a series of tasks (refer to Tables 3-4 and 3-5 and the content task analyses in Tables 3-6, 3-7, and 3-8). Tests that measure performance against established criteria are either normative-referenced or criterion-referenced. *Normative-referenced* means an individual's performance can be compared with that of others of the same age and gender. Most physical fitness test items are normative-referenced. Criterion-referenced tests are designed to provide information about a person's mastery of a specific skill or behavior. An example of a criterion-referenced test item is the following: from a running start, kick a stationary $8\frac{1}{2}$-inch playground ball 30 feet.

Test items that are designed to measure components that make up a task are content-referenced. That is, the ability of an individual to demonstrate all of the content (task components) of a skill or pattern is what is observed. An example from the Test of Gross Motor Development–2 is the content task analysis of the locomotor pattern of running shown in Table 3-9.

Some tests include both criterion-referenced and content-referenced scoring techniques. For example, the task of kicking a playground ball 30 feet from a

---

Table 3-3	Types of Assessments for School-Age Students

Curriculum-based—Competency Testing for Adapted Physical Education (Louisiana), Motor Activities Training Program (National); Moving into the Future: National Standards for Physical Education (National), Skill Tests (Local)

Physical fitness—Brockport Physical Fitness Test: A Health-Related Test for Youths with Physical and Mental Disabilities; Physical Best and Individuals with Disabilities

Functional skills—Mobility Opportunities via Education (MOVE); Test of Gross Motor Development (TGMD); Ohio State University Scale of Intra Gross Motor Assessment (OSU-Sigma)

Sport skills—Methods of Assessing Motor Skills, 1999 (NASPE); Special Olympic Sport Skill Guides (Special Olympics)

Perceptual/motor skills—Purdue Perceptual Motor Skills Survey

Sensory-motor skills—Southern California Tests of Sensory Motor Integration; DiGangi-Berk Test of Sensory Integration; Sensory Input Systems Screening Test

Table 3-4	Norms for the Standing Long Jump in the AAHPERD Physical Fitness Test			
	Test Scores (Meters)*			
Percentile Rank	**11 Years**	**12 Years**	**13 Years**	**Percentile Rank**
100th	2.56	2.26	2.59	100th
95th	1.87	1.98	2.15	95th
90th	1.82	1.90	2.08	90th
85th	1.77	1.85	2.03	85th
80th	1.75	1.82	1.95	80th
75th	1.70	1.80	1.90	75th
70th	1.67	1.75	1.87	70th
65th	1.67	1.72	1.82	65th
60th	1.65	1.70	1.82	60th
55th	1.62	1.67	1.77	55th
50th	1.57	1.65	1.75	50th
45th	1.57	1.62	1.70	45th
40th	1.52	1.60	1.67	40th
35th	1.49	1.57	1.65	35th
30th	1.47	1.54	1.60	30th
25th	1.42	1.52	1.57	25th
20th	1.39	1.47	1.52	20th
15th	1.34	1.44	1.47	15th
10th	1.29	1.37	1.39	10th
5th	1.21	1.26	1.32	5th
0	0.91	0.96	0.99	0

Source: From the American Alliance for Health, Physical Education, Recreation and Dance, Reston, VA.

*To convert to centimeters, move the decimal point two places to the right (1.95 m = 195 cm).

running start could also require the evaluator to indicate whether the student demonstrated the following key elements of the task: backswing of the leg from the knee, contact with the foot, forward swing of the arm opposite the kicking leg, and follow-through by hopping on the nonkicking foot.

Checklists and ecological inventories are content-referenced because they are used to determine whether specific key elements of a task or a series of tasks are demonstrated. Checklists are frequently developed and used to delineate critical aspects of motor coordination and sport skills. The content task analysis of a softball throw is an example of such a checklist (see Table 3-6). Checklists are useful for screening one student or a whole class before beginning a unit of instruction. Through the use of the checklist, the teacher can determine which tasks need to be taught. Hyde[4] developed an instrument for screening kindergarten children for developmental delays (see Table 3-7). Ecological inventories are developed to identify the behavioral contents (demands) of an environment. An example of an ecological inventory is shown in Table 3-8. That ecological inventory is a content analysis of a series of tasks that need to be mastered to participate in the activity of bowling in the community. Ecological inventories are particularly helpful when designing a transition program for students 16 years and older. A community-based ecological inventory completed by a teacher will identify what activities are available in the community and the series of tasks a student needs to master to participate in those activities.

Table 3-5	Isometric Push-Up, Bench Press, Extended Arm Hang, Flexed Arm Hang, and Dominant Grip Strength: Specific Standards for Youngsters with Intellectual Disabilities

Age	Isometric Push-Up[a] (s)	Bench Press[a] (# Completed)	Extended Arm Hang[b] (s)	Flexed Arm Hang[a] (s)	Dominant Grip Strength[c] (kg)
Males					
10	20		23		12
11	20		23		14
12	20		23		16
13		10		6	19
14		16		8	22
15		20		8	24
16		23		8	28
17		25		8	32
Females					
10	13		15		11
11	13		15		12
12	13		15		14
13		5		4	16
14		6		4	17
15		7		4	19
16		7		4	19
17		8		4	19

Source: Adapted with permission from The Cooper Institute for Aerobics and Research, 1992 and 1999, FITNESSGRAM, Dallas, Texas: Cooper Institute for Aerobics Research.

[a]Specific standards reflect a 50% adjustment to minimal general standards.
[b]Specific standards are 75% of minimal general standards.
[c]Specific standards are 65% of minimal general standards.

Evaluating Physical Fitness

There are at least four prevalent measures to assess the health of children and youth in special education that are related to participation in physical activity. These four tools are (1) the Body Mass Index, (2) physical examinations to assess readiness for participation in activity, (3) health risk instruments, and (4) health screenings.

The Body Mass Index (BMI) is a ratio of weight and height. It is calculated by dividing a person's weight in pounds by his or her height in inches squared and multiplying the answer by 703. (BMI = weight in pounds/height in inches [squared] × 703.) BMI in

children is compared with children of the same gender and age. A child's BMI of less than the 5th percentile is considered underweight; a BMI of greater than the 95th percentile is considered overweight. In Arkansas, children are provided with calculators to assess if they have a healthy weight for their gender and age. The calculator automatically adjusts for differences in height, age, and gender.

Physical examinations are required for some children and youth who participate in sport activity. For instance, every athlete who participates in Special Olympics is to have a physical examination. Usually, a primary care physician examines the

Table 3-6	**Content Task Analysis of a Softball Throw**

1. Demonstrate the correct grip 100 percent of the time.
   a. Select a softball.
   b. Hold the ball with the first and second fingers spread on top, thumb under the ball, and the third and fourth fingers on the side.
   c. Grasp the ball with the fingertips.
2. Demonstrate the proper step pattern for throwing the softball three out of five times.
   a. Identify the restraining line.
   b. Take a side step with the left foot.
   c. Follow with a shorter side step with the right foot.
3. Demonstrate the proper throwing technique and form three out of five times.
   a. Grip ball correctly.
   b. Bend rear knee.
   c. Rotate hips and pivot left foot, turning body to the right.
   d. Bring right arm back with the ball behind the right ear and bent right elbow leading (in front of) hand.
   e. Bend left elbow and point it at a 45-degree angle.
   f. Step straight ahead with the left foot.
   g. Keep the right hip back and low and the right arm bent with the ball behind the ear and the elbow leading.

h. Start the throwing motion by pushing down hard with the right foot.
i. Straighten the right knee and rotate the hips, shifting the weight to the left foot.
j. Keep the upper body in line with the direction of throw and the eyes focused on the target.
k. Whip the left arm to the rear, increasing the speed of the right arm.
l. Extend the right arm fully forward, completing the release by snapping the wrist and releasing the ball at a 45-degree angle.
m. Follow through by bringing the hand completely down and the right foot forward to the front restraining line.

4. Throw a softball on command three out of five times.
   a. Assume READY position between the front and back restraining lines with feet apart.
   b. Point the shoulder of the nonthrowing arm toward the restraining line.
   c. Focus eyes in the direction of the throw.
   d. Remain behind the front restraining line.
   e. Throw the softball on command.
   f. Execute smooth integration of skill sequence.

Permission for the Special Olympics Sports Skills Instructional Program provided by Special Olympics, created by The Joseph P. Kennedy, Jr., Foundation. Authorized and accredited by Special Olympics, Inc., for the Benefit of Mentally Retarded Citizens.

---

youngsters (1) to determine the type and degree of abilities and disabilities, (2) to review medications affecting strength and endurance, and (3) to act as a liaison with the athletes' parents and coaches.

Health risk assessments are a critical component of any wellness program. They take the form of a detailed health questionnaire that includes questions on lifestyle issues, such as exercise and weight. They provide information on health status and suggest areas for improvement. An overall risk score is provided.[3] Health screenings include measurements of height and weight, cholesterol levels, blood sugar levels, blood pressure, and/or BMI.[3]

TEST SELECTION CRITERIA

As indicated earlier in this chapter, depending on the purpose for the assessment, both standardized tests and less formal instruments are useful when working with students with disabilities. Once the purpose of the assessment has been decided, an appropriate assessment instrument is selected. Factors that must be considered to select the right test are (1) the need for utilizing a standardized test; (2) the adequacy of test standardization; (3) administrative feasibility; and (4) the student's type of disability. Each of these factors will be discussed.

Table 3-7	Motor Development Checklist		

Name _____   Examiner_____

Birthdate _____ Sex _____   Date_____

Category	Special Notes and Remarks		
Static balance	___ does not attempt tasks	___ heel-toe stand, 5 sec ___ balance on preferred foot, arms hung relaxed at sides ___ 5 sec ___ 10 sec	___heel-toe stand, eyes ___closed, 5 sec ___balance on preferred foot, arms hung relaxed at sides, eyes closed ___ 5 sec ___ 10 sec
Hopping reflex	___ no response ___ no righting of head ___ trunk no step in direction of push ___ right ___ left ___ forward ___ backward	___ head and body right themselves ___ step or hop in direction of push ___ right ___ left ___ forward ___ backward	
Running pattern	___ loses balance ___ almost ___ twists trunk ___ leans excessively ___ jerky, uneven rhythm	___ elbows away from body in arm swing ___ limited arm swing ___ short strides	___ full arm swing in opposition with legs ___ elbows near body in swing ___ even flow and rhythm
Jumping pattern	___ loses balance on landing ___ no use of arms ___ twists or bends sideways	___ arms at side for balance ___ legs bent throughout jump	___ arms back as legs bend ___ arms swing up as legs extend ___ lands softly with control
Throwing pattern	___ pushing or shoving object ___ loss of balance ___ almost	___ body shifts weight from back to front without stepping	___ steps forward with same foot as throwing arm ___ steps forward with foot opposite throwing arm
Catching pattern	___ loses balance___almost ___ shies away ___ traps or scoops	___ arms stiff in front of body	___ arms bent at sides of body ___ arms "give" as catch ___ uses hands
Kicking pattern	___ misses ___ off center	___ arms at sides or out to sides ___ uses from knee down to kick	___ kicks "through" ball ___ arm opposition ___ uses full leg to kick ___ can kick with either foot

Courtesy Beverly Hyde.

Table 3-8	Content Task Analysis of a Series of Tasks Needed to Bowl Independently

1. Can determine when bowling lanes are available.
   a. Finds the number of the bowling establishment in the phone book.
   b. Calls the bowling establishment to determine when open bowling is available.
2. Can get from home to the bowling establishment.
   a. Knows which bus to take to the bowling establishment.
   b. Walks to the nearest bus stop.
   c. Waits at the bus stop until the bus arrives.
   d. Checks the bus sign to make sure it is the correct bus.
   e. Gets on the bus.
   f. Checks with the bus driver to be sure the bus goes to the bowling establishment.
   g. Drops the fare into the box.
   h. Asks the driver to let him or her know where to get off.
   i. Moves to an empty seat and sits down.
   j. Listens for the driver's announcement of the correct stop.
   k. Pulls the cord to alert the driver that he or she wants to get off at the next stop.
   l. After the bus stops, departs from the bus.
   m. Checks to determine where the bus stop is for the return trip home.
3. Can reserve a lane, rent shoes, and select the appropriate ball.
   a. Goes to the counter and tells the clerk how many games he or she wants to bowl and asks for the correct-size bowling shoes.
   b. Pays for the games and shoes and receives the correct change.
   c. Takes a seat behind the lane that has been assigned and changes from street to bowling shoes.
   d. Searches for a ball that fits his or her hand span and is the correct weight.
   e. Selects a ball that fits and is not too heavy.
   f. Places the ball on the ball-return rack of the correct lane.
4. Can correctly deliver the ball.
   a. Picks up the ball with both hands.
   b. Cradles the ball in the nondominant arm while placing his or her fingers in the ball.
   c. Positions self in the center of the approach approximately 15 feet from the foul line.
   d. Holds the ball in both hands and aims.
   e. Walks to the line, coordinating the swing of the dominant arm and the walking pattern of the feet.
   f. Releases the ball from behind the foul line.
   g. Follows through with the dominant arm.
   h. Watches the ball move down the lane and strike pins.
5. Can retrieve the ball and continue bowling.
   a. Walks back to the ball-return rack.
   b. Awaits the ball's return.
   c. Continues to aim and deliver the ball, being careful not to throw the ball while the pins are being reset.
6. Stops bowling when the electronic scoring device indicates that three games have been completed.
   a. Returns the ball to the storage rack.
   b. Changes back into street shoes.
   c. Returns the rented shoes to the counter.
   d. Exits the bowling establishment.
7. Can return home from the bowling establishment.
   a. Goes to the bus stop and awaits the bus.
   b. Checks the bus sign to verify it is the correct bus.
   c. Gets on the bus.
   d. Asks the bus driver if the bus goes to the street he or she is seeking.
   e. Drops the fare into the box.
   f. Asks the driver to let him or her know where to get off.
   g. Moves to an empty seat and sits down.
   h. Listens for the driver's announcement of the correct stop.
   i. Pulls the cord to alert the driver that he or she wants to get off at the next stop.
   j. Waits for the bus to stop before rising from the seat and departing the bus.
   k. Walks home.

Table 3-9	Content Task Analysis of a Locomotor Pattern—Run

1. Arms move in opposition to legs with the elbows bent
2. Brief period where both feet are off the ground
3. Narrow foot placement landing on heel or toe (i.e., not flat-footed)
4. Nonsupport leg bent approximately 90 degrees (i.e., close to buttocks)

From Test of Gross Motor Development–2.
Courtesy of Dale Ulrich

Need for Utilizing a Standardized Test

IDEIA (2004) specifies that, in order to determine a child's eligibility for special services—in this case, special (adapted) physical education—a variety of assessment tools and strategies must be utilized. Although the requirement of utilizing standardized tests is not clearly stated, in IDEIA the intent is implicit. That is, whereby many types of information may be used *in addition to* standardized tests, standardized tests indicating that a student's performance significantly lags behind his or her peers are still required.[10] What is clear in the most recent amendments is that if an instrument is used for eligibility purposes, the adequacy of the person administering the test and the fact that the instrument is technically sound must be demonstrated. That is, the person administering the test must be adequately trained in administration and interpretation, and the test itself must be valid, reliable, and objective for the purposes it is being used.

Standardization

To standardize a test means to give the test to a large group of persons under the same conditions to determine whether the test discriminates among ages and populations. When a test is going to be used for diagnostic purposes, adequacy of the standardized process must be verified. Questions that must be answered include the following: (1) Were the appropriate procedures used to select the population used to standardize the instrument? (2) Did the author(s) demonstrate an appropriate type and level of validity? (3) Did the author(s) establish an appropriate type and level of reliability? (4) Did the author(s) verify the objectivity of the instrument?

Selecting the Standardization Sample

Ideally, the sample that is used for the standardization of an instrument should include the same percentage of individuals in the socioeconomic groups, geographic locations (South, East, North, Northeast, etc.), ages, genders, and races represented in the general population according to the latest population census. Hence, if the year 2005 U.S. census reports that 51 percent of the population is female and 49 percent is male, those percentages should be duplicated in the test sample. If, in the same census, it is reported that the U.S. population is 12 percent African American, 74 percent Anglo, 18 percent Hispanic, 4 percent Native American, 4 percent Asian, and 6 percent other, then those percentages should be used to select the makeup of the sample to be tested. In addition, the test sample should include the ages of the persons with whom the test will be used selected at random from all areas of the country. Because few, if any, motor tests meet these stringent criteria, tests should be selected that come as close to the ideal as possible.

Establishing Validity

Test validity is a measure of how truthful an instrument is. A valid instrument measures what the authors claim it measures. There are three acceptable types of validity: (1) content-related, (2) criterion-related, and (3) construct (see Figure 3-1).

Content-related validity is the degree to which the contents of the test represent an identified domain (perceptual motor, physical fitness), body of knowledge, or curriculum. Content-related validity pertaining to a domain or a body of knowledge is often determined by verifying that experts in the field agree about the components of the domain. To demonstrate content validity, first the author must provide a clear definition of what is being measured. Then, literature that supports the content is identified or the test is examined by a panel of judges selected

TRANSITION: FROM WALKING TO STANDING	GRADE LEVEL	LEVEL I	LEVEL II	LEVEL III
I.1 Can stop walking and maintain a standing position without assistance.	☐ DATE			
I.2 Can stop walking and maintain a standing position when another person helps the participant maintain balance.		☐ DATE		
I.3 Can stop moving legs reciprocally and maintain hip and knee extension for standing while in a front leaning walker or while another person helps maintain balance.			☐ DATE	
Can tolerate fully prompted reciprocal leg movements while being supported in a front leaning walker or by another person. SEE: G.6.				☐ DATE
Can tolerate fully prompted extension of hips and knees. SEE: C.5.				☐ DATE
Can tolerate being placed in a vertical position. SEE: C.6.				☐ DATE

Figure 3-1   Move™ Top-Down Motor Milestone Test™
Used with permission from MOVE International, Bakersfield, CA.

according to a predetermined set of criteria (i.e., five or more publications in the field, recommended by three or more professionals as an authority in the field, etc.). The panel members independently review the items in the test to determine whether they are appropriate, complete, and representative. In the case of content-related validity pertaining to a curriculum, the test is usually constructed by a districtwide, statewide, or nationwide committee made up of professionals in the field. Those professionals select items to include in the tests that they believe are appropriate, complete, and representative of the physical education curriculum at each level (elementary, middle school, junior high, and senior high).

Appropriateness means that the most knowledgeable professionals would agree that items measure what it is claimed they measure. For example, if a test designer claims that the 50-yard dash measures cardiovascular function, few professionals would agree that the test content is appropriate.

Completeness is determined by whether there is a wide range of items or only a select few. To be complete, a test that is purported to measure physical fitness would be expected to sample cardiovascular endurance, upper body strength, abdominal strength, leg power, lower back and hip flexibility, and percent body fat. If only one measure of strength and one measure of cardiovascular endurance were included, the test would be deemed incomplete.

For a test to be declared representative of a given domain, several levels of performance would be sampled. This is accomplished by including a range of items from simple to complex or allowing a set amount of time to complete as many of the same tasks as is possible. In physical fitness tests, the representative requirement is frequently met by allowing the student to perform to the best of his or her ability within a given period of time. That is, the number of sit-ups executed in 30 seconds is counted. Students with well-developed abdominal muscles will perform more sit-ups than those who are less well developed. The content validity of a test is frequently as strong as the literature cited and/or the knowledge base of the professionals selected to evaluate and or develop the test. The broader the literature base and the more knowledgeable and critical the professionals, the stronger the content validity.

Criterion-related validity indicates the test has been compared with another acceptable standard, such as a valid test that measures the same components. There are two types of criterion-related validity—concurrent and predictive. Concurrent criterion-related validity is achieved when the test scores on one test accurately reflect a person's score on another test at a point in time. For instance, if a student performs strongly on a 2-mile run, a strong performance on a bicycle ergometer test is expected. Predictive content-related validity means that the test scores can be used to predict accurately how well a student will perform in the future. Thus, if a student performs well on a motor ability test, the student should do well in a variety of sport activities.

Construct validity is the degree to which a test does what the author claims it will do. To establish this type of validity, an author sets out to develop a test that will discriminate between two or more populations. After identifying which populations the test should discriminate among, a series of studies is completed, measuring each of the identified groups with the test. For example, an author might claim that students with learning disabilities will do significantly more poorly on the test than will students with no learning problems. After the test is designed, it is administered to two groups of students who have been matched on age and gender. One group has verified learning disabilities; the other does not. Each group's scores are compared to determine whether they are significantly different. If the group with learning disabilities scores significantly lower than the group with no learning disabilities, construct validity is claimed.

Different statistical techniques are used to evaluate validity. In the case of content validity relating to a domain or a body of knowledge, percentage of agreement among the judges on the panel is reported. Acceptable content validity can be declared when the judges agree on the appropriateness of items included in the test at least 90 percent of the time. Content validity relating to a curriculum is generally achieved by majority vote of the professionals developing the test. Criterion validity is usually reported as a coefficient that is derived from correlating the sets of scores from the two tests being compared. Ideally, a correlation coefficient of between $+.80$ and 1.00 is desirable. However, few motor tests reach this level of agreement. Construct validity is generally demonstrated by using a statistic that measures differences between the mean scores of each group. Thus, when construct validity is claimed at the $.05$ level of significance, it means that it is expected that the test will accurately classify an individual as belonging to one group rather than another 95 times out of 100.

Determining Reliability

Test reliability is a measure of an instrument's consistency. A reliable test can be depended on to produce the same scores at different times if no intervention, learning, or growth has occurred between test sessions. The two test reliability techniques used for most physical and motor tests are test-retest and alternate forms.

The test-retest technique is the most frequently used method for demonstrating reliability of physical and motor performance instruments. To establish test-retest reliability, the same test is administered to the same group of people twice in succession, and then the scores are correlated to determine the amount of agreement between them. The interval between administrations of the test should be carefully controlled. Never should a period of more than two weeks lapse between test administrations.

The alternate form reliability technique is also referred to as equivalent form reliability. When two tests are identified that are believed to measure the same trait or skill and have been standardized on the same population, they can be used to determine alternate form reliability. To estimate the degree to which both forms correlate, the tests are divided in half and administered to the same population. Half of the group will be tested by using Test A first and Test B second. The other half of the group will be tested with Test B first and then with Test A. The scores from Test A will be correlated with the scores from Test B to determine the amount of consistency (equivalency) between the tests.

Determining the extent to which sets of scores achieved during the testing sessions correlate is the most frequently used statistical method for estimating reliability. The stronger the correlation coefficient, the more reliable the test. A reliability coefficient between $+.90$ and $+1.00$ is most desirable because it means that 90 percent of the two test scores were the same; however, the larger the sample tested, the smaller the size of reliability coefficient that is acceptable.

Determining Objectivity

Objectivity means freedom from bias and subjectivity. The clearer and more concise the instructions, the more objective the instrument. Test objectivity is determined by having two or more scorers independently evaluate the performance of a subject being tested. The scorers' results are then correlated to determine amount of agreement. The greater the amount of agreement between the scores, the higher the correlation coefficient. An objectivity coefficient beyond $+.90$ would be considered an acceptable level of objectivity because it would indicate that all scorers agreed on the scores given 90 percent or more of the time.

Administrative Feasibility

Administrative feasibility means how practical and realistic the test is. Several factors must be considered when attempting to determine whether a given test is administratively feasible to use for a given purpose:

Cost. Resources available to purchase test manuals and equipment must be carefully considered. Costs of tests continue to increase; it is not uncommon for motor tests to range in cost from $250 to $1,000. To conserve resources, needed tests may be stored at a central source and made available for individuals to check out for brief periods of time.

Equipment. The amount and kind of equipment needed to administer tests vary widely. Frequently, it is possible to build, rather than purchase, equipment; however, some items, such as bicycle ergometers, may be out of the practitioner's price range. Standardized instruments will outline very specific guidelines for equipment use or include specific equipment with the purchase of the assessment kit. Many criterion-referenced, curriculum-based tests require equipment that is part of most physical education equipment inventories. School districts vary on their policy regarding homemade equipment because of liability issues.

Level of training to administer the test. Some tests require extensive training for accurate administration; indeed, some tests require evidence of professional training and certification of capability before the tests can be used. Other tests simply require practice and familiarity with the items. Professionals familiar with test administration, such as university professors who teach assessment courses, can be contacted to provide workshops for practitioners who are responsible for testing.

Level of training to interpret the test. Professional training in interpretation of test results is required for most tests. Educators should select tests they understand and can interpret accurately. Again, professionals can be retained to provide workshops in test interpretation.

Purpose of the test. How a test is to be used will determine which test to select. As indicated earlier, different types of tests are used for screening, diagnosing, and programming purposes. For a test to be useful, it must provide the needed information.

Length of time to administer. Limited time is available in school settings for test administration. However, too frequently a test selected because it can be administered in a short period of time yields little usable information. On the other hand, tests that require more than 45 minutes to an hour of administration time are unrealistic for school settings. Tests need to be selected that provide the needed information yet require a minimum of time to administer.

Personnel needs. Some tests can be used if adequate personnel are available to administer and score them. When paraprofessionals and/or volunteers are available, they must be carefully trained, particularly if they do not have a strong background in motor and physical development.

Standardization population. If the test information is going to be used to diagnose a student's movement problems to determine whether special services are required, the test must be standardized on a population the same age as the student being tested. Practitioners sometimes avoid using the appropriate standardized test because they are aware that their student cannot adequately perform the items in the test. One of the purposes of a standardized test is to establish that the student is performing significantly below same-age peers.

Type of Disability

The type of disability a student has greatly impacts the assessment process. There are some tests available that have been developed for use with individuals with specific types of disabilities. These tests obviously should be used for diagnostic purposes to determine whether a student qualifies for special services. Other tests, both formal and informal with minor modifications, can be used to provide the information needed for developing the IEP and determining intervention programs. An overview of tests appropriate for use with individuals with disabilities is presented in Table 3-10. More information about tests that are appropriate for use with specific types of disabilities, as well as suggestions about how they might best be used, will be presented in the chapters in which distinctive populations are discussed (see Figure 3-2).

Care must be exercised to select the assessment tool that is most appropriate and administratively feasible. Once appropriate assessment instruments have been selected, it is critical that the administration, interpretation, and recommendations from the tests produce the type of information that can be used to design a physical education program that will contribute to the growth and independence of students, particularly those with disabling conditions. General guidelines for ensuring that the procedure results in appropriate educational programming are presented in the next section.

THE TESTING PROCESS

Although selecting an appropriate test is a critical step in gathering meaningful assessment information, the most important phase of the process is to ensure that the information gathered is truly representative of the student's capability. The effective evaluator fully prepares for the testing session, conducts the testing with care, and analyzes the information gathered as soon after the session as possible.

Preparations for Testing

After an appropriate instrument has been selected, it is important to give careful thought to the testing

Table 3-10   Selected Motor Tests Appropriate for Use with Individuals with Disabilities

Test	Source	Population	Components	Scoring Type
Adapted Physical Education Assessment Scale II (APEAS II)	AAHPERD Publications 1900 Association Drive Reston, VA 20191	Students qualifying for special education services, ages 5–18 yrs	Motor development, perceptual motor function, motor achievement, posture, fitness	Criterion-referenced
A recently updated standardized test that includes a DVD showing how to administer the items.				
Brockport Physical Fitness Test for Youths with Physical and Mental Disabilities (1999)	Human Kinetics Publishers Box 5076 Champaign, IL 61820	Visually impaired, auditory impaired, orthopedically impaired, ages 10–17 yrs	Body composition, muscular strength and endurance, speed, power, flexibility, coordination, cardiorespiratory endurance	Criterion-referenced
A standardized physical fitness test that includes modifications for different types of disabilities				
Bruininks-Oseretsky Test of Motor Proficiency (BOT II) (2003)	http://ags.pearsonassess ments.com	Normal, mentally retarded, learning disabled, ages 4–21 yrs	Speed and agility, balance, bilateral coordination, strength, fine motor, response speed, hand-eye coordination, upper limb speed and dexterity	Normative-referenced
A standardized test composed of subtests that can be administered individually to determine underlying sensory input and ability level delays				
Competency Testing for Adapted Physical Education (CTAPE) (1995)	Louisiana Department of Education Office of Spec Educ Ser PO Box 94064 Baton Rouge, LA 70804 www.doe.state.la.us/lde/ uploads/2674.pdf	Ambulatory individuals 6 yrs and older	Locomotor, manipulative, balance, sport, fitness, gymnastic, spatial relations	Content- and criterion-referenced
A task analyzed curriculum-imbedded program for all students with disabilities except for the most severely involved				
Computer Assisted Adapted Physical Education Assessment Instruments	Dan Cariaga PC Consulting Service PO Box 1332 Pismo Beach, CA 93448 http:a-ape.com			
Worksheets for 21 of the most commonly used APE assessment tools; input raw scores and receive a statistically interpreted written report				

Name (Year)	Publisher/Address	Population	Skills	Reference Type
I CAN (1978)	Hubbard Scientific Co. PO Box 104 Northbrook, IL 60062	Ambulatory individuals of any age	Preprimary motor and play skills; primary skills; sport, leisure, and recreation skills	Criterion- and content-referenced
A task analyzed curriculum-imbedded program for moderate-to-low-functioning individuals				
Mobility Opportunities Via Education (MOVE) (1990)	Kern County Superintendent of Schools 1300 17th St. —City Centre Bakersfield, CA 93301-6683	Nonambulatory, severely and profoundly involved of any age	A sequence of motor skills that lead to independent self-management	Content- and criterion-referenced
A task analyzed curriculum-imbedded program to promote head, trunk, and limb control of severely and profoundly involved individuals				
Motor Activities Training Program: Special Olympics Sports Skill Program (1997)	Special Olympics Intern 1325 G Street, NW Suite 500 Washington, DC 20005	Severe handicaps of any age	Mobility, dexterity, striking, kicking, aquatics, manual and electric wheelchair	Content-referenced
A task-analyzed program designed for persons with severe mental retardation who are not yet able to compete in a rigorous sports program				
Movement Assessment Battery for Children (Movement ABC–2) (2007)	http://pearsonassess.com	Motor development delays, ages 3–12 yrs	Balance, fine motor, object-control, locomotor	Normative- and content-referenced
A standardized, updated version of the Stott-Henderson Test of Motor Impairment; designed to detect, quantify, and correct motor development delays				
Moving into the Future: National Standards for Physical Education	National Assoc. for Sport and Physical Education AAHPERD 1900 Association Dr. Reston, VA 22091	School-age individuals	Locomotor, balance, object-control, gymnastics, health-related, fitness, sport skills	Normative-referenced
A national curriculum-based assessment developed by physical education professionals in the United States				
Ohio State University Scale of Intra Gross Motor Assessment (OSU–SIGMA) (1979)	Mohican Publishing Co. PO Box 295 Loundonville, OH 44842	Normal, ages 2½–14 yrs	Basic locomotor skills, ladder and stair climbing, throwing, catching	Content- and criterion-referenced
A test to identify critical components of basic locomotor, climbing, and object-control skills				

(Continued)

Table 3-10 (Continued)

Test	Source	Population	Components	Scoring Type
Physical Best and Individuals with Disabilities: A Handbook for Inclusion in Fitness Programs (1995)	AAHPERD 1900 Association Dr. Reston, VA 22091	Mild and moderate retardation, Down syndrome, nonambulatory, cerebral palsy, visual impairment, 5–17 yrs	Aerobic capacity, body composition, flexibility, upper and lower body strength and endurance	Criterion- and normative-referenced
A standardized test for measuring and developing the physical fitness levels of persons with disabilities				
Physical Fitness and Motor Skill Levels of Individuals with Mental Retardation (1991)	Illinois State Printing Service Illinois State University Normal, IL 61761-6901	Mild and moderate mental retardation and Down syndrome, ages 6–21 yrs	Balance, body composition, muscular strength and endurance, power, flexibility, cardiorespiratory endurance, hand-eye coordination	Normative-referenced
A standardized physical fitness test with norms for persons with mental retardation				
Project M.O.B.I.L.T.E.E. Curriculum Imbedded Assessment (1981)	www.tahperd.org/LINKS/ links_physical_ed.html	Moderately and low functioning, ambulatory and nonambulatory, any age	Cardiovascular, speed, agility, power, strength and endurance	Content- and criterion-referenced
A task-analyzed, curriculum-imbedded program for ambulatory and nonambulatory individuals (available at no charge from address provided)				
Test of Gross Motor Development II (TGMD II)	PRO-ED Publishing Co. 8700 Shoal Creek Blvd. Austin, TX 78757-6897 www.devprosoftware.com	Motor Development Delays, ages 3–10 yrs	12 gross motor patterns, including locomotor and manipulative	Criterion- and normative-referenced
A test that can be used to identify critical components of locomotor and manipulative skills				

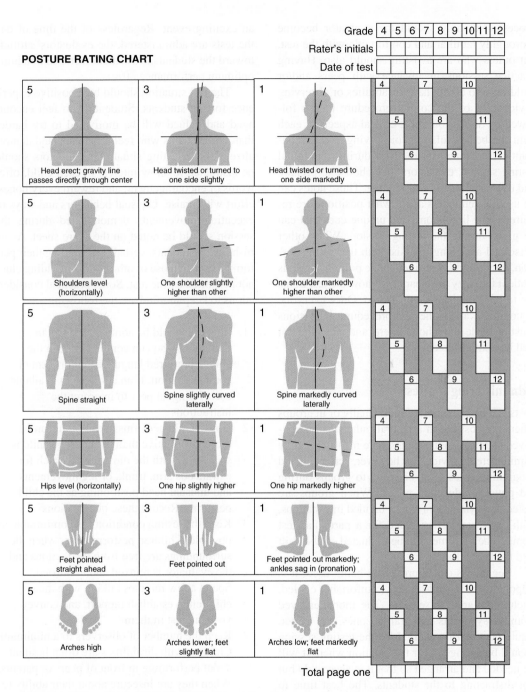

POSTURE RATING CHART

	Grade	4	5	6	7	8	9	10	11	12
	Rater's initials									
	Date of test									

Figure 3-2 New York State Postural Survey

Courtesy New York State Education Department.

process. Not only should the evaluator become thoroughly familiar and comfortable with the test, but others who are assisting should also. Having practice sessions in advance with peers and/or children who do not have disabilities or observing a videotape of the correct procedure to use followed by discussion of the critical aspects of each item can be helpful. To avoid having to refer constantly to the test instructions during the actual testing session, evaluators may choose to prepare and use "crib" notes while testing. These notes can be used as reminders about what positions are required, time limitations, and unique cues that can be given during the testing session. When other personnel are going to assist with the testing session, they should be trained to the point where it is evident that they are clear about how the test items are to be administered and scored. Once everyone is confident about the test procedures, decisions must be made about how, where, and when the test will be administered.

Administering the Test

Tests can be administered individually or in groups whenever possible in a natural rather than a contrived setting. Diagnostic tests are most frequently administered individually; however, screening and programming tests can be given to groups during the physical education period. When groups are tested, the gymnasium can be divided into stations, with each station designated for a particular test item, or the movements to be evaluated can be built into the lesson for the day.

Regardless of the procedure being used, it is important that a well-lighted, comfortably cooled, uncluttered area be selected. The more removed from noisy events and traffic zones, the better. Equipment that is required for the testing session should be arranged near the location where it will be needed and arranged so that it is accessible but not distracting to the students. The best time to administer tests is midmorning or midafternoon. Whenever possible, avoid administering tests early or late in the day, just before or after lunch, after a student has been ill, or prior to or just after

an exciting event. Regardless of the time of day the tests are administered, the evaluators' attitude toward the students is a critical factor in obtaining optimum performance efforts.

The test situation should be a positive experience for the students. Students who feel encouraged and valued will be motivated to try harder than will students who feel threatened and demoralized by the testing situation. Evaluators should be instructed to show interest in each child, offer words of encouragement, and reward every honest effort with praise. Unusual behaviors and ways of executing movements demonstrated during the session should be noted on the score sheet. Avoid rushing the students, verbally comparing their performance with those of others, and providing clues not permitted by the test. Some practical considerations to keep in mind are the following:

1. The test should be administered by an individual who can communicate in the child's preferred language and/or form of communication. If an adult is not available, use a bilingual peer to interpret the instructions

2. How a child performs a task often can be more informative than whether the child is successful with the movement. Watch for extraneous arm, trunk, or leg movements and unusual head positioning as the child performs. Record these observations

3. Keep the testing conditions as comfortable as possible. Children perform better when the surroundings are free from distractions and the evaluator is relaxed and unhurried. Spend a few minutes talking with the children to establish rapport, and convey your interest in them

4. Keep the number of observers to a minimum. Children with disabilities are often hesitant about performing in front of peers or parents. When they are insecure about their ability to perform, they will try too hard or fail to give their best effort if people are watching them

5. Repeat trials when you think the child might be able to perform adequately if given more time

or is less tense. If a child is having difficulty with a given task, go on to easier tasks until he or she regains some confidence. Then go back to a task that was failed earlier and try again

6. Observe the child on different days if possible. Children are just like adults—they have their good days and their bad days. If the testing can be spread over two or three days, the child will have the opportunity to show different performance levels

7. Limit testing time to reasonable periods. Children will perform best for a period of 30 to 60 minutes. If the time is too brief, the child does not have time to get warmed up and into the procedure. If you go beyond an hour of testing time, fatigue and distractibility often interfere with performance

A sensitive evaluator keeps the child's best interest in mind at all times. Focusing on the test rather than the child distorts test results and gives an inaccurate picture of the child's true capabilities. On completion of the testing session, observations and scores must be recorded, organized, and interpreted.

Organizing and Interpreting the Test Results

Once you have the test results in hand, it is important to analyze them as soon as possible. The shorter the time lapse between administering and interpreting the results, the easier it is to remember how the student performed individual tasks in the test. To facilitate reporting and interpreting the data, the test results should be organized. Actual test data for Adam P. are presented in Figures 3-3, 3-4, and 3-5.

Test performance can be charted, grouped according to strengths and challenges, or reported according to subset or subtest scores. Examples of each of these organizational techniques are presented in Figures 3-6 and 3-7 and Tables 3-11 and 3-12. As will be seen by studying these examples, there are advantages and disadvantages to each.

Charted data provide a simple visual record of how the student performed in comparison with established normative standards. This form of reporting can be accomplished in a brief period

of time; however, little information from which to establish goals and to develop an intervention program is available (see Figures 3-6 and 3-7). For instance, by viewing the charted test results, it appears that Adam's strength is not a problem area because his composite strength score is 8 years, 11 months (10 months beyond his age). However, when one reviews the actual test item scores in his comprehensive report, it is apparent that shoulder girdle strength score was very strong, but both abdominal and hip strength scores were very low. Thus, when using a charting method of reporting for individuals, deficiencies within a general area may be masked by one or two item scores. This form of reporting test results can be very helpful when large numbers of students are being tested with the same instrument more than once. The student's performance can be recorded in a different color each time, so that quick comparisons from one test period to the next can be made.

Highlighting Adam's strengths and challenges without providing subtest scores provides more information than simply charting the test results. Grouping test information according to strengths and challenges provides ready reference to areas of concern while acknowledging the student's stronger points (see Table 3-11). However, the evaluator must be trusted to determine accurately what constitutes a strength and a challenge. With this form of reporting, it is possible to determine what Adam can and cannot do, but his performance cannot be compared with that of others his age.

Reporting test results according to subtest scores and including a narrative describing performance on tasks within the subtests give the reader the greatest amount of information (see Table 3-12). Subtest scores reported in percentiles or age equivalency provide both the parent and teacher with a comparative picture of how the student is performing in relation to his or her age group. The narrative report gives the reader insight into what parts of the domain the student is having difficulty with, which will be very helpful in setting goals as well as designing the intervention program. Reporting of this sort facilitates communication between the evaluator and others who will read and use the information; however, it is

TGMD–2

Test of Gross Motor Development–Second Edition

Profile/Examiner Record Form

Section I. Identifying Information

Name: Adam P.
Male ☒ Female ☐ Grade: 3RD
Date of Testing: 10-16-07
Date of Birth: 8-27-99
Age: 8-1

School: BORMAN ELEMENTARY
Referred by: PARENTS
Reason for Referral: COMPLETE EVALUATION
Examiner: JEAN PYFER
Examiner's Title: C.A.P.E

Section II. Record of Scores

First Testing

	Raw Score	Standard Score	Percentile	Age Equivalent
Locomotor	41	9	37	7-3
Object Control	27	5	5	4-9
Sum of Standard Scores		14		
Gross Motor Quotient		82	12	

Second Testing

	Raw Score	Standard Score	Percentile	Age Equivalent
Locomotor				
Object Control				
Sum of Standard Scores				
Gross Motor Quotient				

Section III. Testing Conditions

A. Place Tested: MCL 908 H

	Interfering				Not Interfering
B. Noise Level	1	2	3	4	(5)
C. Interruptions	(1)	2	3	4	5
D. Distractions	1	2	3	4	(5)
E. Light	1	2	3	4	(5)
F. Temperature	1	2	3	4	(5)

G. Notes and other considerations: VERY, VERY TALKATIVE – TESTING TIME EXTENDED BECAUSE OF HIS TALKATIVE NATURE

Section IV. Other Test Data

Name of Test	Date	Standard Score	TGMD–2 Equivalent

Section V. Profile of Standard Scores

Standard Scores	Locomotor	Object Control	Standard Scores	Quotients	Gross Motor Quotient	Quotients
20			20	150		150
19			19	145		145
18			18	140		140
17			17	135		135
16			16	130		130
15			15	125		125
14			14	120		120
13			13	115		115
12			12	110		110
11			11	105		105
10			10	100		100
9			9	95		95
8			8	90		90
7			7	85		85
6			6	80		80
5			5	75		75
4			4	70		70
3			3	65		65
2			2	60		60
1			1	55		55

1

Additional copies of this form (#9262) may be purchased from PRO-ED, 8700 Shoal Creek Blvd., Austin, TX 78757-6897 800/897-3202 Fax 800/397-7633

Figure 3-3 Test of Gross Motor Development

Bruininks-Oseretsky Test of Motor Proficiency

Robert H. Bruininks, Ph. D.

INDIVIDUAL RECORD FORM
Complete Battery and Short Form

NAME _Adam P._   SEX: Boy ☒ Girl ☐   GRADE _3_

SCHOOL/AGENCY _____   CITY _____ STATE _____

EXAMINER _J. Pyfer_   REFERRED BY _PARENTS_

PURPOSE OF TESTING _____

Arm Preference: (circle one)
(RIGHT)   LEFT   MIXED

Leg Preference: (circle one)
(RIGHT)   LEFT   MIXED

	Year	Month	Day
Date Tested	2001	10	18
Date of Birth	1999	8	27
Chronological Age	8	1	

TEST SCORE SUMMARY

Complete Battery:

SUBTEST	POINT SCORE Maximum	POINT SCORE Subject's	STANDARD SCORE Test (Table 23)	STANDARD SCORE Composite (Table 24)	PERCENTILE RANK (Table 25)	STANINE (Table 25)	OTHER
GROSS MOTOR SUBTESTS:							
1. Running Speed and Agility	15	0					—
2. Balance	32	20	10				6-2
3. Bilateral Coordination	20	8	13				7-5
4. Strength	42	18	18				8-11
GROSS MOTOR COMPOSITE				41 SUM			
5. Upper-Limb Coordination	21	12	8				6-8
FINE MOTOR SUBTESTS:							
6. Response Speed	17	11	21				13-11
7. Visual-Motor Control	24	18	15				8-5
8. Upper-Limb Speed and Dexterity	72	32	12				7-5
FINE MOTOR COMPOSITE				48 SUM			
BATTERY COMPOSITE				97 SUM			

*To obtain Battery Composite: Add Gross Motor Composite, Subtest 5 Standard Score, and Fine Motor Composite. Check result by adding Standard Scores on Subtests 1-8.

Short Form:

	POINT SCORE Maximum	POINT SCORE Subject's	STANDARD SCORE (Table 27)	PERCENTILE RANK (Table 27)	STANINE (Table 27)
SHORT FORM	98				

DIRECTIONS

Complete Battery:

1. During test administration, record subject's response for each trial.

2. After test administration, convert performance on each item (item raw score) to a point score, using scale provided. For an item with more than one trial, choose best performance. Record item point score in circle to right of scale.

3. For each subtest, add item point scores; record total in circle provided at end of each subtest and in Test Score Summary section. Consult *Examiner's Manual* for norms tables.

Short Form:

1. Follow Steps 1 and 2 for Complete Battery, except record each point score in box to right of scale.

2. Add point scores for all 14 Short Form items and record total in Test Score Summary section. Consult *Examiner's Manual* for norms tables.

AGS® Published by American Guidance Service, Inc., Circle Pines, MN 55014-1796

Printed on recycled paper

A 0 9 8 7 6

Figure 3-4   Bruininks-Oseretsky Test

Form T-1R

BIOPTOR®
VISION TESTS

No._____

Name   *Adam P.*   Date *10 - 16 - 01*

Address   Age *8 - 1*

                                                 Sex: M ☒ F ☐

Occupation   *STUDENT*

Glasses
Worn: No ☒   Always ☐   Near Only ☐   Far Only ☐   Multi-Focal ☐   Other

Difficulty with Vision: No ☒   Yes ☐   Last Exam by Doctor *SUMMER, 2001*

Comments:

	Test No.		Low Score					High Score	
FAR POINT TESTS 0	1	Vertical Phoria	R. Hyper ★	→ ★	→ ◆		⊙	⊖	
			L. Hyper ■	→ ■	→ ▲				
	2	Lateral Phoria	Over CONVERGENCE 1 ② 3 4 5				6 7	8	
			Under 15 14 13 12 11				10 9		
	3	Central Fusion	Two • • Four Far Apart	Four Close Together	• •	Four Then Three • •• •	Three Boxes •• •		
		Acuity	1	2	3	4	5	6	
	4	Left	(ECDBF)	(TPCDB)	(CEZFL)	EPCFZ	TZOLF	(TCLDZ)	
		Both	LDZTC (OETFL)		(DZEOP)	(LPTOB)	ELTDC	OFLCT	
		Right	(TPEOB)	BFZDL	(TCPBO)	ELDZF	BCZOE	DZEOF	
	5	Stereo	L-R only Forward runner			A 2	B 5	C 3	
	5a	Stereo	L-R only	A 4	B 2	C 5	D 3	E 1 F 2	
	6	Color	A 8	B 15	C 5	D 35	4 out of 6 All Correct		
NEAR POINT 10	7	Lateral Phoria	Over CONVERGENCE 1 2 3 ④ 5				6 7	8	
			Under 15 14 13 12 11				10 9		
	8	Central Fusion	Two • • Four Far Apart	Four Close Together •	• •	Four Then Three • •• •	(Three Boxes •) •		
		Acuity	1	2	3	4	5	6	
	9	Left	(DCF)	(FZDL)	(DZEBO)	LPCFZ	(DCELT)	LDZOF	
		Both	(BPE)	(PCDB)	(FLTCP)	DTFEP	(LFZOE)	LGTDZ	
		Right	(OTB)	OETF	(OPCEZ)	(ELTOB)	TZODC	EDFYG	

Test taken: With ☐   Without ☒   Glasses.

Referred: No ☐   Yes ☒

Tester _____

Stereo Optical Company, Inc.
3539 N. Kenton Avenue
Chicago, Illinois 60641-3879

0 = CORRECT
1 = INCORRECT

Printed in U.S.A.

Figure 3-5   Bioptor Vision Tests

very time consuming. If there are designated professionals whose major responsibility is testing students in a district, they may wish to use this form of reporting at least once every three years and just provide progress reports during the intermittent years.

When the test results are going to be used to determine whether a student's performance is significantly delayed to require special services, comparison with age-expected results is necessary and required by law. Usually, any total or subtest score that falls beyond one standard deviation below the mean or below the 25th percentile or one year below the performance expected for the age of the child is considered a deficit area. But do

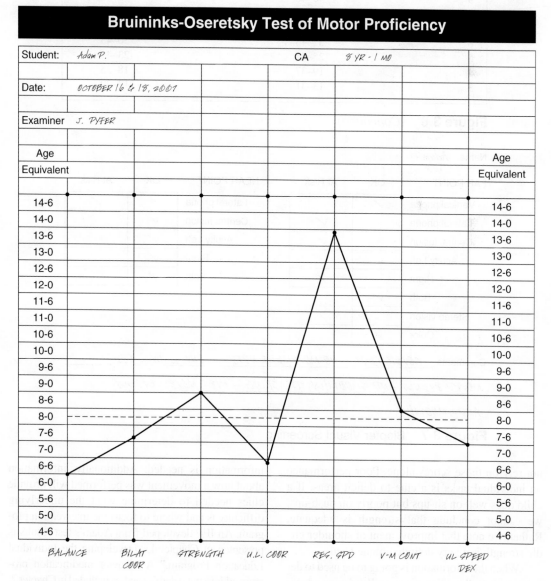

Figure 3-6

TEST OF GROSS MOTOR DEVELOPMENT
Raw Score Expectations for Ages 3 to 10 Years
(25th to 75th Percentile)

Age	Locomotor 25th–75th	Object Control 25th–75th
10	40–46	42–47
9	40–46	42–47
8	(39–45)	41–47
7	35–44	36–46
6	32–43	30–45
5	25–41	(23–41)
4	19–37	18–35
3	13–31	12–29

Figure 3-6   (*Continued*)

Name: *Adam P.*

FAR POINT	OK	At Risk
Vertical phoria	✓	
Lateral phoria		✓
Central fusion		✓
Acuity Left	✓	
Right		✓
Both	✓	
Stereo vision		✓
Color	✓	

NEAR POINT	OK	At Risk
Lateral phoria		✓
Central fusion	✓	
Acuity Left	✓	
Right	✓	
Both	✓	

Comments   *COVER TEST — NO MOVEMENT NOTED; CONV — DIV — EYES*
MOVED EVENLY AND SMOOTHLY; TRACKING — EYES MOVED EVENLY
AND SMOOTHLY

Figure 3-7   Biopter Visual Screening

not rely on those scores alone. Poor performance on individual tasks is a clue to deficit areas. If a child does well on sit-ups but poorly on push-ups, we cannot conclude that strength is adequate. Rather, we note that improvement of shoulder girdle strength is a very definite unique need.

When the information is going to be used to develop an IEP, determine goals, and/or design educational programs, descriptive rather than comparative information is needed. Additionally, information about how a movement was performed will provide clues needed to determine what the underlying difficulty is and where to focus the intervention program. An IEP developed from Adam's test results is presented in Chapter 4, "Developing the Individual Education Program." A behavior modification program addressing Adam's needs is included in Chapter 7, "Enhancing Student Behavior."

Table 3-11	**Adapted Physical Education Evaluation**

NAME: Adam P.   DOB: 8-27-99   CA: 8 years, 1 month

TEST DATES: October 16 & 18, 2007

EXAMINER: Dr. Jean Pyfer, CAPE, Adapted Physical Education Specialist

Adam, who is diagnosed with Asperger syndrome, was referred to the TWU Institute for Clinical Services and
   Applied Research by his parents for a complete motor evaluation and a visual examination. The Test of Gross
   Motor Development–2 and the visual screening tests were administered the first day. The visual screening
   tests included a cover test, a convergence/divergence tracking test, lateral and diagonal tracking tests, and the
   Biopter (an instrument that measures visual acuity, depth perception, and color vision). The Bruininks-
   Oseretsky Test of Motor Proficiency was administered during the second day of testing. All testing took place
   in a small room adjacent to MCL 908. Testing began at 2:30 on each day; no observers were present.

STRENGTHS
 1. Running
 2. Galloping
 3. Sliding
 4. Leaping
 5. Sliding to the left
 6. Stopping the response stick
 7. Tracing mazes
 8. Cutting out a circle
 9. Color vision
10. Visual acuity at near point
11. Central fusion at near point
12. Vertical phoria at far point

CHALLENGES
 1. Hop 3 times in succession
 2. Follow through when jumping, striking, kicking,
    throwing, and rolling
 3. Trapping the ball against the chest
 4. Dribbling a ball
 5. Sit-ups
 6. Long jumps
 7. Balance on one foot, eyes open and closed and stepping
    over a stick
 8. Synchronizing limbs on opposite sides of the body
 9. Lateral visual phoria at near and far point, central fusion
    and stereo vision at far point, and acuity of right eye at far point

GENERAL OBSERVATIONS—Adam was a nonstop talker. He went into great detail about every type of
   dinosaur that ever walked the earth. Because of his insisting that he describe so many dinosaurs, on both days
   it took almost three times the normal amount of time to test. On the second day he appeared to be somewhat
   irritated at me because I did not remember the names of the dinosaurs he told me about the previous day. As a
   result, he went through his entire repertoire again. He sometimes hurried through test items and did not score
   well. When I had the sense he could perform to a higher standard, I asked that he slow down and repeat the
   item. He did improve his performance on those items. He is an only child who lives with his mother and father
   in a metropolitan area in the Southwest.

CONCLUSIONS
1. Adam's ability to stop the response stick quickly indicates he comprehends cause and effect, and has well
   above average reaction time.
2. The scores he attained on maze tracing and cutting out a circle suggest appropriate visual motor control at
   close point.
3. His inability to do sit-ups indicates lack of abdominal muscle strength.
4. His low performance on the long jump indicates lack of explosive strength.
5. His inability to hop on his nonpreferred (left) leg, utilize both arms when jumping, and execute slides to the
   right suggests delayed development on the left side of the body. (Note: Sliding to the right requires the ability
   to hold one's balance momentarily on the left side of the body.)

(Continued)

Table 3-11	*(Continued)*

6. Adam's inability to synchronize movements of limbs across the center of his body, transfer weight while striking, rolling, and throwing indicates cross-lateral coordination is delayed.
7. His lack of visual central fusion, inability to balance on one foot for 10 seconds with eyes open, step over a stick while walking on a balance beam, control his dribble, catch a thrown ball consistently and/or trap the ball between his arms and chest, and contact a ball when kicking suggest lack of depth perception at a distance.

RECOMMENDATIONS
1. An exercise program to strengthen abdominal muscles and extensor, abductor, and adductor hip muscles
2. Gross motor activities wearing weighted cuffs on his left wrist and ankle to assist with increasing kinesthetic feedback and muscular development on the left side of the body
3. A swimming program to promote cross-lateral coordination
4. An examination by a visual developmental specialist to determine depth perception and remediation

Table 3-12	**Texas Woman's University Adapted Physical Education Evaluation**

NAME:	Adam P.
DOB:	August 27, 1999
CA:	8 years, 1 month
TEST DATE:	October 16 & 18, 2007
EXAMINER:	Dr. Jean Pyfer, CAPE
	Adapted Physical Education Specialist

Adam, who is diagnosed with Asperger syndrome, was referred to the TWU Institute for Clinical Services and Applied Research by his parents for a complete motor evaluation and a visual examination. The Test of Gross Motor Development–2 along with the visual screening tests were administered the first day. The visual screening tests included a cover test, a convergence/divergence tracking test, a lateral and diagonal tracking test, and the Biopter (an instrument that measures visual acuity, depth perception, and color vision). The Bruininks-Oseretsky Test of Motor Proficiency was administered during the second day of testing. All testing took place in a small room adjacent to MCL 908. Testing began at 2:30 on each day; no observers were present.

TGMD-2

	Score/Possible Score
1. Locomotor Subtest	
a. Run—Adam demonstrated all performance criteria.	8/8
b. Gallop—Demonstrated all aspects of the skill.	8/8
c. Hop—Adam demonstrated all performance criteria except he did not take off and land three consecutive times on the nonpreferred foot.	8/10
d. Leap—Adam demonstrated all performance criteria.	6/6
e. Horizontal jump—Adam met all performance criteria except he extended his arms forcefully upward, one out of two times, and did not thrust his arms downward during landing.	5/8
f. Slide—Adam demonstrated all performance criteria except the ability to slide to the right.	6/8
Subtest total:	41/48
2. Object Control Subtest	
a. Striking a stationary ball—He demonstrated all performance criteria except he did not transfer his body weight to his front foot when throwing.	8/10

(Continued)

Table 3-12	*(Continued)*

b. Stationary dribble—Adam contacted the ball with one hand at belt level once. He slapped rather than pushed the ball; the ball did not contact the surface near the feet. He did not maintain control of the ball for 4 consecutive bounces.   1/8

c. Catch—Adam extended his arms and hands in preparation to catch the ball and flexed his elbows. He did not catch the ball with hands only (he trapped the ball against his chest).   4/6

d. Kick—When kicking a stationary ball, Adam rapidly approached the ball and placed his nonkicking foot slightly behind the ball. He did not demonstrate an elongated stride prior to ball contact, nor did he kick the ball with the instep or toe.   4/8

e. Overhand throw—Adam used a windup and rotated his hip and shoulders, but he did not transfer his weight to the opposite foot nor did he follow through diagonally across the body.   4/8

f. Underhand roll—Adam demonstrated all performance criteria except he did not stride forward with foot opposite the preferred hand.   6/8

   Subtest total   27/48

VISUAL SCREENING

1. Cover tests—No extraneous eye movement was noted in either eye when each was covered and uncovered.

2. Convergence-Divergence—Adam's eyes moved evenly and smoothly when tracking an object moved toward his nose from a distance of 16 inches to a distance of 4 inches and back.

3. Tracking—His eyes moved evenly and smoothly when tracking an object moved laterally and diagonally about 16 inches from the bridge of his nose.

BIOPTOR TESTING

1. Far Point
   a. Scored above average on vertical phoria and color vision
   b. Scored average on visual acuity with the left eye and with both eyes
   c. Scored below average on lateral phoria (eyes overconverged), central fusion (saw 4 boxes far apart), and visual acuity with his right eye, and stereo vision

2. Near Point
   a. Scored above average on central fusion and acuity with each eye individually and with both eyes together
   b. Scored below average on lateral phoria (eyes overconverged)

BRUININKS-OSERETSKY TEST OF MOTOR PROFICIENCY

Age Equivalency
(Years-Months)

1. Gross Motor
   a. Running Speed and Agility   Did Not Administer
   b. Balance—Adam walked forward on the balance beam and floor for 6 steps;   6-2
   heel to toe on the floor 6 steps and on the beam 5 steps; he did not demonstrate the ability to step over a stick while walking down the the beam. He held his balance on one foot on the floor for 8 seconds and on the beam 5 seconds with his eyes open; he balanced on the beam on 1 foot with his eyes closed for 3 seconds.
   c. Bilateral Coordination—Adam demonstrated the ability to tap his feet alternately   7-5
   while making circles with his fingers and to synchronize finger and foot tapping on the same side of the body. He did not demonstrate the ability to synchronize tapping foot and finger on opposite sides of the body nor to synchronize leg and arm on the same side of the body or opposite sides of the body while jumping. He clapped 2 times while jumping and drew 6 lines and crosses simultaneously; he did not demonstrate the ability to touch his heels while jumping.

(Continued)

Table 3-12   *(Continued)*

d. Strength—He long-jumped 20 inches (below 5th percentile) and completed 16 push-ups (75th percentile); he did not complete any sit-ups (below 5th percentile).	8-11
2. Upper Limb Coordination	
a. Upper Limb Coordination—Adam caught 5 balls with both hands and 4 balls with 1 hand when bouncing the ball to himself; he caught 1 tossed ball with 2 hands and 1 with 1 hand. He hit a target with a tossed ball 3 out of 5 tries and touched a swinging ball 4 out of 5 times. He demonstrated the ability to touch his nose with his fingertip with eyes closed but did not touch his thumb to fingertips with eyes closed, nor did he pivot his thumb and index fingers to standard.	6-8
3. Fine Motor Subtests	
a. Response Speed—Adam stopped the response stick each trial and scored a median score of 11.	13-11
b. Visual-Motor Control—He cut out a circle with no errors and drew a line through a crooked path and a straight path with no errors, but he made 2 errors when drawing a line through a curved path. He drew a triangle with no errors and a circle and overlapping pencils with 1 error, and he did not accurately replicate a horizontal diamond.	8-5
c. Upper Limb Speed and Dexterity—Adam placed 14 pennies in a box with 1 hand and placed 7 pairs of pennies in 9 seconds. He opened a box with 1 hand and placed 7 pairs of pennies in 9 seconds. He sorted 11 cards, strung 3 beads, and displaced 10 pegs in 15 seconds each. He drew 8 vertical lines, placed 21 dots inside circles, and made 65 dots within 15 seconds.	7-5

GENERAL OBSERVATIONS—Adam was a nonstop talker. He went into great detail about every type of dinosaur that ever walked the earth. Because of his insisting that he describe so many dinosaurs, on both days it took almost three times the normal amount of time to test. On the second day he appeared to be somewhat irritated at me because I did not remember the names of the dinosaurs he told me about the previous day. As a result he went through his entire repertoire again. He sometimes hurried through test items and did not score well. When I had the sense he could perform to a higher standard, I asked that he slow down and repeat the item. He did improve his performance on those items. He is an only child who lives with his mother and father in a metropolitan area in the Southwest.

CONCLUSIONS
1. Adam's ability to stop the response stick quickly indicates he comprehends cause and effect and has well above average reaction time.
2. The scores he attained on maze tracing and cutting out a circle suggest appropriate visual motor control at close point.
3. His inability to do sit-ups indicates lack of abdominal muscle strength.
4. His low performance on the long jump indicates lack of explosive strength.
5. His inability to hop on his nonpreferred (left) leg, utilize both arms when jumping, and execute slides to the right suggests delayed development on the left side of the body. (Note: Sliding to the right requires the ability to hold one's balance momentarily on the left side of the body.)
6. Adam's inability to synchronize movements of limbs across the center of his body, transfer weight while striking, rolling, and throwing indicates cross-lateral coordination is delayed.
7. His lack of visual central fusion, inability to balance on one foot for 10 seconds with eyes open, step over a stick while walking on a balance beam, control his dribble, catch a thrown ball consistently and/or trap the ball between his arms and chest, and contact a ball when kicking suggest lack of depth perception at a distance.

(Continued)

Table 3-12	(*Continued*)

RECOMMENDATIONS

1. An exercise program to strengthen abdominal muscles and extensor, abductor, and adductor hip muscles
2. Gross motor activities wearing weighted cuffs on his left wrist and ankle to assist with increasing kinesthetic feedback and muscular development on the left side of the body
3. A swimming program to promote cross-lateral coordination
4. An examination by a visual developmental specialist to determine depth perception and remediation

SUMMARY

Assessment has become an integral part of the educational process. Students are evaluated for the purpose of (1) identifying those who have developmental delays, (2) diagnosing the nature of the student's problem or delay, (3) providing information to use to develop the student's IEP, (4) developing instruction specific to the student's specific needs, and (5) evaluating student progress. Evaluation instruments can be classified as informal or formal. Informal evaluation involves observing movements in a variety of settings, gathering information from parents, and/or using a checklist or clinical test. Formal evaluation involves using a standardized test instrument. Tests can be used to measure mastery of a general or specific curriculum, mastery of a functional or sport skill, level of physical fitness, perceptual motor development, or sensory-motor status. Performance is measured using a criterion or content reference. Criterion-referenced tests measure performance against a standard, whereas content-referenced tests are used to determine whether all components of a task or a series of tasks are demonstrated.

Which instrument is selected depends on established policy, whether standardization is required, administrative feasibility, and the student's type of disability. A variety of tests are available that are very useful for fitness and motor programming for students with disabilities. Evaluators should be trained in test administration and interpretation. Information gathered from assessment must be organized, interpreted, and reported in ways that facilitate communication and program development.

REVIEW QUESTIONS

1. What is the difference between a formal and an informal test?
2. What are the purposes of assessment?
3. When must a standardized test be used?
4. What is curriculum-based assessment?
5. What is administrative feasibility?
6. Describe, compare, and contrast three techniques for organizing test data.

STUDENT ACTIVITIES

1. Identify five assessment tools. Analyze and classify each according to whether the scoring method used is content- or criterion-referenced.
2. Using test results from a physical fitness test, identify present levels of performance.
3. Divide the class into small groups. Using made-up test results, have each group organize the test results by graphing, according to strengths and weaknesses and according to subtest scores. Have the students discuss the advantages and disadvantages of each type of data presentation.
4. Observe teachers assessing learners. Indicate the types of assessment used.
5. Make a list of behaviors/skills a person with disabilities would need to successfully use a fitness center in your community.

REFERENCES

1. Dattilo, J, Williams, R, Cary, L: Effects of computerized leisure education on knowledge of social skills of youth with intellectual disabilities, *Ther Rec J* 37(2):142–155, 2003.

2. de Bildt, A, Kraijer, D, Systema S, Minderas R: The psychometric properties of the Vineland Adaptive Behavior Scales in children and adolescents with mental retardation, *J Autism &38; Dev Dis* 5(1):53–62, 2005.

3. Ferrera, M, Grudzien, L: Impact of ADA and IDEA on wellness program design, *J Deferred Compensation* 11(2):48–57, 2006.

4. Hyde BJ: *A motor development checklist of selected categories for kindergarten children.* Unpublished thesis, Lawrence, University of Kansas, 1980.

5. Jansson L, Sonnander K, Wiesel F: Needs assessed by psychiatric health care and social services in a defined cohort of clients with disabilities, *Euro Arch of Psych* 255:57–64, 2005.

6. King G, Law M, King S, Hurley B, Rosebaum P, Hanna S, Kertoy M, Young N: *Children's assessment of participation and enjoyment (CAPE) and preferences for activities of children (PAC).* San Antonio, TX, Harcourt Assessment, 2004.

7. Leff S, Costigan, T, Power T: Using participatory-action research to develop playground-based prevention programs, *J of Sch Psy* 42:3–21, 2004.

8. Leff S, Lakin R: Playground-based observational systems: A review and implications for practioners and researchers, *Sch Psy Rev* 34(4):475–488, 2005.

9. Meisels SJ: Designing meaningful measurements for early childhood. In Malory BL, New RS, editors: *Diversity and developmentally appropriate practices.* New York, Teachers College, Columbia University Press, 1994.

10. Silverstein R: *A user's guide to the 1999 regulations.* Washington, DC, ERIC, 1999.

11. Waterman BB: Assessing children for the presence of a disability, *National Information Center for Children and Youth with Disabilities (NICHCY) News Digest* 4:1–24, 1994.

SUGGESTED READINGS

Gallo AM, Sheehy D, Patton K, Griffin L: Assessment benefits and barriers: What are you committed to? *JOPERD,* 77(8):46–50, October 2006.

Stewart A, Elliot S, Boyce BA, Block M: Effective teaching practices during physical fitness testing, *JOPERD,* 76(1):21–24, January 2005.

Tripp A, Zhu W: Assessment of students with disabilities in physical education: Legal perspectives and practices, *JOPERD,* 76(2):41–47, February 2005.

Vehrs P, Hager R: Assessment and interpretation of body composition in physical education, *JOPERD,* 77(7):46–51, September 2006.

RECOMMENDED WEB SITES (WWW)

Please keep in mind that these Web Sites are being recommended in the winter of 2007. As Web Sites often change, they may have been moved, reconfigured, or eliminated.

Dan Cariaga's adapted physical education assessment information and goals and objectives, http://a-ape.com

RECOMMENDED VIDEOS

Human Kinetics www.humankinetics.com/products
Brockport physical fitness test, video (NTSC), 1999.

AAHPERD Publications
1900 Association Drive

Reston, VA 20191
www.aapar.org/apeas

APEAS test administration, DVD, 2007.

Developing the Individual Education Program

Photo by Carol Huettig.

■ **O B J E C T I V E S**

Briefly explain educational accountability.

List the specific components of the individual education program (IEP).

Write a measurable annual goal for an IEP; the goal should be appropriate for a physical education program.

List the individuals who should attend the IEP/multidisciplinary team meeting. Describe their function within the IEP/multidisciplinary team meeting.

Explain the essential nature of the individual transition plan and the role of the physical educator in its implementation and development.

Explain some strategies a professional can use to encourage parents to take an active role in the IEP meeting.

Briefly describe the heightened role of the parents in the IEP process.

Thirty years after the passage of the Education of the Handicapped Act (1975), the educational needs of children and young adults with disabilities are still not being met. And the Congress of the United States continues to compromise the very nature of special education in/through the enactment of the

CASE STUDY

Adam

Please review the assessment of Adam in Chapter 3. Then, carefully review the individual physical education programs in Chapter 4.

APPLICATION TASK

Would you have included any other objectives on the IEP? Would you have added or eliminated any instructional modifications?

Individuals with Disabilities Education Improvement Act (IDEIA) and the No Child Left Behind (NCLB) Act of 2001 (NCLB).

Every child in the United States is entitled to a free, public education. This is true of every child with a disability, as well. However, each child with a disability has unique abilities and unique needs. The very nature of a disability simply enhances that uniqueness and requires that the child be taught more carefully.

The 108th Congress of the United States determined that many children with disabilities were not eligible for special education services in IDEIA. Specifically, in order to be eligible for special education a child must have a "clinical definition" of disability, determined by multidisciplinary testing, and must exhibit "adverse educational performance."[57] This has broad-based and significant implications for children with mild disabilities. Literally, children with mild intellectual disabilities, mild learning disabilities, or mild emotional disturbances may now be deprived of their access to an education modified to meet their unique needs. For a child with a disability to qualify for physical education, that service must be specified on the IEP.

To ensure that every child with a disability receives an appropriate education, the Education of the Handicapped Act of 1975 (P.L. 94-142) mandated that an individual education program (IEP) be developed for each student with a disability. The IEP should be the cornerstone of the student's education. It should be a living, working document that the teacher and parents use as the basis for the instructional process. (See Table 4-1.) IDEIA significantly compromises the intent of the educators who initially wrote the law. (See Table 4-2.) Congress eliminated the need for short-term objectives or benchmarks as part of the process of guaranteeing that a child's educational needs are met except when the child takes an alternative assessment. They did, however, retain the requirement that the IEP be reviewed at least annually.

> The IEP is not a piece of paper; it is a process in which parents, educators, and the student work together to ensure that the student is able to achieve his or her designated goals.[59]

The IEP requires that educators and administrators be accountable for the education of the child with a disability. The IEP process, through which a child's education is planned and delivered, requires a specific education program to be developed for each child with a disability. The federal mandates regarding the development of the IEP and the content of the IEP necessitate accountability. (See Table 4-3.)

Educators and administrators must be able to document the child's need, based on a comprehensive assessment and evaluation, and to outline, specifically, the methods, techniques, and procedures that will be used to educate the child, while keeping in mind the child's specific and unique needs. Many educators are, however, deeply concerned that the intent of the law regarding the IEP has virtually been ignored. The IEP has too often become paperwork completed for the sake of doing paperwork. *All too often, the IEP is neither individualized nor special.* Espin et al. wrote,

> Although most special educators would agree that an individual focus is what makes special education special and that the IEP is the key to tailoring individual programs, questions have been raised recently regarding the extent to which individual programming remains central to special education. Most specifically,

Table 4-1	Individual Physical Education Program, as Mandated by IDEIA

Name: Adam P.
Date of Birth: August 27, 1999
Assessment Dates: October 16 and 18, 2007
Chronological Age: 8 years, 1 month
School: Walnut Hill Elementary
Evaluator: Dr. Jean Pyfer, CAPE, Adapted Physical Education Specialist

Tests Administered
Bruininks-Oseretsky Test of Motor Proficiency
Test of Gross Motor Development–2
Bioptor Visual Test (acuity, color, and central fusion)

Present Level of Performance
- Adam was unable to hop on his nonpreferred leg (left).
- Adam was unable to synchronize movement of his limbs across the center of his body, transfer weight while striking, rolling and throwing; these are indicators of a delay in cross-lateral coordination.
- Adam was unable to complete a sit-up.

Annual Goal
Adam will be able to hop 5 times, consecutively, on his left leg, independently.

Annual Goal
Adam will be able to throw a tennis ball 20', 3 of 5 times, while stepping forward with the leg opposite the throwing arm (contralaterally).

Annual Goal
Adam will be able to perform 5 regular sit-ups, with feet on the floor and arms crossed on the chest.

Annual Service Learning Goal
Adam will spend 1 hour/week as an assistant coach in a youth sports program for children with physical disabilities.

Recommended Physical Education Placement
Adam will do well in the general physical education program for 3rd graders, with a physical educator sensitive to his unique strengths and capabilities. An adapted physical education consultant will help the teacher with specific strategies to meet Adam's needs.

Modifications/Adaptations
Modifications and strategies to facilitate participation in the general physical education program are included in Table 4-8.

Duration of Services
August 15, 2008, to May 15, 2009

concerns have been raised regarding the extent to which the same degree of individual tailoring occurs in inclusive settings—general education classrooms where students with disabilities are educated with their peers—as in non-inclusive settings—where students receive special education outside the general education classroom.[16]

Table 4-2	Individual Physical Education Program: A Plan a General Physical Educator or Paraeducator Could Implement

Name: Adam P.
Date of Birth: August 27, 1999
Assessment Dates: October 16 and 18, 2007
Chronological Age: 8 years, 1 month
School: Walnut Hill Elementary
Evaluator: Dr. Jean Pyfer, CAPE, Adapted Physical Education Specialist

Tests Administered
Bruininks-Oseretsky Test of Motor Proficiency
Test of Gross Motor Development–2
Bioptor Visual Test (acuity, color, and central fusion)

Present Level of Performance
• Adam was unable to hop on his nonpreferred leg (left).
• Adam was unable to synchronize movement of his limbs across the center of his body, transfer weight while striking, rolling and throwing; these are indicators of a delay in cross-lateral coordination.
• Adam was unable to complete a sit-up.

Annual Physical Education Goals [and objectives to ensure that the service provider can help Adam achieve those goals]

Annual Goal
Adam will be able to hop 5 times, consecutively, on his left leg.
    Objectives [to ensure Adam will accomplish his goal]
    Adam will be able to hop 3 times, on his left leg, while holding his teacher's hands.
    Adam will be able to hop 2 times, independently, on his left leg.
    Adam will be able to hop 3 times, independently, on his left leg.

Annual Goal
Adam will be able to throw a tennis ball, with his right hand, a distance of 20', 3 of 5 times, while stepping forward with the leg opposite the throwing arm (contralaterally).
    Objectives [to ensure Adam will accomplish his goal]
    Adam will be able to assume a front-back stride, with left foot lead, and throw a tennis ball, with his right hand, a distance of 10', 3 of 5 times.
    Adam will be able to transfer his weight, from his right foot to his left foot, and throw a tennis ball, with his right hand, a distance of 15', 3 of 5 times.
    Adam will be able to throw a ball, contralaterally, with his right hand, with a follow-through across his body, a distance of 15', 3 of 5 times.

Annual Goal
Adam will be able to perform 5 sit-ups, independently.
    Objectives [to ensure Adam will accomplish his goal]
    Adam will be able to perform 3 reverse sit-ups, lowering his body from a flexed position, feet on the floor, arms crossed over the chest, to a half-lying position on a mat.
    Adam will be able to perform 5 reverse sit-ups, lowering his body from a flexed position, feet on the floor, to a half-lying position on a mat.
    Adam will be able to perform 3 sit-ups, arms crossed over the chest, to a half-lying position on a mat.

(Continued)

Table 4-2	**(*Continued*)**

Annual Service Learning Goal

Adam will spend 1 hour/week as an assistant coach in a youth sports program for children with physical disabilities.

Recommended Physical Education Placement

Adam will do well in the general physical education program for 3rd graders, with a physical educator sensitive to his unique strengths and capabilities. An adapted physical education consultant will help the teacher with specific strategies to meet Adam's needs.

Modifications/Adaptations

Modifications and strategies to facilitate participation in the general physical education program are included in Table 4-8.

Duration of Services

August 15, 2008, to May 15, 2009

Table 4-3	**Contents of the Individual Education Program**

The IEP must include the following:

- A statement of the child's present level of performance
- How the child's disability affects involvement and performance in the general physical education class
- How the disability affects the child's involvement and progress in the general curriculum
- A statement of goals
- A statement of how progress toward the annual goals will be measured
- Indications of how the child can be involved and progress in the general curriculum
- A statement describing how each of the child's other needs that result from the child's disability will be met
- A statement describing special education and related services
- A statement describing supplementary aids and services
- A statement of program accommodations or modifications or supports for school personnel that will advance the child toward attaining educational goals
- A statement of services needed for the child to participate in extracurricular and other nonacademic activities
- A statement describing how the child is to be educated so he or she can participate with other children with and without disabilities
- An explanation of the extent, if any, to which the child will participate with children without disabilities in the general class
- A statement describing how the child's parents will be regularly informed, at least as often as parents of children without disabilities, of their child's progress
- A statement that provides information of the extent to which progress is sufficient to enable the child to achieve his or her goals by the end of the year
- Beginning at age fourteen, a statement of transition service needs that focuses on the student's course of study
- Beginning at age sixteen, a statement of needed transition services of interagency responsibilities or any needed linkages
- A plan for positive behavioral management if the child is disruptive

The emphasis on education within the general education program may have had a significant negative impact on the individualization long associated with quality special education programs. Teachers serving children with disabilities in "inclusive settings" are less likely than teachers in resource or self-contained classrooms to develop IEPs that meet the intent and specifications of the law.[16]

PROFESSIONAL PERSONNEL WHO MAY BE INVOLVED IN THE INDIVIDUAL EDUCATION PROGRAM AND/OR THE INDIVIDUAL TRANSITION PLAN

The variety of personnel who provide both direct and related services and who may be involved in the initial evaluation and in the child's subsequent individually designed education program are described in this section. Direct services are those to be provided as part of the child's special education. These include (1) instruction conducted in the classroom, in the home, in hospitals and institutions, and in other settings and (2) instruction in physical education. The personnel involved in the provision of these services are described in the following paragraphs.

Direct Service Providers

Special Educators

Special educators are professional personnel who have received specific training in the techniques and methodology of educating children with disabilities. In the past, special educators were trained primarily to provide instruction to children with one particular disability. For example, special educators received training and subsequent certification in "mental retardation," "emotional disturbance," or "deaf education." Today, most professional preparation programs provide training that leads to a general special education certification. This training and certification may better prepare educators to serve children who have more than one disability.

The level and type of instruction provided to children with disabilities depend on the child's present level of performance and expectations for future performance. For example, special educators working with children who have profound intellectual disorders and who are medically fragile require sensory stimulation experiences and health care (e.g., catheterization, tube feeding, medication) need to meet their unique sensory and developmental needs. Special educators working with children who are autistic and developmentally delayed need to provide a very structured prevocational, self-care program. Special educators teaching children with a history of abuse and subsequent emotional disorders may use a pre-academic or academic curriculum within the framework of a structured, positive behavior management program. The special educator, a classroom teacher, has primary responsibility for the child with disabilities.

Generally, as the child's primary teacher, the child's special educator is responsible for the implementation and monitoring of the IEP. The special educator should work closely with other professionals, including the physical educator and the adapted physical educator, to ensure that the child acquires developmentally appropriate motor skills. The physical educator should regularly communicate with the classroom teacher.

Hospital/Homebound Instructors

Hospital/homebound instructors are trained professionals who provide special education instruction to children who are hospitalized or who, because of severe medical disabilities, cannot be educated within the typical school setting. The education is the same, only the setting is different. Increasingly, parents of children with disabilities are opting to provide home-based instruction. Educators will need to provide services in the home.

Instructors in Institutions and Other Settings

For a variety of reasons, some children, particularly those with profound developmental delays and multiple disabilities, and increasingly those with severe emotional and behavioral disorders, receive their education within an institutional setting. Within recent years, court mandates have significantly improved the quality of both instruction and care within these facilities.

Adapted Physical Educators

The art, the science, and the profession of adapted physical education are described throughout this text. The role of the adapted physical educator, as part of the IEP/multidisciplinary team, is summarized in this section.

Adapted physical educators are physical educators with specialized training. Specifically, these professionals have training in the assessment and evaluation of motor behavior and physical fitness, the development of the child's individual physical education program (IPEP), the implementation of the child's IPEP, and the processes of teaching and managing the behavior of children with disabilities in a venue that emphasizes play, leisure, recreation, sport, and physical fitness skills.

Due, specifically, to the incredible work of Dr. Luke Kelly, University of Virginia, a certification in adapted physical education is now available to trained professionals who meet rigorous standards of professional preparation and who complete/pass a comprehensive examination. Fulfilling the criteria mandated by The Adapted Physical Education National Standards (APENS) allows the adapted physical educator to use the title "certified adapted physical educator," or "CAPE." Many states, however (California, Louisiana, and Minnesota, for example), have extensive certifications, which indicate a significant professional commitment and comprehensive training, as well.

Physical education is mandated by law as a direct education service, not a related service. Adapted physical educators with specific training and knowledge in the neurodevelopmental process may intervene at a variety of levels, depending on the extent of their training and commitment (see Table 4-4).

The initial passage of P.L. 94-142, 1975, mandated that physical education is to be a vital part of each child's special education program. In fact, physical education was the only curricular area designated specifically as a required, direct service. The intent of the law was that specially trained adapted physical educators would provide quality, direct, hands-on, daily physical education instruction to children with disabilities. A lack of financial and personnel resources, as well as a lack of commitment to physical education, in general, has made this scenario a dream, rather than a reality.

Table 4-4	Adapted Physical Education Levels of Intervention

Adapted physical educators with specific training and knowledge in the neurodevelopmental process may intervene at a variety of levels:
- Reflex integration
- Equilibrium development
- Sensory stimulation and sensory discrimination
- Sensory-motor development
- Body image and body cathexis
- Motor planning
- Locomotor and nonlocomotor skills
- Object-control skills
- Patters for leisure, recreation, and sport skills
- Skills and knowledge related to physical fitness

General Physical Educators

The intent of those who carefully crafted the wording of P.L. 94-142 was for physical educators with special training and certification to meet the unique motor needs of children with disabilities as part of their comprehensive education.[45] Increasingly, general physical educators are being asked to provide direct physical education instruction to learners with disabilities. General physical education professionals are, typically, professionals with a state certification or license in physical education. In many states, the educator has an all-level certification that indicates the individual has the necessary education and skills to provide physical education instruction for learners from kindergarten through high school.

The general physical educator, typically, has specific training in the following:

- Motor development
- Motor learning
- Pedagogy, particularly as it relates to human movement
- Anatomy and physiology
- Exercise physiology
- Biomechanical analysis of movement
- Leisure, recreation, and sport instruction
- Coaching

More and more learners with disabilities are receiving their physical education instruction from general physical education teachers within the general curriculum. This is effective only if the general physical educator has access to the personnel (adapted physical education consultant), aids, and resources necessary to provide quality instruction.

Vision Specialists

Historically, a child with a severe visual impairment received educational services within a segregated environment. Typically, educational services were delivered in a separate residential school facility or within a self-contained room in a given school building. In that setting, the child's primary teacher was a vision specialist, a teacher specially trained to meet the educational needs of the child with a severe visual disability.

The increased emphasis on inclusion of learners with disabilities in the general curriculum has changed that scenario. Specifically, the learner with a visual impairment, whenever possible, is educated in his or her home school with support from vision specialists and orientation and mobility specialists. Children who are totally blind, legally blind, or partially sighted and those who have multiple disabilities (whose visual loss is only one of their impairments) may be educated with support within the regular education classroom in school districts embracing the concept of inclusion.

Vision specialists have the skills necessary to complete a visual evaluation and educational assessment to determine the extent of visual disability and the types of intervention that will make possible a successful educational experience. The vision therapist/teacher focuses on modification of instruction, which may include specific visual, tactile, and auditory learning techniques. Other modifications also may be required for the child to learn in the designated education setting. The therapist may suggest augmentative aids, such as a computer with auditory input/output capability, or a text enlarger, to meet the unique needs of the child.

Orientation and Mobility Specialists

Orientation and mobility was added to the Amendments to IDEA of 1997 as a direct educational service. Orientation and mobility means services provided to students who are blind or visually impaired to enable them to use skills systematically to orient them within their environments in the schools, home, and community.[57]

Orientation and mobility services help students improve spatial and environmental concepts and use information received by the senses, such as sound and vibrations. Travel training is often an integral part of the individual transition plan, the special education program that is designed to prepare students for postschool activities. The orientation and mobility specialist works with the child and his or her general or special educators to help the child develop the skills necessary, for example, to use a cane or to successfully ascend and descend school bus stairs. The orientation and mobility specialist focuses on helping the learner develop the skills necessary to access his or her environment.

Related Service Providers

The law also specifies and defines related services. As indicated earlier in the chapter, these are services that must be provided to the child with disabilities so that the child can benefit from instruction. There are several related services that may assist the child to benefit from special education. The list of related services is not exhaustive and may include other corrective or supportive services, such as music or dance therapy, if they help the learner benefit from special education. The related service providers are described in the following paragraphs.

Audiologists

Audiologists are trained to complete a comprehensive evaluation of a child's hearing capabilities. This includes an evaluation of the child's response to the qualities of sound—intensity, pitch, frequency, and timbre. Based on the results of the evaluation, the audiologist makes recommendations to school personnel. The audiologist may suggest, for example, simple modifications in the educational environment of the child with a mild hearing impairment to facilitate learning; specifically, the child may be placed close to the teacher for instructional purposes. The audiologist may recommend that a hearing aid be provided for the child with a more severe hearing disability and may work closely with trained special educators who will help the child develop total communication skills, including sign language, speech reading, and oral language.

In addition, the audiologist may create and administer programs for prevention of hearing loss, as well as counsel parents and teachers regarding hearing loss. The audiologist may also determine children's needs when selecting and fitting an appropriate hearing aid and evaluating the effectiveness of amplification.[57]

Counseling Services

Counseling services are provided by a qualified social worker or other qualified personnel, such as psychologists and guidance counselors.[57] Counseling services are becoming increasingly important in the total education process for all children, particularly children with disabilities. The school-based counselor may serve children with disabilities by implementing programs designed to enhance self-esteem, to teach children to identify and avoid sexual abuse, to share techniques for values identification and clarification, or to teach techniques and methods for dealing with grief.

Children with disabilities living within dysfunctional families may need more comprehensive intervention. These children may need individual counseling services in order to benefit from educational services. Because the family unit must be addressed if counseling is to be of value and have long-lasting effects, the most effective programs involve each member of the family in the counseling process.

Medical Diagnostic Service Personnel

Medical diagnostic services must be provided for a child who needs these services in order to benefit from his or her education. Many school districts have working partnerships with a hospital or rehabilitation facility, so that children who require medical diagnostic services can be referred to medical diagnostic service personnel at that hospital or center. It is important to note, however, that the law does not mandate medical services, just medical diagnostic services.

To be eligible for special education services, a child with an orthopedic impairment or another health impairment must be diagnosed as having a disability; this diagnosis must be made by a licensed physician. For a child to be identified as "emotionally disturbed," a licensed psychologist or psychiatrist must confirm the diagnosis.

Occupational Therapists

Occupational therapists improve, develop, or restore functions impaired or lost through illness, injury, or deprivation, so that individuals can function independently.[57] Occupational therapy must be made available to a child with a disability who requires this service in order to allow the child to be successful in the educational environment. The American Occupational Therapy Association has adopted occupational therapy performance areas[6] that are the focus of occupational therapists in all settings. See Table 4-5 for a description of the services they provide.

Occupational therapists working within the educational setting have had to define their role and focus in relation to special education. As a result, the school-based therapist has had to develop a strategy to function within the educational model rather than the medical model. This is, primarily, due to the lack of funding promised by the Congress when P.L. 94-142 was passed. The American Occupational Therapy Association has described the occupational therapist serving in the schools in the following way:

> Registered occupational therapists in education systems are considered to be related service personnel. The occupational therapist is responsible for assessment, planning, and goal development and for providing appropriate intervention services designed to enhance the student's potential for learning. The occupational therapist assists the student in acquiring functional

Table 4-5	Occupational Therapy Performance Areas as Defined by the American Occupational Therapy Association[5]

1. Activities of daily living
   • Grooming
   • Oral hygiene
   • Bathing
   • Toilet hygiene
   • Dressing
   • Feeding and eating
   • Medication routine
   • Socialization
   • Functional communication
   • Functional mobility
   • Sexual expression
2. Work activities
   • Home management
   • Care of others
   • Educational activities
   • Vocational activities
3. Play or leisure activities
   • Play or leisure exploration
   • Play or leisure performance

American Occupational Therapy Association: Uniform terminology for occupational therapy, ed 2, Rockville, Md, 1989, The Association.

performance skills needed to participate in and benefit from the educational environment, and to help the student function independently.[5]

According to Orr, Gott, and Kainer[43] the occupational therapist in the school setting must focus on the student role. Within the schools, these professionals concentrate on activities of daily living that are part of the process of going to school. In addition, the school-based occupational therapist defines "school" as a child's "work." The occupational therapist is responsible for ensuring that the student with a disability can assume the role of student and benefit from instruction within the school setting. Orr, Gott, and Kainer define behaviors and activities that constitute the role of the student and then develop strategies to allow the child to be successful in the student role.[43]

The school-based occupational therapist contributes to the child's school success in a number of ways. The therapist may help wheelchair-enabled students move independently within the school by teaching them to carry a lunch tray on their lap, manage a ramp to and from the playground, and move through crowded halls without running into classmates. The therapist may assist a learning-disabled student by providing sensory-motor training to ready the child to receive instruction. The occupational therapist usually has significant education and training in the skills necessary to promote sensory integration.

The occupational therapist will often work in cooperation with the physical educator, particularly to ensure student success in managing travel around the gymnasium or playground, in developing strategies to maximize the development of appropriate social skills and play behavior, and in contributing to the physical education individual exercise plan.

Paraeducators

Paraeducators are education support professionals (ESP) who are hired to provide direct or indirect services in schools. They perform many of the routine duties that used to be required of teachers. Three-fourths of these individuals work with special education students. Their roles include instructional and noninstructional assistants, teacher or program aides; preschool caregivers; building, bus, and playground monitors; crossing guards; and nonmanagerial supervisors.[41]

Parent Counselors and Trainers

Parents of children with disabilities are very important participants in the education of their children. This echoes the mandates of P.L. 105-17 that the parent is the child's first and primary teacher. Helping parents gain the skills that will enable them to help their children meet the goals and objectives of the IEP or the individual family service plan (IFSP) is critical.[57] The services provided by parent counselors and trainers are vital to those facing the reality of raising a child with a disability. This counseling and training are even more crucial for a single parent raising a disabled child. The grief, financial struggles, loneliness, and fears are often overwhelming.

Parent counseling and training also focus on helping the parent(s) develop appropriate expectations regarding the child's growth and development. The parent must be helped to develop realistic, yet hopeful, goals for the child.

Physical Therapists

The physical therapist is trained to provide services that address range of motion, maintenance, and development of muscle tone, gait therapy, and mobility assistance with and without physical aids or equipment. The physical therapist can be a vital and integral part of the motor development team. The therapist brings to the child with disabilities a vast wealth of information regarding human motion.

One of the major problems facing the public schools that are attempting to meet the mandates of the federal law is that it is increasingly difficult to hire a physical therapist to work within the schools. The services of physical therapists are sought by hospitals, rehabilitation facilities, and nursing homes. Generally, the public schools cannot compete financially to hire and retain physical therapists.

Psychologists

Psychological services for children with disabilities, and if necessary for their parent(s), have been designated as a related service. Their responsibilities include

- Administer psychological and educational tests
- Interpret assessment results
- Interpret information about the child's behavior and condition related to learning
- Consult with other staff members in planning school programs to meet the special needs of children
- Conduct behavioral evaluations
- Plan and manage a program of psychological services
- Provide psychological counseling for parents and children

- Assist with developing positive behavior-intervention strategies

Many school districts provide these services by hiring a psychologist or psychiatrist as a consultant or on a per-child basis. Larger school districts may hire school-based psychologists as part of the assessment and intervention team.

These professionals are involved in the assessment of children with disabilities referred because of conduct, behavioral, or emotional disorders; aggressive behavior toward other children or their parent(s); severe depression; suicidal tendencies or attempted suicides; or reports of sexual or physical abuse or serious neglect.

Recreation Therapists

Therapeutic recreation specialists usually play their significant role in hospital and rehabilitation programs. Few school districts have the resources to hire and retain these personnel. The school-based recreation therapist has the following responsibilities: "(a) assessment of the interests, resources, level of participation, social capability, and physical limitations of a person with a disability, (b) education for leisure activities, (c) increasing the independence of a person with a disability, and (d) providing recreation activities that are nonstructured and more suited to the wants and needs of the person with a disability."[49]

The school-based recreation therapist provides instruction so that individuals with disabilities will be able to make wise choices in the use of leisure time. The intent is to provide instruction so students will be able to participate in community-based leisure activities. Because of the commitment of recreation therapists to community-based, lifetime activity development, these professionals may play a vital role in the development of the child's Individual transition plan (ITP). The child's IEP in middle school and high school must include specific goals and objectives related to community-based leisure and recreation activities.

Rehabilitation Counselors

Rehabilitation counselors provide services in individual or group sessions that focus specifically on career development, employment preparation, and achievement of independence and integration in the workplace and community. These services include vocational rehabilitation services funded under the Vocational Rehabilitation Act of 1973 as amended.[57]

The rehabilitation counselor focuses on helping the learner with a disability gain the confidence and learn the skills necessary to function as typically as possible. Most rehabilitation counseling and rehabilitation services address the needs of the learner with adventitious injuries or disabilities; these are injuries or disabilities that occur after the child has already experienced typical development.

Rehabilitation counseling addresses grief; specifically, the individual with a new injury or disability must grieve the loss of function or ability before he or she can get on with life. It also addresses strategies for the reestablishment of self-esteem. Techniques are taught so that the child can adapt or compensate for the injury or disability and live a full life. Play, games, leisure, recreation, and sports have been found to be effective tools in the rehabilitation process. Indeed, most major rehabilitation facilities encourage participation in these activities to facilitate recovery and development.

Assistive Technology Service Personnel

In this time, it is increasingly important for all our people to have access to the remarkable technology that is available for communication, interaction, and access to information. The Assistive Technology Act of 1998 defined assistive technology in the following way:

- "any item, piece of equipment, or product system, whether acquired commercially off the shelf, modified, or customized, that is used to increase, maintain, or improve functional capabilities of individuals with disabilities." (Assistive Technology Act of 1998)
- "any service that directly assists an individual with a disability in the selection, acquisition, or use of an assistive technology device." (Assistive Technology Act of 1998)

- Examples typically found in school settings include computers, communication devices, tape recorders, and personal devices, such as wheelchairs, hearing aids, and eyeglasses.[60]

Educational personnel who provide assistive technology services perform any service that directly assists an individual with a disability in the selection, acquisition, or use of an assistive technology device, including

(A) the evaluation of the needs of an individual with a disability, including a functional evaluation of the individual in the individual's customary environment;

(B) purchasing, leasing, or otherwise providing for the acquisition of assistive technology devices by individuals with disabilities;

(C) selecting, designing, fitting, customizing, adapting, applying, maintaining, repairing, or replacing of assistive technology devices;

(D) coordinating and using other therapies, interventions, or services with assistive technology devices, such as those associated with existing education and rehabilitation plans and programs;

(E) training or technical assistance for an individual with disabilities, or, where appropriate, the family of an individual with disabilities; and

(F) training or technical assistance for professionals (including individuals providing education and rehabilitation services), employers, or other individuals who provide services to, employ, or are otherwise substantially involved in the major life functions of individuals with disabilities.[27]

The Washington Assistive Technology Alliance outlined "best practices" in the individual education program:

- Potential benefits of assistive technology should be documented by every child's IEP team.
- The student's assistive technology needs should be assessed by someone with

expertise in the particular assistive technology relevant to the child's disability.

- Teaching the student, family, and school staff how to use the assistive technology during school activities should be addressed in the IEP. In addition to academic classes, these may include school-sponsored clubs and sport teams, band or orchestra, field trips and other school-sponsored events.
- The IEP should include information about who will pay for warranties, insurance, and repairs to the assistive technology device.
- The student's postsecondary assistive technology needs should be considered as an integral part of the transition planning process.
- An IEP should address the types of ongoing services needed to support the use of the assistive technology and the circumstances under which the assistive technology will be sent home.[60]

As the availability of technology to the general public has escalated dramatically, so have the nature and types of technology available to students with disabilities. For example, Microsoft Windows has a feature called "Sticky Keys," which makes it easier to push a designated computer key. Xybernaut and IBM have developed computer systems with touch screens, voice recognition, and icons that are touch-activated.[54] A remarkable technology available for students with disabilities is universal design. A student using this technology is able to have text materials highlighted; the text changed to a different, more readable font; or the particular material presented at a lower reading level. The use of personal data assistants (PDAs) may be very useful for learners with mild disablties to help them coordinate their learning.[54]

School Health Service Personnel

School health services must be provided to students with disabilities. In most school districts, the school health service personnel are nurses. These health services include monitoring immunization records and monitoring and/or completing health

procedures, such as catheterization or tracheostomy tube suction. School health services for children with disabilities become more complex as more children who are medically fragile pursue their right to a free, appropriate public education as mandated by IDEA and Section 504 of the Rehabilitation Act.

Social Workers

Some of the specific tasks done by social workers include

- Prepare social or developmental histories of children with disabilities
- Conduct group or individual counseling with parents and children
- Work in partnership with parents regarding aspects of the child's living situation that affect the child's adjustment to school
- Assist in developing positive behavior-intervention strategies

The licensed social worker intervenes within the family, seen as part of the total community, and helps the child with disabilities and his or her family deal with issues that directly relate to the disability—discrimination, fear, guilt, substance abuse, child abuse, medical expenses, and the intrusion of well-meaning professionals into their lives. The social worker is trained to assist the family in coping with the vast and often complex system designed to provide support for families in trouble. The social worker can, for example, help a parent apply for Aid for Dependent Children or, if necessary, unemployment compensation.

In some large school districts, community social service agencies have opened offices within the schools to improve access to needed social services. This strategy has proved valuable in providing assistance to non-English-speaking children and their families.

Speech Therapists

Speech and language therapy has as its goal the improvement of communication behaviors of students whose speech and/or language deficits affect educational performance. Haynes[25] has identified four speech and language components that must be addressed by the speech therapist:

- Semantics (language content or meaning)
- Syntax (language structure or grammar)
- Pragmatics (language use or function)
- Phonology (the sound system of language)

Service delivery in speech and language programs was historically based on a medical model in which the speech therapist provided therapy to children with speech and language deficits in a clinical, isolated setting. That is, the clinician provided speech and language programming in a setting removed from the child's regular education or special education classroom. That practice is changing.

Current, innovative practice in speech and language programs is based on the notion that speech and language are a basic and integral part of the child's total life experience. As Achilles, Yates, and Freese[1] have suggested, the child uses speech and language throughout the day, in a variety of environments, in response to a variety of stimuli, and in interaction with many different people; as such, speech and language use is an ongoing process. Therefore, speech and language therapy must be embedded within the total academic and nonacademic curriculum.

To allow classroom-based therapy to occur, the speech therapist functions collaboratively with the child's regular educator and/or special educator. A smart, motivated therapist is eager to collaborate with the adapted physical educator and general physical educator because the distinct advantages identified in classroom-based language instruction pertain to the physical education "classroom" or adapted physical education "classroom," as well. In fact, the nature of physical education makes it an exciting, language-rich opportunity. Children involved in dance, play, and games are functioning within their most natural environment; this environment demands communication in a variety of forms—gestures, signs, expressive facial behaviors, and expressive/receptive speech.

In addition, the therapist collaborates with the physical educator or adapted physical educator because of the obvious relationship between gross and fine motor development and the development of speech and language. Indeed, movement is speech; speech is movement.

Transportation Specialists

In *Alamo Heights v. State Board of Education* (1986), the court mandated that transportation, like other related services, must be included on the child's IEP.[3] The Office of Civil Rights has decreed that a child with a disability should not have to ride the school bus longer than other children. The Office of Civil Rights has also indicated it is a violation of civil rights if a child with a disability has a shorter instructional day than other children because of the school bus schedule. In addition, the child with a disability should have the same access to extracurricular, before-school, or after-school programs as any other child.[42] If the child needs an aide (transportation specialist) on the bus during transportation to and from school, litigation indicates it should be included on the IEP as well.

Transition Service Personnel

One of the major transition services offered by transition service personnel is vocational education. A quality vocational education program includes a comprehensive assessment of vocational potential and capabilities. The student with a disability is given the opportunity to demonstrate his or her unique skills and talents, so that appropriate job training can be provided. As the student enters middle school and high school, the focus of the education provided is vocational, if appropriate. Special education instruction focuses on the skills necessary to function within a workplace. Actual work-related opportunities are provided in "work production" or "work simulation" classes. Some progressive school districts have job placement opportunities for children with disabilities in the last years of their special education career. In fact, some provide "job coaches" to work "shoulder to shoulder" with a student with a disability at the actual job site to assist the student with the technical aspects, as well as the social nuances, of the job. For example, if the student is being trained as a maid for a major hotel chain, the job coach accompanies the student to the hotel, both wearing the same uniform as every other employee, and helps the student learn the day-to-day routine and processes involved in being a successful employee.

Each of the professionals described above brings a special expertise to the child with a disability. Seldom does one child require the services of all these specialized professionals. However, the intent of the law is that these personnel must be made available, if necessary, for the child to benefit from the educational process.

Seldom are all these professionals on-staff personnel within a given district. Small school districts may rely on a special education center to provide such services. These centers are called by different names in different states. In Kansas, the term *cooperative special education center* is used. In Michigan, the title *intermediate school district* is given to centers that provide specialized services. In Texas, regional education service centers work in close cooperation with local school districts. When this type of special education center is not available, school districts hire their own specialized personnel on a contractual basis or refer children to private practitioners and/or hospitals or rehabilitation centers for assessment/evaluation services and/or programming.

DESCRIPTION OF EACH COMPONENT OF THE IEP

Present Level of Educational Achievement

The IEP must include a statement of the present level of educational achievement, including the "academic" and "functional performance" of the child. The focus on "academic" competency continues to discriminate against children with disabilities, particularly severe disabilities, and children with English as a second language. It is important that the statement of the child's present level of educational achievement be based on

current, relevant information about the child. Information should be obtained from a variety of sources:

1. Information from the child's parents. There is an increased emphasis on parental involvement in every phase of the child's education. Increasingly, the emphasis in the public schools is on involvement of the parent and/or extended family in the decisions made with/for a child with a disability
2. The most recent evaluation of the child
3. Districtwide assessment results
4. Input from the child's general physical educator and/or adapted physical education teacher

The statement describing the present level of educational achievement, including academic and functional performance, must include how the child's disability affects the child's involvement and progress in the general educational curricula or, in the case of infants, toddlers, and preschoolers age three to five years, their participation in appropriate activities. Appropriate activities are age-relevant developmental abilities or milestones that typically reflect the development of children of the same age.

One of the purposes of assessment is to determine the child's present level of educational achievement and need for specially designed education and physical education. These assessments are needed to ensure the child's involvement and progress in the general education and physical education curriculum and any needed adaptation or modifications to the general curriculum.

The comprehensive determination of a student's present level of educational achievement should include the following:

1. Intellectual assessment
2. Educational assessment
3. Developmental needs
4. Sociological information
5. Emotional/behavioral assessment
6. Physical examination or health update
7. Speech and language assessment
8. Language dominance assessment

9. Motor and play assessment
10. Community-based leisure/recreation/sport and fitness assessment
11. Vocational or prevocational assessment
12. Related services assessment(s)
13. Functional assessments. It appears to be critical that the adapted physical educator and the physical educator remember the focus of the curriculum—play, movement, leisure, recreation, sports, and fitness—and not be forced into a position to deliver services to enhance "functional" skills associated with those of daily living

The statement describing the learner's present level of achievement in physical education must always be based on the results of more than one assessment instrument in order to ensure reliability and validity. A comprehensive statement of the student's present level of performance in physical education may include a description of

1. Motor output that may cause one to suspect a sensory-input system dysfunction
   a. Inappropriate reflex behavior
   b. Equilibrium dysfunction
   c. Sensory integration deficit
   d. Motor-planning deficit
2. The learner's locomotor and nonlocomotor competency
3. The learner's physical and motor fitness level
4. The learner's ability to participate in a variety of play, games, leisure, recreation, and sport and fitness activities
5. The learner's ability to participate in a variety of rhythms, dance, and aquatic activities
6. The learner's ability to use community-based resources to enable participation in play, games, leisure, recreation, sports, and fitness activities

The comprehensive assessment that determines the present level of performance is critical to the development of the IEP. A valid and extensive understanding of the student's present abilities and skills is the basis for the development of the child's annual goals.

Goals

Measurable annual goals are critical to the strategic planning process used to develop and implement the IEP for each child with a disability.

Once the IEP/multidisciplinary team has determined measurable annual goals, the team can develop specific strategies that will be most effective in achieving those goals. The annual goals should address the child's needs that result directly from the child's disability if the disability interferes with the child's ability to make progress in the general curriculum.

Edelen-Smith[14] has suggested that only if the service provider (teacher or related service personnel) and parents believe a goal on an IEP is valid and meaningful will that individual make a concerted effort to help the student achieve that goal. Edelen-Smith suggests eight elements that are vital if the goals are to be perceived as being valid by professionals, parents, and the student (see Table 4-6). The annual goals must include four concepts:

- An action (what?)
- Conditions under which the action should occur (how?)
- A criterion for mastery of a specific task (at what level?)
- A performance better than the child's present level of educational performance

The annual goals must include the "action concept," the "conditions," and criterion of "mastery" that may have been included in the past in the short-term objectives or benchmarks.

Action Concept

The action portion of the annual goal indicates what the learner will do when performing the task. It is important that the action be stated in verb form, such as "throw," "strike," "kick," "do a sit-up," "serve a volleyball," "walk a mile," or "complete a 30-minute aerobic dance work-out."

Conditions

The conditions under which the action should occur describe how the learner is to perform at the

Table 4-6	Edelen-Smith's Criteria for Establishing Valid Goals

1. *Conceivable:* If all parties can conceive of the *outcome* that will result if these particular goals are met, the goals will have particular value for the student.
2. *Believable:* The student, parent, and professionals must believe the goal can be met. To be believable, the goal must also be consistent with family, cultural, and societal value systems.
3. *Achievable:* The comprehensive assessment, if done well, will provide data that make it possible to suggest goals that will be challenging but achievable.
4. *Controllable:* The student must feel as if he or she has had input in decisions regarding personal goals; if the student has had no control, the student will feel unempowered.
5. *Measurable:* The goal must be written so it can be measured.
6. *Desirable:* The goal must be something the student wants to achieve and the parent(s) and teacher(s) wants him or her to achieve.
7. *Stated with no alternative:* In order for a student, parent, or teacher to take a goal seriously, it must be perceived as a significant target, not one that will be adjusted without demonstrated effort.
8. *Growth facilitating:* The goals must seek desirable behaviors instead of seeking to eliminate undesirable behaviors.

Data from Edelen-Smith P: Eight elements to guide goal determination *Intervent School Clin* 30(5):297–301, 1995.

task. It is important to be exact. Changing the conditions makes a task easy or more difficult, inefficient or efficient, simple or more complex. Examples of conditions are

- "With eyes closed and nonsupporting leg bent to 90 degrees, the student will be able to . . ."
- "From a prone position, the learner will . . ."
- "Keeping the back straight and arms at the side of the body, the student will . . ."
- "Floating on her back, the swimmer will . . ."

If the conditions are not specified, it is impossible to determine the student's true capability and what

activities are needed to make progress. If the conditions are not precise, it is unclear how the student is to perform the task, and once again the value of the goal is lost.

Well-written goals include what, how, and at what level the behaviors are to be performed. Inappropriate objectives fail for several reasons:

- "Run as fast as you can."
  Conditions: The condition, distance, or environmental arrangements are not specified. Criterion: Neither an objective, a measurable distance, nor a specified time has been included in the goal. "As fast as you can" is subjective. The students may believe they are running as fast as they can, but the teacher may have a different opinion.
- "Walk on a balance beam without falling off."
  Conditions: The width of the balance beam and the position of the arms make the task more or less difficult. Neither of these is specified.
  Criterion: The distance to be traveled or distance over time is not specified.
- "Swim to the end of the pool."
  Conditions: The stroke is not specified.
  Criterion: Swimming pools are different lengths. It is unclear the exact distance the student is to swim.

Criterion of Mastery

The criterion for mastery of a task in the annual goal is the standard at which the task should be performed. Being able to perform the task to criterion level indicates mastery of the task and, hence, student progress. Reaching a criterion serves notice that one prerequisite in a series has been mastered and that the student is ready to begin working toward the next step. Measures for task mastery can take several forms (see Table 4-7):

- Number of repetitions (10 repetitions)
- Number of repetitions over time (20 repetitions in 15 seconds)
- Distance traveled (8 feet on a balance beam without stepping off)

Table 4-7	Measurable Goals, Including Action, Condition, and Criteria

The student will be able to run 1 mile in 10 minutes 30 seconds.
    Action: Run
    Condition: 1 mile
    Criteria: 10 minutes 30 seconds

The student will be able to walk on a balance beam, 4 inches wide, heel to toe, with eyes closed and hands on hips, for 8 feet.
    Action: Walk
    Condition: A balance beam 4 inches wide
    Criteria: Heel to toe, eyes closed, and hands on hips for 8 feet

The student will be able to swim the breaststroke 50 meters in 1 minute 30 seconds.
    Action: Swim
    Condition: Breaststroke 50 meters
    Criteria: 1 minute 30 seconds

The learner will be able to roll his or her wheelchair through a 5 cone, figure 8 obstacle course in less than 2 minutes.
    Action: Roll wheelchair
    Condition: Through a 5 cone obstacle course
    Criteria: Less than 2 minutes

- Distance traveled over time (200 yards in 25 seconds)
- Number of successive trials without a miss (4 times in a row)
- Specified number of successful responses in a block of trials (3 out of 5)
- Number of degrees of movement (flexibility in degrees of movement from starting to ending positions)
- Mastery of all the stated conditions of the task

Although not required in all situations by IDEIA, it is critical that the adapted physical educator provide short-term objectives for the general physical educator or the paraprofessional who is responsible for providing physical education services to the child. These are vital if effective instruction is to occur. These objectives make it possible for the general physical educator and the paraprofessional to implement the IEP and ensure that progress toward the goal is occurring. The content of short-term instructional objectives meant to enhance instruction includes those of the annual goal.

Specific Educational Services

The dates of the initiation, the duration, the frequency, and the location of all services and supports must be made clear. In the broadest sense, the "specific educational services to be rendered" means what professional services (e.g., adapted physical education, remedial reading, speech and language therapy) will be made available to the student. Every professional service and educational activity should be chosen/designed to help the child attain the annual goals.

The services to be provided must be clearly stated on the IEP, so that the extent of the commitment of school district resources, personnel, equipment, and facilities will be clear to parents and other IEP team members.[57] The specification of the extent of services should include

- Dates of initiation of services
- Duration of services
- Number of minutes a particular service will be delivered to the child per day, week, or month.
  For example: Speech and language therapy, 30 minutes, two days per week

The services may be specified by a range—for example, the student will participate in general physical education three times a week for 30–45 minutes[57]

- Location at which the services will be provided—for example, the adapted physical education services may be provided at the local fitness center, so that the student has the opportunity to learn the skills necessary to enjoy, use, and benefit from the services available in the community

Related Services

Related services are intended to help the student with disabilities benefit from special education—that is, adapted physical education. The goals and objectives of related service personnel may be a vital part of the child's IEP and should be consistent with those of direct service personnel. These services should focus on offsetting or reducing the problems resulting from the child's disability that interfere with learning and physical education performance in school.

Depending on the unique needs of the child, other developmental, corrective, or supportive services may be required to help a child with a disability benefit from special education. Such services include nutrition services and service coordination between school-based physical education services and community-based agencies for health promotion purposes.[57]

Extent to Which the Student Will Not Participate in Regular Education

Increasingly, there are litigative and legislative emphases on the provision of educational services for children with disabilities in the general education program. The IEP/multidisciplinary team's determination of how each child's disability affects the child's involvement and progress in the general curriculum is a primary consideration in the development of the child's IEP. (See Table 4-8.)

If the general physical educator has reason to believe that a child with a disability should not participate in the existing physical education program—for example, because the child is very disruptive—it is vital for the teacher to document aids and services, accommodations, and modifications attempted before suggesting an alternative placement at the IEP/multidisciplinary team meeting. It appears the intent of Congress is that educators try to help a student with a disability succeed in the general program and curriculum before suggesting alternative placements and programs.

Modifications/Accommodations Needed for the Child to Participate in Statewide and Districtwide Achievement Tests

Consistent with congressional mandates regarding participation in the general curriculum is an increased emphasis on the participation of children with disabilities in state- and district-mandated achievement tests.[9] The No Child Left Behind Act clearly places the emphasis on the "academic" curricula.[41]

However, the ramifications for physical education and health are clear, as well. For example, if the local education agency requires a physical fitness assessment of every student, accommodations must be made to include students with disabilities in this assessment, as well. If the IEP/multidisciplinary team believes that the student cannot participate in this assessment, it is the responsibility of the team to explain why the test is inappropriate and to offer an alternative.

Statement of Needed Transition Services

The individual transition plan (ITP) is the very foundation of the educational process for learners with disabilities. Clearly, the existing education process makes absolutely no sense if it is not designed to provide students with the skills necessary to live well and with integrity after their graduation from high school and entrance into the community. *In fact, it appears that one of the major problems of the existing education system is there appears to be no relationship between the IEP of children with disabilities and expectations of "outcomes" that will enable them to thrive and enjoy their lives after graduation.* For example,

Table 4-8 Instructional Modification/Supports

Page _____ of_____

*Instructional modifications/supports determined by ARD committee

Name of student ___Adam P._____   Campus ___WALNUT HILL ELEMENTARY___

The ARD committee has determined that the following modifications are necessary for the student to succeed:

Special language programs[1]

☐ Bilingual   ☐ ESL

Behavior management plan	Regular discipline plan
☐ Yes	☑ Yes
☑ No	☐ No
Assistive technology devices	☐ Modifications not needed or not applicable
☐ Yes	
☑ No	

Goal & objective/subject

	MATH	ENGLISH	P.E.	SOCIAL ST.	MUSIC			
Alter assignments by providing:								
Reduced assignments								
Taped assignments								
Extra time for completing assignments								
Opportunity to respond orally	✓	✓	✓					
Emphasis on major points								
Task analysis of assignments								
Special projects in lieu of assignments								
Other:								
Other:								
Adapt instruction by providing:								
Opportunity to leave class for resource assistance								
Short instructions (one or two steps)								
Opportunity to repeat and explain instructions	✓	✓	✓	✓	✓			
Encouragement to verbalize steps needed to complete assignment/task								
Opportunity to write instructions								
Assignment notebooks								
Visual aids (pictures, flash cards, etc.)								
Auditory aids (cues, tapes, etc.)								
Instructional aids								
Extra time for oral response								
Extra time for written response								
Exams of reduced length								
Oral exams	✓	✓	✓	✓	✓			
Open book exams								
Study carrel for independent work								
Frequent feedback								
Immediate feedback								
Minimal auditory distractions								
Encouragement for classroom participation	✓	✓	✓	✓	✓			
Peer tutoring/paired working arrangement	✓	✓	✓	✓	✓			
Opportunity for student to dictate themes, information, answers on tape or to others								
Other:								
Other:								

[1]Special language programs are required for all students who are limited English proficient.
*Denotes required items.

3/97
ARD-4

(Continued)

Table 4-8	(*Continued*)

*Instructional modifications/supports determined by ARD committee (continued)

Goal & objective/subject

(Column headers, handwritten, angled): MATH, ENGLISH, P.E., SOCIAL ST., MUSIC

Adapt materials by providing:

	MATH	ENGLISH	P.E.	SOCIAL ST.	MUSIC				
Peer to read materials									
Tape recording of required readings									
Highlighted materials for emphasis									
Altered format of materials									
Study aids/manipulatives									
ESL materials									
Large-print materials									
Braille materials									
Color transparencies									
Other:									
Other:									

Manage behavior by providing:

	MATH	ENGLISH	P.E.	SOCIAL ST.	MUSIC				
Clearly defined limits	✓	✓	✓	✓	✓				
Frequent reminders of rules	✓	✓	✓	✓	✓				
Positive reinforcement	✓	✓	✓	✓	✓				
Frequent eye contact/proximity control									
Frequent breaks									
Private discussion about behavior									
In-class time-out									
Opportunity to help teacher									
Seat near the teacher									
Supervision during transition activities			✓						
Implementation of behavior contract									
Other:									
Other:									

Required equipment/assistive technology devices:

	MATH	ENGLISH	P.E.	SOCIAL ST.	MUSIC				
Calculators									
Word processors									
Augmentative communication device									
Note taker/note-taking paper									
Interpreter									
Decoders for TV and films									
Access to equipment:									
Other:									

*Criterion–referenced assessment (TAAS):[1]

✓ Will take reading   _____ Exempt in all areas

✓ Will take mathematics   _____ Will take science

✓ Will take writing   _____ Not offered for this student's grade placement

✓ Will take social studies

Modifications as defined in test administration materials:

_____

_____

End-of-course examinations:[2]

_____ Not enrolled in Algebra I or Biology I

_____ Will take Algebra I

_____ Will not take Algebra I

_____ Will take Biology I

_____ Will not take Biology I

Modifications as defined in test administration materials:

_____

_____

[1]Until Spanish TAAS tests are available, LEP students exempt from the English TAAS must be tested with the alternative measures of accountability.

[2]The only students not required to test are students receiving content modifications resulting in an "S" on the transcript, as stated in test administration materials. These materials also provide information about testing these students for local purposes.

*Denotes required items.

3/97

ARD-5

few IEPs and ITPs address the sport skills necessary so the learner may make a good transition into adult sport programs for individuals with disabilities— United States Association of Blind Athletes, U.S. Cerebral Palsy Sports, National Wheelchair Basketball Association, and so on.

A statement that describes the process by which a child with a disability will make the transition into community-based living must be included on the IEP of each child no later than age 16 years, or earlier if the IEP team determines it to be nessary. All children with disabilities should have appropriate physical education to prepare them for independent living, which includes quality leisure, recreation, sports, and physical fitness experiences. Beginning at the age of 16 years, the IEP/multidisciplinary team, in determining appropriate measurable annual goals and services for a student, must determine the planned instructional and educational experiences that will prepare the student for transition from secondary education to postsecondary life.[57] The physical education component of the student's IEP, after the child is sixteen years of age, must focus on providing instruction and experiences that prepare the student for independent living, which include participation in leisure, recreation, sports, and physical fitness activities in community-based programs.

Roth[46] and Shepherd[50] found that the parents of individuals with disabilities felt as if they weren't allowed to be active participants in the process of determining and developing the ITP, particularly as it related to community-based leisure, recreation, sports, and fitness activities. As important, the parents felt that once their student graduated from high school their support system ended. Clearly, there is a need for more effective interaction between the schools and community personnel and there is a critical need for ongoing support for adults with disabilities who make a transition into community programs.

Increasingly, special educators and others that serve individuals with disabilities are beginning to understand that they must acknowledge and honor the inherent right of all individuals to determine their own fate. The term being used is *self-determination*. Agran developed a model that encourages transition-aged learners to be actively involved in the process of determining their own future. Agran stresses the process of teaching students a strategy to prepare them for transition. IPLAN includes

> I: Inventory your strengths, weaknesses, goals, and choices for learning.
> P: Provide your inventory information.
> L: Listen and respond.
> A: Ask questions.
> N: Name your goals.[2]

Ingraham and Anderson indicate that an opportunity to have an active part in the IEP/ITP process is empowering and helps reduce the sense of helplessness that learners with disabilities often experience.[29]

Positive Behavior Management

Many advocates of persons with disabilities have viewed the rights of the public schools to expel or suspend a student with a disability as an attempt to deny the student his or her entitlement to a free, appropriate public education (FAPE). And, indeed, the Congress has supported that sense in IDEIA. Positive behavior management strategies have proven to be successful in preventing and controlling disruptive behavior in the schools. Appropriate positive behavior management strategies should be included in the contents of the IEP when the student's behavior interferes with his or her learning or disrupts the learning of others.[57]

There are a number of very creative ways to help establish the behavior management plan, as part of the IEP process. Comic strip conversations increase the likelihood that a student with behavior problems will be able to identify problem behavior and develop strategies to react with more appropriate behavior.[21] Essentially, the comic strip conversations use simplistic communication forms—stick figures, drawings—to allow the student the opportunity to discuss and consider inappropriate/appropriate behavior. Tournaki and

Criscitello have suggested that another way to enhance the behavior of children who struggle to behave appropriately is to use reverse-role tutoring; students with disabilities become tutors for students without disabilities.[56] In that role, the students with disabilities demonstrate improved behavior in the classroom. Another strategy that has proven successful is the use of dialogue journals that allow the student and the teacher to share feelings and emotions without direct, personal communication.[47] It appears that the students are more likely to share their feelings within a context that does not require face-to-face communication. These strategies, and others, should be included in the child's IEP.

According to IDEIA, all students with a disability who violate a code of student conduct may be removed from his or her current placement and placed in an appropriate interim alternative educational setting, placed in another setting, or suspended for not more than 10 consecutive school days. If the student has a disability, within those 10 days the child's IEP team must review all relevant information in the student's file to determine if the conduct in question was a result of the child's disability or was a direct result of the LEA's failure to implement the IEP. If the disability or the LEA is found to be at fault, immediate steps must be taken to remedy the situation.

If the conduct was a result of the student's disability, the IEP team must conduct a functional behavioral assessment and implement a behavioral intervention plan for the child. If a plan was already in place, that plan is reviewed and modified to better address the behavior.

School personnel also have the right to move a student with a disability to an alternative educational setting for not more than 45 days if the child knowingly possesses or uses illegal drugs; sells or solicits the sale of a controlled substance; carries a weapon to or possesses a weapon at school, on school premises, or to a school function; or has inflicted serious bodily injury upon another person while at school or a school event.[57]

Special educators (including adapted physical educators), related service personnel, general educators, school administrators, school counselors, and parents need to work in concert to develop and implement a positive behavior management plan. The focus, as in any good behavior management plan, needs to be on prevention of disruptive or inappropriate behavior. Schoolwide implementation of a positive behavior management plan that is consistent throughout the school building is the most effective strategy and has been implemented successfully in many schools and school districts.

Projected Dates for Initiation and Termination of Services

The projected dates for beginning and terminating educational and related services must be included on the IEP. This is just one more technique intended to ensure accountability. All IEPs must include a date when services should begin and an anticipated date when goals will be reached.

Appropriate Objective Criteria and Evaluation Procedures

Each IEP must include a description of the techniques/strategies used to determine the child's present level of performance and to determine whether the child accomplishes each of the goals on the IEP. These must include how the child's progress toward meeting the goals will be measured and when periodic reports on the progress will be provided.

Additional Components of Most School-Based IEP Documents

It is important for the physical educator to be aware that there are many other pieces of information included in most school-based documents. Because the IEP document has often become the basis of litigation by parents and/or advocacy groups and is highly scrutinized by review teams from the state department of public instruction and/or federal grant agencies, the actual document has become increasingly complex. It is not unusual for this document to be between 25 and 50 pages long. This additional information, often kept as records within the principal's office, but often included on the IEP, includes

1. Information about the student:
   a. Name
   b. Identification number
   c. Birthdate
   d. Native language/mode of communication
2. Information about the parent or guardian:
   a. Address
   b. Phone numbers (work, home, emergency)
   c. Contact person/phone for parent without access
   d. Native language/mode of communication
3. Determination of eligibility statement (i.e., does the child have a disability as determined by federal mandates?)
4. Determination of placement or placement options along the service delivery continuum
5. Assurance of placement close to home and/or home school and a specific explanation if the child must receive services in a different setting
6. Waiver/nonwaiver status for state education agency–mandated examinations and specific techniques that will be used to ensure the student every opportunity to participate in state and local education agency assessments and, if that is not possible, modifications of assessments that will be provided
7. Specific modifications in instructional strategies to ensure learning throughout placement continuum
8. Goals for extended-year service (summer school) if it is feared that regression may occur without such service
9. Modified standards for participation in extracurricular activities, if necessary
10. Assurances that
    a. Placement in special education is not a function of national origin, minority status, or linguistic differences
    b. Placement in special education is not directly attributable to a different culture

or lifestyle or to lack of educational opportunity
c. Education will be provided in the student's least restrictive environment

PARENT/GUARDIAN RIGHTS

The often cumbersome IEP document is only one way in which school districts meet federal and state regulations regarding the rights of the child with a disability. In addition, there are specific mandated parent/guardian rights that must be made clear to the parent(s) or guardian(s) before a child is evaluated and either admitted to or dismissed from a special education program.

Most school districts distribute a parent rights manual developed by their state education agency when the child is first referred by the parent or guardian, members of the extended family, classroom teachers, physical education teachers, social workers, day care personnel, medical personnel, child protective services personnel, and/or workers in homeless shelters. Usually, the parent rights manual is given to the parent by a case manager or transition specialist.

Children need to be evaluated in their native language or mode of communication and parents and guardians need to be advised of their rights in their native language or mode of communication. While most state education agencies have parent rights manuals developed in at least two languages (English and Spanish), translators must be used to explain parent rights to those parents who use another language. It should be noted, though, that this process has become overwhelming, particularly for many large, urban school districts.[15] It is not unusual for children and parents within a given school zone to speak hundreds of different languages/dialects and represent that many different cultures.

In addition, the law is clear in its intent—it is not enough to simply hand parents a booklet explaining rights that they may or may not be able to read, much less understand; it is crucial that they really do understand, and a professional must use parent-friendly language to make these rights clear.

In the comprehensive assessment process, the parent or guardian has the right to

- Receive written notice (in native language) before the school assesses the child
- Receive information about the abilities, skills, and knowledge that are to be assessed
- Give or refuse consent for that assessment
- Inspect and review all assessment records before the IEP meeting
- Expect that the assessment information will be considered at the IEP meeting
- Expect that tests and other assessment materials will be in the child's native language or mode of communication
- Expect that no single procedure will be used as the sole basis for admission, placement, or IEP decisions
- Seek one external assessment, an independent educational evaluation, within reason, at the school district's expense, if the parent or guardian disagrees with the results of the evaluation
- Request mediation or a due process hearing if agreement on assessment procedures or results cannot be reached

In regard to the IEP meeting, the parent or guardian also has the right to

- Receive written notice of the IEP meeting before the meeting that explains the purpose, time, and location of the meeting and who will attend
- Receive written notice of what the school proposes for the child as a result of the meeting
- Have the IEP meeting scheduled at a time that is convenient for the parent or guardian and the school. It is considered best practice for the school administrator to make every effort to schedule at a time when both parents, or a parent and grandparent, can attend the meeting together. (If the parent or guardian is unable to attend, the school must contact the parent or guardian via a visiting teacher or personal conference.)
- Have an interpreter present if the parent or guardian is deaf and/or uses a language other than English

- Bring others to the meeting for support or advocacy
- Be an active and important participant in the IEP meeting and discuss any service the parent or guardian thinks the student needs
- Have the meeting reconvened at a later date if the parent or guardian disagrees with the recommendations of the committee
- Seek judicial intervention (due process) if the parent or guardian and school continue to disagree regarding the student's assessment, placement, or services
- Obtain an independent evaluation at public expense and to know where it may be obtained. For example, if the parent disagrees with the assessment report provided by the district's adapted physical educator, the parent may request an independent assessment.
- A written notice at a reasonable time before the school proposes and changes identification, evaluation, or educational placement
- An impartial hearing officer from the state education agency
- Be accompanied and advised by counsel and/or individuals with special knowledge or training with respect to children with disabilities
- Appeal if aggrieved by the findings and decisions made in the hearing

In order for the IEP to be a living, breathing document that ensures educational progress and specifies the focus of the education program, it must be reviewed consistently. The law requires that this be done at least annually, or more frequently, if necessary.

It is absolutely critical that the parent understand the critical role he or she plays in the IEP/multidisciplinary process. Table 4-9 addresses the strategies the parent can use to ensure the child's educational rights are honored.

PARTICIPANTS IN THE IEP/ MULTIDISCIPLINARY TEAM MEETING

The IEP meeting must be attended by the following individuals:

1. The parents or legal guardian of the child

Table 4-9	Strategies for Parents to Ensure the Educational Rights of Children with Disabilities

1. Maintain "business" records of your interaction with district personnel. Communicate only in writing and save a copy of everything. Do not rely on regular mail—hand deliver or send important materials "certified" mail.[13]
2. Get support letters from your child's pediatrician, therapist, or other professional if you believe your child's needs are not being met.
3. Reevaluate your child's educational classification. Some services, such as home-based instruction, are available to children with some diagnoses and not available to others.[13]
4. Cooperate with the school district's reasonable evaluation system. If you disagree with an evaluation, review it carefully. Was your child sick that day? Was the child in transition from one medication to another? Was the evaluator trained to complete the evaluation? If you disagree with the district's evaluation, your child is entitled to an independent evaluation at district expense.[13]
5. An independent evaluation of your child's ability is critical because often the school-based evaluator is pressed by the school district to limit the scope of services available to children with disabilities.
6. Keep your own portfolio of your child's work. Include samples of the child's best work.
7. Demand IEP accountability. Make sure every professional who actually works with the student reads and understands the IEP. Make sure you know who is responsible for follow-up.
8. Be particularly careful to communicate with the teachers of the "extra" subjects, physical education, art, library, and computers. These are the teachers most often responsible for the "inclusive" process.
9. Be wary of proposals regarding inclusion. "Sometimes a school district will include a child without providing needed services. Too often, this is a cost-cutting maneuver which sabotages the child's placement . . ."[13]
10. "Treat the annual review as your most important business meeting of the year."[13]

2. Not less than one regular education teacher of the child (if the child is or may be participating in the regular education environment). This may be the general physical educator if the child is to participate in the general physical education program
3. Not less than one special education teacher of the child or, where appropriate, not less than one special education provider of the child
4. A representative of the school administration. This person must have the authority to allocate school district resources. In most school districts, the principal or the principal's designee fills this role in the meeting
5. An individual who can interpret the instructional implication of evaluation results and who also might be one of the other listed members
6. At the discretion of the parent or the school district, other individuals who have knowledge or special expertise regarding the child, including related services personnel as appropriate
7. Whenever appropriate, the child with a disability[57]

When a child is in transition, whether from preschool to elementary school, elementary school to middle school, middle school to high school, or high school into the community, it is absolutely critical that there are representatives from the child's present and eventual placements if the transition process is to be "seamless" and appropriate.[62] Without participation of the professionals at both schools or placements, precious time will be lost in the education of learners with disabilities.

In addition, the following personnel should be part of this IEP meeting:

1. Any direct or related service personnel who have assessed the student (adapted physical education specialist, occupational therapist, speech-language pathologist, etc.). The

IDEIA regulations do not expressly mandate that the IEP/multidisciplinary team include related services personnel. However, it is critical that those individuals attend the meeting if a particular related service is to be discussed at the meeting

2. The school nurse, particularly if the student has a chronic and/or serious medical condition (e.g., asthma, AIDS, cancer) and/or requires special medical procedures (e.g., tube feeding, catheterization) in order to function in the school environment
3. An interpreter, as required
4. Representatives of the community agencies that will be responsible for implementing individual transition plans (after the student reaches age 16 years)[9]

It is important to note that The American Academy of Pediatrics has taken an active interest in the role of the physician in the IEP process. The academy has particularly identified its role as a member of the IEP/multidisciplinary team for students who have been identified as "other health impaired." The academy recommends that pediatricians ensure that every child with a disability served by their practice have access to the following services:

• A medical home that provides care that is accessible, continuous, comprehensive, family-centered, coordinated, and compassionate
• Comprehensive screening, surveillance, and diagnosis, particularly to check for the risk or existence of a disability or developmental delay
• Appropriate referral to early intervention and special education programs
• Active participation in the multidisciplinary assessment process
• Consultation with the IEP/multidisciplinary team regarding the development of the IEP
• Pediatrician's advocacy for improved community and educational services for children with disabilities[4]

The commitment of The American Academy of Pediatrics, the Committee on Children with Disabilities, is heartening. Certainly, a partnership among the pediatrician, school-based professionals, community agencies, and parents can only improve the quality of the IEP and the delivery of appropriate educational services.

Difficult and occasionally adversarial relationships between parents and school districts have created situations in which a parent may bring an advocate or a lawyer to an IEP meeting. If a student or parent advocate is present, the meeting should continue as scheduled; the advocate is representing the best interests of the student and/or parent and usually represents a nonprofit agency devoted to ensuring rights for children and adults with disabilities. The advocate may be helpful to the parent and other members of the IEP team as strategies for developing and implementing the best possible IEP are discussed. If the parent brings a lawyer without providing appropriate prior notice to the school district, so that the district's counsel can also attend, the meeting must be terminated and rescheduled, so that both sides (the student and/or parent and the school district) are represented by counsel.

The intent of the IEP meeting is that every individual who cares about the child and who has data regarding the child's performance should meet with every other individual with important information about the child and share this information, so that, in the end, the child receives the best possible education. Unfortunately, in the real world this is not always possible. For example, an adapted physical education specialist may be serving as a consultant for over 300 children. There may be only one physical therapist serving an entire district. As a result, not all the people who actually tested the child or who may ultimately be serving the student can attend every meeting. The argument is made that it is neither expedient nor necessary for all evaluators and teachers to be present if those who do attend can interpret the test results and are qualified to develop an appropriate IEP. Adapted physical education teachers who find themselves in this situation should be certain that the person making the physical education report understands the evaluation results and why it is important to follow the physical education recommendations.

DISCIPLINE CONCERNS

The increase in violence and disruptive behavior in the schools has caused many school districts to adopt zero-tolerance statements, which indicate that a student will be expelled or removed to an alternative school for the following behavior:

- Hitting a teacher or another student
- Selling or otherwise distributing drugs
- Taking a weapon into the school building or near school grounds
- Continuing verbal aggression toward a teacher or another student

A student served by special education is subject to the district or school's student code of conduct unless specific exceptions are noted on the student's IEP. The parent has a right to expect that his or her child's IEP will include, if necessary, a positive behavior management plan that outlines disciplinary options to be used in addition to, or instead of, certain parts of the district code. This is to protect a student with a disability from being expelled, or seriously reprimanded, for behavior that is a direct result of his or her disability.

This is an increasingly serious issue in the schools. Escalating violence, murders, and assaults within the schools have caused many administrators and educators to endorse this zero-tolerance stance. Students with severe conduct, emotional, or behavioral disturbances may, for example, exhibit behaviors that are inconsistent with school conduct codes and may be unable to control that behavior. Nevertheless, violent and aggressive behavior cannot be tolerated in a learning environment, much less in the larger society. While the reauthorization of IDEA honored the fact that children with disabilities may, literally, be unable to control their behavior, IDEIA[57] has fostered the notion that any child can/should be removed from the school district if his or her behavior is not consistent with school policies.

THE IEP MEETING AGENDA

A productive IEP meeting should proceed as follows:

1. The principal or meeting leader welcomes all participants and thanks them for attending. This sets the tone for a cooperative effort.
2. Individuals attending the meeting either are introduced by the meeting leader or introduce themselves.
3. Meeting participants review the agenda for the meeting. Although an agenda is not required by federal mandates, it has proven very useful in keeping meeting participants on task. In addition, it helps create the proper mind-set in the participants; *the IEP meeting is a business meeting* and should be treated as such.
4. At this point, the committee members should also agree on an individual who will take minutes of the meeting. These minutes are invaluable in the IEP process and in the maintenance of records. In IEP meetings that last three to four hours, it is almost impossible to remember what was said and by whom, and while the IEP document should reflect committee consensus, it often does not address important concerns regarding the student's education. In addition, in the event that a professional serving the student was unable to attend, the minutes will bring that person "up to speed" about the committee's decisions. These minutes should become a valuable part of the student's comprehensive educational record and an attachment to the IEP.
5. The principal or meeting leader should begin the meeting by expressing a personal interest in the student and commenting on at least one of the student's strengths.
6. The principal or meeting leader should explain the reason for the meeting. This may include
   a. Admission to special education: initial assessment/evaluation
   b. Review of assessment and/or the program
      1. Three-year comprehensive reevaluation
      2. Annual review
      3. Parent's request to reconsider any component of the existing IEP for any reason

4. Disciplinary review

c. Dismissal from special education

7. Each participant then addresses the student's present level of educational performance. It is vital that the parents be encouraged to begin that discussion and to provide their insight into their child's progress. This is consistent with mandates that the parents be much more involved in the total education of their child. Asking the parents to start the discussion validates the parents and increases the likelihood that they will be active participants in the meeting. Then, each professional reports on the student's present level of performance within that person's area of expertise. This includes a concise report that includes the names of the tests administered, the results of the testing (including strengths and deficits demonstrated by the child), and the goals that should be set for the child. Whenever possible, the physical educator should relate findings to results found by other professionals (e.g., poor balance often can be tied to fine motor delays; visual problems can be tied to reading difficulties; poor self-concept can be associated with motivational problems in the classroom). If the meeting has been called at the parent's request or is a result of an ongoing disciplinary problem, the involved participants should indicate specific behaviors that have necessitated the meeting.

8. An open discussion among the people present at the meeting is the next step. During this discussion, the needs of the student and strategies for meeting these needs are explored. At this point, the true multidisciplinary nature of the meeting should surface. Each person must be willing to recognize the value of the services that other persons, particularly the parents, have to offer, as well as the value of his or her own expertise. The knowledgeable adapted physical educator or general physical educator will understand and appreciate services that can be provided by other professionals; however, he or she

must also recognize that many activities in physical education can accomplish the physical and motor goals of the child in an interesting, novel fashion unique to the discipline.[36]

9. The committee must then determine appropriate annual goals. Agreement must be reached among the participants about which of the child's needs are most pressing and which goals should take precedence over others. Most states have determined specific expectations for their students at given age levels and within specific content areas. Whenever possible, the annual goals developed for the student with a disability should be similar to those expected by state department of education policies; the regulations regarding the use of benchmarks make this possible.

10. After determining appropriate annual goals, the committee must consider the educational services that will be required for the student to meet goals and accomplish objectives. When contributing to these decisions, the physical educator should focus on the present level of educational performance evidenced by the child in the physical and motor areas. If, through testing, the child is found to have significant deficits, such as reflex abnormalities, vestibular delays, or range-of-motion limitations, and the physical educator does not believe the child can be included in the general physical education program, referral to a related therapy may be the best recommendation. Such a recommendation does not mean the child should not or cannot participate in some type of physical education class. It simply means that the related therapies should focus on the immediate low-level deficits while the child continues to participate in a physical education program that is designed to reinforce the intervention programs provided by the other services. *None of the related service therapies should replace physical education; however, they should be used to help the student take a*

more active role in the physical education class.

11. The committee must then consider the extent to which the student will be educated in the regular education program. Given increased emphasis on education in the general education curriculum/program, this is often one of the most difficult and potentially confrontational parts of the IEP meeting. Once again, the physical educator must remember that his or her services are valuable, regardless of the child's demonstrated functioning levels. Under no circumstances should the physical educator agree that the child should automatically be included in a regular physical education class or that motor services can better be implemented by an occupational or a physical therapist. Unfortunately, some parents and school personnel continue to perceive physical education as supervised "free play." Their perception that physical education is a nonacademic experience causes them to devalue physical education.

12. Transition must be considered in three situations:
    a. If the child has just turned three years of age and is entering a public school preschool program
    b. If the child is turning six and will be leaving preschool for a school program
    c. If the student is approaching his or her 16th birthday and decisions need to be made to prepare the student for community transition when leaving school

    Note: Enlightened educators understand the need for consideration of transition during every phase of the student's life when major changes are to be encountered, including, in addition to those listed above, a child's transition from elementary school to middle school and the student's transition from middle school to high school. Whenever possible, a significant meeting regarding transition should also occur when the student's family is moving into another school zone, school district, or state. The

technology is available to make such communication easy and inexpensive.

13. The committee must agree on dates for initiation and review of services.

14. The members of the committee must discuss and agree on the criteria for evaluating the student's progress toward IEP goals.

15. The minutes of the meeting should be read, carefully, so that any participants can ask for clarification.

16. The meeting leader should briefly summarize the meeting and ask if any member of the committee has any additional questions or comments. All participants should sign the IEP document.

If the parents do not concur with the recommendations made by school personnel and refuse to sign the IEP, the IEP/multidisciplinary team must be reconvened—in most cases, within 10 school days—to address the issues. If the parents ultimately continue to disagree, the parents then have the right to secure counsel.

Each state is responsible for ensuring the following:

- Mediation is a voluntary process and is not used to deny a parent the right to due process.
- The mediation process is conducted by a qualified, impartial mediator who is well trained.
- A list of trained and qualified mediators is available to the school and parents.
- The schools are prepared to assume the cost of the mediation.

ENCOURAGING AND MAXIMIZING PARENT PARTICIPATION IN THE IEP PROCESS

Parents must be a significant part of the IEP process, that is, part of

- The team that determines what additional data are needed in an evaluation of their child
- The team that determines the child's eligibility
- The team that makes decisions on the educational placement of the child[57]

In addition, the concerns of parents and the information they provide, with their unique perspective, must be considered in developing and reviewing IEPs. Parents must also be informed about the educational progress of their children, at least as often as are parents of children without disabilities, particularly as the information relates to progress in the general curriculum. This is particularly important for the general physical educator, who is usually expected to provide a report card or progress report every six weeks for all the children he or she teaches. If the parents of children without disabilities get a physical education progress report every six weeks, the parents of children with disabilities must also receive a progress report every six weeks.

As a lawyer representing parents in "special education matters," Ebenstein[13] has provided strategies for parents of students with disabilities to use when dealing with a school district in order to guarantee the learner's rights and to maximize his or her educational opportunities (see Table 4-9).

Table 4-10 lists several things that parents have indicated they want at the IEP or ITP meeting. In addition, consider some of the reasons parents of a student may not attend or participate in the IEP meeting

Table 4-10	What Parents Want at the IEP Meeting

- Meetings held in comfortable, homelike places
- Simple refreshments
- Furniture that allows all participants to sit in a circle
- Input into the time/date of the meeting
- An organized, well-planned meeting with an agenda
- An opportunity to prepare for the meeting
  - Information regarding the purpose of the meeting
  - Notice regarding invited participants
  - An opportunity to add agenda items
- Open, respectful, honest communication
- Clarity (avoidance of jargon)

Salembier GR, Furney KS: Speaking up for your child's future, *Except Parent* July:62–64, 1998.

(see Table 4-11). Understanding these reasons helps identify strategies for increasing the likelihood the parents will participate. Parents of a learner with a disability may miss the IEP meeting, or fail to participate actively, if present, for a number of reasons.

To enhance parent participation in the IEP meeting, the climate of the meeting must be

Table 4-11	Obstacles to Parental Attendance at or Participation in the IEP Meeting

- The parent may be in one of several stages of the grief cycle, which makes it difficult, if not impossible, to address his or her child's specific education needs.
- The parent is overwhelmed by the educational system and chooses to avoid interacting with professionals. This is common, particularly when the parent has not been treated, at previous IEP meetings, as a valuable member of the team of individuals seeking to educate the child.
- The parent, despite repeated attempts at notification, is unaware of the meeting. Difficulty notifying parents is typical in non-English-speaking families. It is also typical if parents are illiterate. Difficulty with notification is a particular issue with homeless families; as a rule, they are so transient it is difficult to maintain contact over the period of time required to complete the evaluation and/or paperwork.
- The parent is unable to attend the IEP meeting at the time it is scheduled. A constantly changing work schedule may be one reason for this problem. This is particularly true of migrant farm workers and other members of a temporary workforce.
- The parent cannot find transportation to the meeting site.
- The parent is unable to find a baby-sitter and is hesitant to take other, younger children to the meeting.
- The parent's cultural background is such that he or she feels obligated to accept the decisions of the professionals involved; as such, the parent feels as if he or she has no input of value.
- The parent may have serious personal problems, developmental disabilities, or emotional disturbances, drug-related or otherwise, that preclude participation, without careful assistance, in the IEP process.

parent-friendly. Following are some specific strategies for ensuring this:

Duties of the Professionals
- Emphasize the positive. All parents want to hear good reports about their child; it is difficult for any parent to be bombarded by what the child cannot do.
- Use parent-friendly language. Explain assessment results and discuss goals and objectives without professional jargon or acronyms. The parents will be better able to make good judgments if they understand what is said.
- Use a parent's exact words, describing the IEP goal. There is nothing more enabling for parents than having their thoughts and words embraced. The other bonus is that the parents will be much more likely to encourage the child to accomplish a goal they have understood and articulated.
- If possible, use audiovisual technology to share information with parents about their child. If it is true that a picture is worth a thousand words, a videotape of the child performing a movement activity may be worth a million words.
- Relate to common experiences whenever possible to enhance communication. The physical educator is in a particularly good position to develop rapport with the parent because most parents can identify with movement, play, leisure, and recreation experiences more readily than with a specific academic curriculum.
- Talk directly to the parent and not to the other professionals at the meeting. This is particularly important if there is an interpreter. Look at the parent and not at the interpreter.
- Listen to the parents. Body language and facial expressions must reflect an openness to their thoughts and feelings. This is often easier said than done. Sitting in an IEP meeting with parents you suspect of abusing their child and trying to validate them as human beings may be the most difficult experience an educator has. Extending your work day for an evening IEP meeting that a parent attends intoxicated makes this very difficult. Enabling a parent

who is being verbally abusive to you is almost impossible but is an indicator of professional maturity.

Duties of the Meeting Leader before the Meeting
- Use every possible contact to ensure that a parent is informed of the IEP meeting, including visiting teachers, a parent who lives nearby to remind him or her, phone calls from a community service provider known to the parent, and a network of professionals serving the homeless.
- Schedule the meeting at a time that is convenient for the parent(s). This is seldom during regularly scheduled school hours.
- Help the parent with transportation difficulties by scheduling two meetings back-to-back and helping the parent carpool with a neighbor who does have transportation.

Duties of the Meeting Leader Immediately before the Meeting
- Have a professional the parent already knows and likes greet the parent at the school office and escort the parent to the meeting room. There is nothing more intimidating for a parent than to enter a roomful of professionals, often strangers, alone.
- Ensure that the meeting table is round, so that all participants are given equal value; specifically, there is no head of the table.
- Ask if the parent cares for a cup of coffee or a soft drink.
- Have name tags and use first names. Titles are confusing and intimidating to most parents.

ENCOURAGING AND MAXIMIZING STUDENT PARTICIPATION IN THE IEP PROCESS

The IDEA Amendments of 1997 contain provisions that greatly strengthened the involvement of students with a disability regarding their own future, particularly to facilitate their movement from school to postsecondary activities. The amendments significantly expand the provisions addition of an annual requirement to invite students, of any age, to attend the IEP meeting if the purpose of the meeting is for transition to "adult" life. Indeed, if more IEP/multidisciplinary team meetings were to emphasize outcome-based learning, every meeting would be about the student's eventual transition to "adult" life. If the student does not attend the IEP meeting, the school must take other steps to ensure that the student's preference and interests are carefully considered.

If at all possible, the student should be involved in the IEP meeting. In actuality, only students with the most severe and profound disabilities would have difficulty participating in some way. After all, it is the student's performance that is being reviewed and the student's plan that is being discussed and developed. Lovitt, Cushing, and Stump[34] interviewed 29 students from two diverse high schools and found that "student opinions concerning IEPs reflected confusion, ambivalence, distance or a lack of interest." Few participated in the IEP process or saw a meaning to the process. One student they interviewed regarding the significance of annual goals said, "It really is pretty stupid because . . . I do my work and everything in school. I did everything that was on my list. . . . And each year the objectives are exactly the same. So, it's . . . just basically learning the same stuff over and over every year. And it's been like that since about eighth grade."

Many of the strategies for making the parent feel like a vital part of the IEP process can also make the student feel like a vital part of the IEP process. For example, professionals must make eye contact with the student while talking, instead of looking at other professionals in the room. In addition, the following are strategies for getting students' input concerning their goals and objectives. Before the IEP meeting,

1. Ask the middle or high school student to meet with his or her teachers and therapists to discuss and write goals/objectives that the student believes will be challenging but attainable. If writing is difficult, the student can record his or her goals and objectives on a tape recorder. Then the student will be prepared with input for the IEP meeting.

2. Ask the elementary school student to express his or her desires regarding goals or objectives in the following ways:
   a. Tell what he or she would like to learn to do.
   b. Draw a hero and describe the qualities he or she likes in that hero.
   c. Describe the things a friend does that he or she would like to be able to do. Use a tape recorder or allow the student to make a magazine collage representing his or her particular skills, abilities, and interests.
   d. Tell a story about his or her favorite character (e.g., Pocahontas, Snow White, Clifford the Big Red Dog, Bob the Builder) and describe the things the character does that he or she would like to do.
   e. Make a list of the things he or she does best.
   f. Describe the things he or she wants to do when he or she grows up.

Finally, and perhaps most important, professionals cannot hesitate to include goals and objectives in the child's language on the IEP. It will help the child and his or her parents/guardians feel intricately involved in the process.

CONCERNS REGARDING THE IEP PROCESS

In some school districts, the IEP has become a paper chase that is unrelated to the actual process of educating the child with a disability. Care and concern for the student ends up being buried underneath mounds of paperwork. Indeed, school personnel are asked, "Are you done with Juan's IEP?" or "Have you written the IEP for Demetric?" The IEP is seen as an end product rather than an ongoing process of evaluation, review, and adaptation of the program to meet the child's unique educational needs.

Smith has criticized the IEP process:

Despite overwhelming evidence that IEPs have failed to accomplish their mission, little has been done to rectify the situation. . . . The IEP should be an essential component of instructional design and delivery that enhances and accounts for students' learning and teachers' teaching. Yet, data support the contention that IEPs are not functioning as designed, including being inept at structuring "specially designed instruction."[51]

Indeed, Gerardi et al.[20] have suggested that the IEP may be the "single most critical detriment to appropriate programming" for children in need of special education services. The researchers have suggested that the IEP process has created a huge, ineffective bureaucracy. It has been viewed as superfluous to the ongoing educational process and an educational burden from which many special educators would like to escape,[35] and it has been perceived as being troublesome and expensive to implement.[33]

While the potential for maximizing educational benefits for children with disabilities through the IEP process is great, there have been problems with IEP implementation. Specific problems and suggested solutions follow:

1. School district personnel write IEPs with goals and objectives that bear little relation to the teacher's instructional plans.[58] On the other hand, and perhaps more potentially devastating, teachers plan instruction that bears little relation to the learner's IEP (or, worse yet, don't plan instruction at all). The good teacher embraces the notion that he or she can and must be able to document carefully the child's progress and, more important, be able to design an instructional environment so that the child can accomplish the specific goals and objectives.
2. Educators fear they will be held accountable if the child fails to achieve the goals of the IEP, so they suggest only goals and objectives that can be met easily. The IEP is not, however, a performance contract.[58]
3. The campus leader, the principal, fails to recognize his or her responsibility to ensure that the IEP is implemented. Perhaps

this will happen only when a principal's performance (and subsequent promotion potential) is measured by student performance on state-mandated standardized tests and by student accomplishment of IEP objectives.

It appears that the IEP process can be used to hide ineffectual and inappropriate education for children with disabilities. The IEP process can, however, be used to carefully plan and monitor the education of children with special needs.

THE INDIVIDUAL TRANSITION PLAN

The individual transition plan (ITP) is an extraordinary idea with a promise and potential yet unfulfilled. The intent of the ITP is that those integrally involved in the life of a student with a disability will help plan and determine the "outcomes" of a lifetime of public education (see Table 4-12). Hasazi et al. wrote, "The Individuals with Disabilities Education Act emphasized the importance of including students and parents as active participants in Individualized Education Program and transition planning, and using collaborative and interagency approaches to developing outcome-oriented plans based on students' needs, taking into account their preferences and interests."[23]

Devlieger and Trach wrote, "The life transition process ultimately should be seen as comprised of intersecting and intertwining individual and social dimensions."[11]

The society should prepare its young people for a productive and meaningful life after school. That is, indeed, one of the purposes of public education. Harold Hodgkinson, while he served as the director of the Center for Demographic Policy at the Institute for Educational Leadership, studied the ability of students to make a meaningful transition into adult life; more specifically, he considered the students most in need of general education reform. He found that the top 20 percent of students graduating from high schools in the United States are "world class"; they would be successful

Table 4-12	Target Areas for Holistic Adult Lifestyle Transition Planning

1. Postsecondary education (choose one)

____ 1.1 College
____ 1.2 Junior college
____ 1.3 Adult education
____ 1.4 Vocational/technical training school
____ 1.5 GED program
____ 1.6 Other _____

2. Employment (choose one)

____ 2.1 Competitive employment—no support
____ 2.2 Competitive employment—transition support
____ 2.3 Supported employment—at or above minimum wage, individual placement
____ 2.4 Supported employment—subminimum wage, individual placement
____ 2.5 Enclave—small group in business setting, ongoing support
____ 2.6 Mobile crew—small group in a variety of businesses, ongoing support
____ 2.7 Sheltered workshop
____ 2.8 Day activity center
____ 2.9 Other _____

3. Living arrangements (choose one)

____ 3.1 Living on own—no support
____ 3.2 Living on own—with support
____ 3.3 With family or relative
____ 3.4 Adult foster care
____ 3.5 Group home—specialized training
____ 3.6 ICF–MR—training, ongoing support
____ 3.7 Adult nursing home
____ 3.8 Other _____

4. Homemaking activities (choose all that apply)

____ 4.1 Independent—needs no services
____ 4.2 Needs personal care assistance
____ 4.3 Needs housekeeping, laundry assistance
____ 4.4 Needs meal preparation assistance
____ 4.5 Needs menu planning, budgeting assistance
____ 4.6 Other _____

5. Financial issues

____ 5.1 Earned wages
____ 5.2 SSI
____ 5.3 SSDI
____ 5.4 SSI/SSDI and earned wages
____ 5.5 Unearned income—gifts, family support
____ 5.6 Trust/will
____ 5.7 Food stamps
____ 5.8 Other _____

(Continued)

Table 4-12 *(Continued)*

6. Community resources (choose all that apply)
____ 6.1 Independent—needs no services
____ 6.2 Needs banking assistance
____ 6.3 Needs shopping assistance
____ 6.4 Needs assistance with identifying and using some resources (day care, voting, etc.)
____ 6.5 Needs assistance to use all or most community activities
____ 6.6 Other_____

7. Recreation and leisure (choose all that apply)

____ 7.1 Independent—needs no services
____ 7.2 Needs assistance—needs support to participate in all or almost all activities
____ 7.3 Participates in family activities
____ 7.4 Attends community recreation activities with disabled peers
____ 7.5 Attends community recreation activities with disabled and nondisabled peers
____ 7.6 Participates in church groups, clubs
____ 7.7 Other_____

8. Transportation (choose all that apply)

____ 8.1 Independent—needs no services
____ 8.2 Needs assistance—uses public transportation
____ 8.3 Needs assistance—uses specialized transportation
____ 8.4 Uses family transportation
____ 8.5 Uses car pool
____ 8.6 Uses group home or residential transportation
____ 8.7 Other_____

9. Medical services (choose all that apply)

____ 9.1 Covered by group insurance—Blue Cross, Medicaid, etc.—and needs no assistance
____ 9.2 Covered by group insurance but needs assistance—monitoring medical needs, appointments, etc.
____ 9.3 Needs extensive medical services and support—regular tests and/or daily monitoring of medicine and/or therapy
____ 9.4 Other_____

10. Relationships (choose all that apply)

____ 10.1 Independent—needs no services
____ 10.2 Desires family-planning assistance
____ 10.3 Desires support group
____ 10.4 Desires counseling assistance
____ 10.5 Desires family respite or family support services
____ 10.6 Desires peer or "buddy" friendship network
____ 10.7 Other_____

11. Advocacy/legal (choose all that apply)

____ 11.1 Independent—needs no services
____ 11.2 Desires some assistance—estate planning, will, etc.
____ 11.3 Desires extensive assistance—guardianship, etc.
____ 11.4 Other_____

Data from Lousiana Department of Education

with or without any educational reform. The next 40 percent are capable of completing a college-level education without educational reform. It is the bottom 40 percent about whom he is worried. He wrote,

> The lowest 40% of students are in very bad educational shape, a situation caused mostly by problems they brought with them to the kindergarten door, particularly poverty, physical and emotional handicaps, lack of health care, difficult family conditions and violent neighborhoods. . . . These are the children who are tracked into the "general" curriculum in high school, which prepares them neither for college nor for a job. . . . The best way to deal with this problem is to provide a seamless web of services, combining education, health care, housing, transportation and social welfare.[26]

Halpern[22] believes that this type of comprehensive reevaluation and reenvisioning of general education, in toto, and of transition, in particular, must occur if students, with and without disabilities, leave the public schools in this country ready to assume a role as a productive member of the society.

Many of the children who are served in special education programs in the United States begin to receive early childhood intervention (ECI) services soon after their birth. They make a transition from ECI into public school programs at age 3 years, and many remain there until graduation at age 22 years. What is the point of 19 years of programming? What is the goal? What are the desired educational outcomes?

Certainly, the physical educator and adapted physical educator can and must play a critical role in the individual transition plan process. Hawkins notes the vital role of leisure activities "to promote health/wellness, life satisfaction, and rewarding personal relationships."[24] Piletic wrote, "Most physical educators are already preparing students to participate in activities offered through city recreation programs, YMCAs [and YWCAs], private gyms, racquet clubs, golf courses, bowling centers, and swimming pools. These are the community-based activities that should be included in transitional services for students with

disabilities."[44] Dummer[12] suggested that, if individual transition plan goals and objectives are selected or modified from the core curriculum, physical educators will be best prepared to use their experience and expertise to teach skills that will be critical in the postschool years.

Educators and parents, working closely with the student, must have a preordained idea of what should be the specific "outcomes" of a lifetime of education.

Critical decisions to be made that should have an impact on the thinking of the adapted and general physical educator include the following:

- What specific social-emotional, cognitive-academic, and gross motor skills should be demonstrated as an adult?
- What vocational competencies does the individual need to guarantee independence and the least restrictive educational or work placement? Depending on the type of vocation planned, the skills can be varied:
  Skills to lift, carry, push, pull
  Skills to do research on the Internet
  Skills to plant, dig, prune, weed, and care for plants
- What survival skills does the individual need to guarantee his or her access to community-based programs, facilities, or activities?
  Skills to manage and use public transit systems
  Skills to navigate bus steps, move through revolving doors, step up and down from curbs, climb on and off a moving escalator
  Skills to send and receive e-mail
  Skills to use a phone for emergencies (dial 911) and for personal/social contact, simply to call and stay in touch with a friend
- What skills does the individual need to enjoy a life full of leisure, recreation, sport, and physical fitness activities?
  Specific locomotor, object-control, and culturally determined patterns of movement to be successful in leisure, recreation, sport, and physical fitness activities

Individuals with Paraplegia Enjoy Snow Skiing
Courtesy of Challenge Aspen, Aspen, CO.

Specific skills to gain access to community-based programs, facilities, or activities—for example,

- Renting cross-country skis
- Going to a local sports club to watch the Green Bay Packers play the Minnesota Vikings

Joining and using a local recreation department health center

Packing a simple picnic dinner to attend a Ballet Folklorico performance in the park

Buying and using shoes for an aerobic dance class

Taking a bus to a mall to participate in an early bird walking program

Certainly, the process of planning for the future of a student, with or without a disability, after graduation from high school is a complex one that demands the efforts of all involved. The intent of the mandate regarding an individual transition plan, beginning at age 16, for students with a disability, is to focus the efforts of the student, parents, and professionals alike on the desired outcome—a full, rich, satisfying life. An individual transition plan must be developed for each student with a disability, no later than his or her 16th birthday. The transition plan must address, specifically, the instructional strategies that will be used to prepare the student for the transition from school to community and work environments.

Certainly, some adolescents with disabilities have a more difficult time making a meaningful transition into the community after completion of school-based programs. Only a small percentage of adolescents with emotional disorders enroll in postsecondary education programs.[8] Adolescents who have conduct, behavioral, or emotional disorders tend to have more difficulty securing a job, keeping a job, and developing or maintaining positive interpersonal relationships than do students with other disabilities.[8]

Like many other states, Minnesota mandates that the individual transition plan address

- Employment
- Community participation
- Home living
- Recreation and leisure
- Postsecondary education[37]

Preparing for a transition into the community and workplace after school requires systematic and careful planning.[19] The State of Minnesota has developed a comprehensive Web site, "A Guide to Plan Your Life after High School."[37]

Four to Five Years before Graduation
- Take a community education class.
- Attend events to learn spectator or audience member skills.
- Learn how to plan recreation and leisure activities (where, when, cost, transportation).
- Establish exercise routines.
- Join a club or an organization in your community.

Three Years before Graduation
- Explore new ways to use your free time.
- Identify supports needed to participate in activities of interest.

Two Years before Graduation
- Try additional recreation and leisure activities.

One Year before Graduation
- Continue to take part in activities of interest.

One to Two Years after Graduation
- Join and participate in adult recreation activities.

Stopka et al.[53] wrote that one of the significant concerns regarding the transition of students with disabilities into the vocational setting may be their lack of physical fitness for basic tasks, which include painting, stocking shelves, and doing basic laundry duties. Perhaps of more concern to the physical educator and/or adapted physical educator

is the significant lack of attention paid to planning for a postsecondary life full of quality leisure, recreation, sport, and fitness activities. Although these goals and physical education programs to attain these goals are significant, leisure, recreation, sport, and fitness goals have been virtually ignored on individual transition plans.[17]

The Louisiana Department of Education has developed a visionary ITP that targets the following areas for holistic adult lifestyle transition planning:

- Postsecondary education
- Employment
- Living arrangements
- Homemaking activities
- Financial/income needs
- Community resources
- Recreation and leisure
- Transportation
- Medical services
- Relationships
- Advocacy/legal needs

The Louisiana plan addresses each of these issues and designates the desired adult outcome for each of the areas (see Tables 4-12 and 4-13). This plan then defines the process required to ensure that the individual meets the goals or desired adult outcomes by stipulating the responsibilities of the school, the family, and adult agencies in meeting these outcomes. Included for each desired adult outcome are

- School action steps
- Family action steps
- Adult agency action steps

An increasing number of leisure, recreation, and sport programs are designed to encourage individuals with disabilities to participate in an active lifestyle after school. For a comprehensive list of these agencies, please refer to the Texas Woman's University Project INSPIRE Web site at www.twu.edu/projectinspire (scroll to Leisure and Recreation).[55]

An increasing emphasis is being placed on effective transition from school-based programs into

Table 4-13	Individual Transition Plan Form

INDIVIDUALIZED TRANSITION PLAN
LOUISIANA DEPARTMENT OF EDUCATION   Page___ of___

Comprehensive transition planning should consider each of the following areas.
Check each area that was addressed for this student in this year's plan.

1. ___ Postsecondary Education	4. ___ Homemaking Needs	7. ___ Recreation and Leisure	10. ____ Relationships
2. ___ Employment	5. ___ Financial/Income Needs	8. ___ Transportation Needs	11. ____ Advocacy/Legal Needs
3. ___ Living Arrangements	6. ___ Community Resources	9. ___ Medical Services	12. ____ Other _____

We, the undersigned, have participated in this transition plan and support its intent and recommendations.

STUDENT	STATE ID #	SCHOOL SYSTEM	DATE
PARENT/GUARDIAN		RELATED SERVICE PROVIDER(S)	
TEACHER			
ITP COORDINATOR		ADULT AGENCY SERVICE PROVIDER(S)	
ODR			

DATE	DESIRED ADULT OUTCOMES	SCHOOL ACTION STEPS	DATE	FAMILY ACTION STEPS	DATE	ADULT AGENCY ACTION STEPS	DATE

Courtesy Louisiana Department of Education.

the community. The physical educator and the adapted physical educator must play a vital role in this process. First and foremost, the physical education program must be outcome-based. The curriculum should prepare students to participate in leisure, recreation, sports, and physical fitness programs as adults. Second, the professional can and must be the liaison between the school and the community agencies. See Table 4-14, Adam's projected ITP at age 16 years, and Table 4-15 for recommended 3-year goals.

The process of planning for the critical transition from school to employment, postsecondary school, community living and access, and participation in community activities is not something that can be managed in an IEP/multidisciplinary team meeting. It appears that the crucial decisions may best be made in the informal but trust-based communications among the learner, the parents, and the professionals who have earned the trust of the learner and parents.[10] The personal futures planning model may be a valid and appropriate

Table 4-14	Leisure, Recreation, Sport, and Fitness Component of Adam's PROJECTED Individual Transition Plan (at Age 16 Years): Designed for Success

Adapted Physical Education
Individual Transition Plan

Name: Adam P.
Date of Birth: August 27, 1999
Chronological Age: 16 years
Test Date: August 27, 2015
School: Martin Luther King Junior High School
Evaluator: Dr. Jean Pyfer, CAPE, APE Specialist

Tests Administered: Louisiana Competency Test for Adapted Physical Education, Level V Family Interview re: Leisure, Recreation and Sport Preferences Community Inventory of Leisure, Recreation and Sport Programs

Present Level of Performance
On the CTAPE, Adam demonstrated some developmental coordination disorders—difficulty motor planning and difficulty performing motor skills in a sequence. Adam was able to throw a softball and football, contralaterally, and with accuracy. He was able to serve a volleyball. He had difficulty with receipt skills, including catching and fielding a ball. His physical fitness skills were similar to those in his evaluation of October 16 & 18, 2007. He continues to have a significant deficit in abdominal strength; he is able to perform only 5 complete sit-ups.
Adam was able to walk a mile in 25 minutes.
The family interview included Adam's mother, Marguerite; his father, William; and his older brother, Mike. The family indicated they enjoyed camping, bicycling, and walking.

Annual Transition Goal
Adam will develop his cardiovascular fitness so he can participate in camping, bicycling, and walking activities with his family. Adam will be able to walk 1 mile in 18 minutes.

Objectives
Adam will be able to walk a mile in 22 minutes.
Adam will be able to walk a mile in 20 minutes.

Annual Transition Goal
Adam will develop his cardiovascular fitness, so that he can participate in camping, bicycling, and walking activities with his family. Adam will be able to bicycle 3 miles, on a circuit around his school, with a peer buddy, in 24 minutes.

Objectives
Adam will be able to stationary cycle for 10 minutes, at a 3-mile-per-hour pace.
Adam will be able to stationary cycle for 15 minutes, at a 3-mile-per-hour pace.
Adam will be able to stationary cycle for 20 minutes, at a 3-mile-per-hour pace.

Annual Service Transition Goal
Adam will serve as a coach, 1 hour per week, of a youth sports program for children with physical disabilities, leading to the acquisition of his Eagle Scout badge.

Table 4-15	Individuals with Disabilities Education Improvement Act—Sample: Recommended 3-Year Goals

Adam will develop his cardiovascular fitness, so that he can participate in camping, bicycling, and walking activities with his family. Adam will be able to walk 1 mile in 18 minutes.

Adam will be able to bicycle 3 miles, on a circuit around his school, with a peer buddy, in 24 minutes.

Adam will serve as a coach, 1 hour per week, of a youth sports program for children with physical disabilities.

Note: The 3-year plan provides teachers and paraprofessionals with little information about how to systematically ensure progress toward the long-term goal.

process to ensure that the intentions of the federally mandated ITP are realized.

PERSONAL FUTURES PLANNING

Personal futures planning (PFP) is a process not unlike the IEP process. In fact, if the IEP and ITP process had evolved as its designers and creators had hoped, there would have been no need for PFP in the education of individuals with disabilities. The intent of the PFP process is to really examine the capabilities, strengths, and interests of the learner with a disability in interaction with family members, neighbors, and friends in the context of the community in which the learner lives. Given this matrix, the individuals involved in the planning process help the learner and his or her family dream about the future, immediate and long-term. Then, the individuals involved in the planning process advocate for the learner, so that the school's instructional program helps the learner and the family realize their dreams.

With the present educational system, this is a voluntary process, usually initiated at the request of a parent, and it involves dedicated individuals willing to make a long-term commitment to the well-being and growth of the learner who is the focus of the plan. This is an extended commitment to the learner and the learner's family and may require meetings several times a year.

Increasingly, community service agencies and residential facilities that serve individuals with disabilities are adopting this personal futures planning model. The disability culture suggests this

is critical as self-determination becomes a more significant issue in the provision of services to individuals with disabilities. This process, however, is often met with resistance by agency personnel because it is time consuming. It may also cause serious conflicts with existing modes of service delivery.[52] For example, leisure and recreation service models in many community service agencies have typically been based on convenience and availability of services:[27] all program participants go bowling on Thursday afternoon from 2–4 P.M.; the bowling alley is empty, the bus is available, and the staff likes to bowl. This type of approach is in direct opposition to the philosophy of personal futures planning. How does the agency respond to the participant who would rather go fishing, go horseback riding, or go for a nature walk?

Leatherby suggests that at least the following persons be included in the initial future planning meeting:

1. Learner
2. Parent(s) and at least one other family member, particularly a sibling
3. At least one friend of the learner
4. At least one community representative who is not a service provider
5. At least one human service agency representative or provider
6. At least one school representative who knows the learner well[32]

The first step in the process is to identify, in a drawing, the individuals who are part of the learner's circle. This maps the learner's relationships.

Like a sociogram, it gives pictorial evidence of those relationships that the learner would like to emphasize and maintain and indicates problem areas if they exist. See Figure 4-1 for Adam's circle of friends.

The second step is to identify the learner's community interests. Critical in this process is the identification of family interests. Only if the family or extended family is interested in sharing and encouraging the activities can community-based participation be a reality.[46] Figure 4-2 is a diagram representing Adam's community interests.

The third step is to develop an action plan that identifies the steps that must be taken to maximize the learner's interaction within the context of his or her greater community. In addition, the action plan identifies a tentative time line for completion of these tasks.

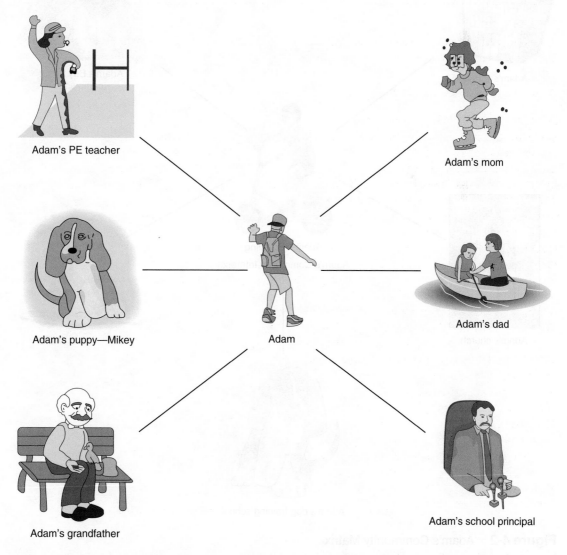

Adam's PE teacher

Adam's mom

Adam's puppy—Mikey

Adam

Adam's dad

Adam's grandfather

Adam's school principal

Figure 4-1   Adam's Circle of Friends

The PFP process is an ongoing, lifelong commitment to the quality of life of the targeted learner, and it contributes to the quality of life of the learner's family and friends.[38] It is a proactive process in which, after the learner's abilities, interests, and skills are targeted, a specific plan is developed to maximize the learner's opportunities to use the skills within the community.

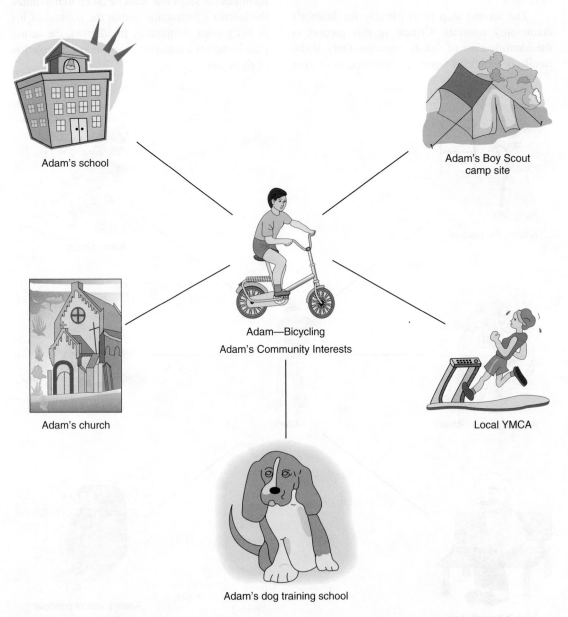

Adam's school

Adam's Boy Scout camp site

Adam—Bicycling
Adam's Community Interests

Adam's church

Local YMCA

Adam's dog training school

Figure 4-2 Adam's Community Matrix

MISSED OPPORTUNITIES

The adapted physical educator could play a critical role in the lives of learners with and without disabilites if he or she became involved and used his or her unique abilities, knowledge, and skills in after-school programs. Increasingly, after-school programs are being used to support the academic needs of children who are having difficulty with state-mandated assessments and those who are at risk for school failure. After-school programs must, inherently, involve children in activity and be experience-based, so that they will attract the students and keep them interested. The adapted physical educator has the significant skills to help design and implement activity and experience-based programs that may meet the needs of students. The National Center for Schools and Communities found that students who are involved in after-school programs can increase their test scores, improve their behavior, improve their participation in school (including attendance and graduation), and reduce high-risk behaviors, such as drug and alcohol abuse.[39]

In addition, the adapted physical educator/physical educator has a unique opportunity to involve learners with disabilities in service learning opportunities that may be very beneficial. When a learner with a disability is given the opportunity to serve others, he or she begins to understand the extent of his or her capabilities and value.[48]

A quality after-school program, in which the adapted physical educator leads and coordinates activities that focus on the needs of children with disabilities and children with other needs, may be a critical part of the total education service delivery process.

SUMMARY

The process of designing individual education programs (IEPs) in physical education for the student with a disability is a basic component of effective programming. The role of the parents in this process has been heightened. In addition, there has been an increased emphasis on the provision of services in the general curriculum and program.

The type of physical education program developed for each student will depend on the student's identified needs. After the student has been assessed to determine specific levels of present performance and needs, goals are determined by the IEP/multidisciplinary team. Not later than age 16, an individual transition plan (ITP) must be developed that ensures the student's ability to function in a community when leaving the school setting.

REVIEW QUESTIONS

1. Explain the importance of and difference among IEP, ITP, and PFP.

2. Explain the role of the adapted physical educator and physical educator in the development and implementation of the IEP, ITP, and PFP.

3. How can the physical educator or adapted physical educator make a parent or a student feel comfortable in an IEP/multidisciplinary team meeting?

4. Describe the potential of involvement in an activity-based after-school program for children with and without disabilities.

STUDENT ACTIVITIES

1. Visit the Web sites of the parent advocacy groups to get a sense of the feelings of parents regarding their rights and needs.
2. Review Adam's IEP, ITP, and the PFP process. Describe other ways the physical educator or adapted physical educator could help Adam and his family, so that they can enjoy community-based leisure, recreation, sport, and fitness experiences together.

REFERENCES

1. Achilles J, Yates R, Freese J: Perspectives from the field: Collaborative consultation in the speech and language program of the Dallas Independent School District, *Lang Speech Hearing Schools* 22:154–155, 1991.
2. Agran M: *Student directed learning: Teaching self-determination skills.* Pacific Grove, CA, Brooks/Cole, 1997.
3. *Alamo Heights v. State Board of Education,* 790 F 2d 1153 (5th Cir 1986).
4. American Academy of Pediatrics, Committee on Children with Disabilities: The pediatrician's role in development and implementation of an individual education plan (IEP) and/or an individual family service plan (IFSP), *Pediatrics* 104(1):124–127, 1999.
5. American Occupational Therapy Association: *Guidelines for occupational therapy services in school systems.* Rockville, MD, 1989.
6. American Occupational Therapy Association: *Uniform terminology for occupational therapy,* 2nd ed. Rockville, MD, 1989.
7. Behrmann M: Assistive technology for students with mild disabilities, intervention, *School Clin* 30(2):70–83, 1994.
8. Bullis M, Cheney D: Vocational and transition interventions for adolescents and young adults with emotional or behavioral disorders, *Focus Except Child* March:1–24, 1999.
9. California Department of Education: *Individualized education program fact sheet,* www.cde.ca.gov/spranch/sed/iep.htm.
10. Caray S: Listening to the voices of deaf students: Essential transition issues. *Teaching Except Child* 35(4):44–48, 2003.
11. Devlieger PJ, Trach JS: Mediation as a transition process: The impact of postschool employment outcomes, *Except Child* 65(4):507–523, 1999.
12. Dummer G: Curriculum revision in adapted physical education, *Palaestra* 15(2):59, 1999.
13. Ebenstein B: IEP strategies: Getting what your child needs from IEP meetings and annual reviews, *Except Parent,* April:62–63, 1995.
14. Edelen-Smith P: Eight elements to guide goal determination for IEPs, *Intervent School Clin* 30(5):297–301, 1995.
15. Elmore RF, McLaughlin MS: *Steady work: Policy, practice, and the reform of American education.* Santa Monica, CA, Rand Corporation, 1988.
16. Espin C et al.: Individualized education programs in resource and inclusive settings: How "individualized" are they? *J Special Ed* 33(3):164–174, 1998.
17. Felix M, Todd B: Transition plans in adapted physical education and recreation: An overlooked need. In Beaver D, editor: *Proceedings of the 6th National Conference on Adapted Physical Activity:* 5–7, Macomb, IL, Western Illinois University Press, 1998.
18. Friedman L: Promoting opportunity after school, *Educational Leadership* 60(4):79–82, 2002/2003.
19. Furney KS, Hasazi SB, DeStefano L: Transition policies, promises, and practices: Lessons from three states, *Except Child* 63:343–356, 1997.
20. Gerardi RJ et al.: IEP—More paperwork and wasted time, *Contemp Educ* 56:39–42, 1984.
21. Glaeser B, Pierson M, Fritschmann N: Comic strip conversations: A positive behavioral support

strategy, *Teaching Except Child,* 36(2):14–21, 2003.

22. Halpern AS: *Transition: Is it time for another rebottling?* Presented at the 1999 Annual OSEP Project Directors' Meeting, Washington, DC, June 14, 1999.

23. Hasazi SB, Furney KS, Destefano L: Implementing the IDEA transition mandates, *Except Child* 65(4):555–566, 1999.

24. Hawkins BA: Leisure and recreational programming. In Stainback W, Stainback S, editors: *Controversial issues confronting special education: Divergent perspectives.* Boston, Allyn & Bacon, 1992.

25. Haynes C: Language development in the school years—What can go wrong? In Mogford K, Sadler J, editors: *Child language disability.* Clevedon, UK, Multilingual Matters, 1989.

26. Hodgkinson H: American education: The good, the bad, and the task. In Elam S, editor: *The state of the nation's public schools: A conference report.* Bloomington, IN, Phi Delta Kappa Foundation, 1993.

27. Holburn S, Vietze P: Acknowledging barriers in adopting person-centered planning, *Mental Retard* 37(2):117–124, 1999.

28. House of Representatives Report No. 105-95, p. 182, 1997; Senate Report No. 105–17, p. 4, 1997.

29. Ingraham C, Anderson H: Self-determination, transition and deaf-blind students, *Odyssey* 2(3):24–25, 2001.

30. Jankowitz W, Cort RH: Transition planning: Will your child be ready for life after high school? *Except Parent* September:83–84, 1999.

31. Johns BH, Crowley P, Guetzloe E: Planning the IEP for students with emotional and behavioral disorders, *Focus on Exceptional Children* 34(9):1–12, 2002.

32. Leatherby J: *Reach for the stars—Planning for the future: Personal futures planning for young children.* Paper presented at the Ninth Annual Statewide Conference on Deaf-Blindness and Multiple Disabilities, Austin, TX, February 1994.

33. Lewis A: Churning up the waters in special education, *Phi Delta Kappan* 73:100–101, 1991.

34. Lovitt T, Cushing S, Stump C: High school students rate their IEPs: Low opinions and lack

of ownership, *Intervent School Clin* 30:34–37, 1994.

35. Lynch E, Beare P: The quality of IEP objectives and their relevance to instruction for students with mental retardation and behavioral disorders, *Remed Spec Educ* 11(2):48–55, 1990.

36. Lytle R, Lavay B, Robinson N, Huettig C: Teaching collaboration and consultation skills to preservice adapted physical education teachers, *JOPERD* 74(4):41–43, 2003.

37. Minnesota Individual Transition Plans at www.disability.state.mn.us/pubs/trans/pyd.html.

38. Mount B: *Dare to dream.* Manchester, CT, Communitas, 1991.

39. National Center for Schools and Communities: *After-school programs: An analysis of need, current research, and public opinion.* New York Fordhan University, 1999.

40. National Education Association, www.nea.org/supportprofessionals.

41. No Child Left Behind Act of 2001, U.S. 107th Congress, Washington, DC.

42. Office of Civil Rights, 1989, EHLR 326.

43. Orr C, Gott C, Kainer M: *Model of student role adaptation: Merging the values of occupational therapy and special education.* Dallas, TX, Dallas Independent School District, 1990.

44. Piletic C: Transition: Are we doing it? *JOPERD* 69(9):46–50, 1998.

45. Pyfer J: Personal communication, fall 1999.

46. Roth K: *Community physical recreation and students with intellectual disabilities: Program evaluation, educational placement comparisons, and post-school outcomes,* Dissertation, Texas Woman's University, 2003.

47. Regan K: Using dialogue journals in the classroom, *Teaching Except Child* 36(2):36–41, 2003.

48. Service learning—Students with disabilities give to others, *Today* (Council for Exceptional Children) 10(4):1, 7, 2003.

49. Shapiro D, Sayers LK: Who does what on the interdisciplinary team regarding physical education for children with disabilities? *Teaching Except Child* 35(6):32–38, 2003.

50. Shepherd D: *Outcomes of leisure/recreation transition planning in adapted physical education.* Dissertation, Texas Woman's University, 2003.

51. Smith SW: Individualized education programs (IEPs) in special education—From intent to acquiescence, *Except Child* September:6–13, 1990.

52. Stone DA: *Policy paradox: The art of political decision making.* Boston, W. W. Norton, 1997.

53. Stopka C et al.: Transition skills for wellness. *Teaching Except Child* 31(1):6–11, 1999.

54. Technology—The great equalizer, *Today* (Council for Exceptional Children) 10(4):1, 5, 2003.

55. Texas Woman's University Project INSPIRE at http://venus.twu.edu/ProjectINSPIRE

56. Tournaki N, Criscitello E: Using peer tutoring as a successful part of behavior management, *Teaching Except Child* 36(2):22–29, 2003.

57. U.S. Department of Education: 34 CFR Parts 300 and 301: Assistance to states for the Education for Children with Disabilities and Preschool Grants for Children with Disabilities, *Federal Register,* August 14, 2006.

58. U.S. Department of Education: Assistance to states for education of handicapped children: Interpretation of the Individual Education Program, *Federal Register,* January 19, 1981.

59. Walsh J: *How to propose an IEP, run an ARD, develop a BIP, and comply with procedural safeguards,* Walsh, Anderson, Brown, Schulze & Aldridge, P. C., Austin, Texas, 1998.

60. Washington Assistive Technology Alliance, http://wata.org/pubs/articles/k_12_flyer.htm.

61. Whitfield C: Transitions and the placement process—It's all about choices, *Exceptional Parent Magazine* August:96–102, 2002.

SUGGESTED READINGS

Davis R, Kotecki J, Harvey M, Oliver A: Responsibilities and training needs of paraeducators in physical education, *APAQ* 24(1):70–83, 2007.

Piletic C, Davis R, Aschemeier A: Paraeducators in physical education, *JOPERD* 76(5):47–55, 2005.

Wasburn-Moses L: Obstacles to program effectiveness in secondary special education, *Preventing School Failure* 50(3):21–30, 2006.

RECOMMENDED WEB SITES

Please keep in mind that these Web sites are being recommended in the winter 2007. As Web sites often change, they may have moved, been reconfigured, or eliminated.

Family Village's information about the IEP and the IEP process
www.familyvillage.wisc.edu/education/iep.html

Information about IEPs and an IEP quiz you can take to see how much you know
www.wrightslaw.com/info/iep.index.htm

A wonderful resource regarding the IEP, with outstanding references to other Web sites as well
www.angelfire.com/ny/Debsimms

List of questions to answer in preparation for a child's individual transition plan (ITP) meeting
www.tsbvi.edu/Outreach/seehear/archive/itp.htm

Adapted Physical Education Standards (APENS), National Consortium for Physical Education and Recreation for Individuals with Disabilities
www.ncperid.org

RECOMMENDED VIDEOS

Insight Media
2162 Broadway
New York, NY 10024
1-800-233-9910
www.insight-media.com

IEPs: How the Law Transforms the Process
TAN3771/VHS tape/2005/17 min/$139.00

A New IDEA for Special Education: Understanding the System and the New Law
UAN4076/DVD/2005/55 min/$119.00

Free Appropriate Public Education for Students with Disabilities
TAN4422/DVD/2004/21 min/$149.00

Teaching to Meet Learners' Needs

The Camden, NJ, Courier-Post, Courtesy National Amputee Golf Association.

■ OBJECTIVES

Recognize the differences between the top-down and the bottom-up teaching approaches.

Discriminate between functional and sport skills.

Give an example of a content analysis.

Identify three functional adaptations a physical educator could make to accommodate students with disabilities.

Explain programmed physical education instruction.

There is no question about the importance of motor development. In addition to its being a critical component of movement efficiency, it is also widely believed to underlie perceptual, cognitive, and affective function.[10] How infants' bodies grow and change has been widely studied in this country since 1920. From that time through the 1940s, child development specialists carefully observed and documented hundreds of motor milestones normally developing children demonstrate during their first few years of life. Those observations became the basis for the majority of motor development screening instruments available to us today (see Chapters 3 and 10 for specific screening instruments). Such instruments are frequently used to determine whether an infant is progressing neurologically at the expected rate because motor milestones are among the first visible indicators of central nervous system maturation.

CASE STUDY

Adam

CRITICAL THINKING TASK

Review Adam's individual education program (IEP) in Chapter 4 (see Figure 4-1). Note the areas of performance that were indicated as weaknesses. As you read this chapter, identify which type of intervention (top-down, bottom-up, or accommodation) could be used to address each challenge.

However, even though motor development screening instruments can be used to identify where a child is performing in comparison with normal expectations, such instruments do not provide information indicating what is interfering with the slowly developing child's progress. That information must be predicted from formal sensory input, sensory integration or psychological tests developed specifically for those purposes, or informal clues provided by the child. More direct, absolute measures are, however, under development.

As we begin a new millennium, developmental psychologists, movement scientists, neuroscientists, and others are joining forces to try to build on the work of the early developmentalists to better understand the processes by which infants and children gain mastery over their bodies. Careful studies are being conducted to determine what aspects of nature and nurture are critical for maximal motor development. Advanced technology is being used to identify and monitor factors that impact favorably on a child's motor competence.

Physical educators who teach individuals with disabilities agree that their primary goal is to facilitate the development of purposeful skills for each student. There are, however, a variety of approaches to programming from which physical educators can select. They range from general physical education activities believed to benefit all children, regardless of degree of function, to developmentally sequenced activities that serve as building blocks of motor development, to activities that enhance very specific skills.

Which approach a physical educator selects depends on the amount of time available, the age and readiness level of the students, the capabilities of the teacher, and the number of individuals available to assist the teacher. In this chapter, the levels of function that contribute to sport and functional skills, ways to facilitate development at each of those levels, and adaptations that can be made to accommodate individuals with special needs will be addressed.

LEVELS OF MOTOR FUNCTION

The ultimate goal of physical education for individuals with disabilities is to equip them with motor skills that contribute to independent living. To plan these programs systematically, it is desirable to distinguish clearly the levels of function that contribute to the acquisition of the many specific sport skills.

Each of these levels makes a unique contribution to independent functioning: (1) basic neurological building blocks, (2) integration processes, (3) functional skills, and (4) sport and recreational skills (see Table 5-1). The physical educator who understands the interrelatedness of these levels and can select intervention activities to facilitate functioning at any given level, depending on a student's needs, will realize success.

The functioning of the basic neurological building blocks depends on the integrity and operation of the sensory input systems. These systems include primitive reflexes, the vestibular system, refractive and orthoptic vision, audition, the tactile and kinesthetic systems, and equilibrium reflexes. Before information can reach the central nervous system for processing, these systems must be intact and functional. The physical educator who automatically assumes these systems are functioning and that adequate stimulation is reaching the central nervous system disregards an important component of purposeful movement.[8]

The second level of functioning is the integration processes. Like the basic neurological building

Table 5-1	Motor Development Model

Motor Output

Sport Skills

Dribbling, shooting, rebounding, spiking, volleying, serving, trapping, pitching, tumbling, punting, diving, skiing, batting

Functional Skills

Locomotor	Object Control
Rolling, crawling, walking, running, hopping, jumping, sliding, galloping, skipping, climbing stairs	Kicking, catching, throwing, striking, bouncing

Integration Processes

Perceptual Motor	Physical Fitness	Motor Fitness
Balance	Strength	Agility
Laterality	Flexibility	Power
Directionality	Muscular endurance	Speed
Body image	Cardiovascular endurance	Coordination
Spatial awareness		
Cross-lateral integration		

Basic Neurological Building Blocks

Equilibrium reflexes
Vestibular, kinesthetic, refractive and orthoptic vision, tactile audition
Primitive reflexes

blocks, these prerequisites enhance the acquisition of skill. If the basic neurological building blocks are functioning, integration processes develop concurrently with quality movement experiences. The integration processes include the perceptual-motor, physical fitness, and motor fitness categories. Examples of perceptual-motor abilities are balance, cross-lateral integration, laterality, directionality, body image, and spatial awareness. Physical fitness prerequisites are strength, flexibility, muscular endurance, and cardiovascular endurance. Motor fitness consists of power, agility, speed, and motor coordination.

The uppermost levels of motor development are functional and sport and recreation skills. Skills are motor behaviors that are specific to either functional living or a sport or recreational activity. Examples of functional skills are the basic locomotor skills, such as walking, running, hopping, and skipping, and the object-control skills, such as throwing, bouncing, and kicking. Sport and recreational skills include shooting a basketball, serving a tennis ball, skiing, and trapping a soccer ball. Functional skills, such as walking and running, usually emerge as the central nervous system prerequisite components mature. Proficiency at specific individual and team sport skills is usually developed through repetitious practice of the skill itself.

INCIDENTAL VERSUS PLANNED LEARNING

Most individuals learn from everyday interaction with the environment. This is particularly true if the environment is varied and the learner possesses all the prerequisites needed to convert environmental stimulation into motor patterns. This is known as *incidental learning*. The more ready an individual is (i.e., the more developed the neurological, cognitive, and motor functions are), the more that can be gained from interaction with the environment. Conversely, the fewer the number of developed prerequisites, the less a person gains from environmental exchanges.

College students need hands-on experience with children of all ability levels

Courtesy of Laurie Zittel.

The individual with a disability is often denied opportunities to interact with varied environments. This is a hindrance because, for the central nervous system to develop normally, a wide variety of stimulation is necessary.[13] Thus, attempts to protect these children from interaction with the environment often delay their development. Because of these delays, learners with disabilities do not always gain as much from incidental learning as do other learners.

Teachers of children with disabilities must be particularly sensitive to the needs of their students. Until a teacher determines the needs of students, appropriate intervention strategies cannot be selected. The physical education teacher must ensure that each student's motor learning improves. The general approach of providing a wide variety of activities to all students gives no assurance that motor learning will result. It is true that the children may have fun and could gain some physical fitness from their activities; however, the students will not make the same gains as would be possible if activities were selected specifically to meet the needs of the learners. There are many activities available that are enjoyable for all children in a class that meet the needs of individual learners. The effective teacher will select those activities that benefit all of the children in his or her class.

FACILITATING SKILL DEVELOPMENT

Children and youth with disabilities frequently demonstrate physical and motor development lags. As a result, they often have difficulty learning chronologically age-appropriate skills. When developmental deficits become apparent, decisions about how to address the deficits have to be made. Questions that need to be answered include whether it is necessary to modify the teaching strategy used or will modifications/adaptations best accommodate the student's needs. In the following sections, three teaching techniques and several functional adaptations that are effective for accommodating the student with special needs will be presented.

Teach Specific Skills: Top-Down

Teaching the skill directly is known as using the task-specific approach. Advocates of this approach stress what skills an individual will need for productive independence as an adult in the community where he or she lives. In the case of the physical educator, the targeted behaviors focus on the functional and recreational sports skills that an individual would have an opportunity to participate in as an adult in the community. The top-down approach places emphasis on the end of the skill sequence, the final motor countdown as an adult, rather than what is to be taught next. When using the top-down approach, it is necessary to monitor carefully the progress of learners with disabilities as they move from elementary to middle schools to high schools and then into adult life. To ensure that functional skills are being taught, it is necessary to gather information about the lesser restrictive environments the individual will function in as an adult. The focus of this approach emphasizes teaching skills and behaviors that are absolutely necessary for a person to function in a community environment.

To determine which skills an individual has in relation to skills that will be needed for ultimate functioning in the community requires the completion of an ecological inventory (community-based assessment). The ecological inventory provides critical information about current and future school and community environments (see Chapter 3, "Determining Educational Needs through Assessment"). Selecting age-appropriate skills tends to maximize the normalization process during the life of a person with a disability. When using ecological assessment data, a major departure from traditional procedures is the need to take students into the community to do part of the instruction. This enables the student to practice the skills in a natural setting.

When using a task analysis approach to assess students' repertoires, the educator can determine which motor skills are present and which are yet to be learned. Once the deficient skills are determined, they are prioritized and analyzed to determine which portions have not yet been mastered, and the specific missing components are taught using a direct teaching method.

In general, there are two types of task analysis, content analysis of discrete tasks and content analysis of continuous skills. Examples of each appear in Table 5-2. An example of a content analysis of a discrete task is given in Table 5-3, and an example of a content analysis of continuous skills is presented in Table 5-4. Once a task analysis is completed and the missing components are identified, a person using a task-specific top-down teaching approach would either teach each of the components found to be lacking or teach the entire movement from beginning to end.

Task analyses can be very formal or quite informal. Tests that are content-referenced are truly sets of analyzed tasks because they provide the components of each task in the test. However, frequently the physical educator relies on observation of performance to determine what parts of the task are inefficient. For example, if the physical educator

Table 5-2	Task Analyses and Educational Performance	
Type of Task Analysis	**Type of Task**	**Examples**
Content analysis of discrete tasks	Discrete tasks broken down into parts that make up the entire task	Dressing, lay-up shot in basketball
Content analysis of continuous skills	Continuous task broken down into components that contribute to the skill	Running, jumping, throwing

Table 5-3	Content Analysis of the Discrete Task of Executing a Lay-Up Shot in Basketball

1. Bounces a basketball with one hand
2. Bounces a basketball at waist height with one hand
3. Runs while bouncing a basketball at waist height
4. Takes a short step and jumps vertically off the foot opposite the shooting hand
5. Times the jump to occur just before the body reaches the area under the basket
6. Releases the ball at the top of the jump
7. Directs the ball to a point on the backboard that will permit the ball to rebound from the backboard into the basket
8. Controls the body when coming down from the jump

Table 5-4	Content Analysis of the Continuous Task of Running

Mature Stage of Running

1. Stride length at maximum, stride speed fast
2. Definite flight phase
3. Complete extension of support leg
4. Recovery thigh parallel to ground
5. Arms swinging vertically in opposition to legs
6. Arms bent at approximate right angles
7. Minimal rotary action of recovery leg and foot

Courtesy of Gallahue, DL, Ozmun, JC (1995), *Understanding Motor Development,* Dubuque: McGraw-Hill.

observes that the student is performing all parts of the basketball lay-up task correctly except timing the jump to occur just before the body reaches the area under the basket and directing the ball to the correct point on the backboard, those are the two components that should be selected to be taught directly.

To correct the jump timing problem, it might be necessary to mark an area on the floor where the jump should be executed for a right-hand lay-up. The student practices approaching the mark and

landing on it consistently with the left foot. When that movement becomes habitual, the student practices the approach and adds a jump off the left foot when reaching the mark on the floor. Then, to direct the student's attention to the correct place to rebound the ball, an area could be marked on the backboard. The student then practices the correct approach, jump, and striking the outlined area on the backboard with the ball in one continuous motion. Minor adjustments may need to be added to modify the amount of force the student uses when releasing the ball.

Once a skill is learned, it should be practiced under a variety of conditions to ensure the learner's ability to use the skill in different situations and environments. Conditions that can be modified include time (fast/slow, even/uneven), space (straight/circular/zig-zag, high/low, alone/with others, inside/outside), force (light/heavy, soft/hard), and flow (synchronized/unsynchronized, run/walk/hop, twist/turn). (See *Gross Motor Activities for Children with Special Needs,* which accompanies this text, for additional examples.)

The task-specific top-down approach is probably the most realistic and expedient type to use with individuals with severe disabilities and higher-functioning individuals in middle school and beyond, but it may be inappropriate for younger children with disabilities. The essential question to ask when trying to decide whether to use this approach is "How much time is available?" Facilitating basic neurological building blocks and integration processes prior to teaching specific skills takes time, perhaps years. Also, there is evidence that children under the age of 12 years respond more readily than do older individuals. When the individual with a disability is older and severely involved and there is a limited amount of time available to develop functional skills needed to live in a natural environment, the task-specific approach is the most efficient intervention strategy.

Eliminate Deficiencies: Bottom-Up

Motor development is a progressive process. For each of us to learn to move efficiently, we must first be able to take environmental information into the central nervous system. Then it must be processed or integrated, so that it can be used to direct movement patterns and skills. Only after the information is received and processed can the brain direct the muscles to work. If anything goes wrong before the information reaches the muscles, movement is inefficient or nonexistent. Advocates of the developmental approach agree that the ultimate goal of education is to produce productive adults who can function independently in their communities. To achieve this goal, the developmentalist would intervene in a child's life as early as possible to determine whether age-appropriate basic building blocks, integration processes, and skills were functional. If any age-appropriate developmental blocks were found to be deficient when the child was tested, then the developmentalist would select activities to promote development of the deficient areas. Thus, if a child were found to have a severe orthoptic (eye alignment) problem that would interfere with eye-hand coordination development, the child would be referred to a visual behavioral specialist for correction of the problem. If a child demonstrated failure to develop equilibrium reactions and/or adequate vestibular (inner ear) function, which are critical for balance development, activities to promote development in those areas would be prescribed.

The developmental approach can be considered a bottom-up teaching strategy because the evaluator tries to determine the lowest level of motor function and correct that problem before addressing specific skills (review Table 5-1). Once the developmentalist determines which basic neurological building blocks and integration components appear to be poorly developed, activities that promote the functioning of each area found to be lacking are selected. The rationale is to ensure that the supporting building blocks and integration processes are fully functioning, so that skill development will be facilitated.

In the following section, each of the basic neurological building blocks and perceptual motor integration processes will be described, clues that

indicate that the systems are not fully developed will be given, and individual activities that promote development will be suggested. Group activities to use to facilitate development of these systems are included in *Gross Motor Activities for Children with Special Needs,* which accompanies this text.

Basic Neurological Building Blocks

The primitive reflexes and the vestibular, visual, kinesthetic, tactile, and auditory systems, as well as the equilibrium reflexes, are considered basic input systems because sensations arising from these systems' receptors provide the basic "stuff" from which integration processes and motor skills are built. These systems normally develop during the first five years of life. After they are functioning, perceptual-motor, physical fitness, motor fitness, and motor skill development occurs. Should any one or a combination of these systems fail to develop fully, all motor development is delayed and/or interfered with in some way.[1,5] For this reason, it is imperative to identify and remediate basic input system delays as early in life as possible. The point at which it becomes too late to attempt to facilitate development of any of these systems is not really known; however, some writers suggest that, if such delays are still present at age 12 years, the educator's time might better be spent teaching the child to accommodate to the delay. See Table 5-5 for an informal screening test that can be used to identify sensory input delays.

Reflexes

Reflexes are innate responses that all normal children develop (see Table 5-6). Reflexes that affect movement are of interest to the physical educator because students whose reflex maturation is delayed have inefficient movement patterns. In general, there is a series of reflexes that should appear and disappear during the first year of life. These early (primitive) reflexes are layered over by (integrated into) voluntary movement patterns. As a child begins to move voluntarily, a different set of reflexes appears. These later automatic patterns

Table 5-5	Sensory Input Systems Screening Test		

Reflex Test Items—Check Pass or Fail		Pass	Fail
1. Tonic labyrinthine supine—(TLS) While lying on back, can bend knees to chest, wrap arms around knees, and touch head to knees. Child should be able to hold position for 10 seconds.			
2. Tonic labyrinthine prone—(TLP) While lying face down on mat with arms at side, child can lift head and upper body and hold off mat for 5 seconds.			
3. Positive support reaction—(PSR) Child is able to jump into air and, on landing, flex ankles, knees, and hips while maintaining balance for 5 seconds.			
4. Equilibrium reactions When placed on a tilt board, child will move hands out to side and maintain balance for 3 seconds when the board is suddenly tipped 15 degrees to one side and then to other side (check each side independently). Check child in each of these positions: a. Seated, start with hands in lap—move right. b. Seated, start with hands in lap—move left. c. On two knees, start with hands on hips—move right. d. On two knees, start with hands on hips—move left. Place child on all fours on tilt board and tip board 15 degrees to one side and then to the other. Child can maintain "all fours" position while holding head in a neutral position. e. When tipped to right. f. When tipped to left.			

Vestibular Test Items—Check Pass or Fail			
1. Seat child in a desk chair that can be rotated 360 degrees. Have child rest hands in lap or on arms of chair. Child should tip head down slightly (30 degrees). Turn chair 10 complete turns in 20 seconds (1 complete rotation every 2 seconds). Stop chair and watch child's eyes. Child's eye should flick back and forth for 7 to 13 seconds. After a 2-minute rest, repeat turning procedure in opposite direction. Check eye movement again. a. Turn to right. b. Turn to left.			

Fixation (Ocular Control)—Check Pass or Fail			
1. Child should sit in a chair facing a seated evaluator. Child can fixate with both eyes on an object held 18 inches in front of the nose at eye level for 10 seconds.			
2. Child should sit in a chair facing a seated evaluator. Cover child's left eye with your hand or a card. Child can fixate with right eye on an object held 18 inches in front of the nose at eye level for 10 seconds.			
3. Child should sit in a chair facing a seated evaluator. Cover child's right eye with your hand or a card. Child can fixate with left eye on an object held 18 inches in front of the nose at eye level for 10 seconds.			

NOTE: Any tendency to turn the head to one side or to blink excessively, or for the eyes to water, could be an indication that the child needs to be referred to a visual developmental specialist for a refractive and orthoptic visual exam.

(Continued)

Table 5-5	(*Concluded*)		
Ocular Alignment (Depth Perception)—Check Pass or Fail		**Pass**	**Fail**

Ocular Alignment (Depth Perception)—Check Pass or Fail

NOTE: On all of the following items start with the child looking at the object with both eyes. Then cover 1 eye and begin your observation.

1. Child is seated in a chair facing a seated evaluator. Child can fixate on an object held 18 inches in front of the nose at eye level without moving right eye as left eye is covered for 3 seconds. (Note whether the right eye moves and in what direction.)
2. Child is seated in a chair facing a seated evaluator. Child can fixate on an object held 18 inches in front of the nose at eye level without moving left eye as right eye is covered for 3 seconds. (Note whether the left eye moves and in what direction.)

Convergence-Divergence Ocular Control—Check Pass or Fail

1. Child is seated in a chair facing a seated evaluator. Child can visually follow with both eyes an object moved slowly from 18 inches directly in front of the nose (eye level), to 4 inches from the eyes (midpoint), and back to 18 inches. (Note whether the eyes move equally without jerking.)

Visual Tracking—Check Pass or Fail

1. Child is seated in a chair facing a seated evaluator. Child can visually pursue with both eyes without moving the head an object held 18 inches from the eyes as the object is moved in the following patterns:
   a. A square (12-inch sides)
   b. A circle (8- to 10-inch diameter)
   c. An *X* (10-inch lines)
   d. A horizontal line (12 inches)
2. Child is seated in a chair, with left eye covered, facing a seated evaluator. Child can visually pursue with the right eye without moving the head an object held 18 inches from the eyes as the object is moved in the following patterns:
   a. A square (12-inch sides)
   b. A circle (8- to 10-inch diameter)
   c. An *X* (10-inch lines)
   d. A horizontal line (12 inches)
3. Child is seated in a chair, with right eye covered, facing a seated evaluator. Child can visually pursue with the left eye without moving the head an object held 18 inches from the eyes as the object is moved in the following patterns:
   a. A square (12-inch sides)
   b. A circle (8- to 10-inch diameter)
   c. An *X* (10-inch lines)
   d. A horizontal line (12 inches)

NOTE: During all tracking tasks, note any tendency for the eyes to (1) jump when the object moves across the midline of the body, (2) jump ahead of the object, (3) jerk while pursuing the object, (4) water, or (5) blink excessively. The watering and/or excessive blinking could be an indicator of visual stress, and such cases should be referred to a visual developmental specialist for a refractive and orthoptic visual exam.

Kinesthesis—Check Pass or Fail

1. Can touch finger to nose 3 times in alternating succession with index fingers while eyes are closed. (Failure if the child misses the tip of the nose by more than 1 inch.)

Courtesy Jean L. Pyfer, Texas Woman's University, Denton, TX, and Robert Strauss, Trinity University, San Antonio, TX.

Table 5-6	**Primitive and Equilibrium Reflex Development**		
Reflex	**Age**	**Age Inhibited**	**Effect on Movement Patterns**
PRIMITIVE REFLEXES			
Flexor withdrawal	Birth	2 months	Uncontrolled flexion of leg when pressure is applied to sole of foot
Extensor thrust	Birth	2 months	Uncontrolled extension of leg when pressure is applied to sole of foot
Crossed extension 1	Birth	2 months	Uncontrolled extension of flexed leg when opposite leg is suddenly flexed
Crossed extension 2	Birth	2 months	Leg adducts and internally rotates, and foot plantar flexes when opposite leg is tapped medially at level of knee (scissor gait)
Asymmetrical tonic neck	Birth	4–6 months	Extension of arm and leg on face side or increase in extension tone; flexion of arm and leg on skull side or increase in flexor tone when head is turned
Symmetrical tonic neck 1	Birth	4–6 months	Arms flex or flexor tone dominates; legs extend or extensor tone dominates when head is ventroflexed while child is in quadruped position
Symmetrical tonic neck 2	Birth	4–6 months	Arms extend or extensor tone dominates; legs flex or flexor tone dominates when head is dorsiflexed while child is in quadruped position
Tonic labyrinthine, supine position	Birth	4 months	Extensor tone dominates when child is in supine position
Tonic labyrinthine, prone position	Birth	4 months	Flexor tone dominates in arms, hips, and legs when child is in prone position
Positive supporting reaction	Birth	4 months	Increase in extensor tone in legs when sudden pressure is applied to both feet simultaneously
Negative supporting reaction	Birth	4 months	Marked increase in flexor tone in legs when sudden pressure is applied to both feet simultaneously
Neck righting	Birth	6 months	Body rotated as a whole in same direction head is turned
Landau reflex	6 months	3 years	Spine, arms, and legs extend when head is dorsiflexed while child is held in supine position; spine, arms, and legs flex when head is ventroflexed while child is held in supine position
EQUILIBRIUM REFLEXES			
Body righting	6 months	Throughout life	When child is in supine position and initiates full body roll, there is segmented rotation of the body (i.e., head turns, then shoulders, then pelvis)

(Continued)

Table 5-6	(Continued)		
Reflex	**Age**	**Age Inhibited**	**Effect on Movement Patterns**
Labyrinthine righting 1	2 months	Throughout life	When child is blindfolded and held in prone position, head raises to a point where child's face is vertical
Labyrinthine righting 2	6 months	Throughout life	When child is blindfolded and held in supine position, head raises to a point where face is vertical
Labyrinthine righting 3	6–8 months	Throughout life	When child is blindfolded and held in an upright position and is suddenly tilted right, head does not right itself to an upright position
Labyrinthine righting 4	6–8 months	Throughout life	Same as labyrinthine righting 3, but child is tilted to left
Optical righting 1	2 months	Throughout life	Same as labyrinthine righting 1, but child is not blindfolded
Optical righting 2	6 months	Throughout life	Same as labyrinthine righting 2, but child is not blindfolded
Optical righting 3	6–9 months	Throughout life	Same as labyrinthine righting 3, but child is not blindfolded
Optical righting 4	6–8 months	Throughout life	Same as labyrinthine righting 4, but child is not blindfolded
Amphibian reaction	6 months	Throughout life	While child is in prone position with legs extended and arms extended overhead, flexion of arm, hip, and knee on same side can be elicited when pelvis on that side is lifted
Protective extensor	6 months	Throughout life	While child is held by pelvis and is extended in air, arms extend when child's head is moved suddenly toward floor
Equilibrium-supine position	6 months	Throughout life	While child is supine on a tiltboard with arms and legs suspended, if board is suddenly tilted to one side, there is righting of head and thorax and abduction and extension of arm and leg on raised side
Equilibrium-prone position	6 months	Throughout life	Same as equilibrium-supine, except child is prone on tiltboard
Equilibrium-quadruped position	8 months	Throughout life	While child balances on all fours, if suddenly tilted to one side, righting of head and thorax and abduction-extension of arm and leg occur on raised side
Equilibrium-sitting position	10–12 months	Throughout life	While child is seated on chair, if pulled or tilted to one side, righting of head and thorax and abduction-extension of arm and leg occur on raised side (side opposite pull)

Table 5-6	(Concluded)		
Reflex	**Age**	**Age Inhibited**	**Effect on Movement Patterns**
Equilibrium-kneeling position	15 months	Throughout life	While child kneels on both knees, if suddenly pulled to one side, righting of head and thorax and abduction-extension of arm and leg occur on raised side
Hopping 1	15–18 months	Throughout life	While child is standing upright, if moved to the left or right, head and thorax move right and child hops sideways to maintain balance
Hopping 2	15–18 months	Throughout life	While child is standing upright, if moved forward, head and thorax move right and child hops forward to maintain balance
Hopping 3	15–18 months	Throughout life	While child is standing upright, if moved backward, head and thorax move right and child hops backward to maintain balance
Dorsiflexion	15–18 months	Throughout life	While child is standing upright, if tilted backward, head and thorax move right and feet dorsiflex
See-saw	15 months	Throughout life	While child stands on one foot, another person holds arm and free foot on same side; when arm is pulled forward and laterally, head and thorax move right and held leg abducts and extends
Simian position	15–18 months	Throughout life	While child squats down, if tilted to one side, head and thorax move right and arm and leg on raised side abduct and extend

Data from Fiorentino MR: *Reflex testing methods for evaluating CNS development.* Springfield, IL, Charles C Thomas, 1970.

are equilibrium reflexes. They help maintain upright posture and should remain with us throughout life.

A child is considered developmentally delayed in reflex development if any of the following conditions exist:

1. The primitive reflexes do not appear during the first year of life.
2. The primitive reflexes appear at the normal time but do not disappear by the end of the first year.
3. The equilibrium reflexes do not appear by the end of the first year of life.

4. Equilibrium reflexes do not persist throughout life.

Primitive Reflexes

Tonic labyrinthine reflexes (supine and prone) help maintain trunk extension when the child is supine and help maintain trunk flexion when prone. If either of these reflexes does not become integrated, the following movement problems will be exhibited:

1. Supine
   a. Difficulty doing sit-ups
   b. A tendency to extend the trunk during the backward roll

c. Rolling over on one side when trying to rise from a back-lying position
2. Prone
   a. Difficulty doing a full push-up
   b. Inability to extend body fully when lying belly down on a scooter

These two reflexes are under the control of the labyrinthine portion of the inner ear. To facilitate integration of these reflexes, the physical educator should have the child perform activities that require lifting the head against the pull of gravity.

To promote integration of the tonic labyrinthine supine reflex, the child should do activities such as the following, which require flexing the head and body from a back-lying position:

1. Hold knees to chest and rock back-and-forth several times
2. Egg rolls
3. V-sits
4. Partial sit-ups

To promote integration of the tonic labyrinthine prone reflex, the physical educator should have the child do activities such as the following, which require extension of the head and body starting in a front-lying position:

1. Wing lifts
2. While lying prone on a scooter, roll down a ramp and toss a bean bag at a target hung overhead.
3. Seal walk while looking at the ceiling.
4. Rock back-and-forth on stomach while holding ankles with hands.

The positive support reflex causes the legs to extend and the feet to plantar flex when the child is standing. Clues to its presence are apparent if there is an inability to bend the knees when attempting to jump or no "give" at the knees and hips on landing.

When the negative support reflex is present, there is flexion of the knees, hips, and ankles when pressure is removed from the feet. Inability to inhibit the expression of the reflex causes the following problems:

1. During vertical jumps, bending of the legs as soon as the weight is taken off the feet; hence, explosive power is lost
2. Inability to maintain extension of the legs while bouncing on a trampoline

Both of these reflexes are caused from pressure to the soles of the feet. A child may have either the positive or the negative support reflex, but not both at the same time. To facilitate integration of these reflexes, the physical educator should use activities that increase pressure on the soles of the feet, while the child controls the position of the legs.

To eliminate the positive support reaction, the child should flex the lower limbs while applying pressure to the soles of the feet. The following activities are suggested:

1. Bounce on an air mat and suddenly stop on landing by bending the knees.
2. Play stoop tag.
3. Bunny hop.
4. Bounce on inner tubes and/or small trampolines (with the child's hands being held to reduce the chance of falling).

To eliminate the negative support reaction, the child should extend the lower limbs while applying pressure to the soles of the feet. The following activities are suggested:

1. While lying prone on a gym scooter, use the feet to push off from the wall; keep legs extended as long as the scooter is moving across the floor.
2. Bounce while sitting on a "hippity-hop" ball.
3. Practice jumping up vertically and putting a mark on the wall.
4. Bounce on an air mat and try to keep legs straight.

Presence of the asymmetrical tonic neck reflex enables extension of the arm on the face side and flexion of the arm on the skull side when the head is turned. Positioning the arms in this fashion when the head is turned is often referred to as the classic fencer's position. Early in life it directs the child's visual attention toward the extended hand. If it persists beyond the 10th month of life, it interferes with bringing the hands to the midline when the head is turned and thus prevents turning the head while creeping and throwing and catching a ball.

Activities that facilitate integration of this reflex include movements that require the child to turn the head toward his or her flexed limbs, such as the following:

1. Practice touching the chin to various parts of the body (e.g., shoulder, wrist, knee).
2. Balance on hands and knees while holding a bean bag between the chin and one shoulder. Then place the hand on the face side of the body on the hip.
3. Hold a bean bag between the chin and one shoulder. Crawl down the mat while keeping the object between the chin and shoulder.
4. Do a no-hands ball relay where the students have to hold a tennis ball between their chin and chest and pass it to one another without using their hands or feet.

When the symmetrical tonic neck reflex is present, the upper limbs tend to flex and the lower limbs extend during ventroflexion of the head. If the head is dorsiflexed, the upper limbs extend and the lower limbs flex. If this reflex does not become fully integrated within the first year of life, the child will demonstrate the following:

1. Instead of using a cross pattern creep, the child will bunny hop both knees up to the hands.
2. If, while creeping, the child lowers the head, the arms will tend to collapse.
3. If, while creeping, the child lifts the head to look around, movement of the limbs ceases.

Activities that require the child to keep the arms extended while the head is flexed, and the arms flexed while the head is extended, will promote integration of this reflex. Examples of such activities include the following:

1. While balancing on hands and knees, look down between the legs; then look up at the ceiling. Keep the arms extended and the legs flexed.

2. With extended arms, push against a cage ball while looking down at the floor.
3. Practice doing standing push-ups against a wall while looking at the ceiling.
4. Do pull-ups (look up when pulling up, and look down when letting oneself down).

Equilibrium Reflexes

The protective extensor thrust causes immediate extension of the arms when the head and upper body are suddenly tipped forward. The purpose of the reflex is to protect the head and body during a fall. The reflex is used during handsprings and vaulting. If the reflex does not emerge, the child will tend to hit the head when falling.

To develop this reflex, the child needs to practice extending the arms and taking the weight on the hands when the head and upper body are tipped toward the floor. The following activities represent ways to accomplish this:

1. While the child is lying prone on a cage ball, roll the ball slowly, so that the head, shoulders, and arms are lowered toward the floor. Roll the ball far enough that the child's weight gradually comes to rest on his or her hands.
2. Practice handstands while someone holds the child's feet in the air.
3. Practice mule kicks.
4. Wheelbarrow with a partner holding the child's knees.

Presence of the body righting reflex enables segmental rotation of the trunk and hips when the head is turned. As a result of this segmental turning, children can maintain good postural alignment and maintenance of body positions. Without it, for example, when doing a log roll, the child will tend to turn the knees, then the hips, and then the shoulders.

To promote development of the body righting reflex, the child should practice turning the head first, then the shoulders, followed by the hips. The child should start slowly and then increase the speed from both a standing position and a back-lying position.

Labyrinthine and optical righting reactions cause the head to move to an upright position when the body is suddenly tipped. Once the head rights itself, the body follows. Thus, these reflexes help us maintain an upright posture during a quick change of position. Without these reflexes, the child will fall down often during running and dodging games and even tend to avoid vigorous running games.

The labyrinthine reflexes are under control of the inner ear, whereas the optical righting reactions are primarily controlled by the eyes. Labyrinthine reflexes are facilitated when the head is moved in opposition to gravity. Any activity requiring the child to move the head in opposition to the pull of gravity will promote development of this reflex (see tonic labyrinthine prone and supine activities). Clinical observation indicates that poorly developed optical righting reactions most frequently accompany orthoptic visual problems (poor depth perception). Once the depth perception problem is corrected, the optical righting reactions begin to appear.

Like the labyrinthine and righting reactions, the other equilibrium reactions help us maintain an upright position when the center of gravity is suddenly moved beyond the base of support. If the equilibrium reactions are not fully developed, children fall down often, fall off chairs, and avoid vigorous running games.

Almost all of these types of equilibrium reactions are the result of the stimulation of muscle spindles and/or the Golgi tendon apparatus. Both muscle spindle and Golgi tendon apparatus reactions result from sudden stretch (or contraction) of the muscles and tendons. To promote these equilibrium reactions, the child should participate in activities such as the following, which place sudden stretch (or contracture) on the muscles and tendons:

1. Bouncing on an air mat while lying down, balancing on all fours, or balancing on the knees
2. Tug of war
3. Crack the whip
4. Wrestling
5. Scooter activities with a partner pulling or pushing the child who is seated on the scooter

Vestibular System

The vestibular receiving mechanism is located in the semicircular canals of the inner ear. As the body moves, sensory impulses from the vestibular system are sent to the cerebellum and to the brainstem. From these two areas, information about the position of the head is sent to the extraocular muscles of the eye, to the somatosensory strip in the cerebral cortex, to the stomach, to the cerebellum, and down the spinal cord. Accurate information from this mechanism is needed to help position the eyes and to maintain static and dynamic balance. When maturation of the system is delayed, students may demonstrate the following problems:

1. Inability to balance on one foot (particularly with the eyes closed)[10]
2. Inability to walk a balance beam without watching the feet
3. Inability to walk heel-to-toe
4. Inefficient walking and running patterns
5. Delays in ability to hop and to skip

Children who demonstrate these clues and who fail to demonstrate nystagmus after spinning are believed to have vestibular development delays and are in need of activities to facilitate development.[10] Concentrated activities to remediate balance problems that result from poor vestibular function should be administered by someone trained in observing the responses of such a child. However, some activities can be done in fun, nonthreatening ways in a physical education class or on a playground with the supervision of parents or teachers.

Anyone who uses vestibular stimulation activities with children should observe closely for signs of sweating, paleness, flushing of the face, nausea, and loss of consciousness. These are all indications that the activities should be stopped immediately. Also, spinning activities should not be used with seizure-prone children. Avoid rapid spinning activities.

The following vestibular stimulation activities should be nonthreatening to most children:

1. Log roll on a mat, changing directions frequently.

2. Spin self while prone on a gym scooter by crossing hand-over-hand; stop and change direction.
3. Lie on a blanket and roll self up and then unroll.
4. Let the child spin himself or herself on a scooter, play on spinning playground equipment, go down a ramp prone on a gym scooter, or engage in other nonthreatening activities that give the child an opportunity to respond to changes of his or her position in space (movement or spinning should not be so fast as to be disorienting or disorganizing).

Visual System

Both refractive and orthoptic vision are important for efficient motor performance. Refractive vision is the process by which the light rays are bent as they enter the eyes. When light rays are bent precisely, vision is sharpest and clearest. Individuals who have poor refractive vision are said to be nearsighted (myopic) or farsighted (hyperopic) or have astigmatism. The following problems are demonstrated by children with refractive visual problems:

1. Tendency to squint
2. Tendency to rub the eyes frequently
3. Redness of the eyes

Orthoptic vision refers to the ability to use the extraocular muscles of the eyes in unison. When the extraocular muscles are balanced, images entering each eye strike each retina at precisely the same point, so that the images transmitted to the visual center of the brain match. The closer the match of the images from the eye, the better the depth perception. The greater the discrepancy between the two images that reach the visual center, the poorer the depth perception. Clues to orthoptic problems (poor depth perception) follow:

1. Turning the head when catching a ball
2. Inability to catch a ball or a tendency to scoop the ball into the arms
3. Tendency to kick a ball off center or miss it entirely

4. Persisting to ascend and descend stairs one at a time
5. Avoidance of climbing apparatus

The physical educator is not trained to test for or correct refractive and orthoptic visual problems. However, a simple screening test that can be used to determine whether the possibility of a serious orthoptic (depth perception) problem exists is described in the screening test for developmental delays (see Sensory Input Screening Test). Individuals who fail the ocular alignment portion of the screening test should be professionally evaluated by a behavioral visual specialist (optometrist or ophthalmologist who has specialized training in orthoptics). Students suspected of having refractive vision problems should be evaluated by either an optometrist or an ophthalmologist.

Kinesthetic System

The kinesthetic receptors are specialized proprioceptors located in the joints, muscles, and tendons throughout the body. Information from the kinesthetic receptors informs the central nervous system about the position of the limbs in space. As these joint receptors fire, sensory impulses are sent to the brain and are recorded as spatial maps. As the kinesthetic system becomes more developed, judgment about the rate, amount, and amplitude of motion needed to perform a task improves. Refined movement is not possible without kinesthetic awareness. Possible signs of developmental delays of the kinesthetic system are

1. Inability to move a body part on command without assistance
2. No awareness of the position of body parts in space
3. Messy handwriting
4. Poor skill in sports that require a "touch," such as golf ball putting, basketball shooting, and bowling

Activities to promote kinesthetic function include any activities that increase tension on the joints, muscles, and tendons. Some activities that have proven useful in promoting kinesthetic function are

1. Games involving pushing (or kicking) a large cage ball
2. Lying prone on a scooter, holding onto a rope, and being pulled by a partner
3. Using the hands and feet to propel oneself while seated on a gym scooter
4. Doing any type of activity while wearing wrist and/or ankle weights

Tactile System

The tactile receptors are located throughout the body and respond to stimulation of body surfaces. Some of the receptors lie close to the surface of the body; others are located more deeply. A well-functioning tactile system is needed for an individual to know where the body ends and space begins and to be able to discriminate tactually among pressure, texture, and size. Children who are tactile defensive are believed to have difficulty processing sensory input from tactile receptors. Behaviors demonstrated by the tactile-defensive child include

1. Low tolerance for touch (unless the person doing the touching is in the visual field of the student)
2. Avoidance of activities requiring prolonged touch, such as wrestling or hugging
3. Avoidance of toweling down after a shower or bath unless it is done in a vigorous fashion
4. Tendency to curl fingers and toes when creeping

Activities believed to stimulate the tactile system and promote sensory input processing should begin with coarse textures and progress (over time) toward finer texture stimulation. A sequence of such activities follows:

1. Present the child with a variety of textured articles (nets, pot scrubbers, bath brushes). Have the child select an article and rub it on his or her face, arms, and legs. (Tactile-defensive children will usually select the coarsest textures to use for this activity.)
2. Using an old badminton net, play "capture me" while crawling around on a mat. The teacher should toss the net over the child as the child tries to crawl from one end of the mat to the other. When the child has been captured, rub the net over exposed parts of the body as the child struggles to escape. Repeat the activity with the child chasing and capturing the teacher.
3. Construct an obstacle course with several stations where the child must go through hanging textures (strips of inner tube, sections of rope) and/or squeeze through tight places.
4. Using a movement exploration teaching approach, have the students find various textures in the gym to rub a point or patch against (e.g., rough, smooth, wavy).

Perceptual Motor Processes

Integration processes, including perceptual motor, emerge after sensory input systems begin to stabilize, usually during the fifth through the seventh years of life. Development of these processes requires not only intact information from the sensory input systems but also the capacity to integrate those signals in the brain. When all sensory input systems are functioning and cortical reception and association areas are intact, integration processes and motor skills emerge and generalize with practice. Weakened, distorted, or absent signals from the sensory input systems will detract from the development of integration processes as well as all other motor performance. This is not to say that specific motor skills cannot be taught in the absence of intact sensory information. Specific motor skills can be taught, but only as splinter skills. A splinter skill is a particular perceptual or motor act that is performed in isolation and does not generalize to other areas of performance. If hard neurological damage or age of the learner prevents development of the sensory input systems, it becomes necessary to teach splinter skills. In such cases, the top-down approach (task analysis) is recommended. If, however, it is believed that sensory input systems are fully functioning and cortical integration is possible, practice in the following activities should promote development of a wide variety of perceptual-motor abilities.

Balance

Balance is the ability to maintain equilibrium in a held (static) position or moving (dynamic) position. Balance ability is critical to almost every motor function. Some literature suggests that, until balance becomes an automatic, involuntary act, the central nervous system must focus on maintaining balance to the detriment of all other motor and cognitive functions.[1,5] Balance, once believed to be a result of combining some sensory input system signals, is now seen as a skill that is learned from using many systems, including all available sensory systems, many muscles, and passive biomechanical elements, as well as many different parts of the brain.[4,12] Clues to poor balance development include

1. Inability to maintain held balance positions (e.g., stand on one foot, stand heel-to-toe) with eyes open
2. Inability to walk heel-to-toe on a line or on a balance beam
3. Tripping or falling easily
4. Wide gait while walking or running

Activities that can be used to promote static balance include

1. Freeze tag—play tag; the child who is caught is "frozen" until a classmate "unfreezes" by tagging the child; "it" tries to freeze everyone.
2. Statues—each child spins around and then tries to make himself or herself into a "statue" without falling first.
3. Tripod—child balances by placing forehead and both hands on the floor; knees balance on elbows to form tripod balance.
4. Child balances bean bags on different parts of the body while performing balancing positions.

Activities that can be used to promote dynamic balance include

1. Hopscotch
2. Various types of locomotor movements following patterns on the floor
3. Races using different types of locomotor movements
4. Walking forward heel to toe between double lines, on a single line, and then on a balance beam; make this more demanding by having the child balance a bean bag on different body parts (e.g., head, shoulder, elbow, wrist) while walking the balance beam

Laterality

Laterality is an awareness of the difference between the two sides of the body. Children who have not developed laterality often demonstrate balance problems on one or both sides. Delays in the development of laterality may be indicated by the following types of behavior:

1. Avoiding the use of one side of the body
2. Sliding sideways in one direction better than the other
3. Using one extremity more often than the other
4. Lacking a fully established hand preference

Laterality is believed to develop from intact kinesthetic and vestibular sensory inputs. If these two input systems are believed to be functioning adequately, then a child will benefit from activities that require differentiation between the two sides of the body. Examples include the following:

1. Wear ankle and/or wrist weights on the weak (unused) side of the body while climbing on apparatus; moving through obstacle courses; and kicking, bouncing, throwing, or catching a ball.
2. Walk a balance beam while carrying objects that weigh different amounts in each hand (e.g., carry a small bucket in each hand, with different numbers of bean bags in each bucket).
3. Push a cage ball with one hand only.
4. Use only one hand in tug of war.

Spatial Relations

Spatial relations concerns the ability to perceive the position of objects in space, particularly as they relate to the position of the body (see Figure 5-1).

Figure 5-1   A Child Must Have Spatial Relationship Abilities to Fit the Body through the Circular Tunnel

Development of spatial relations is believed to depend on vestibular, kinesthetic, and visual development. Problems may be indicated by

1. Inability to move under objects without hitting them or ducking way below the object
2. Consistently swinging a bat too high or low when attempting to hit a pitched ball
3. Inability to maintain an appropriate body position in relation to moving objects
4. Inability to position the hands accurately to catch a ball

If it has been determined that none of the prerequisite input systems are delayed, spatial relations can be facilitated by practice in the following activities:

1. Set up an obstacle course with stations that require the child to crawl over, under, and through various obstacles.
2. Place a 10-foot taped line on the floor. Give the child a bean bag and ask him or her to place the bean bag halfway down the line. If the child makes an error, ask him or her to walk from one end of the line to the other, counting the number of steps. Then have the child divide the number of steps in half, walk that far, and place the bean bag down at that point. The child should then stand to the side of the line and look from one end of the line to the bean bag. Continue practicing until the child is successful at estimating where, on several different lengths of line, the midpoint is.

3. Repeat Activity #2 with the child wearing ankle weights.
4. Place several chairs around the room with varying distances between them. Ask the child to point to the two chairs that are closest together, farthest apart, or a given distance from one another (e.g., 3 feet, 10 feet, 6 feet). If the child makes an error on any task, have him or her walk the distance between the chairs and/or measure the distance with a measuring tape.

Ocular-Motor Control

Ocular-motor control includes the ability to fixate on and visually track moving objects, as well as the ability to match visual input with appropriate motor response (see Figure 5-2). Observed deficiencies might include

1. Failure to locate visually an object in space
2. Failure to track visually a softball when attempting to hit it
3. Failure to track visually a fly ball or ground ball
4. Failure to keep a place when reading
5. Difficulty using scissors or tying shoelaces
6. Poor foot-eye coordination
7. Messy handwriting

Ocular control can be improved with practice if a child does not have serious orthoptic (depth perception) problems. If an individual does have depth perception problems, participation in ocular control activities can worsen the visual difficulties. Once it is ascertained that no depth perception problems exist, the following activities can be used to promote ocular control of the eyes:

Fixation

1. Child sits and rocks back-and-forth while keeping his or her eyes on a tape on the wall directly in front of him or her.
2. Child lies on back with eyes fixated on a point on the ceiling. Child then stands up (or does a series of stunts) while continuing to fixate on the spot.
3. Child is in a standing position, fixating on a designated point on the wall. Child then

jumps and turns 180 degrees and fixates on a designated point on the opposite wall.
4. Child is in a standing position, fixating on a designated point on the wall. Child then jumps and turns completely around (360 degrees) and again fixates on the original point.

Convergence/Divergence

1. Draw two *X*s on the chalkboard (at shoulder height of child) approximately 36 inches apart. Have the child stand centered about 2 inches in front of the board and move his or her eyes back and forth between the two *X*s.
2. Have the child sit at a table and look from an object on the table to an object on the wall directly ahead; continue back-and-forth 10 times. The table should be about 15 inches from the wall.
3. The child sits with arms extended and thumbs up, looking back-and-forth from one thumb to the other.
4. The child sits with one arm extended and the other flexed, so that the hand is about 6 inches from the nose with thumbs up. Have the child look back-and-forth from one thumb to the other 10 times.

Visual Tracking

1. The child lies on his or her back. Have the child visually track lines, pipes, or lights on the ceiling, without moving the head.
2. The child lies on his or her back. Attach a small ball to a string and swing the ball horizontally above the child's head. The child should track the swinging ball with his or her eyes and then point to it as it swings. (The ball should be suspended approximately 16 inches above the child's head.)
3. The child throws a ball up in the air and follows the path of the ball with his or her eyes until it hits the floor. Repeat several times and encourage the child not to move his or her head while tracking the ball.
4. The child either sits or lies on his or her back, then hits a suspended ball with the hand and visually tracks the movement of the ball.

Figure 5-2   Activities That Contribute to the Development of Visual Systems

Figure 5-2 (*Continued*)

Cross-Lateral Integration

Cross-lateral integration is the ability to coordinate the use of both sides of the body. It normally follows the development of balance and laterality. A child who has not developed cross-lateral integration by age eight years is said to have a midline problem because there is difficulty using the hands efficiently at and across the center of the body. Teachers will note the following problems demonstrated by a child with a midline problem:

1. Difficulty using both hands to catch a ball
2. Tendency of eyes to jump when trying to track visually an object that is moving from one side of the body to the other
3. Inability to master a front crawl stroke with breathing while trying to swim
4. Inability to hop rhythmically from one foot to the other
5. Tendency to move the paper to one side of the body when doing paper-and-pencil tasks

Activities that will promote cross-lateral integration are as follows:

1. The child crawls down a rope or line on the floor, crossing hands back-and-forth over the line (rope) going forward, then crossing feet back-and-forth while crawling backward.
2. The child picks up objects (from right side of body) with the right hand and places them in a container on the left side of the body. This should be repeated using the left hand, picking up one object at a time.
3. The child plays pat-a-cake.
4. The child practices swimming the front crawl with breathing.

Body Image

Body image is a broad concept that includes how people picture their body, attitude toward their body, and knowledge of personal bodily capabilities and limitations. Body image develops from all sensory input system information as well as from experiences with the body. Indications of a poorly developed body image are

1. Lack of knowledge of where body parts are located
2. Distorted drawings of self
3. Lack of knowledge about what specific body parts are for
4. Poor motor planning

Activities that can be used to facilitate a child's body image include

1. Give verbal commands to the child (e.g., touch your knees, touch your ankles, touch your ears, touch your shoulders).
2. Have the child stand with eyes closed. The teacher touches various body parts, and the child identifies them. Then have the child touch the same part that the teacher touches and name the part.
3. Trace an outline of the child's body on a large piece of paper or with chalk on the floor. Then have the child get up and fill in the details (e.g., facial features, clothes, shoes). Perhaps make an "own self" body

puzzle. After the child is finished drawing, laminate the body shape; cut it into pieces for the child to reassemble.
   a. Have the child name all the body parts.
   b. Leave out a part and see if the child notices.
   c. Have the child trace around the teacher and name all the body parts.
   d. Have the child trace certain body parts on the drawing with different colors (e.g., yellow for feet, blue for arms).
4. Draw an incomplete picture of a person on the chalkboard and have the child fill in the missing parts.

Studies have shown that children who experience an early rich and varied environment demonstrate increased cognitive and scholastic performance at age 11.[9] Frequently, children with disabilities have not had that opportunity. For this reason, the physical educator is in an ideal position to provide a rich movement experience to promote these youngsters' development.

When attempting to determine whether to use a bottom-up approach in the adapted physical education program, the teacher must again ask, "How much time is available?" The younger the child and the more time available to the teacher, the more appropriate it is to use this strategy. Examples of how each of these two teaching methods are applied to achieve the same principles are given in Tables 5-7 to 5-11.

Physical Fitness

A full discussion of the various components of physical fitness appears in Chapter 8. In general, physical fitness is composed of strength, flexibility, muscular endurance, and cardiovascular endurance. *Strength* refers to muscular strength, which is the ability to contract a muscle against resistance. Flexibility is the range of motion possible at any given joint. Muscular endurance is the ability to continue to contract a muscle against resistance. Cardiovascular endurance is the ability of the heart and vessels to process and transport oxygen from the lungs to muscle cells for use. It has been demonstrated that good nutrition and a high

Table 5-7	Teaching Approaches and Their Relation to Growth and Development Principles		
Principle	**Implication**	**Bottom-Up Teaching Approach**	**Top-Down Teaching Approach**
Each individual is unique.	Every child has a different motor profile.	Test for sensory input deficits and intervene to eliminate those before testing and programming for higher-level abilities and skills.	Test for specific functional motor skill deficits. If some are found, probe down into specific abilities that contribute to those skills. If deficits are found, probe down into sensory input areas.
	Every child learns at his or her own rate.	Select activities that appeal to the child and use those until the deficits are eliminated.	Program activities at the highest level of dysfunction. If the child does not learn quickly, probe down into contributing components for deficits.
Children advance from one stage of development to a higher, more complex stage of development.	Activities are selected appropriate to the level of development.	Select activities that are appropriate for the stage of development the child demonstrates.	Select activities specific to the skill deficits the child demonstrates. Begin an intervention program at the developmental level the child demonstrates.
	Progression to the next stage of development depends on physiological maturation and learning.	When a child appears to have mastered one stage of development, select activities appropriate for the next level of development.	When a child masters lower levels of a specific skill, select activities to promote learning of a more complex aspect of that skill.
Children learn when they are ready.	As neurological maturation takes place, we are capable of learning more.	Test from the bottom up and begin instruction with the lowest neurological deficit found.	Analyze a specific task from the top down until the present level of educational performance is found.
	There are critical periods of learning.	It is assumed the child will learn fastest if instruction is begun at the developmental stage at which the child is functioning.	The level of instruction determined by empirical testing verifies that the child is ready to learn.
Development proceeds from simple to complex.	Development begins with simple movements that eventually combine with other movements to form patterns.	Eliminate reflex and sensory input delays before teaching higher-level abilities and skills.	Functional skill deficits are identified. The pattern of the skill is analyzed to determine contributing components. Behavioral programs are constructed and implemented to develop pattern deficits.

(Continued)

Table 5-7	*(Concluded)*		
Principle	**Implication**	**Bottom-Up Teaching Approach**	**Top-Down Teaching Approach**
	Development progresses from large to small movements (from gross to fine patterns).	Promote reflex and vestibular development to stabilize balance. Once balance becomes automatic, control of the limbs will follow.	Program to synthesize patterns that contribute to a specific skill.

level of physical fitness contribute to one's health and enjoyment of life. Because an active lifestyle is critical for persons with disabilities, an exemplary adapted physical education program continually promotes physical fitness.

Techniques for evaluating various aspects of physical fitness and teaching strategies to use are discussed in Chapter 8. As you read that material and observe individuals performing activities to evaluate or promote physical fitness, keep in mind the impact of the primitive reflexes as well as the kinesthetic system on performance. Recall that individuals who have difficulty demonstrating a sit-up may have a persisting trace of a tonic labyrinthine supine reflex, which interferes with flexion of the head and trunk. Individuals having difficulty with a push-up may have a persisting trace of a tonic labyrinthine prone reflex, which promotes flexion when a person is in a "belly down" position.

A well-functioning kinesthetic system is critical to muscle tone. If the muscle spindles are not continually firing and sending impulses to the central nervous system, definition (firm shape) of the muscle will be lacking.

Motor Fitness

Agility, power, speed, and coordination are the four components of motor fitness. Agility, the ability to change position in space quickly and accurately, is dependent on the visual, kinesthetic,

and vestibular systems. Should any of these systems be delayed, agility is compromised.

Power, or explosive strength, requires the ability to rapidly contract and coordinate muscles to perform to maximum effort.[4] Power is frequently evaluated by using a standing long jump. Thus, strength is a primary contributor to power. When the standing long jump is used to measure power, the physical educator

Children need positive movement opportunities
Courtesy of Laurie Zittel.

Table 5-8	Teaching Approaches and Their Relation to the Generalization Process*		
Principle	**Implication**	**Bottom-Up Teaching Approach**	**Top-Down Teaching Approach**
Generalization procedures	Activities to promote generalization are selected in particular ways.	Activity is selected to develop sensory input systems, reflexes, and abilities that are believed to be prerequisite to many skills that could be used in a variety of environments.	Functional age-appropriate activities are selected to promote appropriate skills in a variety of natural environments.
Generalization process	There is a degree to which the learning environment matches the natural environment.	At the basic levels (reflexes, sensory inputs, and abilities), the environment is controlled only to ensure that the basics are learned. No attention is paid to the type of environment the eventual skills will be used in.	Skills are practiced in environments that correspond closely to the environment in which the skill will be used (e.g., practice shooting baskets in the gym).
Retention	The more meaningful the skill, the longer it is remembered.	It is believed that, once basic reflexes, sensory input systems, and abilities emerge, they remain stable (unless the child is traumatized in some way).	Activities are reviewed immediately after a lesson and then periodically to ensure retention.
Overlearning	Overlearning occurs when a skill or an activity is practiced after it has been learned.	Overlearning occurs as the basic levels are interwoven into higher skill levels.	Ability levels prerequisite to skills should be substantially greater than minimum entry requirements needed to fulfill the needs of the task.

*A task is not considered learned until it can be demonstrated in a variety of environments.

is reminded that strength of the hip adductor and abductor muscles, as well as the quadriceps, greatly impacts that movement. The stronger the hip stabilizers and flexors, the greater the distance jumped. In addition to muscular strength, good kinesthetic and vestibular information, as well as the absence of the negative support primitive reflex, is critical to jumping performance.

Speed is the ability to move quickly in a short period of time. Speed is dependent on reaction time and movement time. Thus, the time it takes to hear and respond to a signal, as well as how quickly a person moves after initiating the movement, is critical to speed. Speed is frequently measured using a 50-yard dash. Obviously, a person will be able to demonstrate greater speed if

		Bottom-Up Teaching	Top-Down Teaching
Table 5-9		**The Relation of Teaching Approaches to Attention of the Learner**	
Principle	**Implication**	**Approach**	**Approach**
Get the attention of the learner.	Help the child attend to relevant rather than irrelevant cues.	Permit the child to participate in a free activity of his or her choice each day if the child enters the room and immediately focuses on the beginning task.	Keep bats, balls, and other play equipment out of sight until time of use.
	Give a signal (sometimes called a "ready signal") that indicates a task is to begin.	Structure each day's lesson the same way, so that the child knows that, when a given activity ends, the next activity will begin.	Teach the child precise signals that indicate a task should begin.
Provide the appropriate stimulation.	Stimulate the child to focus on the desired learning task.	Make the activities enjoyable, so that the child will want to continue the task.	Use precise, detailed instruction that is designed around eliciting attention through the use of the following hierarchy: 1. Visual or verbal input only 2. Combined visual and verbal input 3. Combined visual, verbal, and kinesthetic instruction

the vestibular, kinesthetic, and auditory systems are fully functioning; the primitive reflexes are integrated; and the equilibrium reflexes are well developed. Speed is also dependent on the number of fast twitch muscle fibers that can be recruited during the movement. Fast twitch muscle fibers are believed to be genetically determined.

Coordination is "the ability to integrate separate motor systems with varying sensory modalities into efficient patterns of movement."[4] To demonstrate coordination, individuals are required to perform a series of moves accurately and quickly. Gross motor coordination involves the whole body; thus, balance, agility, and rhythm must be synchronized to enable a smooth, efficient movement pattern. Hand-eye and foot-eye coordination requires the ability to use visual information, muscular control, and kinesthetic information while maintaining balance. Should any one of the visual, kinesthetic, or vestibular systems or the primitive or equilibrium reflexes be compromised, the efficiency of the movement is impacted.

Table 5-10	Managing the Instructional Environment through Teaching Approaches		
Principle	**Implication**	**Bottom-Up Teaching Approach**	**Top-Down Teaching Approach**
Impose limits for use of equipment, facilities, and student conduct.	Children should learn to adhere to rules that are necessary in a social context.	Students are not permitted access to equipment and areas unless they have been given permission by the teacher.	The equipment and facilities a student has access to are specified in the behavioral program.
Control the social interaction among children.	Inappropriate social behavior among children may disrupt class instruction.	The teacher must consider the performance level and emotional stability of each child when grouping children for activities.	Tasks and environments are structured to reduce adverse interaction with peers.
Do not strive for control in all situations.	Children with disabilities must develop social skills that will promote social interaction in the natural environment. For this to occur, students must have an opportunity to adjust to situations independent from supervision or with minimum supervision.	Select activities that will meet the long-range goals of the students and promote social interaction. Pair children so that their interaction contributes to both students' objectives—for example, a child who needs kinesthetic stimulation might be given the task of pulling a child who needs to ride a scooter for tonic labyrinthine prone inhibition.	The students are permitted to interact with others as long as progress toward short-term objectives is occurring.

PROGRAMMED INSTRUCTION

Instructional strategies are the ways to arrange an educational environment so that maximum learning will take place. Instructional strategies discussed thus far are the task-specific, top-down approach and the developmental, bottom-up approach. A third approach, which will be discussed in this section, is programmed instruction. Factors that affect the type of instructional strategy selected include the amount of time available, the age and readiness level of the learner, the capabilities of the physical education teacher, and the number of persons available to assist in the educational process. An instructional strategy that meets the needs of a wide range of learners and that can be delivered by a limited number of personnel is more valuable for ensuring that individual needs are met than is a strategy that presumes homogeneous grouping. For learners with disabilities who have heterogeneous needs, an instructional strategy that promotes individualized learning is

Table 5-11   Nature of Activity and Quality of Experience as They Relate to Two Teaching Approaches

Principle	Implication	Bottom-Up Teaching Approach	Top-Down Teaching Approach
Learning occurs best when goals and objectives are clear.	Clear goals provide incentives for children to learn.	The desired outcome is clear to the teacher (e.g., 5 seconds of postrotatory nystagmus). The child may be advised of another goal (e.g., stay on the spinning scooter until it stops).	The goal and ongoing measurement of the attainment of the objectives that lead to the goal are shared by the teacher and the child.
Actively involve the student in the learning process.	The more learning time and the less dead time, the more learning will occur.	The child stays active because activities that are enjoyable to the child are selected.	When and if the child learns to self-instruct and self-evaluate or do so with the help of peer tutors, the student will be active throughout the period. The well-managed class will have children work on nonspecific activities when not participating in behavioral programs.
Discourage stereotyped play activities that develop rigid behaviors.	Permitting children to participate in the same activity day after day deters learning.	The teacher must initiate new activities as soon as lack of progress is evidenced.	The ongoing collection of data makes lack of progress immediately apparent to the teacher and the child and serves notice that the activity should be changed.
Program more for success than failure.	Every satisfying experience decreases anxiety and increases confidence.	The teacher selects activities the child enjoys and from which the child gains a feeling of accomplishment.	The increment of the step sizes in the behavioral program is constantly modified to match the ability of the learner.

not only desirable but absolutely necessary. See Table 5-12 for an example of a standard teaching sequence.

Individualization of instruction can be realized through the use of programmed instruction. The major goals of programmed instruction are to promote students' abilities to direct their own learning and to develop a communication system between the student and teacher that enables them to become independent of each other. The teacher's primary goals are to guide and manage instruction according to the student's individual needs and learning characteristics. The programmed instruction approach enables a teacher to cope with heterogeneous groups of children and to accommodate large numbers of children in the same class without sacrificing instructional efficiency.

Table 5-12	Standard Teaching Sequence

The system requires only that the teacher note the child's progress using the following symbols: X = the steps (activities) in the standard teaching sequence that can be mastered by the student, in this case step nos. 1, 2, 3, and 4; / = immediate short-term instruction objective, in this case no. 5; ★ = goal, in this case no. 18. All behaviors between the present level (/) and the goal (★) are potential objectives (6 to 18).

Walks unsupported (step no.): X̶ X̶ X̶ X̶ 5̶ 6 7 8 9 10 11 12 13 14 15 16 17 18★ 19 20 21 22 23 24 25 26

Two-Footed Standing Broad Jump

Type of program: Shifting criterion
Conditions
1. Both feet remain behind restraining line before takeoff.
2. Take off from two feet.
3. Land on two feet.
4. Measure from the restraining line to the tip of the toe of the least advanced foot.
Measurement: Distance in inches

Two-footed standing broad jump (inches)	60	62	64	6̶6̶	6̶8̶	7̶0̶	7̶2̶	74	76	78	80	82★	84
Date mastered				9/7	9/21	10/5							

The scoring procedure of the ongoing development of the person would be explained as follows. The program that the child is participating in is the two-footed standing broad jump. The child began the program at an initial performance level of 66 inches on September 7 and increased performance by 4 inches between September 7 and October 5. Thus, the present level of educational performance is 70 inches (note the last number with an X over it). The child will attempt to jump a distance of 72 inches (immediate short-term objective) until he or she masters that distance. The child will continue to progress toward the goal, which is 82 inches (note the asterisk). It is a mistake in the applications of learning principles to ask the child to jump the 82 inches when it is known that the goal far exceeds the present level of educational performance. Unreasonable instructional demands from the learner by the teacher violate the principle of learning in small steps, which guarantees success for the child.

The same procedure could be used when teaching a child to throw a ball for accuracy. In the following example, a shifting condition program is used. For instance, two hierarchies that are known in throwing for accuracy are the size of the target and the distance between the thrower and the target. Thus, a standard teaching sequence might be similar to the following sequence of potential objectives: demonstrate the ability to throw a 4-inch ball a distance of _____ feet and hit a target that is _____ feet square five out of five times.

Throwing for Accuracy

Type of program: Shifting condition
Conditions
1. Remain behind the restraining line at all times.
2. Complete an overhand throw (ball released above the shoulder).
3. If the ball hits any part of the target, it is a successful throw.

(Continued)

Table 5-12	(*Continued*)

The previous information would be contained in a curriculum book. However, the specific standard teaching sequence would be placed on a bulletin board at the performance area in the gymnasium. This would enable the performer to read his or her own instructional objective. The measurement of the performer's placement in the standard teaching sequence would be indicated on the prescription sheet.

Criterion for mastery: Three successful hits out of three

DISTANCE OF THROW	SIZE OF TARGET	DISTANCE OF THROW	SIZE OF TARGET
Step 1. 6 feet	3 feet square	Step 10. 18 feet	2 feet square
Step 2. 9 feet	3 feet square	Step 11. 21 feet	2 feet square
Step 3. 12 feet	3 feet square	Step 12. 24 feet	2 feet square
Step 4. 15 feet	3 feet square	Step 13. 27 feet	2 feet square
Step 5. 18 feet	3 feet square	Step 14. 30 feet	2 feet square
Step 6. 21 feet	3 feet square	Step 15. 21 feet	1 foot square
Step 7. 24 feet	3 feet square	Step 16. 24 feet	1 foot square
Step 8. 27 feet	3 feet square	Step 17. 27 feet	1 foot square
Step 9. 30 feet	3 feet square	Step 18. 30 feet	1 foot square

The steps of the standard teaching sequence can be reduced and tasks can be added that are more or less complex as the situation requires.

STUDENT RECORDING SHEET

Throwing for accuracy (step no.)	✗	✗	✗	✗	✗	✗	7	8	9	10	11	12	13	14★	15	16	17	18
Date mastered																		

The most expeditious way to manage an average-size class in a public school, using the individualized approach, is by using a variety of stations arranged around the gymnasium, with a different activity performed at each station. Each activity is graduated from simpler moves to more demanding requirements. The needs of individual children are determined ahead of time, and each child performs only the level of the activity that is appropriate for that student. Self-instructional and self-evaluative materials composed of a pre-arranged series of objectives help students develop skills at their own rates.

Specific examples of techniques to provide appropriate inclusive environments for students with disabilities are included in Chapter 6, "Delivering Services in the Most Inclusive Environment."

EVIDENCE-BASED PRACTICE

An approach receiving increased attention in educational circles is evidence-based practice. *Evidence-based practice* refers to utilizing instructional procedures and curricula that have been validated as effective by scientific research. The current focus is a direct result of language in the No Child Left Behind (NCLB) Act, which requires that educators use practices that have proven to promote high rates of achievement. The basic concept has always been a part of the Individuals with Disabilities Education Act

(IDEA). Prior to IDEA and NCLB, educational decisions often were made at the whims of policy makers, administrators, and elected school board members who often did not consider research findings. Teachers used instructional procedures and curricula that they were comfortable with or were mandated by the school district or local school administrators. The Reauthorization of IDEA and enactment of NCLB attempted to rectify these problems by requiring that educators use scientifically based strategies and methods as primary tools to allow schools to make meaningful changes in instruction.

Validated instructional practices include (1) using strategies for teaching that have proven results, (2) continuously monitoring, (3) encouraging family involvement, (4) providing feedback, and (5) engaging in positive behavior support in the classroom.

The essence of an evidence-based curriculum is objective measurement of a child's progress in response to intervention (RTI). If RTI has not resulted in satisfactory progress toward the annual goals, changes must be made, so that learning does occur. Continuous measurement is ongoing from where the child begins (present level of performance) to what is to be learned over a period of time (annual goal).[2] The continuous measurement occurs by routinely monitoring progress toward

short-term objectives (the steps to be acquired between present level of performance and the annual goal). Modification of the teaching approach should occur when there is no demonstrated progress toward the short-term objectives. The characteristics of an evidence-based curriculum are presented in Table 5-13.

Adapted physical educators who have used the practices and procedures advocated in this textbook over the years are already using evidence-based practice because they have monitored their students' responses to intervention by examining progress as demonstrated by achievement of the short-term objectives. When the short-term objective is not achieved in a timely fashion, instruction should change. This is why we have included both the top-down and bottom-up instructional strategies for the last several editions. Physical educators frequently use a top-down teaching strategy because that is what they were taught to use in their methodology courses. The bottom-up teaching strategy was born when a physical education teacher became frustrated because half of her students were not progressing satisfactorily when she used a top-down teaching strategy. Years of hands-on research with children with disabilities led to the identification of underlying neurological delays that, when addressed, broke the cycle of no progress and enabled the children to perform to the level

---

Table 5-13	**Characteristics of an Evidence-Based Curriculum**

- Objectives are clear, specific, and stated in behavioral terms.
- The behaviors are sequenced or in a hierarchical order, so that each objective builds on the preceding behavior.
- Students can proceed with little outside help.
- There are small increments of learning.
- A student's performance level along the sequence moves upward toward the annual goal at the student's own rate.
- Students are actively involved.
- Immediate feedback is provided concerning adequacy of performance.
- The curriculum accommodates the ability range of many students, thus enabling continuous progress.
- Instructional practices are continually studied and modified in light of the students' progress.
- Assessment is part of instruction.
- Assessments provide valid data.

The National Sports Center for the Disabled, Winter Park, Colorado, Has an Extraordinary Equestrian Program

The National Sports Center for the Disabled.

adaptations in accordance with a child's needs may enable immediate participation in age-appropriate activities selected to enhance specific skills. Following is a list of functional adaptations for children with physical, sensory, or motor deficits:

• Children who are blind can receive auditory or tactual clues to help them locate objects or position their bodies in the activity area.
• Individuals who are blind read through touch and can be instructed in appropriate movement patterns through manual kinesthetic guidance (i.e., the instructor manually moves the student through the correct pattern) or verbal instructions.
• Children who are deaf can learn to read lips or learn signing, so that they understand the instructions for an activity.
• Children with physical disabilities may have to use walkers, wheelchairs, or crutches during their physical education classes.
• A child with asthma may be permitted to play goalie in a soccer game, which requires smaller cardiovascular demands than the running positions.
• Rules may be changed to accommodate the variety of ability levels demonstrated by children in the class (see Chapter 6, "Delivering Services in the Most Inclusive Environment").
• A buddy, peer tutor, or paraprofessional may be assigned to help the student with special needs execute the required moves or stay on task.

In these examples, functional adaptations are necessary for the student with a disability to participate in chronologically age-appropriate physical education activities. The approach is most beneficial when the only motor prerequisites lacking are those that are a result of the student's disabling condition or when including the student to promote social interaction.

of children without disabilities. As they say, necessity is the mother of invention. That physical education teacher thought it was necessary that she enable her students to move efficiently, regardless of their disability. As a result, we now have an alternative teaching strategy that has been scientifically validated to use with children who have disabilities.

FUNCTIONAL ADAPTATIONS

Functional adaptations are modifications, such as using an assistive device, changing the demands of the task, or changing the rules to permit students with disabilities to participate. Making functional

GENERALIZATION TO COMMUNITY ENVIRONMENTS

Time spent teaching skills in physical education training settings is wasted if the individual with disabilities cannot demonstrate competency in

Modified Sports Equipment Opens the World to Individuals with Disabilities
Courtesy of Challenge Aspen, Aspen, CO.

sport and recreation settings other than the schools and in the presence of persons other than the original teachers. To ensure that generalization to community environments and activities does occur, simulated training conditions need to be developed. Although there are few studies in physical education that have examined the generalization of motor skill and sport performance from instructional to community environments, it is known that when accommodations and opportunities are provided for persons with disabilities to interact in the community with persons without disabilities the programs are successful. The American Youth Soccer Organization's VIP (very important person) program is an outstanding example of a creative way to include players with disabilities in regular leagues. The rules used by VIP teams are modified somewhat and the fields they play on are smaller. Peer Buddies may be included initially; however as the persons with disabilities gain in skills and knowledge of the game, use of Peer Buddies is gradually lessened.[7]

On the other hand, the literature on simulated settings versus training in the applied settings on nonphysical education tasks is mixed. It is critical that instruction not cease until the individual uses the new skills spontaneously and correctly in the community.

COMMERCIAL PROGRAMS

Since 1980, several physical and motor programs have been made available commercially. The achievement-based curriculum development in physical education (I CAN),[11] the Data-based Gymnasium,[3] and Mobility Opportunities Via Education (MOVE)[6] are excellent examples of commercial programs specifically developed to promote physical and motor capability.

A Creative Teacher Helps a Child with No Fingers Enjoy Arts and Crafts

Courtesy Dallas Independent School District.

REPORTING THE RESULTS TO PARENTS

Parents should always be informed of their children's educational performance levels and the goals and objectives of the school curricula. IDEA requires that the parents be apprised of the educational status of their children and approve the IEP that has been designed for them. When the procedures described in this chapter are followed by the teacher and the information shared with the parents, there will be no question about the educational process. Parents may question whether appropriate goals have been selected for their children, but usually, when evaluation results and the importance of their child's achieving as normal a performance level as possible are explained, parents agree with the professional educator's opinion.

It is important to point out to the parents their child's specific deficiencies and how those deficiencies interfere with the child's functional ability. Wherever possible, basic level and integrative process deficiencies should be linked to skill performance. That is, the educator should explain not only what deficits exist but also how those deficits relate to the child's present and future levels of performance ability. Once parents understand these relationships, they usually endorse the school's efforts on behalf of their children. In addition to pointing out a child's deficiencies, it is important to tell the parent about areas of strength their child has demonstrated. Parents of children with disabilities need to hear positive reports as frequently as possible. Do not overlook that need.

SUMMARY

Physical educators have traditionally included exercises, individual stunts and tumbling, games, sports, rhythmic activities, and gymnastics in their curricula. Often these activities are selected according to teacher bias. More recently, teachers have been sensitized to the need to provide appropriate learning environments for students who demonstrate a wide range of abilities. These teachers are exercising greater care in selecting meaningful activities to include in their programs. Even when following a set curriculum, more attention is being paid to selecting activities that will meet a variety of learners' demonstrated needs.

The goal of a physical education program for students with disabilities is the development of motor behaviors that assist ultimate functional responses in the community environments. Maximizing performance of the many specific skills of the physical education curriculum is the unique role of the adapted physical educator. Individuals with disabilities often possess limited motor skills. Thus, the physical educator must determine which skills are needed and select appropriate intervention strategies to ensure that learning occurs. Teaching specific skills, fostering developmental sequences, and using programmed instruction are three acceptable intervention strategies. The amount of time available, the age and readiness of the learner, the capabilities of the physical education teacher, and the number of persons available to assist with the class dictate which intervention strategy to use. Regardless of the teaching approach used, functional adaptations may need to be made to enable the student to gain from the intervention strategy.

REVIEW QUESTIONS

1. Identify three perceptual-motor abilities.
2. What are the differences between bottom-up (developmental) and top-down (task-specific) approaches?
3. Name two sensory input systems, two categories of integration processes, and two specific skills.
4. What is incidental learning? Why are some children with disabilities unable to learn as much through incidental learning as children without disabilities?
5. What is programmed instruction?
6. What is evidence-based practice?

STUDENT ACTIVITIES

1. Observe a physical education class that includes students with and without disabilities. Make a list of the functional adaptations used during the class. Select the two adaptations you believe aided the children most and tell why those adaptations were so helpful.
2. Conduct a content analysis of one functional skill and one sport skill. Identify each component required to successfully perform each of the skills.
3. Break the class into small discussion groups and have them share their bottom-up and top-down teaching approach suggestions for Adam's class with one another. Have each group agree on two suggestions for each teaching approach, and share them with the rest of the class.
4. Develop a task analysis of a specific sport skill.

REFERENCES

1. Abbruzzese G, Berardelli A: Sensorimotor integration in movement disorders, *Mov Disord* 18(3):231–140, 2003.
2. Clayton J, Burdge M, Denham A, Kleinert H, Kerns J: A four-step process for assessing the general curriculum for students with significant cognitive disabilities, *Teach Except Child* 38(5):20–27, 2006.
3. Dunn JM, Frederick H: *Physical education for the severely handicapped: A systematic approach to*

a data based gymnasium, Austin, TX, PRO-ED, 1985.

4. Gallahue DL, Ozmun JC: *Understanding motor development: Infants, children, adolescents, adults.* New York, McGraw-Hill, 2006.

5. Horak FB, Henry SM, Shumway-Cook A: Postural perturbations: New insights for treatment of balance disorders, *Physical Therapy* 77:517–533, 1997.

6. Kern County Superintendent of Schools: *Mobility opportunities via education,* Bakersfield, CA, 1990.

7. Lavay B, Semark C: Everyone plays—Including special needs children in youth sport programs, *Palaestra* 17(4):40–43, 2001.

8. Quiros JB, Schrager OL: *Neuropsychological fundamentals in learning disabilities.* San Rafael, CA, Academic Therapy, 1979.

9. Raine A, Reynolds C, Venables PH, Mednick SA: Stimulation seeking and intelligence: A perspective longitudinal study, *J Pers Soc Psychol* 82:663–674, 2002.

10. Thelen E: Motor development: A new synthesis, *American Psychologist* 50:79–95, 1995.

11. Wessel JA, Kelly L: *Achievement-based curriculum development in physical education.* Philadelphia, Lea & Febiger, 1986.

12. Westcott SL, Lowes LP, Richardson, PK: Evaluation of postural stability in children: Current theories and assessment tools, *Physical Therapy* 77:629–645, 1997.

13. Wright-Ott CA, Escobar RJ, Leslie S: Encouraging exploration, *Rehab Manage,* June 2002, www.rehabpub.com.

SUGGESTED READINGS

Cheatum BA, Hammond AA: *Physical activities for improving children's learning and behavior: A guide to sensory motor development.* Champaign, IL, Human Kinetics, 2000.

Davis RW: *Inclusion through sports.* Champaign, IL, Human Kinetics, 2002.

Seaman JA, DePauw K, Morton KB, Kathy O: *Making connections from theory to practice in adapted physical education.* Scottsdale, AZ, Holcomb Hathaway, 2003.

6

Delivering Services in the Most Inclusive Environment

Partnering peers promotes friendships
Courtesy of Tara McCarthy

■ OBJECTIVES

Define inclusion.

Compare and contrast inclusion and the least restrictive environment.

Suggest strategies for preparing the school and community for inclusion.

Describe the nine instructional variables that can be modified to accommodate a learner with a disability in the least restrictive environment.

Evaluate an existing physical education program to determine its appropriateness for students with disabilities.

Describe inclusive community-based leisure, recreation, and sports programs.

INCLUSION: THE CONTROVERSY CONTINUES

There are strong and passionate voices that support the inclusion of students with disabilities in the general education program and equally strong and passionate voices that believe the concept of least restrictive environment (LRE), if appropriately implemented, better addresses the unique needs of learners with disabilities. Judith Heumann, then assistant secretary of the Office of Special Education and Rehabilitation Services (OSERS), an individual who has experienced firsthand discrimination because of her disability, spoke at the 15th National Institute on Legal Issues of Education for Individuals with Disabilities, May 1994. One of the most outspoken and articulate advocates of inclusion for individuals with disabilities at all levels, she paraphrased the famous words of Dr. Martin Luther King, Jr.:

> Let us never succumb to the temptation of believing that legislation and judicial decree play only a minor role in solving problems. Morality cannot be legislated . . . but behavior can be regulated. Judicial decrees may not change the heart . . . but they can restrain the heartless. The law cannot make an employer love an employee or a teacher love a student . . . but it can prevent him/her from refusing to hire me or teach me because of the color of my skin or my disabilities.[27]

The ARC, formerly the Association for Retarded Children, has a strong position on the inclusion of individuals with intellectual disabilities that has significant implications for the adapted physical educator and the general physical educator because the statement addresses community recreation and leisure activities:

> Children should:
> Live in a family home.
> Grow up enjoying nurturing adult relationships both inside and outside a family home.
> Learn in their neighborhood school in a regular classroom that contains children of the same age without disabilities.
> Participate in the same activities as children without disabilities.

CASE STUDY

Adam

Review Adam's IEP in Chapter 4 and the suggested modifications/adaptations that the general physical educator might use to teach Adam and help him accomplish his IEP goals.

APPLICATION TASK

Consider the strategies the general physical educator might use to help train the support personnel that would work with Adam in the general physical education program.

> Play and participate with all children in community recreation.
> Have the opportunity to participate in an inclusive spiritual life.
>
> Adults should have the opportunity to:
> Have maximum control over their lives.
> Have relationships that range from acquaintances to life partners.
> Live in a home of their choice, with whom they choose.
> Engage in meaningful work in an inclusive setting.
> Enjoy inclusive recreation and other leisure activities.
> Participate in inclusive spiritual activities.[3]

TASH, the vocal and primary advocate for students with severe disabilities, formerly The Association for Individuals with Severe Handicaps, strongly supports inclusive education:

> THEREFORE BE IT RESOLVED, THAT TASH, an international advocacy association of people with disabilities, their family members, other advocates and people who work in the disability field, affirms that all students with disabilities shall be provided a quality, inclusive education that assures full and meaningful access to the general education curriculum. To achieve such an education, support services must be provided as

needed, programs and curricula must be modified as needed, and students must receive such supports, supplementary aids and services as are necessary in an inclusive setting. The expectation shall be that every school community shall provide a quality, inclusive education for all students with disabilities that is predicated on a shared vision of high expectations for all students and a commitment to a set of learning goals or standards that are strong, clear, understood, and put into practice.[74]

The intent of the law was, and continues to be, that there must be a *continuum of services* and service delivery models, so that the unique needs of every learner with disabilities can be met. The least restrictive environment is a *civil right* that was guaranteed to all children in *Brown v. Board of Education* in 1954. See Table 6-1 for the courts' interpretation of LRE.

The recent position statement of the American Association for Physical Activity and Recreation (AAPAR) supports the position that each child, with and without a disability, has the right to be a physically educated person. AAPAR's powerful position statement, "Physical Education for Infants, Children, and Youth with Disabilities," 2003, begins as follows:

> Physical activity provides meaningful movement experiences and health-related fitness for all individuals in order that they may have the opportunity to acquire the motor skills, strategies, and physical stamina necessary for a lifetime of rich leisure, recreation and sport experiences to enhance physical fitness and wellness. A quality physical education program provides the foundation for a healthy, happy, and physically active lifestyle. Infants, children and youth with disabilities have the right to receive the full range of benefits from physical education just as their able bodied peers. Benefits include the development of motor skills and physical fitness, as well as the opportunity to participate in play, active leisure, aquatics, recreation, outdoor adventure, and sport experiences.[1]

Table 6-1	Least Restrictive Environment Determination, as Mandated by the Courts[83]

School district determinations regarding the LRE should be based on the following:

- Has the school taken necessary steps to maintain the child in the general classroom?
  What supplementary aids and services were used?
  What interventions were attempted?
  How many interventions were attempted?
- Benefits of placement in general education (with supplementary aids and services) vs. special education
  Academic benefits
  Nonacademic benefits (e.g., social, communication, peer-model)
- Effects on the education of other students
  Is the education of other students adversely affected (e.g., if the student is disruptive)?
  Does the student require a great deal of attention from the teacher, compromising the education of the other children?
- If the student is being educated in a setting other than the general classroom, is he or she interacting with peers without disabilities to the maximum extent appropriate?
  In what academic settings is the student integrated with peers without disabilities?
  In what nonacademic settings is the child integrated with peers without disabilities?
- Is the entire continuum of alternative services available?

EMPHASIS ON EDUCATION WITHIN THE GENERAL EDUCATION PROGRAM

The emphasis of the Office of Special Education and Rehabilition Services (OSERS) has been on the education of learners with disabilities within the general education program. According to IDEIA, 2004,

> Access to the general education curriculum means that students with disabilities are actively engaged in learning the content and

skills that define the general education curriculum. It isn't enough to simply be *placed* in the general education classroom—students must be actively engaged in learning the content and skills that define that curriculum.[11]

The inclusion movement has evolved because of the significant efforts of parents, professionals, and advocates devoted to the right to educational equity of children with disabilities. Federal law continues to indicate that children with disabilities should be educated in the least restrictive environment. That is, children with disabilities have the right to be educated with typically developing children whenever appropriate. But that means that a continuum of service delivery options should be available for the IEP team to consider. However, the majority of students with disabilities still spend at least 40 percent of their day in general education classrooms.[58]

Certainly, the LRE mandate has had a huge impact on the general physical educator, the librarian, the art teacher, and the computer teacher in the schools because, typically, children who may not be able to be included with children without disabilities in the so-called academic programs are included in physical education, library, art, computer, and recess times.

The courts continue to assert the rights of learners with disabilities to be educated in inclusive environments.

THE IMPACT OF INCLUSION

According to Giangreco et al.,

> Inclusive education provides opportunities for teachers to model acceptance of human diversity in its many forms (e.g., culture, race, gender, disability). If we are to encourage the next generation to accept and value diversity, what better opportunity than welcoming students with disabilities into the classroom as full, participating members? The expanding diversity of the student population reflects the corresponding expansion of diversity in our communities, which highlights the need for

students to learn how to live, work, and play harmoniously with people who have an ever-widening range of personal characteristics.[26]

Inclusive education has been defined as education in which the following are true:

- All students are welcomed into the general education classes in their home/neighborhood school.
- Students are educated in groups that represent the greater society (i.e., approximately 10 percent of the students in any class/school have identified disabilities).
- A zero-rejection philosophy is in place, so that no student, regardless of the nature or severity of the disability, is excluded.
- Students with varying abilities share an educational experience, with specific modifications and accommodations to meet individual needs.
- Special education support is provided within the context of the general education program.[26,47]

Because of the growing national movement toward acceptance of the philosophy of inclusion and the implementation of educational practice to promote inclusion, this text includes a variety of strategies for meeting the needs of students with disabilities in an inclusive setting. Our decision to provide this information is not intended to imply an endorsement of the notion that all students' needs can best be met in the general physical education setting. We are deeply committed to the notion that the least restrictive environment mandates better protect the individual rights and ensure a quality physical education experience. General guidelines, including types of activities that will meet the needs of all students in various school levels, are included in this chapter, and more specific strategies are addressed in each of the chapters dealing with specific disabilities.

Inclusion and Physical Education

Inclusion is a philosophy in which "all individuals can participate in physical activities that enable them to be motorically, cognitively, and affectively successful within a community that embraces diversity."[75]

It is clear that a carefully administered comprehensive assessment, a skillfully designed individual education program, systematic and qualified instruction, and continual monitoring of student progress are critical factors that positively impact motor performance and physical development.

Initially, assumptions were made that significant resources, including personnel, equipment, and assistive technology, would be available to the general physical educator to make inclusion a possibility. Even physical educators judged to be highly effective elementary school teachers found the process of trying to include children with disabilities to be frustrating and guilt-producing, and it caused the children to feel inadequate.[42]

It is critical to remember that the law remains clear. The IEP or multidisciplinary team is responsible for determining the appropriate education for the student. Block and Burke wrote, "The IEP team should decide what constitutes an appropriate physical education program, as determined by each child's age, unique needs, interests, parental interests, and what is available and popular in physical education and community recreation programs."[4] Unfortunately, a widespread, not child-based, inclusion model is typical in physical education. In fact, it is not uncommon to have children with disabilities in the general physical education program.

Inclusion and Developmentally Appropriate Practice in Physical Education

As mentioned earlier, the law remains clear—there should be a continuum of placement and instructional opportunities for learners with disabilities. If children with disabilities are to be included in the general physical education program, the physical educator must be using developmentally appropriate practices. That is, the physical educator engages the learners in the class in activities that are age and interest appropriate for the learners. For

example, learners with disabilities can most effectively be included in the general physical education curriculum for 1st and 2nd graders if the emphasis in the program is the acquisition and refinement of basic locomotor and nonlocomotor patterns, movement exploration, cooperative play activities, and elementary rhythms and dance. If inappropriate practices are being used—for example, team sports and competitive games—children with disabilities, like all young learners who are not "superstars," are doomed to failure and frustration.

The same is true of general physical education at the high school level. If the general physical educator concentrates on instruction in leisure and recreation skills for use as adults in postschool years and emphasizes the development of physical fitness, for example, most learners with disabilities can be successful in the general physical education environment.

PREPARING FOR INCLUSION—A PROACTIVE APPROACH

All too often, inclusion was something that "happened" within a given school community. Any change, particularly a dramatic change, in an educational environment must be preceded by careful and systematic preparation to ready all involved in the process. A model blue-ribbon school, Marvel Springs School established an entire school culture in its efforts to be inclusive. According to Stockall and Gartin,

> A learning community was established that embraced children with disabilities and students at risk and created a school world that embodied specific cultural rules. First, no child was excluded from opportunities to socially interact with others. Second, school faculty modeled ways to mark signs of ability in all children and actively searched for positive markers of success. Finally, they established a context of caring and cooperation among all students. These subcultural rules guided teachers' actions and decisions about their teaching practices. The consciously attended to and marked signs of social interaction supported these beliefs.[73]

For inclusion to be effective within a given community and school, significant preparation must occur. Unfortunately, all too often inclusion "happens" without forethought, consensus building, values modification, or comprehensive in-service education. In this section, suggestions are made for ensuring that inclusion is successful by preparing the community, administrators, parents, children, teachers, and paraprofessionals.

Preparing the Community

An increased emphasis on school-community partnerships necessitates a broad-based public relations campaign to help focus community interest on issues tied to the quality of life of individuals with disabilities. Within a given community, visible, capable, and effective individuals with and without disabilities need to be part of a public relations campaign to educate and motivate its citizens to embrace appropriate inclusion in the schools. It is particularly critical that the school board—elected representatives of the public—has

adopted a philosophy that emphasizes appropriate inclusion.[34] The school board—representatives of the taxpayers who continue to be overwhelmed with the financial responsibility of educating their children—must be able to communicate carefully and effectively to all its citizens the benefits of appropriate inclusion. This is particularly important if learners with disabilities are to have the opportunity to make a meaningful transition into the community.

The Building Principal: The Key to Effective Instructional Programs

Without a primary building administrator who is deeply committed to the philosophy and ideal of quality instruction for ALL learners, including those with special needs, schoolwide education programs for children with disabilities, particularly inclusion programs, can be poorly applied and practiced. See Table 6-2 for a summary of the practices of principals who encourage inclusion. Unfortunately, all too often children with disabilities are

---

Table 6-2   **The Building Principal: The Key to Successful Inclusion in Physical Education**

An administrator who values and supports the education of diverse learners is absolutely critical to successful inclusion.[76] The administrator committed to inclusion will do one or more of the following to ensure that quality physical education is received by all:

1. Decrease the class size by hiring additional professional personnel or arranging alternate scheduling patterns
2. Decrease the student–teacher ratio by assigning trained paraprofessionals to assist the teacher and ensuring they do their job
3. Decrease the student–teacher ratio by assigning school volunteers to assist the physical educator in the gymnasium
4. Use creative alternative scheduling patterns for service delivery. Perhaps it is more prudent to have students attend a quality physical education class three times a week if the class size is limited to 30 students than to have them attend a large, ineffective baby-sitting service daily if class size is in excess of 80 students
5. Arrange for university/community college interns to provide vital extra hands

In addition to limiting the student–teacher ratio in physical education, the campus administrator must also provide support for the physical educator by addressing other concerns:

1. The physical educator must be encouraged to attend classes and in-service presentations that address the education of children with disabilities in the regular physical education program.
2. The physical educator must be given release time to participate actively as part of the motor development team or the multidisciplinary team in the assessment/evaluation of the child's gross motor skills and in the creation and implementation of the child's individual motor education plan (IMEP) or individual physical education plan (IPEP).

included in general physical education, art, music, library, and computer classes without careful regard to the unique needs and abilities of the child or the unique needs and abilities of the teacher.

The IEP/multidisciplinary team may provide inclusion experiences—based solely on the social needs of the child—in the so-called special education program in order to meet parental demands for placement with typical children without jeopardizing student performance in the so-called academic components of the curriculum.

Administrative support for the appropriate inclusion of children with disabilities in general education, including general physical education, is vital if a nurturing educational environment is to be created. If the principal believes some children with disabilities may be integrated effectively into the general physical education program, and that meets the child's social, physical, or motor needs, then the administrator must support the physical educator in a number of ways.

The local campus administrator cannot expect a physical educator to create a nurturing, supportive environment for a child with a disability—for any child, for that matter—if saddled with huge class sizes. It is not uncommon in some school districts for a physical educator to have a class size in excess of 80 students. It is impossible to address the needs of each child in a class of this size, and it is ridiculous to assume that even the best teacher could meet the needs of a child with a disability.

The federally mandated participation of students with disabilities in state and district assessments may redirect school administrators to focus their efforts on the performance of students in special education. Unfortunately, many school administrators believe physical education and adapted physical education are simply peripheral or so-called special activities and focus their energies on test scores in the "general" education program.

Preparing Parents

Perhaps the most important phase of a successful inclusion program is the education and preparation of parents of children with and without disabilities. Certainly, a broad-based public relations campaign

within the community is a good start, but carefully designed parent education programs are vital. Brochures like the one published by the National Consortium of Physical Education and Recreation for Individuals with Disabilities (NCPERID), entitled "Physical Education for Children with Disabilities: A Guideline for Families and Educators," provide parents with basic information about the physical education their children should be receiving.[55] Parents of children with disabilities are often the primary advocates of inclusion programs. However, some parents of children with disabilities are fearful of the general education program. Parents fear their child may be teased or hurt, laughed at, and ridiculed by typically developing children. The best way to deal with these types of fears is to invite parents to visit the general physical education program before the IEP/multidisciplinary team considers the possibility of the child's attending the class. If the parents have the opportunity to see a caring, nurturing teacher and a well-organized, child-centered physical education program, their fears will be reduced.

Preparing the parents of children without disabilities for inclusion may be the most difficult part of the development of an inclusion education program. Most parents of children without disabilities are supportive of inclusion efforts if, and only if, they believe their children's education will not be compromised. Parents of children without disabilities are concerned that

- The teacher's time and energy will be exhausted dealing with a learner with disabilities.
- School resources and tax dollars will be allocated disproportionately for learners with disabilities.
- Their child's learning will be disrupted by a child with inappropriate learning behaviors— aggressive, acting out, and refusal behaviors, in particular.
- Their child will begin to mimic inappropriate behaviors demonstrated by children with disabilities.
- Their child's safety will be compromised by a child with physically aggressive behavior.

Achilles Track Club Sponsors a Summer in Central Park for Disabled Children, Which Promotes Family Involvement
Courtesy Achilles Track Club, New York, NY.

- Their child's emotional well-being will be compromised by a child who is verbally aggressive or who uses inappropriate language.
- Their child's health will be compromised by a child who vomits, drools, spits, is not toilet trained, or has a communicable disease (e.g., AIDS, syphilis).

The single most important strategy for preparing parents of children without disabilities for inclusion is gradual and thoughtful inclusion of children with mild disabilities, at first. It appears that this is particularly effective if very young children with disabilities are included with their peers. If parents of children without disabilities can see that their children's education is not compromised, and, in fact, if they learn some important social skills about dealing with others, they will be more likely to support inclusion.

Another significant strategy is to give parents of children with and without disabilities the opportunity to discuss their mutual and independent concerns in a carefully designed open forum. Often, if a parent becomes aware of the fears, needs, dreams, and hopes of another parent, an avenue of communication is opened that will transcend discriminatory practice.

If infants, toddlers, and preschoolers grow up learning together, as young adults there will be no question of "who belongs." In fact, if a school district is deeply committed to effective, inclusionary practice with a minimum of heartbreak, the district would begin inclusion in their preschool program; then children would grow up together into elementary school, then junior high school and, later, high school. Although the total transformation would take up to eight years, at the end of that time the school district would be a place in which all children could learn together.

In fact, if inclusion is well done, there are innumerable benefits for all children. According to Rogers,

- The presence of an included classmate should provide opportunities for growth for the entire class.
- Classmates can develop a sense of responsibility and the enhanced self-esteem that results from such responsibility.
- Classmates' understanding of the range of human experience can be enhanced.
- Children can benefit from their classmates with disabilities as role models. As a result of advancements in medical science that allow most people to live even longer lives, most of those children without disabilities will survive to become persons with disabilities themselves one day.
- Classmates are enriched by the opportunity to have had friends with disabilities who successfully managed their affairs and enjoyed full lives.[68]

Lockhart, French, and Gench reported that a number of factors have been identified as those that promote positive attitudes and improve social interaction in physical education:

- A conducive social climate
- An equal status contact
- An intimate, rather than casual, contact
- Pleasurable and satisfying contact
- Cooperative activity that engages all students in a common goal[48]

To ensure that this is a positive experience for all children, helping children without disabilities to understand what it is like to have a disability is an excellent first step.[46] Children respond well to empathy experiences in which they have the opportunity to feel what it is like to have a disability. These empathy experiences help a child, in a concrete way, learn and accept.

In the physical education classroom, empathy experiences designed to help learners without disabilities understand the person with a disability might include the following:

1. Navigate an obstacle course in a wheelchair.
2. Wear mittens when trying to play catch with a friend.
3. Play in the gymnasium and on the playground using only gestures or sign language for communication.
4. Wear a headset to cut out hearing and attempt to play in a game.
5. Wear eye patches.
6. Kick a ball while supporting self on crutches.
7. With a yardstick splint on the dominant arm, catch, throw, and dribble with the nondominant hand and arm.
8. Participate in a pool exercise/game using blindfolds.

One of the most significant means of preparing an environment for a learner to be successfully included is to identify and encourage a circle of friends to be in place before the inclusion experience is attempted.[57] This helps provide a vital, caring, and humane transition into general education services. (See Table 6-3, which addresses peer friendships.) A child with a disability is given the opportunity to make friends in a controlled, reverse mainstream setting before attempting to move into the general education/physical education setting. For example, if a six-year-old girl with Down syndrome is hoping to participate in the general education/physical education program, several six-year-old girls are asked to meet and play with the child in her classroom, preferably during a time in which interaction might occur (e.g., center time). Then, after the child has made friends, she is included in the general education/physical education program, more comfortable because of her friends.

Table 6-3	Improving Friendships between Children with and without Disabilities

The teacher must
- Model friend-first behavior.
- Provide opportunities at the beginning of the school year and intermittently throughout the year for children to get to know one another.[71]
- Use books, videos, and songs/dances that encourage friendship.[71]
- Teach specific skills for being "friends." Increasingly, students go to school without the interpersonal skills necessary to create and maintain friendships.
- Ensure opportunity to practice the specific skills for being "friends." The skills are specific and "learned" and need to be practiced.
- Reinforce and reward "friendly" behaviors.
- Teach children specific skills for handling a peer's rejection.
- Provide structure, if needed, at lunch or recess to encourage appropriate social interactions.[71]
- Stipulate annual goals and objectives directly tied to learning appropriate social skills (e.g., friendship skills) in the child's IEP.[24]
- Identify and assign roles in a "cooperative learning" experience to foster friendship. For example, one child in the group could be specifically charged with being a "cheerleader" for the other group members.
- Help children create a "circle of friends" before moving into a new educational environment. For example, if a child is going to begin participating in general physical education, *before* the child starts he or she should already have a "circle of friends" in place, ready to welcome the child into the learning environment.

Preparing older students, middle and high school age, for inclusion needs to be approached altogether differently. These students are more likely to be accepting of an individual with a disability if they are able to understand the disability on an intellectual level. Honest communication of information regarding the nature of a disability will reduce fear. They are also more likely to interact with a classmate with a disability if given a leadership role (e.g., as a peer tutor or personal assistant). Only the truly mature adolescent is able to deal with peer pressure issues to only "hang with the in crowd." Selective assignment and recruitment of tutors and personal assistants must be used.

Preparing Professionals, Including the General Physical Educator

Clearly, undergraduate and graduate professional education programs need to be restructured to focus on real-world applications. An increased emphasis on the skills necessary to provide services to students with very diverse characteristics/needs is critical. The general educator must be prepared to meet the diverse needs of children representing a wide variety of cultures, races, languages, socioeconomic classes, abilities, and disabilities.[37] And an increased emphasis needs to be placed on the professional skills necessary to work in collaboration with other professionals.

Parent panels have been used effectively in the preparation of professionals who will be serving children with disabilities. The parent panel would consist of meetings between parents and the instructional staff to discuss information about disabilities and effective intervention strategies.[19]

For a child with even a mild disability to be educated in the general physical education class, careful preparation must be made. There are three variables that must be considered before deciding to place a child in the general education/physical education program:

1. The professional preparation of the educator to teach a child with disabilities

2. The attitude of the educator toward learners with disabilities

3. The nature of the educator's previous experience working with learners with disabilities

Table 6-4 addresses teachers' perceptions of the support they need if inclusion is to be successful.

The first variable to be considered in the decision to include children with disabilities in general education/physical education programs is the professional preparation of the teacher. An introductory-level adapted physical education class at the undergraduate level that addresses the attitudes and feelings of preprofessionals is the basis of such preparation.[28,37] It is particularly critical that the preparation include hands-on experiences with children with disabilities in the physical education setting.[21,44] It appears that the nature of the practicum is critical in the quality of the experience as well. The controlled practicum, on a university campus, is characterized by the following:

- The faculty member is actively involved in ongoing supervision.
- Students are served in small teacher–student ratios.
- Students with disabilities are carefully selected for participation.

If the physical educator did not acquire knowledge of ways to accommodate a learner with disabilities in the general curriculum during undergraduate or graduate professional preparation, the educator must be provided access to this information through in-service preparation before a child with a disability is included in the general program. Subsequent, ongoing in-service training is vital in order to keep professional staff on the cutting edge in the provision of services to learners with disabilities in a general physical education setting. The second variable that must be considered before placing a child with a disability in the general classroom is the teacher's attitude toward teaching those with disabilities. If the teacher has a negative attitude about including a learner with a disability in the class, the learner will know it

Table 6-4	Teachers' Perceptions of the Day-to-Day Support Required If Inclusion Programs Are to Be Successful

- Personalized, ongoing, specific training to meet the needs of a particular child[22, 78]
  - Training designed to complement the teacher's learning style
  - Training components developed for use when the teacher has time
- Training and opportunity to develop a collegial staff[34]
- Goals and activities for the child that are tied to the general goals and activities of the classroom[33]
- Training that addresses the following:[37]
  - Cooperative teaching
  - Curriculum-based assessment
  - Behavior management techniques
  - Multiple intelligences[60]
  - Trust building[82]
  - Conflict resolution[82]
- Opportunities to observe in other classrooms where inclusion programs are successful
- Opportunities for practice of specific techniques until a comfort level emerges[37]
- Support from a team of professionals
- In-class assistance[78]
- Administrative support
- Time to work with support team, parents, and the child
- Smaller class size[33, 62]
- Additional money for class materials and supplies[22]
- The option/right to remove the child to another place (e.g., resource room or self-contained classroom) if significant misbehavior continues
- Reconfigured "roles" of personnel to allow flexibility in meeting children's needs[33]
- Schoolwide consensus on a set of values that affirms inclusion[33]
- Organizational and role flexibility[82]

instantly and be devastated by it; the learner with a disability simply cannot be placed in a classroom or gymnasium in which he or she is not valued.

Teachers may have negative attitudes toward students with disabilities for a variety of reasons, but attitudes are learned behaviors that, when necessary, can be changed.[64] According to Clark, French, and Henderson,[8] it is important to find ways to teach physical educators the knowledge and skills necessary to work effectively with students with disabilities in the general classroom and increase positive attitudes toward them. These are not mutually exclusive. Teachers may have negative attitudes toward students with disabilities because they do not know how to teach them.

Clark, French, and Henderson[8] have recommended preservice or in-service training that includes empathy experiences, volunteerism,

experiences with learners with disabilities, group discussions, and lectures as vehicles for attitude change. The following techniques are suggested to enhance the attitudes of physical educators toward learners with disabilities.

Empathy Experiences

The general physical educator can be provided experiences that simulate the experience of being disabled. For example, the individual can be asked to spend a day teaching in a wheelchair or to spend a night at home with his or her family while wearing a headset. Or the educator/physical educator can be asked to wear eye patches and a blindfold and allow a student to take him or her on a tour of the playground.

The same type of experience that might help a child understand the phenomenon associated with having a disability can help the professional as well. A truly remarkable account of an empathy experience is the true story of an entire football team, players and coaches, who shaved their heads to commiserate with a teammate who had lost his hair as a side effect of chemotherapy for cancer.

Illumination Experiences

The educator/physical educator can be exposed to information about the potential and the performance of individuals with disabilities. The physical educator might be asked, for example, to compare his or her running performance with the national marathon record of male and female racers who use wheelchairs. Better still, the physical educator can be given the opportunity to compete against an elite athlete with a disability. The teacher might have a chance to play tennis against a tennis player who uses a wheelchair. Or the teacher might have the opportunity to bowl against a member of the American Wheelchair Bowling Association or to play golf against a low-handicap player of the National Amputee Golf Association.

Observation Experiences

The physical educator can be invited to attend a local or regional sports competition for individuals with disabilities. These include events sponsored by, for example, the Special Olympics, the National Wheelchair Athletic Association, or the National Association of Sports for Cerebral Palsy. If this is not possible, the teacher can be given the opportunity to view tapes, for example, of a recent Special Olympics or Paralympics competition.

Volunteer Experiences

The physical educator can be given the opportunity to volunteer to work with learners with disabilities. The mere act of volunteering does not cause a change in attitude, but a positive experience, one in which the educator perceives his or her work to be of value—one that allows for important and honest communication between the educator and the individual with a disability—can alter an attitude for a lifetime.

Perhaps the most significant experience for a physical educator with hesitations about educating a student with a disability in his or her class is the opportunity to observe another professional physical educator teaching children with disabilities in the general program. This may have a positive effect on attitudes and may help the educator develop specific strategies for teaching learners with disabilities. Within a given school district, a mentor teacher could be identified, so that new or hesitant teachers could observe and learn effective strategies for including learners with disabilities in the general physical education program.

Preparing the Paraprofessional or Teacher Assistant

The nature and role of the paraprofessional/paraeducator in the public schools have been compromised by the No Child Left Behind Act (NCLB), 2001.[56] The NCLB mandates significant training/education for individuals who serve in the public schools as paraprofessionals/paraeducators. Specifically, NCLB mandates that the individual have training in the instruction of reading, mathematics, science, and social studies. While it is, of course, obvious that the more training the educators and paraeducators of our children have the better outcomes for our children, this act compromises the availability of these very special educators. Increasingly, school administrators will pull these individuals from their roles in special education in order to increase school test scores.

The paraprofessional or teacher assistant is often the key to the success of a learner with a disability in the general physical education program.[45] Paraprofessional personnel are often willing, but grossly underpaid, members of the teaching staff. Increasingly, however, paraeducators who work within special education are involved in significant instructional behaviors. These include tutoring, gathering and maintaining data, implementing behavior management plans, preparing instructional materials, and collaborating with teachers.[61] These staff members can be the single most important force in the school life of a child with a disability. If

Table 6-5	Paraeducator Roles

A dedicated and well-trained paraeducator may serve in the following roles:

- Ensuring access to the general physical education setting
- Providing physical and emotional support for the learner with a disability
- Serving as an advocate for the learner
- Implementing the IEP
- Supplementing instruction by providing individualized learning experiences
- Being the child's "best friend"
- Communicating with the other professionals serving the child[18]
- Communicating with the child's parents/caregivers
- Documenting intervention and the child's progress[18]

a paraprofessional is given specific training, he or she can better meet the needs of the child. With success in intervention, the paraprofessional will be enabled and reinforced to continue (see Table 6-5).

In-service training needs to be concrete and specific to the needs of the individual children the paraprofessional is expected to serve. The single most important part of the training is the management of the learner's behavior. If the paraprofessional can help the learner behave appropriately, the general educator/general physical educator will be more likely to embrace the learner in the gymnasium and on the playground.

VARIABLES AFFECTING INSTRUCTION IN PHYSICAL EDUCATION IN THE LEAST RESTRICTIVE ENVIRONMENT

It is critical that instruction, not placement, be the deciding factor in the process of educating a learner with a disability. Unfortunately, all too often learners with disabilities are "placed" in a particular educational setting and left there to learn or fail.

The most critical factor in the instruction of learners with disabilities is a comprehensive

assessment. The assessment drives and is the basis for the development of the individual education program. Then, and only then, should decisions be made regarding instruction and placement in the least restrictive environment.[30]

In complete disregard of the LRE mandates of the federal law, a huge majority of our children are receiving their physical education services in the general physical education program. Decker and Jansma[15] have cautioned that federal mandates to provide education in the least restrictive environment have been largely ignored, and, indeed, many school districts have as few as two "service delivery options." Their research in 452 schools throughout the United States indicated that "the most widely used continuum (50.7 percent) was not a continuum at all, but rather a single placement option: full-time general class in a general school."[15] It seems logical to concur that this widespread abuse of the least restrictive environment alternatives has escalated. Careful consideration must be given to the variables that affect instruction in physical education in the least restrictive environment:

- Accessibility
- Curriculum
- Program participation
- Support personnel
- Teaching style
- Management of behavior
- Grading
- Assessment
- Equipment

It is impossible to determine what is the "least" or "most" restrictive when considering instruction. Generalizations regarding what is least or most restrictive are inappropriate when considering individual instruction for learners with disabilities. The determination of least or most restrictive must be carefully considered by the IEP/multidisciplinary team. Each of the variables can be considered on a continuum (see Figure 6-1). However, the determination of least or most restrictive is an individual decision that must be made by the IEP/multidisciplinary team.

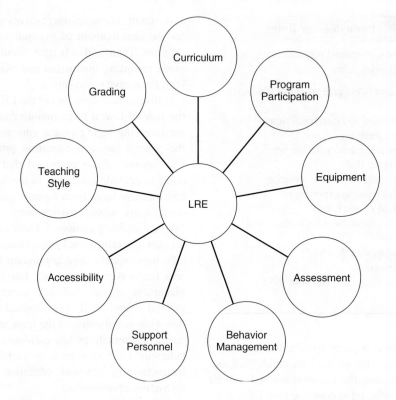

Figure 6-1   Least Restrictive Environment Considerations

Accessibility and the LRE

Accessibility is a critical issue in the determination of the least restrictive environment. Facilities for physical education at the elementary, middle, and high school level vary extensively from district to district and from state to state. Most schools have an indoor gymnasium/play area and an outdoor playground area available for class use. Some school districts have no gymnasium and rely entirely on outdoor facilities. Some inner-city schools, however, have no viable (safe, weapon-free, gang-free) playground area, and often the gymnasium is too small to allow appropriate activities.

It is, of course, necessary to evaluate the facilities with regard to the appropriateness for all learners. In addition, it is vital that the physical educator critically evaluate the facility with the unique needs of learners with disabilities in mind.

The physical educator must ask the following questions regarding the learning environment:

- Is the indoor gymnasium/play area architecturally accessible for a student who uses a wheelchair, a walker, or crutches?
- Can the student with a physical or neurological disability make an easy transition from the indoor gymnasium/play area to the outdoor playground area?
- If the gymnasium/play area is not architecturally accessible, what accommodations can be made to ensure that a student is not limited by a disability?
- If the student is unable to make an easy transition from the indoor to the outdoor play area—because of stairs, for example—what accommodations can be made to ensure that the child is not limited access to the program by the disability?

- Can the play areas be modified to provide a safe, secure, and nurturing learning environment for all learners?
- Are there accessible washrooms close to the indoor gymnasium/play area and the outside playground area?
- Can all learners, including those with disabilities, be safely evacuated from the indoor gymnasium/play area in the event of a fire?

It is important for the teacher to understand that Section 504 of the Rehabilitation Act of 1973 and subsequent legislation—specifically, the Americans with Disabilities Act of 1990—mandate that all new public facilities be built to ensure access for individuals with disabilities. In the event, however, that the teacher is serving in an old building, the law mandates that a "reasonable accommodation" must be made to ensure that the student has access to programs offered to others. For example, if the primary pathway from the gymnasium to the playground is down a set of stairs, a student using a wheelchair may be unable to get to the playground by that route. A reasonable accommodation is for the physical education teacher to have the entire class take an accessible route—one with a ramp, for example—so that the learner using the wheelchair feels part of the group. The gymnasium and playground areas can be modified to make them more user-friendly for learners with disabilities:

- A constant sound source could be placed in the gymnasium or on the playground to allow the student with a visual impairment to orient himself or herself in both settings.[2]
- A "safety strip" made of a material different from that of the major play area could surround the gymnasium or playground area to warn the visually impaired or blind student of walls or fences.
- The playground area must be completely surrounded by fences if a learner with a conduct disorder, a student with autism, or a "wanderer" or "runner" is to be allowed to play and/or recreate outside. Actually, given the present climate in the society, it is critical that

all school property is surrounded by a fence with gates that can be locked or supervised to control access to the school.
- The gymnasium should be well lighted to ensure use by a student with a visual disability.
- The gymnasium should have good acoustics to ensure that a learner with a hearing impairment can hear the teacher's instructions. Materials to absorb sound and prevent it from bouncing around the environment are critical for the learner with Asperger syndrome or autism.
- The teacher should have access to a microphone to speak at levels that can be heard by a student with a hearing impairment.
- Major equipment should always be stored in the same place in the gymnasium to provide consistency for learners with visual impairments or autism.

Curricular Variables Affecting Instruction in the LRE

The adoption of a given curriculum for use by some or all students within a given district is a critical variable affecting instruction in the creation of an inclusive learning environment. Increasing emphasis is being placed on the use of universally designed materials, so teachers need to teach only one flexible curriculum in order to meet the needs of all of their students.

> In terms of learning, universal design means the design of instructional materials and activities that allows the learning goals to be achievable by individuals with wide differences in their abilities to see, hear, speak, move, read, write, understand English, attend, organize, engage, and remember. Universal design for learning is achieved by means of flexible curricular materials and activities that provide alternatives for students with disparities in abilities and backgrounds.[59]

The curriculum must be considered when determining instruction in the least restrictive environment:

- *NASPE National Standards for Physical Education as the basis of the school curriculum.* The National Association for Sport and Physical Education has determined the standards of performance in physical education. If possible, learners with disabilities should participate in this curriculum.

- *State education agency "essential elements" in physical education as the basis of the school curriculum.* Most states have developed their own standards or "essential knowledge and skills" for all curricular areas, including physical education. These essential elements may not be as global as those outlined by NASPE.
- *Local education agency physical education curriculum.* Many local districts have developed their own curriculum. Curricula developed at the local level tend to reflect the interests and attitudes of local school and community personnel.
- *Modified physical education curriculum.* According to Kelly,

> Physical educators must examine how they as professionals and their content area of physical education contribute to an inclusive school. This may involve issues such as revising the physical education curriculum so that it reflects the needs and interests of all the students and the community at the expense of what the physical education staff has traditionally taught or valued in the past.[36]

Program Participation Variables Affecting Instruction in the LRE

In determining the least restrictive environment, there are many alternatives that may be considered by the IEP committee (see Figure 6-2):

- *Full, independent participation in general physical education.* In actuality, the general physical educator has coped with the notion of inclusion for years. It has been relatively standard, albeit inappropriate, practice to give students the opportunity for "socialization" in art, music, and physical education to pacify parents interested in having their child educated with typically developing peers.
- *Full, independent participation in general physical education with younger students.*

Occasionally, it may be appropriate to integrate children with disabilities into physical education classes with younger children. This strategy, viable only at the elementary school level, may be appropriate with children with delayed social and play skills. Under no circumstances, however, should a child with a disability be integrated into a physical education class serving children more than two years younger. To place a 1st grader with a mild conduct disorder into a physical education class with kindergartners may be a humane and creative way of allowing the child to develop the social and play skills he or she lacks. However, it would be inappropriate to place a 4th grader in a kindergarten class. The child is not "included" in that learning environment; the child is set apart for ridicule by the very nature or differences in size and interests.

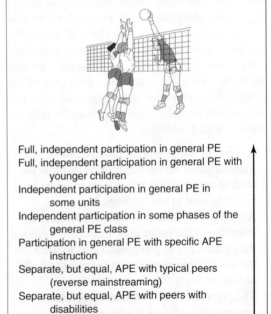

Full, independent participation in general PE
Full, independent participation in general PE with younger children
Independent participation in general PE in some units
Independent participation in some phases of the general PE class
Participation in general PE with specific APE instruction
Separate, but equal, APE with typical peers (reverse mainstreaming)
Separate, but equal, APE with peers with disabilities
APE in home, hospital, or institution

Figure 6-2   Program Participation Variables Affecting Instruction in the LRE

- *Full, independent participation in some units in general physical education.* On occasion, a decision about instruction in the least restrictive environment must be made on a unit-by-unit basis. For example, a learner with a behavior disorder may be able to participate independently in individual activities, such as bowling, bocci, or inline skating, but would be overwhelmed by a large-group game or sport activity.
- *Full, independent participation in some phases of the daily lesson in general physical education.* A learner with mild autism, for example, may be able to participate in the structured warm-up/fitness phase of the physical education class but would be unable to handle a group game or sport.
- *Participation in general physical education with specific APE instruction.* A student with Duchenne muscular dystrophy, for example, may be able to participate in the "relaxation" phase of the daily lesson. However, when the rest of the class is involved in a group game or competitive sport activity, the student should receive specific instruction in leisure and recreation activities, such as fishing or bocci.
- *Adapted physical education in the school building with typically developing peers.* In the event that a student requires a program participation limitation—separate, but equal, adapted physical education—a reverse mainstreaming model may be adopted. In that model, with parental permission, students without disabilities may be invited to participate in a physical education program specifically designed for students with disabilities. This is the basis of the Special Olympics Unified Sports concept. The intent of that instructional, recreation, and sports program is to allow individuals with mental retardation to be taught with, to recreate with, and to compete with individuals without disabilities.
- *Separate, but equal, adapted physical education in the school building with peers with disabilities.* Students with severe disabilities and/or delays may need to receive

their physical education within a separate, adapted physical education class. This may, in fact, be the least restrictive environment for a student with severe behavior disorders, Rett syndrome, or severe/profound intellectual disability.

- *Adapted physical education in the home, hospital, or institutional setting.* Students with profound disabilities and/or chronic, terminal illness may need to receive physical education, as well as the rest of their educational services, in an institutional setting, the hospital, or their home. Students with an illness or injury that requires hospitalization or causes them to be homebound for more than four weeks (this timeline may vary from state to state) require educational services, including physical education, in the hospital or home.

Assessment Variables Affecting Instruction in the LRE

Legislation mandates that learners with disabilities be included, whenever possible, in state-mandated assessments. As an alternative to more traditional assessments, the State of Kentucky implemented the use of portfolio assessments for those students whose disabilities were so severe they could not participate in the state-mandated assessments.[35]

The challenge of including students with disabilities in state and districtwide assessments is great. Generally, students receiving special education services may participate in the education process in three ways: (1) in standard tests administered to all other students; (2) through the use of approved accommodations; and (3) through an alternative assessment designed to measure the progress of students who cannot participate, meaningfully, in the standard assessment process.[20]

Support Personnel Variables Affecting Instruction in the LRE

The IEP/multidisciplinary team must carefully consider the learner's need for instructional support from a teacher, paraprofessional, volunteer, or peer buddy (see Table 6-6). In addition, the IEP/multidisciplinary team must assess the child's need for support from a highly trained adapted physical educator as a consultant or as a direct service provider.

- *No support required.* The least restrictive environment in terms of support is that in which the general physical education teacher requires no support in order to provide services. An IEP, however, is required if a student is to receive services in adapted physical education.
- *General physical educator with adapted physical education consultant support.* The general physical educator provides instruction and relies on an adapted physical education consultant for assessment/evaluation, IEP development, and program recommendations.
- *Same-age peer buddy.* Often, the only accommodation that must be made to allow a learner with a disability to function effectively within the general physical education class is to ask another child to be a special buddy. The buddy is asked to include the learner in play, games, or activities. Often, this is the only "ice-breaker" necessary to allow the student to thrive in the general program. Trained peer

Table 6-6	Support Personnel Variables Affecting Instruction in the LRE

Student requires no support.
General PE teacher has APE consultant.
Same-age peer buddy
Older peer buddy
Older student as teacher assistant
Adult volunteer as teacher assistant
PE paraprofessional provides support.
Special education paraprofessional provides support.
APE teacher provides support in general PE program.
APE specialist as teacher

Table 6-7	Peer Tutor Instructions

Job description: peer buddy
Peer buddy: Molly Pyfer
Student: Cole Huettig
Physical education teacher: Dave Auxter

Physical education: Monday, Wednesday, and Friday, 8:00 to 8:45

Every time your class goes to PE,

1. Walk behind Cole in line. Take his hand if he starts to get out of line. Tell him, "Cole, walk with me, please." If he says, "No," drop his hand.
2. Sit next to Cole in the gymnasium.
3. Follow Mr. Auxter's direction so that Cole can watch you and learn from you.
4. If Cole is not doing what the class is doing, tell Cole, "Watch me."
5. During free play, ask Cole, "Will you play with me?" If he says, "No," leave and go play with other friends.
6. If Cole does play with you, tell him, "I like playing with you, Cole."
7. If Cole hits, spits, or tries to wrestle with you, leave him and tell Mr. Auxter.

tutors appear to be effective in improving the motor performance of learners with disabilities in integrated physical education classes.[29,54] (See Table 6-7.)

Peers are powerful facilitators of learning.[77] Once instruction becomes specific, it is not difficult for students to learn what it is they are to do and then communicate information to their peers. The peer instruction or modeling can be done by students with and without disabilities. Buddies must know what is to be done and have the ability to communicate with the learner.

The buddies should receive the same type of preservice and in-service training as does the professional, although the learning needs to be adapted, so that it is developmentally appropriate. A classwide peer tutoring model that has proven successful is presented in Table 6-8.

Empathy experiences are particularly valuable in the training of peer buddies. Also, just like

Table 6-8	Classwide Peer Tutoring Model[39]

The beauty of the classwide peer tutoring model is that children with and without disabilities alike can serve interchangeably as peer tutors, depending on the activity. The following steps are recommended to teach the classwide peer tutoring model:

1. Develop specific task sheets with criteria for successful performance for discrete skills.
2. Provide a model—teacher demonstration, demonstration by skilled student, or videotape.
3. Allow the students an opportunity to practice the skill.
4. Distribute the specific task sheets and criteria.
5. Provide a demonstration of the peer tutoring process.
6. Review the process.

paraprofessionals, the buddy should have a specific job description (review Table 6-7). In close cooperation with the student's classroom teacher, this experience can be valuable for the peer buddy, as well as for the child with a disability.

- *Older peer buddy.* A student who is unable to function within the general physical education class with a same-age buddy may thrive if given the opportunity to work with an older buddy. This buddy should be carefully trained to help meet the special needs of the student without interfering with instruction and without setting the child apart from the others. This older, more mature student should receive training in the nature of the disability, in techniques for communicating effectively with the learner, and in methods of helping the learner (to move his or her wheelchair, for example, or, if blind, to orient himself or herself in the gymnasium). Older students may serve as excellent models and, if carefully chosen, may serve as a magnet to draw other students toward the student with a disability (see Table 6-9).
- *Older student as teacher's assistant.* Teacher's assistants in physical education can be

indispensable in individualized learning environments. They can assume several responsibilities that contribute to class management and record progress in physical education, such as setting up and storing equipment before and after class, collecting data on themselves and others, and assisting with the instruction of younger students. These students are often honor students who are released from school or are scheduled with younger and slower-learning children. These students need to be thoroughly familiar with the programming if their assistance is to be valuable.

- *Adult volunteer as teacher's assistant.* The adult volunteer must be carefully trained to meet the needs of the student with a disability in the general physical education classroom. This may be a more effective instructional environment (the least restrictive one) for a learner with a behavior disorder that another child could not manage but a trained adult could manage.

As funds become increasingly scarce, administrators and teachers are becoming more and more dependent on the use of volunteer resources to continue or improve programs. The effective recruitment and retention of volunteers is enhanced by effective communication. However, it is important for the general physical education teacher or adapted physical education teacher to understand the nature of the volunteer to effectively use the volunteer to meet program goals (see Table 6-10).

Parents may take an active role as adult volunteers within the physical education program.[17] As with other volunteers, it is critical that parents receive training for their task. Downing and Rebollo wrote, "Parental roles as support personnel and/or adjunct educators of their children can only be as effective as their preparation to serve in these capacities."[17]

Schools and school districts have begun the process of actively recruiting volunteers to work with children within the schools. Schools may be

Table 6-9	Strategies for Developing Student Support Programs in General Physical Education

1. Discuss student support programs (peer buddy and older student assistant) in adapted physical education with the local campus administrator. At the request of the campus administrator, usually the principal, present program guidelines to the site-based management school committee.
2. Discuss the student support plan with the classroom teachers whose students will be affected. Suggest that the program be used as a reinforcer for good work in the classroom. For example, those students who have turned in homework assignments each day of a given week would be given the opportunity to serve as "peer buddies" or "student assistants" in the following week.
3. Secure permission of parents of students without disabilities in order for them to participate in the program. Outline potential benefits of participation in the program for students involved:
   a. Opportunity to learn responsibility
   b. Opportunity to assume a leadership role
   c. Chance to interact with children with different needs and abilities
4. Schedule a preservice orientation meeting for all teachers, students, and their parents. Include
   a. A description of the program
   b. Roles/responsibilities of all involved
   c. Characteristics of children with disabilities (use empathy experiences)
5. Provide in-service training for all teachers and students involved in the program. Invite parents to attend as well.
6. Develop a specific schedule for each classroom teacher whose children will be involved in the program.
7. Plan ongoing in-service education during each class period. Spend a few moments before each class reminding the student support personnel of their roles and responsibilities.
8. Informally evaluate the performance of the student support personnel; provide positive feedback whenever possible.
9. Honor the student support personnel at the end of the year in the student award assembly. *The greater the student perception of program importance, the greater the participation and personal investment.*

Table 6-10	Strategies for Increasing Volunteer Support in the Gymnasium

1. Develop a poster recruiting campaign that features the fact that it is "fun" and a great "change of pace" to work with children with disabilities in a play, leisure, recreation, or sport setting.
2. Actively recruit volunteers on the basis of their athletic skills; it is easier to recruit someone who has the perception of being needed because of particular skills.
3. Form a "dad's club" that allows fathers to contribute to their child's education in a format in which they may be comfortable.
4. Indicate the potential for learning new skills, particularly those that might be marketable. This is particularly valuable in recruiting individuals who are unemployed or seeking alternative employment opportunities.
5. Share program goals and objectives with the volunteer. Share specific goals and objectives for specific children the volunteer serves.
6. Write a specific job description for the volunteer. This is the key to successful volunteer recruitment and retention. The volunteer needs to understand his or her role within the program.
7. Ensure that the volunteer is recognized for his or her efforts. Help the children in the program express their thanks. This is perhaps the most valuable form of recognition for most volunteers. Develop a systematic strategy for recognizing the volunteer. This includes "volunteer highlights" in the adapted physical education newsletter, thank-you notes, plaques, and/or recognition dinners.

"adopted" by a corporation or a civic organization. Corporate employees or members of a civic group may each serve the school in a unique way as a part of the "adopt a school" program.

The use of volunteers in the schools can greatly enhance the opportunities that can be given to children with disabilities. The physical educator can provide a chance for children to thrive and grow through the encouragement and help of program volunteers.

Physical Education Paraprofessional to Provide Support

The student's least restrictive physical education environment may be the general physical education class with the support and assistance of a physical education paraprofessional. This paraprofessional literally serves as a second physical education teacher, who focuses interest and efforts on the children with special needs. Many paraprofessionals contribute greatly to the successful inclusion of a child with a disability in the general education setting. (See Table 6-11.) In some instances, the general physical education teacher should insist that, if one or more learners with disabilities are to be included in the physical education class, a paraprofessional must be available (see Table 6-12).

Table 6-11	Perceptions of Paraprofessionals Regarding Their Role in Inclusion Programs

- Paraprofessionals assumed an advocate role for "their" students being included.[51]
- Paraprofessionals sought to make the experience positive for the general education teacher with whom they worked.[51]
- They felt responsible for controlling all student behaviors to avoid disruption in the classroom.[51]
- They believed they were a critical liaison among parents, the general education teacher, and other school personnel involved with the child (school nurse, etc.).
- They believed themselves to be "experts" regarding the student to whom they were assigned.

Table 6-12	Example of Specific Responsibilities for a Special Education Paraprofessional

Class 1, 8:00–8:45

7:55
Go to Room 109 to accompany Michelle to the gym. Insist she push her own chair.

8:00–8:15
Roam throughout the gymnasium while children are doing warm-up exercises, encouraging all the children to do well. If necessary, remind Michelle to do her modified warm-ups, which are posted on the wall.

8:15–8:40
Monitor Michelle's interactions with others in the class. Record and describe any inappropriate interactions on her behavior chart in the teacher's office. Refer to the description of appropriate and/or inappropriate behaviors on her chart.

8:40–8:45
Accompany Michelle to her room.

In many school districts, paraprofessionals or teacher's aides are assigned to assist a teacher in a given program without regard to their training or background in physical education. As such, it is possible that the physical education teacher will need to ensure that the paraprofessional attend preservice and in-service programs regarding physical education and, if students with disabilities are to be served, regarding physical education for children with disabilities.

At the very least, the paraprofessional must have the opportunity to share the same types of learning experiences recommended for teachers. One of the most significant aspects of the supervision of a paraprofessional is the description of the paraprofessional's role and responsibilities. Most school districts have a generic job description for the paraprofessional. This description is, however, often vague regarding the specific role and responsibilities of the paraprofessional. In addition, the job description for the paraprofessional is usually prepared for the individual who will assist a classroom teacher. The duties and responsibilities of the paraprofessional working in the gymnasium are different from the duties and responsibilities of the paraprofessional in the classroom.[14] As such, the general physical education teacher or adapted physical education teacher must work closely with the building principal to design a specific job description, particularly if the paraprofessional is to help teach children with disabilities.

A specific job description significantly alleviates potential problems. If respective roles and responsibilities are clear to both the physical education teacher and the paraprofessional, they can work together as a professional team, serving children in the best possible way. In addition, the wise physical educator should take every opportunity to reinforce the efforts of the paraprofessional. For example, the physical educator should write a letter to the principal praising the efforts of the paraprofessional. A copy should be shared with the paraprofessional. Or the physical educator should routinely orchestrate a class "thank-you" for the paraprofessional with cards, cake, and punch.

Special Education Paraprofessional to Provide Support

The presence of a special education paraprofessional in the gymnasium is more restrictive than if the student works with a physical education paraprofessional because of the stigma attached to having a "special ed" teacher accompany the learner to class. Every bit of information that applied to the physical education paraprofessional applies to the special education paraprofessional as well (review Table 6-12).

The paraprofessional may play a particularly important role within the school as a liaison between the community and the school. The paraprofessional who lives within the school feeder system may be of critical value to the physical educator who seeks to provide a physical education program that is meaningful not only to the students but also to the community at large.[23]

Adapted Physical Educator to Provide Student Support

For a student to function within the general physical education program, it may be necessary for an adapted physical education specialist to intervene with the student in the gymnasium. Unfortunately, few school districts (except in California and Louisiana) have adapted physical educators who actually provide direct instructional service to students. In some school districts, an adapted physical education specialist may be able to provide hands-on services once a week or once a month. A good model lesson may be helpful for the general physical educator and the paraprofessional, however.

Adapted Physical Educator as Teacher

Many school districts have not made a strong commitment to quality adapted physical education programming. In some schools, for example, the caseload of the adapted physical educator may be more than 200 students; there is no way that quality service can be delivered in that situation. A separate, but equal, service for students with disabilities, who may be unable to benefit from general physical education, has become a luxury, not a reality.

The adapted physical educator may provide direct service in some institutions or with a very specific type of student—those with traumatic brain injuries, for example—but, in general, staff priorities cause this form of direct service to students with disabilities and their parents to be rare.

Teaching Style as a Variable Affecting Instruction in the LRE

The teaching style of the general physical educator must be considered carefully if a learner with a disability is to be taught in the general physical education class. It is clear that most teachers have a set teaching style and are unwilling or unable to change that style; in fact, an adapted physical educator serving as a consultant is wise to make recommendations and suggestions that fit into the teacher's typical behavior and rhythm.[30] For example, there may be two physical educators in the same large high school. The IEP committee may need to evaluate the teaching style of both teachers to determine in which class the learner is likely to succeed. Certainly, a willingness to work with a student with a disability and a commitment to educating all are necessary and desirable traits in a teacher selected to work with a learner with a disability.

The selection of an instructional approach appears to be based heavily on the teacher's experience. Professional preparation training programs continue to produce teachers who are most likely to teach the way they have been taught. This cycle, unfortunately, continues to place teachers who remain teacher-directed and teacher-focused and who believe themselves to be the "givers of knowledge" in direct contact with students who would be more successful if given the opportunity to direct their own learning, to discover, and to take responsibility for their own learning. Following are different types of instructional strategies.

- *Learner's individually designed program.* The essence of this teaching style is that the focus is on each student and his or her needs. A teacher who is already focusing on individual students can easily accommodate and serve a student who just happens to have a disability. The learner is empowered to design and develop a series of tasks and activities that meet his or her needs, and the teacher serves essentially as a consultant—the teacher helps the student by asking important questions, reinforcing appropriate tasks and activities, and redirecting the student's efforts if the tasks or activities are not developmentally appropriate.
- *Guided discovery.* In this teaching style, the teacher asks questions, chooses and develops activities, and plans events to lead a student to a predetermined answer or solution.[53] The most common guided discovery teaching style in physical education is movement exploration. For example, a student who uses a wheelchair may be guided through the following activities at the same time as his or her ambulatory peers:

"When You Adjust the Height of the Basket, I Can Be Successful"

Picture by Carol Huettig.

1. Can you move in a large circle on the floor?
2. Can you move in a large circle on the floor in a different way?
3. What can you do to make the circle smaller?
4. What can you do to make the circle even smaller?

This type of approach empowers all movers and respects the individual's unique responses to movement problems and challenges. This teaching style is one in which learners with disabilities can be easily included.

- *Self-check.* In this teaching style, the teacher shares with the learner the skills needed to perform a task or an activity individually.[53] The teacher has established criteria for successful accomplishment of a given task, so that the individual learner can evaluate his or her own success. If the teacher is serving a student with a disability, the teacher can help the student establish challenging, yet attainable, standards for success. Once again, the emphasis on meeting the needs of individual students facilitates the inclusion of students with disabilities.
- *Reciprocal style.* This teaching style is characterized by the establishment of learning partnerships.[53] While the teacher determines the activity or task and establishes the criteria for success, students work in partnership to

provide each other feedback regarding performance. This teaching style easily accommodates learners with disabilities, even those who require the support of a same-age or older peer buddy to be successful. If every student has a learning buddy, it is easy for the learner with a disability to have a buddy as well.

- *Command style.* This teaching style has often been called the traditional teaching approach.[53] The teacher explains an activity, demonstrates it, and expects each learner to replicate it. The teacher-controlled atmosphere allows little individual variation in performance. Though this sounds restrictive, this teaching style may be exactly what a learner with a conduct disorder or autism needs in order to learn. The structure may prove very helpful.

The needs of learners demand that teachers of children, with and without disabilities, examine strategies to meet those needs. Most certainly, teachers have to focus on active rather than passive learning. Children, like adults, learn by doing, not by watching and certainly not by listening. And it is critical that teachers honor and respect the various ways that children learn.

Management of Behavior as a Variable Affecting Instruction in the LRE

The behavior of students with and without disabilities in a general education setting is often the major factor that determines the students' success or failure within that setting. Carpenter and McKee-Higgins wrote,

> A classroom climate characterized by learning and cooperative interactions with groups of students who are motivated, responsive to traditional authority figures and systems (e.g., teachers and schools), and compliant with established rules and routines may be jeopardized by the presence of students who have not learned or adopted behaviors that are compatible with performing within a community of learners.[7]

A proactive, positive behavior management program is the key to the successful inclusion of students with disabilities in the general education program.[43] Increasingly, inappropriate behavior is a critical problem in the public schools. Children with and without disabilities are exhibiting inappropriate behavior. There are a myriad of reasons, but the result is that it is difficult for the teacher to teach and difficult for the learner to learn.

Identical Behavioral Expectations

Inappropriate behavior in the physical education classroom is the reason most often given that physical education teachers do not want a learner with a disability in the gymnasium. If a learner with a disability is to be readily accepted in the general physical education program, by the teacher and students alike, the learner must be able to meet the behavioral expectations and standards set for every other learner. Too often, a learner with a disability is excluded from the physical education environment, not because of a motor delay but because of the learner's inability to follow class rules (see Table 6-13).

Slightly Modified Behavioral Expectations

General physical educators are often willing to include a learner with a disability in the general physical education program if it requires making only minor changes in behavioral expectations.

Table 6-13	**Skills Needed for Success in the General Program**

One of the keys to the inclusion of children with disabilities in the general physical education program is teaching *all* the children the skills they need to be successful within the program. These specific behaviors include

- Following directions
- Asking and answering questions
- Beginning and completing tasks
- Getting, using, and returning equipment
- Sitting, standing, and walking in line

For example, if a student with an attention deficit disorder is unable to sit on a given spot while listening to directions, the teacher may accommodate the student by allowing the student to stay within a larger space (e.g., a free-throw circle).

Individually Designed Reinforcement System

As an example of this behavior management system, a deeply committed physical educator teaching a high school student with Down syndrome was willing to abide by the recommendations of the IEP committee and completed a behavior checklist each week to be sent home to the student's parents. When the student willingly participated in class activities more than 50 percent of the time, she earned a coupon, which she could use to rent a video on the weekend.

Individually Designed Behavior Management Plan (BMP)

The most restrictive environment is one in which the student with a disability has an individual behavior management plan (BMP) that is different from the plans of his or her classmates. The physical educator, often teaching large classes, will find it almost impossible to implement a specific behavior management plan.

An individual behavior management plan is almost impossible to implement in a physical education class without the support of an additional trained adult in the gymnasium. Under no circumstances should a student, even an older student, be put in the position of implementing a behavior management plan for another student. The ethical and legal implications of a student's being given the responsibility of managing the behavior of another student are frightening.

According to IDEIA 2004, schools have a responsibility to provide appropriate behavioral supports, individualized where necessary, to children who require them. Supports may include a functional behavioral assessment (FBA) and related behavior intervention plan. Conducting individualized FBAs and intervention plans is the job of the administration and teachers. Professional

development will be necessary to be certain assessments and plans are completed accurately.[6]

Grading as a Variable Affecting Instruction in the LRE

If the school district has made a commitment to parents of children without disabilities to provide report cards every six weeks (six report cards per academic year), parents of children with disabilities have a right to have a report card explaining their students' progress every six weeks.

Grading is one of the most difficult issues facing the general physical educator (any educator, for that matter). All too often, children with disabilities are "placed" in the general physical education program, and the IEP/multidisciplinary team has made no recommendations regarding modifications/accommodations in grading.

Same Expectations in Grading and Reporting Grade

In terms of instruction, the least restrictive environment in the physical education program is one in which learners with disabilities are able to meet the same expectations in all phases of the grading process. That includes the motor, physical fitness, knowledge, and behavioral components of grading. The teacher is able to use the same state or local assessments for the learner with a disability as he or she uses for other children and is able to report the results on the same instrument.

Modifications of Expectations in Grading and Reporting Grade

Occasionally, a learner with a disability participates in the general physical education program successfully with basic modifications in expectations for grading and in the way that grade is reported to parents. For example, a student with severe dyslexia may need to have written tests administered verbally. A high school student with a mild intellectual disability may be required to answer only every third question on a written test. Or a student with spina bifida who uses a wheelchair may be asked to "roll" instead of "run" in the cardiovascular-respiratory endurance phase of the physical fitness test. The modifications made must be reported on the standard school report card.

Individual Plan for Grading and Reporting Grade

A grade in any subject should promote educational goals and should reflect educational aims and objectives. For programs to be most effective, established objectives must indicate the desired goals of instruction, so that they become the criteria on which grades are based. If the criteria are valid, successful measurement will result in valid evaluation. The grade, if one desires to translate behavioral performance, could reflect how well these criteria have been met.

The complexity of grading in physical education classes is magnified when an attempt is made to evaluate the performance of students with disabilities. The one common denominator among all students is the mastery of individual performance objectives. If students are graded on the basis of how well they meet their IEP objectives, a student with poor posture, a student with a cardiac disorder, an obese student, and a student who has just had surgery can all be properly evaluated for their grades in the class. In the case of a student with a disability, the student's IEP may be used as the tool for reporting progress (grade) to parents.

Equipment as a Variable Affecting Instruction in the LRE

Making instructional modifications for students with disabilities in physical education may be as simple as finding a different type of equipment for the student to use while learning.

- *Same equipment.* Every learner within the class shares and uses the same equipment.
- *Similar but different equipment.* It is possible to improve instructional modifications simply by changing the type of equipment available for student use. For example, a student with

juvenile rheumatoid arthritis may not be able to participate in a volleyball game with a real volleyball but may be successful in a "volleyball" game that uses a beach ball instead. A child with a visual impairment may experience difficulty tracking a typical playground ball but would be able to participate in a game of catch if the ball were a bright, fluorescent color.
- *Specially designed equipment.* It is possible to enhance opportunities for inclusion by providing the learner with a disability with specially designed equipment to meet his or her needs. For example, a student with cerebral palsy may be able to bowl by using an "automatic grip release" or a ramp. A student with a below-the-knee amputation may be able to participate in a downhill skiing unit with an "outrigger" ski pole.

Instruction within the least restrictive environment is a dynamic and evolving process. Unlike a determination of "placement," in which a student receives services without regard for acquisition of motor behaviors, social behaviors, or self-abusive behavior, carefully designed instruction requires the physical educator to evaluate constantly the student's needs within each continuum.

WORKING DOCUMENT FOR THE IEP COMMITTEE: LEAST RESTRICTIVE ENVIRONMENT IN PHYSICAL EDUCATION

The Irving, Texas, Independent School District designed a special education program design matrix for the IEP/multidisciplinary committee in its consideration of the least restrictive environment within the general education program. The strength of this document is that it provides the members of the IEP committee with a working document that emphasizes a student's strengths and considers the realities of the general education experience. The committee members then try to match the student's strengths with the educational opportunity that will be provided.

This type of proactive effort in determining the least restrictive environment for learners with disabilities may be modified for use in physical education as well. Examples of matrixes for a unit and a daily plan are presented in Figures 6-3, 6-4, and 6-5. Figure 6-4 is an illustration of how the student's strengths are matched by unit(s) in which the student is likely to experience success. Focusing on the student's strengths is of particular value in the IEP/multidisciplinary team meeting. Parents are often much more receptive to the ideas of the committee members if the emphasis is on what the student can do, rather than what the student cannot do. In Figure 6-5, the student's strengths are matched with each phase of the daily lesson plan in the 1st grade physical education program.

If an IEP/multidisciplinary team is truly focused on providing the best possible instruction for a student, within the federally mandated least restrictive learning environment, accommodations can and must be made to ensure success. Careful consideration of the student's abilities, the schedule and plan of the general physical educator, and the availability of support can all influence decisions involved in the construction of an appropriate learning environment.

Specific Strategies for Including Learners with Disabilities

In the following sections, specific instructional strategies for instructing learners with disabilities in the general physical education program are

---

Program Design Matrix

To facilitate positive and constructive admission, review, and dismissal meetings (ARDs) for all students, this program design matrix was developed at Irving Independent School District. It was during a difficult ARD that this matrix was scratched out for all participants to see a "picture" of the student. Because it focused on the strengths of the student, the ARD was able to maintain a proactive focus that generated an individual education program (IEP) for the student's needs. The successful and positive ARD supported the need for this matrix.

The following is a guide to implement the matrix.

1. The matrix is given to the teacher before the ARD to fill in the schedule of a regular school day. Copies are to be made to hand to all those attending the ARD.
2. After review of student's testing, progress, etc., you could begin the use of the matrix, explaining that this will help develop the IEP and programming for the student.
3. Next, identify strengths of the student. Everyone should participate and feel comfortable with the identified strengths before doing a cross-check with the classroom schedule.
4. As you do a cross-check, mark an *X* in the appropriate box and column to signify the student's specific strength(s) that could allow the student to be able to be successful in the classroom. It does not mean that the child could not get support if needed.
5. Empty boxes could indicate areas of concern that the ARD committee needs to address or that a box is not applicable. Circling an activity identified as an area of need will alert the committee to be sure to develop strategies to meet the student's needs in that area. Through ARD discussion, areas that could provide support through modification, consultation, pullout, collaboration, etc., could be identified. It is not to be assumed that support services are to be provided at the specific time scheduled for an activity identified as an area of need. The time assigned will allow the ARD committee to see how much time during the day is needed to program for special education support. The bottom boxes allow times to be totaled, which will help transfer information onto the time sheet.
6. Support suggestions can include equipment, peer tutor, buddy classmate, modifications to the lesson or activity, support personnel, etc.

A

Figure 6-3   Special Education Program Design Matrix to Facilitate Inclusion Based on Student's Strengths   (*continued*)

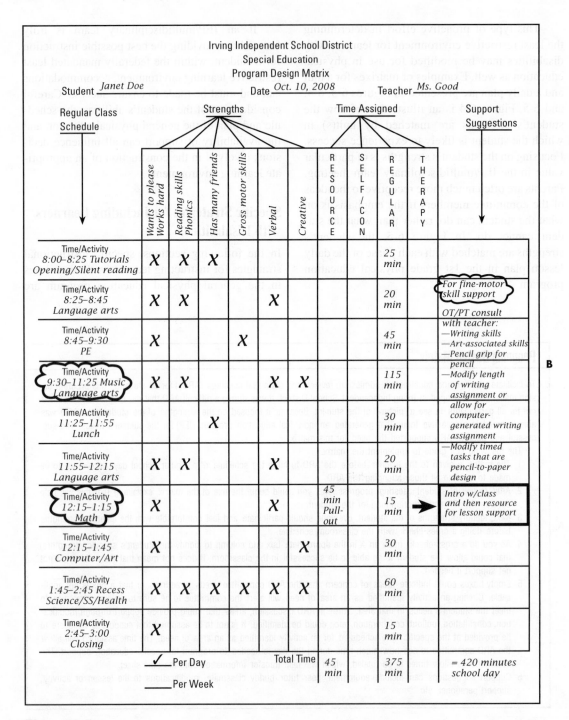

B

Figure 6-3

Courtesy Irving (Texas) Independent School District.

Least Restrictive Environment Design Matrix (Unit)
High School Physical Education
First Semester

Student _Julia Hernandez_ _____ Date_____ _1/6/08_ _____

Adapted Physical Education Teacher _Brett Favre_ _____

Physical Education Teacher ____ _Mr. Garcia_ _____

Activity/ Unit	Student Strengths					Support Suggestions
	Good runner	*Excellent flexibility*	*Works well independently*	*Responds well to music*	*Follows directions*	
September, Weeks 1 & 2 Fitness Evaluations	✓	✓			✓	
September, Weeks 3 & 4, October, Weeks 1 & 2 Individual Fitness	✓	✓			✓	
October, Weeks 3 & 4 Archery			✓		✓	
November, Weeks 1 & 2 Flag Football						*Remove for separate, but equal program with low*
November, Weeks 3 & 4 Soccer						*pupil-staff ratio*
December, Weeks 1 & 2 Volleyball						
December, Week 3 Creative Dance			✓	✓		

Figure 6-4 Example of Least Restrictive Environment Design Matrix (Unit) to Facilitate Humane Inclusion in High School Physical Education Class

Least Restrictive Environment Design Matrix
First Grade Physical Education
Daily Lesson Plan

Student _____ *Dione Haley* _____   Date _____ *9/7/08* _____

Adapted Physical Education Teacher _____ *Emmitt Smith* _____

Physical Education Teacher _____ *Cassandra Williams* _____

Activity/ Unit	Student Strengths				Support Suggestions
	Basic locomotor skills	Balance	Rhythmic ability	Responds well to 1–1 instruction	
9:40–9:45 Roll				✓	*Pair with a buddy for roll/ directions*
9:45–9:55 Warm-Ups to Music			✓		
9:55–10:10 Movement Exploration	✓				
10:10–10:20 Large-Group Activity				✓	*Pair with a buddy for parallel activity*
10:20–10:25 Relaxation				✓	*Pair with a buddy for relaxation activity*

Figure 6-5   Example of Least Restrictive Environment Design Matrix (Daily Lesson Plan) to Facilitate Humane Inclusion in 1st-Grade Physical Education Class

considered at the elementary, middle, and high school levels.

Elementary Physical Education

According to Ratliffe, Ratliffe, and Bie,[65] effective learning environments allow teachers to provide learning tasks, refine students' performance, and focus on students' skill and knowledge rather than on their behavior. Until such a learning environment has been established, most of the teacher's time is spent attending to students' behavior and trying to keep students on task. Although the strategies outlined by these authors (see Table 6-14) were designed for organizing instruction in the general elementary physical education class, they are appropriate for any physical education setting. The teacher approaches classroom organization proactively and creates a situation that enhances learning and prevents inappropriate behavior.

Williams[81] addressed the fact that many activities typically used in elementary physical education programs are inappropriate, not only for children with disabilities but for any child. He identified the "Physical Education Hall of Shame" to help physical educators take a close look at decisions regarding games that are inappropriate for any learner (see Table 6-15). The intent of the 1996 Hall of Shame is to encourage educators to focus on developmentally appropriate activities to avoid the following:

- Embarrassing a child in front of his or her peers
  One student performing while the others watch[80,81]
  One line, one ball, one chance to participate[80,81]
- Eliminating students from participation to allow only one "winner"
- Low participation time and low activity time
- Placing learners at serious risk for injury and harm
- "Rolling out the ball"[80]
- Inappropriately sized equipment, such as 10-foot high basketball hoops in elementary schools
- Using exercise as punishment

Table 6-14	Strategies for Reinforcing Appropriate Behavior

1. Reward appropriate behavior (e.g., smiley faces, stars, "happy-grams," stickers, hugs, smiles, or free time).
2. Remove distractions from the area before starting a lesson.
3. Provide equipment of the same type and color for all children to help prevent fights.
4. Strategically place students who are likely to exhibit inappropriate behavior in designated spots within the gymnasium (e.g., close to the teacher or near children who will be good models).
5. Have students practice "stopping" an activity by placing equipment on the floor in front of their feet. Have students practice returning equipment to the original storage place.
6. Develop a strategy for transition from the classroom to the gymnasium that allows maximum control. For example, have the students practice walking in a line with hands behind the back.
7. Consider an immediate individual activity when students sit on their designated spot, waiting for further instruction. For example, have the children join in singing a song while waiting for the entire class to be seated.
8. Reward students who listen and cooperate by letting them choose equipment first and take turns first.
9. Stand near a disruptive student. Make your immediate presence known by placing your hand firmly on the student's shoulder.
10. Provide a designated time-out area separate from the group but easily monitored.

Data from Ratliffe T, Ratliffe L, Bie B: "Creating a learning environment: class management strategies for elementry physical education teachers" *J Phys Educ Rec Dance* 62:24–27, 1991.

- Allowing students to choose teams[80,81]

Young children who are still in the process of developing their basic sensory systems and their perceptual-motor integration processes are best served by using the bottom-up developmental model. Types of activities that have proved to be effective in resolving delays frequently demonstrated by young children whose development was

Table 6-15	Activities Included in the Physical Education Hall of Shame[80]

- Dodgeball
- Duck, Duck, Goose
- Giants, Elves, and Wizard
- Kickball
- Musical Chairs
- Relay races
- Steal the Bacon
- Line Soccer
- Red Rover
- Simon Says
- SPUD
- Tag

compromised before, during, or after birth are discussed at length in Chapter 5.

As often as possible, activities that address specific areas of development should be incorporated into the activity of children demonstrating those delays. When programs for these youngsters are delivered in a general physical education program, it is possible to address their specific needs and still benefit other students within the class.

Games and activities that promote development in specific areas and are enjoyed by all children, regardless of ability level, are included in *Gross Motor Activities for Young Children with Special Needs.* Over 200 group activities to promote reflex and equilibrium development; vestibular, tactile, proprioceptive, auditory, and visual sensory stimulation and discrimination; body image; motor planning; object-control skills; locomotor and non-locomotor patterns; cross-lateral integration; fitness; and relaxation are included.

The Middle and High School Physical Education Program

One of the most successful techniques for designing physical education classes that appeal to and accommodate a wide range of ability levels is described in the book *Changing Kids' Games,* by Morris and Stiehl.[52] These authors suggest that an excellent way to pique students' interest and

involvement in a physical education class is to engage them in a process that puts them in control of many aspects of the games included in the curriculum. They propose using a games' analysis technique in classes to enable students and teachers to identify and modify any aspect of a game or sport. Using a chalkboard or a flip chart, a teacher can lead the students through a process of systematically identifying the components that are included in the six categories that constitute a game.

The six categories included in every game are purposes, players, movements, objects, organization, and limits. Each category includes several components that have the potential to be changed, depending on the wishes of the group. The categories and their components are as follows:

1. *Purposes.* The purposes of a game include developing motor skills, enhancing self-worth, improving fitness, having enjoyment, gaining satisfaction, and developing cognitive skills. When deemed necessary, the components may be subdivided to identify specifics, such as which motor skills, aspects of fitness, and cognitive skills are included in the game.

2. *Players.* Analysis of the players category yields characteristics such as the number of players required, whether individual performance or group cooperation is needed, and the makeup of the groups. To create greater opportunities for students to be involved in a game, the number of team members could be increased, all teams could be made coeducational, efficient and inefficient movers could be placed on the same team, and students with disabilities and/or different cognitive levels could be included.

3. *Movements.* The components of the movements category include types (body awareness, locomotor versus nonlocomotor, reception versus propulsion, and physical attributes); locations, including personal space (levels, directions, and pathways) and general space; quality (force, flow, and

speed); relationships (objects, players, and group); quantity (number, unit of time, distance, and location); and sequences (task order within an episode). Students should be given the opportunity to alter the types of movement demands, so that everyone has a chance to participate fully. Individual games could be changed to partner or small-group efforts, and a variety of pathways from which players could choose could be built into the game. Players could be given the opportunity to play for a predetermined score rather than for time or vice versa.

4. *Objects.* The discussion of objects will center around the types and uses of the objects, the quantity needed, and their location. A game that requires everyone to use the same implements does not require much imagination. Why not give everyone the opportunity to use a batting tee, or to swing at a slow pitch rather than a fast pitch, or to catch with the mitt of choice rather than the one the rules call for?

5. *Organization.* Organizational patterns include patterns in the game (lines, circles, or scattered), number of players in the pattern, and locations of the players (close to one another or far apart, etc.). Differences among students can become less discouraging if the students are given opportunities to change things, so that they can be successful. Permitting the volleyball server to stand as close to the net as he or she chooses, designating specific players who have a difficult time keeping up to execute all of the throw-ins in soccer, working with peer partners who can help interpret written personal fitness program instructions, or allowing a hit after two bounces of the tennis ball can turn a dreaded class into a positive, uplifting experience.

6. *Limits.* Limits in games have to do with what is expected of players (the kind of participation and the movements that are necessary) and the environmental conditions (boundaries, time limits, scoring, and rules).

Wider boundaries, modified rules, shoulder instead of forward rolls, spotting instead of executing a cartwheel, smaller goals to defend, and more than one chance to execute a correct serve can include students who might never have had the opportunity to participate in a game with their classmates.

Students can be wonderfully creative when they are given an opportunity to analyze the components in a familiar game and are invited to invent ways to alter it by changing one or more components. In the beginning, the teacher may have to provide some examples—such as, if the game requires the use of one ball, what changes to the game would be necessary if two or more balls were used? How could the rules be changed if three rather than two teams were included in the game?

Participation in Interscholastic Sports

The Americans with Disabilities Act makes it clear that students with disabilities have the right to participate in interscholastic sport activities sponsored by the school. Most coaches would agree that students with disabilities have a right to participate in interscholastic sport experiences. Most, however, also feel inadequately prepared to address the specific needs of individuals with disabilities in interscholastic sport settings.[39,67] Essentially, opportunities for learners with disabilities to participate in interscholastic sports at the middle and high school levels are extremely limited.[39,40]

A variety of factors influence the lack of formalized opportunities for students with disabilities to participate in interscholastic sports in segregated programs, let alone a placement continuum:

- State interscholastic athletic agency policies
- Coach, administrator, and parent concerns regarding athlete safety
- Athletic program emphases on winning
- A lack of preparation, "infusion" of material regarding coaching athletes with disabilities in the undergraduate professional preparation curriculum[16]

Rizzo et al.[67] has suggested that, if coaches had opportunities to coach young athletes with disabilities in integrated youth sport settings, the coaches would be better prepared to meet their unique needs at the middle and high school levels.

Collaboration and Inclusion

The collaborative process, one in which two or more professionals share responsibilities and, subsequently, thoughts and ideas, is often difficult for educators. It is particularly distressing to some professionals when the need for collaboration is thrust on them by programs or administrators. The most successful collaborations are those that spring from grassroots, teacher-based efforts and that emerge naturally as professionals learn to trust each other and themselves. Sands wrote,

> Just as animals claim, enhance and protect their territories, so do disciplines assume ownership of particular bodies of knowledge, skills, or modes of intervention and, once established, promote and defend their turfs.[70]

According to Giangreco, Baumgart, and Doyle,

> The inclusion of students with disabilities in general education classrooms can serve as a catalyst to open classroom doors and change staffing patterns so that teachers can build collaborative alliances with other teachers and support personnel in order to have ongoing opportunities to engage in professional dialogue, problem solving, and various forms of co-teaching.[25]

Shared responsibility necessitates significant communication and specific delineation of responsibilities. General, ongoing team meetings are necessary if this type of communication is to work. In addition, there must be a way for team members involved in the collaboration to communicate with others generally. Many teachers have found shared lunch periods and common planning periods to be good times to discuss common problems and to create solutions.

Maguire[50] noted that there are four types of skills necessary for collaboration between educators in the school setting:

1. Exchanging information and skills
2. Group problem solving
3. Reaching decisions by consensus
4. Resolving conflicts

Exchanging Information and Skills

All professionals involved in collaboration must be able to share information and skills in a nonthreatening, nurturing way. As is true of all collaborative efforts, a teacher who is confident of his or her ability is delighted to share and receive information and skills from others. While this type of information sharing can be accomplished in formal, in-service training experiences, often the most effective information sharing occurs in small doses as professionals work together on an ongoing basis. This type of mutual learning occurs when teachers learn from watching another's behavior (modeling), observe another teacher's portfolio assessment, and share assessment/evaluation data.

Group Problem Solving

Historically, teachers have had their own autonomous classroom or gymnasium. Decisions made within their rooms have been made independently. Collaborative teaching necessitates that teachers learn to make group decisions and solve problems together. The skills required for group problem solving include

- Identifying the problem
- Stating the problem
- Listing solutions
- Comparing solutions
- Deciding on the solution to the particular problem
- Reaching decisions by consensus

Reaching Decisions by Consensus

Although it is a more time-consuming process than making decisions by a vote, the collaborative process necessitates that all team members feel comfortable with group decisions. To reach consensus requires open and honest communication and, by necessity, a willingness to give and take for the sake of the program. For example, if a local campus received a small grant allocation and needed to determine how best to use the money to serve its students, the teachers (and, in the best educational environment, the students) would meet to discuss and prioritize needs. Together, all involved would come to a decision that all could accept.

Resolving Conflicts

As is true of any human community, conflicts may arise among members of that community. Teachers involved in a collaborative effort may find that there are times when disagreements occur and conflicts arise. One of the most important aspects of a collaborative effort is the willingness of those involved to address disagreements and conflicts openly and honestly. Left to fester, disagreements and conflicts will grow out of proportion. This type of open discussion requires professionals who are secure in their own skills and competencies. In the event that professionals cannot solve a dispute by themselves, a negotiator may be required to help find resolution.

THE CONSULTANT AND INCLUSION

The significant impetus toward including learners with disabilities in general physical education has drastically and dramatically changed the nature of adapted physical education in the schools and, at the same time, the nature of services provided by the adapted physical educator. Many adapted physical educators have been thrust into the role of consultant. For many physical educators specially trained to provide services to children and adults with disabilities, the process of changing roles from direct service provider to that of consultant has been difficult.[49] Thrust into the often unwanted role, the adapted physical education consultant must create an educational environment that can be maintained without daily supervision.[30] The general physical educator can indeed provide an excellent program for students with disabilities if their

adapted physical education consultant provides the following services:

- Assessment and evaluation of motor performance
- Evaluation of the learning environment
- Collaborative development of the IEP
- Monitoring of student progress toward annual goals and benchmarks
- Collaboration in the development of a portfolio assessment
- Help in solving student-related problems, particularly related to behavior
- Grading of modifications
- Curriculum modifications
- Activity modifications
- Demonstrations of teaching behavior[34]
- Work with parents to foster their participation in program development
- Communication skills
- Provision of specialized equipment

With this type of comprehensive support, a student with disabilities may be able to learn and thrive in the general physical education setting, and the general physical educator will be willing to serve children with special needs.

In the event that the student is unable to participate successfully without additional personnel support, the adapted physical education consultant may play a crucial role in the creation of a successful inclusion program. The adapted physical education consultant can

1. Create a personnel support program
2. Identify student needs
3. Determine the least intrusive personnel continuum that will meet the student's needs (e.g., a peer buddy is much less intrusive than a full-time paraprofessional)
4. Develop a training program
5. Write specific job descriptions for support personnel

It is vital that important communication be established with the principal, teachers, and parents of students with and without disabilities if a successful student support program is to be implemented. (Specific strategies to follow when initiating student support programs in physical education were presented in Table 6-9.) In addition, communications with building personnel are a vital part of this process.

Perhaps the most important thing a quality adapted physical education consultant can do is honor the role of the general physical educator. The general physical educator has specific, usually state-based, mandates regarding the curriculum, the essential knowledge and skills that are expected by the state education agency. The APE consultant, while focused on the child with a disability, must make sure that the recommendations made to the general physical educator are consistent with the curriculum and class format.[32]

Creating concise job descriptions may be the single most important part of the process of serving as a consultant to the general physical educator. Specifically, a job description allows the adapted physical education consultant to ensure some quality control and takes a huge load off the shoulders of the general physical educator. The job description should include specific task requirements, dates/time involved, the extent of responsibility, the hierarchy of authority, and allowance for "storms." (Sample job descriptions used in a large, urban school district adapted physical education consultancy are presented in Tables 6-7, 6-16, and 6-17.)

Each job description is written in very different terms, using different language, depending on the sophistication of the service provider. It is vital that the information in the job description also be shared verbally for the support person who is unable to read. A translator may be required to communicate the components of the job description to a student, volunteer, or paraprofessional who uses a language not used by the consultant.

The job description can be used informally, as a simple method of communicating with support personnel. If it is determined that the job is not being done well—that is, the student with disabilities is not being served well—several options exist, including

1. Evaluate job performance in relation to the job description and provide supervisory

---

Table 6-16	**Job Description for an Adult Volunteer in an Elementary Physical Education Program**

Volunteer: Beth Ann Huettig
Students: Alex, Talitha, Lashundra, and Jesus
Physical education teacher: Jean Pyfer
Physical education: Tuesday and Thursday, 10:10 to 10:50 A.M.

■ Provide instructional support for Alex, Talitha, Lashundra, and Jesus.
■ Please use the following strategies for encouraging appropriate behavior:
   1. Praise the child if "on task."
   2. Praise another child, in close proximity, who is "on task."
   3. Remind the child verbally regarding the task— for example, "Alex, we are all doing warm-ups now" *or* "Alex, I'd like you to join the other children and do your sit-ups."
   4. Physically assist the child with the task. For example, sit down next to Talitha and help her hold on to the parachute handle.
■ If the child demonstrates "off-task" or disruptive behaviors after using the four steps, request the teacher's assistance.
■ Beth, remember you are responsible solely to me. If one of the children is abusive or aggressive, please let me intervene.

---

support. Revise the job description if necessary.
2. Find another peer buddy, older student assistant, or volunteer.
3. Use the job description as a type of contract, and ask school personnel to sign the contract in the presence of the building principal.

A letter written to motivate, as well as educate, a general physical education teacher is a great tool. This type of letter is extremely effective for building cooperative teams with school personnel because it is personal and it compliments the physical education teacher. This is particularly important in school settings in which the teachers feel unempowered (most schools, unfortunately). An adapted physical education consultant willing to

Table 6-17	Job Description for a Paraprofessional for Middle School Physical Education

To: Mr. Chen, special education assistant, self-contained classroom, Carthage Middle School
From: Jean Pyfer, adapted physical education consultant

Responsibilities for: Alejandro Moreno
Physical education: 11:00 to 11:50 A.M. every day

- Allow Alejandro to wheel himself to the gymnasium every day. Please leave 5 minutes before passing time, so that Alejandro will not be late.
- Please watch quietly as Alejandro does his modified warm-ups with the class. Please note that his exercises are posted in the coach's office on the back of his door. He knows his exercises, but he may "pretend" he doesn't to avoid them.
- As the class begins their group activity, please use another student (one who hasn't dressed for activity) to work on skills with Alejandro. For example, if the class is playing basketball, demonstrate to the student how to bounce pass to Alejandro. Carefully monitor the activity to ensure that his peer is not too rough.
- When the class begins laps at the end of class (outside or inside), Alejandro should start his as well. At the beginning of the year, he was able to roll 2 times around the gymnasium in 10 minutes. Build, please, throughout the year by adding 1 lap per month. I would like him to be able to roll 6 times around the gymnasium in 10 minutes. Reward good effort with the football cards I gave you.
- You are responsible for Alejandro's safety and well-being in the gymnasium. If you have difficulty with his behavior, call me and we will develop a specific behavior management plan. If he has a "bad" day (swearing, refusing, etc.), report it to his classroom teacher.

take the time to thank and honor a general physical educator for service to students with disabilities will have created a strong support network. A letter, at once thanking the teacher and reminding

him or her of the needs of his or her students, also provides a summary and review of communication that is important documentation of one's program and efforts. Copying the letter to the physical educators' principal and any other administrative "higher-ups" is reinforcing to the teacher and reminds the administrators of the importance of adapted physical education.

Remembering to take the time to thank school personnel who serve students well is important. A simple handwritten or computer-generated thank-you note is a marvelous tool for reinforcing good efforts and developing a team of individuals willing to serve students with disabilities. Perhaps most effective is a note, voice tape, or work of art created by the student (with the help of the classroom teacher or art teacher) to thank his or her peer buddy, older student assistant, volunteer, or paraprofessional. This type of thank you is also very important for the general physical educator. A sample of a note sent to a paraeducator who served children very well is presented in Table 6-18. Sending a copy to building principals, district physical education coordinators, and area special education coordinators enhances their impact.

One of the most difficult aspects of being an adapted physical education consultant is having a great deal of responsibility and very little, if any, authority. The consultant must be accountable for his or her actions and for the supervision provided to school personnel. Job descriptions, letters that outline responsibilities and summarize conversations, correspondence regarding support personnel programs, and copies of thank-you notes help document efforts. As important, the adapted physical education consultant must do the following:

1. Keep a copy of original assessment data, as well as the written report shared with the IEP committee.
2. Attend as many IEP meetings as possible. There is simply no substitute for face-to-face communication with parents, general educators, building personnel, and related service personnel.

Table 6-18	"Thank-You" Memo Sent to a Paraprofessional

MEMO

To: Sharon Black
From: Carol Huettig, adapted physical education consultant
Subject: Deundrae Bowie, Dunbar Learning Center
Date: December 1, 2008

I can't thank you enough for your efforts on Deundrae's behalf. He is so lucky to have you as a mentor and friend. Your willingness to provide him with special help has truly enhanced the quality of his life. His dribbling skills have really improved, as has his ability to maneuver his wheelchair.

I thank you, once again, for your professionalism, dedication, and concern for your students.

cc: Mr. Moore, principal, Dunbar Elementary School
Dr. Pittman, area coordinator

---

3. Keep a copy of the IEP and carefully document visits to campus sites to monitor achievement of goals/objectives.
4. Maintain careful logs that document
   a. Direct student contact, including the date, length of time spent with the student, and the purpose on that date (e.g., assessment, team teaching, or modeling teaching behavior)
   b. Time spent in consultancy, including the date, length of time spent in collaboration, personnel with whom he or she consulted, and the purpose on that date (e.g., modifying grading, modifying activities, or developing a behavior management program)
   c. The nature and extent of parent communication
   d. The nature and extent of any communication with the student's physician and/or related service personnel
5. Be visible on the local school campus. In addition to signing in at the office, make a point of speaking to the building principal, the office secretary, the child's general and/or special educator, and the physical educator.
6. Send a note home to the student's parent if the student has made progress or has accomplished a goal/objective and leave copies with the child's general and/or special educator and the physical educator.
7. Keep transportation logs to verify campus visits.

One of the unique difficulties associated with the consultancy is demonstrating, in a systematic way, the efficacy of the program and the effect it has on the lives of students with disabilities. As more and more school districts and school systems demand accountability of their staff members, the responsibilities of the consultant become more clear—the consultant must keep and maintain a paper trail to document service delivery.

TRANSITION

The activities and skills learned in the physical education class should be applicable to community leisure and recreation activity. The intent of the physical education program from kindergarten through the senior year of high school must be to prepare all students, particularly those with disabilities, for a life enhanced and enriched by quality leisure and recreation experiences. According to Dattilo and Jekubovich-Fenton,

The trend toward inclusive leisure services focuses attention on participants' strengths as opposed to weaknesses, thus providing all participants—including people with mental retardation—with choices of age-appropriate recreation activities in which they can participate with their peers.[13]

Active participation in leisure and recreation activities after leaving the school-based setting is only effective if the student has had the opportunity to learn, while in school, the skills needed to function with success in the community. Because few school districts hire therapeutic recreators to help in the transition process, the role of the adapted physical educator and general physical educator becomes ever more important. Their role in interaction with the parents and family members of the learners with disabilities is critical in the "outcomes" of adapted physical education. If the adapted physical educators have not been an integral and critical part of the transition process, individuals with disabilities, as adults, tend not to be active participants in community leisure and recreation experiences.[69] Krebs and Block[41] outlined eight responsibilities of the adapted physical educator in the transition process, which are summarized in Table 6-19.

A model inclusive leisure, recreation, and sports program, Promoting Accessible Recreation Through Networking, Education, Resources and Service (PARTNERS), has demonstrated success in providing transition from rehabilitation services to a community-based leisure, recreation, and sports program. The multidimensional program includes the following components:

- AIM for Independence—activity instructional program. The quality instructional program is designed to give individuals with disabilities and their families and friends an opportunity to explore a variety of activities, including skiing, scuba diving, canoeing, kayaking, water skiing, stunt kite flying, sledge hockey, and weight training.
- Equipment rental program. The specially designed equipment necessary for an individual with a disability to participate in some leisure and recreation activities is often prohibitive financially. PARTNERS makes equipment such

Table 6-19	Transition Responsibilities of the Adapted Physical Educator

1. Identify accessible community-based resources and programs in which an individual with a disability would be made welcome.
2. Provide instructional and technical support to personnel within local leisure and recreation facilities.
3. Analyze the environments in which learners could participate in leisure and recreation programs and identify specific skills required for participation. These include gaining access to the facility, making choices regarding participation, skills required to prepare for the activity (changing into swimwear, for example, and using a locker), equipment necessary for participation, and motor skills and fitness levels required to participate.
4. Determine levels of support required.
5. Identify personnel who may be available to provide support.
6. Participate actively in the individual transition plan (ITP) meeting.
7. Implement the program.
8. Conduct ongoing program evaluation.

Data from Krebs P, Block M: Transition of students with disabilities into community recreation: The role of the adapted physical educator *Adapt Phys Act Q* 9:305–315, 1992.

as sit-skis, bi-skis, and mono-skis available for rental.
- Sports development program. While providing a youth sports development program, PARTNERS is designed to be sensitive to groups of individuals with an interest in a particular activity. For example, if a number of individuals wish to explore winter camping, the staff mobilizes to provide needed instruction and to help find accessible facilities and necessary equipment.
- Education and advocacy. PARTNERS provides education and advocacy to enhance the likelihood that an individual with a disability who chooses to participate in a leisure, recreation, and sports program will be extended the hospitality and welcome that any individual has a right to expect.

The Denver Parks and Recreation Program provides a program called Transition to Recreation Activities in the Community (TRAC), in which a certified therapeutic recreator provides direct services and support to individuals making a transition from a hospital or rehabilitation program into the community.

It is only through a comprehensive school-based adapted physical education program that emphasizes community-based programming based on individual and community needs and resources, paired with a dynamic leisure and recreation program, that a learner can make a successful transition into the community as an active participant, making independent choices regarding activities that meet his or her needs.

Inclusion in Leisure, Recreation, and Sports

Historically, society has tended to isolate and segregate individuals with disabilities, and, despite some improvements, such forms of discrimination against individuals with disabilities continue to be a serious and pervasive social problem. Discrimination against individuals with disabilities persists in such critical areas as employment, housing, public accommodations, education, transportation, communication, recreation, institutionalization, health services, voting, and access to public services. Individuals with disabilities continually encounter various forms of discrimination, including outright intentional exclusion; the discriminatory effects of architectural, transportation, and communication barriers; overprotective rules and policies; failures to make modifications to existing facilities and practices; exclusionary qualification standards and criteria; and segregation and relegation to lesser services, programs, activities, benefits, jobs, and other opportunities.

Kozub and Ozturk[38] discussed the implications of *Joshua D. v. SISD,* in which the IEP committee decided to assign a young man with an intellectual disability a role as the manager of the girls' tennis team. The authors' major ethical question is what possible motor/physical education benefits could be gained by this 16-year-old student as a "manager" of a team rather than as a participant in an activity that addressed his own motor and fitness needs. Unfortunately, LRE considerations are far too often made based on the potential social benefits of participation in an activity or a class rather than on the "physical education" benefits.

In essence, the Americans with Disabilities Act of 1990 expands the mandates of Section 504 of the Rehabilitation Act of 1973. That law mandates that no individual can, solely on the basis of a disability, be denied access to publicly supported facilities and programs. The Americans with Disabilities Act of 1990 expands that to include privately owned public facilities. The law states that

> No individual shall be discriminated against on the basis of disability in the full and equal enjoyment of the goods, services, facilities, privileges, advantages or accommodations of any place of public accommodation by any person who owns, leases (or leases to), or operates a place of public accommodation.[63]

In addition, the law mandates that individuals with disabilities be able to participate in the programs and activities of the public facility in the most integrated setting appropriate to the needs of the individual. A reasonable accommodation must be made to ensure access. A reasonable accommodation may include modifications of rules and policies, provision of assistive devices, or provision of support personnel.

However, despite federal and state mandates regarding access to community leisure, recreation, and sports programs, many adults with disabilities continue to face challenges related to participation in sport and recreation activities.

Four-hundred thirty-four athletes participating in Wheelchair Sports USA, U.S. Association for Blind Athletes, and U.S. Cerebral Palsy Athletic Association national competitions completed a survey addressing disability-related problems that made it difficult for individuals with disabilities to participate in sports.[25] The athletes identified the following nonmedically oriented problems: lack of transportation, lack of equipment or equipment failure, lack of support personnel (guides), and difficulty with orthotics or prostheses. They identified the following medically oriented problems: general medical problems, pressure sores or skin breakdown, difficulties with medication, and seizures.

One of the most serious obstacles for sports and recreation programs for individuals with disabilities is "critical mass." Simply, it is difficult for individuals with disabilities to find individuals with similar disabilities with whom to compete.[9]

In some cases, integration requires creative strategies. Special Olympics International has developed several creative programs designed specifically to enhance integration of individuals with and without disabilities into sports programs. The Partner's Club Program is designed to encourage high-school-age students to seek coaching certification and to be actively involved as coaches of athletes who have intellectual disabilities. The Unified Sports Program is designed to foster the integration of individuals with and without disabilities into training and competition programs by matching participants on the basis of age and ability. Then, children with and without disabilities can train and compete together, being mutually dependent on each other for the outcome of the event.

Part of the growth of leisure, recreation, and sports programs is due to an increased desire of individuals with disabilities to participate in leisure and recreation activities and to their willingness to serve as self-advocates in finding resources and programs that will address their needs. One of the major developments in leisure and recreation programs nationally is the trend toward participation by individuals with and without disabilities in programs with an emphasis on outdoor, environmental experiences. The Breckenridge Outdoor Recreation Center in Breckenridge, Colorado, is known for exceptional wilderness programming for challenged individuals. The innovative program includes the following winter activities: downhill and cross-country skiing, sit-skiing, mono-skiing, helicopter skiing, ice sledding, winter camping, backpacking, solo trips, and ropes courses. More and more community-based leisure and recreation programs are being made available to individuals with disabilities.

A Student Who is Learning to Transition into a Community Facility
Courtesy Doma Lovetro, Mesa, Arizona Public Schools.

Many exciting and innovative programs encourage individuals with disabilities to participate with individuals without disabilities. Wilderness Inquiry of Minneapolis, Minnesota, has a model program that includes wilderness canoeing, backpacking and hiking, cross-country skiing, and dog sledding. The Wilderness Inquiry mission is to "make adventure travel accessible to everyone, regardless of age, background, or ability."[79] Wilderness Inquiry has adopted a philosophy called "Universal Program Participation," which is the basis for all decision making regarding accessibility and programming. Wilderness Inquiry should particularly be recognized for its emphasis on family-based programming and services that meet the needs of the entire family (see Table 6-20).

Table 6-20	Universal Program Participation Skill

Wilderness Inquiry staff receive intensive training to prepare them for Universal Program Participation:

- Techniques for making the wilderness accessible without altering it
- Strategies for using adapted equipment
- Skills to communicate with individuals with and without disabilities
- Skills to ask a person regarding his or her specific needs
- Techniques for determining what each person can bring to the group

Challenge Aspen has a beautiful program that provides recreational, cultural, competitive, and educational experiences for individuals who have mental or physical disabilities. Activities include nature hikes, climbing wall activities, an archery course, and a ropes course. The H.S.A. International provides a variety of excellent programs to train scuba instructors to teach individuals with disabilities and provides an opportunity to develop dive buddy skills and open-water skills. Camp ASCCA-Easter Seals, Adaptive Aquatics, Inc., has a recognized program that focuses on water skiing and includes special instruction in slalom, barefoot, jumping, and trick skiing. Desert Breezes, Balloon Adventures, Inc., has developed a balloon basket customized and certified to fly passengers with disabilities. The Vinland Center has developed a comprehensive program for children and adults with disabilities. Vinland's programs are whole-person and focus on wellness, positive lifestyles, fitness, and productivity.

The Wisconsin Lion's Camp focuses on the development of individual competency through the use of a challenging ropes course, canoeing, hiking and climbing. Other camping-based programs focus on the unique needs of the chronically ill child. Camp John Marc Myers, for example, in Texas, has been designed to give children with special health needs the chance to learn new skills, form peer relationships, and develop greater independence and self-esteem. Camp John Marc Myers is based on the following philosophy:

> Chronic disease and physical disability can rob children of the chance to just be kids, leaving them to spend the precious years of their youth watching from the sidelines. In lives that are filled with doctors, hospitals, and the painful awareness that they are not like other children, the chance to be a "normal" kid is rare. Going away to camp gives children with special health needs that chance. The feeling of freedom experienced through camping provides an invaluable opportunity for these children to overcome preoccupation with illness and feelings of isolation.[6]

Other programs offer children with disabilities the opportunity to learn more community-based leisure and recreation skills. Kathy Corbin's "Never Say Never" program is a nonprofit organization that teaches golf to physically challenged individuals. The National Amputee Golf Association provides clinics in local schools and community centers to teach golf skills and golf-teaching skills to those with amputations. The U.S. Tennis Association offers a series of clinics in the public schools to teach beginning tennis to children with and without disabilities. The American Wheelchair Bowling Association works in close cooperation with the American Bowling Association to develop integrated bowling leagues.

Increasingly, more sophisticated sports and recreation equipment for individuals with disabilities is available to encourage participation and ensure access. Deming Designs has created wheelchairs with supersize tires to allow individuals using wheelchairs access to beaches, woods, and other outdoor environments. Endolite has created sophisticated prostheses to allow individuals with amputations access to track and field, golf, and other leisure and sport experiences.

The Orthopedic and Prosthetic Athlete Assistance Fund, Inc., helps provide equipment for athletes that allows access to leisure, recreation, and sports activities. Orthomerica has designed prosthetics and braces to encourage and foster independent mobility and access to leisure and recreation activities. The

Table 6-21	Strategies the General Physical Educator Can Use to Demonstrate a Commitment to a Quality Education for All Children

- Know and use each child's name. This is a fundamental requirement if the teacher is to communicate the fact that the child is valued.
- Do not jump to conclusions regarding a child's behavior, particularly if the child represents a different culture. For example, children from many Asian cultures have been taught to lower their heads and their eyes to show respect to adults. A teacher insisting that the child, "Look at me when I'm talking to you" is literally asking the child to show disrespect.
- Ensure that there is someone available to translate if the teacher does not understand the language or dialect of the student. Often, another student can help communicate. While it would be wonderful for the teacher to be familiar with basic phrases in the native language or mode of communication of each child in his or her classes, it is not unusual in a large urban district for children to use more than 90 different languages and dialects.
- Minimize the use of verbal language and rely heavily on demonstrations.
- Use posters that reflect a diverse community.
- Recognize "heroes" that reflect a diverse community.
- Learn to read the student. Body language, gestures, and facial expressions can often communicate intent and feelings better than verbal language can.
- The teacher should select and use music that represents a variety of cultures.
- Invite parents and members of the community to teach dance, games, and other activities that represent the cultures of the children served.
- Honor diverse religious and cultural celebrations. Ask parents and other members of the community to share that diversity to celebrate, for example, Juneteenth, Cinco de Mayo, Rosh Hashanah, and the Chinese New Year.

Cure Our Children Foundation is a great resource for articles and Web links related to sports and recreational activities for children with physical disabilities.[12]

Embracing ALL Our Students

Clearly, one of the major opportunities and challenges facing the physical educator is teaching ALL of our children. Our schools are a microcosm of a society that is increasingly diverse. Certainly, educating ALL of our students becomes increasingly difficult as our children and their families represent culturally and linguistically diverse populations. Teachers dedicated to serving all our children can find resources, notably the Culturally and Linguistically Appropriate Services (CLAS, http:// clas.uiuc.edu), that will enable them to teach ALL our children (see Table 6-21). There is a great deal of information available, however, as Corso, Santos and Roof note:

> Thus, on our journey to intercultural competence, we can engage in the deeper process of selecting and adapting materials that are respectful of the diverse cultural values and beliefs of the children, families, and communities with whom we work.[10]

SUMMARY

Adapted physical education has changed dramatically since inclusion was widely embraced as an educational philosophy and practice. General physical educators are becoming increasingly responsible for providing instruction to students with disabilities. There are instructional strategies and procedures that can be used to ensure that appropriate services are provided.

Physical educators deeply committed to providing quality adapted physical education services have to cope with, adjust to, and create new collaborative and consultative procedures for providing services in inclusive settings. Careful preparation, communication, and documentation are needed for the process to work.

The physical educator can also use a variety of strategies to ensure that all students are embraced in the learning environment.

REVIEW QUESTIONS

1. What are the nine instructional variables that can be addressed to accommodate learners with disabilities in the least restrictive environment?

2. How can the least restrictive environment design matrixes included in this chapter be used to evaluate appropriate physical education services for a student with disabilities?

3. What are the characteristics of a quality inclusive, community-based leisure, recreation, and sports program?

STUDENT ACTIVITIES

1. Consider each of the instructional variables that can be used to accommodate a learner with a disability in the general curriculum. Describe which accommodations would need to be made to include Adam in the general physical education program.

2. Write a job description for a peer buddy assigned to work with Adam in a general physical education class.

REFERENCES

1. AAHPERD at www.aahperd.org. 2003.

2. American Foundation for the Blind at www.afb.org/education/jtlipaper.html. 2003.

3. ARC at www.thearc.org/posits/inclusionpos.htm. 2003.

4. Block ME, Burke K: Are children with disabilities receiving appropriate physical education? *Teaching Except Child* 31(3):12–17, 1999.

5. Breckenridge Outdoor Recreation Center, Breckenridge, CO, at http://boec.org. 2003.

6. Camp John Marc Myers, Special Camps for Special Kids, Dallas, TX.

7. Carpenter SL, McKee-Higgins E: Behavior management in inclusive classrooms, *Remedial Spec Educ* 17(4):195–203, 1996.

8. Clark G, French R, Henderson H: Attitude development of physical educators working with the disabled, *Palaestra* 1:26–28, 1986.

9. Colon KM: Sports and recreation: Many rewards, but barriers exist. *Except Parent,* March:56–60, 1998.

10. Corso RM, Santos RM, Roof V: Honoring diversity in early childhood education materials, *Teaching Except Child,* January/February 2002:30–36, 2002.

11. Cortiella C: *NCLB and IDEA: What parents of students with disabilities need to know.* The Advocacy Institute, Minneapolis, MN, University of Minnesota, National Center on Educational Outcomes, 2006.

12. Cure Our Children Foundation at www.cureourchildren.org/sports.html. 2007.

13. Datillo J, Jekubovich-Fenton Q: Trends: Leisure services for people with mental retardation, *Parks and Recreation* May:46–52, 1995.

14. Davis RW, Kotecki JE, Harvey MW, Oliver A: Responsibilities and training needs of paraeducators in physical education, *APAQ* 24:70–83, 2007.

15. Decker J, Jansma P: Physical education least restrictive environment continua used in the United States, *APAQ* 12:124–138, 1995.

16. DePauw KP, Goc Karg G: Integrating knowledge of disability throughout the physical education curriculum: An infusion approach, *APAQ* 11:3–13, 1994.

17. Downing JH, Rebollo J: Parents' perceptions of the factors essential for integrated physical education programs, *Remedial Spec Ed* 20(3):152–159, 1999.

18. Doyle MB: *The paraprofessional's guide to the inclusive classroom: Working as a team.* Baltimore, MD, Paul H. Brookes, 2002.

19. Duckworth SV, Kostell PH: The parent panel: Supporting children with special needs. *J Assoc Childhood Education International* 75(4):199–203, 1999.

20. Erickson R et al.: Inclusive assessments and accountability systems: Tools of the trade in educational reform, *Teaching Except Child* November/December:4–9, 1998.

21. Folsom-Meek SL, Groteluschen W, Nearing RJ: Influence of academic major and hands-on experience on college students' attitudes toward learners with disabilities, *Brazilian Int J of Adapted Phys Ed Re* 3(1):47–66, 1996.

22. Fox NE, Ysseldyke JE: Implementing inclusion at the middle school level: Lessons from a negative example, *Except Child* 64(1):81–85, 1997.

23. French NK, Pickett AL: Paraprofessionals in special education: Issues for teacher educators, *Teacher Education and Special Education* 20(1):61–73, 1997.

24. Gelzheiser LM et al.: IEP specified peer interaction needs: Accurate but ignored, *Except Child* 65(1):51–65, 1998.

25. Giangreco M, Baumgart D, Doyle M: How inclusion can facilitate teaching and learning, *Intervent School Clin* 30(5):273–278, 1995.

26. Giangreco M et al.: Problem-solving methods to facilitate inclusive education. In Thousand J, Villa R, Neven A, editors: *Creativity and collaborative learning: A practical guide to empowering students and teachers.* Baltimore, MD, Paul H. Brookes, 1994.

27. Heumann J, Hehir T: *Questions and answers on the least restrictive environment requirements of the Individuals with Disabilities Education Act.* U.S. Department of Education, Office of Special Education and Rehabilitative Services, November 23, 1994.

28. Hodge SR, Jansma P: Effects of contact time and location of practicum experiences on attitudes of physical education majors, *APAQ* 16:48–63, 1999.

29. Houston-Wilson C, Lieberman L, Horton M, Kasser S: Peer tutoring: A plan for instructing students of all abilities, *JOPERD* 68(6):39–44, 1997.

30. Huettig C: *But I didn't want to be a consultant.* Presentation at the 28th National Conference on Physical Education for Individuals with Disabilities, Costa Mesa, CA, October 1999.

31. Huettig C, Simbeck C, Cravens S: Addressing fears associated with teaching all our children. *Teach Elem Physical Education* May 2003: 14(3):7–12

32. Huettig C, Roth K: Maximizing the use of APE consultants: What the general physical educator has the right to expect, *JOPERD* 73(1):32–35.

33. Hunt P, Goetz L: Research on inclusive educational programs, practices, and outcomes for students with severe disabilities, *J Spec Ed* 31(1):3–29, 1997.

34. Idol L: Key questions related to building collaborative and inclusive schools, *J Learn Dis* 30(4):384–394, 1997.

35. Kearns JF: Principal supports for inclusive assessment: A Kentucky story, *Teaching Except Child* November/December:16–23, 1998.

36. Kelly L: Preplanning for successful inclusive schooling, *JOPERD* 65(1):37–39, 1994.

37. King-Sears ME, Cummings CS: Inclusive practices of classroom teachers, *Remedial and Spec Ed* 17(4):217–225, 1996.

38. Kozub F, Ozturk M: A reexamination of participation for individuals with disabilities in interscholastic sport programs, *JOPERD* 74(2):32–35, 51, 2003.

39. Kozub FM, Poretta D: Interscholastic coaches' attitudes toward integration of adolescents with disabilities, *APAQ* 15:328–344, 1998.

40. Kozub FM, Poretta D: Including athletes with disabilities: Interscholastic athletic benefits for all, *JOPERD* 65(3):19–32, 1996.

41. Krebs P, Block ME: Transition of students with disabilities into community recreation: The role of

the adapted physical educator, *APAQ* 9:305–315, 1992.

42. LaMaster K, Kinchin G, Gail K, Siedentop D: Inclusion practices of effective elementary specialists, *APAQ* 15:64–81, 1998.

43. Lavay B, French R, Henderson H: *Positive behavior management in physical activity settings.* Champaign, IL, Human Kinetics, 2006.

44. Lavay B, Lytle R, Robinson N, Huettig C: Teaching collaboration and consultation skills to preservice and inservice APE teachers, *JOPERD* 74(5):13–16, 2003.

45. Lieberman LJ: *Paraeducators in physical education: A training guide to roles and responsibilities.* Champaign, IL, Human Kinetics, 2007.

46. Lieberman LJ, Houston-Wilson C: *Strategies for inclusion: A handbook for physical educators.* Champaign, IL, Human Kinetics, 2002.

47. Learning Disabilities Association of America at www.ldnatl.org/positions/inclusion/html. 2007.

48. Lockhart RC, French R, Gench B: Influence of empathy training to modify attitudes of normal children in physical education toward peers with physical disabilities, *Clinical Kines* 52(2): 35–41, 1998.

49. Lytle RK, Hutchinson GE: Adapted physical educators: The multiple roles of consultants, *APAQ* 21:34–49, 2004.

50. Maguire P: Developing successful collaborative relationships, *JOPERD* 65(1):32–36, 1994.

51. Marks SU, Scharder C, Levine M: Paraeducator experiences in inclusive settings: Helping, hovering or holding their own? *Except Child* 65(3):315–328, 1999.

52. Morris GS, Stiehl J: *Changing kids' games,* 2nd ed. Champaign, IL, Human Kinetics, 1999.

53. Mosston M, Ashworth S: *Teaching physical education.* New York, Macmillan, 1994.

54. Murata NM, Jansma P: Influence of support personnel on students with and without disabilities in general physical education, *Clin Kinesiology* 51(2):37–46, 1997.

55. National Consortium for Physical Education and Recreation for Individuals with Disabilities (NCPERID): Physical education for children with disabilities: A guide for families and educators, www.uwlax.edu/sah/ncperid. 2007.

56. No Child Left Behind Act, January 8, 2002, www.edu.gov/nclb/landing.html.

57. O.A.S.I.S.: Circle of Friends, www.udel.edu/bkirby/asperger/socialcircle.html. 2003.

58. Office of Special Education and Rehabilitation Services, 26th Annual Report to Congress, 2004.

59. Orkwis R, McLane K: *A curriculum every student can use: Design principles for student access.* ERIC/OSEP Special Project. The ERIC Clearinghouse on Disabilities and Gifted Education, Reston, VA, Council for Exceptional Children, Fall 1998.

60. Pankake AM, Palmer B: Making the connections: Linking staff development interventions to implementation of full inclusion, *J Staff Development* 17(3):26–30, 1996.

61. Paraeducators: Providing support to students with disabilities and their teachers, *Research Connections in Special Education,* Spring: 2003.

62. Pearman EL, Huang AM, Mellblom CI: The inclusion of all students: Concerns and incentives of educators, *Ed and Training in MR and Developmental Disabilities* March:11–20, 1997.

63. Petersen JC, Piletic CK: Facility design and development: Facility accessibility, *JOPERD* 77:38–44, 2006.

64. Prom M: Measuring perceptions about inclusion, *Teaching Except Child* 31(5):38–42, 1999.

65. Ratliffe T, Ratliffe L, Bie B: Creating a learning environment: Class management strategies for elementary physical education teachers, *JOPERD* 62:24–27, 1991.

66. Ravensberg JD, Tobin TJ: *IDEA 2004 final regulations: The reauthorized functional behavioral assessment.* Educational and Community Supports, College of Education, University of Oregon, 2006.

67. Rizzo T, Bishop P, Tobar D: Attitudes of soccer coaches toward youth players with mild mental retardation: A pilot study, *APAQ* 14:238–251, 1997.

68. Rogers J: The inclusion revolution, *Research Bulletin,* Phi Delta Kappa, Center for Evaluation, Development and Research, May:2–3, 1993.

69. Roth K, Pyfer J, Huettig C: Transition in physical education and students with cognitive disabilities: Graduate and parent perspectives, *Educ and Train*

Mental Retardation and Dev Disabilities
42(1):94–106, 2007.

70. Sands RG: "Can you overlap here?" A question for an interdisciplinary team, *Discourse Processes* 16:545–564, 1993.

71. Searcy S: Friendship interventions for the integration of children and youth with learning and behavior problems, *Preventing School Failure* 40(3):131–134, 1996.

72. Shepherd D: *Outcomes of leisure/recreation transition planning in adapted physical education.* Texas Woman's University, Denton, TX. 2003.

73. Stockall N, Gartin B: The nature of inclusion in a blue ribbon school: A revelatory case, *Exceptionality* 10(3):171–188, 2002.

74. TASH at http://tash.org/inclusion/ res02inclusiveed.htm. 2003.

75. Texas Woman's University Project INSPIRE at www.twu.edu/INSPIRE. 2003.

76. Thousand J et al.: The evolution of secondary inclusion, *Remedial Spec Ed* 18(5):270–306, 1997.

77. Ward P, Ayvazo S: Classwide peer tutoring in physical education: Assessing its effects with kindergartners with autism, *APAQ* 23:233–244, 2006.

78. Werts et al.: Teachers' perceptions of the supports critical to the success of inclusion programs, *JASH* 21(1):9–21, 1996.

79. Wilderness Inquiry at www.wildernessinqiry.org/ programs/alp/index.php.

80. Williams N: The physical education hall of shame, part 2, *JOPERD* 65(2):17–20, 1994.

81. Williams N: The physical education hall of shame, part 3, *JOPERD* 67(8):45–48, 1996.

82. Wood M: Whose job is it anyway? Educational roles in inclusion, *Except Child* 64(2):181–196, 1998.

83. Yell ML: Least restrictive environment, inclusion and students with disabilities: A legal analysis, *J Spec Ed* 28(4):389–404, 1995.

SUGGESTED READINGS

Block ME, Conatser P: Consulting in adapted physical education, *APAQ* 16:9–26, 1999.

Block ME, Obusnikova I: Inclusion in physical education: A review of the literature from 1995–2005, *APAQ* 24: 103–124, 2007.

Davis RW: *Inclusion through sports: A guide to enhancing sport experiences,* Champaign, IL, Human Kinetics, 2002.

Kozub FM, Lienert C: Attitudes toward teaching children with disabilities: Review of the literature and research paradigm, *APAQ* 20: 323–346, 2003

RECOMMENDED WEB SITES

Please keep in mind that these Web sites are being recommended in the winter of 2007. As Web sites often change, they may have moved, been reconfigured, or eliminated.

National Resource Center for Paraprofessionals
www.nrcpara.org

Inclusive Playgrounds
http://ncaonline.org/index.php?q=taxonomy/term/136/all

Inclusion Education Web Site: The Renaissance Group—the What and How to of Inclusive Education
www.uni.edu/coe/inclusion

Inclusion: School as a Caring Community
http://www.ualberta.ca/~jpdasddc/incl/intro.htm

Circle of Inclusion
www.circleofinclusion.org

Family Village
www.familyvillage.wisc.edu/recreat.htm

Building the Legacy: IDEA 2004
http://idea.ed.gov

CAST Universal Design for Learning
www.cast.org/research/udl/index.html

RECOMMENDED VIDEOS

Insight Media
2164 Broadway
New York, NY 10024-0621
1-800-233-9910
www.insight-media.com

Enlisting the Help of Parents
#UAP4350/DVD/2005/35 min/$179

How to Involve All Parents in Your Diverse Community
#UAP5116/DVD/2007/15 min/$159

The Paraprofessional's Guide to the IDEA and Special Education Programs
#TAP4132/DVD/2005/22 min/$179

Enhancing Student Behavior

Give the four fundamental assumptions about behavior management.

Describe techniques that can be used to identify behaviors that need to be learned or changed.

Name and describe five techniques that can be used to facilitate performance of a skill or behavior.

Differentiate between behavior management techniques for reducing disruptive behaviors in a group setting versus with individuals.

Give three examples of techniques to facilitate generalization.

Identify the characteristics of effective classroom management rules.

Name five critical mistakes a teacher cannot afford to make.

Identify the circumstances that permit school personnel to suspend or expel a student with a disability.

Expose Children to Water at a Young Age
Picture by Carol Huettig.

Discipline is the number one concern in the schools in the United States.[40] Behavior problems, lack of discipline, student safety, and violence in schools are among the top concerns.[42] More and more children are going to school from homes where socially acceptable behavior is not taught. Children who are raised in homes

CASE STUDY

Adam

CRITICAL THINKING TASK

In Chapter 3, one of the behaviors Adam demonstrated while being tested was constantly talking. He talked so much it took a very long time to test him. As you read this chapter, identify at least three ways you, as the physical educator, could reduce Adam's constant chatter and keep him focused during class.

where cultural, religious, and ethnic expectations differ vastly from the expectations of the schools cannot expect to thrive in school settings. Children from homes where patterns of abuse, verbal and physical, are the norm cannot be expected to demonstrate kindness and consideration for others, let alone wait quietly in line and take turns. Their everyday world has taught them to look out for themselves first and to mistrust adults. How do teachers manage the behavior of children who are being raised in environments that, instead of meeting their basic needs, constantly threaten their safety and well-being?

In the past, teachers who became overwhelmed with a student's behavior would refer the "problem" to special education or to the school psychologist to be fixed. However, more recently, educators are coming to understand that the problem may not rest solely with the child. It is becoming clear that the structure of the learning environment, the types of behaviors that are taught directly, and the kinds of interactions that are allowed to routinely occur in that environment are critical factors that impact the behavior of students.

Leading educators and recent legislation address the need to maximize positive learning environments while minimizing problematic behavior. Rather than using negative behavior management techniques that have been used in the past, positive behavioral support plans are being promoted.[3]

Negative intervention strategies, such as verbal reprimands, time-outs, corporal punishment, and denial of privileges, may solve immediate problems, but are rarely effective in eliminating undesirable behaviors.[17] School administrators, teachers, and staff have important roles in creating and maintaining a learning environment and providing the support necessary to enable all students to learn and benefit from their educational experience. The person in most direct contact with the student, the teacher, has the primary responsibility for ensuring positive student outcomes.

Effective teachers are emotionally stable, flexible, and empathetic toward students, as well as proactive rather than reactive. The most effective teachers plan in advance, give clear instructions, demonstrate consistency, teach to learners' strengths, model behavioral expectations, follow through on consequences, affirm positive behavior, and teach students developmentally appropriate behaviors and socialization skills.[13] These teacher behaviors result in improved student performance levels and lead to reduction of undesirable behaviors.

In this chapter, we will discuss effective discipline practices, ways to identify problematic performance and behavior, and techniques for maximizing student performance.

ASSERTIVE, EFFECTIVE DISCIPLINE

Establishing the Rules

As a teacher you have the right to teach, you have the right to ask for help, and you have the right to be safe. Students have the right to learn, the right to ask for help, and the right to be safe. Teachers who establish clear and positive rules for the learning environment honor these basic premises.[3] These teachers are consistent, establish clear and concise rules and expectations, and have clear and concise consequences tied to the behavior. Their classroom management rules are positive, specify proper student behavior in observable terms, and have specific, observable consequences.[2] The management rules should be developed at the beginning of the school term and involve the students. The number of rules should be limited to five to seven and be written in terms the students can understand. Consequences for breaking the rules should also involve the students and be clearly stated. The rules should be displayed in a prominent place and the students should frequently be reminded about them. An example of a good set of classroom rules is presented in Figure 7-1. Consequences for not following the rules appear in Figure 7-2.

It is important that the teacher remember that a child has a right to choose to misbehave. When those occasions arise, the student must be reminded that his or her behavior was his or her choice, and then the consequence must always be offered as a choice. A proven way to ensure that students follow the rules is to catch students being good and then praise them for following the rules. Other proven strategies are staying close to the student, providing signals when the rules are not followed, giving verbal redirection, and remaining unemotional but firm when intervening.

Several mistakes a teacher must avoid are listed in Table 7-1. These mistakes must be avoided because they communicate very negative messages to students. It is imperative that teachers honor students' individuality and treat all students equally. Inconsistency sends a definite message that some students are "better" than others. Demonstrating anger informs the student that acting out is an acceptable behavior. Criticizing students in front of others is demeaning and demoralizing. Asking a child to do something like

Gymnasium Rules

Sit Quietly on Your Spot While Waiting for Instructions

Use Your Hands and Feet Only to Do Good Work

Put Your Equipment Away When You've Finished

In the Gymnasium, Use Your "Indoor" Voice

Figure 7-1   Example of Classroom Rules

"Jon, will you sit down?" gives the student the opportunity to refuse. Once that happens, the teacher has few positive options left. Comparing students publicly through the use of posted charts and grades enables other students to observe who has

---

If You <u>Choose</u> to Break the Rules . . . You Have <u>Chosen</u> the Consequences

1st Time	√	√ by your name on the board
2nd Time	√√	5 minute time-out in the gymnasium
3rd Time	√√√	30 minutes cleaning equipment
4th Time	√√√√	Phone call home to adult family member
5th Time	√√√√√	Removal from gym to alternative education placement for 1 week

If You <u>Choose</u> to Swear, Hit/Kick/Bite Someone, Use Drugs, or Bring a Weapon to the Gym, You Have <u>Chosen</u> to Be Suspended from School.

Figure 7-2   Consequences

Table 7-1	Critical Mistakes a Teacher Cannot Afford to Make

- Be inconsistent in expectations, demeanor, and behavior
- Treat children differently
- Be volatile
- Criticize a child in front of others
- Ask a child to do a particular task
- Compare students using posted charts and grades
- Be sarcastic
- Make vague, negative statements about the student
- Use corporal punishment
- Use consequences that are disproportionate to the act
- Use consequences that are unrelated to the act
- Select consequences that you can't administer evenly, calmly, and without anger
- Ignore inappropriate behavior when you are too exhausted to deal with the student and the behavior
- Delay consequences to meet your schedule
- Threaten
- Threaten without being able to follow through
- Use exercise as punishment
- Punish the whole class for the misbehavior of one child

performed more poorly than others (a public put-down). Sarcasm should not be used because students frequently do not understand sarcasm, and it is a clear sign the teacher is unable to positively control the situation. Vague, negative statements such as "I can't believe you just did that," "What a stupid thing to do," and "What did you just say?" do nothing to convey to the student what is expected. Using corporal punishment teaches the student that physically abusing another is acceptable behavior. Selecting consequences that are disproportionate, unrelated to the act, and can't be administered evenly, calmly, and without anger communicates to students very mixed and negative messages that can be interpreted in a variety of ways. When you ignore behavior that is dangerous to the student or others, you inadvertently inform the student that the behavior is acceptable. For consequences to be effective, they must be immediate. Threats such as "Just you wait, young man," "So help me, you're going to regret doing that," "Don't make me come over there," and "That's it, you're dead meat" convey nothing to the student except you do not know how or you choose not to deal with the problem immediately. Using exercise

as punishment teaches the student exercising is negative rather than positive. Punishing the whole class for one child's misdeeds may lead to disapproval and possible retaliation by the child's peers. The teacher who understands and avoids making these critical mistakes is a teacher who has successfully created a positive learning environment in which all students feel valued, know they can expect answers to their questions, and feel safe to learn.

In addition to creating a positive learning environment, the teacher who serves children with various physical, mental, and emotional disabilities frequently needs several methods for identifying problematic performance and behavior as well as strategies to systematically structure the learning environment to enhance those students' opportunities to learn. Students with disabilities who have ongoing behavior problems must have a formal behavior management plan that has been developed in conjunction with the parents.[31] Methods for identifying problematic behaviors and strategies for structuring the environment are described in the following section.

Courtesy of Tara McCarthy.

IDENTIFYING PROBLEMATIC PERFORMANCE AND BEHAVIOR

Need to Assess and Monitor Performance and Behavior

According to Cowart,[5] an experienced adapted physical education teacher, "Good teaching practices include instructional strategies matched to each student's learning style, curriculum appropriate for that student, and applying good reinforcement practices." The two most common techniques for assessing and monitoring a student's progress are through actual testing and observation. The initial assessments and observations are used to determine present levels of performance, so that the student's individual educational plan can be developed. Once that plan is implemented, ongoing observation is necessary to determine whether the student is benefiting from the intervention strategies selected. In addition to monitoring physical and motor performance, the student's behavior must also be noted because, if a student misbehaves, instruction slows until the teacher is able to address that problem. When, for whatever reason, it is observed that learning is not occurring, the teacher must determine why. That is to say, the problem must be identified and addressed.

Define the Problem

The teacher is alerted to the existence of a problem when any of the following occurs: (1) no progress

is being made toward the instructional objectives, (2) tasks are not being completed in a timely manner, (3) the teacher is having to spend an inordinate amount of time with one student, (4) a student is disrupting other students, or (5) a student is behaving in a nonacceptable fashion. At this point, the teacher must evaluate the situation to determine exactly what the problem is and why it is occurring.[4]

After determining what problem is occurring, it is critical that the problem be clearly stated in observable terms that convey what is occurring, when, where, how often, and the strength (intensity). Examples are "When Thomas attempts to perform a basketball lay-up shot, he misses the basket because he always overruns the point at which he should be releasing the ball" and "At the end of her first week in class, when Marquitta arrived at the jump rope station, she picked up one end of a rope and began swinging it rapidly around her head endangering other students at that station." Each of these examples is a description of what is occurring, when, where, how often, and at what intensity. Once the problem has been identified, the possible cause for the behavior must be determined.

Determine Why the Problem Is Occurring

When trying to determine why a problem is occurring, the teacher asks himself or herself several questions that address instruction, the curriculum, and reinforcement.[5] Instructional questions would center on whether the student understands the task, whether the student needs additional assistance, and/or whether the demonstration of the task was sufficient for the student to replicate the skill. In the case of Thomas, the instructional question might be "Does Thomas require some specific cues to understand when to jump and how to release the ball?" In Marquitta's case, the question might be "Are the types of jump rope activities that we expect to be performed at that station understood by Marquitta?"

An example of a curricular question is "Has Thomas been taught the lead-up skills necessary to be successful with his lay-up shots?" To address Marquitta's behavior, we might ask ourselves whether she has recently transferred from a school where jumping rope was not included in the physical education program.

Reinforcement questions should address whether the student is trying to obtain something, avoid something, or both obtain and avoid something; to access sensory stimulation; and/or to communicate.[4] In Thomas's case, the question might be "Is Thomas deliberately dribbling past the basket to avoid trying to make a successful shot, so that he will get more individual attention from me?" In the case of Marquitta swinging the rope around her head, we might wonder if she is attempting to avoid a jumping task or whether she is trying to communicate something to other students.

Address the Problem

The answers to the questions will determine the next steps the teacher will take to impact the performance of the student. Sometimes quickly thinking through your observations of the student experiencing the problem will help with the solution. However, there are times when more information must be gathered before the nature of the problem is understood, and yet immediate action must be taken. As we think about Thomas's problem, we are reminded that he doesn't usually misbehave to get extra attention, so we can assume that there is something about the way the skill is performed that needs to be corrected. A task analysis of the skill components will help pinpoint the error as occurring because Thomas is not timing his jump correctly or he does not understand where the ball must contact the backboard to rebound into the basket. Potential solutions to this problem were discussed in Chapter 5 of this text, "Teaching to Meet Learners' Needs." But when a student's behavior is disruptive to the class, immediate intervention is required and solutions thought out later.

Because Marquitta's behavior is endangering others, the teacher needs to immediately tell Marquitta to stop and possibly redirect her to another task, such as being one of two turners of the long

jump rope. If she chooses not to cooperate, she is given other options that are included in the class rules. By intervening, the teacher has solved the immediate problem; however, to prevent similar problems in the future, the reason Marquitta chose to misbehave in the first place must still be determined. Frequently, talking privately with the disruptive student will provide insight into the problem. In Marquitta's case, she may tell you that one or more of the students in her group made fun of the way she dressed or talked and she just got "mad" and decided to hurt them back. In this case, the effective teacher will (1) find a way help Marquitta understand that striking out at others in anger is never productive in the long run, (2) restructure the class to separate her temporarily from those who were teasing her, and (3) praise Marquitta's good behavior (or dress or bilingual ability) in the presence of the class.

Usually, experienced teachers who have worked with hundreds of students are able to intuit the right intervention strategy more readily than inexperienced new teachers. But the primary goals for all teachers are to maximize student performance and minimize distractions.

MAXIMIZING STUDENT PERFORMANCE

As Cowart[5] reminds us, "Good teaching practices include instructional strategies matched to each student's learning style, curriculum appropriate for that student, and applying good reinforcement practices." In this section, these three practices will be discussed.

Solid instructional practices include clarity of instruction, appropriate intervention, and provision for feedback.[5] The most effective teachers keep their instructions to a minimum. Clear and concise directions are a must in the physical education setting. The less time spent with the teacher talking and the more time spent with the students practicing, the better. When it is noted that several students are experiencing difficulty, the activity should be halted and additional instruction given. When additional assistance is needed by a few students to enable them to perform effectively, physical

Using a balloon, a foam paddle, and physical assistance when teaching striking

Courtesy of Kristi Roth, University of Wisconsin Stevens Point.

assistance can be provided and/or verbal and/or sign clues can be used until the task is mastered.

Effective physical education curricula include activities and skills that are age appropriate and consistent with students' needs, material and equipment appropriate for the students' capabilities, and a learning environment that supports what is being taught.[5] Sometimes students misbehave because the activities are too difficult, too easy, or too boring, or they require too much standing around. Novice learners, whether because of age or inability to understand, cannot be expected to be successful if the balls, the standards, and other activity equipment cannot be easily managed by them. Frequently students with physical disabilities can participate in most activities if the activity or the equipment is modified to meet their unique needs. Learning environments that are uncluttered, clearly marked, and accessible to all learners are inviting places that make participation enjoyable.

Applying Good Reinforcement Practices

As stated earlier, positive reinforcement practices are good reinforcement practices. When students feel safe, valued, and successful, their performance improves and their misbehavior decreases. The discussion that follows focuses on positive reinforcers because they yield the most lasting results. Positive reinforcers include teacher or peer praise, stickers, a paper certificate, positive notes to parents, sports equipment, medals, first in line and squad leader privileges, selection of activities a student enjoys doing, and success on a task. Positive reinforcement is constructive because it helps individuals feel good about themselves.

Selection of Reinforcers

Reinforcers may be intrinsic (internal) or extrinsic (external). Intrinsic reinforcement comes from within the learner. Often, knowledge of success on a task or the satisfaction of participating is sufficient reinforcement. Extrinsic reinforcement comes from outside the learner. Examples of extrinsic reinforcement are praise and other rewards from a person who acknowledges the learner's achievement. One objective of a reinforcement program is to move the learner from dependence on extrinsic reinforcers to a search for intrinsic reinforcers. Once learners no longer have to rely on teachers for feedback, they can direct their own learning. It is important that both the learner and the teachers agree on what the reinforcer will be and how the system of reinforcement will work.

Reinforcement Procedures

Contingency management is a way of controlling the use of reinforcers. A contingency agreement is an agreement between the student and the teacher that indicates what the student must do to earn a specific reward. A token economy is a form of contingency management in which tokens (external reinforcers) are earned for desirable behavior. This type of system can be used with a single student, selected groups of students, or classes of students. Lewis and Doorlag[22] suggest the following procedure for setting up a token economy:

1. Specify the behaviors that earn tokens.
2. Use tokens that are appropriate for the student.
3. Pose a menu (list) of the types of available reinforcers.
4. Allow students to suggest reinforcers for the list.
5. Revise the menu regularly.

6. Use a clear recording system (of distributing the tokens) that is accurate.
7. Give students frequent opportunities to cash in their earned tokens.
8. The cash-in system should take a minimal amount of time.
9. Provide clear rules to staff and peer tutors for distribution of tokens.
10. Gradually reduce the value of the tokens to increase reliance on more natural reinforcers.

Token economy systems that have proved successful in the physical education program include those that allow students to cash in their tokens to buy the following:

A given number of minutes of supervised free play

The right to lead class warm-up exercises

Equipment That Enables Participation Motivates a Child's Desire to Persist at a Task

Courtesy Dallas Independent School District.

The right to choose a class activity for 5 to 10 minutes on a given day

The privilege of being the "assistant" teacher for a given class

The privilege of 5 to 10 minutes of uninterrupted one-on-one play time with the physical education teacher

The right to eat lunch with the physical education teacher

A poster of a sports star

Recreation and sport equipment

Relatively inexpensive recreation and sport equipment can be purchased to support the token economy system. Children love having the privilege to earn jump ropes, balls, juggling scarves, and hackey-sacs. Parent-Teacher Associations often are willing to help with fund-raising to help provide the physical education teacher with this type of equipment. There are corporations that have fund-raiser/promotional campaigns (e.g., Campbell Soup Company) that may help the physical education teacher secure this type of equipment without buying it out of an already small budget or an equally small personal salary.

Frequency of Reinforcement

The frequency of distributing reinforcers should be carefully controlled, so that the student continues to strive toward desirable goals. The frequency that reinforcers are given is called the reinforcement schedule. Schedules of reinforcement should move from continuous (a reinforcer every time the desirable behavior occurs) to a fixed ratio (e.g., one reinforcer for every three instances of desirable behavior). Interval reinforcement schedules provide reinforcement after an established period of time. The schedule should be changed eventually to a variable-interval ratio (e.g., one reinforcer for every three instances of desirable behavior followed by one reinforcer for every five instances of desirable behavior, or one reinforcer every minute followed by one reinforcer every three minutes). The variable-interval ratio is the most effective because, when students are unable to predict when they will be reinforced, they tend to persist at a task.

Peer Tutoring

Peer tutoring has been shown to increase instructional effectiveness for persons with disabilities. Peer tutoring involves using same-age peers or (older) peers to interact with children with disabilities to keep them on task. Both the child with a disability and the peers benefit from the interaction.[24] The benefits to students with disabilities include (1) sustained positive interactions and friendships, (2) increased opportunities to practice needed skills, (3) age-appropriate role models, (4) development of social behaviors and communication skills, and (5) discovery of hidden strengths. Peer tutors gain from the experience by (1) increasing acceptance of individual differences, (2) developing a deeper sense of social justice and advocacy for others,[10] (3) increasing self-esteem,[12] and (4) developing a better understanding of how to communicate with and provide assistance to people with disabilities.[37]

Minimizing Distractions

Much of the previous discussion concerns the uses of reinforcement to increase efforts toward learning tasks. Very often, reinforcement procedures are used to decrease undesirable behaviors. The undesirable behaviors must be eliminated or substantially reduced, so that the student can focus attention and effort on positive learning habits.

Because of self-concept and attention deficits, children with disabilities may disrupt classrooms and make it difficult for themselves and others to learn meaningful motor skills. When behavior management strategies are applied to classroom management, they must be systematic, consistent, and concerned with both preventing disruptive behavior and promoting positive behavior. There are two levels of classroom management: one for the group and another for individuals within the group.

CONTROLLING GROUP BEHAVIOR

There are some techniques for managing behavior that are particularly effective for groups. These include positive teacher attitudes, prevention, establishment and enforcement of class rules, teacher intervention, flexibility in planning, appeals to values, control of the environment, and student leadership opportunities.

Positive teacher attitudes have a powerful impact on the learning of social behavior and physical skills. Some behaviors a teacher can demonstrate that will motivate a class to perform to their maximum include

1. Be positive. Students work harder to gain rewards than they do to avoid punishment.
2. Teach enthusiastically. Use a comfortable verbal pace, varied inflection, and an encouraging tone of voice.
   a. Set realistic expectations. Students will strive toward goals they believe they can accomplish.
   b. Inform students about their progress. Students need to know they are on track and improving.
   c. Reinforce every legitimate effort. Students are more motivated to persist when their efforts are noticed and reinforced.[36]

The single most effective method for controlling behavior is prevention. The most significant technique for controlling behavior is to "catch 'em being good." This proactive teaching response, in which the teacher consistently and enthusiastically embraces "good" behavior, allows the teacher and the students to focus on good behavior. It is crucial that, when addressing the behavior of a child or children, the focus is on behavior. When praising a child for good behavior, it is necessary that other children understand that it is the behavior that is being praised, so that those not being praised do not get the unintentioned message that they are somehow "bad." Examples of appropriate responses include the following:

- "Juan, thank you for being such a good listener."
- "I really like the way Thelma is following directions."
- "Carlos, I'm really proud of you for putting your ball away."
- "Way to be, Jason! I like the fact that you shared your toy with Julianna."

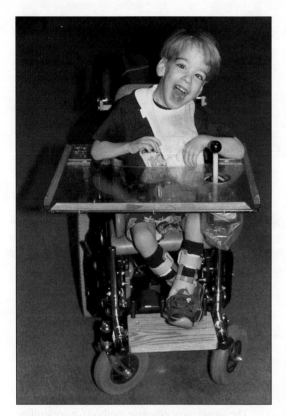

Children Who Enjoy Activity Are Internally Motivated
to Continue Participation
Courtesy Dallas Independent School District.

The good teaching technique of "catch 'em being good" is one of the basic elements of preventive planning, which consists of establishing class rules and enforcing them in the least intrusive ways possible. Rules for class conduct should communicate to students the behavior expected by the teacher. Effective class rules should (1) be few in number, (2) be a statement of behavior desired from the student, (3) be simple and clearly stated in a positive way, and (4) explain guidelines that the teacher can enforce. For example, a well-stated rule is "When lined up at the door waiting to pass to the next class, keep your hands to yourself." Clearly stated expectations lead to appropriate classroom behavior. They provide learners with rules of conduct and identify behavior that will be rewarded. It is suggested that a list of rules be placed where students can observe it each day. The consequences for breaking rules should also be made clear to the students. These must be posted in the native languages of the children served. For example, if a school serves a large number of Hispanic students, rules and consequences should be posted in both English and Spanish. When serving young children or nonreaders, rules and consequences must be reviewed before each class period; in some situations, rules and consequences may need to be repeated periodically throughout the class.

Rules cannot take care of every situation; often, there is disruptive behavior not covered by the rules. The difficult decision each teacher must make is whether to intervene and stop the disruptive behavior. Teachers have a responsibility to interfere with behaviors that

Present a physical danger to self or others
Are psychologically harmful to the child and others

Modifying Equipment to Enable Everyone to Play
Is a Reinforcer to the Child
Courtesy Orthotic & Prosthetic Athlete Assistance Fund, Inc.

Lead to excessive excitement, loss of control, or chaos

Prohibit continuation of the program

Lead to destruction of property

Encourage the spread of negativism in the group

Lead to conflict with others outside the group.

Compromise the teacher's mental health and ability to function[35]

If the teacher does decide it is necessary to intervene to control disruptive behavior, several techniques are effective. Some specific techniques that have been identified by Redl to manage disruptive students in a physical education setting are as follows:

- **Planned ignoring.** Much of children's behavior is designed to antagonize the teacher. If this behavior is not contagious, it may be wise to ignore it and not gratify the child.
- **Signal interference.** The teacher can use nonverbal controls, such as hand clapping, eye contact, frowns, and body posture, to indicate to the child disapproval and control.
- **Proximity control.** The teacher can stand next to a child who is having difficulty. This is to let the child know of the teacher's concern regarding the behavior.
- **Interest boosting.** If a child's interest is waning, involve the child actively in class activities of the moment and let him or her demonstrate the skill that is being performed or discussed.
- **Reduction of tension through humor.** Humor is often able to penetrate a tense situation, with the result that everyone becomes more comfortable.
- **Hurdle lesson.** Sometimes a child is frustrated by the immediate task. Instead of asking for help, the child may involve his or her peers in disruptive activity. In this event, select and structure a task in which the child can be successful.

- **Restructure of classroom program.** If the teacher finds the class irritable, bored, or excited, a change in program might be needed.
- **Support from routine.** Some children need more structure than others. Without these guideposts, they feel insecure. Structure programs for those who need it by clearly defining the rules, boundaries, and acceptable limits of behavior, as well as adhering to the same general routine each day.
- **Direct appeal to value areas.** Appeal to certain values that children have internalized, such as a relationship between the teacher and the child, behavioral consequences, awareness of peer reaction, and appeal to the teacher's power of authority.
- **Removal of seductive objects.** It is difficult for the teacher to compete against balls, bats, objects that can be manipulated, and equipment that may be in the vicinity of instruction. Either the objects have to be removed or the teacher has to accept the disorganized state of the group.[33]

In addition, whenever possible, students should be given opportunities to provide leadership within the class,[32] be given opportunities to select activities,[36] and engage in planning sessions on ways to modify games to include a wide range of student abilities (see Chapter 6).

Handling the Disruptive Student

The behavior problems of students with disabilities frequently contribute to their placement in special physical education programs. When students with special needs are placed in the physical education class, teachers are often concerned that their problem behaviors will interfere with the operation of the classroom.

Behaviors that interfere with classroom instruction, impede social interaction with the teacher and peers, or endanger others are considered classroom conduct problems. Examples of inappropriate classroom behaviors are talking out, fighting, arguing, being out of line, swearing, using equipment or facilities inappropriately, being noncompliant, and

Success with Challenge Courses Promotes Self-Confidence
Courtesy of Donna Louctro, Mesa, Arizona Public Schools.

avoiding interactions with others. Breaking of the rules of the game, poor sportsmanship, and immature and withdrawn behaviors also fall under this category. Behaviors that interfere with the special student's motor skill development are considered skill problems. Typical skill problems result from poor attending behavior and failure to attempt tasks with a best effort.

Problem behaviors are exhibited in one of three ways: (1) there is a low rate of appropriate behaviors, (2) there is a high rate of inappropriate behaviors, or (3) the appropriate behavior is not part of the student's repertoire. Knowing the characteristics of the behavior is important, since different management strategies are linked to each.

1. *Low rate of appropriate behaviors.*
   Students with low rates of appropriate behaviors do exhibit appropriate behaviors,

but not as frequently as expected or required. For example, a student may be able to stay on task only 50 percent of the time. Also, students may behave appropriately in one setting but not in another. For instance, the special student may work well on individual tasks but find it difficult to function in group games. To alleviate these problems, the teacher sets up a systematic program to generalize on-task behaviors from one situation to another. An example of facilitating the generalization of on-task behavior toward functioning in a group setting is to gradually move a student from an individual task to a task that is paralleled by another student, to a task where two students assist each other in being successful (such as taking turns spotting one another during free weight lifting).

2. *High rate of inappropriate behaviors.* Inappropriate behaviors that occur frequently or for long periods are troublesome to teachers. Examples are students who do not conform to class rules 30 to 40 times a week, those who talk during 50 to 60 percent of class instruction, those who use profanity 5 to 10 times in one class period, and those who are off task 70 to 75 percent of the class period. To overcome these high rates of inappropriate behavior, the physical education teacher attempts to decrease the frequency or duration of the undesired behavior by increasing appropriate behaviors that are incompatible. For instance, to decrease the incidence of hitting a peer while in class, the teacher can increase the rate of performing tasks or decrease the time between tasks.

3. *Appropriate behavior not part of the student's repertoire.* Students may not yet have learned appropriate behaviors for social interaction or classroom functioning. For instance, they may not know sportsmanship conduct in class games. Teachers must provide instruction to help students acquire new behaviors. Behavior problems do not occur in isolation. Events or actions of others can initiate or reinforce inappropriate behaviors. To understand and manage classroom problems, the teacher should examine the student in relation to the target behavior. For example, classmates who laugh at clowning or wisecracks tend to reinforce that type of disruptive behavior; as a result, the disruptive student continues to exhibit the undesirable behavior. Students show inappropriate behavior when they have not learned correct responses or have found that acting inappropriately is more rewarding than acting appropriately. These behavior problems do respond to instruction.

Several methods for decreasing inappropriate behavior are available. Walker and Shea have proposed the following continuum of behavior modification interventions:

1. *Reinforcement of behavior other than the target behavior.* A reinforcer is given at the end of a specified period of time, provided that a prespecified misbehavior has not occurred during the specified time interval.

2. *Reinforcement of an appropriate target behavior.* A reinforcer is given following the performance of a prespecified appropriate target behavior.

3. *Reinforcement of incompatible behaviors.* A reinforcer is given following the performance of a prespecified behavior that is physically and functionally incompatible with the target behavior.

4. *Extinction.* The reinforcer that has been sustaining or increasing an undesirable behavior is withheld.

5. *Stimulus change.* The existing environmental conditions are drastically altered to ensure that the target behavior is temporarily suppressed.

6. *Reprimand.* This is a form of punishment that involves verbally chastising a student for inappropriately exhibiting a target behavior. The reprimand should
   - Be specific to the inappropriate behavior
   - Address the behavior, not the child
   - Be firm and administered immediately
   - Be accompanied by loss of privileges
   - Include a statement of appropriate behavior
   - Be done in a calm voice privately followed by observation of the child's reaction, so that the effect of the reprimand can be evaluated

7. *Nonexclusionary time-out*
   a. Restriction to a place in a separate area of the gymnasium but able to observe activities
   b. Removal of materials (work, play)

8. *Physical restraint.* Physical restraint may be used only if it is included on the child's behavior management plan. If the child loses control or becomes violent, physical restraint

may be used by a person trained in the proper technique. Following the incident the parents must immediately be contacted.

9. *Negative practice or satiation.* The target behavior is eliminated by the continued and increased reinforcement of that behavior.

10. *Overcorrection.* This punishment procedure requires the individual who misbehaves to improve the environmental effects of the misbehavior and/or repeatedly perform the appropriate form of the target behavior in the environment in which the misbehavior was exhibited.

11. *Exclusionary time-out*
   a. Temporary distraction. When a student's behavior has reached the point at which he or she will not respond to verbal controls, the student may have to be asked to leave the room (to get a drink, wash up, or deliver a message—not as punishment, but to distract the student).
   b. Quiet room/think station. Some schools provide quiet spaces for students to use when it becomes necessary to remove oneself from a group setting to ponder about the misbehavior. The student should be continuously monitored, and the length of time should be limited to 2 to 10 minutes.
   c. In-school suspension

12. *Response cost lottery.* Students are given a predetermined number of slips of paper. Each time the student violates a class rule, he or she must relinquish one slip of paper. The names of the students are written on the slips of paper the students still have at the end of a given time period and are placed in a hat for a lottery drawing. The winner of the drawing receives a prize.[41]

Consistent Management Techniques

There is consensus that successful schools use systems of firm, consistent management. Research confirms that clearly structured, secure environments permit students to master the objectives of the program. Haring indicates that "teaching . . . necessitates finding a method of instruction which allows the child to learn."[11]

The preconditions for the application of learning principles are that there must be a precisely defined short-term instructional objective, and there must be incentives for the learner to master the objective. If either of these preconditions is not satisfied, the effect of the program is minimized. Effective learning is the result of mutual understanding between the student and the teacher. The student must understand what is expected and the consequences of not performing to expectations. Homme[14] provides nine rules to follow when using behavior management techniques:

1. Praise the correct objective.
2. Praise the correct objective immediately after it occurs.
3. Praise the correct objective after it occurs and not before.
4. Objectives should be in small steps, so that there can be frequent praise.
5. Praise improvement.
6. Be fair in setting up consequences for achieving objectives.

Encouragement by a Teacher Is Critical to Developing Risk-Taking Behaviors
Picture by Carol Huettig.

7. Be honest and provide the agreed-on consequences.
8. Be positive, so that the child can achieve success.
9. Be systematic.

Praise the Correct Objective

To implement this principle effectively, persons involved with instruction (teachers, school administrators, parents, and related service personnel) must know precisely the objective or behavior that the learner is to carry out. That behavior must be praised only if it is achieved. The application of this principle must be consistent among all persons who work with the child.

There are two ways that this learning principle can be violated by a teacher, parent, or school administrator. First, he or she may provide praise even though the objective has not been achieved; second, he or she may neglect to provide praise even though the objective has been achieved. In the first case, the learner is being reinforced for doing less than his or her best and consequently will have a lessened desire to put forth maximum effort on subsequent trials. In the second case, if the teacher does not deliver the agreed-on consequence (explicit or implicit), the student's desire to perform the instructional task again will be reduced.

Praise Immediately after Completion of the Task

Learners need to receive feedback immediately after task performance. Homme[14] indicates that reinforcing feedback should be provided 0.05 second after the task for maximum effectiveness. Immediacy of feedback on task performance is particularly important with children functioning on a lower developmental level. If there is a delay between task performance and feedback, the child may be confused as to what the praise is for. For example, if a child walks a balance beam correctly but confirmation of task mastery is provided late (for instance, as the child steps off the beam), the behavior of stepping off the beam may be strengthened to a greater degree than the desired objective of walking the beam. Thus, the timing of the feedback (immediately after the task has been completed) is important.

Praise at the Appropriate Time

If a child is praised for performing an objective before it is completed, there is a good chance that he or she will expend less effort to meet the objective.

Make Sure Objectives Are in Small Steps

If the step size is small, there will be a greater rate of success. As has been indicated, disruptive behavior may be triggered by lack of success. This principle may therefore be applied in attempts to control disruptive behavior in the classroom. Thus, if a child often exhibits many different types of disruptive behavior, objectives can be postulated to reduce the occurrence of these disruptive behaviors in small steps. For children with disabilities, learning by small steps permits much needed success.

Praise Improvement

The acquisition of skill toward an objective should be praised. Providing appropriate consequences for improvement may in some instances violate the principle of praising the correct objective. However, on tasks that cannot be broken into small steps, it is necessary to praise improvement. To do so, the instructor must know precisely the student's present level of educational performance. When the performance reflects an improvement on that level, the student must be reinforced with praise. Improvement means that the learner is functioning on a higher level than before. Therefore, it is unwise to praise or provide positive consequences to students who perform at less than their best effort, since to do so may encourage them to contradict their potential.

Be Fair in Setting Up Consequences

When there are specific objectives to be achieved to develop skill or appropriate classroom behavior, specific consequences can be arranged to support the development of these objectives. However, if such arrangements are to be made between the learner and the teacher, there must be equity between the task and the incentives. If the learner does not have sufficient incentive to perform the tasks or to behave appropriately, he or she is unlikely to do so. This learning principle operates at very early ages.

In one clinical experience, a target objective was set up for an 18-month-old boy with Down syndrome to learn to walk. The task involved walking from one chair to another, which was placed 8 feet away. If the child walked the full distance, he was allowed to play for 15 seconds with the toys that were placed on top of the chairs. When this period elapsed, he would return to the task of walking a prescribed distance of 8 feet 1 inch, a short distance farther than the previous time. After a time, the child refused to participate in the activity. The child's mother suggested that he be permitted to play with the toys for 30 seconds rather than 15 seconds. This procedure was used, and the child again engaged in the instructional task. It was inferred that the child would participate in tasks if the opportunity to play was commensurate with the effort put forth to master the objective. This is an example of equity between incentive and performance.

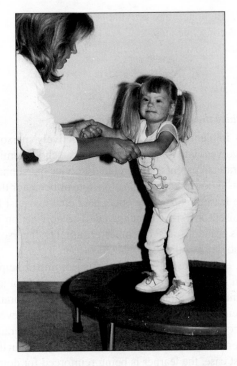

Equipment for the Home Provides Play Opportunity for Child and Parent
Source unknown.

Be Honest

Agreements between teachers and learners must be honored by both. If there is an implicit or explicit arrangement between the teacher and the learner and the teacher does not follow through with the arrangement when the learner has upheld his or her end of the bargain, then the learning conditions will be seriously weakened. It is not uncommon for teachers to inadvertently forget the arrangements that have been made. Therefore, it is important for teachers to have records of arrangements between themselves and learners. Forgetting the preconditions between learner and teacher may have a negative impact on the pupil's learning at a subsequent time.

If the teacher requests that a learner perform a specific task, the teacher must not provide the desirable consequences unless the learner achieves the proper objective. Honest delivery of the agreed-on consequences is similar to praise for the correct behavior. However, praise for the correct

behavior usually connotes a specific short-term task, whereas an agreed-on consequence may involve a contractual arrangement between two parties. Principals and teachers who set policies may achieve positive results with the application of this principle.

Be Positive

The objective should be phrased positively, so that the learner can achieve the stated objective (e.g., "Walk to the end of the balance beam"). An example of a negative statement is "Don't fall off of the balance beam." In the negative instance, the child is avoiding failure, and there can be little value in mastering the desired behavior.

Be Systematic

To make the greatest positive impact on children with disabilities, it is necessary to apply all the learning principles all the time. Inconsistency confuses the learner with regard to the material to be learned and the type of behavior to maintain during class. The consistent use of behavior management strategies enhances a child's ability to learn desirable behaviors. This learning principle is the most difficult one for teachers of children with emotional disturbances to master.

Contingency Contracting

A contract is an agreement, written or verbal, between two or more parties, that stipulates the responsibilities of the parties concerning specific items or activities.[41] Contingency contracting is a method used to individualize instruction to respond to the interests, needs, and abilities of children. When the students satisfactorily complete the conditions of their contracts, they receive something they have identified. Contingency contracts can be used to teach a new behavior, maintain existing behaviors, and decrease inappropriate behaviors. The values of this type of contracting are that (1) the technique can be used with fairly large groups of students, (2) they allow for delay of reinforcement during busy periods, (3) they allow one reinforcer for reinforcing many behaviors, and (4) reinforcers can be given without interruption of teaching the class.

TECHNIQUES TO ENSURE PERSISTENCE OF LEARNING OR CHANGE

Maintenance is perpetuation of a trained behavior after all formal intervention has ceased. To determine whether a trained behavior is being maintained, it can be formally assessed, observational data can be gathered, and/or individuals who interact with the student can be interviewed. The most powerful indication that behavior has really been impacted and is being maintained is the extent to which the behavior has been generalized to other settings.

Maintenance is the degree to which a behavior change is maintained over time. Generalization is the ability to use a learned skill or way of behaving in places other than the instructional setting. The

success of instruction can be measured by the extent to which a learned way of behaving can be used in a variety of practical settings. Such generalization assists with independence and adds to the quality of life for persons with disabilities.

In the past, generalization was an expected, yet unplanned, outcome of instructional programs;[38] however, during the past 25 years generalization has been more systematically planned and evaluated. Studies have documented that generalization of motor skills can be taught successfully. More recently, studies have been conducted to determine the process and variables that control the generalization of all types of behaviors to applied settings. LeBlanc and Matson[21] have developed a social training program that helps preschool children with disabilities generalize behaviors to other social settings. The program uses protocols for modeling, feedback, and time-out from reinforcement. Other instructional packages directed at self-management, self-modeling, self-assessment, discrimination training, and cooperative efforts can be used for physical skill development.[1,25]

Although a number of considerations are a part of the development and application of generalization techniques, two are of paramount importance: (1) the techniques should support the generalization of functional motor skills to nontraining settings, such as recreational environments in the community and the home and (2) the techniques should be reasonably efficient. Efficiency is the use of a skill in an applied setting with a minimum amount of training or assistance to produce the desired results. To ensure the transfer of learning to applied settings, it is critical that specific generalization goals be incorporated into the student with severe disability's educational program.[34]

Morris[28] describes three types of generalization: (1) response maintenance, (2) situation or setting, and (3) response:

1. Response maintenance generalization includes changes that are maintained even after the behavior modification has stopped.
2. Situation or setting generalization includes changes that occur from one environment to another and/or from one person to another.

3. Response generalization includes changes in behavior that was not targeted for intervention.

Generalization Variables

There are two basic forms of generalization in the curriculum content of physical education: (1) generalization of the acquired motor skills and (2) generalization of the cognitive and social dimensions that enable participation with others. Clearly, if the skills of a physical sport (e.g., basketball, soccer, or softball) are acquired but the social skill is inappropriate for participation in culturally acceptable environments in the community, then the person with a disability will not have the opportunity to express the attained skills.[43]

When using generalization procedures, the adapted physical educator should consider the cognitive and social ability levels of the student, the acquired level of proficiency of the target skill, and the features of the natural environment. The cognitive and motivational levels of the individual with disabilities and his or her attitude toward the skill are other dimensions of generalization. Also, it is important to understand the student's attitude toward competition. Some individuals do not enjoy participating in activities in which there are winners and losers. If these individuals participate in competitive sports, they may be motivated by focusing on the importance of their contributions to the team effort rather than on bettering their opponents.[8,23]

Considerations for Generalization

At least two types of environments are associated with the process of generalization. One is the instructional environment, and the other is the natural environment. Instructional environments are settings where the education of students with disabilities is of explicit concern. Natural environments are those settings where the motor skills that are learned in school are actually used (e.g., community environments). Natural environments are those in which individuals without disabilities function and in which individuals with disabilities should be taught

to function. To facilitate generalization from educational to community environments, it is recommended that the teacher (1) develop a management system to assess the generalized effect of the motor skill training program in nontraining environments, (2) determine the effects of training on the motor function of persons with disabilities, (3) analyze the ecological variables (i.e., community situations in which the motor skills will be used), and (4) manipulate environmental variables to facilitate the generalization of the use of the motor skills.[43]

Generalization is an important issue for students with severe disabilities because they typically do not learn motor skills sufficiently to enable participation in natural environments. Some persons with disabilities have difficulty generalizing newly learned motor behaviors to other settings, persons, and stimuli because of their limited motor capabilities. It is desirable to establish a comprehensive repertoire not only of motor behaviors that will permit sufficient immediate opportunities for participation in the community but also of motor skills that can be recombined to permit other opportunities to participate in an expanding number of recreational activities in the natural community. Fostering the ability to generalize across similar events in dissimilar settings is essential. A person can be aided in generalizing to new environments if he or she is taught the cues and correction procedures used in natural settings.

Cues and Correction Procedures

Cues and correction procedures are used to increase the probability that a skill learned in one setting will generalize to a second setting. The procedures range from those that provide maximum assistance to those that offer minimum guidance and those that occur exclusively in instructional environments to those that occur exclusively in natural environments.[9] There are three important considerations in the use of cues and correction procedures for generalization:

1. Know the cues and correction procedures that persons without disabilities typically use

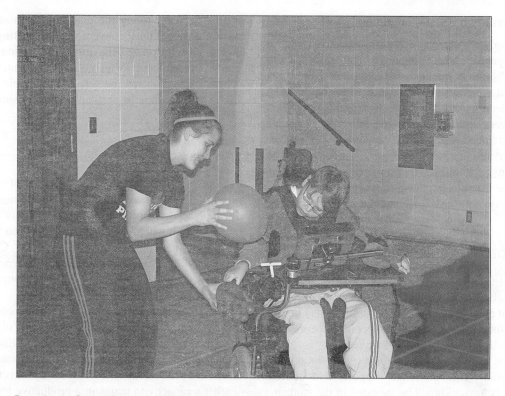

Prompting the Student Ensures Initial Success
Courtesy of Kristi Roth, University of Wisconsin Stevens Point.

when performing a specific motor skill in the natural environment.

2. Know the specific motor response required to perform the particular skill.

3. Know how to use the environmental cues and correction procedures that shape and develop motor responses.

All three components of the instructional process must be fully comprehended, and detailed attention must be given to these three essential aspects of instruction.

Self-Management

Self-management of behavior should be taught to persons with disabilities.[29] The technique requires that the control over behavior be shifted from the teacher or parent to the student. Self-management has been used to teach individuals with disabilities play and social skills, as well as to lessen disruptive behavior.[18,19] The effectiveness of a variety of self-management procedures has been demonstrated in classroom settings. It has been shown that students can regulate their behavior by selecting appropriate goals; by self-instructing; and by self-monitoring, reinforcing, and evaluating responses.[7,15,29] Self-management procedures consist of one or more of the following strategies:

- *Goal setting.* Teaching students to select numerical targets to achieve leads to higher performance than not selecting goals or selecting vague goals.[16,39]

- *Self-instruction.* Teaching individuals to direct their own task performance is critical for independent functioning.

- *Self-evaluation.* Teaching individuals to observe, record, evaluate their performance according to a standard, and reward their own successes promotes ongoing growth and independence.[29]

Learning by Self-Correction

A mode of behaving that contributes to successful independent functioning in the community is learning by self-correction. Adults must learn to think about the effectiveness of their behaviors in order to identify aspects in need of change. Obviously, it is necessary that the individual have the cognitive ability needed to reflect on his or her performance and determine where or how errors occurred. The ability to learn by self-correction varies according to the learner's cognitive capabilities and the complexity of the task being attempted.

VIOLATIONS OF SCHOOL CONDUCT RULES

The 1997 IDEA amendments clearly indicate to what extent students with disabilities may be disciplined. The amendments reemphasize the fact that, if a student's undesirable behavior is related to the child's disability, positive behavioral interventions, strategies, and supports that address that behavior should be included in the student's IEP. However, the student with a disability may be suspended or expelled from the school setting for any infringement of the school's rules of conduct to the same extent as students without disabilities. When a child with a disability has been disciplined by removal from school for more than 10 days, the school must convene an IEP meeting and develop a functional behavioral assessment plan. After developing the plan and the assessment, the school must convene an IEP meeting to determine appropriate behavioral interventions to use with the student. When necessary, an interim alternative setting will be selected to enable the student to continue to participate in the general curriculum.

DISCIPLINE

Teachers report behavior problems as one of their greatest school-related concerns and challenges.[6] Spending classroom time managing students' behavior has a negative impact not only on the teacher but also on student performance.[20] Children exhibiting problem behaviors experience a type of school day that is vastly different from that of their typical peers.[27]

Severe problem behavior, such as aggression and self-injury, may compromise the quality of life for persons with disabilities and others.[26] Disruptive classroom behavior is a major factor in teacher stress and discontent and significantly affects a teacher's capacity to maintain a productive learning environment. Student interactions with teachers as a result of problem behavior command twice the amount of attention than do those of nondisruptive students.[27]

The teacher who uses the assertive effective discipline techniques presented in this chapter can significantly reduce behavior problems and, in so doing, contribute to a positive learning environment.   ✍

SUMMARY

Learning is facilitated and changes in behavior occur when a systematic process is used. New skills and behaviors can be learned and inappropriate behaviors can be diminished when appropriate procedures are followed. First, the behavior to be learned or changed must be identified. Second, intervention strategies and appropriate reinforcers must be selected. Finally, reinforcement must be consistently applied and change in behavior validated. The maintenance of a learned skill or behavior can be verified through reevaluation in the educational or community setting. The true measure of learning is the extent to which the skill or behavior generalizes across several environments and contributes to independent functioning. Students with disabilities who are expelled or suspended from school must be provided a functional assessment and an intervention program that will be implemented in an alternative setting.

REVIEW QUESTIONS

1. What techniques can be applied to maximize student achievement in motor skill development?
2. What are some positive teacher techniques that can be used to adapt instruction to the needs of the learner?
3. Name and describe some behavioral techniques for facilitating the development of positive behavior.
4. What are some techniques that can be used to manage disruptive classroom behavior?
5. List some types of reinforcers.
6. What are some of the characteristics of a teacher that can maximize the development of motor and social skills for individuals with disabilities?
7. What is generalization, and how does it apply to independent recreational sport and physical activity in the community?
8. What are some principles that may guide the physical educator to generalize the physical education activities learned in a class setting to activity outside class?
9. Under what circumstance can a student with a disability be expelled or suspended from school?

STUDENT ACTIVITIES

1. Working in small groups, identify three ways to reduce Adam's talking and keep him focused in class.
2. Make a list of class rules, other than those suggested in this chapter, that would minimize disruptive behavior in a physical education class.
3. Working in small groups, describe a scenario of a student who needs a behavioral intervention plan. Then exchange the scenarios, and assign each group the responsibility of developing an intervention plan that could be used to correct/improve the performance of the student described in the scenario.
4. Conduct an ecological assessment of the community to determine what activities should be included in physical education programs for individuals with disabilities in your community.

REFERENCES

1. Berg WK et al.: A demonstration of generalization of performance across settings, materials, and motor responses with profound mental retardation, *Behav Modif* 19:119–143, 1995.
2. Bicard DF: Using classroom rules to construct behavior, *Middle School J* 31(5):37–45, 2000.
3. Canter L, Canter M: *Assertive discipline: Positive behavior management in today's classroom* (3rd ed.). Los Angeles, Lee Canter and Associates, 2002.
4. Collier D, Reid G: Preventing and coping with difficult behaviors, *Palaestra* 19(3):36–45, 2003.
5. Cowart J: Managing student misbehavior in adapted physical education by good teaching practices, *Palaestra* 16(1):40–45, 2000.
6. Darling-Hammond L: Keeping good teachers: Why it matters what leaders can do, *Educ Leadership* 60(8):6–13, 2003.
7. Ellis DN, Cress PJ, Spellman CR: Training students with mental retardation to self-pace while exercising, *APAQ* 10:104–124, 1993.
8. Ellis ES: The role of motivation and pedagogy on the generalization of cognitive training by the mildly handicapped, *J Learning Disabil* 19:66–70, 1986.
9. Falvey MA: *Community-based curriculum: Instructional strategies for students with severe handicaps.* Baltimore, MD, Paul H. Brookes, 1986.

10. Falvey M, Gage S, Eshilan L: Secondary curriculum and instruction. In Falvey M, editor: *Inclusive and heterogeneous schools: Assessment, curriculum and instruction.* Baltimore, MD, Paul H. Brookes, 1995.

11. Haring N, editor: *Developing effective individualized programs for severely handicapped children and youth.* Washington, DC, U.S. Office of Education, Bureau of Education for the Handicapped, 1977.

12. Helmsmetter E, Peck C, Giangreco M: Outcomes of interactions with peers with moderate or severe disabilities: A statewide survey of high school students, *J of Assoc for Persons with Severe Handicaps* 19:180–286, 1994.

13. Hester P, Gable RA, Manning M: A positive learning environment approach to middle school, *Childhood Education* 79(3):130–136, 2003.

14. Homme L: *How to use contingency contracting in the classroom.* Champaign, IL, Research Press, 1970.

15. Hughes CA, Korinck L, Gorman J: Self-management for students with mental retardation in public school settings: A research review, *Educ Train Ment Retard* 26:271–291, 1991.

16. Kahle AL, Kelley JL: Children's homework problems: A comparison of goal setting and parent training, *Behav Ther* 25:275–290, 1994.

17. Kennedy CH: Toward a socially valid understanding of problem behavior, *Education and Treatment of Children* 25(1):142–153, 2002.

18. Kohler FW et al.: Promoting positive supportive interactions between preschoolers: An analysis of group oriented contingencies, *J Early Intervention* 14:327–341, 1990.

19. Kohler FW et al.: Using group-oriented contingency to increase social interactions between children with autism and their peers, *Behav Modif* 19:10–32, 1995.

20. Lambert MC, Cartledge G, Heward WL, Lo YY: Effects of response cards on disruptive behavior and academic responding during math lesson by fourth-grade urban students, *J of Positive Beh Interv* 8(2):88–99, 2006.

21. Leblanc LA, Matson JL: A social skills training program for preschoolers with developmental delays, *Behav Modif* 19:234–246, 1995.

22. Lewis RB, Doorlag DH: *Teaching special students in the mainstream.* Columbus, OH, Charles E. Merrill, 1983.

23. Licht BC, Kistner JA: Motivational problems of learning-disabled children: Individual differences and their implications for treatment. In Torgesen JK, Wong BYL, editors: *Psychological and educational perspectives on learning disabilities.* New York, Academic Press, 1986.

24. Longwill AW, Kleinert HL: The unexpected benefits of high school peer tutoring, *Teach Except Child* March/April:60–65, 1998.

25. Lonnecker C et al.: Video self-monitoring and cooperative classroom behavior in children with learning and behavior problems: Training and generalization effects, *Behav Disord* 20:24–34, 1994.

26. McLaughlin DM, Carr EG: Quality of rapport as a setting event for problem behavior, *J of Positive Behav Interv* 7(2):68–91, 2005.

27. Morgan PL: Increasing task engagement using preference or choice making, *Remed Spec Educ* 27(3):176–187, 2006.

28. Morris RJ: *Behavior modification with exceptional children.* Glenview, IL, Scott Foresman, 1985.

29. Nelson RJ, Smith DJ, Colvin G: The effects of a peer-mediated self-evaluation procedure on the recess behavior of students with behavior problems, *Remed Spec Educ* 16:117–126, 1995.

30. Nelson RJ et al.: A review of self-management outcome research conducted with students who exhibit behavioral disorders, *Behav Disord* 16:169–179, 1991.

31. *Neosho School District v. Clark* (8th circuit district court of appeals), 2003.

32. Pierangelo RA: *A survival kit for the special education teacher.* West Nyack, NY, Center for Applied Research in Education, 1994.

33. Redl F: Managing surface behavior of children in school. In Long HJ, editor: *Conflict in the classroom.* Belmont, CA, Wadsworth, 1965.

34. Sailor W, Guess D: *Severely handicapped students: An instructional design.* Boston, Houghton Mifflin, 1983.

35. Silverstein R: *A user's guide to the 1999 IDEA regulations.* Washington, DC, Center for the Study and Advancement of Disability Policy, George Washington University School of Public Health and Health Services, 1999.

36. Spodek B, Saracho ON: *Dealing with individual differences in the early childhood classroom.* New York, Longman, 1994.

37. Staub D, Hunt P: The effects of social interaction training on high school peer tutors of school mates with severe disabilities, *Except Child* 60:41–57, 1993.

38. Stokes TF, Baer DM: An implicit technology of generalization, *J Appl Behav Anal* 10:349–367, 1977.

39. Swain A, Jones G: Effects of goal-setting interventions on selected basketball skills: A single subject design, *Res Q Exerc Sport* 66:51–63, 1995.

40. U.S. Office of Special Education Programs: *Research connections in special education.* Washington, DC, Center for effective collaboration and practice, 1997.

41. Walker JE, Shea TM: *Behavior management: A practical approach for educators.* Columbus, OH, Charles E. Merrill, 1999.

42. Warger, Eavy & Associates: *Prevention strategies that work.* Wager, Eavy & Associates Reston, VA, 1999.

43. Warren SF et al.: Assessment and facilitation of language generalization. In Sailor W, Wilcox B, Brown L, editors: *Methods of instruction for severely handicapped students.* Baltimore, MD, Paul H. Brookes, 1985.

SUGGESTED READINGS

Farmer TW, Goforth JB, Hives J, Aaron A, Jackson F, Sgammato A: Competence enhancement behavior management, *Preventing School Failure* 50(3):39–44, 2006.

Lavay, B, French R, Henderson HL: *Positive behavior management in physical activity settings,* 2nd ed. Champaign, IL, Human Kinetics, 2006.

Stopka C: *Teacher's survival guide: Adaptations to optimize the inclusions of students of all ages with disabilities in your program,* www.pecentral.org, 2006.

RECOMMENDED WEB SITES

Please keep in mind that these Web sites are being recommended in the winter of 2007. As Web sites often change, they may have moved, been reconfigured, or eliminated.

Fitzsimmons, M: *Functional behavioral assessment and behavior intervention plans,* ERIC/OSEP Digest E571, Reston, VA, 1998, Eric Clearinghouse on Disabilities and Gifted Education http://ericec.org

National Information Center for Children and Youth with Disabilities, *Positive behavioral support:*

A bibliography for schools, Washington, DC, 1997 www.nichcy.org

PE Central: *Creating a positive learning environment* http://pecentral.org/climate

Rehabilitation Research Training Center on Positive Behavioral Support: *Facilitator's guide: Positive behavioral support* http://rrtcpbs.fmhi.usf.edu

RECOMMENDED VIDEOS

Insight Media
2162 Broadway
New York, NY 10024-0621
1-800-233-9910
www.insight-media.com
1-2-3 Magic: *Managing Difficult Behavior in Children*
17AN4392/DVD/2001/120 min/$109.00

Managing Non-compliance: Effective Strategies for K–12 teachers
UAN4473/DVD/2005/20 min/$159.00

The Behavior Education Program: A Check-in, Check-out Intervention
TAN4586/DVD/2005/25 min/$119.00

Children and Youth at Risk

Today, more than any other time in our history, an increasing number of children are entering our schools with significant physical, social, and psychological disadvantages. Many arrive in this world addicted to drugs and/or malnourished; spend their first few years without having their basic physical, safety, and affection needs addressed; and have little exposure to activities beyond their home and culture. Their at-risk status continues to escalate when they enter school because they lack adequate skills, knowledge, and resources to benefit fully from what education has to offer. Fortunately, a quality physical education program has the potential to address and ameliorate the majority of these delays using powerful experiential strategies not available to the classroom teacher. In the gymnasium setting, fun activities are used to promote physical, motor, social, and intellectual development; physical educators provide opportunities for children to build self-esteem by mastering their bodies in their own time at their own speed; physical educators help them learn to take responsibility for their own actions by allowing them to establish and honor rules that apply equally to everyone; and physical educators give them the opportunity to experience the deep satisfaction that comes from working with others by using cooperative learning initiatives. The challenges these children represent to themselves and society will be addressed in this part, as will the programmatic strategies the physical educator can use to help all children grow and reach their full potential.

CHAPTER

8

Physical Fitness and Sport Conditioning

■ O B J E C T I V E S

Identify five of the national standards for physical education.

Cite at least five values to persons with disabilities of participating in a regular physical activity program.

Identify the potential dangers of a sedentary lifestyle.

Identify the unique problems that persons who are undernourished or overweight present for the physical educator.

Identify at least three types of physical fitness tests.

Construct a circuit training program that addresses a wide range of physical fitness levels.

Identify three ways to involve students' families in an active lifestyle.

Compare and contrast a general and a specific sports conditioning program.

Proper Training Yields Successful Performance

Courtesy of Jason Wening. Gold Medal winner 400M Free (World Record) IPC World Swimming Championships, New Zealand, 1998.

An issue that is gaining greater attention at federal and state levels is the dramatic increase in obesity, which is associated with a host of chronic health conditions that consume half of the medical expenditures in the United States. Adapted physical educators have a role to play in the prevention and amelioration of obesity with children and youth in special education. This chapter places emphasis on obesity and addresses (1) the relationship among food insecurity, proper diet, exercise, and obesity and (2) increased opportunities for sport competition for children and youth with disabilites.

CASE STUDY

Adam

APPLICATION TASK

Review Adam's test results (see Chapter 3) to determine what physical fitness deficiencies he demonstrated. As you read this chapter, identify potential activities other than calisthenics that you could build into your physical education program that Adam and his classmates would enjoy while in school and after school. What are some ways you could involve Adam's parents in his physical activity program?

One of the objectives of physical educators is to assist students in developing an activity repertoire that will promote life-long physical activity. Individuals who are physically fit are healthier, are able to perform motor skills competently, and are able to perform daily living activities without undue fatigue. During a child's early years, activity is an intregral part of living—most young children love to move. However, the biological drive for physical activity declines as we grow, and extrinsic factors affecting activity levels become more important motivators. This reliance on extrinsic motivation peaks in adolescence, when the need for peer acceptance, sexual attractiveness, self-concept, and physical capabilities become prominent influences on whether an individual participates in regular physical activity.[45] Obviously, the individual who is physically gifted will use sports as a primary source for attention getting. Those individuals less gifted will turn to other activities. Those less gifted movers present the greatest challenge to the physical educator. Without assistance, these are the persons who are at risk for becoming sedentary adults.

The Centers for Disease Control and Prevention reports that being overweight is one of the nation's serious health problems. One in five American adults engages in a high level of overall physical activity and about one in four American adults engages in little or no regular physical activity.[64] Persons with disabilities, in general, are less physically active than persons without disabilities. Participation in regular physical activity promotes health and reduces the risk of developing many debilitating conditions.

Participation in a regular physical activity program is as important, if not more important, for persons with disabilities. The lack of physical development and low vitality of persons with disabilities constitute a major concern of physical education. Inadequate physical activity may be a precursor of a host of chronic health disorders. Chronically ill persons with debilitating conditions are particularly prone to poor physical vitality and development. Persons with cardiorespiratory conditions, such as chronic bronchitis and various heart defects, also show a tendency toward poor physical fitness. Increasing numbers of children who are medically fragile are being educated in the public schools. Children with disabilities and children without disabilities often lack the physical and motor abilities that are prerequisite to successful participation in sports and the activities of daily living. It is of primary importance that the physical educator take responsibility for identifying the physical fitness needs of all students and for designing interesting, fun, and challenging programs that will motivate students to adopt a healthy, active lifestyle. This chapter includes a discussion of physical fitness and special problems demonstrated by persons who are undernourished, obese, visually impaired, and/or mentally and physically impaired. To assist the coach who becomes involved with sport programs, the chapter also discusses sport conditioning.

DEFINITION OF PHYSICAL FITNESS

The American Alliance for Health, Physical Education, Recreation and Dance (AAHPERD) describes physical fitness "as a physical state of well-being that allows people to perform daily activities with vigor, reduce their risk of health problems related to lack of exercise, and establish a fitness base for participation in a variety of activities."[1] In 1995 the National Association for Sport and Physical

Education (NASPE), a member of AAHPERD, developed national standards for physical education. Those standards were presented in Chapter 1.

Developing and maintaining an appropriate level of physical fitness is critical for persons with disabilities because, frequently, the disabling condition itself interferes with the ability to move efficiently. The problem is compounded when physical fitness levels are not adequate, because appropriate levels of muscular strength, joint flexibility, muscular endurance, and cardiovascular endurance are requisite for movement efficiency. A sedentary lifestyle that results from inadequate levels of fitness can lead to chronic disorders that diminish health and limit mobility, ability to work, and other major life functions. The types of health problems that can result include obesity, hypertension, low back pain, osteoporosis, coronary heart disease, diabetes, colon cancer, anxiety and depression, and premature death.[28]

The primary value of physical activity for persons with disabilities is that it increases the number of years of quality living.[28,44] However, there are additional values for persons with disabilities, including (1) prevention of secondary disabling conditions, (2) independent living, (3) physical fitness, (4) biological measures, and (5) general health and quality of life. A list of the benefits of physical activity in each of these areas follows.

Prevention of Secondary Disabling Conditions
- Decreases the risk of diabetes[47]
- Decreases the risk of depression and anxiety[10,47]
- Prevents hypertension[5,57]
- Reduces the risk of colon cancer[30]
- Lessens backaches[7]
- Enhances insulin production in persons who have diabetes[7]
- Prevents or delays the onset of osteoporosis[7]

Independent Living
- Improves functional independence[22,52]
- Increases pain-free weight-bearing capacity[55]
- Reduces medical expenditures[54]
- Reduces potential falls of persons with balance and ambulatory problems[34]
- Contributes to mobility[17]

Physical Fitness
- Allows maximal muscle power[8]
- Improves aerobic fitness[33,61]
- Prevents physical reconditioning[48]
- Increases and maintains muscular strength and endurance and contributes to mobility[28,44]
- Improves hand function, reaction time, tapping speed, and coordination[26]
- Enables a person with severe disabilities to lift the head, roll over, and maintain a sitting position[35]

Biological Measures
- Improves efficiency in ventilatory capacity[37]
- Improves stroke volume[49]
- Diminishes fluid retention in varicose veins[7]

General Health and Quality of Life
- Improves psychosocial health[38]
- Reduces depression[10]
- Improves sleep patterns[7]
- Facilitates weight reduction[7]
- Enhances postural stability[17]
- Enables a person with moderate to mild disabilities to engage in leisure-time activities in the community

Thus, participating in activities to improve physical fitness enhances a person's attitude about life, enhances ability to perform the activities of daily living, enhances sport and leisure skills, improves and maintains health, and reduces the chances of developing secondary disabling conditions.

Once minimum levels of physical fitness are achieved, development and use of motor fitness can contribute to additional physical fitness development. That is, once an individual begins to use agility, balance, and coordination in daily living activities, as well as in games and sports, physical fitness levels continue to rise and health continues to improve.

PHYSICAL ACTIVITY IN THE UNITED STATES

Although the United States appears to be having a fitness boom, there is evidence that the general population is not as active as one would believe.

Less than 50 percent of the adults in the United States participate in the recommended amount of physical activity each week. Twenty-five percent report no weekly physical activity.[64] Other alarming facts about U.S. citizens that have recently been reported are

- The rates of obesity have doubled for preschool children and tripled for adolescents in the past 25 years.[68]
- In 2004 approximately 60 percent of obese children between 5 and 10 years of age had at least one cardiovascular disease risk factor and 25 percent had two or more.[62]
- Seventeen percent of children and youth 10 to 17 years of age are overweight or obese.[62]

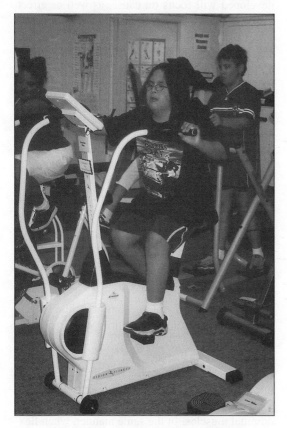

Activities to Promote Cardiovascular Endurance Also Help Control Weight

Courtesy of Donna Louctro, Mesa, Arizona, Public Schools.

- Overweight adolescents have up to an 80 percent chance of becoming obese adults.[68]
- Sixty-six percent of adults are overweight and 32 percent of adults are obese.[63]

Furthermore, there is evidence that women and persons of minorities and of less education are at considerable health risk because they are less likely than Caucasian males to participate in leisure-time physical activity.[47] Major cardiovascular diseases account for almost 40 percent of the leading causes of death in this country.[43] Because conditions that contribute to cardiovascular disease begin in childhood, there is renewed concern about the activity level of children. This concern is justified because (1) the nation's schoolchildren have become less active and fatter during the last 25 years; (2) if this trend continues, these children will be at greater risk for illness when they become adults; and (3) less than one-half (46 percent) of physical education teachers have as their major goal the improvement of the physical fitness of students.[23] It is apparent that children in the United States are not as physically fit as experts believe they should be, and it is evident that youth with disabilities are less fit than their peers without disabilities. The No Child Left Behind initiative, which impacts 85 percent of the children and youth with disabilities who are in inclusive classroom settings, focuses on academic achievement. Fortunately, the Physical Education Progress Act, which was added to the No Child Left Behind Act, provides federal funds to local schools to promote physical activity.[39] However, funding for this program must be approved each year by the legislature.

All physical fitness test results that have been normed using children and youth with disabilities have shown lower physical fitness levels than results normed using children who lack disabilities.[13,53,59] Individuals with moderate intellectual disabilities do more poorly on cardiorespiratory function tests than do those without mild intellectual disabilities.[13] Males and females between the ages of 6 and 18 years who have intellectual disabilities are heavier than individuals the same age who do not have an intellectual disability.[13] Individuals between the ages of 10 and 17 years who have visual impairments and those with spinal neuromuscular conditions have higher percentages of body fat than those the same age with no disabilities.[59] Males and females between the ages of 10 and 17 who have visual impairments,[59] moderate intellectual disabilities, or Down syndrome[13] have less flexibility (sit-and-reach test) than youth without those disabilities. An in-depth study on the health status of individuals with intellectual disabilities was conducted by Special Olympics International. In general, it was reported that the more severe the intellectual disability, the poorer the health status.[21] It is evident that physical educators who serve children and youth with disabilities must address the physical fitness deficiencies these youngsters demonstrate.

CAUSES OF POOR PHYSICAL FITNESS

Several factors contribute to poor physical fitness, including health status, developmental delays, lack of recreational opportunity, lack of confidence by the child or the caregiver, and poorly designed physical education programs. Examples of health status problems include obesity; asthma and other chronic respiratory problems; susceptibility to infectious diseases, including the common cold; poor nutrition; inadequate sleep; motor limitations, such as paralysis, muscular dystrophy, and cerebral palsy;[4] cardiopulmonary or metabolic limitations, including advanced cyanotic heart disease, cystic fibrosis, scoliosis, and undernutrition;[4] minority status; low income;[47] sensory and motor impairment in the lower limbs;[31] use of psychoactive medications; risk-taking behavior;[34] mobility impairments;[31] and balance or gait abnormalities.[32]

Developmental delays that can impact physical fitness levels include abnormal reflex development, delayed vestibular function, poor vision, delayed cross-lateral integration, inadequate spatial awareness, poor body image, and any other factor that limits the ability to move efficiently. Lack of opportunities to participate in physical fitness activities results from environmental barriers, such as limited access to community, group, or private exercise facilities;[10] insufficient programs as a result of inadequate testing procedures; lack of instructor knowledge; and limited curriculum offerings in the school system.[60]

Caregivers, including parents, medical personnel, and educators, sometimes encourage children to "take it easy" because they fear the children will overdo or hurt themselves during activity participation.[4] Also, some individuals with disabilities may be exceptionally self-conscious, and they may lack self-confidence. Their fear of failure may result in avoidance of both instructional and extracurricular physical activity.[41] It is important to determine why a person's fitness is low (i.e., why the person is avoiding physical activity), so that the physical fitness program that is developed will focus on cause, as well as effect.

The quality of the physical education program being offered in the school setting is critical to students with and without disabilities. Poorly managed physical education programs result in 60 percent of the class time being spent standing or sitting, and only 8 percent of the time devoted to vigorous physical activity.[18] Well-designed physical education programs offer a variety of activities and keep the students moving and motivated to participate.

The physical educator is the ideal person to address the deterrents to exercise; however, before a program can be implemented, the student's present level of performance must be ascertained. With those results in hand, a physical activity program can be established to benefit the student.

EVALUATING PHYSICAL FITNESS

The full evaluation of the physical fitness of a child with a disability requires comprehensive assessment of ability areas identified through research (see Chapter 3). One does not just measure strength as a single entity. Rather, one measures the strength of specific muscle groups, such as the knee extensors, elbow flexors, or abdominal muscles. In the same manner, when flexibility is evaluated, it is necessary to determine range of motion at specific joints in the body. A severe loss of strength in any muscle group or limited range of motion in any joint could seriously affect the attainment of specific daily living or sport skills. Thus, a full evaluation of physical education needs would involve assessing the strength of major muscle groups, range of motion of many joints, and factors that affect cardiovascular efficiency.

It should be obvious that there is seldom enough time or personnel in a school system to assess every child comprehensively. Therefore, the physical educator usually samples only some physical and motor fitness components. Which components are measured is usually determined in one of two ways. Either a specific test (e.g., Physical Best and Individuals with Disabilities)[53] is administered or test items that measure specific aspects of a given daily living skill or motor skill are selected and administered.

Remarkable Hippocampe Wheelchairs, Developed by Spokes in Motion, Make It Possible for Boys to Play in the Ocean

Courtesy of Spokes in Motion.

The ultimate purpose of preevaluation in the areas of physical fitness is to determine which activities will meet the unique needs of the child with disabilities. The procedures to be used for determining the needs in the areas of physical fitness are as follows:

1. Identify motor skills to be taught in the physical education program that contribute to physical fitness and can be expressed as recreational skills and activities of daily living for independence in the community.
2. Select physical fitness areas associated with the skills needed for independent living in the community.
3. Identify levels of physical fitness necessary for independent recreation and activities of daily living in the community.
4. Test for present levels of educational performance in the physical fitness domain.
5. Compare the child's performance with normative community standards to determine whether there is sufficient discrepancy to indicate an educational need.
6. If it is determined that there are physical fitness needs, establish long-range goals and short-term objectives that lead to those goals.

There are at least four orientations to physical fitness testing. One type is "health-related fitness," which refers to the components of physiological functioning that are believed to offer protection against such degenerative diseases as obesity, disk degeneration, and coronary heart disease.[25] A second type includes tests designed to develop aspects of physical fitness, such as optimal strength, endurance, and flexibility, to be used in sport activities. A third orientation, which is preferred by Evans and Meyer[14] for individuals with disabilities, is a function-specific type of physical fitness that relates to independent functioning in the community. The American College of Sports Medicine recommends a fourth type of testing, problem-oriented exercise management.[36] Problem-oriented exercise management involves five steps: (1) collection of subjective data, (2) collection of objective data, (3) assessment and generation of a problem list,

(4) formulation of a diagnostic or therapeutic plan, and (5) periodic reassessment.[36]

Health-related tests include measures of cardiovascular/cardiorespiratory endurance, abdominal strength, percentage of body fat, and flexibility. The performance of children and youth with disabilities has been measured using items included in the Health-Related Physical Fitness Test and the Prudential FITNESSGRAM. These types of tests are meaningful when individuals with mild or moderate cognitive and physical disabilities are being evaluated. AAHPERD has incorporated those test items into its Physical Best and Individuals with Disabilities evaluation (see Chapter 3). Winnick and Short's[59] Brockport Physical Fitness Test is an excellent criterion-referenced health-related test that can be used with children and youth with different types of disabilities. Nonambulatory severely and profoundly involved students would benefit from the test items and curriculum presented in Mobility Opportunities Via Education (MOVE) (see Chapter 3).

Individuals with severe disabilities who are ambulatory require functional physical fitness tests that relate specifically to what an individual needs to meet the daily demands of the environment. Examples of such test items are walking to develop the endurance to walk to and from one's home from designated areas in the neighborhood, developing sufficient balance to remedy a wide shuffling gait, and performing specific heel-cord stretching exercises to lengthen tight heel cords, so that the entire foot will strike the ground when walking. The type of fitness test selected depends on the goals and objectives of the physical education program. Inactive persons frequently cannot sustain exercise for more than 5 minutes. Therefore, the physical educator must use good judgment when selecting test items. For the sedentary person, heart rate after a 6-minute or 12-minute walk may be the best indicator of cardiovascular endurance.

PROGRAMMING FOR PHYSICAL FITNESS

Physical fitness encompasses muscular strength and endurance, flexibility, body composition, and cardiovascular endurance. Each of these factors must be addressed in the training program. When physical fitness tests have been conducted, the information for the tests can be used for programmatic purposes. If it is the intent to improve physical fitness through programs, then the content of the physical fitness program should be aligned with specific components of the physical fitness test.

Muscular Strength

Muscular strength is the ability to contract a muscle against resistance. Types of contraction include

- Concentric. Muscle tension is greater than the amount of applied resistance, so the muscle shortens and movement occurs.
- Eccentric. Resistance is greater than the muscle tension, so the muscle lengthens without relaxing.
- Isotonic. Movement occurs but the tension in the muscle remains the same.
- Isokinetic (motion). The speed of the muscle contraction is controlled throughout the range of motion of the joint.
- Isometric (static). Muscle tension equals the amount of applied resistance, so no movement occurs.

Muscular strength can be improved by using the overload principle. The overload principle is applied by gradually increasing the resistance (load or weight) used over time (days or months). Most workouts include isotonic, isokinetic, or isometric exercises. Isotonic exercises use progressive resistance with free weights or Nautilus or Universal weight machines. When isotonic exercises are being performed, the greatest resistance is during the start or finish of the movement. Isokinetic exercises provide resistance throughout the entire range of motion. Isokinetic exercise machines include the Cybex and Orthotron. When isometric exercises are being performed, the resistance is so great that the contracting muscles do not move.[43] The physical educator is cautioned to be sure to include instruction about proper breathing during both isotonic and isometric exercises. The person involved in exercise should be instructed to breathe out while executing an exercise such as a sit-up or a bar press and to breathe in when returning to the starting position.

Muscular Endurance

Muscular endurance is the ability to continue to contract a muscle against resistance. Muscular endurance is developed by gradually increasing the number of repetitions completed during an exercise period.

Flexibility

Flexibility is the range of motion possible at any given joint. Flexibility can be improved through the use of static stretching, which is accomplished by slowly lengthening a muscle group that surrounds a joint and then holding the extended position for 30 to 60 seconds.

Body Composition

Body composition refers to the muscle, bone, fat, and other elements in the body.[43] Usually in a discussion of physical fitness, the term is used to express the percentage of body fat in comparison with lean tissue. Overweight and obese individuals have high percentages of body fat. There is controversy as to what percentage of body fat is most desirable; however, most fitness experts agree that levels less than 30 percent are healthiest.

Cardiovascular Endurance

Cardiovascular endurance is the ability of the heart and vessels to process and transport oxygen from the lungs to muscle cells for use. The greater the cardiovascular endurance, the longer a person is able to continue exercising. Cardiovascular

Peer Tutors Help Students with Moderate Intellectual Disabilities Perform Stability Ball Exercises
Courtesy of Donna Louctro, Mesa, Arizona, Public Schools.

endurance can be improved by persisting at activities that increase the heart rate to between 60 and 90 percent of maximum.

PRINCIPLES OF TRAINING

In 1990 the American College of Sports Medicine (ACSM) made recommendations in the following five areas for achieving and maintaining physical fitness:

1. *Mode of activity.* It is recommended that any continuous physical activity that uses large-muscle groups and that can be rhythmic and aerobic be used.[43] Activities such as walking, running, inline skating, hiking, rowing, stair climbing, swimming, dancing, and cycling are suggested.

2. *Frequency of training.* Frequency of training is the number of times per week a person should exercise. Rest periods are interspersed between training sessions to permit the body to recover.[15] The surgeon general's report on physical activity and health recommends that people of all ages include a minimum of 30 minutes of physical activity of moderate intensity most, if not all, days of the week.[66]

3. *Intensity of training.* Intensity is the magnitude (percentage of one's capacity) of exercise during one exercise session. Usually, the higher the intensity, the greater the benefit from the activity. In aerobic activity, the faster the pace, the greater the intensity. In resistance training, the heavier the weight, the greater the intensity.[27] Individuals with disabilities who have been sedentary should begin their exercise program with a short duration of moderate intensity and gradually increase the duration or intensity until the preset goal is reached.[66] Low to moderate intensity will provide these advantages: (1) less chance of cardiovascular problems, (2) possibly fewer injuries, and (3) a greater probability that the individuals will continue their exercise programs after formal instruction.

4. *Duration of training.* Duration is the length of time a person exercises at a given time.

Duration of exercise applies primarily to cardiorespiratory endurance development. The surgeon general recommends setting a goal of 30 minutes of sustained activity.[66] High-intensity activities (80 to 90 percent of maximum heart rate) require shorter periods of time; activities that generate a lower level of intensity (less than 70 percent of maximum heart rate) require longer periods of time. The duration time should include at least a 10-minute warm-up period and a 5- to 10-minute cool-down period that includes stretching and reduced exertion exercise (e.g., walking more slowly). When one is working with students who have disabilities, it is better to begin with a shorter duration of less intense activity and gradually work toward lengthening the time and intensity of the activity. There is some evidence that cardiorespiratory fitness gains are similar when persons engage in several short sessions of activity (e.g., 10 minutes) as when they participate in a 30-minute session.[66]

5. *Resistance training.* The goals of resistance training are to improve muscular tone or overall muscular strength and/or endurance. The intensity of exercise will vary, depending on the condition of the individual; however, in general, to develop and maintain a healthy body composition, it is recommended that moderate-intensity strength training be used.[20] The workout should begin with 2 or 3 repetitions initially and eventually build to 3 sets of 8 to 12 repetitions 3 times weekly. Isotonic or isokinetic exercises of major muscle groups should be included. See Table 8-4 later in the chapter for recommended programs to build muscular endurance, muscle tone, or strength. The number of times the weight is moved depends on the repetition continuum selected. Once a student can repeat the exercise 8 times in a row with ease, the number of sets should be increased by 1. As the amount of resistance is increased, the number of repetitions is decreased and then

The Kili-Kart Is an Off-Road All-Terrain Cart to Provide Persons with Physical Disabilities Access to Outdoor Activities

Courtesy of Clark James Mishler Photography for Disability Options, Inc. Palmer, AR.

gradually increased. Rest ranging from 30 seconds to 5 minutes should always occur between the sets.

DEVELOPING TRAINING PROGRAMS

Resistance training is well established as an effective method for developing musculoskeletal strength. Major health organizations, including the American College of Sports Medicine,[3] the American Heart Association,[2] and the surgeon general,[66] recommend strength training to improve strength, endurance, and health and have developed resistance exercise guidelines for health promotion. Their recommendations are 1 set of 8 to 12 repetitions of 8 to 10 exercises 2 or 3 times per week for persons under 50 years of age.

Fitness instruction for students with disabilities should be conducted in conformance with the individual education program (IEP). This means that there should be measurable, observable objectives and that present levels of educational performance should be determined for each student when the activity program is begun. To accommodate the changing demands of the ability level of each learner, the following principles are suggested:

1. *Individual differences.* Every student's IEP should be based on specific assessment data that indicate the unique needs for alleviating deficits in prerequisites for living and leisure physical activity that contribute to health, worthy use of recreational time, and self-sufficiency.

2. *Overload/shaping principle.* Increases in strength and endurance result from small increments of workload greater than the present ability. Overload can be achieved in the following ways:

   a. Increase the number of repetitions or sets.
   b. Increase the distance covered.
   c. Increase the speed with which the exercise is executed.
   d. Increase the number of minutes of continuous effort.
   e. Decrease the rest interval between active sessions.
   f. Implement any combination of the above.

3. *Maintenance or development of physical fitness.* Training sessions can be used to maintain or develop physical fitness. The data on the performance levels of training will indicate whether the training results maintain or develop physical fitness levels.

4. *Physical fitness for a purpose.* Values gained from exercises should be relevant to the development of functional skills and/or health benefits. Exercises are highly specific; they need to be done at intensity levels commensurate with the ability of the student.

5. *Active/voluntary movement.* Benefits are greatest when the exercise is active (done by the student) rather than passive (done by the therapist or teacher). When the student performs the activity, it is possible to provide behavioral measurement and apply learning principles from research and demonstration.

6. *Recovery/cool-down.* Students should not lie or sit down immediately after high-intensity exercise. This tends to subvert return of blood to the heart and cause dizziness. Cool-down should entail continued slow walking or mild activity.

7. *Warm-up.* At least 10 minutes of warm-up exercises using movements specific to training should precede high-intensity exercise sessions or competitive games. The warm-up is particularly important for persons with chronic respiratory problems or cardiovascular conditions. Warm-ups should emphasize stretching exercises that facilitate range of motion (flexibility) rather than ballistic (bouncing) exercises.

Examples of ways to write behavioral physical fitness goals are provided in Table 8-1.

Contraindications

Physical educators should know what exercises and activities are contraindicated for each individual. Lasko-McCarthey and Knopf[29] recommend avoiding the following movements during exercises:

- Head circles that involve circumduction/hyperextension of the cervical spine
- Trunk circling that involves flexing the spine from a standing position with the legs straight
- Shoulder stands
- Hyperextension of the spine from a prone (face-down) position
- Standing toe touches with straight legs
- Bilateral straight-leg raises
- Sit-ups with feet held and hands behind head
- Sit-ups with straight legs
- Trunk twists from a standing position
- Deep knee bends (squats)
- Bench press performed with the feet on the floor
- Hip flexor stretches from a prone or kneeling position
- Hurdle stretches
- Prone flies from a standing position
- Military presses with head extended (dorsiflexed)
- Isometric exercises for individuals over age 40 or those with a history of cardiovascular disease
- Immediate rest after intense exercise

In addition, the medical records of individuals with disabilities should always be reviewed to determine whether specific exercises and activities have been identified as contraindicated by medical personnel.

Table 8-1	Behavioral Statements for Development of Physical Fitness

Many physical fitness tasks are measurable. Usually, if measure can be incorporated into a task, performance difficulty can be prescribed for the individual learner. The following are statements that involve physical and motor tasks requiring specifications of measurement to be ascribed to the tasks. Many children with disabilities will be able to participate in these tasks at their ability level if objectives are sequenced.

1. Walk a specified distance at a heart rate of 120 beats per minute.
2. Jog and walk alternately 50 steps for a specified distance.
3. Run in place, lifting the foot a specified distance from the floor a specified number of times for a specified period of time.
4. Run in place 100 steps in a specified amount of time.
5. Run a specified distance in a specified period of time.
6. Perform a modified push-up a specified number of times.
7. Perform a modified chin-up a specified number of times.
8. Climb a rope a specified distance in a specified amount of time.
9. Perform toe raises with a specified amount of weight a specified number of repetitions.
10. Perform a sit-up (modified if necessary) a specified number of repetitions; sit-up difficulty can be modified by performance on an incline, where gravity assists with the sit-up.
11. Perform a specified number of dips on the parallel bars (lower and raise the body by straightening and bending the arms) with a specified amount of weight attached to a belt; if one dip cannot be done, reduce the range of motion of the dip.

12. Perform arm curls with a specified weight and a specified number of repetitions.
13. Curl the toes and pick up a specified number of pencils or sticks of the same size; move them a specified distance to a target of a specified size over a specified time frame.
14. Perform a wrist roll in which a rope of specified length has a weight of specified pounds attached to it a specified number of repetitions over a specified time frame.
15. Perform toe curls with a towel with the heels flat on the floor; bunch up the towel under the feet and put a weight of a specified number of pounds on the towel a specified distance from the toes.
16. Perform a wrist curl in which the wrist is over the edge of a table or a chair; then bend and straighten the wrist, holding a weight of a specified amount a specified number of repetitions.
17. Jump and reach a specified height.
18. Throw a medicine ball of specified weight from a sitting position a specified distance.
19. Run a specified distance over a specified period of time.
20. Run around a hoop 4 feet in diameter a specified number of times over a specified time frame.
21. Leap over a rope placed at a specified height.
22. Leap over 2 lines on the floor that are a specified distance apart.
23. Step up and then down on a bench of a specified height a specified number of repetitions over a specified time frame.
24. Run in a figure-eight fashion around a specified number of cones set a specified distance apart a specified number of times during a specified time frame.
25. Perform a shuttle run in which the parallel lines are a specified distance apart a specified number of trips in a specified amount of time.

Static Stretching Exercises

Adapted physical education requires that tasks be adapted to the ability level of each learner. When this occurs, each student with a disability can be accommodated. Usually, individuals with disabilities have tight muscles and connective tissue, which limits joint range of motion. Stretching is an important activity for increasing movement of desired joints. Lasko-McCarthey and Knopf[29] recommend the following practices for achieving a permanent increase in flexibility: (1) engage in a 5- to 10-minute warm-up before stretching; (2) do not apply too much force to the stretch; (3) hold the stretch for 30 to 60 seconds; (4) do not perform stretching if pain, infection, or edema is present; and (5) incorporate stretches at the end of the cool-down to prevent adaptive shortening and promote relaxation of muscles.

Walk-Run Program for Cardiovascular Endurance

A walk-run program has at least two variables that can be manipulated to make it more or less difficult: (1) the distance that the individual should run and (2) the length of time permitted to travel the prescribed distance. Suggested distance intervals are 1/4 mile, 1/2 mile, 3/4 mile, and 1 mile. Suggested criterion times for each distance could be 5 minutes for 1/4 mile, 11 minutes for 1/2 mile, 17 minutes for 3/4 mile, and 23 minutes for 1 mile.

Jumping Rope for Cardiovascular Endurance

When a cardiovascular fitness program is being conducted for individuals with disabilities, each individualized program should have specific objectives tailored to the student's present level of ability. A continuum of exercise activities can be used to accommodate individual differences. A procedure for constructing an individualized physical fitness program of rope jumping may be as follows:

1. Make a 4-minute musical tape recording that uses a cadence of 70 jumps per minute.
2. Test the students to determine how long they can jump without a rest interval.
3. Prescribe each individual to continue for 2 seconds longer each day.
4. When an individual can jump continuously for 4 minutes, substitute another tape that uses a cadence of 80 jumps per minute.

Under these conditions, there are two stations of different frequencies, but each person at each of those stations is performing for specific lengths of time commensurate with his or her present level of ability. Increasing cadences could be added to the program as cardiovascular endurance increases. Another factor that could be introduced into the program to make it more or less difficult is the length of the rest intervals between repeated bouts of exercise.

Exercise in Water

Exercise in the water is an excellent activity for persons with disabilities.[11] In the water the body weighs 50 to 90 percent less than when on land. Because of this, cardiovascular endurance and strength benefits from walking, running, and jumping can be realized without undue stress on joints. A water temperature of 82 to 88 degrees F is recommended.[46]

Accommodation of Individual Differences

Physical fitness activities for students with disabilities must be tailored to abilities and to the severity of the condition. The goals of the exercise program for persons with disabilities will vary, depending on the type of impairment, and will differ from those of individuals with no disabilities.[36]

Exercises can be modified to accommodate the ability level of each student with a disability:

1. The number of repetitions can be modified to make the task easier or more difficult. The fewer the repetitions, the less difficult the activity.
2. The position of the body in relation to gravity during the activity can be modified. Strength exercises done using gravity for assistance are the least demanding (e.g., executing a sit-up on a slant board with the head higher than the feet). Strength exercises done in a side-lying position will eliminate the effect of gravity (e.g., going from a full body extension to a crunch position while in a side-lying position). Exercises done against gravity are the third most demanding (e.g., executing a sit-up from a supine position or on a slant board with the head lower than the feet). The most demanding

strength exercises are those done with resistance and against gravity (e.g., individual leg extensions from a sitting position while wearing ankle weights).

3. The time that it takes to complete a set of repetitions can be shortened or lengthened. The shorter the time interval for completing the work, the more difficult the exercise task.

4. The number of sets of repetitions can be modified. Greater numbers of sets are associated with more intense and difficult training regimens. The number of sets can be decreased to accommodate the individual's present level of ability.

5. Theraband, surgical tubing, and sections of inner tubes can be used for strengthening specific muscle groups. These types of exercises are particularly valuable for individuals with physical disabilities who do not have access to weight-training equipment.

6. The use of flotation devices in the pool for the nonswimmer will enable that person to realize the benefits of moving in the water.

7. Stationary bikes, recline cycles, and arm cranking devices can be used by individuals with balance difficulties and those who are nonambulatory.

8. Large therapy balls can be used to develop trunk and abdominal strength.

9. For the sedentary person, the distance to be traveled and the time to engage in the activity can be shortened.

10. Self-selected rest periods can be allowed during the class time.

11. Relaxation practice can be built into each class period.

12. Low-impact exercises can be done.

Circuit Training

Accommodation for individual differences for most students with disabilities can be easily accomplished if a circuit training program is used. Circuit training uses a series of stations with different types of activities at each station. Individual

differences can be accommodated by altering the intensity and workload required of each student. To meet the individual physical needs of each student in circuit training, the following modifications can be made:

1. Develop a wide variety of activity levels, the lower of which can accommodate most individuals with disabilities.

2. Assign students with disabilities to only those stations in the circuit that meet their assessed needs.

3. Modify the nature of the activity at each station, so that each student can participate at the appropriate ability level.

4. Provide peer assistance, if available, and special instructions for the use of specific apparatus or equipment.

5. Provide verbal encouragement.[50]

6. Pair higher-functioning individuals with lower-functioning persons who need assistance at each station.[50]

Accommodating for Specific Types of Disabilities

Students with varying types of disabilities may need specific accommodation in circuit training exercises. Visually impaired and deaf students need assistance with communication systems that provide them with instructional information, whereas students with physical disabilities need accommodation for impaired motor functioning. Students who have intellectual disabilities or who have a specific learning disability, on the other hand, may need assistance in comprehending the task. Youngsters with autism need a structured environment with as few distractions as possible. The following are suggestions for accommodating students with a variety of disabilities.

Visual Disabilities

Students with visual impairments need confidence to cope with training programs. They may need the exercise environment to be modified, or they may need help from others to participate in training activities. Some environmental aids and supplemental assistance that may enable the student with a visual disability to benefit from circuit training can be found in Table 8-2.

Physical Disabilities

Students with physical disabilities may need accommodations to move physically through the environment and to manipulate exercise equipment. Some accommodations to enable these individuals to participate in circuit training follow:

1. Select activities that involve functional body parts (e.g., if the legs are impaired, prescribe activities for the arms).

Table 8-2	Circuit Training: Environmental Aids and Supplemental Assistance for Students with Visual Disabilities

1. Provide boundaries that define the general exercise area to facilitate mobility of the student within the exercise area.
2. Use boundaries to define the location of each specific exercise station.
3. Use sighted peers, if available, to help the student with visual disabilities move from station to station and to comprehend each task.
4. Provide a complete explanation of the way to use specific apparatus or equipment.
5. Arrange the exercise area the same way every time, so that the student with visual disabilities will be able to move through a familiar environment.
6. Arrange for enlarged type or Braille descriptions of the activity at each session.
7. Physically move the student through the exercise several times.
8. Plan the circuit so that movement to different areas for exercise is minimized.
9. Provide initial reference points that indicate where the student starts in the circuit.
10. Use brightly colored objects as boundaries to assist students with residual vision.

2. If an individual has limited function of the wrists and fingers, place pads on the forearms and select activities that will enable the individual to move the weights with the padded forearms.
3. If necessary, attach weights to the body or attach a body part to a piece of equipment with Velcro straps (e.g., if the student has difficulty keeping the feet in bicycle stirrups, attach the feet to the pedals with Velcro straps).
4. Establish an exercise environment that is accessible for students using wheelchairs.

Cognitive Disabilities

Students who are learning disabled or who have intellectual disabilities can benefit from pictures of exercises that are to be practiced at each station on the circuit. Rimmer[50] suggests that a variety of cardiovascular endurance activites be used when working with individuals with short attention spans. Specifically, the following 2-minute stations would be included in a training circuit: walk briskly around the track, jump on a mini trampoline, step up and down the bleachers, pedal a stationary cycle, perform jumping jacks, and use the rowing machine. A 30- to 60-second rest should occur between each station. Because a study by Roth reported that the primary source of exercise for adults with intellectual disabilities was Special Olympics,[51] their families should be encouraged to join their youngsters in a walk after dinner, use community-based fitness centers as often as possible, and perform light calisthenics between commercials while watching TV.[50]

SELECTED FITNESS PROBLEMS

As mentioned earlier in this chapter, the problems of underdevelopment and low physical vitality are closely associated with a great number of organic, mental, physiological, and emotional problems, which are discussed throughout this book. However, the major problem areas are malnutrition and eating disorders, overweight, and obesity.

Malnutrition and Eating Disorders

The term *malnutrition* means poor nutrition, whether there is an excess or a lack of nutrients to the body. In either instance, the malnourished individual has relatively poor physical fitness and other serious disadvantages. There are approximately 30 million persons from impoverished families in the United States who are food insecure (suffer from limited access to safe, nutritious food).[40] In the last 10 years access to nutritious food has been limited for low-income families.[69]

It is important that the cause of physical underdevelopment be identified. One is a lack of physical activity, which does not provide an opportunity for the body to develop its potential. However, some children are physically underdeveloped partially because of undernutrition. When a person's body weight is more than 10 percent below the ideal weight, indicated by standard age and weight tables, undernutrition may be a cause. Tension, anxiety, depression, and other emotional factors may restrict a person's appetite, causing insufficient caloric intake and weight loss. The most severe emotional disturbances causing insufficient caloric intake and weight loss are anorexia nervosa and bulimia nervosa. Individuals with anorexia nervosa have an intense fear of gaining weight. As a result, they severely limit their caloric intake. Individuals with bulimia nervosa have frequent episodes of uncontrolled overeating, followed by inappropriate compensatory behavior to prevent weight gain, such as vomiting, purging, or excessive exercise.[40] Eating disorders are commonly associated with substantial psychological problems, including depression, substance abuse, and suicide.

Impairment in physical development may also ensue. In culturally deprived areas, common in the urban inner city, children may lack proper nutrition

The Successful Athlete Devotes Many Hours to General and Specific Training
Courtesy of College Park, For Disability Options, Inc., Palmer, AR.

as a result of insufficient food resulting from poverty, the use of money for other priorities (e.g., drugs), easy access to fast food outlets, or loss of appetite caused by an organic problem. Proper nutrition and exercise go hand in hand in growing children. One without the other may cause lack of optimum physical development. The role of the physical educator in dealing with the underweight person is to help establish sound living habits with an emphasis on proper diet, rest, and relaxation.

Students from affluent families should be encouraged to keep a three-day food intake diary, after which, with the help of the teacher, a daily average of calories consumed is computed. After determining the average number of calories taken in, the student is encouraged to increase the daily intake by eating extra meals that are both nutritious and high in calories.

The physical educator must be sensitive to the unique problems of the child who is homeless, the child living in poverty, and the child who is nutritionally abused. A change in caloric intake is not a simple matter of the child's understanding the relationship between caloric intake and health. Often, the child is a victim, unable to control the powerful forces around him or her. The physical educator may take the lead in arranging for the child to have a federally or state-subsidized free breakfast or lunch. This may be the only meal the child eats during the day. In addition, the physical educator may use fresh fruit as a reward, always seeking an opportunity to allow the hungry child to earn the reward.

Overweight and Obesity

Overweight and obesity are serious nationwide health problems, requiring urgent attention. Risk factors, such as inadequate nutrition and inadequate physical activity, that result in overweight and obesity can lead to chronic conditions. Obesity, particularly in adults, is considered one of the great current medical problems because of its relationship to cardiovascular problems and other diseases. The frequency of overweight among patients with angina pectoris, coronary insufficiency, hypertension, and coronary occlusions is considerable.

Overweight can be defined as any excess of 10 percent or more above the ideal weight for a person, and obesity is any excess of 20 percent or more above the ideal weight. Obesity constitutes pathological overweight that requires correction. Several factors must be considered in determining whether a person is overweight. Among these are gender, weight, height, age, general body build, bone size, muscular development, and accumulations of subcutaneous fat.

The most recent report of the incidence of overweight in children and youth is as follows:

- 14 percent of children ages 2–5 years
- 19 percent of children ages 6–11 years
- 17 percent of adolescents[63]

More than one-third of young people do not meet the recommended guidelines for physical activity.[68] Obesity originates in childhood. Children in households with incomes under 200 percent of the poverty level are more likely than those living in higher-income households to be overweight or obese.

In the past, sufficient attention was not given to the diagnosis of overweight among many children in our society. Overweight persons are at greater risk for being diagnosed with diabetes, high blood pressure, high cholesterol, asthma, arthritis, and structural foot conditions.[65]

The basic reason for overweight is that the body's caloric consumption is greater than the energy expended to use the calories. Consequently, the excess energy is stored in the body as fat, leading to overweight. In many instances, overeating is a matter of habit. Thus, the body is continually in the process of acquiring more calories than are needed to maintain a normal weight.

Overweight and obesity have many causes. Among them are (1) caloric imbalance from eating incorrectly in relation to energy expended in the form of activity; (2) dysfunction of the endocrine glands, particularly the pituitary and thyroid, which regulate fat distribution in the body; and (3) emotional disturbance.

Social environment definitely influences obesity. The time youngsters spend in front of the TV or computer has greatly increased in the past decade. In inner cities where gangs, crimes, and violence are prevalent, it is simply not safe for children to play outside. In the past 30 years, the percentage of young people who are overweight has more than doubled.[67] Unless appropriate intervention is provided, these youngsters will grow up to be obese, sedentary adults.

Adverse Effects of Obesity

Many obese children exhibit immature social and emotional characteristics. It is not uncommon for obese children to dislike the games played by their peers, since obesity handicaps them in being adept at the games in which their peers are adequate. Many of these children are clumsy and slow, are objects of many stereotypical jokes, and are incapable of holding a secure social position among other children. Consequently, they may become oversensitive and unable to defend themselves and thus may withdraw from healthy play and exercise. This withdrawal from activity decreases the energy expenditure needed to maintain the balance that combats obesity. Therefore, in many instances, obesity leads to sedentary habits. It is often difficult to encourage these children to participate in forms of exercise that permit great expenditures of energy.

Obesity may be an important factor as children form ideas about themselves as persons and about how they think they appear to others. The ideas that they have about themselves will be influenced by their own discoveries, by what others say about them, and by the attitudes shown toward them. If the children find that their appearance elicits hostility, disrespect, or negative attention from parents and peers, these feelings may affect their self-concept, since children often assess their worth in terms of their relationships with peers, parents, and other authority figures.

When children pass from the child-centered atmosphere of the home into the competitive activities of the early school years, they encounter social stresses. They must demonstrate physical abilities, courage, manipulative skill, and social adeptness in direct comparison with other children

their age. The penalties for failure are humiliation, ridicule, and rejection from the group. Obesity places a tremendous social and emotional handicap on children. Therefore, educators should give these children all possible assistance and guidance in alleviating or adjusting to obesity.

Programming for the Obese Child

Since children who are overweight often cannot efficiently perform the activities of the physical education program, it is not uncommon for them to dislike many of these activities. As a result of their inability to participate in the program, they are often the objects of practical jokes and disparaging remarks from other children. In such an environment, boys and girls who are obese become unhappy and ashamed and often withdraw from the activity to circumvent emotional involvement with the group. The physical educator should attempt to create an environment that will enable the obese child to have successful experiences in the class, thus minimizing situations that could threaten the child's position as a person of worth. The physical educator is also challenged in regard to developing the attitudes of other students in the classes. Consequently, proposing to the class the acceptance of children who are different is an important and worthwhile goal of the physical educator.

Conducting a Weight-Control Program

A weight-control program should follow the basic procedures according to the instructional process of the Education of the Handicapped Act. First, there must be a goal—a desirable body weight that the individual is to achieve. Next, the weight of the person should be measured. Third, short-term instructional objectives that lead from the present weight to the eventual goal must be developed. For instance, if the present body weight is 100 pounds and the desirable body weight is 90 pounds, then the series of short-term objectives can be in 1- or 2-pound increments. The weight-loss goal will be reached most quickly if diet control is practiced while the exercise program is conducted. Appropriate goal setting will contribute not only to immediate weight loss but also to changes in lifelong diet and exercise habits.

The use of behavior management techniques contributes to success in weight-control programs by controlling the positive influences and minimizing the negative variables of the program. Some of the positive aspects of behavior management that will strengthen weight-control behaviors are (1) encouragement by the instructor, (2) a safe environment that keeps the student free from injury, (3) a variety of activities to reduce boredom, (4) a regularly scheduled routine, (5) a compatible, supportive social group, (6) feedback about progress toward short-term objectives, and (7) social reinforcement when weight losses occur. Punishing features that should be minimized are (1) poor program advice, (2) inconvenient time and place, (3) muscle soreness and/or injury, (4) lack of progress, and (5) disapproval about participation in the program by peers and family.

There can be no one program for the remediation of children who are obese. The true cause of the problem must be found. When the cause of obesity is known, several avenues are available for treatment. Some rules to be applied for successful weight control are provided in Table 8-3.

Table 8-3	Guidelines for a Safe and Effective Weight-Control Program

1. Know your desirable weight.
2. Count calories.
3. Try to calculate the energy expenditure through controlled workouts.
4. Do not cut out the food you like; cut down on the amounts you eat.
5. Seek medical treatment in the case of a glandular dysfunction.
6. Seek counseling when emotional causes are at the root of the problem.
7. Seek counseling on the consequences of obesity to the total personality.
8. Disrupt sedentary ways of living.

Courtesy Canadian Association of Athletes with a Mental Handicap.

Obese students should be guided into activities that can be performed safely and achieved successfully. This will tend to encourage them to participate in more vigorous activities. Some of the activities that can be used to combat obesity are general conditioning exercises, jogging, dancing, rhythmical activities, swimming, and sports and games. Much can be done for these children through individual guidance, encouragement, and selection of the proper developmental experiences. Loss of weight results in a decrease in the amount of stored adipose tissue; however, which stores of adipose tissue will decrease cannot be predicted. Therefore, it is impossible to spot reduce.

FAMILY INVOLVEMENT IN ACTIVE LIFESTYLES

Lifestyles of physical activity are shaped in part within the school setting and in part within the home. The family unit provides the primary social learning environment for the child. Parents serve as role models for children's attitudes and practices, and the extent to which the parents participate in physical activity impacts their child's attitude and behavior.[24] When family members support and cooperate with teachers, participation in physical activity is reinforced. For this reason, teachers should routinely reach out to the home to communicate their program goals and seek support.[9]

Effective collaboration of schools and families to facilitate physically active leisure lifestyles for persons with disabilities involves a blend of convenience, acceptability of information sent to the home, home-based curricula, and family learning opportunities. When these factors are controlled, the vast majority of families participate with the school to enhance their child's well-being.[19] Some successful components of a parent training program follow:

- *Home packets* that list the values of exercise, suggest types of activities, identify community resources, and highlight upcoming special physical activity events can be distributed to students on a regular basis by the physical education teacher.

- *Family fun nights* can be used to generate interest in the physical program, raise awareness of the value of exercise, and inform all members of the family about the joy and benefits of regular participation in physical activity. The evening should be a mini-health fair aimed at improving health habits. Events can be structured that demonstrate games and activities that individuals and families should participate in to enhance their health.
- *Family scorecards* should be distributed to families to allow them to record the amount and frequency of physical activity in which the child with a disability and the family participate. The scorecard should include specific activities for which points can be earned, the activities and points earned by the student, and the activities and points earned by the family as a whole.[24]

IMPLICATIONS FOR PHYSICAL EDUCATION

Physical education has emerged with new importance as awareness of the deleterious effect of inactivity on the sedentary adult population has increased. Through the efforts of many disciplines, the public is beginning to realize that proper exercise can be a deterrent to many characteristics of premature physiological aging, as well as to their concomitant diseases.

Research has yielded new concepts about the type of physical fitness activities best suited for adults. Acquisition of motor skills in physical education could encourage participation in ongoing physical activity, which in itself assists in maintaining physical fitness and controlling weight. Continuity of well-planned activities can serve as a preventive conditioner.

A multidisciplinary approach has resulted from medicine's concern for premature cardiovascular disease and the positive effects of proper exercise. The physician, physical educator, exercise physiologist, sports nutritionist, and many other professionals are lending their skills to help solve the problem of lack of physical fitness among adults. With the implementation of many medically oriented adult physical education programs, there is an increased need for trained teachers of adapted physical education who understand the problems and needs of the adult population. Establishing individual physical education programs for adults is one of the greatest challenges of our time.

SPORT CONDITIONING

There are provisions in IDEIA for equal opportunities for participation in extracurricular activities, which includes participation in competitive sports. Competitive sports for persons with disabilities provide opportunities for an active, healthy lifestyle, as well as the development of wholesome human values. Boys and girls alike should be provided these opportunities.

Opportunities in top-level competitive sports for persons with disabilities are increasing,[6] particularly in the area of physical disability.[42] Competition is designed to bring out the best performance qualities of individuals with and without disabilities. Many competitions have been arranged for persons with disabilities at the local, state, national, and international levels. Athletes who are serious about competition strive to participate at the highest level. Qualifying for participation at the upper levels of competition requires effective training and conditioning programs. Middle school and high school special education students should be encouraged to participate in sport competition. The value of intensive conditioning has been demonstrated by the Manitoba Special Olympics Medallian Program, which will be described in Chapter 11, and by the Paralympic performances of dedicated elite athletes with disabilities. In this section, we will examine sports conditioning components and procedures that maximize physical performance.

Match Program to Abilities, Needs, and Interests

Sports conditioning programs for persons with disabilities should be designed to match their abilities, needs, and interests. The challenge in designing effective sports conditioning programs is to select activities that promote general conditioning, as well as activities that maximize transfer to improved performance in competition. *General conditioning* refers to developing the prerequisite physical, motor, and perceptual factors that generalize across many sporting activities for many persons. *Specific conditioning* refers to developing the muscular strength and endurance and movements that are critical for success in the event of choice. Stopka reminds us that effective training involves attention to duration, intensity, and frequency.[56] She goes on to say, "We must train within, not beyond" our limitations.[56] The goal of conditioning is improvement in both overall and sport-specific strength, endurance, flexibility, power, and relaxation.

Year-Round Training Regime

Whereas the recreational athlete focuses on training in the weeks just prior to competition, elite athletes train year-round. Typically, the first two or three months of the training year are dominated by laying a base for what is ahead. Early season goals include improved strength, endurance, flexibility, power, and aerobic capacity. The strength goals are aimed at muscle groups specific to the sport. Weight lifting and Theraband or surgical tubing exercises target the muscle groups used in the sport. For swimmers, exercises may emphasize development of the biceps, triceps, and latissimus dorsi muscle groups, as well as simulate the arm-pulling patterns in the types of strokes used in competition.[12] Runners may focus on developing

their quadriceps, hamstrings, gastrocs, and hip abductors and adductors, as well as abdominal strength. Sprinters might add explosive strength to give them an advantage when coming out of the blocks. Muscular and cardiovascular endurance activities should be done five to seven times per week, with a focus on movements specific to the sport performance (e.g., stroke and turning techniques, lay-ups, wheelchair mobility). The types of activities that can be used to promote muscular endurance, muscle definition, and strength are presented in Table 8-4.

The mid-year training regime usually lasts four months and involves more frequent and intense practices, with a focus on building a strong aerobic base as well as improving range of motion and upper body, limb, and abdominal strength. Interval training that involves mixing slow with faster exercises is built into each workout. For sports requiring explosive moves, plyometric training is frequently used. Plyometric exercises involve rapid stretching of a muscle, which is undergoing stress while lengthening, followed by a rapid contraction of that muscle. The rapid stretching of the muscle results in the storing of energy in the muscle, which will be used immediately when the muscle is contracted.[16] An example of a plyometric exercise appropriate for gymnasts, divers, and high jumpers is pike jumping. In pike jumping, the person starts in a standing position with the feet shoulder width apart. The action involves swinging the arms backward, then forward, and bending the knees while jumping vertically. The person straightens the legs while in the air until they are parallel to the floor, then moves the legs to under

Table 8-4	Variations in Resistance Exercise Programs[20]		
Result	**Resistance**	**Frequency**	**Rest**
Muscular endurance	Light loads (less than 70 percent of 1 maximum repetition)	12–20 reps × 2–4 sets	30–90 sec
Muscle tone	Moderate loads (60 to 80 percent of 1 maximum repetition)	8–12 reps × 1–3 sets	30–90 sec
Strength	Heavy loads (95 to 100 percent of 1 maximum repetition)	1–6 reps × 4–8 sets	2–4 min

the body for landing. The activity is immediately repeated. To reduce the potential for injury, coaches frequently have the athletes practice plyometric exercises in the water. For the plyometric training program to be effective, it should be specific to the activity the athlete competes in. Resistance training combined with plyometric training has been shown to increase sports performance more than either resistance or plyometric training alone.[58]

The next few months prior to one month before competition are generally known as the in-season training program. Focus is on maintaining fitness and refining performance skill. A constant effort should be made to improve the efficiency and accuracy of the movements involved in the competition. Overpracticing skills is recommended to reinforce the efficiency of the motor units involved in specific skills.

Workouts during the last few weeks prior to competition differ according to the sport. All sports require continual work on timing, concentration, and mental imagery. However, endurance sports require ongoing endurance training. Specific training regimes used by world-class elite athletes with disabilities appear in each issue of *Palaestra*. Refer to those issues for more specific information about sports conditioning.

SUMMARY

Americans are underexercised. As a result, we are at high risk for developing a number of health problems, including obesity, hypertension, low back pain, osteoporosis, coronary heart disease, diabetes, colon cancer, anxiety and depression, and premature mortality. AAHPERD defines physical fitness as a physical state of well-being that allows people to perform daily activities with vigor, to reduce their risk of health problems related to lack of exercise, and to establish a fitness base for participation in a variety of activities. Physical educators have a unique and important role in encouraging active lifestyles for all individuals.

Because each person possesses a unique composition of physical and motor abilities, individual assessments should be used to determine the needs of each person. Activity programs should be constructed so that the physical and motor fitness tasks can be adapted to the ability level of each learner. Circuit training can be used to develop a wide range of performance levels. Fitness training should include both resistance training and aerobic activities. Programs of activity should specify mode of activity, frequency of training, intensity of training, duration of training, and resistance training.

Although collectively persons with the same disability may be similar, each student with a disability needs to be in a program that benefits his or her unique needs.

Undernourished and obese students present a challenge to the physical educator. The physical educator must be sensitive to the environmental conditions that contribute to these students' sedentary lifestyle and eating problems. A carefully designed exercise program guided by an appropriate behavior-modification plan should be developed and implemented for each child with a weight problem.

Family interest and involvement in physical activity enhance the probability that a child will have a positive attitude toward and will participate in an active lifestyle. Teachers should reach out to the home to encourage the understanding of and participation in healthful activities.

Sports conditioning regimes can be used to improve the performance of athletes with disabilities. The serious elite competitor participates in year-round general and sport-specific conditioning programs designed to enhance strength, agility, endurance, flexibility, relaxation, and specific sport skills.

REVIEW QUESTIONS

1. What is a physically educated person?
2. What are the values of exercise for persons with disabilities?

3. How would one determine a unique physical fitness need for a specific functional skill?

4. Why do some people choose not to participate in regular physical activity?

5. What special challenges do students with eating problems present to the physical educator?

6. What are the critical components of general and sport-specific conditioning programs?

STUDENT ACTIVITIES

1. In small groups or individually, identify selected group activities that could be used in a regular physical education class that would be fun for the class and would address Adam's physical fitness deficiencies (see Chapter 3).

2. Working in small groups, with each group assigned a muscle group (e.g., abdominals, quadriceps, biceps), develop four levels of strengthening exercises (with, without, and against gravity and against gravity with resistance) for your assigned muscle group.

3. Construct a circuit training program that includes three levels of activities to promote shoulder girdle strength, abdominal strength, quadricep endurance, and cardiovascular endurance.

4. Design and implement a weight-reduction program of exercise and diet that incorporates behavior management principles.

5. Develop a general and specific sports conditioning program for a specific sport. Reference the activities included in the conditioning program from the literature.

REFERENCES

1. American Alliance for Health, Physical Education, Recreation and Dance, National Association for Sport and Physical Education, www. aahperd.org.

2. American Association of Cardiovascular and Pulmonary Rehabilitation: *Guidelines for cardiac rehabilitation programs,* 2nd ed. Champaign, IL, Human Kinetics, 1995.

3. American College of Sports Medicine: *Resource manual for guidelines for exercise testing and prescription,* 3rd ed. Baltimore, MD, Williams and Wilkins, 1998.

4. Bar-Or O: Importance of differences between children and adults for exercise testing and exercise prescription. In Skinner JS, editor: *Exercise testing and exercise prescription for special cases.* Philadelphia, Lea & Febiger, 1993.

5. Bove AA, Sherman C: Active control of hypertension, *Physician Sportsmed* 26:45–53, 1998.

6. Campbell E, Jones G: Precompetition anxiety and self-confidence in wheelchair sport participants, *APAQ* 14:95–107, 1997.

7. Carlucci D et al.: Exercise: Not just for the healthy, *Physician Sportsmed* 19(7):47–54, 1991.

8. Coelho CW, Velloso CL, Brasil LO, Conceicao FL, Vaisman M, Arajo GS: Six-week home-based resistance training improves muscle power in adult patients with GH-deficiency, *Medicine and Science in Sports and Exercise,* Supplement 31:S268, 1998.

9. Cooper P: *Update on comprehensive school health programs in West Felciana Parish.* Paper presented at the Louisiana Association for Health, Physical Education, Recreation and Dance, New Orleans, LA, 1992.

10. Coyle CP, Santiago MC: Anaerobic exercise training and depressive symptomatology in adults with physical disabilities, *Arch Phys Med Rehabil* 76:647–652, 1995.

11. Dowzer CN, Reilly T, Cable NT: Maximal physiological responses to deep and shallow water running, *J of Sports Science* 16:514–515, 1998.

12. Dummer GM, Anderson NE: Focus on training, *Palaestra* 8:50–53, 1992.

13. Eichstaedt C et al.: *Physical fitness and motor skill levels of individuals with mental retardation.* Normal, IL, Illinois State University, 1991.

14. Evans IM, Meyer L: *An educative approach to behavior problems.* Baltimore, MD, Paul H. Brookes, 1985.

15. Fleck SJ, Kraemer WJ: Resistance training: Basic principles, *Physician Sportsmed* 16:160–171, 1988.

16. Haff GG: Explode with plyometrics, *Muscular Development* 36:92–98, 1999.

17. Hamdorf PA et al.: Physical training effects on the fitness and habitual activity patterns of elderly women, *Arch Phys Med Rehabil* 73:603–607, 1992.

18. Heath EM, Coleman KJ, Pope RP, Hernandez D, Alcala I, Jewell SL: Characterization of elementary physical education in a predominantly Mexican-American culture, *Medicine and Science in Sports and Exercise* Supplement 31:S175, 1998.

19. Hearn MD et al.: Involving families in cardiovascular health promotion: The CATCH feasibility study, *J Sch Health* 23:22–31, 1992.

20. Hesson JL: *Weight training for life.* Belmont, CA, Wadsworth/Thomson Learning, 2003.

21. Hortwitz SM, Kerker BD, Owens PL, Zigler E: *The health status and needs of individuals with mental retardation.* Unpublished paper, Washington, DC, Special Olympics International, 2001.

22. Huany Y, Macera CA, Blair SN, Rill NB, Kohl HW, Kroenenfeld JJ: Physical fitness, physical activity, and functional limitations in adults aged 40 and older, *Medicine and Science in Sports and Exercise* 31:1430–1435, 1998.

23. Humphrey JH: *An overview of childhood fitness.* Springfield, IL, Charles C Thomas, 1991.

24. Johnson CC et al.: CATCH: Family process evaluation in a multicenter trial, *Health Educ Q* 2:S91–S106, 1994.

25. Katch FI, McArdle WS: *Nutrition, weight control and exercise,* 2nd ed. Philadelphia, Lea & Febiger, 1983.

26. Kauranen KJ, Siira PT, Vanharanta HV: A 10-week strength training program: Effects on the motor performance of an unimpaired upper extremity, *Archives of Physical Medicine and Rehabilitation* 79:925–930, 1998.

27. Kraemer WJ, Fleck SJ: Resistance training: Exercise prescription, *Physician Sportsmed* 16:69–81, 1988.

28. Kujala UM, Kaprio J, Sarna S, Koskenvuo M: Baseline leisure physical activity and future mortality in twins, *J of Sports Science* 16:508–509, 1998.

29. Lasko-McCarthey P, Knopf KG: *Adapted physical education for adults with disabilities,* 3rd ed. Dubuque, IA, Eddie Bower, 1992.

30. Lee IM, Paffenbarger J, Hsieh E: Physical activity and the risk of developing colorectal cancer among college alumni, *J of the National Cancer Institute* 83:1324–1329, 1991.

31. Luukinen H, Koski K, Kavella SL: Predictors for recurrent falls among the home-dwelling elderly, *Scandinavian J of Primary Health Care* 13:294–299, 1995.

32. Maki BE, Holliday PJ, Topper AK: A prospective study of postural balance and risk of falling in an ambulatory independent elderly population, *J of Gerontology* 49:M42–M49, 1994.

33. McMurray RG, Ainsworth BE, Harrell JS, Griggs TR, Williams OD: Is physical activity or aerobic power more influential on reducing cardiovascular disease risk factors? *Medicine and Science in Sports and Exercise* 31:1521–1529, 1998.

34. Means KM, Rodell DE, Sullivan PS: Obstacle course performance and risk of falling in community-dwelling elderly persons, *Archives of Physical Medicine and Rehabilitation* 79:1570–1576, 1998.

35. Modell SJ, Cox TA: Fitness activities for children with severe profound disabilities, *Teaching Exceptional Children,* January/February:24–29, 1999.

36. Moore GE, Durstine JL: Framework. In Durstine JL, editor: *Exercise management for persons with chronic diseases and disabilities.* Champaign, IL, Human Kinetics, 1997.

37. Myers J, Dziekan G, Goebbels U, Dubach P: Influence of high-intensity exercise training on the ventilatory response to exercise in patients with reduced ventricular function, *Medicine and Science in Sports and Exercise* 32:929–937, 1999.

38. Nacher S, Valenzuela J, Nogues J, Rodriguez FA: The effects of self-administered swimming and walking programmes on health and fitness in previously inactive adults, *J of Sports Science* 16:508–509, 1998.

39. *National Coalition for Promoting Physical Activity Newsletter,* Washington, DC, May 15, 2003.

40. National Institutes of Health: *Eating disorders.* Washington, DC, National Institute of Mental Health, www.nimh.nih.gov/eating disorders, 2007.

41. Pagenoff SA: The use of aquatics with cerebral palsied adolescents, *Am J Occup Ther* 38:469–473, 1984.

42. Pensgaard AM, Roberts GC, Ursin H: Motivational factors and coping strategies of Norwegian Paralympic and Olympic winter athletes, *APAQ* 16:238–250, 1999.

43. Payne WA, Hahn DB: *Understanding your health,* 4th ed. St. Louis, Mosby, 1995.

44. Pommering TL et al.: Effects of an aerobic program on community-based adults with mental retardation, *Ment Retard* 32:218–226, 1994.

45. President's Council on Physical Fitness and Sports: Adolescence: A "risk factor" for physical inactivity, *Research Digest* 3:1–8, 1999.

46. Quarta C: Exercise options: Consider water or a chair, *Disabled Sports USA* 5(2):18, 2001.

47. Ransdell LB, Wells C: Physical activity in urban white, African-American, and Mexican-American women, *Medicine and Science in Sports and Exercise* 31:1608–1617, 1998.

48. Raven PB, Welch-O'Conner RM, Shi X: Cardiovascular function following reduced aerobic activity, *Medicine and Science in Sports and Exercise* 31:1041–1052, 1998.

49. Raymond J, Davis GM, Climstein M, Sutton JR: Cardiorespiratory responses to arm cranking and electrical stimulation leg cycling in people with paraplegia, *Medicine and Science in Sport and Exercise* 32:822–828, 1999.

50. Rimmer JH: *Fitness and rehabilitation programs for special populations,* Madison, WI, Brown & Benchmark, 1994.

51. Roth K: *Community physical recreation and students with disabilities.* Unpublished dissertation, Denton, TX, Texas Woman's University, 2003.

52. Sandstrom RM, Mokler PJ, Hoppe KM: Discharge destination and motor function outcome in severe stroke as measured by the functional independence measure function-related group classification system, *Archives of Physical Medicine* 79:762–765, 1998.

53. Seaman JA, editor: *Physical best and individuals with disabilities: A handbook for inclusion in fitness programs.* Reston, VA, American Association for Active Lifestyles and Fitness, 1995.

54. Shepard RJ, Emter M, Finne M, Stalenheim G: A 3-year follow-up of asthmatic patients participating in a 10-week rehabilitation program with emphasis on physical training, *Archives of Physical Medicine and Rehabilitation* 79:539–544, 1998.

55. Shepard RJ: Do work-site exercise and health programs work? *Physician and Sportsmed* 27:48–72, 1999.

56. Stopka C: Managing common injuries in individuals with disabilities; prevention comes first, *Palaestra* 12:28–31, 1996.

57. Trudeau F, Laurencelle L, Tremblay J, Rajic M, Shepard RJ: Daily primary school physical education: Effects on physical activity during adult life, *Medicine and Science in Sports and Exercise* 32:111–117, 1999.

58. Waller MA, Piper TJ: Plyometric training for the personal trainer, *J of Strength and Conditioning* 21:9–14, 1999.

59. Winnick JP, Short FX: *The Brockport physical fitness test manual.* Champaign, IL, Human Kinetics, 1999.

60. Wiseman DC: *Physical education for exceptional students: Theory to practice.* Albany, NY, Delmar, 1994.

61. Woolf-May K, Kearney EM, Jones DW, Davison RC, Coleman S, Bird SR: The effects of two different 18-week walking programmes on aerobic fitness, selected blood lipids and factor XIIa, *J of Sport Science* 16:701–719, 1998.

62. U.S. Department of Health and Human Services: *Physical activity among adults.* Atlanta, GA, Centers for Disease Control and Prevention, 2003.

63. U.S. Department of Health and Human Services: *National health and nutrition examination surveys.* Atlanta, GA, Centers for Disease Control and Prevention, National Center for Health Statistics, www.cdc.gov/nchs/about/major/nhanes/nh3data.htm, 2003.

64. U.S. Department of Health and Human Services: *Overweight and physical activity among children: A portrait of states and the nation chart book.* Washington, DC, Health Resources and Services Administration, http://nschdata.org/documents/overweight, 2005.

65. U.S. Department of Health and Human Services: *New state data show obesity and diabetes are still on the rise.* Atlanta, GA, Centers for Disease Control and Prevention, 2002.

66. U.S. Department of Health and Human Services: *Physical activity and health: A report of the surgeon general.* Atlanta, GA, National Centers for Chronic Disease Control and Prevention, 1996.

67. U.S. Department of Health and Human Services: *Promoting lifelong physical activity.* Atlanta, GA, National Centers for Chronic Disease Control and Prevention, March 1997.

68. U.S. 109th Congress, S. 799, The Prevention of Childhood Obesity Act, Washington, DC, 2005.

69. U.S. 109th Congress, S. 1325, Improved Physical Activity and Nutrition Act, Washington, DC, 2005.

SUGGESTED READINGS

American Association of Cardiovascular and Pulmonary Rehabilitation: *Guidelines for cardiac rehabilitation and secondary prevention programs,* 4th ed. Champaign, IL, Human Kinetics, 2004.

American College of Sports Medicine: *Exercise management for persons with chronic diseases and disabilities.* 2nd ed. Champaign IL, Human Kinetics, 2003.

Stopka C: *The teacher's survival guidebook: Adaptations to optimize the inclusion of students of all ages with disabilities in your program,* www.pecentral.org, 2006.

Stopka C, Bowie L: *Adapted equipment ideas to facilitate inclusionary teaching,* 2nd ed. Boston, Pearson, 2000.

RECOMMENDED WEB SITES

Please keep in mind that these Web sites are being recommended in the winter of 2007. As Web sites often change, they may have moved or been reconfigured or eliminated.

Canadian Wheelchair Basketball Association
www.cwba.ca

Family Fitness Programs
www.kidnetic.com

International Wheelchair Basketball Federation
www.iwbf.org

Sports Disabilities
http://edweb6.educ.msu.edu/kin866

United States Handcycling
www.ushf.org

United States Quad Rugby Association
www.quadrugby.com

Wilderness Inquiry Outdoor Adventures
www.wildernessinquiry.org

RECOMMENDED VIDEOS

Insight Media
2162 Broadway
New York, NY 10024-0621
1-800-233-9910
www.insight-media.com

Exercise as an Antidote for Obesity: Considerations Regarding Fitness and Mortality
YAN2696/DVD/40 min/2006/$119.00

The New Physical Education: Promoting Healthy and Active Lifestyles
YAN2727/DVD/50 min/2006/$109.00

Physical Activity Recommendations for Youth: What Fitness Professionals Should Know
YAN2723/DVD/50 min/2005/$119.00

Children at Risk:
Psychosocial Issues

A Child Engaging in Solitary Play

Courtesy Callier Center for Communications
Disorders, Dallas, TX.

■ OBJECTIVES

Describe the nature of infant mortality in the United States.

Explain the impact of prenatal exposure to drugs on children with and without disabilities.

Describe the nature of abuse and neglect of children with and without disabilities.

Explain the relation of poverty and homelessness to inadequate psychosocial development in children with and without disabilities.

Describe some of the causes of violence in our society.

List some of the signs/symptoms that a child or an adolescent may be a gang member or a gang member "wannabe."

Describe cooperative learning and the New Games approach to physical education.

Describe Hellison's physical education programs, and explain why they are effective.

Marion Wright Edelman, president of the Children's Defense Fund, wrote,

> We can build a nation where families have the support they need to make it at work and at home; where every child enters school ready to learn and leaves on the path to a productive future; where babies

are likely to be born healthy and sick children have the care they need; where no child has to grow up in poverty; where all children are safe in their community and every child has a place to call home—and all Americans can proudly say, "We Leave No Child Behind."[11]

Educators must respond to the increased psychosocial needs of the infants, children, and adolescents they serve. Children with and without disabilities are entering the public school system unprepared, understimulated, abused, abandoned, homeless, unloved, frightened, distrustful, tired, hungry, unkempt, and angry, as well as members of gangs and gang member "wannabes." The school, as a microcosm of the society, reflects and mirrors the larger society.

A child fortunate enough to be born without an identifiable disability is entering a society in which the deck is "stacked" against the child. Our society is taking children with the potential for normalcy and, perhaps, giftedness and destroying that potential (see Table 9-1). Societal priorities and federal and state legislative decisions are creating children with disabilities. Obviously, that is directly related to the numbers and types of children served in special education.

Many special educators are exceptional, talented, and dedicated teachers. However, it is particularly frightening to note that children with disabilities receiving special education services are the most likely to be taught by emergency-licensed teachers

Table 9-1	The Nature of Children's Lives in the United States

When compared with other industrialized countries the United States ranks

1st in military technology
1st in the number of millionaires and billionaires
11th in the proportion of children living in poverty
18th in the gap between rich and poor children
22nd in infant mortality
Last in protecting its children against gun violence

With grateful appreciation to the Children's Defense Fund in their efforts to protect our children. (Adapted from The State of America's Children, 2001).

CASE STUDY 9-1

Lashone

Lashone entered a public school at age four years. His mother was overwhelmed with his behavior and, subsequently, appeared to be very honest with school personnel regarding his background. She admitted she had abused just about every known drug during pregnancy. Lashone was born addicted to crack cocaine and, presumably, to the other drugs that had affected his system in utero. He started school with a violent, uncontrollable temper, no sense of cause-effect, and no apparent social conscience. At age three, in a Preschool Program for Children with Disabilities classroom, Lashone had already required a one-on-one "behavior coach."

APPLICATION TASK

The prekindergarten- and kindergarten-age students all go to the gymnasium for physical education at the same time. Develop a list of specific tasks you want Lashone's one-on-one aide to perform while he is in the gymnasium, so that you, as the physical educator, are free to teach and the other children are safe.

with no background in education, much less special education. Zahn and Schultze wrote, "A severe shortage in fully trained special education teachers has resulted in an increasing number of emergency-licensed teachers 'who have the least amount of training' assigned to the most challenging students."[71] The children who most need support and nourishment are the very children most in jeopardy. The physical educator, standing in a gymnasium full of 60 children, can assume that at least 20 of those children are at significant risk for school failure because of overwhelming poverty, homelessness, abuse, and inappropriate parenting/caregiving.

INFANT MORTALITY

In 2007 the United States ranked 22nd among industrialized nations in infant mortality.[34] This continues to be a reflection of racial prejudice and is tied directly to poverty. The gap remains frightening among infant mortality figures for Caucasian infants, African American infants, and Native American/Alaska Native infants. U.S. Surgeon General Dr. David Satcher noted that African American babies are more than twice as likely as Caucasian babies to die before their 1st birthday and that the stresses of racism, including environmental toxins, violence, discrimination, and other stress, may be to blame.[44] School-aged children are affected by environmental toxicity as well. Thousands of schools in poverty-affected areas have been built on or near toxic waste sites; this compromises the health and well-being of the students and teachers.[54] The students are more likely to develop asthma, cancer, and learning disorders than those not exposed.

ALCOHOL AND OTHER DRUG ABUSE

According to Greer,

> We are facing the emerging of what some are now calling a bio-underclass; a frightening

proportion of the next generation of school children will have impairments which, in the words of Dr. Harold Nickens of the American Society of Addiction Medicine, may require the medical community to define an entirely new, organic brain syndrome based on the physical and chemical damage done to fetal brains by drug-abusing mothers.[24] In fact, physicians are, increasingly, referring to Fetal Alcohol Syndrome as "alcohol-related developmental disorder" and "alcohol-related birth defects."[4]

Recently, fetal alcohol syndrome has been included in a classification titled fetal alcohol spectrum disorders (FASD). This umbrella term encompasses a range of physical, mental, behavioral, and learning disabilities that can occur in an individual whose mother drank alcohol during pregnancy. Fetal alcohol syndrome is the most severe effect of alcohol consumption during pregnancy.[49]

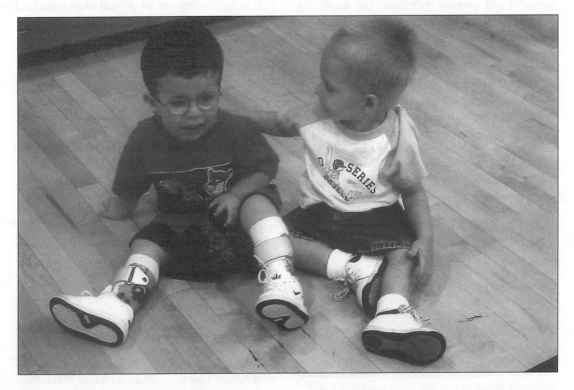

Inclusion Experiences Should Begin at an Early Age
Courtesy of Dr. Linda Hilgenbrink, Northern Illinois University.

The escalation of the use and abuse of alcohol and other drugs has had a profound impact on the quality of life of millions of infants, children, and adolescents with and without disabilities. It is estimated that between 10 and 12 percent of babies born in the United States today are exposed in utero to alcohol and illicit drugs.[52] Over 1 million women in the United States who use and abuse alcohol, nicotine, marijuana, cocaine, or other drugs and continue to abuse the drugs during pregnancy give birth to babies with significant developmental delays.[16]

Fetal alcohol exposure is now the nation's leading known cause of intellectual disabilities, surpassing Down syndrome. Five in 1,000 children are born with fetal alcohol spectrum disorders.[49] The damage done by maternal ingestion of alcohol appears to be represented by a continuum from severe damage to the central nervous system (cerebellum atrophy and dysgenesis of the corpus callosum) to minor neurotransmitter dysfunction.[12] The effects of in utero exposure to alcohol on infants are summarized in Table 9-2.

CASE STUDY 9-2

Charlie

Charlie is a 10-year-old child with fetal alcohol syndrome. He has significant learning disabilities, poor fine motor coordination, gross motor awkwardness, and difficulty with social-emotional issues. He has a particularly difficult time following rules and is unable to deal with "no." He has been in trouble at school since he entered kindergarten.

APPLICATION TASK

Design an after-school physical education program, based on Hellison's four-level model of behavior/value development, that would encourage Charlie to make good decisions about his behavior. In particular, describe the major activities that will be emphasized and outline a "typical" day.

Table 9-2	Effects of in Utero Exposure to Alcohol (Fetal Alcohol Syndrome)[14,16,60,69]	
Infancy	**Early School Years**	**Adolescence**
Low birthweight	Gross motor deficit	Significant social deficit
Short stature	Fine motor deficit	Social withdrawal
Craniofacial defect	Attention deficit disorder	Difficulty with friendships
Cleft palate	Hyperactivity	Dependency
Lip palate	Delay in spoken language	Difficulty in group settings
Small eye openings	Difficulty with verbal comprehension	School and work
Extra skin fold at eyes	Poor impulse control	Difficulty with attention
Low-set ears	Poor visual motor memory	
Receding chin	Difficulty with social skills	
CNS dysfunction	Aggressive behavior	
Abnormal reflexes		
Sleep disorder		
Tremors		
Hypertonia		
Hypotonia		
Heart defects		
Spinal defects		
Difficulty ignoring sensory stimuli		

Tarr and Pyfer[61] found that the use and abuse of illicit substances, alcohol, or both by the mother significantly affect the physical and motor development of neonates/infants exposed in utero (see Table 9-3). Table 9-4 briefly describes the effects of crack cocaine on infants and children. The child protective service agencies, child welfare agencies, and foster care systems are being bombarded because of this abuse. Not only have these infants been abused during the prenatal experience, but often these infants are subsequently abandoned on the streets and in dumpsters, bathrooms, and hospitals. The women who give birth to these infants commonly continue to be drug abusers and often are unable to care for themselves, much less an infant.

POVERTY AND HOMELESSNESS

Dr. Lillian Parks, superintendent of the East St. Louis schools, said, "Gifted children are everywhere in East St. Louis, but their gifts are lost to poverty and turmoil and the damage done by knowing they are written off by their society."[39] A young child's risk for living in poverty appears to depend on three major factors:

1. Single parenthood; single-parent families, headed by women, represent 40 percent of the homeless population[40]

Table 9-3	Motor and Physical Consequences for Infants Exposed to Drugs in Utero[61]

- Decreased birthweight
- Decreased birth length
- Decreased head circumference
- Decreased Apgar scores (measures of the neurological integrity of the infant) at 1 and at 5 minutes after birth
- Decreased gestational age (preterm birth)
- Increased irritability
- Increased tremors and convulsions
- Increased hypertonicity or hypotonicity
- Decreased Bayley Motor Development Index Scores on the Psychomotor Development Index at 6 months, 12 months, 18 months, and 24 months

2. Low educational attainment of the parent
3. Part-time or no employment of the parent[47]

In 2004, 37 million people in the United States were living in poverty. That is an increase of 1 million over the previous year. One in every five children in the United States is living in poverty.[33] In fact, 44 percent of children under the age of six are living in poverty if neither parent is employed and if neither parent has a high school diploma. However the demographics are changing. It is important to note that nearly 80 percent of all young children in poverty

Table 9-4	Characteristics of Infants and Children Exposed Prenatally to Crack Cocaine[23,56,59,63]	
Infants	**Young Children**	**Adolescents**
Poor body state regulation	Passivity	Continued difficulty
Tremors	Passivity in learning	Learning
Chronic irritability	Difficulty learning	Social skills
Poor visual orientation	Hyperactivity	
Small head	Desperate need for structure	Pathological conscience
Missing bowels	Inappropriate social behavior	Tendency toward
Malformed genitals	Tendency toward aggression	aggression
Prone to strokes	Lack of social conscience	Lack of social conscience
Prone to seizures	Lying and stealing	
Difficult and serious withdrawal behavior	Speech and language delays	

live in a family in which at least one parent is employed.[33] Parents, struggling and working to make a life for their children, remain in poverty because of the nature of the employment available to them—minimum-wage and below-minimum-wage jobs.

The significant gap between the rich and the poor continues to grow, and it appears that the gap between the extremely rich and the "middle class" is growing as well. Victor Sidel, M.D., noted, "Hunger, even if there are no direct signs of malnutrition, can affect children's health, can affect their ability to learn."[36] Clearly, a child whose basic needs are not being met—and one of those needs is adequate and nutritious food—cannot be free to learn, to grow, and to move toward self-actualization. The primary concern of a child who is hungry is food, and this dominates thought.

Poverty may also be tied to substandard housing, if the family has housing. Significant dangers to children inherent in substandard housing include (1) faulty wiring, which can lead to fires; (2) overcrowding, which helps spread infectious disease; (3) cockroach infestations, which can exacerbate allergies and asthma; (4) rat infestations; and (5) chipped or flaking lead paint, which can cause lead poisoning.[13] It should be noted that refugee children are more likely than U.S.-born children to be affected by lead poisoning.[22]

Poverty and Access to Technology

Certainly not as critical, in terms of life and death, as many of the other issues tied to poverty and race but nevertheless a very real problem associated with poverty is the ever-escalating gap between those who have the means to access the Internet and other technology-based information and those who do not. A 2003 report by the U.S. Census Bureau study showed that Caucasians are 66 percent more likely to own computers than are African Americans and Hispanics, and Caucasians are roughly twice as likely to have Internet access as are African Americans and Hispanics.[62] Larry Irving, an administrator of the National Telecommunications and Information Administration, said, "There is a gap, it is widening and what should be done is not only a civil rights issue but a matter of public policy."[26] While it is difficult to determine if it is an issue related to poverty, race, or education, the result is the same. Individuals without access to Internet technology are being put at a significant disadvantage for acquiring information critical to living in a contemporary society that requires access to information.

Homelessness

The number of people who are homeless in this country is escalating dramatically. "In the United States 3.5 million people will experience homelessness in a given year. Children under the age of 18 years account for 39% of the homeless and 42% of these are under the age of 5."[40]

Griffin writes, "Tonight, like any other, more than a million children will sleep in shelters, abandoned buildings, cars, or public parks."[25] Homeless children experience more acute and chronic medical problems than do poor children who have homes. Health care workers find high incidences of diarrhea and malnourishment, as well as asthma and elevated blood levels of lead, in children who live in shelters.

Inconsistent health care, inadequate nutrition, and inadequate rest cause significant health risks for the child who is homeless. The Children's Defense Fund, an active child advocate agency, has reported that children who are homeless are three times more likely to have missed immunizations than are poor children with apartments, trailers, or houses.[11]

Children who are homeless are at high risk not only for health problems but also for problems in psychosocial development. In addition to a chaotic family life, homeless children frequently also experience a loss of friends, a loss of familiar neighborhood surroundings, school disruptions, exposure to strangers, and threatening situations on the streets and in the shelters.

These children's lives are in jeopardy. Of significant concern is the fact that, in the past, homeless children had difficulty gaining access to one of their fundamental rights—a free, public education. Those who make it to school are frightened, exhausted, hungry, and disenfranchised. The

CASE STUDY 9-3

Anthony

Anthony is a 4-year-old boy who lives with his mother, Lisa, in a shelter for women who are victims of domestic abuse. Lisa finally left her husband after he physically abused Anthony as well. Lisa, 22 years old, is seeking employment but struggling to secure care for Anthony while at work. She is trying to get him admitted to a school near the shelter, but school officials have not been particularly helpful. Since the shelter is not a permanent address, school officials hesitate to invest a great deal of time in Anthony's enrollment. His enrollment status is further compromised by the fact that Anthony has been diagnosed as having ADD/ADHD. When Anthony takes his medication, he functions well within the shelter and in community settings. However, his mother finds it impossible to get to the community-based medical center, where she can receive free medication. As a result, his behavior is unpredictable, and, more often than not, he is in trouble at the shelter and difficult to manage in community settings.

APPLICATION TASK

As you read this chapter, consider the multiple factors that affect Anthony's potential for success in school. Describe a kindergarten physical education program that would meet Anthony's needs. Specifically, describe five noncompetitive, cooperative activities in which Anthony would be likely to succeed.

children feel unempowered and overwhelmed by the uncertainty of their lives. They are often embarrassed because they have difficulty getting access to showers and baths, as well as to washers/dryers, to keep them and their clothes clean. They are also embarrassed because they lack the basic materials required for school—school supplies and so on. Children who are homeless are among those most at risk for delays in psychosocial development because they are denied the most basic of human rights—to be warm, protected, and safe. See Table 9-5 for information about how the physical

educator can help children who are homeless and poor within the school setting.

The education subtitle of the McKinney-Vento Homeless Assistance Act includes a more comprehensive definition of homelessness. This statute states that the term "homeless child and youth" (A) means individuals who lack a fixed, regular, and adequate nighttime residence and (B) includes (i) children and youth who lack a fixed, regular, and adequate nighttime residence and children and youth who are sharing the housing of other persons due to loss of housing, economic hardship, or a similar reason; are living in motels, hotels, trailer parks, or camping grounds due to lack of alternative adequate accommodations; are living in emergency or transitional shelters; are abandoned in hospitals; or are awaiting foster care placement; (ii) children and youth who have a primary nighttime residence that is a private or public place not designed for or ordinarily used as a regular sleeping accommodation for human beings; (iii) children and youth who are living in cars, parks, public spaces, abandoned buildings, substandard housing, bus or train stations, or similar settings; and (iv) migratory children who qualify as homeless for the purposes of this subtitle because the children are living in circumstances described in clauses (i) through (iii).[59]

This federal law, the McKinney-Vento Homeless Assistance Act, enacted by Congress July 1987, and its amendments of 1990, mandates that all children, including homeless children, have a

Courtesy of Laurie Zittel.

Table 9-5	Strategies the Physical Educator Can Use to Help Homeless Students and Those Living in Poverty

- Provide healthy snacks as rewards and create situations where hungry students get the "rewards" often:
  - Fresh fruit
  - Fresh vegetables (most supermarkets will gladly donate fruit and vegetables to teachers for use in the school)
  - Peanut butter crackers
  - Crackers and cheese
- If you bring your lunch to school, bring two and share it with a student who needs it. If you buy your lunch, buy an extra sandwich, piece of fruit, etc., and share it.
- Allow *supervised* locker room use by students needing to shower, shave, brush teeth, etc. Ask other faculty and PTA members:
  - To save the "stuff" they find in their hotel/motel rooms—shampoo, soap, hand and body lotion
  - To donate toothbrushes given them by their dentists and ask their dentists to donate toothpaste samples
  - To donate the travel kits given them on international and long domestic flights
- Be one of the faculty who volunteer to help wash and dry clothes.
- Keep a box of clean clothes, socks, and shoes that have been left in the gym for use by students who need them.
- Use school supplies as "rewards," and create situations in which the learners win and get the rewards.

right to access a free, appropriate public education and that school residency laws may not be used to prevent homeless children from attending school[59] (see Table 9-6). In the past, homeless children were often denied access to school because of a lack of address as a "legal and permanent resident" of a district, and/or because parents were unable to locate or provide health records. In addition, parents of homeless children may fail to register their child for school because of the seemingly impossible obstacles of providing transportation from shelters, abandoned cars, or empty buildings to school; of sending the child to school clean and in clean clothes; and of securing needed school supplies. In addition, the parents may be fearful that their children will be reported by school authorities and taken away from them by social service agencies.

PARENTAL INSTABILITY

One of the major issues in the psychosocial development of infants, young children, and adolescents, with and without disabilities, is the presence of a stable, caring, nurturing primary adult in their lives. Without the security of a stable, caring, and nurturing adult, children are not free to explore the world around them and, subsequently, are at significant risk for developmental delays.

While a slight majority of children still live in nuclear families, a rising number live with single parents, with other relatives, in foster homes, in

Table 9-6	The McKinney-Vento Homeless Assistance Act[59]

Teachers must help parents understand their rights:
- Parents do not need a permanent address to enroll a child in school.
- Parents have a choice of school placement. A child may remain at the same school he or she attended before becoming homeless or may enroll at the school serving the attendance area where he or she is receiving temporary shelter.
- A homeless child cannot be denied school enrollment just because school records or other enrollment documentation are not immediately available.
- The homeless child has the right to participate in all extracurricular activities and all federal, state, and local programs for which the child is eligible, including food programs, before- and after-school programs, vocational education, and Title I and other programs for gifted, talented, and disadvantaged learners.
- The child cannot be isolated or separated from the mainstream school environment solely due to homelessness.

institutions, in homeless shelters, or on the streets. In 2005 it was reported that, in the United States, more than 6 million children live in households headed by grandparents.[5] Of particular concern is the fact that single grandmothers who head households are at significant risk of being poor.[45] But those children would be even more in crisis had not these grandparents stepped up and assumed roles as caregivers for the children of their children.

One in every four children in this country lives in a single-parent household, and most of these single parents are women living in poverty. While single parents can be very effective parents, when the process is complicated by lack of money and a lack of education, parenting becomes a very difficult process.

Babies are having babies, in hopes that they will "have someone who loves me." These young teenagers, often incapable of caring for themselves, certainly lack the parenting skills necessary to raise a child, particularly if that process is made more difficult because of a lack of support from the father, poverty, insufficient education to seek and keep a good job, and lack of access to appropriate, affordable child care.

SCHOOL VIOLENCE AND THE GANG CULTURE

The schools are a microcosm of the greater society, which that is characterized by escalating violence and rage. Hatred, intolerance, bullying, racism, homophobia, and the noxious presence of gangs haunt this society.

Children and adolescents are faced with violence on a daily basis. It is estimated that as many as 10 million children may witness or be victims of violence in their homes or communities on any given day.[47] Studies routinely report that over 90 percent of youth living in urban areas have been exposed to one violent event or were familiar with someone who had been involved in violence.[19] Watching violent television programs (including Saturday morning cartoons) and playing violent video games contribute to increased acceptance of aggressive attitudes and increased aggressive behavior.[2] According to Funk,

Baldaccia, Pasold, and Baumgardner's 2004 article, "In order to succeed at a violent video game, players must identify and then choose violent strategies. Repeated violent choices result in a continuous cycle of reward. Violence is presented as justified, without negative consequences, and fun."[19]

A bulletin board, made by a prekindergarten class in a core, inner-city elementary school in Dallas, celebrated Martin Luther King's birthday. Each four-year-old child in the class was asked to complete the statement "I have a dream . . ." Eighteen of the 22 children in the class responded with statements such as "I have a dream . . . the shooting will stop" and "I have a dream . . . my momma won't get dead." These four-year-old children, and other victims like them, experience symptoms like those of posttraumatic stress disorder: (1) anxiety; (2) heightened sense of hearing, smell, and sight; and (3) hypervigilance or "tuning out" the environment.[66] While these symptoms prepare the child for "fight or flight" reactions in stressful situations in the streets or in their homes, they interfere significantly with learning in school. Unable to tune out the environment, or tuning it out completely, makes it difficult for these children to learn.

School Violence

Rene Girard, a French scholar, has developed a theory regarding human violence. His theory of "scapegoating" suggests that humans lash out when they feel threatened or harmed. They exhibit a powerful, often unconscious, need to maintain order and unity among the groups with which they identify. This is consistent with the work of Dawn Perlmutter, who suggests that schoolyards are "sacred grounds" where popular students—notably, athletes and cheerleaders—are idolized.[57] Increasingly, school violence appears to be tied to young Caucasian men who feel disenfranchised and feel like outcasts within the school society (see Tables 9-7 and 9-8). It appears that school violence may be escalated, even caused, by situations that make students feel there is no justice and no fairness.

Gang Culture

Many children and adolescents in this society do not feel secure, loved, wanted, needed, or respected. The gang, as a sociological phenomenon, has always been present in cultures in which individual members of that culture feel unempowered and disenfranchised (see Table 9-9). In many ways, the gang replaces the family as the primary source of security.

In addition, participation in a gang may provide the gang member with a sense of power and recognition that is missing in other relationships. *Gang* has been defined as a formal or an informal association of three or more persons who have a common name or identifying signs, color, or symbols and who individually or collectively engage in a pattern of criminal activity involving felony crimes and violent misdemeanor offenses.[21] The gang culture has a profound influence within the schools. Though only 10 percent of young people join gangs,[7] their presence in schools significantly increases the likelihood that students and teachers will be affected negatively by fear and violence.

CHILD ABUSE AND NEGLECT

In 2005 approximately 6 million children were reported for child abuse to the child protective services. There were just under 900,000 confirmed victims of child maltreatment.[1] It is frightening to note that these are the substantiated cases; child abuse and neglect are often unreported and may be very difficult to prove. Most child abuse is an abuse of power. Children under the age of three have the highest rate of victimization.[1] Our littlest and most defenseless children are a major target.

Shaken baby syndrome is the most common cause of mortality of infants in the United States. A baby's brain, along with the blood vessels and other support tissues connecting the skull to the brain, are fragile and underdeveloped. If a baby is shaken, the brain rebounds around the skull, causing brain damage, which may result in intellectual disabilities, speech and learning disabilities, paralysis, seizures, hearing loss, and even death. The diagnosis of

Table 9-7	Early Warning Signs That a Student Is at Risk for Committing School Violence[17]

The following signs are indications that there is reason for concern. However, viewed individually none of these is an indication the student will actually commit a violent act.

- Social withdrawal
- Excessive feelings of isolation and aloneness
- Excessive feelings of rejection
- Being a victim of violence
- Feelings of being teased, bullied, and picked-on
- Poor academic performance
- Little interest in school
- Expression of violence in writing, drawing, Web sites, or music
- Uncontrolled anger
- Constant hitting, intimidating, and bullying
- History of discipline problems
- History of violent/aggressive behavior
- Intolerance for difference and prejudices
- Alcohol and other drug use
- Affiliation with gangs
- Inappropriate access to, possession of, and use of firearms
- Serious threats of violence

The following are signs that violent behavior is imminent.

- Serious physical fighting with peers/family
- Severe destruction of property
- Severe rage for seemingly minor reasons
- Detailed threats of lethal violence
- Possession and/or use of firearms/weapons
- Self-injurious behavior/threats of suicide

Modified from Early Warning, www.air.org/cecp.

shaken baby syndrome is based on the triad of subdural hematoma (bruising), cerebral edema (swelling), and retinal hemorrhage.[55]

Wang and Daro[64] noted the following types of abuse:

1. Physical abuse (16 percent). Physical abuse is the physical battery of a child[1] (see Table 9-10).

CASE STUDY 9-4

Marie

Marie, a 16-year-old junior high student, was wounded in a gang drive-by shooting. The bullet did so much damage that Marie will probably need a wheelchair to ambulate the rest of her life.

APPLICATION TASK
List five specific strategies the physical educator could use to encourage Marie to become an active participant in wheelchair sports.

---

2. Sexual abuse (9 percent). Sexual abuse includes oral-genital, genital-genital, genital-rectal, hand-genital, hand-rectal, or hand-breast contact. It includes showing pornography to a child and using a child in the production of pornography. Sexual intercourse includes vaginal, oral, or rectal penetration[9] (see Table 9-11).

3. Neglect (62 percent). Neglect includes failure to meet a child's basic physical needs (e.g., food, clothing, shelter) and health needs (e.g., adequate medical intervention, regular physical examinations, and needed inoculations against childhood disease)[21] (see Table 9-12).

4. Emotional maltreatment (7 percent). Emotional abuse includes intentional verbal or behavioral acts that result in adverse emotional consequences. Emotional neglect occurs when a caregiver intentionally does not provide the nurturing verbal and behavioral actions that are needed for health development[9] (see Table 9-13).

5. Other (6 percent). Behaviors included in this category are abandonment, medical and

---

Table 9-8	Checklist of Characteristics of Youth Who Have Caused School-Associated Violent Deaths[8]

The following characteristics should alert school administrators, teachers, counselors, and parents that a student is troubled and may engage in violent behavior:

1. ___ Has a history of tantrums and uncontrollable angry outbursts
2. ___ Characteristically resorts to name calling, cursing, and abusive language
3. ___ Habitually makes violent threats when angry
4. ___ Has previously brought a weapon to school
5. ___ Has a background of serious disciplinary problems at school and in the community
6. ___ Has a background of drug, alcohol, or other substance abuse or dependency
7. ___ Is on the fringe of his or her peer group with few or no close friends
8. ___ Is preoccupied with weapons, explosives, or other incendiary devices
9. ___ Has previously been truant, suspended, or expelled from school
10. ___ Displays cruelty to animals
11. ___ Has little or no supervision and support from parents or a caring adult
12. ___ Has witnessed or been a victim of abuse or neglect in the home
13. ___ Has been bullied and/or bullies or intimidates peers or younger children
14. ___ Tends to blame others for difficulties and problems he or she causes himself or herself
15. ___ Consistently prefers TV shows, movies, or music expressing violent themes, rituals, and abuse
16. ___ Prefers reading materials dealing with violent themes, rituals, and abuse
17. ___ Reflects anger, frustration, and the dark side of life in school essays or writing projects
18. ___ Is involved with a gang or an antisocial group on the fringes of peer acceptance
19. ___ Is often depressed and/or has significant mood swings
20. ___ Has threatened or attempted suicide

Printed with permission from The National School Safety Center.

Table 9-9	Signs and Signals of Gang Involvement[20,30]

- Has a sudden drop in grades and loss of interest in school
- Begins to hang around with new friends who are of "questionable" character
- Is defensive about activities
- Separates from the family
- Loses interest in normal activities
- Uses hand signs with friends
- Has issues with police
- Engages in out-of-control behavior (ignores curfew, is defiant)
- Begins wearing a particular color or style of clothes
- Has symbols on his or her personal property
- Changes his or her nickname
- Possesses weapons
- Possesses drugs or other controlled substances
- Gets unexplained threats/messages from callers who refuse to identify themselves to parents
- Is unable to account for time spent away from home

Table 9-10	Indicators of Possible Physical Abuse the Physical Educator Should Know[3,9,32,35,37,43,70]

Affective disturbances
  Low self-esteem
  Hopelessness
  Depression
  Nonresponsiveness
  Flat affect
  Anxiety
  Aggressive behavior
  Posttraumatic stress disorder
  Increased suicide risk
  Substance abuse

Soft-tissue damage (most common site—buttocks, hips); soft-tissue bruises, particularly multiple bruises

Bruise colors in different stages of healing
- Days 1–2   Red/blue
- Days 3–5   Blue/purple
- Days 6–7   Green
- Days 8–10   Yellow/brown

Burns
  Burns in areas child could not reach
  Burns shaped in patterns of objects used to inflict burn (curling iron, steam iron, lightbulb, immersion)

Head trauma
  Cephalohematoma
  Skull fracture
  Intercranial soft-tissue damage

Joint dislocations, abdominal trauma, spiral fractures

educational neglect, substance and alcohol abuse, and lack of supervision or bizarre discipline.

Wang and Daro[64] also identified the causes of child abuse and neglect. The three primary causes are (1) substance abuse; (2) poverty and economic strains, including inadequate housing and unemployment; and (3) lack of parenting skills. Other significant factors are a history of abuse, homelessness, and inadequate parental education.

Unfortunately, society perpetuates and allows the abuse of children. Child abuse and neglect must be considered within the societal context. Child abusers are most often parents, siblings, other relatives, or people entrusted with the care of the child—baby-sitters, child care workers, and youth group leaders, for example. One of the most tragic issues surrounding child abuse and neglect is that the abuser is almost always someone the child trusts or someone on whom the child is dependent.

Child abuse must be considered within the context of a society that endorses the notion that children are the property of the parent. The courts typically have supported the notion that the best possible place for a child to be raised is with the natural parents. The efforts of professionals involved in child protection are often thwarted by the interpretation of laws that continue to support the notion that the parents "own" their child and, subsequently, have the right to treat the child, the "property," as they see fit. Teachers who report suspected child abuse are often dismayed to learn

Table 9-11	Indicators of Sexual Abuse the Physical Educator Should Know[9,18,32,35]

Clinical manifestations of sexual abuse
  Pregnancy
  Sexually transmitted disease
  Vaginal, penile, or rectal injuries, lesions, or pain;
    redness of area of a discharge with or without
    bleeding
  Soft-tissue injuries on/around the mouth and breasts
  Pain and irritation during urination or defecation

Behaviors associated with sexual abuse
  Seductive behavior
  Activity of a sexual nature with peers, animals,
    or objects
  Preoccupation with age-inappropriate sexuality
  Prostitution

Affective disorders associated with sexual abuse
  Deficit with age-appropriate play behaviors
  Deficit in age-appropriate social skills
  Fearfulness of adults
  Sleep disorders
  Regression
  Aggression
  Feelings of hopelessness and despair, suicide
    attempts
  Self-mutilation
  Poor school performance (especially if it had been
    good)
  Eating disorders

Table 9-12	Indicators of Neglect the Physical Educator Should Know

Failure to thrive
  Below-average height for age
  Underweight for age

Malnutrition
  Poor physical fitness levels
  Low energy levels
  Complaints of hunger

Inappropriate clothing for weather (e.g., no socks
  in winter)

Table 9-13	Indicators of Psychological Abuse the Physical Educator Should Know[21]

Long-term psychological deprivation, the absence
of appropriate nurturing, can have long-term effects
on the mental, social, and emotional health of the
child. The indicators of psychological abuse are[21]

Affective disturbances
  Flat affect
  Volatility, or "acting-out" behaviors
  Inability to maintain significant relationships
  Inability to participate in age-appropriate play

Physical indicators
  Failure to thrive
  Malnutrition
  Frequent illness

that an abused child has been returned to the home, the place where abuse occurs, after investigation.

The percentage of children with disabilities may be at greater risk of abuse and neglect than children who do not have disabilities.[15] Sobsey[58] found that more boys are physically abused and neglected, but more girls are sexually abused, and that boys with disabilities are overrepresented in all categories of abuse. In fact, the very characteristics of some children with disabilities put them in jeopardy. Children particularly at risk are those with intellectual disabilities, behavior disorders, attention problems, or difficulty maintaining reciprocal relationships; premature infants (particularly colicky and crying babies); and children with behavioral problems (see Tables 9-14 and 9-15).

Children who are abused or neglected are at greater risk of becoming emotionally disturbed, language-impaired, intellectually disabled, and/or physically disabled than are children who are not abused. In fact, adolescents who have been physically abused are much more likely to have difficulty with internalizing issues (depression, suicide, withdrawal, attentional problems) and externalizing issues (aggression, delinquent behavior, and aggressive behavior) than are adolescents who have not been abused.[38] Once a child is abused or neglected, it increases his or her likelihood of arrest as a juvenile

Table 9-14	Children with Disabilities and Their Susceptibility to Abuse[68]

Children with disabilities may have one or more of the following characteristics, which make them more susceptible to child abuse and neglect than children without disabilities.[68]

- Need for expensive medical intervention/therapy and the pressure that puts on the caregiver
- Inability to follow expected developmental patterns in motor, speech, social, and play skills
- Dependency on others to take care of basic daily living needs
- Dependency on others to take care of social/friendship needs
- Inability to take control of own life, which causes long-term need for caregiver
- Inability to effectively communicate needs and wants
- Inability to participate in reciprocal relationships
- Lack of knowledge about sex and misunderstanding of sexual advances
- Inability to differentiate between acceptable and nonacceptable touch
- Inability to defend self

Table 9-15	Characteristics of the Parents of Children with Disabilities That May Make the Parents More Prone to Abuse Their Children

The parents of children with developmental disabilities may be more prone to abuse their children because of the following:

- The parents' obligation to provide constant care
- Significant financial and time obligations and restraints
- The parents' guilt, denial, and frustration[68]
- The parents' lack of understanding regarding the developmental sequence of the learner with a developmental delay
- The tendency to compare the child's development with that of nondelayed children
- Failure to develop appropriate expectations regarding the child's behavior
- Frustration because of intervention, and perceived intrusion, by care providers, such as teachers, therapists, and social workers
- Frustration because of the child's lack of reciprocal relationship capability
- Frustration due to the child's lack of ability to express needs and wants
- Feelings of helplessness
- Disputes between parents regarding care of the child with a disability
- Alcohol and other drug abuse[68]
- The parents' own developmental delay
- The parents' own history of abuse

and as an adult and for committing a violent crime. In addition, these children are more likely to have mental health concerns, educational problems, occupational difficulties, and public health and safety issues (such as prostitution and alcohol problems).[72] Having suffered from abusive behavior as a child not only tends to create a scenario in which abusive behavior continues, but the abused individual seeks alcohol, marijuana, and other drugs to escape the feelings associated with the abuse.[27] The impact of the cycle of abuse of our most precious resource, our children, has yet to be fully understood. It is clear, however, that our children must be protected.

TEACHING STRATEGIES FOR PHYSICAL EDUCATORS WORKING WITH CHILDREN WHO HAVE BEEN ABUSED

The physical educator is in a unique position to see the indications of child abuse. In addition, the physical educator is more likely than other school personnel to see children and adolescents who are not fully clothed. A child with legs badly bruised from being kicked may be able to hide them in the regular classroom but may have difficulty hiding the bruises if the required dress is shorts, for example. A child whose back has been beaten may be able to sit in a chair in the classroom by adjusting his or her posture; that child may find it impossible to lie on a mat to do a sit-up.

If a physical educator suspects abuse, he or she must report it. It is a felony to suspect child abuse or neglect and not report it.

Most school districts have policies that outline the steps the teacher should take to report abuse. Referrals are usually made to child protective service agencies or the police through the school principal. However, if those responsible for reporting the suspected abuse do not do so, the teacher must take the responsibility to ensure that the child's rights are protected.

The physical education program should be adjusted to accommodate the abused child's physical, social, and motor needs. Children who can't keep up with their classmates because of underdevelopment, malnourishment, or behavioral problems must be able to learn in an environment in which it is possible for them to succeed. The preschool and elementary school programs should focus on the development of age-appropriate play behavior. The middle school and secondary physical education programs should be used to help these students develop self-responsibility.

Because the young child who has been abused may be delayed socially as well as physically, placement in a physical education setting with younger children might allow the child to function best. That placement should never deviate more than two grades from the child's age-appropriate placement.

Garbarino identified eight elements that children need in order to overcome the social toxicity in their environment.[21] It is crucial that physical educators honor these needs and ensure that their actions and programs meet these needs: (1) stability; (2) security; (3) affirmation of worth; (4) time with teacher; (5) belief in ideology; (6) access to basic resources; (7) community; and (8) justice.

Stability

The single most important variable in maintaining stability in the physical education environment is a professional educator able to exhibit consistent, calm, and nurturing behavior; there is no room for volatility when teaching children whose lives are in chaos.

- Class rules need to be posted, in clear view, and must remain consistent. They should be posted in the primary languages of the children whenever possible.

- Rules need to be written in specific, behavioral terms. For example, "Be good!" has little or no meaning to young children who have been raised in chaos, but "Listen when the teacher talks" gives the children the specific information they need to follow directions.
- Class rules need to be written in positive terms, rather than in negative terms. For example, "Keep your hands and feet to yourself" conveys a much more positive message than "No hitting or kicking."
- There should be rewards for following the rules, as well as consequences for breaking them. Consequences for breaking the rules need to be provided as choices to help the children learn cause-effect and must be the same for every child, every time.

Security

It must be clear to all children that verbal and physical abuse of others will not be tolerated (as made clear by the rules). Verbal or physical abuse of children is never a consequence of misbehavior. Even in districts and states in which corporal punishment is allowed, the physical educator must never allow that to be part of the program. By its nature, it perpetuates the violence and chaos that have caused the children to be at risk in the first place.

Affirmation of Worth

The following strategies are effective in affirming each child's worth.

- Know and use each child's name.
- Expect excellence from all your students.[53]
- Always "catch 'em being good" and acknowledge that behavior.
- Praise often and well.

The emphasis in the physical education setting, at all levels (elementary school, middle school, junior high school, and high school), must be on cooperative, not competitive, experiences. At-risk children have difficulty experiencing success even in cooperative experiences. Competition causes some children to lose; these children don't need to lose any more than they already have.

Time with Teacher

While it may be difficult for the physical educator to find time every day for each child, warm-up time, station time, and relaxation time offer excellent opportunities for interpersonal communication—a compliment, a question, or a pat on the back will be significant for the student. (But be sure to ask for permission to touch a child until you know he or she will be receptive to your touch.)

Belief in Ideology

The student must be given the opportunity to feel that his or her life matters and that there is some sense in the "big picture." This is desperately hard for many children who have come to believe that their only option is prison or death. The physical educator can help with this process in a small but significant way. Give students specific responsibilities as part of the class experience. Develop a system, so that all children have the opportunity to assume responsibility and be rewarded for performing the given task. Load the gymnasium with pictures and posters that represent ethnic, cultural, gender, and ability diversity. Invite role models, such as area athletes and professional or college or university athletes, including those with disabilities, to participate in your program as guest speakers or mentors.

Access to Basic Resources

Playground areas are often disregarded in school planning, particularly in urban, poor school districts. Organize a community/parent campaign to design and build a playground area. Use inexpensive and homemade equipment, so that, when appropriate, each child has access to his or her own piece of equipment. (Many children have never had even a balloon to play with.)

Community

The focus in play, games, leisure/recreation, and sport must be based on the adoption of the philosophy espoused in the "New Games" movement.[46,51]

Children Need to Experience Success When Participating in Age-Appropriate Activities
Photo by Carol Huettig.

In this philosophy, individuals have an opportunity to learn to move while learning cooperative, rather than competitive, behaviors. There is no winner and, subsequently, no loser in the New Games, or Cooperative Play, movement.

Use ethnic and culturally diverse music for warm-ups and rhythm/dance activities. Expand the curriculum to include ethnic and culturally diverse play, games leisure/recreation, and sports.

Justice

Every child must be treated the same way as every other child, all the time, if children are to believe the physical educator to be just.

MODEL PHYSICAL EDUCATION AND RECREATION PROGRAMS FOR AT-RISK CHILDREN AND YOUTH

The physical educator is in a unique position to address some of the issues that plague at-risk children and youth, with and without disabilities. In fact, the physical educator can help children who have psychosocial delays by providing an opportunity to develop the social skills necessary to function within play, games, leisure/recreation, and sport. Many of the skills necessary to participate successfully in the physical education program are those necessary to participate successfully within the schools and society at large. Sometimes, however, it is difficult to address the social skills of at-risk students because the skills necessary for their street survival are not those necessary to survive in "middle-class" society.

Hellison and his associates at the University of Illinois–Chicago Circle have developed a beautiful, innovative model physical education and sports program for at-risk children and youth that honors their street skills and builds on those skills.[29] Hellison and his associates have based their program on the notion that the physical education class, or a team within a class, is a microcosm of the greater society and that children can learn to develop values and behaviors necessary to participate in play, games, leisure/recreation, and sport; those social skills are at the foundation of an individual's ability to function within the society at large.[31] The intent of the program is to develop the child's self-responsibility and social responsibility:

> Self-responsibility is conceptualized as empowering at-risk youth to take more control of their own lives, to learn how to engage in self-development in the face of a variety of external forces, including socialization patterns, peer pressure, self-doubt, lack of concepts and skills, and limited vision of their own options. Social responsibility is conceptualized as the development of sensitivity to the rights, feelings, and needs of others. Indicators include movement beyond

The Development of Trust Is Often Difficult for Children
Courtesy Wisconsin Lions Camp, Rosholt, WI.

egocentrism and ethnocentrism, recognition of the rights and feelings of others, caring and compassion, service to others, and concern for the entire group's welfare.[29]

Hellison's program has been based on the notion that children, even those who are most seriously at risk, can learn the social and emotional skills necessary to function in play, games, leisure/recreation, and sport and, perhaps more important, can generalize those skills to participation in the larger society. Hellison suggests a four-level model of behavior/value development for the physical education program (see Table 9-16).[30]

At-risk children and youth are given the opportunity in Hellison's program to develop the fundamental skills necessary for human interaction.

Table 9-16	Hellison's Four-Level Model of Behavior/Value Development

Level 1: sufficient self-control to respect the rights and feelings of others
Level 2: participation and effort in program activities
Level 3: self-direction with emphasis on independence and goal setting
Level 4: caring about and helping others

Data from Hellison D: "Teaching PE to at-risk youth in Chicago: a model" *JOPERD* 61:38–39, 1990.

Indeed, many children and youth have not been taught the necessary skills for communicating basic needs, for negotiating, and for expressing emotions that are socially appropriate. The children's models have used verbal and physical aggression to communicate; young people mirror what they have learned and what they have seen. Specific strategies for modifying games to better meet students' needs are presented in Chapter 6. Hellison and his associates have used student logs and diaries in which students explain behavior and indicate their progress on skills at each of the four levels of social development.[28,30] The culmination of the acquisition of socially desirable behaviors includes students' efforts to provide help, care, and support for others. Hellison and his colleagues provide the opportunity for children to learn the skills that are expected within the larger society, in a structured environment, which allows the children to self-test and grow.

Martinek and Hellison[41] have suggested that an effective way to foster resiliency, the ability to survive and thrive despite the circumstances, is an extended day program. They suggest that before-school, after-school, and evening programs provide an opportunity for at-risk children and youth to develop the social competence, autonomy, optimism, and hope required to succeed. Martinek and Hellison suggest that a successful extended day program must follow these guidelines:

1. Treat the children and youth as resources with potential, not as problems.

Children Participating in Parallel Play
Photo by Carol Huettig.

2. Focus on the whole child or youth, addressing emotional, social, educational, and economic needs.
3. Respect the individuality of the child or youth, including his or her cultural, developmental, and behavioral characteristics.
4. Encourage participation in the program by fostering active participation and allowing a decision-making voice in the program.
5. Ensure there are clear expectations and values associated with the program.
6. Help the child or youth envision and plan a future (other than death or prison).
7. Ensure a physically and psychologically safe environment.
8. Foster and nurture links with community leaders—ministers, business leaders, parents, and teachers.

Children Participating in Cooperative Play
Photo by Carol Huettig.

Horseback Riding Develops Spenser's Balance and Confidence

Courtesy of Roxanne and Randy Roberson, Spenser's Mom and Dad.

9. Conquer the system obstacles.
10. Help ensure that the child or youth has regular contact with an adult who is a mentor.

Physical activity programs provide the most logical opportunity for the development of the skills required for resiliency: social competence, autonomy, and optimism. Martinek and Hellison have found that goal-setting skills, particularly significant in physical activity programs, are critical in the development of resiliency and autonomy. They note, however,

> Certain barriers must be negotiated before any kind of goal-setting can take place. These barriers are: (1) the school culture, (2) combative values, (3) dysfunctional home life, and (4) fear of making choices.[42]

Essentially, Martinek and Hellison, both with extensive experience working with at-risk youth, have found in their "club" system and extended school day programs that many at-risk youth are not able or willing to participate in traditional, school-based goal-setting experiences because they perceive the school culture as that of the "enemy"; they prefer fighting to problem solving; their models may have been abusive; and they may avoid making choices

because it requires a commitment and accountability. Martinek and Hellison, writing to physical education professionals, said,

> You have to value this work, to have a passion for it. Without sufficient internal drive, we would have given up long ago. When we do workshops for teachers and youth workers, we always make the point: "You have to outlast them!" We refer not only to the children, who reflect the influences in the community, but also to all attempts to derail your efforts. We often say that our most important goal is to hang in there (white-knuckled) through thick and thin—all the rest is details.[42]

Psychosocial Goals and Objectives on the IEP

Psychosocial goals and objectives are a crucial part of the IEP. A carefully developed physical education program that includes developmentally appropriate play, games, leisure/recreation, and sport gives the physical educator the opportunity to focus on the attainment of psychosocial goals and objectives. Certainly, the physical educator can be a critical person in increasing the school connectedness of children and adolescents by encouraging involvement in intramurals, after-school programs, and developmentally appropriate athletic programs. School connectedness appears to be a major factor in the health and well-being of young people.[6] (See Chapter 4 for more information on IEP goals and objectives.)

John Hope Franklin, an African American scholar who wrote *From Slavery to Freedom: A History of African Americans,* speaking before the North Carolina Assembly, July 22, 1997, said,

> It surely is not enough for the most powerful nation in the world to have an educational system that is impoverished not only in terms of its dilapidated physical facilities but also in terms of inequities along racial and class lines among schools and school districts. I hope that you will agree that it is not enough for us to move at a snail's pace in wiping out the remnants of racial and ethnic strife. In doing so, we merely add to the burdens we must bear in leading the world toward a lasting peace, devoid of the sentiments and enmities that have already brought on huge wars time and time again. We can do better than that, and I hope that you agree.[65] (See Table 9-17.)

With Just a Little Help and Encouragement a Child Can Succeed
Laurie Zittel.

Table 9-17	In the Three Hours It Took You to Study This Chapter[10]

300 children in the United States were abused or neglected
300 children were born into poverty
180 children were born without health insurance
9 children died before their first birthday
1 child or teen was killed by gunfire

Modified from the Children's Defense Fund: *Moments in America 2007* With grateful appreciation to the Children's Defense Fund for their advocacy efforts on behalf of our children.

SUMMARY

Children with and without disabilities in this society are at serious risk. Children are among the most ignored and neglected of our people. Children with and without disabilities are entering the public school system unprepared, understimulated, abused, homeless, unloved, fearful, tired, hungry, and unkempt. All of these factors have an impact on the psychosocial development of children. In combination, the effect is devastating. Psychosocial development can be promoted through participation in developmentally appropriate play, games, leisure/recreation, and sport in a well-designed physical education program. The physical education program must carefully address the student's needs, play skills, and motivations for social interaction and must create a nourishing, nontoxic learning environment.

REVIEW QUESTIONS

1. Explain the long-term effect of in utero maternal abuse of alcohol or other drugs on the school performance of children.

2. List some of the reasons that children with disabilities are more at risk for child abuse and neglect than other children.

3. Describe the impact of poverty and homelessness on infants, children, and their families.

4. Describe the turbulent nature of the schools in contemporary society.

5. Describe Martinek and Hellison's model physical education programs for at-risk children and youth.

6. Describe the nature of a New Game.

STUDENT ACTIVITIES

1. Work in small groups. Choose one game typically played in elementary physical education—kindergarten through 6th grade—and modify it so it becomes a *cooperative* game, not a competitive game.

2. Volunteer in an after-school program for children at risk for school failure.

3. Volunteer in a homeless shelter or shelter for abused women and children.

4. Work in small groups and develop IEP goals and objectives that address psychosocial behavior for each of the children highlighted in the four case studies in this chapter.

5. Write a letter to your local newspaper voicing concerns, if you share them, about federal, state, and local spending priorities.

REFERENCES

1. Administration for Children and Families: *Child Maltreatment Summary for 2005,* www.acf.hhs.gov/programs/cb/pubs/cm05/summary.htm.

2. Adults and Children Together Against Violence, http//:actagainstviolence.apa.org/mediaviolence/index.html, 2007.

3. Allen DM, Tarnowski KJ: Depressive characteristics of physically abused children, *J Abnorm Child Psychol* 17:1–11, 1989.

4. American Academy of Pediatrics, Committee on Substance Abuse and Committee on Children with Disabilities: Fetal Alcohol Syndrome and alcohol related neurodevelopmental disorders, *Pediatrics* 106(2):358–361, 2000.

5. American Seniors/TodaysSeniorsNetwork.com: Grandparent caregivers, www.todayssenior network.com/grandparent-caregivers.htm.

6. Bonny A, Britto M, Klostermann B, Hornung R, Slap G: School disconnectedness: Identifying Adolescents at risk, *Pediatrics* 106(5):1017–1021, 2000.

7. Burnett G, Walz G: Gangs in schools, *Clearing-house on Urban Education Digest,* http://eric-web.tc.columbia.edu/digests/dig99.html. 2003.

8. *Checklist of characteristics of youth who have caused school-associated violent deaths,* National School Safety Center, www.NSSC.org/reporter/checklist.htm. 2003.

9. *Child abuse,* www.childabuse.com. 2003.

10. Children's Defense Fund: *State of America's children yearbook, 1999.* Boston: Beacon Press, 1999.

11. Children's Defense Fund: *Moments in America for children,* www.childrensdefense.org/site, February 2007.

12. Clark C, Li D, Conry J, Conry R, Loock C: Structural and functional brain integrity of Fetal Alcohol Syndrome in nonretarded cases, *Pediatrics* 105(5):1096–1099, 2000.

13. Dangerous homes: Substandard housing is a health risk for kids, *Dallas Morning News,* April 13, 1999.

14. D'Entremont DM: *Intervention strategies for school age children,* Report # CG023529, University of Southern Maine (ERIC Document Reproduction Service # ED 334514).

15. Diamond LJ, Jaudes PK: Child abuse in a cerebral-palsied population, *Dev Med Child Neurol* 1:12–18, 1987.

16. Dodge NN: *Effect of legal and illegal substances used by women during pregnancy.* Paper presented at "Understanding the Impact of Alcohol and Other Drugs on Young Children and Their Families," Region 20 Education Service Center, Richardson, TX, April 16–17, 1999.

17. *Early warning, timely response: A guide to safe schools,* www.air.org/cecp/guide/files.3.htm. 2003.

18. Elliott DJ, Tarnowski KJ: Depressive characteristics of sexually abused children, *Child Psychiatry Hum Dev* 21:37–47, 1989.

19. Funk JB, Baldaccia HB, Pasold T, Baumgardner J: Violence exposure in real life video games, television and the Internet: Is there desensitization? *J of Adolescence* 27:23–39, 2004.

20. *Gang culture and parent awareness,* http://gangsgang.com/index.html, 2007.

21. Garbarino J, Garbarino AC: *Emotional maltreatment of children.* Chicago, National Committee for Prevention of Child Abuse, 1986.

22. Geltman P, Brown M, Cochran J: Lead poisoning among refugee children resettled in Massachusetts, 1995–1999, *Pediatrics* 108(1):158–162, 2001.

23. Green C: Infant mortality rate may rise: Poverty, drug use, AIDS among factors cited in panel's report, *Dallas Morning News,* February 27, 1990.

24. Greer JV: The drug babies, *Except Child* February:382–384, 1990.

25. Griffin L: Welfare cuts leaving more families homeless, study finds, *Dallas Morning News,* July 1, 1999.

26. Hadnot I: Digital divide: Experts wonder how to close gap between whites and minorities in computer use, *Dallas Morning News,* July 27, 1999.

27. Harrison PA, Fulkerson JA, Beebe TJ: Multiple substance abuse among adolescent physical and sexual abuse victims, *Child Abuse Neg* 21(6):529–539, 1997.

28. Hellison D: Making a difference: Reflections on teaching urban at-risk youth, *JOPERD* 61:33–45, 1990.

29. Hellison D: Physical education for disadvantaged youth, *JOPERD* 61:37, 1990.

30. Hellison D: Teaching PE to at-risk youth in Chicago: A model, *JOPERD* 61:38–39, 1990.

31. Hellison D, Templin T: *A reflective approach to teaching physical education.* Champaign, IL, Human Kinetics, 1991.

32. Huettig C, DiBrezzo R: *Factors in abuse and neglect of handicapped children.* Paper presented at American Alliance of Health, Physical Education, Recreation and Dance National Convention, Las Vegas, April 1987.

33. *Income, poverty, and health insurance coverage in the United States.* Washington, DC, U.S. Census Bureau, www.census.gov/prod/2005 pub/p60-229pdf, 2005.

34. *Infant mortality and life expectancy for selected countries.* Pearson Education, publishing as infoplease, April 11, 2007.

35. Jason J: Child abuse or maltreatment. In Conn RB, editor: *Current diagnosis,* 7th ed. Philadelphia, WB Saunders, 1985.

36. Jasperse P: Four million U.S. kids hungry, *Milwaukee Journal Sentinel,* July 20, 1995.

37. Johnson CF: Inflicted injury versus accidental injury, *Pediatr Clin North Am* 37:791–814, 1990.

38. Kaplan S, et al.: Physically abused adolescents: Behavior problems, functional impairment, and comparison of informants' reports, *Pediatrics* 104(1):43–50, 1999.

39. Kozol J: *Savage inequalities: Children in America's schools.* New York, Crown, 1991.

40. Los Angeles Homeless Services Coalition: *United States homeless statistics,* http://lahsc.org/wordpress/educate/statistics/united-states-homeless-statistics April 12, 2007.

41. Martinek TJ, Hellison D: Fostering resiliency in underserved youth through physical activity, *Quest* 49:34–49, 1997.

42. Martinek T, Hellison D: Values and goal-setting with underserved youth, *JOPERD* 69(7):47–52, 1998.

43. McClelland CQ, Kingsbury GH: Fractures in the first year of life: A diagnostic dilemma, *Am J Dis Child* 136:26–29, 1982.

44. *Minority health: Racism linked to high infant mortality rate.* Kaiser Family Foundation Reproductive Health Report, http://report.kff.org/repro/db2/1999/03/kr990322.4.html, March 22, 1999.

45. More children being raised by grandparents, Census Bureau finds, *Dallas Morning News,* July 1, 1999.

46. *More new games and playful ideas from the New Games Foundation.* Garden City, NY, Headlands Press, 1981.

47. National Center for Children Exposed to Violence, www.nccev.org/violence/index.html, 2007.

48. National Center for Children in Poverty: *Basic facts about low-income children birth to age 6.* New York, Columbia University, www.nccp.org/pub_ycp06b.html, 2006.

49. National Center on Birth Defects and Developmental Disabilities: *Fetal alcohol*

spectrum disorders. Atlanta, GA, Centers for Disease Control and Prevention, www.cdc.gov/nchddd/fas/fasask.htm, 2007.

50. National Survey on Drug Use and Health, Office of Applied Studies, Department of Health and Human Services, www.oas.samha.gov/2K3/pregnancy/pregnancy.htm.

51. *New games.* Garden City, NY, Headlands Press, 1976.

52. Office of Applied Studies: *National survey on drug use and health.* Washington, DC, Department of Health and Human Services, 2004.

53. O'Neil J: Transforming the curriculum for students "at-risk," *Curr Update* Vol. 1–3, 6, 1991.

54. Pianin E, Fletcher M: Study: Thousands of students at risk: Report on 45 states says almost 1,200 schools built on, near toxic sites, *Dallas Morning News,* January 21, 2002.

55. Reese RM, Kirschner RH: *Shaken baby syndrome/shaken impact syndrome.* National Center for Shaken Baby Syndrome, www.dontshake.com. 2003.

56. Rotholz D, et al.: A behavioral comparison of preschool children at high and low risk from prenatal cocaine exposure, *Educ Treat Child* 18(1):1–18, 1995.

57. Sieder JJ: Scholars take look at anatomy of violent acts, *Dallas Morning News,* June 12, 1999.

58. Sobsey D, Randall W, Parrila RK: Gender differences in abused children with and without disabilities, *Child Abuse Negl* 21(8):707–720, 1997.

59. Stewart B McKinney Homeless Assistance Amendment Act, P.L. 100-645, 1990 U.S. Code., Cong. & Ad. News (104 Stat.) 4673, 1990.

60. Streissguth A, et al.: Fetal Alcohol Syndrome in adolescents and adults, *J Amer Med Assoc* 265:1961–1967, 1991.

61. Tarr S, Pyfer J: Physical and psychomotor development of neonates/infants prenatally exposed to drugs: A meta-analysis, *APAQ* 13(3):269–287, 1997.

62. U.S. Census Bureau: *Computer and Internet use in the United States: 2003.* Washington, DC, U.S. Department of Commerce, 2005.

63. Waller M: Helping crack-affected children, Mount Carmel, IL: Corwin Printing, 1994.

64. Wang CT, Daro D: *Current trends in child abuse reporting and fatalities: The results of the 1997 annual fifty state survey.* Chicago, Prevent Child Abuse America, 1998.

65. Washington V, Andrews JD, editors: *Children of 2010.* Washington, DC, National Association for the Education of Young Children, 1999.

66. Wasserman J: Surviving the mean streets, *Dallas Morning News,* January 12, 1995.

67. Wehling D: The crack kids are coming, *Principal* May:12–13, 1991.

68. Westcott H: The abuse of disabled children: A review of the literature, *Child Care Health Dev* 17:243–258, 1991.

69. Williams B, Howard V, McLaughlin T: Fetal Alcohol Syndrome: Developmental characteristics and directions for future research, *Educ Treat Children* 17(1):86–97, 1994.

70. Wilson EF: Estimation of the age of cutaneous contusions in child abuse, *Pediatrics* 60:750–752, 1977.

71. Zahn M, Schultze S: Children with special needs often get teachers with little training, *Milwaukee Journal Sentinel,* May 24, 1998.

72. Zero to Three: *Research summary: Children exposed to violence,* www.zerotothree.org/site/docserver/courtteam_children_violence.pdf, 2001.

SUGGESTED READINGS

Hellison D: *Teaching responsibility through physical education,* 2nd ed. Champaign, IL, Human Kinetics, 2003.

Kozol J: *Rachel and her children: Homeless families in America.* Meza, AZ, Three Rivers Press, 2006.

Kozol J: *The shame of the nation: The restoration of apartheid schooling in America.* Mesa, AZ, Three Rivers Press, 2006.

RECOMMENDED WEB SITES

Please keep in mind that these Web sites are being rec-ommended in the winter of 2007. As Web sites often change, they may have moved or been reconfigured or eliminated.

National Center for Children in Poverty
  www.nccp.org

National Coalition for the Homeless
  www.nationalhomeless.org

Shaken Baby Syndrome
  www.dontshake.com

Children's Defense League
  www.childrensdefense.org

RECOMMENDED VIDEOS

Insight Media
2162 Broadway
New York, NY 10024-0621
1-800-233-9910
www.insight-media.com

Addiction and Depression
#50AN4507/DVD/2005/23 min/$109

Child Abuse: How I See It, How I Stop It
#74AN3823/DVD/2002/25 min/$149

Child Abuse: Neglect and Sexual Abuse
#74AN4315/DVD/2005/30 min/$129

Suicide: A Guide for Prevention
#50AN4945/VHS tape/200/30min/$129

RECOMMENDED WEBSITES

Please keep in mind that these Web sites are being recommended in the winter of 2007. As Web sites often change, they may have moved or been reconfigured or eliminated.

National Center for Children in Poverty
www.nccp.org

National Coalition for the Homeless
www.nationalhomeless.org

Shaken Baby Syndrome
www.dontshake.com

Children's Defense League
www.childrensdefense.org

RECOMMENDED FILMS

Insight Media
2162 Broadway
New York, NY 10024-0621
1-800-233-9910
www.insight-media.com

Addiction and Depression
#SDANA580/DVD/2003/$23 min/$100

Child Abuse: How I See It; How I Stop It
#TRAN338/DVD/2002/29 min/$149

Child Abuse: No Longer and S Part Three
#TRAN313/DVD/2005/50 min/$129

Suicides: A Guide for Prevention
#SDAN885/VHS/1996/30 min/$129

PART

IV

Needs of Specific Populations

In this part, specific types of disabilities and suggestions for intervention strategies are described. While we recognize that each person has unique qualities and needs, for ease of communication we have grouped similar conditions together. Each condition is defined, characteristics are given, means of testing are suggested, and specific programming and teaching techniques are detailed. The conditions addressed in each chapter have been organized to be consistent with the 2004 amendments to IDEA. Expanded coverage has been given to categories of conditions that are increasing in incidence. These include pervasive developmental disorders, conduct disorders, speech impairments, traumatic brain injuries, and spinal cord injuries.

CHAPTER

10

Infants, Toddlers, and Preschoolers

■ **OBJECTIVES**

Explain the difference between IDEA mandates for early childhood intervention (ECI) birth to three years and preschool programs for children three to five years.

List and describe Howard Gardner's eight forms of intelligence and explain the implications for assessment and intervention.

Describe the infant-family interaction process.

Explain effective modeling techniques for parents who are trying to improve motor and play skills in their infant or toddler.

Describe developmentally appropriate practice in assessment and intervention in preschool learning environments, including preschool movement programs.

Discuss strategies for identifying a child's anger and helping the child deal with the anger.

Design an active learning center for indoor and outdoor play.

Describe strategies to develop an antibias active learning center.

Courtesy Dallas Independent School District.

Early and developmentally appropriate intervention during the crucial years in which central nervous system development is "plastic," marked, and pronounced has a profound impact on cognitive, language, social-emotional, and motor performance. Attention

Caleb

Caleb and his twin sister were born 3 months prematurely. They received remarkable medical care in the neonatal intensive care ward of a major hospital. Caleb and his twin spent the first several months of their lives in the hospital. Caleb was the smaller and weaker of the two infants. His respiratory system was particularly compromised; he continues to be very susceptible to colds. As a 16-month-old toddler, he has very low muscle tone, hypotonia. The Early Childhood Intervention Program has recommended that Caleb participate in an aquatics program.

APPLICATION TASK

Explain the kinds of play activities Caleb could participate in to foster the development of his muscle tone in the aquatic environment.

to these factors is important for all children; however, it is critical for children who are born with disabilities or developmental delays or who are at risk for failure.

In this chapter we examine the most recent theories of intellectual development, as well as the gross motor, cognitive, receptive and expressive language, symbolic play, drawing, fine motor, constructive play, self-help, and emotional characteristics of the typically developing child from birth through five years. Techniques for identifying the developmental level of young children and intervention strategies to facilitate their developmental processes are explained. In addition, federal mandates that address required services for at-risk infants, toddlers, and preschoolers are discussed. The central role of the parents and other family members, including the extended family, in this process is emphasized. The characteristics and importance of developmentally appropriate learning environments designed to facilitate the primary learning tool of the young child—play—are highlighted.

THE POTENTIAL OF QUALITY EARLY INTERVENTION

There is a window of opportunity in which quality, family-based early intervention can make a significant difference in the lives of an infant, a toddler, or a preschooler and, subsequently, his or her family and the greater community.[72] During the early years of a child's life there are incredible opportunities to enhance central nervous system function. A quality early childhood intervention program can have lasting positive results: higher scores on intelligence tests, higher scores on reading and mathematics tests, and an increase in the probability that the individual will study at the college level and be employed. This type of program can reduce the likelihood that the individual will require special education, will become pregnant as a teenager, and will be incarcerated or served by the juvenile justice system.[47]

THE EIGHT TYPES OF INTELLIGENCE—THE PHILOSOPHICAL FOUNDATION OF EFFECTIVE AND APPROPRIATE EARLY INTERVENTION

A socially valid physical education program for preschoolers at risk, with developmental delays or disabilities, is based on the premise that professionals, parents, and other family members acknowledge, recognize, accept, and embrace the notion that there are eight types of intelligence.

Howard Gardner,[23] in his classic work *Frames of Mind: The Theory of Multiple Intelligences,* suggests that, if educators are to conceptualize cognition, it must be considered in a far broader realm than that typically used to identify or quantify an individual's ability to think and learn. Specifically, Gardner suggests that the instruments used typically to assess and evaluate intelligence tend to ignore many types of human intelligence in lieu of measuring those that are easiest to measure—namely, linguistic and mathematical abilities.

Gardner's theory of multiple intelligences has been widely embraced by enlightened educational communities. His theory continues to be ignored by those satisfied with the status quo.

Gardner defines intelligence as the ability to solve problems or create products valued within one or more cultural settings. His emphasis on multicultural settings is of particular value in consideration of the philosophy. His work is gaining recognition as educators seek to explore and define strategies to evaluate the intelligence of children representing a wide variety of cultures and as they seek educational intervention strategies that meet their diverse needs.

Widely used norm-referenced linguistic and mathematically based "intelligence tests" have widespread cultural, racial, socioeconomic, and gender biases. Historically, these tests have been used to include children in learning environments and experiences, as well as to exclude them. The tracking of African American and poor children, which provided the impetus for *Brown v. Board of Education* (Kansas), 1954, is a practice that, unfortunately, still exists. If Gardner's theory of multiple intelligences were widely embraced and practiced, educational assessment would more appropriately and equitably evaluate the performance and potential performance of all children. Educational intervention would be more appropriate and equitable, and more children would love school and want to stay in school to learn. Movement and play programs would be embraced as a vital and integral part of the total education process. Movement and play would be recognized for their significant potential in the lives of young children.

Educators, lawmakers, voters, school board members, and state education agency personnel must acknowledge that there are at least eight types of intelligence. In order to thrive and grow, our society needs individuals with each of these types of intelligence. The educational system must nurture each child and honor the child's intelligence. Each of Gardner's theorized intelligences is considered in the following sections with examples of the behaviors of infants, toddlers, and preschoolers that reflect these intelligences.[23]

Linguistic Intelligence

Linguistic intelligence is expressed in and through the use of oral language (receptive and expressive) and written language (reading and writing). It represents a sensitivity to and interest in the use of words, the sound and rhythm of words, and the functions of language—to express wants and needs, to convince, to share, and to explain. The young child demonstrates this intelligence by cooing and babbling, scribbling and drawing, asking questions, repeating nonsense rhymes, telling stories, listening to stories, identifying simple words or signs, and rote counting.

Logical-Mathematical Intelligence

Logical-mathematical intelligence is an individual's ability to group and sequence objects, to order and reorder them, to describe their quality and quantity, and to see and understand patterns. The young child demonstrates this intelligence by separating dinosaurs from zoo animals; stacking rings, diminishing in size, on a base; collecting sticks and separating the long ones from the short ones; sequencing blocks in patterns, such as three blue, two red, and three blue; and arranging balls from the largest to the smallest.

Musical Intelligence

Musical intelligence is an individual's ability to recognize sounds and distinguish one from another, identify and see patterns in music, be sensitive to rhythm and time variables, know and appreciate timbre and tone, and express feelings and emotions through music. The young child demonstrates this intelligence by seeking one "favorite" musical instrument; moving the body to a beat; using pots and pans as drums; turning off the CD player if he or she does not like the music; asking to sing a favorite song, over and over; clapping or toe tapping to a particular rhythm or beat; singing or humming; and "rapping" a favorite song.

Spatial Intelligence

Spatial intelligence includes the ability to identify shapes and differentiate between objects in terms of size, to see commonalities in shape or size, to perceive the visual world accurately, to perform simple transformations of visual images, and to recreate a graphic image of a visual representation, such as a map or graph. The young child demonstrates this intelligence by putting puzzles together, building a block structure, building a "Lego" bridge, drawing self, sorting objects by shape and size, copying a given figure, drawing a particular shape in a variety of positions,[23] identifying a child who is larger or smaller than self, and identifying a child who is taller or shorter than self.

Bodily-Kinesthetic Intelligence

Bodily-kinesthetic intelligence is characterized by the ability to use the body in highly differentiated and skilled ways, for expressive and goal-directed purposes. The young child demonstrates this intelligence by crawling, creeping, and walking in, around, and between objects; using gestures to express needs and wants; using facial expressions to convey emotions; reaching to get a favorite toy; rolling over; hurling a ball; catching a rolled ball; jumping over a set of blocks, arranged in an ever-taller sequence; kicking a ball; using the body to pretend to be "mad," "sad," or "glad"; and carrying a toy from the toy box to the play area.

Interpersonal Intelligence

Interpersonal intelligence is one in which an individual can identify and empathize with the feelings and emotions of others. The young child demonstrates this intelligence by crying if another child cries, telling a parent or another caregiver if a friend is hurt or sad, comforting a friend who is upset, noticing that the parent or caregiver is having a "bad day," and engaging in cooperative play.

Intrapersonal Intelligence

Intrapersonal intelligence is one in which the individual is able to identify his or her own feelings, emotions, and motives and is basically inner-directed (i.e., internally driven). The young child demonstrates this intelligence by seeking solitary play experiences; judging his or her own art project; keeping a journal of pictures, drawings, or symbols that reflect feelings; expressing emotion in housekeeping play experiences; and preferring an independent plan-do-review process to a group process.

Naturalist Intelligence

In later works, Gardner identified the 8th form of intelligence. At first, he suggested that it might be a "spiritual" intelligence.[28] In more recent works he has called it "naturalist" intelligence. In fact, it appears that this intelligence is probably a combination of "spirituality" and a profound sense of "nature." The young child demonstrates this intelligence by collecting and sorting leaves or taking loving care of a class rabbit.

DEVELOPMENTALLY APPROPRIATE ASSESSMENT OF INFANTS, TODDLERS, AND PRESCHOOLERS

While the move toward assessment that acknowledges multiple forms of intelligence has been embraced by some educators, there is a desperate need for assessment that is sensitive to the unique needs of infants, toddlers, and preschoolers (i.e., developmentally appropriate practice). This is critical because assessment drives eligibility. Eligibility drives decisions regarding goals and objectives on the IEP and individual family service plan. Goals and objectives drive placement and programming decisions.

In this section, we address developmentally appropriate assessment of movement and play for infants, toddlers, and preschoolers, with an emphasis on play-based, transdisciplinary assessment practices and the development of a movement/play portfolio assessment process to follow the child from infancy through adulthood.

Shepard[61] has suggested three basic principles to guide the assessment of young children:

1. Only testing that can be shown to lead to beneficial results should take place.
2. Assessment methods, particularly the language used, must be appropriate to the development and experiences of the children being tested.
3. Assessment features, including content, form, evidence of validity, and standards for interpretation, must be tailored to the specific purpose of the assessment.

Mandates specific to screening and assessing the "little ones" are included in P.L. 99-457:

1. Using a multidisciplinary approach to screen and assess children from birth through five years of age
2. Identifying infants and young children with known disabilities and developmental delays and, at states' discretion, identifying children from birth through two years of age who are at risk for developmental delays (including physical delays)
3. Planning comprehensive services for young children with special needs, including a model of periodic rescreening and reassessment
4. Involving the family in all levels of assessment, identification, and intervention

Levels of services included in the law are

1. Child Find activities
2. Developmental and health screening, including administration of screening instruments, questioning of parents, and administration of medical, vision, and hearing examinations
3. Diagnostic testing, including formal testing, parent interviews, and home observation
4. Individual program planning[41]

The expansion of services mandated by P.L. 99-457 has enabled the physical educator to become more fully involved in identifying and remediating delays evidenced by a wider range of young children. This provides a significant opportunity to have a positive impact on the lives of growing numbers of at-risk children in those critical early periods of life to help ready them for school.

GUIDELINES FOR SCREENING AND ASSESSMENT OF INFANTS, TODDLERS, AND PRESCHOOLERS

The following guidelines for screening and assessing young children are recommended by Meisels and Provence:[42]

1. Screening and assessment are services—as part of the intervention process—and not only a means of identification and measurement.
2. Processes, procedures, and instruments intended for screening and assessment should be used only for their specified purposes.
3. Multiple sources of information should be included in screening and assessment.
4. Developmental screening should take place on a recurrent or periodic basis. It is inappropriate to screen young children only once during their early years. Reassessment should continue after services have been initiated.
5. Developmental screening should be viewed as only one path to more in-depth assessment. Failure to qualify for services based on a single source of screening information should not become a barrier to further evaluation for intervention services if other risk factors (e.g., environmental, medical, familial) are present.
6. Screening and assessment procedures should be reliable and valid.
7. Family members should be an integral part of the screening and assessment process. Information provided by family members is critical for determining whether to initiate more in-depth assessment and for designing

appropriate intervention strategies. Parents must give complete, informed consent at all stages of the screening process. Suen and colleagues write eloquently of the need for significant parent input in the screening and assessment process:

> Parents . . . have more longitudinal evidence of their child's development. While their ideas of child development may not be as rich in formal theory, the sheer amount of time spent with their own child over multiple situations lends a great deal of credence to their observations. Indeed, some newer approaches emphasize ecological/authentic information collection and rely on periodic parent appraisals of their children, especially when professional in-site assessment is not feasible.[63]

8. During screening or assessment of developmental strengths and problems, the more relevant and familiar the tasks and setting are to the child and the child's family, the more likely it is that the results will be valid.
9. All tests, procedures, and processes intended for screening and assessment must be culturally sensitive.
10. Extensive and comprehensive training is needed by those who screen and assess very young children.

Selected motor assessment instruments that are appropriate for use with infants, toddlers, and preschoolers are included in Table 10-1.

TRANSDISCIPLINARY, PLAY-BASED ASSESSMENT

The Individuals with Disabilities Education Improvement Act (IDEIA, 2004) mandates a comprehensive assessment, for children from birth to three, and three to five, to determine eligibility and to serve as the basis for the development of the individual family service plan or the IEP. The standard within the profession is transdisciplinary, play-based assessment (TPBA), described by Linder as follows:

> Transdisciplinary play-based assessment involves the child in structured and unstructured play situations with, at varying times, a facilitating adult, the parent(s), and another child or children. Designed for children functioning between infancy and 6 years of age, TPBA provides an opportunity for developmental observations of cognitive, social-emotional, communication and language, and sensorimotor domains.[35]

The assessment process must be transdisciplinary; that is, it should be done by a team of individuals with a commitment to infants, toddlers, and preschoolers representing various disciplines. The child's parents are the most important members of the team—the parents are the best source of information about the child.

Professionals with unique abilities and skills in one or more of the domains are a vital part of the team as well. These professionals include, but are not limited to, (1) an educational psychologist, (2) a speech and language therapist, (3) an occupational therapist, (4) a physical therapist, (5) an adapted physical educator with specific training and experience working with little ones, (6) a play therapist, and (7) a music therapist. A transdisciplinary approach to assessment with infants, toddlers, and preschoolers allows the team members to gain vital information about the child's development and to share that information with other professionals.

The adapted physical educator may add a unique perspective to the transdisciplinary team because of specific competencies. Cowden and Torrey[11] suggest the "adapted motor developmentalist" should have the following competencies:

- Knowledge of normal and abnormal motor development
- Curriculum- and judgment-based assessment techniques
- Appropriate response-contingent toys and materials for sensory stimulation and physical and motor development
- Strategies for relaxation, socialization, and play

Table 10-1	Selected Motor Assessment Instruments for Infants, Toddlers, and Preschoolers			
Test/Description	**Source**	**Age**	**Motor Components**	**Reference**
Alberta Infant Motor Scale (AIMS) (1994) A tool for assessing the early postures of the developing infant	Piper & Darrar: Motor Assessment of the Developing Infant W.B. Saunders Company 6277 Sea Harbor Drive Orlando, FL 32821	Birth–19 mos	Prone, supine, sit, stand postures	Content-referenced
Bayley Scales of Infant Development III (2005) This revised scale is sensitive to differences between children who are at risk for developmental delay and those who are not.	Harcourt Assessment 3052 Smidmore Street Marrickville, NSW 2204	1–42 mos	Posture, locomotor, fine motor	Norm-referenced
Brigance Diagnostic Inventory—Revised (2005) A widely used, teacher-friendly scale that also includes speech and language, general knowledge and comprehension, social and emotional development, reading readiness, basic reading skills, manuscript writing, and basic math assessment techniques	Curriculum Assoc., Inc. 5 Esquire Road North Billerica, MA 10862	Birth–7 yrs	Preambulatory, motor skills, fine motor, gross motor, self-help skills	Content-referenced
Callier-Azusa Scale (1978) A developmental scale designed to aid in the assessment of deaf-blind and profoundly disabled children. It also includes daily living skills, cognition, communication and language, and social-developmental milestones.	The University of Texas at Dallas The Callier Center for Communication Disorders 1966 Inwood Road Dallas, TX 75235	Birth–7 yrs	Postural control, locomotion, fine motor, visual-motor and visual, auditory, and tactile development	Content-referenced

Table 10-1	*(Continued)*			
Test/Description	**Source**	**Age**	**Motor Components**	**Reference**
Denver Development Scale II (DDST II) (1990) This easy-to-use screening tool also includes screening for language and personal-social skills (self-help).	Denver Developmental Materials, Inc. PO Box 371075 Denver, CO 80237-5075	Birth–6 yrs	Gross motor skills, fine motor–adaptive skills	Content-referenced
Hawaii Early Learning Profile (HELP) (1995) A curriculum-embedded developmental checklist that also includes cognitive, language, social, and self-help skills	VORT Corp. PO Box 601321 Palo Alto, CA 94306	Birth–6 yrs	Gross motor, fine motor, self-help	Content-referenced
Miller Assessment for Preschoolers (1988 Rev.) An instrument that also includes evaluation of a child's speech and language and cognitive abilities and provides guidance in determining whether a child's behavior during testing ranges from severely dysfunctional to normal	The Psychological Corp. 555 Academic Court San Antonio, TX 78204-2498	2.9–5.9 yrs	Sense of position and movement, touch, basic movement patterns, gross motor, fine motor	Content-referenced
Movement Assessment of Infants (1980) An instrument that enables the evaluator to determine whether a child is developing normally during the first year of life	Movement Assessment of Infants PO Box 4631 Rolling Bay, WA 98061	Birth–12 mos	Muscle tone, primitive reflexes, equilibrium reflexes, volitional movement	Content-referenced
Peabody Developmental Motor Scales (2000) A curriculum-embedded assessment tool that is widely used by preschool teachers	Harcourt Assessment 19500 Bulverde Road San Antonio, TX 78259	Birth–6 yrs	Fine motor, gross motor	Norm-referenced

(Continued)

Table 10-1	(*Continued*)				
Test/Description	**Source**	**Age**		**Motor Components**	**Reference**
SMART START (1995) A preschool movement curriculum designed for children of all ability levels	PRO-ED 8700 Shoal Creek Boulevard Austin, TX 78757-6897	2.5–6 yrs		Gross motor, play	Content-referenced

The assessment process is sensitive to the child's unique needs and allows flexibility in order to see the child's very best. In and through play—the most natural phenomenon of early childhood—the assessment team has the opportunity for developmentally appropriate observations within the cognitive, social-emotional, communication and language, and sensory-motor domains (see Table 10-2).

The more traditional assessment/evaluation model is inappropriate for infants, toddlers, and preschoolers for a number of reasons:

- Infants, toddlers, and preschoolers are not comfortable with strangers. It is frightening to meet a stranger, much less be asked to leave a parent or "more comfortable" adult to go with a stranger into a room to "play."
- Young children are uncomfortable outside of their natural setting—their home, their neighborhood, their child care setting—and will not behave naturally when asked to perform outside of their natural setting.
- A young child may be asked to play with an evaluator, but the child does not control the situation—the unfamiliar adult does. The child is asked to play without favorite toys and, to facilitate evaluation, the child may find a toy he or she enjoys playing with and then be asked to return the toy to move on to another task.
- Assessment protocols often discriminate against a child with a disability. For example, most "intelligence tests" rely heavily on language and prelogical/mathematical skills;

the child's performance may be significantly negatively affected by a dialect unfamiliar to the examiner.
- Many developmental assessment scales assume that there is a typical developmental sequence; many children with disabilities do not acquire developmental milestones in a typical way.
- Many of the tasks that infants, toddlers, and preschoolers are asked to perform have little or no meaning for the child or the child's parents. Unfortunately, this has been part of the clinical "mystique," which has presumed that the professionals have the answers and the parents are dependent on the professionals for information.

In order for the assessment process to yield meaningful information, the infant, toddler, and preschooler and his or her family members must be honored and respected. Neither the child nor the family members should be put in an uncomfortable situation.

COMPREHENSIVE MOTOR ASSESSMENT

The assessment of movement and play behaviors in infants, toddlers, and preschoolers requires a special sensitivity to the fact that major developmental changes occur during the crucial years from birth to age five.

ECOLOGICAL ASSESSMENT

Whenever possible, the assessment and evaluation of an infant, a toddler, or a preschooler

Table 10-2	Motor Development Delay Indicators: Three Years and Older*

I. Muscle tone status (check all that apply):
   a. Low tone (proprioceptive problems):
      Difficulty holding up head _____
      Slumped posture _____
      Tendency to put legs in a W position when sitting _____
   b. High tone (overflow/tension):
      Stiff body movements _____
      Fisting of one or both hands _____
      Grimacing of mouth or face when concentrating _____

II. Strength and endurance—demonstrates any of the following:
      Tires during play before other children _____
      Gets out of breath before other children _____
      Has breathing difficulties sometimes _____

III. Equilibrium/extensor muscle control (check all that apply):
   a. Does not raise and control head when:
      Lying face down _____
      Balancing on hands and knees _____
      Sitting _____
   b. Does not roll from front to back _____
   c. Does not prop on forearms _____
   d. Does not reach for a toy when:
      Lying face down _____
      Balancing on hands and knees _____
      Sitting _____
   e. Cannot remain standing without support _____

IV. Equilibrium/flexor muscle control (check all that apply):
   a. Has difficulty with the following moves from a back-lying position:
      Rolling from back to front _____
      Sitting up _____
      Standing up _____
      Reaching for toy _____

V. Equilibrium when moving (check all that apply):
      Does not use sequential movement when rolling (head, shoulders, hips, followed by legs) _____
      Stands/walks/runs on balls of feet _____
      Uses a wide base of support during walk/run _____
      Loses balance when suddenly changing directions _____
      Does not put arms and hands out to break fall _____
      Avoids walking on narrow supports (balance beam, curb) _____

VI. Visual status (indicators of depth perception problems)—demonstrates any of the following:
      Both feet are not off ground momentarily when running _____
      Does not jump down from bottom step _____
      Watches feet when moving on different surfaces _____
      Marks time when ascending and descending stairs _____

(Continued)

Table 10-2	(*Continued*)

Avoids climbing apparatus   _____

Turns head when catching ball   _____

Cannot bounce and catch playground ball with both hands   _____

Misses ball when kicking   _____

(NOTE: Children demonstrating three or more of the preceding eight behaviors should be referred to a visual developmental specialist for an orthoptic visual examination.)

VII. Coordination (check all that apply):
   a. Does not bring the hands together at midline when:
      Lying down   _____
      Sitting up   _____
   b. Does not demonstrate the following:
      Uses arms in opposition to legs when crawling   _____
      Uses arms in opposition to legs when walking   _____
      Uses arms in opposition to legs when running   _____
      Arms are bent at waist height when running   _____
      Use of both arms to assist during jump   _____
      Slides leading with one side of body   _____
      Gallops   _____
   c. Does not demonstrate the following when kicking:
      Swings kicking leg behind body when preparing to kick   _____
      Follows through with kicking leg after contact   _____

VIII. Additional information
   a. What are the primary means of moving during play? _____

_____

   b. What motor skills does the child avoid? _____

_____

   c. Can the child imitate a movement pattern that is demonstrated? _____
   d. Can the child demonstrate a sequence of movements when requested to do so? _____

_____

   e. Check the stages of play the child demonstrates: _____
      Solitary (onlooker or ignores others)   _____
      Parallel (plays alongside or with similar toys)   _____
      Associative (follow the leader)   _____
      Cooperative (social interaction)   _____

IX. Comments/observations/concerns: _____

_____

_____

*Activities that can be used in preschool and elementary grades to promote motor development can be located in the handbook *Gross Motor Activities for Young Children with Special Needs,* which instructors can download for distribution to students from the book's Web site, www.mhhe.com/auxterlle.

should be completed in the child's most natural environment—the child's home, child care setting, or neighborhood play area. In addition to being sensitive to the child's natural environment, the assessment must be culturally, linguistically, socioeconomically, and gender sensitive.

THE PORTFOLIO ASSESSMENT PROCESS

Sensitivity to the fact that assessment is not, and should never be, a six-month, annual, or three-year comprehensive event but, rather, a day-to-day, ongoing process has led educators to the portfolio assessment. Just as caring parents have historically saved documentation of their child's progress—pictures, drawings, height/weight information, "new" words, and so on—caring educators must begin to save, carefully, documentation of the progress of the children they teach.

Danielson has identified three types of portfolios:

1. Display, or showcase, portfolio. The display portfolio captures, usually with photos, the many activities in which children engage in a classroom. It is a picture of what goes on in the classroom but does not document a child's performance or development. A display portfolio shows only a child's best work and, subsequently, does not accurately reflect actual consistent performance.

2. Working portfolio. One way to get more accurate documentation of how a child is growing and developing is in a working portfolio. It shows the process of learning new concepts and applying new understanding to tasks. Gronlund suggests that a collection of work samples that pertain to a child's goals and objectives is key in the assessment of educational progress:

> The work samples document the child's strengths and weaknesses in meeting certain goals or learning objectives. The work is not representative of the child's best work, but rather is evidence of her typical, everyday performance. In this way a teacher can really look at the child's work samples and decide on teaching strategies to help that child grow and develop in her skills and knowledge. And, on a practical level, if the teacher collects only work samples that pertain to goals and objectives, s/he

significantly limits the number of things that will be collected and stored.[26]

3. Assessment portfolio. An assessment portfolio is a collection of student work that represents what the student has learned. The most effective portfolios also contain the student's reflection about what he/she has gained from the assignment. Danielson and Abrutyn wrote, "Documentation for assessment purposes must be more than photos and work samples. Teacher commentary becomes an essential source of information for evaluating the work. . . . Identifying what makes a quality piece of work or an informative work sample for portfolio collection is critical."[16]

The portfolio assessment process allows educators to address each of the eight types of intelligence to carefully document and monitor the progress of the infants, toddlers, and preschoolers they serve.[32] If the parent and teacher are sensitive to the fact that their role should not be intrusive but, rather, supportive—not as the director of learning but as the facilitator of learning, the portfolio is a natural and obvious conclusion. If the educator is actively watching and learning—from the children, the teacher will become adept at documenting each child's progress.

The adapted physical educator has a great deal to contribute to the child's total portfolio. In fact, this specialist may contribute information and data to the portfolio for all eight types of intelligence. Sharing these type of data with the early childhood educator helps validate the active play and learning process and encourages teachers and parents to perceive the adapted physical educator as a professional who can and does make a significant contribution. The following are examples of movement and play data that can be collected to reflect each of the eight types of intelligence.

Linguistic Intelligence

- A toddler says, "Ball," when he or she wants the teacher to roll the ball to the child; the teacher records the utterance on the child's daily log.
- The child sings a simple "rap" song while jumping; the teacher videotapes the child.

Logical-Mathematical Intelligence

- A child builds a tower with giant soft blocks, and the teacher takes a picture of the structure.
- A group of children line up to form a "train," and the teacher videotapes the group performing to the song "Chug-a-Long Choo Choo."

Musical Intelligence

- Several children dance to Hap Palmer's "What a Miracle"; the teacher videotapes the child being assessed.
- A child walks to the beat of a drum; the teacher notes the progress.

Spatial Intelligence

- A toddler can trap a 13-, 10-, 8-, or 6-inch ball rolled to the child sitting in a V-sit position; the parent notes the ability and shares the information with other team members.
- An infant crawls toward and reaches a toy; the preschool movement/play specialist records that on the ongoing motor development assessment instrument.

Bodily-Kinesthetic Intelligence

- A two-year-old toddler hurls a ball; the teacher records the progress on the child's portfolio.
- A five-year-old with Down syndrome climbs up and down a set of five stairs, holding the railing; the teacher records the milestone.

Interpersonal Intelligence

- A child engages in parallel play in a sandbox; the teacher videotapes the play.
- A child identifies the children he or she likes to play with and those he or she does not like to play with; the teacher records this on a sociogram.

Intrapersonal Intelligence

- A child describes the way he or she feels when playing a simple game with a friend; the teacher catches this on audiotape.

Naturalist Intelligence

- A child names a flower on a nature walk; the teacher notes it.
- A child describes how he or she feels chasing his or her shadow; it is recorded on audiotape.

Contemporary communication, technology, and computer capabilities make it possible for parents and teachers to save vast amounts of information about the development of young children. Baby-boomers have sepia photographs of their grandparents as children. The children of the 2000s have audio and visual memories stored on CD-ROM or on personal Web sites.

The technology exists to begin a portfolio for every infant that can follow the child throughout his or her development. The beauty lies in the capability to store information that could increase the likelihood that infants, toddlers, and preschoolers grow and learn in the best possible way. When an infant makes the transition into a toddler program, when that toddler makes the transition into a preschool program, and when that preschooler makes the transition into 1st grade, his or her teachers will have a comprehensive record of the child's progress.

The most significant questions related to the assessment process with infants, toddlers, and preschoolers include, but are not limited to, the following:

1. Does the assessment process yield important information that relates to eligibility, placement, and programming?
2. Does the assessment process do no harm? That is, can the infant, toddler, or preschooler be hurt in any way by the process? If so, it should not be done under any circumstance.
3. Does the assessment discriminate against children on the basis of culture, socio-economic base, or gender? It must not.
4. Does the process provide information that the parents and other practitioners can use?

Assessment can be intrusive. A transdisciplinary, play-based approach to assessment completed in the child's natural ecosystem reduces the potential for the assessment to frighten the child or parent. Assessment can also be discriminatory. Recognizing eight types of intelligence and monitoring progress using a portfolio assessment minimize that possibility as well.

AGES AND STAGES—UNDERSTANDING TYPICAL AND ATYPICAL DEVELOPMENT

It is vital that the physical educator be aware of the development of the whole child. It is also necessary for the educator to embrace the notion that there is no such thing as a "typical" child. Each child is a unique being who develops in a unique way.

The description of the approximate ages at which a child usually acquires a new skill is charted in Table 10-3. Certainly, the educator must know what is typical in order to work with a child with delays or disabilities. But it must be understood that each child develops uniquely. For example, it is not uncommon for an abused or neglected child to demonstrate typical gross and fine motor development yet show marked delays in social-emotional, cognitive, receptive, and expressive language development. It is not uncommon for a child struggling to learn English as a second language to demonstrate typical gross and fine motor development but show delays in play behavior and receptive and expressive language development.

An understanding of typical development allows the educator to better meet the needs of the child in early childhood intervention and preschool programs for children with disabilities.

EARLY CHILDHOOD INTERVENTION PROGRAMS—BIRTH TO THREE YEARS

Infants, Toddlers, Preschoolers, and Their Families

Federal mandates (IDEA Reauthorization, 2004) to provide educational services to infants, toddlers, and preschoolers have opened a window of opportunity for adapted physical education professionals. However, the strategies for intervention with infants, toddlers, and preschoolers are significantly different from those used in traditional educational programs. Consistent with the direction of the Office of Special Education Programs (OSEP), legislation has emphasized the importance of the family unit in providing early services to infants and young

children. The family takes a central role in providing for young children, particularly those children with high probability for lagging in their developmental process.

The shift toward embracing the family in the early intervention process represents philosophical and pedagogical shift from past practices. The growing societal awareness of the importance of early intervention for positively impacting the quality of children's lives and the current national emphasis on parental involvement in programs for at-risk children can dramatically modify the educational experiences of all children.

Strategies for fostering the participation of parents in ECI programs are summarized in Table 10-4.

Central to early childhood intervention is a respect for the family unit—in whatever form that takes. The child must be seen as part of that dynamic unit with the parent (or parent substitute) as the child's primary and most significant teacher. Dawkins and colleagues[15] acknowledged that there has been a wonderful transformation in the provision of services to infants, toddlers, and preschoolers:

The "family-centered approach" has become the foundation of early intervention. Families are seen as having enormous strengths and making the critical difference that enables a child to reach his or her potential. In the family-centered approach, families are allowed to choose their role at each stage and professionals are there not to direct but to support the family and provide services.[15] Given the large number of children being raised in poverty who are in need of early intervention services, it is important to note that "parents as teachers" programs have been found to have some success, particularly with very poor families.[67]

The 25th Annual Report to Congress indicates that 71.8 percent of infants and toddlers receive early intervention services in the home. Approximately 10 percent of children in the same age group receive services in programs designed for young children with developmental delays and/or disabilities.[69]

To consider movement and play intervention with an infant or a young child, it is vital that the adapted physical educator be sensitive to

Table 10-3	Ages and Stages of Typical Child Development			
Months	Typical Gross Motor Development	Typical Play Development	Typical Fine Motor/ Constructive Play	Typical Cognitive Development
0–3	Optical righting (2 mos)—child uses vision to align head when body is tilted; labyrinthine righting prone (2 mos)—when body is tilted, head orients to normal position	Gets excited when a toy is presented; shakes rattle if placed in hand	Puts fist in mouth; brings hands to chest and plays with hands and fingers; refines movements that satisfy needs (e.g., thumb sucking)	Follows object with eyes; continues actions to produce interesting reactions (e.g., kicks, coos, babbles)
3–6	Labyrinthine righting supine (6 mos)—when body is tilted, head orients to normal position; body righting (6 mos)—when body is tilted, body orients to normal position	Smiles, laughs in response to parent's speech, smile, or touch; enjoys simple songs, tickling, vocal games	Early grasping patterns emerge; plays with hands and feet; rubs, strikes, and shakes things to make noise; develops reaching patterns; uses both hands together; reaches for and grasps objects	Uncovers partially hidden object; imitates simple familiar actions
6–12	Supine and prone equilibrium reactions (6 mos); crawling (6–7 mos); hands and knees equilibrium reactions (8 mos); creeping (7–9 mos); sitting equilibrium reaction (10–12 mos); cruises holding on to furniture	Likes to bang things together; begins to imitate social games; prefers play with a parent to play with a toy; bites/chews toys; explores environment with adult help	Imitates simple actions (e.g., clapping, lying down; thumb begins to help with grasp; loves to shake and bang toys; begins to move intentionally; real pincer emerges at 12 months; begins to release objects)	Uncovers hidden object; imitates somewhat different actions; puts familiar actions together in new combinations; moves to get toy
12–18	Standing equilibrium (15 mos); walks up stairs, marking time; stands alone; walks alone with wide base of support; starts and stops walking; pushes a playground ball back and forth with a partner; makes a whole-body response to music; pulls or pushes a toy while walking	Enjoys piling objects and knocking them down; engages in solitary play; swings on a swing; plays alone contentedly if near an adult; likes action toys but plays with a variety of toys; uses realistic toys on self (e.g., pretends to brush hair with brush)	Stacks hand-sized blocks; combines objects; puts on/takes off pan and jar lids; takes objects out of a container; begins to scribble; holds crayon in hand with thumb up	Modifies familiar actions to solve new problems; imitates completely new actions; activates toy after adult demonstration

Table 10-3	(Continued)		
Typical Social-Emotional Development	**Typical Development of Receptive Language**	**Typical Development of Expressive Language**	**Typical Development of Self-Help**
Begins to find ways to calm and soothe self (e.g., sucking); draws attention to self when distressed; learns adults will answer (if, indeed, an adult answers); likes face-to-face contact; responds to voices	Notices faces of others; coos in response to pleasant voice; may stop crying when someone enters room	Cries and makes vowel-like sounds; uses "different" kinds of cries; makes pleasure sounds	Depends on parent for everything
Cries differently in response to adults; shows excitement when adult approaches to lift, feed, or play; regards adult momentarily in response to speech or movement; smiles when parent smiles; laughs and giggles; smiles at mirror image	Turns eyes and head toward sound; responds to sound of own name	Varies tone to express feelings; makes new sounds; stops making sounds when adult talks; begins vocal play; squeals; babbles; coos; "talks" to toy or pet	Depends on parent for everything
Asserts self; demonstrates curiosity; tests relationship with caregiver; exhibits anxiousness over separation; shows awareness of difference between parent and "stranger"; gives hugs and kisses; likes to play simple adult-child games; exhibits sensitivity to other children (e.g., cries if another child cries); demonstrates emotions—joy, fear, anger	Shows interest in sounds of objects; understands and recognizes own name; understands "no" and "stop"; imitates simple sounds; gives objects on request	Makes same sounds over and over; uses gestures; imitates adults' sounds; enjoys simple games, such as "peek-a-boo"; appears to sing along with familiar music; asks for toys/food by pointing and making sounds; says "da-da" and "ma-ma"	Pulls off own socks; feeds self finger foods; holds bottle independently to drink
Demonstrates initiative; imitates; "me do it" attitude; explores (if feels safe; exploration inhibited if child feels insecure); begins to comply with simple requests; resists change; demonstrates affection with parent; follows simple 1-step directions; initiates interactions with other children	Recognizes names of people and some objects; points to some objects; responds to a simple command; points to 1 to 3 body parts when asked; acknowledges others' speech by eye contact, speech, or repetition of word said	Jabbers; understands simple turn-taking rules in simple play; tries to communicate with "real words"; uses 1 to 3 spoken words; calls at least 1 person by name	Spoon-feeds and drinks from cup with many spills; sits on toilet, supervised, for 1 minute

(Continued)

Table 10-3	**(Continued)**			
Months	Typical Gross Motor Development	Typical Play Development	Typical Fine Motor/ Constructive Play	Typical Cognitive Development
18–24	Walks down stairs, marked time, 1 hand held; walks backward; hurls a tennis ball while standing	Engages in parallel play; likes play that mimics parent's behavior; adds sounds to action (e.g., talks to a teddy bear); play themes reflect very familiar things (e.g., sleeping, eating); engages in play beyond self (e.g., child holds doll and rocks it)	Builds tower of 4 blocks; turns a key or crank to make a toy work; fits simple shapes into form boards; pours/dumps objects out of a container; scribbles vigorously; begins to place scribbles in specific place on paper	Points to pictures of animals or objects; chooses pictures to look at; points to mouth, eyes, nose; looks for familiar person who has left room; uses stick to get out-of-reach toy
24–30	Runs; jumps over a small object; stands on tiptoes momentarily	Likes rough and tumble play; pretends with similar objects (e.g., a stick becomes a sword); uses a doll to act out a scene; imitates adult activity in play (e.g., pretends to cook or iron)	Stacks 5 or 6 objects by size; nests cups by size; puts together simple puzzles; dresses/ undresses dolls; strings objects; turns doorknob; scribbles begin to take on forms and become shapes; imitates circular, vertical, and horizontal strokes; rolls, pounds, and squeezes clay	Points to and names pictures; likes "read-to-me" books; loves stories that include him or her; points to arms, legs, hands, fingers; matches primary colors
30–36	Walks to and kicks a stationary playground ball; climbs on/off child-sized play equipment	Shares toys with encouragement; plays with other children for up to 30 minutes; pretend play reflects child's experience; pretends with dissimilar objects (e.g., a block becomes a car)	Draws a face; makes pancakes with clay; moves fingers independently; snips on line using scissors	Understands "front"/"back" and "in"/"out"; matches objects that have the same function (e.g., comb, brush)
36–48	Stands on 1 foot for 5 seconds; walks up stairs, alternating feet; runs contralaterally; hops on "best" foot 3 times; catches a bounced playground ball; throws a ball homolaterally; does a simple forward roll	Plays with an imaginary friend; prefers playing with other children to playing alone; pretends without any prop (e.g., pretends to comb hair with nothing in the hand); pretends after seeing, but not experiencing, an event; assumes "roles" in play and engages others in theme; acts out simple stories	Builds 3-D enclosures (e.g., zoos); makes specific marks (e.g., circles, crosses); draws a simple face; drawings represent child's perceptions (adult should not try to name/label); makes balls and snakes out of clay; cuts circles with scissors	Fills in words and phrases in favorite books when an adult reads; corrects adult if adult makes an error in reading (or tries to skip part of the story); points to thumbs, knees, chin; matches brown, black, gray, white; names red and blue when pointed to; matches simple shapes; understands "over"/"under"; classifies animals, toys, and modes of transportation

Table 10-3	**(Continued)**		
Typical Social-Emotional Development	**Typical Development of Receptive Language**	**Typical Development of Expressive Language**	**Typical Development of Self-Help**
Expresses emotions by acting them out; likes cuddling; follows simple rules most of the time; begins to balance dependence and independence; "no" becomes a favorite word; remains unable to share	Recognizes common objects and pictures; follows many simple directions; responds to "yes" or "no" questions related to needs/wants; listens as pictures are named; points to 5 body parts when asked; understands approximately 300 words	Uses simple 2-word phrases (e.g., "Bye-bye, Daddy" or "Cookie, more"); uses simple words to request toys, reject foods, or answer simple questions; favorite word may be "no"; names familiar objects; has an expressive vocabulary of at least 25 words; refers to self by name	Chews food; begins using fork
Separates easily from mother in familiar situations; exhibits shyness with strangers; has tantrums when frustrated; imitates others' actions; may be bossy and possessive; identifies self with children of same age and sex	Understands simple questions; understands pronouns ("I," "me," "mine"); follows a related 2-part direction; answers "what" questions; understands approximately 500 words	Begins to put together 3- and 4-word phrases; says first and last name; uses "I" and "me"; asks simple questions; uses "my" and "me" to indicate possession	Uses spoon, spills little; takes off coat; puts on coat with help; washes and dries hands with help; gets drink from fountain; helps when being dressed; tells adult regarding need to use toilet in time to get to toilet
Comforts others; relates best to 1 familiar adult at a time; begins to play with others with adult supervision; is conscious of and curious about sex differences	Listens to simple stories; follows a 2-part direction; responds to simple "yes" or "no" questions related to visual information; points to pictures of common objects by use (e.g., "Show me what you eat with"); understands approximately 900 words	Begins to tell stories; plays with words/sounds; has 300-word vocabulary; asks "why" and "where" questions; adds "ing" to words	Stabs food with fork and brings to mouth; puts on socks and shirt
Begins to say "please" and "thank you"; shows affection for younger siblings; enjoys accomplishments and seeks affirmation; begins to form friendships	Answers "who," "why," and "where" questions; responds to 2 unrelated commands; understands approximately 1,500 words	Begins to use tenses, helping verbs; uses simple adjectives—"big," "little"; uses language imaginatively when playing; uses 3- or 4-word sentences; repeats simple songs; asks lots of questions; uses speech to get/keep attention of others; has 900- to 1,000-word vocabulary; repeats simple rhymes	Eats independently, with little help; brushes hair; spreads with knife; buttons/unbuttons large buttons; washes hands independently; uses tissue, with verbal reminder; uses toilet independently, with assistance to clean and dress self; puts on/takes off shoes and socks (Velcro closures); hangs up coat (child-sized cubbies)

(Continued)

Months	Typical Gross Motor Development	Typical Play Development	Typical Fine Motor/ Constructive Play	Typical Cognitive Development
48–60	Walks down stairs, alternating feet; walks to an even beat in music; jumps forward 10 times consecutively; hops on nonpreferred foot; catches using hands only; gallops with 1 foot leading; slides in 1 direction; throws contralaterally; swings on a swing and self-propels	Plays a table game with supervision; acts out more complex stories; creates stories that reflect that which child has not experienced; plays cooperatively with 2 or 3 children for 15 minutes	Prints first name; repeats patterns in structure (e.g., 3 red blocks, 3 blue, 3 red); draws self with primary and secondary parts; creases paper with fingers; begins to distribute shapes/objects evenly on paper; begins to draw bodies with faces; completes 8-piece puzzle; threads small beads on string	Follows along in a book being read; tries to read book from memory; names green, yellow, orange, purple; names circle and square when pointed to; understands "forward"/"backward," "above"/"below"; classifies food/people
60–72	Gallops with either foot leading; may skip; bounces and catches tennis ball	Plays several table games; engages in complex sociodramatic play	Combines drawings of things the child knows (e.g., people, houses, trees); draws pictures that tell stories; folds paper diagonally and creases it; colors within the lines; pastes and glues appropriately	Retells story from a picture book; reads some words by sight; names triangle, diamond, rectangle when pointed to; understands "right"/"left"; classifies fruits and vegetables; matches letters

Table 10-3 (Continued)

(Continued)

the unique needs of the child within the family unit and to the needs of the parent(s) in response to the child. The interactions of the child and parent may be seriously compromised if the infant has a disability or if the parent is ill prepared for the role.

Klemm and Schimanski wrote,

Parents have to adjust emotionally to the fact that our experiences with our child are different than we thought they would be, and that we have been thrust into a whole new world. This world contains professionals we never knew existed, words and acronyms that are unfamiliar, reactions from friends and family that we never would have anticipated. We must learn about the disability itself and what

this will mean for our child and our family. We often feel scared, alone, lost.[32]

Stern has described a representational model that helps explain the complexities of the infant-parent interaction.[17] It is vital that the educator who hopes to intervene successfully understand the nature of the interaction. Every attempt must be made to see every parent as an individual of value—as one who wants the best for the child (see Figure 10-1).

The interaction between the infant and the parent is complex because the actions of the infant and the parent may represent hopes, fears, and dreams that the parent finds difficult, if not impossible, to

Table 10-3	*(Continued)*		
Typical Social-Emotional Development	**Typical Development of Receptive Language**	**Typical Development of Expressive Language**	**Typical Development of Self-Help**
Begins to describe feelings about self; acknowledges needs of others and may offer assistance; starts to initiate sharing; tends to exaggerate; shows good imagination	Understands approximately 2,500 words; knows words associated with direction (e.g., "above," "bottom")	Uses adjectives; uses past tense; can retell a story; defines simple words; can describe differences in objects; can describe similarities in objects; uses 5- to 6-word sentences	Cuts easy food with knife; does laces; buttons smaller buttons; uses toilet independently; uses zipper
Asks for help from adults; cares for younger children; waits for turn for adult attention; has "best friend"; seeks autonomy	Participates in conversation without dominating it; understands words related to time and sequence; understands approximately 10,000 words; understands opposites	Participates in give-take conversation; uses words related to sequence; uses "tomorrow" and "yesterday"	Dresses self completely; makes simple sandwiches; brushes teeth alone; likes to make simple purchases; can assist in setting table, making beds; has complete independence in bathing

Table 10-4	**Fostering Parents' Participation in Early Childhood Intervention Programs**[39,52]

- The emphasis should be on families, not children alone.
- Program practices should be directly tied to the characteristics and circumstances of the families served.
- The emphasis should be on expanding on the parents' strengths.
- Frequent, personal, and enabling conversation appears to be the key to parent-faculty relations.
- Parents must be honored in and for their lives and roles separate from that of "parent."

articulate and may be a result of learned behavior. Subsequently, the infant's and parent's actions may be grounded in representations that are often difficult to understand. The relationship between the infant and parent, and their unique representations, are considered here.

The initial actions of the infant are reflex behaviors (rooting, for example) and responses to basic physiological needs (crying when hungry, for example). Subsequent actions are a result, at least in part, of the primary caregiver's responses to the initial actions. The infant's life is driven by the need to create a "global pattern perception," in which there is constancy and a predictable routine. Indeed, if the parent is able to make a natural

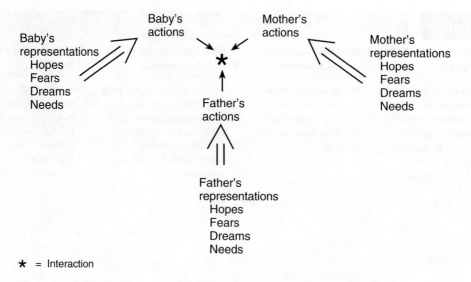

★ = Interaction

Figure 10-1　Stern's Model for Infant-Parent Interaction Analysis before Caregiving

response to the baby's natural needs, the baby will have a regular, schedule-based, and predictable routine, which, as with older children, is the critical basis for the infant's development.

Stern described the "motherhood constellation,"[17] a complex of hopes, fears, dreams, and needs that have an impact on the mother and the way the mother acts and reacts to her child:

Survival and growth. The mother believes that her primary responsibility is to keep the baby alive and growing. The mother's major fear is that something will happen to the baby. This shared instinct is one of the reasons members of this society react so violently to mothers who abandon their infants in trash bins or kill their children.

Fear regarding competence. The mother fears that she will be unable to fill her role as a mother, that she lacks the basic skills required for meeting the needs of the infant. Unfortunately, all too often this fear is well grounded. Consider the example of one child who was born naturally, full-term, and healthy. The very young mother took the

child home but did not understand she needed to feed her child, who was hospitalized with severe malnutrition and dehydration four days after being released into the mother's care. The child now has a profound intellectual disability and severe quadriplegic spastic cerebral palsy as a result of the profound deprivation. And, as one would expect, the mother is guilt-ridden.

Primary relatedness. The mother fears she will be unable to love the baby or that the baby will be unable to love her. The mother knows that society expects that the infant and mother will have a natural bond and that the mother will be the primary and most important person in the infant's life. The significant bond between the infant and the mother is relatively set by 12 to 18 months. These bonds tend to take one of three forms: (1) secure attachment pattern, (2) insecure attachment pattern, or (3) disorganized attachment pattern. Insecure and disorganized attachment patterns are typical in very young mothers and in mothers who are abusing drugs. Insecure and disorganized attachment patterns are also typical in the mothers of children with infantile autism and those born addicted to drugs. The infant may be unable to make the responses expected by the mother. Thus begins a vicious cycle in which the infant-mother connection evolves into one that is confusing and frightening for both.

Validation as caregiver. The mother, particularly if the child is her first, is in desperate need of validation. That is, the mother needs to have other women perceive her to be a good mother. The new mother, in particular, needs validation from her own mother. If her relationship with her own mother has been secure, she is more likely to be able to form a secure attachment with her new baby. If her relationship with her own mother has been insecure or a disorganized, she is more likely to form an insecure or a disorganized attachment pattern with her new baby.[15]

Identity reorganization. The process of becoming a mother causes a vast reorganization of a woman's identity. The woman goes from being her mother's daughter to being her child's mother and, usually at the same time, moves from being a partner in a committed relationship to being a parent. This causes significant adjustments in her perception of herself. The same type of identity reorganization occurs in professional women who have a first child; the woman may have been validated as a professional in the workplace and now seeks validation in the role of parent. This process may be complicated by the fact that job requirements are often relatively basic—do this, and you will be perceived to be a good employee. Being a parent is not that easily defined, and that may result in confusion.

The mother's perception of the baby is complex and is formed, at least in part, by seeing the baby in diverse roles:

- Baby as individual being
- Baby as son or daughter
- Baby as partner's son or daughter
- Baby as grandchild
- Baby as sibling
- Baby as niece or nephew

The mother's perception of the baby begins while the fetus is still in utero, and these perceptions are heightened by seeing a sonogram and feeling the baby move and kick. The mother's expectations of the infant are heightened, as well, when the infant achieves basic milestones related to growth and development. For example, when the child first sits up independently and manipulates an object (at approximately 7 to 8 months), the mother's expectations may change, and the child may be envisioned as a pianist or an author. When the child first walks independently (at 11 to 13 months), the mother's expectations may change, and the child may be envisioned as an architect or a firefighter.

Not as much research has been done on the role of the father in this process. But the father, who is critical in this process, has many of the same questions and fears regarding validation as a parent and, most certainly, shares expectations regarding the child and the child's future. And there is a great deal of evidence that the father suffers from a significant period of confusion when the infant replaces the father as the primary focus of attention. The father may experience the following:

- Concern regarding his ability to care for and support the infant and mother—financially and emotionally
- Fear regarding his ability to assume the role of father
- Concern with the loss of primary importance in his partner's life
- Expectations regarding his child's future

Being sensitive to the families of infants, toddlers, and preschoolers with disabilities is much more complex, given the vast diversity in the families served in early childhood intervention programs and their ethnic, cultural, linguistic, and economic characteristics. And, certainly, although there are a myriad of educational materials available to the professional serving learners with disabilities and their families, the most difficult process is selecting and using materials that are appropriate for each child and his or her family.[9] Suggestions for providing culturally competent services are outlined in Table 10-5.

Infant-Parent Relationships in Families with an Infant with a Disability

The myriad of actions and representations of the infant and parents, especially when complicated by actions and representations of members of the extended family, are difficult enough in the growth and development of an infant or a child who develops typically. The process is much more

Table 10-5	Cultural Competence[13]

- The family, in whatever form, must be the focus of treatment and services.
- Many Americans with diverse racial/ethnic backgrounds are bicultural or multicultural. As a result, they may have a unique set of needs.
- Families make choices based on their cultural backgrounds. Service providers must respect and build on their own cultural knowledge as well as the families' strengths.
- Cross-cultural relationships between providers and consumers may include major differences in worldviews. These differences must be acknowledged and addressed.
- Cultural knowledge and sensitivity must be incorporated into program policy making, administration, and services.
- Natural helping networks, such as neighborhood organizations, community leaders, and natural healers, can be a vital source of support to consumers. These support systems should be respected and, when appropriate, included in the treatment plan.
- In culturally competent systems of care, the community, as well as the family, determines direction and goals.
- Programs must tailor services to their consumers—the family.
- When programs include staff who share the cultural background of their consumers, the programs tend to be more effective.

complex when the infant or child has a developmental delay or disability.

There are early indicators that an infant may be at risk for delay and/or disability. Typically, these infants present one of two profiles: the "model" baby or the "irritable" baby. The model baby is lethargic, prefers to be left alone, and places few demands on parents. These behaviors, which cause these babies to be perceived to be "good" babies, may be due to neurological or neuromuscular pathology. A typically developing infant seeks contact with the parents, particularly the mother, engages in social interaction (at seven weeks the infant seeks to make eye contact), and makes his or her needs known.

The irritable baby cries excessively, sleeps fitfully, is difficult to console (does not respond to rocking or caress), and has difficulty nursing or eating. Mothers of infants later diagnosed as having attention deficit disorder or attention deficit hyperactivity disorder have suggested that the fetus is irritable within the uterus and that the kicking and other fetal movements are not like those of other children. Again, these behaviors may have a neurological or neuromuscular basis.

Other behaviors associated with atypical infant development (potential indicators of developmental delay or disability) are the following:

- Lack of response to sound (parent's cooing or singing)
- Lack of response to parent's presence (face or smile)
- Limited imitation of parent's expressions, gestures, or vocalizations
- Difficulty with gaze behavior (avoiding eye contact or staring)
- Limited response to parent's play attempts
- Unnatural attachment to objects

Comprehensive and early medical evaluation of infants makes it possible for a child with a potential for developmental delay or disability to be identified early in many cases. In fact, many potential delays or disabilities can be identified when the fetus is in utero.

Early identification of an at-risk fetus or infant provides the parents with early warning and may

Parents Are the Child's Most Important Teachers

give them the opportunity to begin the grief process. However, this grief process is as complex and multidimensional as the actions and representations of the infant, parents, and members of the extended family. Typically, the grief process is similar to that described by Kübler-Ross in her classic works regarding death and dying. The grief of parents and others when confronting the delay or disability of an infant is often much more profound than that of an individual dealing with the death of someone who has lived a long and purposeful life.

The contrast between the expectations and dreams for the infant and the reality is often vast. The parent who dreams of his or her child's being the first female president of the United States grieves unbelievably when the parent learns that that is most probably not an option for her daughter with Down syndrome. The father who dreams of his son as a professional hockey player grieves terribly when he learns his son has Duchenne muscular

dystrophy and that, unless there is a cure soon, playing professional hockey is probably not an option.

The stages of grief that a parent may experience in response to an infant with a delay or disability are detailed in Table 10-6. Also presented is a range of appropriate responses from the professional educator. The parent moves through these phases of grief in a fluctuating way—simple events may cause the parent to experience all these feelings all over again. For example, if the infant is still unable to walk at age three years, the parent may begin the grieving process all over again. If the child requires placement in a preschool program for children with disabilities at age three, the parent may need to envision the dream all over again. If the child can't make a transition into kindergarten on entering school, the parent may face denial and anger all over again. The professional working with the parent must consistently focus on honest, open communication and redirect the parent to focus on the child's abilities rather than disabilities.

One of the primary issues of the new millennium is the critical mental health crisis that has a global and pervasive effect on individuals in the society. It has become clear that mental health and well-being begin in infancy; indeed, it may begin in utero. While it is critical for professionals to address the mental health issues of family members, it is also important for professionals to address the mental health of the infants being served. Lieberman identified principles associated with infant mental health:[34]

1. The baby's primary relationships must support the baby's developmental needs. These relationships are "the core of the baby's capacity to love well and grow well."
2. Each parent and each baby is unique. Acknowledging the uniqueness will help in understanding the parent-child relationship and identify causes of conflict.
3. The environmental context affects the parents and the baby. Parents often cannot control their circumstances and what they can offer to their children. "Understanding a child, therefore, needs to involve an understanding of the psychological and sociological configuration created by the parent's culture and specific circumstances."

Table 10-6	Stages of Parental Grief and the Educator's Role in Response to Infants with Developmental Delays or Disabilities	
Stage	**Parent's Behavior**	**Role of the Educational Professional**
Denial	The parent does not acknowledge that the infant has a delay or may have a disability. In the initial stages of grief, this is a self-protective mechanism that keeps the parent from being totally destroyed by this information.	During this time, the professional working with the parent may help in the following ways: • Share information about the infant and the infant's progress; far too often, the parent is exposed only to what the infant cannot do rather than what the infant can do. • Deal with the present rather than projecting the future. • Express a willingness to listen. Use open-ended questions to allow the parent to discuss feelings and thoughts. • Share information in simple, direct writing, so that the parent can review the information in private and on the parent's terms.
Negotiation	During this stage, parents may try to negotiate, or "make a deal" with, their God or a force in the universe. The parents may promise to "do good works" in order to have their infant cured.	The professional working with the infant and the parent should continue to work with the parent as if in denial.
Guilt/grief	During this stage, the parent may experience tremendous guilt and grief. This is particularly true if the cause of the delay or disability is genetic or a result of parental alcohol or other drug abuse. This is often a time in which parents blame each other for the child's disability. This is difficult if there is no blame to be had; it is devastating if one of the parents' behavior did, indeed, have a cause-effect relationship in the disability.	The professional working with the infant and the parent should • Encourage parents to express guilt and "get it in the open" • Encourage parents to examine their belief system • Help parents meet other parents who have experienced the same thing—contact existing support groups or help parents make contact with parents of other infants • Share realistic expectations regarding their infant's development • Reinforce any parental attempt to play or interact with the infant
Depression	The parent may become overwhelmed with the contrast between the expectation and the reality. Stern described a mother's reaction to having a severely disabled infant as a narcissistic wound.[15] The depression, ultimately, allows parents to abandon their dream and may help the parent move to self-acceptance.	The professional dealing with the parent who is depressed must do so with great care, since the parent is very fragile at this time. The professional must keep an open line of communication that is nonjudgmental and caring.
Anger	Though this may be the most difficult stage for the professional to deal with, when the parent finally gets angry, the parent is on the way to healing (a process that may take a lifetime).	During this time, the professional must • Acknowledge that anger directed toward him or her may be displaced (or the parent may simply be angry with the motor specialist) • Encourage the parent to express anger • Encourage the parent's effort to play with the child and help the parent develop skills to avoid directing the anger toward the child

The Adapted Physical Educator as an Advocate for Infants, Toddlers, and Preschoolers with Disabilities and Their Families

Low-income children with disabilities are eligible for Supplemental Security Income (SSI). SSI disability determination personnel gather evidence to make a judgment as to whether these children with disabilities are eligible for SSI. Eligibility hinges on the fact that the school provides relevant information about developmental motor delays of children with disabilities to the Social Security Administration (SSA). This is critical because it enables them to acquire health insurance (e.g., Medicaid) and have access to other public health programs (e.g., Women, Infants, and Children).

The adapted physical educator is in an excellent position to provide data to the Social Security Administration that will enable families to receive federal resources that are vital to the health and well-being of their infant, toddler, or preschooler with a disability. Unfortunately, only approximately 15 percent of children in special education receive Supplemental Security Income (SSI).[3] The most critical information the adapted physical educator can provide to SSA is information regarding significant motor development delays and delayed social functioning. This information, transmitted to the SSA, can help families of children with severe disabilities receive financial and public health resources.

Early Childhood Intervention in Natural Settings

Best practices in early childhood intervention (ECI) acknowledge that infants and toddlers between birth and three years of age must be educated in their most natural environments. In fact, an amazing number of infants and toddlers spend time outside the home in regulated and unregulated child care centers.[33] Specifically, increasing numbers of children receive care outside the home because of the following:

- Increased numbers of parents/families unable to provide care within the home
- Increased numbers of parents/families unwilling to provide care within the home
- Increased numbers of parents/families living in poverty and the subsequent need for both parents (if there are two parents) to work
- Increased requirements for job training and work for parents receiving social support services
- Increased numbers of single parents, particularly young women, trying to support their children
- Increased numbers of children with significant developmental delays and disabilities with special needs because of improved medical technology that allows infants to survive who would have died in the natural selection process in earlier civilizations

The Division of Early Childhood of the Council for Exceptional Children has developed well-documented and carefully validated[40] recommendations regarding best practices in early intervention and early childhood special education.[58] The ECI natural settings initiative is in direct response to programs that in the past served typically developing infants and toddlers as well as infants and toddlers with developmental delays or disabilities, in training/school centers or provided programs in hospital-based or university-based clinical settings. Advocacy groups, such as Advocacy Incorporated and the Association for Retarded Citizens, have lobbied actively for service provision in the most inclusive and natural setting. According to Crais,

> The suggested changes involve moving from client-centered to family-centered services, from professionally-driven to family-driven decision making, and from focusing on problems to identifying and developing family and child strengths.[12]

Specifically, the focus is on a family-centered approach, in which the family and its culture are honored. Winston[71] and Crais[12] have suggested that the following underlying principles must be the crux of the family-centered, natural setting initiative:

1. Families are the constants in their children's lives, whereas service systems and professionals may only be sporadic.
2. Services should be ecologically based and therefore focus on the mutual influence of the contexts surrounding the child and family.
3. Families should be equal partners in the assessment and intervention process.
4. Services should foster families' decision-making skills and their existing and developing skills while protecting their rights and wishes.
5. Professionals need to recognize the individuality of children and their families and to modify their own services to meet those needs.
6. Services must be delivered using a coordinated, "normalized" approach.

It has also been established that quality intervention to prepare parents as "teachers" can be effective, particularly if the program is well defined, if parents are reinforced for effective behavior and educational intervention, and if the training was generalized into the home environment.[27] This has resulted in ECI mandates, at the federal and state levels (in most states), that expect the family-centered individual family service plan (IFSP) process—including assessment, IFSP development, and service delivery (see Chapter 4)—to relate to the family's ability to choose services that reflect and support the child in the family's natural settings. Natural settings include

- Home
- Family and for-profit or nonprofit agency child care settings
- Church and synagogue programs and activities
- Community playgrounds
- Park and recreation department programs and activities
- Library "reading times"
- Grocery stores

The assessment and the IFSP must provide information regarding the infant's or child's eligibility and the level of functioning in the following areas:

- Cognitive development
- Physical development, including vision and hearing, gross and fine motor skills, and nutrition status
- Communication development
- Social-emotional development
- Adaptive development or self-help skills[48]

In addition, the assessment must include the child's unique strengths and needs "in relation to the child's ability to function in settings that are natural or normal for the child's peers who do not have disabilities, including home and community settings in which children without disabilities participate."[48]

Recent mandates also require parent input regarding their child's functional abilities and the extent of their participation in settings that are natural or normal for their child's age peers without disabilities. The focus is on the family's perception of their needs if they are to provide quality parenting in natural environments.

Mandates ensure that each family has a plan of services that meets the unique needs of the child and family and reflects and supports the collaborative partnership between parents and professionals. The program must provide service coordination and an IFSP for all eligible children. The IFSP must

- Be written within 45 days of referral
- Be jointly developed through a face-to-face meeting of a team of professionals that includes the parents
- Be based on information from a comprehensive evaluation and assessment performed by an interdisciplinary team
- Be developed to include the services to be provided, the child's ability to function in natural environments, and the family's ability to meet the child's needs
- Coordinate services with all other providers, including child care providers
- Address the need for assistive technology assessment, services, and devices

- Include a statement that describes the child's health and medical history
- Include a statement that describes the present level of development
- Contain major outcomes and strategies for achieving outcomes
- Include frequency, intensity, location, and method of delivering services (FILM)
- Contain a summary of opportunities for inclusion in family and community life and life with peers
- Address starting dates and expected length of services
- Include medical and other services required and the method of payment
- Include a transition plan, beginning at two years, into preschool programs[48]

The Reauthorization of IDEA makes it possible for educators in preschool programs for children with disabilities to extend the IFSP into the child's preschool years and potentially into the school years. This is certainly a direct reflection of Congress's commitment to the provision of services to the family.

Active Start: Recommendations Regarding Activity for Infants, Toddlers, and Preschoolers

The childhood obesity epidemic is *the* critical health issue of this century. Second only to tobacco abuse, obesity is the most preventable and avoidable cause of illness and death in the United States.[2] Childhood obesity is now prevalent in infants, toddlers, and preschoolers; thus, it is critical that professionals and parents committed to the health and well-being of young children address childhood obesity in their homes and classrooms. The National Association of Sport and Physical Education of the American Alliance of Health, Physical Education, Recreation and Dance released recommendations regarding activity for infants, toddlers, and preschoolers in the hope that their health would be maximized and obesity prevented. Titled "Active Start: A Statement of Physical Activity Guidelines for Children Birth to Five Years," the recommendations as

- Infants should be in settings that encourage physical movement and do not restrict movement for prolonged periods of time. Infants should move in/through basic activities, such as rolling, crawling, and creeping.
- Toddlers should get at least 30 minutes of activity every day. The activities should include early movement skills, such as running, jumping, and throwing.
- Preschoolers should get at least 60 minutes of activity every day.
- Toddlers and preschoolers should not be sedentary for more than one hour at a time, except, of course, when sleeping.[1]

The adapted physical educator is critical in the process of helping parents develop activity programs for their infant, toddler, or preschooler with a disability in the child's natural setting. Critical to this process is ensuring that children are engaged in developmentally appropriate PLAY, not participating in exercise regimens.[57]

The Movement Program and the ECI Natural Settings Initiative

It is no longer appropriate to pull infants, toddlers, and preschoolers out of their natural settings to provide intervention, including intervention with parents, in a clinic based in a service agency, on a public school campus, or on a university campus. Far too often in the past, an infant or a toddler was removed from the familiar home and neighborhood environment and taken into an enhanced learning environment (e.g., a clinical setting with all the necessary materials and equipment [toys, for example]).

The opportunity for learning and development is great while the child receives services within the clinical setting. Cowden, Sayers, and Torrey,[10,60] reported significant success in motor intervention for infants and toddlers with disabilities in a university-based clinical setting that focused on the following:

- Increase or decrease of muscle tone to facilitate effective movement
- Inhibition of primitive reflexes

- Reciprocal innervation
- Neurodevelopmental repetitive facilitation of movements
- Stimulation of automatic equilibrium reactions
- Tactile stimulation for warm-up, flexibility, range of motion, and relaxation
- Positioning for increasing muscle tone, strength, and balance of specific muscles
- Coordination of stability and mobility
- Resistance training

However, university-based clinical experiences provide little or no opportunity for transfer of the learning experience into the home or neighborhood. Cheatum and Hammond[8] address that in their text, a recommended reading. Also, parents are often overwhelmed by the clinical setting and become observers rather than leaders in the learning process.

The adapted physical educator must be prepared to provide services in settings described as "natural" for children from birth to age three years:

- Home
- Child care or family day care
- Neighborhood recreation center
- Community playground

Intervention within a child's natural setting has many advantages. The first, and most important, is that an infant or a toddler will be most at ease in the familiar environment. The specialist will have the opportunity to see the child moving in his or her most natural play environment and will be able to develop a movement/play program designed to work within that context. The second advantage is that the specialist will have an opportunity—in the home, in the child care setting, in the neighborhood recreation center, and on the community playground—to provide meaningful intervention with the parent in a context familiar to the parent or other caregiver. Strategies can be developed to help the parent develop skills for facilitating the child's development in the environment most familiar to both the parent and the child. The likelihood that the parent will become an active participant in the child's learning is enhanced.

There are, however, some disadvantages and problems associated with the provision of services in the natural setting. These disadvantages and problems, which are increased in inner-city and other poverty-stricken areas, including Native American reservations and camps for transient migrant workers, include the following:

- The safety of the professional may be compromised within a community, particularly in the late afternoons and evenings. Unfortunately, there are some homes and neighborhoods in which the lives of professionals (even when traveling in pairs) are in jeopardy.
- The health of the professional may be compromised in homes in which basic health care standards are not met (lack of cleanliness or appropriate immunizations).
- The provision of services in a clinical setting provides professionals the opportunity, if only for a brief time, to meet an infant's or a toddler's basic health and safety needs. For example, infants and toddlers are often bathed and fed nutritious meals while attending the clinic. That type of opportunity is not readily available in some homes and neighborhoods.
- The professional feels as if he or she has no base and only limited connection with other early childhood professionals.

Movement and Play in the Individual Family Service Plan

The single most important factor in the development of the IFSP is that the goals and objectives must reflect the family's preferences, hopes, dreams, and realities. The trend toward intervention within the natural context can be effective only if the goals and objectives (and the specific strategy for accomplishing these objectives) are functional, can be generalized, can be integrated within the natural setting, are measurable, and reflect a hierarchical relationship between long-range goals and short-term objectives. It is critical to put real-life skills into the IFSP.[49] This is true of movement and play, as well. The following are examples of real-life goals and objectives:

- *Functionality.* Will the movement or play skill increase the child's ability to interact with people and objects in the environment? For example, facilitating the development of sitting equilibrium increases the likelihood that a child will be able to sit and play with a toy. An appropriate annual goal may be "The child is able to retain sitting equilibrium while being bounced on a mattress with hands held."
- *Generality.* Can the movement or play skill be used in several different settings? For example, if a child is able to grasp and release small objects, the child can (1) at home—help pick up toys and put them in a bucket, (2) at child care—build with large Duplo blocks, and (3) on the playground—collect and stack twigs. An appropriate annual goal may be "The child is able to grasp and release a variety of small objects."
- *Integrated into natural setting.* Can the movement or play skill be used within the child's daily environment? For example, if a child is able to participate in parallel play, he or she can (1) at home—sit and look at a book while the parent looks at a newspaper, (2) at child care—share a water table with another child, and (3) on the playground—share a sandbox and engage in filling and pouring like another child. An appropriate annual goal may be "The child is able to engage in parallel play with adults and peers."
- *Measurable.* Can the movement or play skill be measured? A goal or an objective is of no use if the educator or parent cannot determine if the objective has been met. For example, "The child will be able to run better" is not an appropriate goal or objective. An appropriate annual goal may be "The child will be able to run, using arms in opposition to the legs."
- *Hierarchical annual goals and objectives.* Can the movement/play goals and objectives be expressed in hierarchical fashion? The only appropriate annual goals and objectives are those in which the objectives can build on one another, leading to an annual goal.[49]

Role of the Adapted Physical Education Specialist with Infants and Toddlers in Natural Settings

The role of the adapted physical educator is the same in each of the natural settings. The first responsibility is the completion of a comprehensive, developmentally appropriate, ecological assessment and the initiation of the portfolio assessment process. The APE specialist is, then, responsible for working closely with the parents or other caregivers to help them understand the importance of play in the lives of their little ones. Most young children learn to play naturally and without specific professional intervention. However, young children with disabilities may need specific intervention. This is particularly true of young children with severe disabilities. Huettig, Bridges, and Woodson wrote,

> While play appears to evolve naturally in typically developing children, children with severe and profound disabilities must often be taught to play. Acquiring play skills is a complex process for children with severe and profound disabilities. . . . These children often have many hours of idle, non-productive time if they are not able to develop play skills.[29]

It is critical that parents be involved in the process of helping their infants, toddlers, and preschoolers, particularly those with severe and profound disabilities, to learn to play. Infants and young children are more responsive to adults who are playful than to those who are not; infants, toddlers, and preschoolers develop stronger bonds with parents who play than with those who do not.[31]

The most effective strategy for introducing developmentally appropriate play to parents is to engage parents, with their children, in activities that are reinforcing to both. The following activities are reinforcing to both the parent and the child and will encourage the development of the child's central nervous system.

Strategies and Techniques for Enhancing Sensory Stimulation
Vestibular Stimulation

1. Hold and rock the infant or toddler in your arms or rock in a rocking chair.

2. Bounce the infant or toddler on your lap with the child lying on his or her stomach, sitting, and standing.
3. Gently pat the bed or couch cushion next to the infant or toddler while the child lies prone.
4. Dance, holding the infant or toddler in your arms.
5. Carry the child in a baby backpack.

Tactile/Proprioceptive Stimulation

1. Do infant massage. Hold (or lie down next to) the infant or toddler and gently stroke the child with the fingertips and fingers. Apply slightly more pressure as the massaging hand moves down the long bones in the arms and legs and down the spine.
2. Play with the child's fingers and toes.
3. Introduce Koosh balls and squishy animals for the child to hold and feel.
4. Grasp the child's feet and gently pump up and down while chanting or singing a simple song: "Molly is kicking, kicking, kicking, Molly is kicking all day long" (sung to "London Bridge").
5. Lift and move the child's arms and legs; stretch and bend.
6. Use different types of materials to rub gently on the child's body—flannel, silk, cotton, fake fur, terry cloth, feathers, sponge, and so on.
7. Wiggle the child's fingers and toes in water, sand, cereal, whipped cream, and so on.
8. Help the child do finger play in a scoop of pudding on the child's high chair tray.
9. Plan simple games, such as "This Little Piggy," while touching and pulling gently on the baby's toes and fingers.
10. Let the child pound on chunks of refrigerated cookie dough.
11. Put pillows on the floor for the child to crawl and creep on or over.
12. Let the toddler push and pull objects, such as laundry baskets.

Auditory Stimulation

1. Talk, coo, and sing to the baby.
2. Read. If the parent cannot read, help the parent select audiotapes or CDs of simple books or, better still, urge the parent to participate in a parent/child literacy program.
3. Tell the child simple stories that include the child. Use the child's name often in the story.
4. Expose the infant or toddler to different types of music—classical, jazz, rock, and country-western.
5. Allow the infant or toddler to stimulate his or her own auditory system using rattles.
6. Attach a large jingle bell to the child's arm or foot using a ponytail holder; help the child kick the foot.

Visual Stimulation

1. Expose the newborn to black/white contrasts.
2. As the infant matures, expose the baby to vibrant, primary colors.
3. Imitate the baby's gestures and expressions.
4. Encourage the child to look at self in a mirror.
5. Jiggle a brightly colored toy or noisemaker in front of the child's face. When the child's eyes locate the object, jiggle it again.

Olfactory Stimulation

1. Hold the child very close to your body, allowing the child to pick up the body's unique odor.
2. Expose the child to the varying odors of perfumes and spices.

Strategies and Techniques for Enhancing the Development of Equilibrium Behaviors

Supine Equilibrium

1. With the infant or toddler supine, jiggle a bright toy or noisemaker above the child's face (no closer than 12 inches to the child's face).
2. With the child supine on your lap, with the head supported by a hand under the head, gently bounce the infant or toddler on your lap.
3. Put a brightly decorated sock on the baby's foot to encourage the child to reach for his or her toes.
4. Lie on your back with the child supine on your chest. Supporting the child's head and body, roll from side to side.

Prone Equilibrium

1. With the infant or toddler in the prone position, place a bright toy or noisemaker in front of the child's head to encourage the child to lift the head.
2. With the infant or toddler in the prone position, walk your fingertips up the child's back, with fingers on each side of the spine.
3. Use textures to stimulate the muscles in the baby's back and neck. Try using a paintbrush, washcloth, and sponge.
4. Lie on your back with the child prone on your chest. Supporting the child's head and body, roll from side to side.
5. Put a rolled-up towel under the child's shoulders, allowing the hands and arms to move freely in front of the child. Blow bubbles for the child to track or use a music box or rhythm instrument to encourage the child to hold the prone position, bearing weight on the forearms.

Sitting Equilibrium

1. Hold the child on your lap, supporting the child's head on your chest, and gently rock from side to side.
2. Hold the child on your lap, supporting the child's head on your chest, and gently bounce the child up and down.
3. Prop the child up in a sitting position using pillows. Put toys or musical wind-ups above eye level to encourage the child to hold the head up.
4. Place the baby in a high chair, an infant seat, or a walker. Hold a toy in front of the child and encourage the child to reach for it.

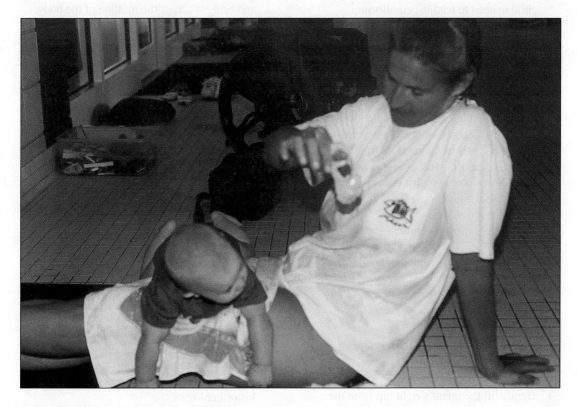

An Activity to Promote Equilibrium in Prone Position
Photo by Carol Huettig.

5. Prop the baby in a corner in a sitting position with pillows for support. Encourage the child to reach for a toy and play with it while sitting.

6. When the child can sit independently, place a number of toys within the child's reach and a number just beyond easy reach, so that the child has to adjust equilibrium to get the toys.

7. Play games such as "Pat-a-Cake."

8. With the child seated on a mattress or pillow, gently pull or push the child to force the child to regain equilibrium.

9. Let the older child sit on a rocking-horse or the like.

10. With the child in a sitting position, put a bucket in front of the child and objects to be placed in the bucket at the sides and near the back of the child.

11. Put a wheeled toy in front of the child and let the child roll it back and forth, causing the child to need to readjust equilibrium.

Standing Equilibrium

1. With the child supine, put the palms of your hands against the bottom of the child's feet and push gently.

2. After the child has head-righting capabilities, hold the child in a standing position with the child's feet on your lap. Bounce the child and gently move the child from side to side, keeping the feet in contact with the lap.

3. Play "Sooooo Big"—lift the child above your head while keeping the child in a vertical position.

4. While supporting the child in standing position, "dance" back and forth, and forward and back, keeping the child's feet in contact with the floor.

5. Let the child stand on your shoes as you dance around the room.

Strategies and Techniques for Developing Simple Locomotor Competency

Rolling

1. Gently lift the infant's right hip from the supine toward the side-lying position; alternate and lift the left hip from the supine toward the side-lying position. Let the return happen naturally.

2. If the infant is supine, place a favorite toy on either side of the child's head to encourage the child to roll the head to look for the toy.

3. Place the child on a blanket or towel on the stomach or back. Gently raise one side of the blanket to assist the child in rolling to the side. (Do not use this activity if the infant arches his or her back during the roll.)

4. Jiggle a favorite toy or noisemaker in front of the child's eyes (never closer than 12 inches) while the child lies supine; when the child focuses on the toy, slowly move it to a position at the side of the child's head on the crib mattress.

5. Place the child on a small incline, so that the child has a small hill to roll down.

6. With the child supine, gently bend one leg and bring it across the midline of the body. Go slowly, so that the child's body follows the movement.

Pull to Sitting

1. Sit with your back against a support and with your knees bent to make an incline for the child to lie on. The baby lies with the head near the knees and the hips cradled by your chest, so that the child faces you. Carefully, and with head support, round the baby's shoulders toward you and lift the baby into a sitting position. As the baby develops strength and sitting equilibrium, gradually reduce the amount of support.

Crawling

1. Sitting on the floor with your legs stretched out, place the child over your leg and shift the child so that the child's hands are in contact with the floor, and gently roll the child toward his or her hands, so that the child gradually takes more weight on the hands.

2. Repeat 1, but this time shift the weight so that the child gradually takes more weight on his or her knees.

3. Place the child on a carpet or mat and remove shoes and socks. Place a favorite toy in front

of the child to encourage the child to move toward the toy. If needed, help the child move by placing a palm against the child's foot, so that the child has something to push off from.

Creeping

1. Place a bolster or rolled-up towel in front of the child and encourage the child to creep over it to get to a favorite toy.
2. Make a simple obstacle course with sofa cushions, pillows, rolled-up towels, and rolled-up newspapers and encourage the child to move through the obstacle course toward a favorite toy.

Pull to Standing

1. Place a favorite toy on the edge of the seat of a sturdy, cushioned chair or sofa; when the child expresses interest in the toy, move it back just a little from the edge.
2. When the child is in a sitting or kneeling position, periodically throughout the day grasp the child's hands and pull gently to standing.

Cruising

1. Put a small, child-sized chair with metal feet on a tile or wooden floor. Help the child pull to stand near the chair and "cruise," holding weight on the chair.
2. Put several well-cushioned chairs close together and increase interest in cruising by placing toys on the chair seats.

Strategies and Techniques for Facilitating/ Scaffolding Symbolic Play Behavior

1. Imitate the infant or toddler's facial expressions and gestures.
2. Demonstrate simple strategies for the child to communicate the following and model parent response:
   a. Behavioral regulation
      1. Requesting objects
      2. Requesting actions
      3. Protesting
   b. Social interaction
      1. Greeting
      2. Calling

   3. Requesting social routine
   4. Requesting permission
   5. Showing off
   c. Joint attention
      1. Commenting
      2. Requesting information
      3. Providing information[54]

Strategies and Techniques for Scaffolding Learning

Pretend play, or symbolic play, is an important part of the child's growth process. The adapted physical educator may help the parent develop the scaffolding skills necessary to gently nudge the child toward more sophisticated symbolic play as he or she moves through the sequence of development of symbolic play skills.[5,25,54,70]

Following is the "typical" sequence in which young children develop "pretend play" skills. Understanding this sequence can make it possible for the teacher and parent to more readily facilitate "pretend play" behavior.

Pre-Pretense or Accidental Pretense The child puts a comb in his or her hair or a telephone to his or her ear. The adult can help scaffold learning by responding, "Emily, you're combing your hair," or the adult can pretend to put a telephone to his or her own ear and say, "Hello, Hannah. This is . . ."

Self-Pretend The child pretends to do familiar things. The most typical are eating and sleeping. The adult can help scaffold learning by saying, "Is it good? Can I have some, too?" or the adult can cover the child and say out loud, "Ssshhhh, Molly is sleeping."

Other-Pretend The child pretends to do things that he or she has seen significant others do. For example, the child may pretend to feed a baby or drive a car. The adult can help scaffold learning by saying, "Lashundra, what a good mommy you are being, feeding your baby." Or the adult may sit down next to the child and make "vvvvvvrooooom" sounds. The adult may facilitate other-pretend play by providing appropriate props after a trip—for example, to the grocery store: garbage bags, boxes of food, an old wallet.

Imaginary Objects and Beings   The child not only uses a variety of real or child-sized replicas of real objects in play but also uses imaginary objects to engage in pretend behavior. For example, the child might ride an imaginary horse or pretend a block is an ice cream cone. The adult may provide support for play by joining in—riding an imaginary horse while twirling a rope or giving the child another "scoop" of ice cream. This type of play is best facilitated when the child has access to props—blocks, for example—that can be anything.

Animated Play   The child uses toy people and toy animals, for example, and assigns them words or actions. The toy horse may gallop across the range while "neeeeiiiiighing." The adult can facilitate play by galloping and then jumping over "fences."

Sequential Play (30 Months or Older)   The child is moving into sophisticated play scenarios, and the play represents a sequence of events. For example, the child may "go to the store, buy groceries, bring them home, and fix dinner." The adult can scaffold learning by asking simple questions about the sequence but should not intrude on or change the child's plan.

Demonstrating How Simple Materials Found in the Home or Other Settings Can Be Used to Facilitate Play and the Development of Gross Motor and Fine Motor Skills

1. Use mattresses as "trampolines."
2. Provide pillows as "mountains" for climbing over and rolling down.
3. Provide wooden spoons, strainers, funnels, and old pans to make music or "cook."
4. With the child lying on a quilt, pick up an edge of the quilt to help the child roll from the stomach to the back.
5. Put a favorite toy just out of reach of the child to encourage crawling, creeping, cruising, or walking to the toy.

Demonstrating the Use of Simple Toys

1. Securely attach objects (large hair curlers, clean jar lids, plastic rings) to a dowel and tie it across the crib.
2. Put dry oatmeal, cereal, or macaroni in film canisters.
3. Make building blocks out of 2×4s (saw and sand the blocks).
4. Recycle empty cereal boxes as building blocks.
5. Use cardboard rolls from paper towels and toilet paper for building and rolling.
6. Make available things to crumple and crinkle—waxed paper, aluminum foil, tissue, used wrapping paper, newspaper, and so on.
7. Clean a 1-liter soda bottle and fill it with water. To enhance the effect, add food coloring. Close the lid tightly and seal with duct tape. To help the child with discrimination of weight, put varying amounts of water in a number of bottles.

Helping the Parent (or Other Caregiver) Select Toys That Facilitate Communication between the Caregiver and the Child

1. Toys that draw attention to the parent's actions
   a. Push toys that make noise
   b. Musical instruments
   c. Rattles
2. Toys that draw attention to the parent's face
   a. Bubbles
   b. Pinwheels
   c. Scarves
3. Toys that facilitate reciprocal interaction
   a. Puppets
   b. Push toys (cars, trains, trucks)
   c. Balls

Helping the Parent Select Toys That Empower the Child

1. Toys that allow the child to see cause-effect (bang pan with spoon and make noise)
2. Toys the child can push and pull
3. Toys with which the child can follow the action (ball is dropped into the top and rolls down the series of chutes)

THE PRESCHOOL PROGRAM FOR CHILDREN AGES THREE TO FIVE YEARS

A comprehensive, family-focused early childhood intervention program based in natural settings has the potential to prepare a three-year-old child for participation in "regular day care" or for continued home/community involvement. If a child deemed at risk for developmental delays exhibits a disability at age three years, the child will usually make the transition into a preschool program for children with disabilities within a community agency or public school program.

The components necessary for children to achieve their potential are

- Health
- Nutrition
- Family and community stability
- Cultural competence
- Self-esteem
- Quality of early learning experience

If a preschooler has each of these six components in his or her life, the child will be more likely to have a quality life. The importance of a quality preschool learning experience has been well documented in the research literature. The most noteworthy of the studies is the Perry Preschool Project,[6] which is a comprehensive, longitudinal study of 123 African American children from families with low incomes—children who were believed to be at risk for school failure.

The results were astonishing and demonstrated lasting benefits of quality preschool education. This is consistent with the findings of the Abecedarian Study of the effectiveness of birth-to-five intervention. When compared with the control group, the individuals in the experimental group demonstrated the following:

- Improved cognitive performance during early childhood
- Improved scholastic performance during school years
- Decreased delinquency and crime

- Decreased use of welfare assistance
- Decreased incidence of teenage pregnancy
- Increased graduation rates
- Increased frequency of enrollment in postsecondary education and vocational training programs
- Increased employment

Not only is this evidence impressive from a human success standpoint, but it is also incredible because the return on the dollar is so significant. "Over the lifetimes of the participants, preschool is estimated to yield economic benefits with an estimated present value that is over seven times the cost of one year of the program."[6] Unfortunately, current legislative thrusts ignore the simple findings. If society spends $1 to educate a three-year-old child, it will save $7 later on costs associated with special education, social services, unemployment, and prisons.

Unfortunately, preschoolers are being bombarded by a host of forces over which they have little or no control. In order for preschool education to be effective, teachers must address the children's anger and fears. Certainly this is most effective if done in concert with the family. The typical causes of anger in toddlers and preschoolers are addressed in Table 10-7. Strategies the teacher can use to help young children deal with their anger constructively are outlined in Table 10-8.

It is also critical that preschool educators help young children deal with the realities of violence in their lives. Strategies a teacher can use to help a preschooler deal with violence in his or her life are listed in Table 10-9.

The preschool educator is also faced with the reality of teaching many children whose language he or she does not share. It is not uncommon for a teacher in a preschool program for children with disabilities to be working with children who represent four or five different linguistic backgrounds. In a typical prekindergarten or kindergarten class in an urban, core area, the children may speak as their first languages as many as 15 languages. When combined with other factors affecting so many children—poverty,

Table 10-7	Typical Causes of Anger in Toddlers and Preschoolers

- Conflict over possessions or space.[38] Children get angry if another child takes a toy with which they are playing or moves into a space, such as a spot at the sand table, that they had "claimed."
- Physical assault. Toddlers and preschoolers get angry if jostled, pushed, or hit.
- Verbal aggression. Toddlers and preschoolers, like other individuals, get angry if teased, taunted, or ridiculed.
- Lack of recognition or acceptance. Children get angry, particularly, if not allowed to participate, if they want to play and peers say "no."
- Compliance issues.[38] Children may get angry when asked to do something they believe interferes with their plans, such as washing their hands, putting away toys, or stopping to go to the bathroom.

Table 10-8	Helping Toddlers and Preschoolers Develop Skills to Deal with Anger

- Create a safe environment for expression of emotion.[38]
- Model responsible anger management[38] and discuss it with the children.
- Help children develop self-regulatory anger management skills.
- Help the children give a name to their anger. Teachers typically encourage children to "use your words. . . ."
- Encourage children to talk about situations that cause anger.
- Read books and talk about books that help children talk about anger.

Table 10-9	Helping Young Children Deal with Violence[62]

Early childhood educators can help young children deal with violence by

- Helping children identify violence, find a name for it, and talk about its consequences
- Talking *with* children about real-world violence
- Recognizing and responding to children's traumatic reactions to violence
- Training young children in basic violence-related safety and self-protection
- Eliminating "disciplinary" violence against children
- Supporting families trying to help children cope with violence
- Providing a safe haven for young children and their families

Table 10-10	Developmental Sequence of Second-Language Acquisition in Young Children[64]

Home Language Use
　Children continue to use their home language, even in settings in which it is not used by others, and seem not to understand that their language is not the one being used by others.

Nonverbal Period in the New Language
　Children realize their home language is not that being used and, in frustration, stop using the home language. Instead, the child uses crying, whimpering, whining, pointing, and other forms of gesturing to communicate wants and needs.

Telegraphic and Formulaic Language
　Children use language that helps them get along—"OK," "yea," "mine," "bye-bye," "I don't know," and so on.

Productive Use of the Language
　At first, it may appear that the child has regressed in the use of language; in actuality, the child is struggling with the nuances of the English language.

abuse, parents with limited parenting skills—the language issue becomes overwhelming. When it is difficult to communicate with a child, it is difficult to teach and to provide support, love, and care. The developmental sequence of second language acquisition is illustrated in Table 10-10. Strategies

Table 10-11	Basic Strategies for the Teacher of Preschoolers with English as a Second Language

- Rely heavily on nonverbal communication.
- Rely heavily on demonstrations.
- Use visual images—pictures, graphics, photographs—to help communicate.
- Combine gestures with the important words in a sentence.
- Use a buddy system to pair an outgoing English-speaking child with a second-language learner.[64]
- Establish and keep a predictable routine in the class.
- Use graphics to help the students anticipate activities.
- Use music and simple dances in which the sequence of movements is very predictable.
- Use favorite music, dances, and movements often.

for the teacher of preschoolers who use English as a second language are outlined in Table 10-11.

The incredible diversity of children creates a situation in which it is difficult for a teacher, school district, or state education agency to determine an effective assessment and curricula to meet their needs. Increasingly, however, preschool programs are using curriculum-based measures to serve children. These include curriculum embedded, curriculum compatible, and normative curriculum compatible programs.[53]

A quality preschool learning environment is one in which expectations for children's performance are high and the learning environment encourages active exploration. A quality learning environment for three- to five-year-old children is play-based.[36] A child's natural drive to play is encouraged, fostered, and respected. Play is a vehicle through which a child's motor, language, social-emotional, and cognitive skills are scaffolded in and through interaction with another child or a gentle, caring adult. Play by any name—symbolic play, fantasy play, make-believe, pretend play, dramatic play, imaginative play—is the foundation or focus of the development of cognition, social-emotional skills, and language.

Vygotsky emphasized the role of representational play, or fantasy play, as a leading factor in child development:

> Play creates a zone of proximal development in the child. In play, the child always behaves beyond his average age, above his daily behavior; in play it is as though he were a head taller than himself. As in the focus of a magnifying glass, play contains all developmental tendencies in a condensed form and is itself a major source of development.[66]

In most child care and preschool settings, this play-based, quality educational environment is one that is centers-based. That is, there are unique, separate, and distinct areas within the classroom that are specifically designed and equipped for active exploration. Dodge and Colker[20] recommend the following centers for the preschool classroom:

Blocks

House corner

Table toys

Art

Sand and water

Library

Music and movement

Cooking

Computers

Outdoors

A center gives children the opportunity to explore and interact with a wide variety of materials that engage a whole spectrum of senses, encourages sensory integration, and allows the children to be involved in an extended process of pretend and real play. For example, a housekeeping center may include the following:

- Child-sized furniture, including a stove, refrigerator, sink, comfortable chair, sofa, kitchen table and chairs, doll bed, and stroller
- Play props, including pots and pans, cooking and eating utensils, a coffee pot, glasses and cups, a broom, and a mop
- Baby dolls reflecting diversity—cultures, genders, and abilities

- Doll clothes
- Dress-up clothes, including hats, scarves, and costume jewelry
- A full-length mirror

A puppet theatre and puppets reflecting a variety of people, animals, and so on may also encourage pretend and real play. An area that can be used to simulate a post office, grocery store, or restaurant and the necessary props to stimulate play may also encourage pretend play.

Given this type of play support, the young child who is just developing pretend play skills will be nudged toward more sophisticated play. Eventually, the child will not need actual objects to stimulate play but will be able to substitute any object for another in play.

Quality Movement, Play, and Wellness Experiences in Preschool Programs

Garcia and colleagues wrote,

> Common sense suggests that happy and successful experiences early in life predispose people to enjoy physical activity. If that is true, school administrators, early childhood educators, motor development specialists, and physical educators have a tremendous opportunity to influence the health of the next generation by providing movement program opportunities to young children.[22]

Certainly, the need for quality movement, play, and wellness experiences exists for ALL children, but there is a critical need for quality programs for children with disabilities. Huettig and O'Connor wrote,

> Creating an environment in which preschoolers with disabilities become "well" and develop early skills tied to a lifelong understanding and practice of wellness requires the educator/caregiver and parent to address physical fitness, nutrition, emotional health, and the other dimension of wellness on a daily basis. Most important, we must remember and recognize the fact that play is the vehicle and the process in and through which a child can embrace wellness.[30]

The key to developing a quality movement, play, and wellness program for young children is dependent on developmentally appropriate practice. Sanders wrote,

> Developmentally appropriate practices in movement programs recognize children's changing capacities to move and promote such changes. A developmentally appropriate movement program accommodates a variety of individual characteristics in children, such as developmental status, previous movement experiences, fitness and skill levels, body size, and age.[59]

The Council on Physical Education for Children of the National Association for Sport and Physical Education developed a position statement regarding developmentally appropriate practice in movement programs for young children. Its recommendations, excellent suggestions for early childhood professionals, include

- Teachers limit the group size in order to provide young children with developmentally appropriate individualized instruction.
- Teachers use activities that do not eliminate children and frequently modify activities to enhance maximum participation.
- Teachers plan and organize movement programs as part of the total educational program.
- Teachers provide a variety of novel learning experiences that emphasize the same motor skill.
- Teachers use both direct and indirect teaching methods.
- Teachers design movement activities for the total development of children.
- Teachers demonstrate positive attitudes toward fitness and recognize the importance of children's valuing physical activity as a lifelong habit.
- Teachers use authentic assessment based on the scientific knowledge of children's developmental characteristics and ongoing observations of students in activities.
- Teachers provide children with opportunities to practice skills at high rates of success, adjusted for their individual skill levels, and within a

"try again" and "effort equals improvement" environment.

- When teachers use games, the game reinforces a planned objective.
- Teachers plan a movement curriculum with a scope and sequence based on appropriate objectives and outcomes for the children's developmental levels.
- Teachers present broad skill areas, such as balancing, rolling, jumping and landing, climbing, and weight transfer.

Unfortunately, developmentally inappropriate practices have emerged in movement programs for young children. A young child cannot be expected to do the following:

- Sit and wait "forever" for a turn
- Sit and listen "forever" to directions given by an adult
- Participate in an activity predetermined by an adult and be given no choice regarding participation
- Participate in large-group activities when the child is not yet able to play with another, one-to-one
- Share equipment before the child is ready to share equipment
- Use modified equipment—mini-basketballs, shortened baskets, large plastic bats—with a stereotypical *adult* expectation regarding the use of the equipment
- Perform skills for which he or she is not ready, because the teacher or parent does not understand developmental sequence (e.g., a five-year-old trying to bat an arched, pitched ball)
- Play cooperatively or compete with other children when the child is developmentally at onlooker, solitary play, or parallel play stage

Given the critical issue of childhood obesity, it is important for the physical educator to understand the need of children, with and without disabilities, to MOVE in order to develop and maintain health and wellness. Not only is movement basic to the child, but movement provides an opportunity for toddlers and preschoolers to equalize calorie intake and expenditure. NASPE (2001) guidelines for toddlers and preschoolers include the following:[18]

1. Toddlers should accumulate at least 30 minutes daily of structured physical activity; preschoolers, at least 60 minutes. Toddlers and preschoolers do not tolerate "structured" activity for more than a few minutes at a time. A creative teacher can provide "structure" for the activity by ensuring the children's play area is safe, the play is well supervised, appropriate equipment is available, and there are enough play units. These are discussed later in the chapter.
2. Toddlers and preschoolers should engage in at least 60 minutes and up to several hours per day of daily, unstructured physical activity and should not be sedentary for more than 60 minutes at a time, except when sleeping.
3. Toddlers and preschoolers should develop movement skills that are building blocks for more complex movement tasks; preschoolers should develop competence in movement skills that are building blocks for more complex movement tasks.
4. Toddlers and preschoolers should have indoor and outdoor areas that meet or exceed recommended safety standards for performing large muscle activities.
5. Individuals responsible for the well-being of toddlers and preschoolers should be aware of the importance of physical activity and facilitate the child's movement skills.

Developmentally appropriate movement, play, and wellness programs for preschoolers with and without disabilities should provide young children access to neurodevelopmentally appropriate activities that enhance the development of equilibrium; sensory discrimination; sensory-motor function (body image and motor planning); basic locomotor and nonlocomotor competency; cross-lateral integration; object-control skills; and fitness. Specific activity suggestions can be found in *Gross Motor Activities for Young Children with Special Needs,* which is available on this book's web site.

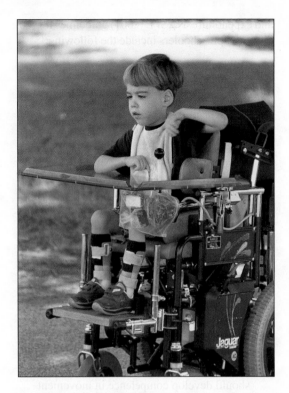

A Motorized Chair Gives a Child the Opportunity to Control His or Her Destiny

THE INDOOR ACTIVE LEARNING CENTER

The active learning center for preschoolers with and without disabilities should provide children with the opportunity to move, self-test, explore, interact, and play. Ideally, the adapted physical education specialist should create the active learning center *with* the children. The educator should be sensitive to the needs of the children and create and re-create the environment on the basis of the materials and equipment to which the children are drawn. The following materials and equipment enhance the learning environment and encourage active exploration and active experiences in movement and play:

- Mats of different types and densities, including "crash-type" mats
- Large, foam-filled forms of different shapes (pyramids, cubes, donut holes, etc.) for kids to

roll on, jump on, and climb in, around, over, and through

- Large, empty boxes for children to climb in, around, over, and through
- Giant tumble balls (17-, 23-, and 30-inch)
- Hippity hops
- Large balls for catching (10- to 13-inch)
- A wide variety of small balls and bean bags to throw
- Tricycles and child-sized safety helmets
- Scooters and child-sized safety helmets
- Wagons and wheelbarrows
- A variety of scooter boards, with and without handles (Sportime has some excellent "huge" scooter boards that two children can share)
- Sheets and blankets to make forts and tunnels
- Steps for climbing and a slide for sliding
- An incline ramp
- Nets and ropes for climbing
- Big trucks, cars, and so on.
- Hula hoops
- Parachutes (6-, 12-, and 20-foot)
- Tug of war rope and shorter ropes for pulling and jumping over
- Cones
- Paper and markers to identify a play area (e.g., Pooh's house)

In the indoor learning center, the children have the opportunity to use their vivid imaginations, while moving:

1. The children may pretend to be people cutting and stacking firewood and shoveling snow.
2. The children may pretend to be ice skaters, skating on pieces of waxed paper on the wood or tile floor.
3. The children can use large building blocks to make snow forts and have a "snowball" fight using yarn balls or rolled-up white socks.
4. The children can ride tricycles and pretend to be snowmobilers.
5. The teacher can fold a large rope between panels of a mat. Several children can ride on the "sleigh" while the teacher and other children are the horses. To make it even more

fun, the children can jingle "sleigh bells" and sing "Jingle Bells."

6. The teacher can push children lying prone on scooter boards, and the children can pretend to be sledding.

Movement is an end in itself. Children need to move, and they must be given every opportunity to do so. It may be easier, however, for the adapted physical education specialist to convince other preschool educators to involve children in gross motor activity if the teachers believe the activity will reinforce learning that occurs in other centers or supports a given "theme." The opportunities for learning that are inherent in the active learning center are endless and meet the needs of young children to use their bodies and to participate in play, all the while reinforcing other learning.

As mentioned earlier, the equipment, materials, and other props simply help the adapted physical educator establish the learning environment. The learning opportunities are endless. They are endless, however, only if each child has adequate play opportunities. There is nothing as sad as seeing a group of young children in a huge, open play space with only two or three balls to share.

Careful preparation of the play environment will maximize learning opportunities and minimize the potential for arguments. The key to the preparation of any learning environment for young children is the creation of at least 2.5 play units (play materials, equipment, and spaces) per child. Sharing is one of the things that preschoolers really struggle with—to force them to do something for which they are developmentally unprepared is to create conflict between children. Fewer play units increase the likelihood that children will argue about materials, equipment, and space.

Wetherby[70] describes the different types of play units:

- Simple play unit: a play area that occupies one child and is not conducive to cooperative interaction

- Complex play unit: a play area that occupies up to four children, such as a sand table with pouring utensils for each child or a puppet stage with puppets for each child

- Super play unit: a play area that occupies up to eight children, such as a dramatic play area with eight costumes or a block area with at least 25 interlocking or 50 unit blocks per child

With young children, the leap from independent, solitary play in a simple play unit to play in a complex play unit may be overwhelming. A "partner" play unit is developmentally appropriate as children learn to deal first with one other child and then with small groups of children. Teachers must create opportunities for play with only one other child as well. A play unit analysis for indoor active play centers is presented in Table 10-12.

THE OUTDOOR ACTIVE LEARNING CENTER

The outdoor play experience for young children with developmental delays or disabilities should be an extension of learning that occurs within the home, day care center, recreation center, neighborhood playground, and active learning center. As in every other setting, the outdoor play of young children needs to be respected and valued, and it may serve as a scaffold for the development of

- More complex and sophisticated play
- Gross and fine motor skills
- Interpersonal skills
- Communication and language

The outdoor active learning center must also provide adequate play units if the environment is to enhance learning. An example of an outdoor active play center play unit analysis is found in Table 10-13.

The opportunity to play and learn outdoors is as vital to a child as the air he or she breathes. Children, as resilient people, will find a way to play—in almost any outdoor setting. Being able to use "outside voices" and to do the things that come naturally to many children—running, jumping, climbing, swinging, hanging—creates the

Table 10-12	Active Learning Center, Indoors: Play Unit Analysis

Following is a sample evaluation of an indoor active learning center that a preschool adapted physical education specialist would complete before involving young children in its use. Required: 2.5 play units per child

Materials, Equipment, Spaces	Number of Play Units
Simple Play Units (1 Point Each)	
5 tricycles	5
3 wheelbarrows	3
2 small slides (height = 6 feet)	2
2 small balance beams (6 inches wide, 6 inches long)	2
6 scooter boards (2 feet × 3 feet)	6
3 wooden trucks	3
3 plastic fire trucks	3
2 "jumpin jiminy"	2/26 play units
Partner Play Units (2 Points Each)	
3 small pull wagons (1 child pulls, 1 rides)	6
2 two-seat rockers	4
6 huge (refrigerator/stove), empty boxes	12/38 play units
Complex Play Units (4 Points Each)	
1 CD player with songs for dancing	4/42 play units
Super Units (8 Points Each)	
1 large parachute with handles for 16	16/58
	68 play units

Play area is adequate to support quality play of 27 children!

Table 10-13	Active Play Center, Outdoors: Play Unit Analysis

Following is a sample evaluation of an outdoor play area that a preschool adapted physical education specialist would complete before involving young children in its use. Required: 2.5 play units per child

Materials, Equipment, Spaces	Number of Play Units
Simple Play Units (1 Point Each)	
5 tricycles	5
3 wheelbarrows	3
2 small slides (height = 6 feet)	2
2 small balance beams (6 inches wide, 6 inches long)	2
6 scooter boards (2 feet × 3 feet)	6
3 wooden trucks	3
3 plastic fire trucks	3
2 "jumpin jiminy"	2/26 play units
Partner Play Units (2 Points Each)	
3 small pull wagons (1 child pulls, 1 rides)	6
2 two-seat rockers	4/10 play units
Complex Play Units (4 Points Each)	
1 water table (with a spoonful of dishwashing detergent)	4/4 play units
2 buckets	
2 measuring cups	
2 watering cans	
4 bubble makers	
Super Units (8 points each)	
1 large sandbox	8
5 buckets	
5 shovels	
4 rakes	
4 pancake turners	
2 sieves	
1 small parachute with handles for 8	8
1 large play structure	8/24 play units
	64 play units

Play area is adequate to support quality play of 25 children!

opportunity for a joyful learning experience. However, as Rivkin reminds us,

> Although no person or government planned it, habitats for children, especially in industrialized countries, have been greatly altered—often destroyed. . . . Children's access to outdoor play has evaporated like water in sunshine.[56]

Unfortunately, this alteration and destruction of play environments for children—the ruination of their habitats—have significantly compromised the quality of young children's lives. In many urban environments, children simply cannot "go out to play" for fear of drive-by shootings or kidnapping, contact with drug paraphernalia, and contact with toxic substances. In fact, many children have the opportunity to play outdoors only under the supervision of teachers and assistants in a day care or preschool program. An integral part of a total early childhood education program, the outdoor play experience should be a part of the daily schedule.[43] Children must have the opportunity to play outside every day. The only exception, of course, is during inclement or dangerous weather, including weather "warnings,"

storms with lightning, severe heat or severe cold, and, particularly for children with asthma and other respiratory problems, ozone and other pollution alerts.

Most preschool educators would agree that the ideal outdoor play setting is one in which the child has the opportunity to interact with and learn from nature. This gives the child with a "naturalistic" intelligence the opportunity to learn and grow and use that intelligence.[28] It not only is vital for the child's physical and social development but may inherently be vital for the development of his or her soul. The ideal preschool outdoor play area is nature-based (Figure 10-2) and includes the following:

• Flowers, bushes, and trees native to the area

Figure 10-2   Natural Outdoor Play Area

- Natural play surfaces: grass (short and tall grasses), dirt, sand, hills, and valleys
- Apparatus for climbing, swinging, and hanging: trees, rocks, vines
- Apparatus for balancing, self-testing: tree stumps, fallen logs
- Play areas for digging and pouring: dirt/mud, sand, stream/pond
- Play materials for building and stacking: rocks, twigs
- Play materials for sorting and classifying: flowers and weeds, leaves, seeds (acorns)

In the event that the outdoor play area is not in a natural setting, there are still ways for the creative adapted physical educator to help design an outdoor play area that meets the fundamental needs of young children (see Figure 10-3). The "asphalt" play area could include the following:

- Flowers, bushes, and trees native to the area (flower boxes, potted trees, potted bushes)
- Play surfaces: wood chips, sand, dirt, pea gravel, incline ramps
- Apparatus for climbing, swinging, hanging, and sliding: net climbers, tire climbers, swings, slides, steps/ladders, horizontal poles, vertical poles
- Apparatus for balancing, self-testing: railroad ties, 4 × 4's
- Play areas for digging and pouring: sandbox, dirt/mud, sand table, sand, water table, plastic swimming pool, sprinkler, garden plots

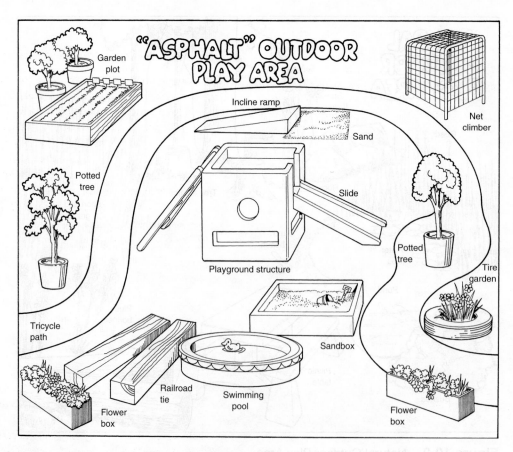

Figure 10-3 "Asphalt" Outdoor Play Area

- Play materials for building and stacking: plastic blocks, rocks, wooden blocks, twigs

In some inner-city areas, it is virtually impossible to maintain a developmentally appropriate outdoor play area because of theft and vandalism. Large play structures that can be cemented into the ground may be the only option to provide any play spaces for children. And educators have to be concerned about parts of those play structures that can be disconnected to be sold to gain recycling dollars. There are some creative play structures that provide access for all children that are difficult to disassemble and difficult to hurt.

Basic Standards for the Preschool Outdoor Play Area

The adapted physical education specialist must determine the safety and developmental appropriateness of the outdoor play area. The following must be considered:

1. Is the outdoor play area large enough to allow children to move freely (75 to 100 square feet per child)? If the play area is not that large, can scheduling patterns be devised to limit the number of children using the outdoor play area at any given time?
2. Can the teachers and assistants see all the children in the outdoor play area without obstruction?
3. Is the area accessible to all children?
4. Is the area adjacent to bathrooms and water fountains? Are those accessible to all children?
5. Is there a phone available in the event of an emergency?
6. Does the outdoor play area provide areas that are sunny and areas that are shaded?[20]
7. Is the area fenced in to provide protection? Is there an area that serves as a buffer between the street and the play area?
8. Are there child-sized places to rest and relax (e.g., child-sized picnic tables or benches)?
9. Is the area free of debris, litter, and broken glass?[20]

10. Are playground structures no taller than twice the height of the tallest preschooler using the play area? Actually, some playground safety experts believe that climbing structures should be significantly limited. A cautious rule of thumb is 1 foot of height for every year of age. A three-year-old can climb a ladder/mound to 3 feet. A five-year-old can climb a ladder/mound to 5 feet.[55]
11. Does any of the equipment have rust, cracks, or splinters?[20]
12. Are there any hazards, such as sharp edges or places where a child can be pinched?

Careful attention should be paid to the safety of the outdoor play area. Careful review of safety standards, on a daily basis, is a vital part of the role of the adapted physical educator.

PRESCHOOL INCLUSION PROGRAMS

If this society is committed to the notion that all individuals should have the opportunity to learn together—a commitment not based on administrative feasibility or perception of cost reduction—the best possible place to begin inclusionary practices is with infants, toddlers, and preschoolers. The 25th Annual Report to Congress reported the following "settings" in which preschoolers with disabilities received educational services during the 2000–2001 academic year:[69]

Early Childhood—35.9 percent

Early Childhood Special Education—31.1 percent

Home—3.1 percent

Part-Time Early Childhood Special Education—15.2 percent

Other—14.6 percent

The decision regarding the extent to which a child should be included, if the child should be included, must be based solely on the child's individual needs.[44]

Young children are, inherently, very accepting of other children. Their curiosity is natural and, if

A Textured Ball Provides a Tactile Experience
Photo by Laurie Zittel.

their questions are answered honestly, they accept their playmates naturally and without hesitation. A child-sensitive inclusion program begins with inclusive infant, toddler, and preschool programs. As children who have played together enter school together, they are able to learn together and, eventually, be citizens together in peace.[37]

Preschool inclusion programs became a major service delivery option for children with disabilities and their families in the 1990s.[50] At present, Bricker[7] suggests that professionals committed to preschool inclusion must focus on the potential benefits of inclusion to ALL children and schools. Perhaps most important, she suggests, "We need a clearly articulated set of outcomes for all children who participate in inclusive programs."[7] When there is so much interest in outcomes tied to the educational process, adapted physical educators need to work closely with parents and other professionals to determine desirable and reasonable outcomes associated with inclusive preschool education.[50]

Odom[50] suggests several critical factors that must be considered in preschool inclusion programs:

1. Preschoolers with disabilities must be given the chance to engage in the regular, daily, scheduled activities of typically developing children.
2. Preschoolers with disabilities will not be included if they only drop in to the activities of typical children periodically throughout the day or week.
3. A number of variables must be considered prior to determining that the inclusive environment is appropriate for the child. These include philosophy of the program, administrative support, faculty/staff training, and professionals' collaborative skills.
4. The child's family must have the ultimate decision-making authority regarding their child's placement.

Odom also notes that the process in and through which children learn to accept one another must be carefully planned. The adapted physical educator has a unique potential in this process because of the emphasis, in a developmentally appropriate program, on play.

It appears that children make play choices, to include or not to include another child, based on behaviors, not disability. Preschoolers do not want to play with children who are aggressive or destructive.[46] Millspaugh and Segelman[45] suggested that preschoolers are so willing to accept other children with disabilities because each preschooler is virtually disabled in the so-called adult-designed world: "Society systematically handicaps all small children by making drinking fountains too high to manage, stairs too deep to climb, and toilet paper dispensers too far (away) to reach." A checklist that can be used to evaluate the extent to which a child with a severe disability is actually included in a preschool activity program is presented in Table 10-14.

A publication written for the W. K. Kellogg Readiness Initiatives, supported by the W. K. Kellogg Foundation in cooperation with the National Association for the Education of Young Children, *Grassroots Success: Preparing Schools and Families for Each Other,*[68] suggested that schools that are ready for children

- Welcome all children and families in the community
- Design curriculum content and daily routines that promote children's self-motivated learning: social, emotional, cognitive, and physical

Physical Educators Must Appraise Play Facilities with the Needs of Students with Disabilities in Mind

Courtesy Collier Center for Communicative Disorders, Dallas, TX.

Table 10-14	Preschool Movement/Play Inclusion Checklist for Children with Severe Disabilities

Student: _____ **Age:** _____ **Date:** _____ **Y/N**

1. Is the child in a position to participate in all phases of the movement/play activity? If the child uses a wheelchair or crutches, is the activity taking place on a surface that is accessible? _____

2. Does the child participate in the same movement/play activities as the other children? If not, are the modifications kept to a minimum? _____

3. Does the child engage in movement/play activities at the same time as the other children? _____

4. Is the child actively involved, or does the child spend a great deal of time watching others move/play? _____

5. Does the child receive physical assistance from an adult only when absolutely necessary? _____

6. Is the adult careful not to interrupt the play of the child? _____

7. Does the child receive only the most unobtrusive prompts from adults to help the child participate in the activity? _____

8. Do other children seek out the child for play (e.g., ask the child to play)? _____

9. Does the child seek out other children for play? _____

10. Does the child have gestures, signs, or pictures to help him or her communicate if the child is unable to communicate verbally? _____

11. Do teachers interact with the child the same way as they do with the other children—the same type of praise, stickers, hugs, etc.? _____

12. Does the child have the same opportunities as other children for responsible roles in the active learning center (e.g., selecting music, distributing equipment)? _____

- Offer challenging, hands-on, relevant learning activities that build on what children already know and prepare them to contribute to a democratic society
- Ensure that staff are well prepared to work with the ages and abilities of the children
- Use appropriate methods to assess children's progress and evaluate possible special needs
- Prepare environments that enable children to construct knowledge and understanding through inquiry, play, social interaction, and skill development

As is true of school-based inclusive adapted physical education programs (see Chapter 2), a great deal of preparation must occur to address attitudes and biases, abilities and skills, and, most important when addressing inclusive learning with preschoolers, the developmental appropriateness of the learning environment. Children with diverse abilities and disabilities can learn and thrive together in developmentally appropriate learning environments with few, if any, modifications in curriculum or pedagogy.

RESPONSIBILITIES OF THE ADAPTED PHYSICAL EDUCATION SPECIALIST

Goodway and Rudisell[24] have provided an incredible challenge to adapted physical educators and other early childhood educators to provide quality motor programming for children with disabilities and those at risk. They found that African American preschoolers who are at risk for school failure or developmental delays start school feeling competent and good about themselves. However, data have shown that by the 3rd grade these feelings of competence and acceptance have declined.[51] Clearly, the adapted physical educator, like every other educator, needs to address the issue.

The responsibilities of the adapted physical educator who works with preschoolers include the following:

1. Address the gross motor and play goals/objectives on the IEPs of each of the children with disabilities

2. Collect data for each child's portfolio assessment, those children with and without disabilities
3. Create a learning environment in which all the children, those with and without disabilities, have the opportunity to work on gross motor and play skills; the key to a successful, developmentally appropriate motor/play learning environment is the work done before the children are present to prepare the learning environment
4. Coordinate and plan the learning experience to support the theme or focus of the child care or preschool program
5. Model appropriate motor and play behavior for all students
6. Encourage and support age-appropriate interaction among all students
7. Provide support for the children with disabilities who are having difficulty with a gross motor or play skill, not by separating the children for individual instruction but by encouraging a small group of children to work together
8. Model and provide consultative support for the early childhood educators and assistants and other preschool regular and special educators and their paraprofessionals
9. Communicate with parents through notes and newsletters (see Tables 10-15 and 10-16).

Table 10-15	Parent Note

PARENT NOTE

It is very important that you know . . .

You can be very proud of _____. Your child did some great things this week:

      Played in a small group

      Caught a bounced 6-inch playground ball

You could help at home by

      Complimenting play at home that doesn't include fighting

      Playing catch with your child

Thank you for sharing your great kid with me.
      Emily Unger, Preschool Motor Specialist

Table 10-16	PPCD Newsletter

PPCD Newsletter
September 2, 2008

Dear Parents,

We are learning a great deal together . . . and want you to know how well we are doing!

We are learning to	Things to do at home
Walk on a 6-inch balance beam	Hold your child's hand while the child practices walking on a curb.
Throw a small ball, overhand, at a target	As you finish looking at the paper, wad up each piece of paper and ask the child to throw it as hard as possible.
Jump	Rake leaves with your child and jump into them.
Act out stories	Tell your child a story and act it out together.
Identify body parts	Ask your child to draw a picture of you and ask the child to explain it to you. Go on a nature walk and collect leaves, seeds, etc.

An example of including all children in a learning center that reflects a child-care or preschool theme is provided in Figure 10-4. In this example, the theme for the week was "transportation," and the adapted physical educator created an active learning center to support that theme. The active learning center, indoor or outdoor, for preschoolers with and without disabilities designed to support a transportation theme would include the following:

- A marked roadway for automobiles, buses, and trucks with tricycles, scooter boards, and wagons, including stop signs and so on

- An incline ramp with crash mat to simulate an airplane takeoff
- Different-sized boxes for the children to decorate as race cars, police cars, firetrucks, and so on
- A roadway created with a series of mats to provide varied surfaces for the cars to move on
- An obstacle course for the automobiles, buses, and trucks to move on, over, between, and through
- A CD including the following songs: "The Freeze" (We All Live Together, Volume 2); "Yellow Submarine" (Mod Marches); "Chug A Long Choo Choo" (Preschool Aerobic Fun, Georgiana Stewart)

Once the active learning center is designed to expand on the theme, the role of the adapted physical educator is that of *facilitator*. Following are examples of techniques that can be used to address IEP goals/objectives and still serve all the children in the program:

- If a four-year-old with Down syndrome is having difficulty with jumping skills and performing a vertical jump[8] using a definite flexion-extension pattern with hips, knees, and ankles is one of her short-term objectives, the teacher may position himself or herself near the "airplane takeoff area" and offer to spot for all the children as they run and jump into the crash pad. All children gravitate to a teacher who is actively supporting and encouraging children. In this way, the teacher can work on the child's IEP goals without singling the child out from the others.
- If a three-year-old child with low muscle tone is having difficulty lifting his head and shoulders when in a prone position, the teacher may sit on the floor and play "super-girl" or "superboy" by letting children get on scooter boards on their stomachs and then push them, so that they race until they run out of gas.
- If a five-year-old with spina bifida is using a manual wheelchair to ambulate and one of her annual goals is "Elaine will be able to stop and

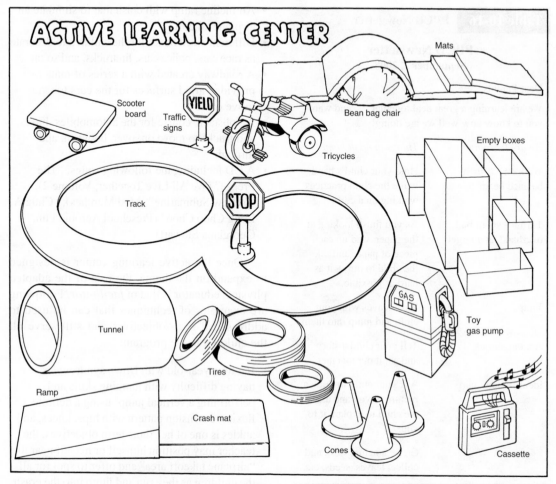

Figure 10-4   Active Learning Center to Support a Transportation Theme

start her wheelchair to avoid bumping into other children in the hallway," the teacher can help her decorate her wheelchair as a police car and then work with all the children on starting/stopping activities in the figure-eight raceway.

- If a four-year-old child with ADHD (who has difficulty playing with other children) has an annual goal that reads "Jeremiah will be able to participate in a small-group cooperative play activity," the teacher may invite three or four children to play "Freeze," an active parallel play experience.

If preschoolers with disabilities are receiving services from an adapted physical education teacher, it is usually as a consultant rather than as a direct service provider. The general physical educator may work with preschoolers who are three, four, or five years old but in many school districts the early childhood educator is responsible for addressing the child's gross motor and play needs. Thus, the major task of the adapted physical education specialist is to help local campus staff follow through and continue the activity and actions throughout the week when the teacher is not present.

Atypical Play Behavior

The adapted physical educator needs to be sensitive to the play behavior of young children because atypical play behavior may be an indicator of developmental delays or reflect problems in the child's personality and social functioning.[14] Bergen stated,

> Most at-risk young children engage in the first stage of play development (sensorimotor/ practice play) although the quantity and quality of the play is influenced by the nature and severity of their handicaps, biological risk, or environmental risk conditions. For example, visually impaired, autistic, and motorically-impaired children have narrower ranges of sensorimotor play behaviors, severely multiply-handicapped children initiate less sensorimotor play, and abused/neglected children may be hypervigilant and less exploratory. Down syndrome and hearing impaired children, however, seem to show sensorimotor play behaviors that are very similar to those of children who are not at risk.[4] [Author's note: No attempt was made to change this quotation to reflect person-first language.]

The preschool movement/play specialist, always a careful observer of young children at play, must be sensitive to the following types of idiosyncrasies in play:

1. Significant preoccupation with a single play theme may be an indicator of a behavior disorder or an autistic-like behavior. Most young children seek repetition as a means of gaining and keeping control of their environment. Any parent who has been urged to read a story "one more time" or any teacher who has grown weary of a particular song or dance understands this phenomenon.
2. Unchanging repetition of a play theme may indicate the following
   a. An emotional disturbance or a cognitive delay

   b. A need for control of part of the child's life, as is typical of children living with abuse and neglect or parental drug abuse
3. Unusual or morbid play themes (drive-by shooting, funeral) may indicate that a child has had the experience and is trying to put it into perspective.
4. Imitation of sexual acts and practices may indicate that the child is being or has been sexually abused or molested.
5. Lack of awareness of other children may indicate
   a. A developmental delay (in children age three or older)
   b. An emotional disorder
   c. Autism or pervasive developmental disorder
6. Fragmentary play—an inability to sustain play—
   a. In children older than three years may indicate a developmental delay or attention deficit disorder
   b. May indicate that a child is unable to cope with a significant, acute, or chronic trauma
7. Difficulty separating self from a play role (e.g., the child is a Power Ranger, not Sally playing "Power Ranger") may be typical of a child who has been treated aggressively.
8. Difficulty joining groups at play without disrupting others may be typical of a child with a developmental delay.
9. A tendency to lash out and spoil the play (knock down the block structure) of other children may indicate the child has a disability that makes it difficult to participate, so the child acts out in frustration.

Management of Behavior in the Preschool Learning Environment

Zittel and McCubbin wrote,

> Best practice in early childhood education, for children with and without developmental delays, calls for the design of environments that are more child- versus teacher-directed.[73]

If educators design a learning environment that is more child-directed, behavior management is simplified. The beauty of the developmentally appropriate, play-based learning environment is that behavior problems are minimized.[21] The following environmental variables encourage appropriate behavior and minimize behavior problems:

- A small student–teacher ratio (young children demand and require the attention and care of adults; a ratio of no more than 8:1 is vital)
- Age-appropriate, child-driven activity
- A routine that the child can count on during the day, every day
- Child choices regarding activity
- A daily schedule sensitive to a child's basic needs—nutritious snack and lunch time, quiet or nap time
- A daily schedule that provides an opportunity for solitary, partner, small-group, and large-group activities
- A daily schedule that allows for a mix of indoor and outdoor play
- A quiet place to which a child can retreat at any time during the day
- An adequate number of play units (there must be a sufficient number of materials, so that children are not expected to share)

If these basic variables are controlled, most children's behavior will be controlled as well. To encourage consistency, just as in any other setting, rules must be clear, concise, brief, and understandable.

The most basic strategy for establishing a positive learning environment in which a preschooler will be successful is to be proactive and to "catch 'em being good" whenever possible.

Cultural Diversity in the Active Learning Centers

The adapted physical education specialist needs to be particularly sensitive to the diverse cultures,

languages, socioeconomic backgrounds, genders, and abilities/disabilities of the children served. Even very young children begin to develop stereotypical notions regarding performance and potential. The wisest responses from educators are to openly address issues related to culture, socioeconomic forces, gender, gender preference, age, and ability/disability and, specifically, to be willing to address the many questions that young children will raise.

According to Derman-Sparks and the Anti-Bias Curriculum (A.B.C.) Task Force, research data reveal that

- Children begin to notice differences and construct classificatory and evaluative categories very early.
- There are overlapping but distinguishable developmental tasks and steps in the construction of identity and attitudes.
- Societal stereotyping and bias influence children's self-concept and attitudes toward others.[19]

To create a learning environment that encourages antibias within the active learning center, the adapted physical educator may do the following:

1. Display posters and photographs of people that reflect a broad variety of cultures, socioeconomic status, gender, age, and ability/disability.
   a. Posters and photographs should empower all children.
   b. Posters and photographs should correctly reflect daily life with an emphasis on movement, sport, recreation, and leisure activities.
2. Use CDs/cassettes of various types of music common to the cultures of the children in the program.
   a. Use a broad assortment of music that features males and females as lead performer.
   b. Choose a broad assortment of music that features young and old performers.

c. Use CDs/cassettes that reflect diversity: "You Are Super the Way You Are" (Joining Hands with Other Lands), "Mi Casa, My House" (Joining Hands with Other Lands), "Somos El Barco" (Head First and Belly Down), "Sister Rosa" (The Neville Brothers), "Native American Names" (Joining Hands with Other Lands), "La Bamba" (Dancin' Magic), "Shake It to the One You Love the Best" (Shake It to the One You Love the Best, Cheryl Mattox)

d. Use CDs/cassettes that honor young children as they are: "Ugly Duckling" (We All Live Together, Volume IV, Greg and Steve), "What a Miracle" (Walter the Waltzing Worm, Hap Palmer), "Free to Be You and Me" (Free to Be You and Me, Marlo Thomas), "Self Esteem" (B.E.S.T. Friends).

3. Use music that includes culturally distinctive instruments.

4. Provide a variety of cultural musical instruments:
    a. Kenyan double stick drum
    b. Zulu marimba
    c. Indian sarangi
    d. Mexican guiro
    e. West African balaphon
    f. Japanese den den
    g. Native American dance bells
    h. Chilean rainstick

5. Teach dances that reflect a variety of cultures and experiences.
    a. Ask parents and grandparents of the children to teach the songs and dances of their childhood.
    b. Provide materials of color that have cultural connotations to enhance celebrations and studies of different cultures (e.g., red and gold to celebrate Chinese festivals; red, white, and green to represent the Mexican flag for Cinco de Mayo celebrations).

6. Introduce simple games that reflect a variety of cultures and experiences. Ask parents and grandparents of the children to teach simple games.

7. Use language that is gender-free when referring to the activities and play of children. If the child, for example, is zooming around the room "pretending to be," be certain the words you use reflect no bias. The child is a "firefighter," a "police officer," or a "postal worker."

8. Read and act out stories of children involved in diverse play, sport, leisure, and recreation experiences.

SUMMARY

The adapted physical education specialist has a unique role to play in the child development process. The professional must be a consultant, or a teacher of teachers—including the parent.

A developmentally appropriate learning environment for infants, toddlers, and preschoolers is one in which adults are sensitive to the unique needs of the children and are responsive to those needs. The learning environment allows active exploration with others and with materials. A developmentally appropriate learning environment for movement reflects the same needs.

A heightened respect for the family unit, in whatever form, has dominated "best practices" in early childhood intervention and preschool education. In addition, the emphasis has been placed on providing intervention within the most "natural" setting—the home, church, child care center, community center, or neighborhood park.

REVIEW QUESTIONS

1. Compare and contrast the behavior of a typically developing infant, toddler, or preschooler with that of an infant, a toddler, or a preschooler who has a delay or disability.

2. Explain the differences between the individual family service plan and the individual education program.

3. List each of Howard Gardner's eight forms of intelligence and give examples of behaviors tied to each.

4. Describe techniques that parents or teachers could use to improve an infant's or a toddler's motor and play skills.

5. Describe developmentally appropriate assessment practices for preschool-age children.

6. Describe developmentally appropriate intervention programs for preschool-age children.

7. Describe a developmentally appropriate preschool learning environment.

8. Explain strategies the physical educator could use to encourage "antibias" in the curriculum.

STUDENT ACTIVITIES

1. Visit a child care center and evaluate the play units in its outdoor play area.

2. Volunteer in a child care center/preschool for children at risk.

3. Working in small groups, design an active learning center for indoor play and one for outdoor play.

Present your group's center to the rest of the class and explain the purpose of each component and why it was included in the plan.

REFERENCES

1. Active Start: *A statement of physical activity guidelines for children birth to five years.* Reston, VA: National Association of Sport and Physical Education, 2001.

2. Albu J, Allison D, Boozer, C, Heymsfield S, Kissileff H, Kretser A: Obesity solutions: Report of a meeting. *Nutrition Review* 50:150–156, 1997.

3. Auxter, D. Temporary assistance for needy family comments: Administration for children and families. Washington, DC: Consortium for Citizens with Disabilities Prevention Task Force, 2003.

4. Bergen D: *Play as the vehicle for early intervention with at-risk infants and toddlers.* Paper presented at the annual conference of the American Educational Research Association, Chicago, April 1991.

5. Berk L: Vygotsky's theory: The importance of make-believe play, *Young Children* November:30–39, 1994.

6. Berrueta-Clement J, et al.: *Changed lives: The effects of the Perry Preschool Program on youths through age 19.* Monographs of the High/Scope Educational Research Foundation, No 8, Ypsilanti, MI, 1985, High/Scope Press.

7. Bricker D: Inclusion: How the scene has changed. *Topics Early Child Spec Educ* 20 (1):14–20, 2000, retrieved online, EBSCO host.

8. Cheatum BA, Hammond AA: *Physical activities for improving learning and behavior: A guide to sensory motor development.* Champaign, IL, Human Kinetics, 1999.

9. Corso R, Santos RM, Roof V: Honoring diversity in early childhood education

materials. *Teach Except Child* 34(3):30–36.

10. Cowden JE, Sayers LK, Torrey CC: *Pediatric adapted motor development and exercise: An innovative, multisystem approach for professionals and families.* Springfield, IL, Charles C Thomas, 1998.

11. Cowden J, Torrey C: A ROADMAP for assessing infants, toddlers, and preschoolers: The role of the adapted motor developmentalist, *APAQ* 12:1–11, 1995.

12. Crais E: *"Best practices" with preschoolers: Assessing within the context of a family-centered approach.* Chapel Hill, NC, Carolina Institute for Research on Infant Personnel Preparation, Frank Porter Grahman Child Development Center, 1991.

13. U.S. Department of Health and Human Services, Substance Abuse and Mental Health Services Administration, Center for Mental Health Services: *Cultural competence in serving children and adolescents with mental health problems.* Rockville, MD, Author, 1999.

14. Curry N, Arnaud S: Personality difficulties in preschool children as revealed through play themes and styles, *Young Children* May:4–9, 1995.

15. Dawkins C, et al.: Perspectives on early intervention, *Except Parent* February:23–27, 1994.

16. Danielson CL, Abrutyn L: *An introduction to using portfolios in the classroom,* Alexandria, VA, Association for Supervision and Curriculum Development, 1997.

17. *A day with Daniel N. Stern, M.D.* Presentation sponsored by the Texas Association for Infant Mental Health, Dallas, February 20, 1995.

18. Council on Physical Education for Children (COPEC): Appropriate practices in movement programs for young children ages 3–5. Position Statement of the National Association for Sport and Physical Education. Reston, VA: NASPE, 2000, 8, 10, 12–14, 15.

19. Derman-Sparks C, A.B.C. Task Force: *Anti-bias curriculum: Tools for empowering young children.* Washington, DC, National Association for the Education of Young Children, 1989.

20. Dodge D, Colker L: *The creative curriculum for early childhood.* Washington, DC, Teaching Strategies, 1992.

21. Dunn L, Kontos S: What have we learned about developmentally appropriate practice? *Young Children* July:4–13, 1997.

22. Garcia C, Garcia L, Floyd J, Lawson J: Improving public health through early childhood movement programs. *JOPERD* 73(1):27–31, 2002.

23. Gardner H: *Frames of mind: The theory of multiple intelligences.* New York, Basic Books, 1983.

24. Goodway JD, Rudisell ME: Influence of a motor skill intervention program on perceived competence of at-risk African American preschoolers, *APAQ* 13:288–301, 1996.

25. Gowen J: The early development of symbolic play, *Young Children* March:75–84, 1995.

26. Gronlund G: Portfolios as an assessment tool: Is collection of work enough? *Young Children* May:4–10, 1998.

27. Hancock T, Kaiser A, Delaney E: Teaching parents of preschoolers at high risk. *Topics in Early Childhood Special Education* 22(4):191–213, 2002.

28. Howard Gardner on the eighth intelligence: Seeing the natural world—An interview, *Dimens Early Child* Summer:5–6, 1995.

29. Huettig C, Bridges D, Woodson A: Play for children with severe and profound disabilities. *Palaestra* 18(1):30–37, 2002.

30. Huettig C, O'Connor J: Wellness programming for preschoolers with disabilities. *Teach Except Child* January/February:12–17, 1999.

31. Hughes F, Elicker J, Veen L: A program of play for infants and their caregivers, *Young Children* January:52–88, 1995.

32. Klemm D, Schimanski C: Parent to parent: The crucial connection. *Except Parent* September:109–112, 1999.

33. Lally J: The impact on child care policies and practices on infant/toddler identity formation, *Young Children* November:34–36, 1995.

34. Lieberman AF: An *infant* mental health perspective, *Zero to Three* 18(3):3–5, 1998.

35. Linder T: *Transdisciplinary play-based assessment: A functional approach to working with young children.* Baltimore, MD, Paul H. Brookes, 1993.

36. Linder T: *Transdisciplinary play-based intervention: Guidelines for developing a*

meaningful curriculum for young children. Baltimore, MD, Paul H. Brookes, 1993.

37. Lubeck S: The politics of developmentally appropriate practice: Exploring issues of culture, class, and curriculum. In Mallory B, New R, editors: *Diversity and developmentally appropriate practices: Challenges for early childhood education.* New York, Teachers College Press, 1994.

38. Marion M: Guiding young children's understanding and management of anger, *Young Children* 52(7):62–67, 1997.

39. McBride SL: Family-centered practices, *Young Children* 54(3):62–68, 1999.

40. McLean M, Synder P, Smith B, Sandall S: The DEC recommended practices in early intervention/early childhood special education: Social validation, *J Early Intervention* 25(2):120–128, 2002.

41. Meisels SJ: Developmental screening in early childhood: The interaction of research and social policy. In Breslow L, Fielding JE, Love LB, editors: *Annual review of public health,* vol. 9, Palo Alto, CA, Annual Reviews, 1988.

42. Meisels S, Provence S: *Screening and assessment: Guidelines for identifying young disabled and developmentally vulnerable children and their families,* Washington, DC. National Center for Clinical Infant Programs, 1989.

43. Miller K: *The outside play and learning book: Activities for young children.* Mt. Ranier, MD, Gryphon House, 1989.

44. Mills PE, Cole KN, Jenkins JR, Dale PS: Effects of different levels of inclusion on preschoolers with disabilities, *Except Child* 65(1):79–90, 1998.

45. Millspaugh F, Segelman M: Neither fear nor pity: Public-service announcements about differences. In Harmonay M, editor: *Promise and performance: Children with special needs.* Cambridge, MA, Ballinger, 1977.

46. Nabors L: Playmate preferences of children who are typically developing for their classmates with special needs, *Mental Retardation* 35(2):107–113, 1997.

47. National Association for the Education of Young Children at www.naeyc.org/naeyc.

48. *"Natural environment" draft policy recommendations.* Texas Interagency Council on Early Childhood Intervention, March 31, 1995.

49. Notari-Syverson A, Shuster S: Putting real-life skills into IEP/IFSP's for infants and young children, TEACHING *Except Child* Winter:29–32, 1995.

50. Odom S: Preschool inclusion: What we know and where we go from here, *Topics in Early Childhood Special Education* 20(1):20–28, 2000.

51. Overby LY, Branta C, Goodway J, Smith Y: *The relationship of parental attitudes to perceived competence, motor development and physical fitness of at-risk youth.* Paper presented at the National Convention of the American Alliance for Health, Physical Education, Recreation and Dance, Denver, CO, April 1994.

52. Powell DR: Reweaving parents into the fabric of early childhood programs, *Young Children* September:60–67, 1998.

53. Pretti-Frontczak K, Kowalski K, Brown R: Preschool teachers' use of assessments and curricula: A statewide examination. *Excep Child* 69(2):109–123, 2002.

54. Prizant, B, Meyer E: Socioemotional aspects of communication disorders in young children and their families, *Am J Speech-Lang Pathol* 2:56–71, 1993.

55. Readdick CH, Park JJ: Achieving great heights: The climbing child, *Young Children* 53(6):14–19, 1998.

56. Rivkin M: *The great outdoors: Restoring children's right to play outside.* Washington, DC, National Association for the Education of Young Children, 1995.

57. Sanborn C, Huetting C, Popejoy A: *The O generation: Our children are at risk for obesity.* Presentation at the Texas Association of the College of Sports Medicine, Houston, TX, March 2003.

58. Sandall S, McLean M, Smith B: *DEC recommended practices in early intervention/early childhood special education.* Washington, DC, Council for Exceptional Children: Division of Early Childhood, 2000.

59. Sanders S: *Active for life: Developmentally appropriate movement programs for young children.* National Association for the Education of Young Children, Washington, DC, in cooperation with Human Kinetics, Champaign, IL.

60. Sayers LK, et al.: Qualitative analysis of a pediatric strength intervention on the developmental stepping movements of infants with Down syndrome. *APAQ* 13:247–268, 1996.

61. Shepard L: The challenges of assessing young children appropriately, *Phi Delta Kappan* November:206–212, 1994.

62. Slaby RG, Roedell WC, Arezzo D, Hendrix K: *Early violence prevention: Tools for teachers of young children.* Washington, DC, National Association for the Education of Young Children, 1995.

63. Suen HK, Logan CR, Neisworth JT, Bagnato S: Parent-professional congruence: Is it necessary? *J Early Intervention* 19(3):243–252, 1995.

64. Tabors PA: What early childhood educators need to know: Developing effective programs for linguistically and culturally diverse children and families, *Young Children* 53(6):20–26, 1998.

65. U.S. Department of Education, Office of Special Education Programs: *Twenty-third annual report to Congress on the implementation of the Individuals with Disabilities Act.* Washington, DC, Author.

66. Vygotsky L: The role of play in development. In Cole R, et al., editors: *Mind in society.* Cambridge, MA, Harvard University Press, 1978.

67. Wagner M, Spiker D, Inman M: The effectiveness of the parents as teachers program with low-income parents and children, *Topics in Early Childhood Special Education* 22(2):67–82, 2002.

68. Washington V, Johnson V, McCracken J: *Grassroots success: Preparing schools and families for each other.* Washington, DC, W.K. Kellogg Readiness Initiatives, National Association for the Education of Young Children, 1995.

69. Westat, Prepared for the Office of Special Education and Rehabilitation Services, U.S. Department of Education: Twenty-Fifth Annual Report to Congress on the implementation of the Individuals with Disabilities Act, *Journal for Vocational Special Needs* 27:22–47, 2004.

70. Wetherby A: *Communication and language intervention for preschool children.* Buffalo, NY, Educom, 1992.

71. Winston P: *Working with families in early intervention: Interdisciplinary perspectives.* Chapel Hill, NC, Carolina Institute for Research on Infant Personnel Preparation, 1990.

72. Zero-to-Three at www.zerotothree.org. 2003

73. Zittel LJ, McCubbin JA: Effect of an integrated physical education setting on motor performance of preschool children with developmental delays, *APAQ* 13:316–333, 1996.

SUGGESTED READINGS

Cheatum BA, Hammond AA: *Physical activities for improving learning and behavior: A guide to sensory motor development,* Champaign, IL, Human Kinetics, 1999.

Dodge D, Colker L: *The creative curriculum for early childhood.* Washington, DC, Teaching Strategies, 1992.

Huettig C, Bridges D, Woodson A: Play for children with severe and profound disabilities. *Palaestra* 18(1):30–37, 2002.

Paciorek KM: *Annual editions: Early childhood education,* 28th ed. Dubuque, IA, McGraw-Hill, 2008.

Paciorek KM, Monro JH: *Annual editions: Early childhood education,* 26th ed. Dubuque, IA, McGraw-Hill, 2006.

Slaby RG, Roedell WC, Arezzo D, Hendrix K: *Early violence prevention: Tools for teachers of young children.* Washington, DC, National Association for the Education of Young Children, 1995.

RECOMMENDED WEB SITES

Please keep in mind that these Web sites are being recommended in the winter of 2007. As Web sites often change, they may have moved or been reconfigured or eliminated.

Culturally, Linguistically Appropriate Services
  http://clas.uiuc.edu

Zero to Three: The Nation's Leading Resource on the First Years
  www.zerotothree.org

National Association for the Education of Young Children
  www.naeyc.org

Council for Exceptional Children: Division of Early
    Childhood: Recommended Practices
    www.dec-sped.org/recommendedpractices.html

Project INSPIRE: Play and Parent Pages
    www.twu.edu/INSPIRE

RECOMMENDED VIDEOS

Films for the Humanities and Sciences
PO Box 2053
Princeton, NJ 08543-2053
www.films.com
1-800-257-5126

Insight Media
2162 Broadway
New York, NY 10024-0621
www.insight-media.com
1-800-233-9910

*Infants and Young Children with Special Health
Needs: Motor Development*
    #GTH8456-A/DVD/VHS/1992/25min/$69.95
*Promoting Cognitive, Social and Emotional
Development*
    #GTH8459-A/DVD/VHS/1992/22min/$69.95
Promoting Family Collaboration
    GTH8457-A/DVD/VHS/1992/24min/$69.95

Infant Motor Development
    #IAM2975/VHS/1998/20 min/$149
Gross Motor Skills
    #31AP1937/DVD/2001/10 min/$189
Infancy: Landmarks of Development
    #78AP4286/DVD/2003/29 min/$139
Physical Development: The First Five Years
    #NAP7988/DVD/1996/29 min/$129

Intellectual Disability

■ **O B J E C T I V E S**

Define intellectual disability as it appears in IDEA.

Explain how the IDEA definition of mental retardation differs from the AAIDD definition of intellectual disability.

Identify three causes of intellectual disability.

Identify typical motor development delays demonstrated by persons with Down syndrome.

Describe how physical education needs might differ for persons with mild intellectual disability and persons with severe intellectual disability.

Describe modifications the physical educator should make when programming exercise for students with intellectual disability.

Beginning with the first edition of this textbook, published in 1969, this chapter has always been titled "Mental Retardation." It has been retitled in this (the 11th) edition to reflect contemporary usage. The term complies with the name change of the American Association on Mental Retardation (AAMR) to the American Association on Intellectual and Developmental Disabilities (AAIDD). The purpose for this change was to move away from "mental retardation," which is a term that many people find offensive and move toward terms that more accurately reflect the intellectual functioning of a large percentage of people. The association continues to be committed to improving the life and support systems of individuals who are classified in key areas of federal and state policy as "mentally retarded."[93]

CASE STUDY

Luther

Luther is a six-year-old boy with Down syndrome. His gross motor skills are significant strengths. He is able to perform the following:

- Run contralaterally, stopping and starting with ease
- Broad jump a distance of 3 feet
- Hop on his left foot 5 times in a row and 2 times on his right foot
- Gallop with ease with a left-foot lead
- Throw a tennis ball, with his right hand, using a contralateral pattern, a distance of 50 feet
- Kick a stationary ball with his left foot, with a good plant and follow through
- Dribble a basketball 10 times using his right hand

At present, he is receiving his instruction in physical education in the general kindergarten class. Luther is having difficulty with behavior problems. Specifically, he hugs and wrestles with other children. Because he is strong, the children are becoming frightened of him.

APPLICATION TASK

Describe the types of low-organized games and activities in which Luther is likely to be successful. Consider the strategies the physical educator might use to help eliminate his inappropriate behaviors.

In keeping with this momentous effort to change public perception about the abilities of persons who require various levels of support systems to fully enjoy the freedoms those of you reading the chapter enjoy, the term "mental retardation" will be used only when referring to definitions from the past and those used in public laws. In other sections, the term "intellectual disabilities" will be used.

Intellectual disability is not a fixed, unalterable condition that condemns an individual to a static, deprived lifetime of failure to achieve. Rather, cognitive, psychomotor, and affective behaviors are dynamic processes that, if properly stimulated, can be developed further than ever before imagined. Early concepts of intellectual disability viewed the condition as an inherited disorder that was essentially incurable. This notion resulted in hopelessness on the part of professionals and social and physical separation of persons who had an intellectual disability. After years of research and innovative programming, it is now recognized that intelligence and other functions depend on the readiness and experience of the child, the degree and quality of environmental stimulation, and the types of support systems provided.

In the late 1960s and early 1970s, institutions that served persons with intellectual disabilities began designing and implementing educational programs intended to help those persons develop independent living skills to enable them to function in community settings. As institutionalized individuals rose to the challenge of these educational programs, a movement began to promote their placement in communities. During the 1970s, thousands of persons with intellectual disabilities were removed from institutions and allowed to take their rightful place as contributing members of communities. As institutions began to develop viable educational programs, public schools took up their responsibility toward young children with intellectual disabilities who lived in the communities. School systems hired professionals trained in appropriate teaching techniques to provide educational opportunities for these children. As a result of efforts by both institutions and public school systems, all except those individuals who are the most severely intellectual disabled are living, going to school, and working in the community. Today these individuals have more opportunities for optimum social interaction than ever before. The social awareness and commitment required to maximize the physical and social community opportunities for individuals with intellectual disabilities are beginning to be understood and implemented.

DEFINITION OF INTELLECTUAL DISABILITY

The labels assigned to different groups of individuals with an intellectual disability vary depending on who is doing the labeling.[45] Traditionally, levels of disability were determined by IQ scores. The 2000 edition of the *Diagnostic and Statistical Manual of Mental Disorders,*[3] while recognizing the importance of adaptive functioning, bases severity of intellectual impairment on the following IQ scores: mild = 50–55 to approximately 70; moderate = 35–40 to 50–55; severe = 20–25 to 35–40; and profound = below 20 or 25. The definition of intellectual disability that was adapted by the American Association on Mental Retardation in 2002 but amended in 2006 reads as follows:

> [Intellectual disability] is a disability characterized by significant limitations both in intellectual functioning and in adaptive behavior as expressed in conceptual, social, and practical adaptive skills. This disability originates before age 18.[2]

The following five assumptions are essential to the application of this definition:

1. Limitations in present functioning must be considered within the context of community environments typical of the individual's age peers and culture.
2. Valid assessment considers cultural and linguistic diversity as well as differences in communication, sensory, motor, and behavioral factors.
3. Within the individual, limitations often coexist with strengths.
4. An important purpose of describing limitations is to develop a profile of needed supports.
5. With appropriate personalized supports over a sustained period, the life functioning of the person with an intellectual disability generally will improve.[77]

The 2006 AAMR system of determining intellectual disability includes IQ test scores with subaverage intellectual functioning considered to be 2 standard deviations below the mean of the instrument being used. In addition to paper-and-pencil tests, it is recommended that several sources of information be used for determining whether a person is declared intellectual disabled.

AAMR (now AAIDD), has taken the position that, if adequate supports (resources and strategies) are provided to persons with intellectual disabilities, their independence, ability to establish and maintain relationships, contributions, school and community participation, and personal well-being will be enhanced. Supports may be needed in the areas of (1) intellectual abilities; (2) adaptive behavior (conceptual, social, and practical skills); (3) participation, interactions, and social roles; (4) health (physical health, mental health, etiological factors); and (5) context (environments and cultures). The level of support required will differ according to the needs of each individual.[2] Those four levels are presented in Table 11-1.

The public schools have not yet adopted the AAIDD definition. Rather, they are adhering to the definition that appears in the rules for implementing the Individuals with Disabilities Education Act (IDEA):

> Mental retardation means significantly subaverage general intellectual functioning existing concurrently with deficits in adaptive behavior and manifested during the developmental period that adversely affects a child's educational performance.[70]

Table 11-1	Levels of Support Required by Individuals with Intellectual Disabilities
Intermittent	Supports are on an as-needed basis. Supports may be high- or low-intensity when needed.
Limited	Supports are needed consistently over time (e.g., employment training, transitional support when moving from school to an adult).
Extensive	Supports are characterized by regular involvement (e.g., daily) in at least some environments (at work or at home).
Pervasive	Supports are constant, high-intensity, provision across environments. They are potentially life sustaining in nature.

Most schools consider an IQ score lower than 70 to be significant subaverage general intellectual functioning. Thus, IQ scores lower than 70 accompanied by deficits in adaptive behavior qualify a student for the mental retardation classification and services.

INCIDENCE OF INTELLECTUAL DISABILITIES

Approximately 3 percent of the total population of the United States is intellectually disabled. The individuals with less severe forms of intellectual disability (those needing intermittent and limited support) are often associated with lower socioeconomic groups. Those individuals with the more severe forms that require extensive or pervasive support are in all levels of socioeconomic groups.[9] During the 2005–2006 school year, the number of children and youth reported to be served under federal requirements was 533,426.[95]

CAUSES OF INTELLECTUAL DISABILITY

Although frequently there is no clear cause of intellectual disabilities,[37] the following are some causes that have been identified:

- Chromosomal abnormalities (e.g., Down syndrome, fragile X syndrome)[9]
- Genetic metabolic and neurological disorders (e.g., phenylketonuria, Tay-Sachs disease, neurofibromatosis, tuberous sclerosis)[9]
- Congenital infections (e.g., rubella, herpes simplex)[9]
- Prenatal drug exposure (e.g., alcohol, cocaine, medications)[9]
- Perinatal factors (e.g., CNS bleeding, high forceps delivery, prematurity, low birthweight, lack of medical referral for intervention services)[2]
- Postnatal factors (e.g., severe malnutrition, asphyxia, lead or mercury poisoning, viral infection, inadequate early intervention and/or special education services)[1,9]

CHARACTERISTICS OF INTELLECTUAL DISABILITY

Although research tends to generalize the characteristics of people who are intellectually disabled, these individuals are diverse in cognitive, social, and physical functions. Almost 87 percent of persons with intellectual disabilities are only a little slower to learn new information and skills. The remaining 13 percent score below 50 on IQ tests. These individuals have more difficulty learning at home, in school, and in the community; thus, they need more support systems to enable them to enjoy a satisfying life.[61] Some athletes with intellectual disabilities are extremely adept at sports. On the other hand, some persons with intellectual disabilities are unable to participate in regular sports events and need modification of the activities to be successful in their efforts to play. Other persons with severe intellectual disabilities may not be ambulatory or have the physical capability needed to participate in play of any sort.

Because of the diversity within the group, it is difficult to generalize a set of characteristics to the total population. However, the cognitive and physical characteristics of this population provide basic guidelines and alert the physical educator to the potential nature of the physical education programs they need.

Cognitive Characteristics Related to Skill

In addition to the considerable variability in intelligence as measured by standardized tests, individuals demonstrate variance in processing information, comprehension, and memory. The cognitive limitations associated with intellectual disabilities are difficulty in organizing thoughts, persistence in using incorrect methods even when they have repeatedly resulted in failure to learn through imitation, and difficulty in evaluating self.[47] However, there are aspects of intelligence that may be superior to many with so-called normal intelligence. For instance, some persons with an intellectual disability have phenomenal memories.

As a group, persons who are intellectually disabled are not as adept in perceptual attributes that relate to motor skills as are comparable nondisabled individuals. They may be clumsy and awkward and lack balance, which affects their ability to perform motor tasks efficiently. A review of the literature reveals that there are many perceptual and cognitive characteristics that may inhibit the learning of motor skills. Early studies reported that individuals with an intellectual disability demonstrated less preparation and slower actual movement times.[90] Also, when compared with other persons, they are less able to spontaneously predict the changing conditions of a motor task. They are slower than others to estimate the amount of time needed to plan activities[38] and to intercept moving objects.[21] Even youngsters with mild intellectual disabilities often inaccurately perceive their competence to perform motor skills. Perceived motor competence relates directly to motivation, self-esteem, and social development.[102] Some studies have demonstrated that, although female adolescents with an intellectual disability improve their athletic performance when involved in integrated sports, their perceived athletic competence suffers.[67] Other studies have shown that poor physical education experiences in high school have a negative impact on the activity levels of adults with intellectual disabilities.[34] Individuals with negative perceptions of their motor competence do not persist at participating in physical activities.[80]

The good news is that, when intervention occurs, even individuals with a severe intellectual disability improve their planning and movement times.[15] Others report that, as individuals with IQs of 40 and above increase in chronological age, their reaction times and individual variability decrease.[100] Thus, it is reasonable to expect individuals who have intellectual disabilities to benefit from appropriate intervention programs. Well-designed physical education programs can promote physical and motor gains.

Persons with severe intellectual disabilities most likely have adverse performance in social, cognitive, language, and motor development. Many students who are severely intellectually disabled have difficulty interacting with others. This may stem from abnormal behavior, including self-abusive acts as well as behavior that is injurious to others. Furthermore, stereotyped behaviors and bizarre acts, such as rocking back and forth, waving the hands in front of the eyes, and making strange noises, may also adversely affect social interaction with others. In addition, those who are severely intellectually disabled may have problems with self-help skills, such as dressing, feeding, and basic motor functioning.

Attention, Memory, and Decision Making

Attention, regardless of how it is defined, is generally considered to be a critical aspect of information processing. As a result, attention plays a prominent role in a wide range of cognitive and behavioral activities.[12] Two important aspects of learning motor skills are the attention that one gives to the instructional task and the ability to remember and respond to movement cues. DePauw and Ferrari[24] indicate that, compared with persons who have intellectual disabilities individuals who are not intellectually disabled have a more difficult time performing tasks when some interference occurs. Thus, once individuals who are intellectually disabled are on task, they are not distracted by extraneous cues and information. Furthermore, Newell[65] found no difference between subjects who were intellectually disabled and those who weren't on adopting memory strategies for the recall of movement cues on a motor task. Thus, it seems that persons with intellectual disabilities can improve their movement accuracy if they are helped to understand and remember essential movement information.

Decision-making capability varies widely among persons with intellectual disabilities. Some persons with an intellectual disability may be able to make decisions that enable independent functioning in the community, while some may be totally dependent on others for cognitive decisions. One unique study, which focused on the impact of exercise on problem-solving skills, reported that moderate-intensity exercise (55 to 60 percent VO_2 max) for 20 minutes resulted in an increase in speed of problem solving in teenagers with average IQ scores of 60.[22] It has also been shown that persons with an intellectual disability can be made aware of exertion levels during physical exercise[6] and can successfully engage in self-management practices.[29]

Many persons who are severely intellectually disabled have impaired cognitive and language development. Many are unable to respond to simple commands. Thus, it is difficult for them to grasp instruction. Furthermore, they may lack the ability to generalize skills learned in one setting to another setting. They often have problems with language. This further makes communication during instruction difficult.

Motor Development Delays

Motor delays are very common among persons who are severely intellectually disabled. Delays in developing postural reflexes[100] impact the ability to perform such basic tasks as grasping objects, holding the head up, sitting, standing, and walking. In addition, these delays, to varying degrees, negatively affect their motor and physical capabilities. They may be less capable in strength, flexibility, agility, coordination, and balance.

Physical Health

There is an increasing frequency of chronic health conditions among persons with intellectual disabilities. They have a higher incidence of infections and cancers, poorer dental health, and a

Even severely involved children can bowl
Courtesy of Tara McCarthy.

greater incidence of motor vehicle accidents than persons with normal intelligence.[42]

Health promotion that involves physical activities directed at persons with intellectual disabilities can significantly improve this group's health status. Individuals who are helped to develop lifestyles that maintain and enhance the state of well-being will frequent community-based programs.[85]

In the past there has been a lack of overall policies regarding health promotion for people with an intellectual disability. Despite the research that has demonstrated significant health and physical fitness benefits for persons with intellectual disabilities, their individual transition plans have consisted mainly of vocational skills and activities of daily living.[82]

The 2004 amendments to IDEA retain both physical education as a direct service and recreation as a related service for persons with disabilities. To enable individuals with an intellectual disability to improve their health status and ability to function well in their job settings, physical educators must make a significant effort to include and promote strength and endurance activities in each person's ITP.

Postural Development

Many individuals who have an intellectual disability have postural abnormalities, including malalignment of the trunk or the legs. One of the most obvious postural deficiencies is that of the protruding abdomen, which may be associated with obesity[73] and/or lack of abdominal strength. In addition, because of depth perception problems and/or delayed vestibular and equilibrium reflex development, there may be a tendency to hold the head flexed, externally rotate the legs, and use a wide base of support when walking and running. Delays in reflex development always result in delays in the appearance of motor milestones.[41]

Physical Fitness Development

In general, individuals with intellectual disabilities are in need of intervention programs to improve their physical fitness levels.[23] In many individuals, regardless of disability level, poor respiration and susceptibility to respiratory infections may accompany the underdeveloped cardiovascular system.[19,35,49] There is, however, strong evidence that physical fitness, including cardiovascular endurance, can be developed through training regimens. Canadian Special Olympics athletes who were given an opportunity to participate in the Manitoba Special Olympics Medallion program demonstrated outstanding improvement in physical fitness and skill performance levels. The six-month-long, intensive, three-times-a-week training program for selected Special Olympics athletes in Manitoba combines fitness and skill-specific training akin to generic sport training, as well as nutritional counseling.[5] Frey and colleagues[35] studied the physical fitness levels of trained runners with mild intellectual disability and those without intellectual disability and found no difference in percentage of body fat, peak oxygen consumption, and lower back/hamstring flexibility. In another study, after a 12-week-long program to improve muscular strength, high school students with mild intellectual disabilities demonstrated a significant improvement in their ability to perform physical work activities.[81] Merriman et al.,[57] using a 12-week, three-times-a-week training program, reported significant improvements in the muscular endurance, cardiorespiratory endurance, and flexibility of 22 adults whose intellectual disabilities ranged from severe to mild. The Canadian program and studies in the United States verify that, when individuals with intellectual disabilities are given appropriate practice opportunities and guidance, they demonstrate high levels of fitness and motor performance.

Individuals with intellectual disabilities who have not been given opportunities to exercise and build work capacity demonstrate low levels of function,[20] as well as low muscle mass and strength.[33] When provided instruction in physical fitness and given opportunities to practice, they demonstrate improvement, but at a slower rate than their peers who do not have an intellectual disability.[19,69] Fernhall[30] indicates that individuals with intellectual disabilities may take between 16 and 35 weeks to show improved VO_2 max; however, functional capacity

gains frequently occur sooner. Investigations using subjects who have intellectual disabilities indicate that it is possible to strengthen all muscle groups when using appropriate training regimes.[5,14,74,103]

Social Development

The social characteristics of individuals who are intellectually disabled also vary greatly. Some persons with an intellectual disability are dependable, are cooperative, and can delay their gratification, while others are self-centered and impulsive.[79]

Competition

Competition is an important motivator to bring out the best efforts of athletes. While evidence exists that persons who have intellectual disabilities can benefit through competition, such as Special Olympics, some of these youngsters who have intellectual disabilities may not understand the concept of competition. The central goal in most sport competition is to win; however, Special Olympics places the challenge on participation rather than winning. Bringing the participants to the starting line is more important than the sport skills that carry the athletes across the finish line.[27] Everyone deserves a chance to do his or her best.[72] The athlete who is severely intellectually disabled may not comprehend "Run as fast as you can," "Jump as high as you can," and "Score more points than your opponent." Also, studies show that besting an opponent is not important to some persons with an intellectual disability;[104] as a result, their competitive performance is not adversely affected by anxiety.[71] In addition, individuals with intellectual disabilities frequently demonstrate lower levels of self-determination than others in the same situations;[96] thus, their workouts must be supervised by individuals willing to motivate them to persist.

TESTING TO DETERMINE FUNCTIONING LEVELS

Development of the individual education program (IEP) requires that present functioning levels be determined. Several formal tests that can be used with students who have an intellectual disability were listed in Table 3-3 of this text. Although there are tests to assess the areas of physical fitness of individuals who are intellectually disabled, there has been increased interest in the validity of using general physical fitness tests with individuals who have an intellectual disability. Some of the studies to validate physical fitness tests have examined VO_2 max as a predictor of aerobic capacity,[31] the walk-run tests of different lengths,[35] and the Eurofit physical fitness test.[54] Preference should be given to measuring physical fitness, locomotor skills, object-handling skills, and balance. Reliable strength measures can be obtained from individuals who have an intellectual disability.[89] When measuring strength, it is suggested that the mean of three trials be used to best represent the individual's capability.[45,46] For individuals who appear to demonstrate poor posture, postural alignment should be assessed and followed by specific programming to correct any abnormalities. Lavay et al.[52] reviewed three physical fitness tests to determine their validity for use with individuals with an intellectual disability and concluded that all three tests were appropriate. The items included in the tests were sit and reach for flexibility; strength measures, including grip strength, sit-ups, isometric push-ups, and bench press (for age 13 years and older); and run, jog, march, walk, exercise bicycle, or propel oneself in a wheelchair or on a scooter board for 12 minutes while maintaining a heart rate between 140 and 180 beats per minute for cardiovascular endurance. Winnick and Short's Brockport Physical Fitness health-related test for youth is an excellent test for use with youngsters between the ages of 10 and 17 years.[95] Other acceptable ways to evaluate the functioning levels of this population are task analysis and observation of the students as they perform a hierarchical sequence of activities. These techniques were described in Chapters 5 and 7.

Fernhall et al.[31] cautions about the importance of determining whether any potential congenital cardiovascular problems exist prior to beginning testing, particularly for individuals with Down syndrome. To help ensure valid testing results, the recommendations presented in Table 11-2 should be followed.

One of the most difficult problems of testing individuals with intellectual disabilities is determining whether poor comprehension or poor motor development is the reason for their inability to perform a specific task. Because it is difficult to determine whether a student who has an intellectual disability understands directions given during test situations, the suggestions presented in Table 11-3 may help the evaluator elicit the best performance possible.

Table 11-2	Practices to Ensure Valid Test Results[30]

During All Testing
- Provide ample time for individuals to become familiar with the test procedures, environment, and staff.
- Tailor the test procedures to the individual. (Allow staff members to adjust the testing procedures to ensure the validity of test results and safety of the person being tested.)
- Provide an environment in which the individual feels like a participating member.

When Using a Treadmill for Testing
- Permit the person being tested to walk at a speed that is comfortable.
- Increase grade, but not speed.
- Use work stages of one to three minutes.

Table 11-3	Techniques for Improving Response to Requests to Perform Test Items

1. If after the student has been told what to do the response is incorrect, demonstrate the position or movement.
2. If demonstration does not elicit the correct performance, manually place the student in or through the desired position or pattern.
3. Use positive reinforcement (praise, tokens, free play) to encourage the student.

Because persons with intellectual disabilities who participate in competitive sports, such as Special Olympics, are more likely than most athletes to experience sport-specific injuries,[91] it is strongly recommended that physical examinations tailored to each athlete be administered prior to participation. Athletes with Down syndrome should always be assessed for atlantoaxial instability prior to participation.

FETAL ALCOHOL SYNDROME, DOWN SYNDROME, AND FRAGILE X SYNDROME

The three most common causes of intellectual disabilities are fetal alcohol syndrome (FAS), Down syndrome, and fragile X syndrome.

Fetal Alcohol Syndrome

Fetal alcohol syndrome (FAS) is the leading known cause of an intellectual disability. Estimates of the number of individuals born with fetal alcohol syndrome range from 2.2 per 1,000 to 1 per 100 live births.[63] It is caused by maternal alcohol use during pregnancy, and it usually results in lifelong consequences, including intellectual disabilities, learning disabilities, and serious behavioral problems.[63] The most severe form of FAS results from the mother's heavy drinking during pregnancy; lesser degrees of alcohol abuse result in milder forms of FAS.[9]

Both anatomical and cognitive modifications can accompany the condition. More than 80 percent of all children with FAS have pre- and postnatal growth deficiencies, microcephaly, and characteristic facial features (saddle-shaped nose and gap between the front teeth). Students with this syndrome have difficulty receiving and processing information. Common characteristics include hyperactivity, impulsivity, attention and memory deficits, inability to complete tasks, disruptiveness, poor social skills, need for constant supervision, and disregard for rules and authority.[64]

Down Syndrome

Down syndrome is the most common chromosomal disorder leading to intellectual disabilities. In about 95 percent of the cases, there is an extra chromosome #21.[9] The incidence rates are about 1 in 800, of whom 80 percent score between 25 and 50 on IQ tests.[8] The following are some physical characteristics of individuals with Down syndrome:

- Small skull
- Slanting, almond-shaped eyes
- Ears slightly smaller than average
- Flat-bridged nose
- Protruding tongue
- Palmar crease
- Short stature
- Short fingers
- Short limbs
- Short neck
- Overweight
- Substantial delays in reflex integration
- Varied levels of intellectual disability
- Looseness of joints
- Lack of muscle tone during infancy

There has been considerable research interest in the specific physical and motor characteristics of individuals with Down syndrome. When compared with the general population, people with Down syndrome may differ in the following ways:

- They demonstrate less power and strength.[78]
- They function lower than average on cardiovascular measures.[49]
- They have deficient leg strength associated with lower cardiovascular measures.[49]
- They begin the aging process earlier than expected.[60]
- They have less capability for decision making that relates to motor control.[51]
- They have difficulty in planning goal-directed movements.[44]
- They have a greater incidence of obesity.
- They have atlantoaxial instability.

It is believed that effective programs of physical activity can significantly impact physical and psychomotor deficiencies. Clinical intervention programs that begin early in life can promote reflex integration, vestibular function, and kinesthetic impulses that affect muscle tonacity. Development of these input systems is critical to gaining locomotor and object-control patterns and skills. Other intervention programs have also been shown to be effective. Ulrich et al.[94] demonstrated facilitation of stable walking patterns through the use of treadmill programming. Once locomotor and object-control skills are developed, the child will be more likely to participate actively with peers and may be less likely to develop obesity.

The atlantoaxial segments of the cervical spine of some children with Down syndrome tend to develop localized anomalies that are in danger of atlantoaxial dislocation. As a result of this potential danger, in 1983 a group of physicians, including experts in sports medicine and the surgeon general of the United States, met at the Joseph P. Kennedy, Jr., Foundation to discuss the perceived dangers of atlantoaxial instability among individuals with Down syndrome. Of particular concern were the thousands of athletes with Down syndrome in Special Olympics.

The incidence of atlantoaxial instability is in question. The range of incidents is reported to be from 10 to 30 percent of the Down syndrome population. However, the American Academy of Pediatrics' Committee on Sports Medicine reports 15 percent.[53]

Atlantoaxial instability is a greater than normal mobility of the two upper cervical vertebrae—C1 and C2—at the top of the neck. The condition exposes the victims to possible serious injury if they forcibly flex the neck, because the vertebrae may shift and thereby squeeze or sever the spinal cord. A dislocation involves an actual displacement of the bone from the normal position in the joint. Awareness of the significance of atlantoaxial instability can aid in the prevention of injuries of the upper cervical spine level. The instability is due to (1) the laxity of the transverse ligament that holds the odontoid process of the axis (C2) in place against the inner aspect of the inner arch of atlas (C1) and (2) abnormalities of the odontoid. These conditions allow

some leeway between the odontoid and the atlas, especially during flexion and extension of the neck. This results in an unstable joint. The atlantoaxial instability can be gradual and progressive.

The two types of symptoms of atlantoaxial dislocation are observable physical symptoms and neurological signs. Some of the physical symptoms are as follows:

• Fatiguability
• Difficulty in walking, abnormal gait
• Neck pain, limited neck mobility, torticollis (head tilt)
• Weakness of any of the extremities
• Incoordination and clumsiness[17]

The following are some of the neurological signs associated with atlantoaxial dislocation:

• Spasticity
• Sensory deficits
• Hyperreflexiveness[53]

Special Olympics has taken the lead in the formulation of policies for the participation of athletes with Down syndrome who may have atlantoaxial instability. Tens of thousands of individuals with Down syndrome have participated in Special Olympics over the past 30 years. However, officials of Special Olympics International believe that none have suffered injury related to atlantoaxial instability while participating in Special Olympics training or competition. However, as a precaution, Special Olympics has developed a policy requiring that all athletes with Down syndrome receive neck X rays before they participate in its nationwide competitive program.

Professionals in physical education need to be aware of the potential injury-inducing activities and situations for persons with atlantoaxial instability. The adapted physical educator should be aware of each student's medical status, including the condition of the atlantoaxial joint. Results of medical examinations should be kept in the student's permanent health file at the school. The American Academy of Pediatrics' Committee on Sports Medicine reported in 1995 that only 3 of the 41 recorded pediatric cases had worsening of atlantoaxial instability during organized sport participation; however, the committee urges pediatricians to follow the Special Olympics policy to conduct lateral neck X rays on all athletes with Down syndrome.[1] The Special Olympics policy and the Committee on Sports Medicine[16] guidelines are presented in Table 11-4.

Fragile X Syndrome

Fragile X syndrome (FXS) is the most common inherited cause of intellectual disabilities, and it is recognized as second only to Down syndrome as a specific chromosomal cause of developmental disability.[9] Prevalence rates are estimated to be 1 in 6,000 births, with males being affected more often than females.[9]

Table 11-4	Guidelines to Follow When Individuals with Down Syndrome Participate in Physical Education and/or Special Olympics

1. Check the medical files to determine which individuals have the atlantoaxial instability condition.
2. If there is no record of neck X-ray results, with the principal's permission, contact the parents and explain the importance of screening.
3. Discuss the medical options and the situation with the student's parents or guardians.
4. Have the parents sign a consent form allowing the child to participate in the physical education program.
5. Restrict participation in gymnastics, diving, the butterfly stroke in swimming, the diving start in swimming, the high jump, soccer, and any warm-up exercises that place pressure on the neck muscles.
6. Design a physical education program with activities that are not contraindicated for those with atlantoaxial instability.
7. Watch for the development of the symptoms indicating a possible dislocation.
8. Adhere to the physician's recommendations.

Cause

FXS is a result of an abnormally long X chromosome, which appears to have "fragile" ends, hence its name.[87] The gene on the X chromosome that causes FXS is called the Fragile X Mental Retardation 1 (FXMR1) gene. This gene makes a protein that is needed for normal brain development.[13] Fragile X syndrome usually expresses itself less fully in females because they have two X chromosomes, one normal and abnormal. Because males have only one X chromosome, the condition manifests itself more fully. In addition, two distinct categories of variation at the fragile X locus have been identified. A mosaic premutation results in milder deleterious features than the fuller, nonmosiac, mutation.[9] The fuller mutation is the one associated with the developmental delays that affect development.[9]

Characteristics

Approximately 95 percent of the males with the full mutation are intellectually disabled (moderate to severe range), whereas only about 50 percent of the females with the full mutation are intellectually disabled; however, those who are not labelled as having an intellectual disability usually demonstrate learning disabilities.

There are several differences in the physical features between the genders, with males being more affected than females. When full expression of the condition prevails, there are several distinct physical features in the newborn male. The baby may be large and have a high forehead; a heavy lower jaw; large, low-set ears; and a large head, nose, hands, and feet. These features become more prominent with age, with the face narrowing and lengthening.[68] Other distinguishing characteristics in males are large testicles (70 percent of the time), strabismus (56 percent), mitral valve prolapse (50 percent), hypotonia, and joint laxity (50 percent).[39] Males demonstrate autistic-like behaviors, such as hand flapping, perseveration, word repetition, body rocking, hand biting, and poor eye contact.[75] Many of these children are hyperactive, have attention deficits, and engage in aggressive outbursts.[97]

Females have an increased prominence of the ears but few of the other physical characteristics that the males demonstrate.[97] They tend to be shy, depressed, anxious, hypersensitive, and somewhat hyperactive as children and socially impaired as adults.[9]

Whereas most young fragile X syndrome boys demonstrate a moderate intellectual disability, some (between 25 and 75 percent) tend to deteriorate cognitively with age. The greatest change in cognitive ability is seen between the ages of 8 and 13 years.[98] By adulthood, most males test in the moderate to severe range of intellectual disability.[9] Interestingly, many of these males have good verbal expressive skills and are socially engaging; however, they tend to avoid direct eye contact during conversation, they have a short attention span, they are hyperactive, and they demonstrate motor delays.[40]

Approximately 33 percent of the females have a mild intellectual disability; those who are not intellectually impaired usually have learning disabilities, particularly in mathematics.[83] Most fragile X syndrome females, regardless of degree of affect, demonstrate deficits in short-term memory for nonverbal information, deficits in mental flexibility, and visual-motor performance deficits.[9]

Both genders frequently have sensory-motor integration deficits, which result in delayed balance (probably related to recurring middle ear infections), poor coordination, motor planning deficits, and tactile defensiveness.[39]

The physical limitations of the males require careful motor programming. Hypotonia and joint laxity could predispose students to a tendency to hyperextend joints during contact sports; strabismus could create depth perception difficulties that limit success in games and sports requiring object control; and a prolapsed mitral valve might limit cardiovascular endurance. Activities such as weight training could contribute muscle tone and greater joint stability, as well as enhanced self-esteem.

Students of both genders should receive sensory integration activities, particularly vestibular, kinesthetic, and tactile stimulation, as early in life as possible. Later in life, when motor skills are being learned, short-term memory lapse and difficulty mastering sequential information will require that attempts be made to teach the whole task in the context where it will be used.[55] The teacher should use pictures and concrete examples whenever possible.[62] The greater the teacher's success at presenting the "whole picture," the easier it will be for the student to learn.

TEACHING STRATEGIES

The capabilities of persons with intellectual disabilities vary widely. About 87 percent of these persons are only a little slower than average when learning new skills and information. They can do well in school; however, some individualized assistance is usually needed. The other 13 percent score below 50 on IQ tests and need more intensive support throughout their lives.[61] A physical educator can make a tremendous difference in every student's life, including those with intellectual disabilities. Because of the individual variation among persons with this condition, it is difficult to make generalizations that may be helpful when providing instruction of activities. However, as a guide, some strategies for teaching physical education to individuals with intellectual disabilities appear in Table 11-5.

Every student, regardless of disability, can learn. The teaching methodology selected to use with the individual who has a severe intellectual disability depends on age. All children who have an intellectual disability should engage in a bottom-up developmental program early in life because they need to develop their sensory-motor and perceptual motor systems, as well as learn the basic elements of fundamental movement skills. A bottom-up approach is critical for persons who are severely or profoundly involved because of the extent to which they are motorically delayed. The Special Olympics Motor Activities Training Program (MATP) is designed for this population.

Older individuals who are severely impaired learn specific skills best with a defined instructional procedure that uses a top-down teaching approach. That procedure includes (1) assessing the

Table 11-5	Strategies for Teaching Physical Education to Persons with Intellectual Disabilities

1. Use methods that are compatible with individualized instruction.

Use strong visual, tactile, and auditory stimuli for the children who are more severely involved, because these often bring the best results.

Have many activities available, because the attention span is short.

Use a systematic style of instruction where the behaviors are defined, measured, modeled, and monitored for acquisition.

Keep verbal directions to a minimum. They are often ineffective when teaching children who are more severely disabled.

Use demonstration as an effective instructional tool. It is particularly effective to use a peer demonstrator.

Use **manual guidance** as a method of instruction. The proprioceptors are great teachers of movement. The less ability the child has to communicate verbally, the more manual guidance should be considered as a tool for instruction.

Help students develop sound self-management procedures, so that they can learn to plan and complete tasks independently, evaluate their own performance, compare their performance with a standard, and make adjustments.[58]

Provide opportunities for choice of activities to foster self-motivation and decision making;[11] these practices decrease social avoidance and reduce problem behavior[34] and noncompliance.[18]

2. Involve students actively in activities they can do successfully.

Structure the environment in which the activity takes place so that it challenges the students yet frees them from the fear of physical harm and gives them some degree of success.

Analyze tasks involved in activities to be sure you are clear about all the components of the skill you are about to teach.

Work for active participation on the part of all the students. Active involvement contributes more to neurological development than does passive movement.

Modify the activity so that each child can participate up to his or her ability level.

3. Facilitate participation in group activities.

Use markers to indicate where students are to participate.

Have students hold hands as they organize for instruction (e.g., in a circle).

Use peer partners during group exercises.[50]

Use a token or point system to reward compliant behavior.[20]

4. Interact appropriately with students.

Be patient with smaller and slower gains of students who are more severely involved. Often, gains that seem small when compared with those of their peers are tremendous for these students.

Do not underestimate the ability of students who have an intellectual disability to perform skilled movements. There is a tendency to set goals too low for these children.

Convey to all students that they are persons of worth by reinforcing their strengths and minimizing their weaknesses.

5. Teach for generalization to community environments.

Remember that children with lower levels of cognition must be taught to play. This means that physical education programs are responsible for creating the play environment, developing the basic motor skills that are the tools of play, identifying at what play level (self-directed, onlooker, solitary, parallel, associative, or cooperative) the child is functioning, and promoting development from that point.

Use effective maintenance and generalization programs to ensure that the skills attained in physical education are used in community settings.[24] If possible, teach the skills within the community-based setting that will be used for leisure, recreation, or sports participation.

Create a safe play environment but do not necessarily provide security to the extent that the students are unduly dependent on you for physical safety.

Children Should Gain Confidence in the Water
Courtesy of Laurie Zittel.

present level of the student in defined target skills; (2) arranging the skills in an appropriate sequence, so that objectives can be identified; (3) providing clear cues during the instructional process; (4) providing precise feedback immediately after the task is completed; (5) including strategies to promote generalization of skills to meaningful community environments; and (6) measuring and evaluating the performance gains to enable appropriate subsequent instructional decisions.

Behavior modification coupled with task analysis is usually recommended when teaching students who have intellectual disabilities.[7] This system involves selecting a signal or a request to cause the desired behavior. After selecting the skill to be taught, divide it into its component parts. Teach the parts using backward or forward chaining. If the task is a continuous one (such as running or jumping), shaping, rather than task analysis, is more appropriate. Once the physical skill has been performed, reinforce the student (see Chapter 7).

The Physical Education Program

Knowledge of the characteristics of persons who have intellectual disabilities provides information about the types of programs that need to be implemented to serve them. However, designing entire physical education programs around these characteristics for the purpose of teaching groups of these persons may not meet the needs of the individuals within

the group. Clearly, the assessed needs of each individual must be taken into consideration when designing the individual physical education program.

Individuals who have an intellectual disabilitiy have developmental lags in intellectual quotients and usually have parallel lags in motor and social development. Table 11-6 shows the mental and chronological ages of individuals who have an intellectual disability with a conversion of motor behaviors one would expect from individuals with delayed mental ages. Children with a chronological age of two to five years who are mildly impaired would be expected to attempt locomotor patterns. Those between six and nine years would be attempting to learn to jump and balance on one foot briefly, as well as learning to throw. This information provides a good basis for constructing curricula for group activity because it is simple and straightforward. However, full assessments of the physical education needs of persons with intellectual disabilities will reveal deviations from the behaviors indicated in Table 11-6.

Every effort must be made to provide each student who has an intellectual disability with an appropriate physical education program that will promote the motor growth and development of that child. Children under the age of nine years will benefit from a physical education program that focuses on promoting sensory input and perceptual-motor integration. Older students should be taught to perform culturally relevant community-based recreational skills that can be used throughout their lives to promote and maintain a healthy lifestyle in social settings.

Numerous studies have demonstrated that individuals who have intellectual disabilities benefit from physical fitness training coupled with reinforcement.[74,92,103] Individualized treadmill exercise regimes have been proven safe and beneficial for improving and maintaining cardiovascular fitness.[4] In addition, training in a modified form of judo is a valuable therapeutic, educational, and recreational tool for persons with an intellectual disability. A biweekly, six-month-long program resulted in gains in physical fitness as well as developmental skills such as walking, stair climbing, running, jumping, and hopping.[36] Appropriate

Table 11-6	Conversion of Behavior in Physical Education Activity Adjusted for Mental Age of Persons with Moderate Intellectual Disabilities		
Chronological Age	**Activities for Normal Children by Chronological Age**	**Activities for Those with Mild Intellectual Disabilities Adjusted for Mental Age**	**Mental Age**
4 to 8 years	Generalization of running, jumping as subroutines into play activity; low organized games (i.e., Follow the Leader, Tag).	Learning to run; balance on one foot; manipulate objects; engage in activity that requires simple directions.	2 to 4 years
8 to 12 years	Can play lead-up games to sport skills that involve throwing and catching. Can play games of competition where there is team organization. Can learn rules and play by them.	May be able to generalize running and locomotor skills into play activity. May be able to play games of low organization and follow simple direction. May socially interact in play; may play by self or may play in parallel.	4 to 6 years
12 to 17 years	Can play games of high organization. Can further develop skills that involve racquet sports and balls and require high levels of skill. Can participate in team games and employ strategies in competitive activity.	Can participate in modified sport activity. Is better in individual sports (e.g., swimming, bowling, and track), where there is a minimum of social responsibility. Can throw and catch balls, but it is difficult to participate in meaningful competitive activity.	6 to 8 years
Over 17 years	Can participate independently in recreational activities in their chosen community.	Can participate in community recreational sport and physical activity in special programs and with assistance from others.	Over 10 years

motivation, high teacher expectations, and carefully designed learning sequences appear to be the keys to promoting learning among individuals who have an intellectual disability.[101]

Stopka et al.[88] report significant results for secondary students with intellectual disabilities when using a twice-weekly program consisting of 5 to 10 minutes of warm-up and stretching, 20 to 25 mintues of resistance training or weight training, and 20 to 30 minutes of sports and recreational skills and games. When determining repetitions, they recommend weight be increased for 17- to 22-year-olds when 8 to 12 repetitions can be easily performed and for 13- to 17-year-olds when 15 to 20 repetitions can be easily performed.

Fernhall[30] recommends that the following modifications be made when working with individuals with an intellectual disability:

1. Exercise intensity should be between 60 and 80 percent of maximal functional capacity.
2. Exercise should be supervised.
3. Provide a longer training duration to achieve the desired effects.
4. Motivational techniques, such as token rewards, may be necessary to maintain adherence to the program.
5. Strength training using machines rather than free-weights should be incorporated whenever possible because this may have

important ramifications for vocational productivity and independence.

Physical education programs should be based on the nature and needs of the learner. As mentioned previously, there is great variability among the individuals who have intellectual disabilities. This is attributable to inherent differences between mild and more severe impairment, the causes of the disability, and the many other disorders that accompany the condition.

Disorders associated with intellectual disabilities are sensory impairments, such as blindness, hard-of-hearing, or deafness; emotional disturbances; and neurological disorders, such as cerebral palsy, muscular dystrophy, and problems in perception. It is apparent that physical education programs for persons who have an intellectual disability must meet a multitude of needs at all age levels and all levels of intellectual and physical development. Programming principles to use for persons with intellectual disabilities appear in Table 11-7.

Whenever possible, students who have an intellectual disability should be integrated with their peers into regular physical education classes. If they cannot participate successfully in regular classes, they should be given special developmental physical education commensurate with their capacity and needs. The regular physical education class may not provide adequate placement for all students who have intellectual disabilities. These children have social and motor deficits that make it difficult for them to participate equally with members of the regular class. Consequently, they often are found on the periphery of activity and do not involve themselves in the games and activities of the physical education class. An effort must be made to integrate persons with intellectual disabilities into regular class activities; however, if this is not possible, special physical education programs should be adapted to the needs of the children.

The physical educator is cautioned against generalizing about the motor functioning level and learning capability of the student who has an intellectual disability. As in all cases of students with disabilities, they should be thoroughly tested for

Table 11-7	**Programming Principles for the Physical Education Program for Persons with Intellectual Disabilities**

1. Select activities that meet the needs of the students in the class.

Select activities to meet the students' interest levels. However, precaution should be taken against participation in one activity to the exclusion of others. Be aware of students' tendency to favor the single activity with which they are most familiar.

Consider individual differences when selecting the activities. There are many games that allow for differences in abilities among class members.

Select activities according to the needs of the students who have an intellectual disability.

2. Include appropriate physical and social opportunities.

Select sensory-perceptual-motor activities to promote specific and general development of the young child who has an intellectual disability and to develop recreational skills of older students to make it possible for these individuals to integrate socially with peers and members of their families now and in later life in community activity.

Select activities primarily on the basis of the development of motor skills; however, chronological ages should bias your selection of activities. Whenever possible, the activities should be age appropriate as well.

Provide a broad spectrum of activities that have recreational and social significance for later life.

Teach specific social skills that are meaningful within a specific social environment, so that the behavioral change results in functional social performance.[56]

Work for progression toward skill development. For young children, use sensory-motor activities that contribute to sensory input system development; for older children, use task analysis with sequential progression methodology.

motor skill functioning level and physical fitness before decisions are made as to what type of physical education program is needed. If testing shows a student to be deficient in areas of motor behavior performance, a thorough task analysis should be completed before the student's program is determined. Program adjustments may be required to ensure maximum benefit for students with intellectual disabilities. In the following sections, ways to meet the needs of students with mild and those with severe intellectual disability in a segregated or inclusive setting are addressed.

Adaptations for Students Who Are Mildly Impaired

The most apparent difficulty for persons with the mildest forms of intellectual disability is comprehension of complex playing rules and strategies. Often, the student who is mildly impaired who is included in the regular physical education class is inappropriately accused of trying to cheat, when, in reality, he or she honestly does not understand what the rules or proper moves are. Such accusations by peers or teachers often lead to momentary or prolonged rejection of the student. Rejection leads to low self-esteem, which contributes directly to withdrawal or retaliation by the student. Acting out then becomes an everyday occurrence, and before long such students are perceived as trouble makers. The vicious cycle can be avoided if the teacher anticipates comprehension difficulties and counters them before they occur. Some suggestions for dealing with a lack of understanding of rules or playing strategies are as follows:

1. Place the student in a less demanding position.
2. Overteach and constantly reinforce cognitive aspects of each game.
3. Help the other students in the class develop an understanding of and sensitivity toward the student's learning difficulties.

If the student who is intellectually impaired has a propensity toward excessive body fat, this problem will be detected when the AAHPERD Health Related Fitness Test or a similar test is given early in the school year to all students. Every student identified as having excessive body fat should be provided with appropriate aerobic activities and, possibly, nutritional counseling to reduce body fat stores. There is a need for routine health-related testing of all students in all schools, at every level. The sooner children learn the importance of controlling body fat levels through diet control and exercise, the higher the chance that these good habits will carry over to adulthood.

To enhance the probability that children with intellectual disabilities will interact with their families and peers in healthful leisure-time pursuits, care must be taken to teach students to play games and sports that are typically pursued in community settings. The child who finds success and enjoyment in vigorous activity at a young age will continue participation as an adult.

Modifications for the Student Who Is Severely Impaired

With the development of instructional technology in the late 1970s, it became possible to demonstrate the competence of individuals who are severely impaired. Project MOVE and the Data Based Gymnasium are examples of programs that use instructional technology for improving the movement capability of persons who are severely involved.[28,59] Through implementation of the available information from research and demonstration (i.e., best practice), it has been shown that it is possible to maximize the potential of this group of individuals for meaningful participation in society. Physical education, which develops the motor capabilities of this group, is an integral part of their education.

It is true that many children who are severely impaired demonstrate delayed motor development milestones early in life and learn more slowly than children who are not impaired. However, the early childhood intervention programs that are gaining in popularity may help offset the marked motor delays that more involved children demonstrate when they reach school age.

When designing the adapted physical education program, the physical educator should work closely with both physical and occupational therapists, who often test students who are severely involved to determine their range of motion and level of reflex development. Consultation with the therapists and creative modification of traditional physical education activities will benefit students who are severely delayed. Some common activities used by physical and occupational therapists with this population are presented in Table 11-8.

Special considerations must be made for the student with profound impairment and developmental delays. Many of these students spend a great deal of the instructional day, or day at home, in wheelchairs, in recliners, or on pillows or bolsters. The aquatic environment can afford a student with profound impairment a singular opportunity for freedom. There are remarkable floatation devices that can help the

student maintain a relatively upright position in the water and allow any cause-effect reaction. *Abilitations,* published by Sportime, is a catalog specifically devoted to aquatics for individuals with disabilities.

Most aquatic educators do not recommend the widespread use of floatation devices when teaching students with disabilities to swim. However, as it is unlikely that the student who is profoundly impaired will learn to swim independently or is independently mobile enough to put himself or herself in jeopardy of falling into a pool, the floatation devices simply increase freedom from restraint. Large floatation mats may be helpful for the student with severe contractures. Massage in a warm-water environment may be very helpful in maintaining circulation and preventing further contractures.

Because many students with profound intellectual disabilities have significant difficulty maintaining thermal equilibrium, care must be taken to watch for signs of overheating—flushed face and rapid respiration—or significant cooling—blue lips, shivering, chattering teeth, goose pimples, and so on. The student must be removed from the pool if these signs exist.

Students with an educational/medical diagnosis of profound intellectual disability may retain significant primitive reflexes that interfere with movement in the water in the same way the reflexes interfere with movement on dry land. The aquatic environment is great for these learners, however, because the viscosity of the water reduces gravity's impact on movement.

Attention must also be given to apparatus attached to the body, as well as the toileting habits of the students. Stomas used for providing oxygen or other nutrients to the body or for removing body water must be covered securely with waterproof tape. Depending on the child's toileting schedule, if necessary, a catheter must wear "Huggies Swimwear" or the like. Adults must wear a "Depend" undergarment specifically designed to prevent disintegration when in contact with water, or secure plastic undergarments must cover the diapers.

Many students with profound delays respond particularly well to music. Music can be calming and

Table 11-8	Activities for Persons with Severe Intellectual Disabilities

- To stretch hip and knee flexors, remove the student who is nonambulatory and has a severe intellectual disability from a sitting position and allow him or her to stretch out on a mat.
- To improve range of motion, encourage the individual to reach for an object held just a few degrees beyond the range of capability. To hold interest, permit the person to reach the object occasionally.
- Place the student face down on the mat and place a pillow or bolster under the upper chest. Encourage the student to look up (lift head) from this position as often as possible.
- Place the student who has a severe intellectual disability face down on a long scooter. Pull the scooter and encourage the individual to try using hands and feet to propel himself or herself.
- Place the student in a supine position on an air mat or a trampoline. Gently bounce the surface around the student.
- Praise every attempt the student makes to initiate movement.
- Hook a light-weight Theraband strip or an elastic loop around each of the student's limbs (one at a time) and encourage him or her to pull against the loop.

encourage relaxation. (For more information about appropriate accommodations, refer to Project INSPIRE Aquatics Pages: http://twu.edu/ INSPIRE.)

Special Olympics International has developed training materials for use with individuals who are severely intellectually impaired.[85] Activites in the Special Olympics Motor Activities Training Program (MATP) are broken down into the following components: dexterity, reaching, grasping, releasing, posture, head control in prone and supine positions, sitting in a chair, rolling, crawling, use of an electric wheelchair, and sensory, visual-motor, auditory-motor, and tactile awareness. Each of these activities is sequenced to maximize the potential for learning. The motor development curriculum promotes improvement in coordination and control of the body when performing a variety of motor activities. It is designed to develop age-appropriate sport and recreation skills as well as physical fitness, sensory awareness, and the sense of being part of a group. Included in the curriculum is a motor activities assessment instrument that should be used to evaluate mobility, dexterity, striking, kicking, and aquatic activity, as well as manual and electric wheelchair mobility skills. Also included are Special Olympics activities specifically adapted for severely intellectually impaired athletes. These include aquatics, track and field, basketball, bowling, gymnastics, softball, volleyball, and weight lifting. Each sport is task analyzed for inclusion of the motor activities in the guide. Criteria and standards are identified to inform the teacher as to when the skill or task has been mastered. Furthermore, data sheets on which to record the types of instruction used (physical assistance, physical prompts, demonstration, verbal cues, and visual cues) are included. Spaces are also provided for recording the type of reinforcement used (e.g., edible, social, token), as well as the schedule of reinforcement (continuous, fixed, or intermittent).

Integration

The ultimate goal of sports and physical activity for persons who have intellectual disabilities is participation in integrated physical activity in natural community environments. For the most part, integration models for acquiring physical skills for persons with intellectual disabilities in the public schools offer a choice of participation in regular or special physical education programs. When including the student with an intellectual disability in the regular class, careful selection of activities, frequent positive feedback, and opportunities to interact successfully with other students are critical.

Individuals with disabilities have a basic right to be provided opportunities that will lead to their full integration into community recreational settings. (Special Olympics has initiated several such integration programs, which will be detailed later in this chapter.) To achieve this integration, the process should include the following opportunities:

1. There should be a continuum of lesser restrictive environments in both instructional settings in the schools and in community recreational environments, and they should be coordinated for the benefit of each individual.
2. Persons with an intellectual disability should be placed in the most appropriate environment that is commensurate with their social and physical abilities.
3. Persons with an intellectual disability should be provided with a support system commensurate with their needs to adapt to present restrictive environments and advance to lesser restrictive environments.

When this procedure to achieve integration is used, individuals with disabilities will have a much greater opportunity to interact successfully in community recreational settings than they now have. Just placing students who have intellectual disabilities in a regular physical education class and hoping they gain all they need has not been successful. The current mainstreaming practice of chance placement must be replaced by a carefully planned integration process.

To enable individuals with disabilities to progress toward integration into community recreation programs, a continuum of lesser and lesser restrictive environments is needed. Three major environments that would promote the participation of individuals with disabilities into a sport activity are (1) a training environment restricted to individuals with disabilities; (2) a mixed, or integrated, athletic competition; and (3) a normal community environment (see Figure 11-1).

A persons-with-disabilities-only training/playing environment, where athletes receive special training from teachers and trained peer tutors, is a critical starting place for many individuals who have an intellectual disability (see Table 11-9). They need opportunities to learn fundamental movement skills before being placed with persons who do not have a disability. The next most appropriate environment is mixed, or integrated, athletic competition, where the composition of the team is at least 50 percent athletes without disabilities. This step is important because, to facilitate functioning in natural settings, athletes who have an intellectual disability need exposure to peers who do not have an intellectual disability and who have specific training in the principles of integration. The next step would be participation in integrated settings with nontrained peers without disabilities who are willing to assist with the integration process. In the fourth step, individuals who have an intellectual disability would participate in integrated leisure, recreational, and sport activities with the assistance of nonparticipants. The ultimate goal is participation without assistance in natural community, school, and recreation environments, such as church, YMCA, YWCA, and community recreation programs. Modifications of the major integration environments may be made to serve the unique needs of each athlete. It is most important that the thrust of integration be a process to move the students through the continuum of restrictive environments in specific sports to lesser restrictive environments to independent recreational functioning in sport activities in communities.

Physical skill is one variable to consider for placement of persons with intellectual disabilities in integrated settings with persons who do not have an intellectual disability. The ability to adapt to others when participating in activity is critical for the successful integration of individuals into leisure, recreation, and sport activity. The ability to cooperate and work harmoniously with others, to compete, to display sportsmanship, to respond to coaching and instruction, and to control one's emotions is necessary if a person is to participate successfully in an integrated leisure, recreation, or sport activity. In addition to considering the physical and social abilities of individuals who have an intellectual disability, the social complexity and the entry level of skill required

Independently integrated	Integrated recreational sports participation
	Integration with nonplayer support
Integrated with assistance	Integration settings in the community where nontraining peers facilitate the integration process
	Integrated training environments where trained peers direct the integration
Nonintegrated settings	Special training and playing environments

Figure 11-1   Continuum of Lesser Restrictive Environments That Enable Progression toward Independent Recreational Participation in a Specific Sport Activity

Table 11-9	Aquatics for Learners with Intellectual Disabilities

- In an aquatic environment, a small teacher–student ratio is necessary. Students with mild intellectual disability can be served safely in/through small-group instruction (one teacher to four to seven children). Students with profound intellectual disability require careful, well-trained, one-to-one instruction.
- A whole-part-whole approach to instruction appears to be most effective particularly when dealing with stroke skills. The use of David Armbruster's (famous coach of the University of Iowa Swimming Team and extraordinary swimming teacher) technique in which the student is introduced to all swimming strokes via the human stroke or dog paddle is particularly viable. Once the student can human stroke (dog paddle) on his or her stomach, each side, and back, the foundation is laid for the development of each of the basic swimming strokes. Then refinement of stroke mechanics and technique can be introduced.
- When possible, use the least invasive/directive strategy to provide instruction. Keep verbal instruction simple. Use one-word and two-word directions. If possible, keep verbal instructions simple but age appropriate. For example, don't ask a teenager to lie on his or her "tummy"; it is much more appropriate to ask the student to lie on his or her stomach. Pair the verbal instruction with a simple physical demonstration to clarify instruction.
- It is vital that the demonstration be done in the same place as the activity should be performed. For example, it is very confusing for a student with an intellectual disability to watch an instructor demonstrate the arm pattern for the back crawl with the instructor standing. Preferably, the instructor demonstrates in the water in the proper position; if that is not possible, the instructor should lie on the pool deck to demonstrate.
- If necessary, pair strong tactile and proprioceptive cues using patterning with a simple verbal (or sign) associative cue. For example, hold the student's hand and move it through a pulling motion, pairing that with the word (or sign) "pull." The student with intellectual disability will find it easier to manage his or her own behavior if given the opportunity to choose a particular activity or activity sequence. For example, the teacher can give the student the opportunity to decide if he or she wants to practice flutter kicking first or practice back float first.
- Using "if then" strategies may be particularly effective in dealing with stubborn students—for example, "If and only if you bob five times will you be allowed to play with the beach ball."
- Repetition is key to learning in the student with an intellectual disability and developmental delays. The instructor can ensure this will happen without boredom by modifying the activity to involve other students and different types of equipment. For example, the student can practice the flutter kick while doing the following:
  Being towed by teacher
  Kicking at a beach ball
  Wearing fins
  Going "fast" and "slow"
  Going as part of a song, "If you're happy and you know it 'kick your feet' "

For more information refer to Project INSPIRE Aquatics Pages: http://twu.edu/INSPIRE.

to participate need to be considered. Individual sports, such as track and field, bowling, and swimming, require less social ability than team sports with complex rules, such as basketball or soccer. Specific examples of integration techniques follow.

Softball Integration

There is a concept in the integration process that is known as reverse mainstreaming. In this procedure, persons who are not intellectually disabled are integrated into activities designed for persons who are disabled. Modification of this technique was initiated in the development of the Massachusetts Special Olympics softball integration project.[10] Special Olympics International subsequently funded the Research Center for Education Achievement to study the effects of Special Olympics' softball integration on coaches and players who were intellectually disabled and those who weren't. (The integrated softball game is composed of teams on which at least 50 percent of the players are not intellectually disabled.) Reverse mainstreaming can be used with individuals with any type of disability.

Integrated softball is a lesser restrictive environment than traditional Special Olympics, where a different social support system is provided to produce positive results. Through the construction of social networks of lesser restrictive environments in which individuals who have an intellectual disability and those who don't participate on the same team, impressive social and physical gains can be made.

Budoff[10] has conducted research on integrated (Special Olympics) softball. In this activity, the individuals who do not have an intellectual disability participate on the same team as an equal number of players who have an intellectual disability. Budoff, in comparing the play of the players who had an intellectual disability in integrated softball with all other softball games made up entirely of players who did not have intellectual disabilities makes the following comments: "The contrast between the mixed (integrated) and all-mentally retarded [SIC] teams is so stark as to make the same slow-pitch softball game look like a dramatically different game."[10] As a result of a three-month season of integrated softball, the athletes who had an intellectual disability demonstrated lateral movement and intelligent positioning for the ball as it was coming toward them. There were few "dead spots," where players were immobile and did not move when a ball was directed to them. The team members worked well together. To explain this phenomenon, Budoff comments that "it seems that playing alongside of non-handicapped players helped to steady their [players with intellectual disabilities] game, even when there were no overt signs of instruction."

An integrated team promotes the playing and understanding of the players who have an intellectual disability because (1) the coach and the players who do not have an intellectual disability are commited to teaching and supporting the players who have an intellectual disability and (2) the players who do have an intellectual disability

serve as models on the field. According to Budoff, "There seems to be no doubt of the individual development observed in the play and sense of the game among players who [have an intellectual disability] during this past season on the integrated (mixed) teams."[10] Thus, there are strong indications that an integrated environment in sport activity benefits individuals who have intellectual disabilities.

Integrated Basketball with Adolescents Who Are Severely Impaired

The previous description of integrated activity with participants who do not have intellectual disabilities was based on modeling procedures and intuitive coaching techniques. Many of the athletes in the integrated softball project had the potential for integrated activity without a highly technical support system. However, there are persons with intellectual disabilities who may always need support systems for integrated play in sports.

Pilot research has been done in integrated basketball play with individuals who were severely mentally impaired.[7] In this activity, an equal number

Recreation and Leisure Activities Provide Opportunities for Joy throughout the Life Span

Courtesy Recreation Services, Division Care and Treatment Facilities, Department of Health and Social Services, Northern Wisconsin Center for the Developmentally Delayed.

of college students preparing for professional roles in human service served as player-coaches. The rules of the basketball game were modified, so that the athletes who were intellectually disabled were required to perform the basic skill aspects of the game. The modified rules were (1) a player who had an intellectual disability could travel and double dribble; (2) players who were not mentally impaired could not dribble, shoot the ball, or pass to a teammate who was not mentally impaired; and (3) only players who had an intellectual disability could shoot. To increase scoring, another modification to the game was to award one point when the ball hit the rim. This modification provided more reinforcement to the conditions of play.

Each player who was not intellectually impaired was paired with a specific athlete with an intellectual disability. This player-coach then provided direct instruction as to when and to whom the ball was to be passed, when to dribble, and when to pass. These specific behaviors were reinforced. Thus, play and technical instruction were combined. When using this procedure, the stimulus cues and reinforcing properties by peer player-coaches are withdrawn as the athlete who has an intellectual disability improves social and physical skills and can perform tasks without the cues. The limitations of this type of integrated play are that the desirable ratio of player-coach volunteers is one to one and prerequisite training is needed for direct instruction by player-coaches.

Roles of Player-Coaches

The roles assumed by the player-coaches in a complex social interactive game (e.g., basketball and softball), which may require direct coaching of social and cognitive strategies, appear to be critical to the integration process. The complexities of the social and cognitive judgment of the athletes in running activities are were not as great as in basketball and softball. Therefore, the demand on the coaches would not be great. Nevertheless, attention by the coach was necessary to adapt integrated environments and training regimens commensurate with the ability of the athletes who had an intellectual disabilities.

In both of the integration environments, there was commitment by those who conducted the coaching. The attitudes of the coaches involved in all of the projects supported the notion that, in an educational setting with teachers who favor integrating individuals with disabilities, mainstreaming has a reasonable chance of success. On the other hand, the evidence also suggests that, where teachers oppose integration, the prognosis for success is not good. Thus, because Special Olympics is a volunteer activity for coaches, it is logical to assume that volunteers bring with them good attitudes toward the integration process.

Competition and Integration

The evidence from these integration programs is that they were beneficial to the performance of athletes with intellectual disabilities. Inasmuch as there is some debate on the values of competition for persons who have intellectual disabilities as compared with play, the preliminary findings from these studies indicate support for the findings of Karper, Martinek, and Wilkerson.[48] Their study investigated the effects of competitive and non-competitive learning environments on motor performance in mainstreamed physical education classes. They found that the performance of the students who had intellectual disabilities dropped during noncompetitive treatment following a competitive one. Although there is no way of knowing whether competition was the cause of the behavioral changes, the effects of competition on the performance of athletes who have intellectual disabilities may be a significant and fruitful avenue for future research.

COMMUNITY-BASED OPPORTUNITIES

Opportunities to learn motor skills and participate in leisure and recreation using learned skills should be available to all persons beyond the normal years of public-sponsored education. After leaving school, individuals must be able to find recreation using the skills and activities they learned in school. Opportunities for such recreation should be available to persons of all ages and capability levels. Those who have not had opportunities to participate and to learn motor skills should be provided with instruction in skills and ways of using leisure time for physical activity. Programs using direct instruction in appropriate warm-up and weight-training techniques report that their "graduates" continue participation in community-operated and commercial health and fitness programs.[88]

Children who have intellectual disabilities need to be taught to play, regardless of their level of impairment. Fine, Welch-Burke, and Fondario[33] propose a three-dimensional model designed to enhance the leisure functioning of individuals with intellectual disabilities. Levels of social play are autistic, solitary, parallel, cooperative, and competitive. Levels of cognitive play are functional, constructive, dramatic, and games with rules. Areas of skill development range from acquisition of prerequisite fine and gross motor skills and functional play to toy-play, art, simplified table games, exposure to the community, self-initiated play, and leisure education. Following is the five-step model designed to promote the achievement of higher levels of play:

1. Assessing current levels of skill and play
2. Setting goals consistent with individual needs
3. Teaching goal behaviors
4. Generalizing newly learned skills to higher levels of skill and to other environments
5. Teaching individuals to apply skills in natural environments

Recreational opportunities for children who have intellectual disabilities should be provided after school, during school vacations, and after formal educational training. There should be adequate provision in the recreation program for vigorous activity, such as sports, dancing, active games, swimming, and hiking. Intramural and community sports leagues should be provided to reinforce skills developed in the instructional program. In addition, winter snow games should be made available. Camping and outdoor education programs are other ways of affording expression of skills and interests.

Recreation

Though at least one study has shown that mildly intellectually impaired adolescents can generalize motor skills from one setting to another,[90] whenever possible, recreational activities for persons with intellectual disabilities should take place in a community-based integrated setting. Recreational activities should be designed to stimulate interaction between individuals who have intellectual disabilities and those who don't.[25] Adults who have intellectual disabilities are more apt to integrate socially when they are given the opportunity to select leisure activities of interest to them.[11]

In conjunction with the recreation program, special events scheduled throughout the school year stimulate interests, motivate the children, and inform the community about the progress of the physical education program and about the abilities of youngsters who have intellectual disabilities. Examples of such events are demonstrations for PTA meetings, track and field meets, swimming meets, play days, sports days, "hoop-it-up," pass-punt-kick contests, hikes, and bicycle races.

Overcoming Barriers to Full Recreational Inclusion

Following are some of the barriers to full inclusion in recreation programs that adults with intellectual disabilities face:

- Restrictive attitudes of parents and family
- Opposition from some members of the community
- Lack of widely available guidelines for planning and implementation of integrated programs
- Lack of skill[47]

Part of the solution to overcoming these barriers is fostering and improving social relationships.[66] What is needed is a community commitment to provide programs for all the citizens. Following are some ways a community can meet the needs of its citizens with intellectual disability:

1. Develop guidelines for planning and implementing integrated recreational programs

2. Provide opportunities for individuals who have an intellectual disability to socialize with persons who are not intellectually disabled
3. Use existing materials to train personnel to work with individuals who have an intellectual disability
4. Change attitudes toward persons with intellectual disabilities by "showcasing" their capabilities at local fairs and festivities

Volunteer Assistants

Individuals who are severely mentally impaired often require individual attention. Volunteers trained in specific duties can be of assistance to the instructional program as well as to after-school and vacation recreation programs. Parents of children who have an intellectual disability, members of high school and college service clubs, and scouting groups are becoming increasingly active as volunteers. Instructors can seek out these people and ask them to become involved with the programs for individuals who have an intellectual disability. A one- or two-hour training session can be planned to teach these volunteers what needs to be done, how to do it, what to expect from individuals who have intellectual disabilities, and how to deal with behavior problems.

The Home Program

The amount of time that the physical educator will be involved personally with students who have intellectual disabilities is relatively small. If maximum benefits are to be derived from programs, follow-up activities must be taught in the form of a home program. An educational program for parents describing the children's program and its purpose should be provided for implementation in the home. Parents should receive direction and assistance in methods for involving their children in physical activity in the neighborhood and the home.

Special Olympics

Probably no single program has done as much to foster the participation of individuals who have intellectual disabilities in physical activities as the Special Olympics program. This program, which is now international in scope, was begun in 1968 by the Joseph P. Kennedy, Jr., Foundation. In 2007 there were 169 countries with accredited Special Olympics programs.[84] Special Olympics includes training in physical fitness and sports and provides competition at the local, district, state, national, and international levels for children and adults who are disabled. A study by Roth emphasized the ongoing importance of the Special Olympics program. Parents from three areas of the United States reported that, regardless of whether their child with an intellectual disability received educational services in a segregated or an integrated setting, after completing their school years Special Olympics was the primary source of physical activity during their adult years.[76] Special Olympics also has been instrumental in developing integration programs for athletes who have intellectual disabilities.

The Special Olympics philosophy is expressed by its motto: "Let me win, but if I cannot win, let me be brave in the attempt." The stated mission of Special Olympics is

> To provide year-round sports training and athletic competition in a variety of Olympic-type sports for all children and adults with [an intellectual disability], giving them continuing opportunities to develop physical fitness, demonstrate courage, experience joy, and participate in a sharing of gifts, skills, and friendship with their families, other Special Olympics athletes, and the community.[86]

The philosophy and mission are supported by four basic programs:

1. *Special Olympics Sports Skill Program.* This program is based on illustrated guides for each sport, which include the rules under which the athletes must compete, task-analyzed skills, goals and objectives, and pre- and posttraining assessments.
2. *Unified Sports Program.* This program uses an equal number of players with and without intellectual disabilities to participate in the sponsored events. Principles that guide this program are age and ability groups. Usually,

unified teams compete with other unified teams.

3. *Special Olympics Motor Activities Training Program (MATP).* This program serves persons with severe intellectual disabilities.[85] It provides a wide range of activities and stresses the following points:
   a. Training should be fun.
   b. Ultimately, athletes should be able to choose their own activities.
   c. Activities should be age appropriate.
   d. Participants should demonstrate their newly developed skills to significant others.
   e. Functioning level guides activity selection.
   f. Even partial participation has value.
   g. Creativity should be used when providing community-based sports and recreational activities.

4. *Demonstration Sports Program.* This program explores and researches the appropriateness of incorporating new sports into the Special Olympics program.

The following are the four Special Olympics International initiatives for persons with intellectual disabilities:

1. *Schools and Youth.* This movement is committed to increasing the participation of youth with intellectual disabilities in Special Olympics (SO) by establishing school-based programs and activities. The goals of this initiative are to
   a. Develop new constituencies and leaders for the SO movement
   b. Promote greater understanding and acceptance of similarities and differences in others among school-age youth
   c. Involve school-age youth in a variety of activities centered on Special Olympics, including Special Olympics sports and events that will enable them to play a positive role in their schools and communities

2. *Special Olympics Young Athletes.* This initiative is an innovative sports play program for children with intellectual disabilities, designed to introduce them to the world of sports prior to Special Olympics at age eight years. The program addresses two levels of play:

   Level 1—includes physical activities focused on developing fundamental motor tracking and eye-hand coordination play

   Level 2—concentrates on application of Level 1 physical activities through a sports skills activity program, which focuses on developing skills consistent with Special Olympics official sports

3. *Athlete Leadership Programs.* This initiative allows athletes to explore opportunities to participate in nontraditional roles, such as serving on boards of directors or local organizing committees and/or being a spokesperson for Special Olympics, a team captain, a coach, or an official.

4. *Camp Shriver.* The newest of the Special Olympics initiatives is a place for persons with intellectual disabilities to come together to learn new sport skills, improve individual sport performance, participate in individual and team sports, build friendships, and have fun with partners who have trained as Camp Shriver volunteers.[84]

In 2007 there were 30 official Special Olympics sports—alpine and cross country skiing, aquatics, athletics (track and field), badminton, basketball, bocce, bowling, cricket, cycling, equestrian sports, figure skating, floor hockey, football (soccer), golf, gymnastics, kayaking, judo, netball, power lifting, roller skating, sailing, snow boarding, snowshoeing, speed skating, softball, table tennis, team handball, tennis, and volleyball. Special Olympics competitions are fashioned after the Olympic Games. World Games are held every two years, alternating between winter and summer.[84]

Some of the rules of the Special Olympics sports program follow:

1. Athletes can participate beginning at age 8 years.
2. Competition is conducted according to age, ability, and gender.

3. Competition must be preceded by at least 10 hours of training within the previous 2 months.
4. Records of performance levels during practice must be submitted prior to competition to establish competition divisions.

5. Head coaches must be formally trained.
6. Event managers must complete formal training.

SUMMARY

Intellectual disabilities are characterized by significant limitations both in intellectual functioning and in adaptive behavior as expressed in conceptual, social, and practical adaptive skills. Intellectual disability begins before age 18 but may not always be of lifelong duration. The prevalence of intellectual disabilities in the population is approximately 3 percent. Persons with an intellectual disability can be expected to learn and develop.

Physical educators can expect to have students with intellectual disabilities in the classes they teach. Those students' motor skills and physical fitness levels may be equal to or lower than those of students who do not have intellectual disabilities. These students can be taught and can improve. Carefully selected teaching strategies and program adaptations will yield positive motor development results. Students should be tested to determine their specific motor strengths and weaknesses, as is true for most performance abilities. Physical education programs should be designed around these test results.

Physical education programs in the public schools should provide assistance for transition of the recreational skills acquired in physical education classes to independent, integrated recreational activity in the community. Participation in recreation, home programs, and Special Olympics should be encouraged. Special Olympics has taken the lead in developing programs to include individuals who have intellectual disabilities in integrated sports activity.

REVIEW QUESTIONS

1. How does the IDEA definition of mental retardation differ from the American Association on Intellectual and Developmental Disabilities' definiton of intellectual disability?
2. What types of physical education program modifications need to be made for individuals with Down syndrome who have atlantoaxial instability?
3. What types of modifications are recommended for use when programming exercises for persons with intellectual disabilities?
4. What are five specific teaching strategies that can be used with persons with an intellectual disability?

5. How are adaptations of physical activity different for persons with mild and severe intellectual disabilities?
6. What accommodations are needed outside of school to enable persons with an intellectual disability to participate in community recreation programs?
7. What Special Olympics programs are available for persons with intellectual disabilities?

STUDENT ACTIVITIES

1. With the class divided into small groups, select appropriate games for Luther's class. When each group reports its selection of games, each group should give its rationale for each selection.

2. Select three behavior management techniques for all of Luther's teachers to use to control his behavior and describe how they would use those techniques in an inclusive physical education class.

3. Locate one of the journals that deals with intellectual disabilities. (Some of these journals are *Adapted Physical Education Quarterly; Palaestra: The Forum of Sport, Physical Education and Recreation for the Disabled; Exceptional Children; Retardation; Education and Training of the Mentally Retarded;* and *Journal of Intellectual Disability.*) Look through recent issues for articles that might be applied to conducting physical education programs for students who have an intellectual disability.

4. Visit classes in which youngsters with intellectual disabilities are included. Compare the performance of these students with that of the other students in the class. List the ways their performance and/or behavior differs.

5. Volunteer to assist in a Special Olympics meet. Describe how the experience affected you.

REFERENCES

1. American Association on Mental Retardation: *Definition, classification, and systems of support.* Washington, DC, Author 2002.

2. American Academy of Pediatrics Committee on Sports Medicine: Atlantoaxial instability in children with Down syndrome, *Pediatrics* 96:151–154, 1995.

3. American Psychiatric Association: *Diagnostic and statistical manual of mental disorders,* vol. 4. Rev., Washington, DC, Author 2001.

4. Anchuthengil JD, Neilsen DH, Schulenburg J, Hurst R, Davis MJ: Effects of an individualized treadmill exercise training program on cardiovascular fitness of adults with mental retardation, *J of Ortho, Sports, and PT* 16:229–237, 1992.

5. ARA Consulting Group: *The Winter Medallion Program of Manitoba Special Olympics: An evaluation.* Winnipeg, Canada, Author 1994.

6. Arnold R, Ng N, Pechar G: Relationship of rated perceived exertion to heart rate and workload in mentally retarded young adults, *APAQ* 9:47–53, 1992.

7. Auxter DM, et al.: *Prediction of playing basketball and basketball skills among persons with severe mental retardation.* Unpublished paper, Special Olympics International, Washington, DC, 1987.

8. Baumgardner TL, Green KE, Reiss AL: A behavioral neurogenetics approach to developmental disabilities: Gene-brain-behavior associations, *Current Opinion in Neurology* 7:172–178, 1994.

9. Beers MH, Berkow R, editors: *The Merck manual of diagnosis and therapy.* Whitehouse Station, NJ, Merck Research Laboratories, 2006.

10. Budoff M: *The evaluation of the mixed teams softball in Massachusetts Special Olympics—coaches' views.* Cambridge, MA, Research Institute for Educational Problems, 1987.

11. Bullock CC, Mahon MJ: Decision making in leisure: Empowerment for people with mental retardation, *JOPERD* 63:36–39, 1992.

12. Burack JT, Enns JA: *Attention, development and psychopathology.* New York, Guilford Press, 1997.

13. Centers for Disease Control and Prevention at www.cdc.gov/ncbddd/single_gene/fragileX.htm, September 2006.

14. Chanias AK, Reid G, Hoover ML: Exercise effects on health-related physical fitness of individuals with an intellectual disability: A meta-analysis, *APAQ* 15:119–140, 1998.

15. Choi S, Meeuwsen HJ, French R, Stenwall J: Learning and control of simple aiming movements by adults with profound mental retardation, *APAQ* 16:167–177, 1999.

16. Committee on Sports Medicine: Atlantoaxial instability in Down syndrome, *Pediatrics* 74:152–154, 1984.

17. Cooke RE: Atlantoaxial instability in individuals with Down's syndrome, *APAQ* 1:194–196, 1984.

18. Cooper LJ, Wacker DP, Thursby D, Plagmann L, Harding J, Millard T, Derby M: Analysis of the effects of task preferences, task demands, and adult attention on child behavior in outpatient and classroom settings, *J of Applied Behav Analysis* 25:823–840, 1992.

19. Croce R: Effects of exercise and diet on body composition and cardiovascular fitness, *Educ and Train in Mental Retard* 25:176–187, 1990.

20. Croce R, Horvat M: Effects of reinforcement-based exercise on fitness and work productivity in adults with mental retardation, *APAQ* 9:148–178, 1992.

21. Croce R, Horvat M: Coincident timing by nondisabled mentally retarded, and traumatic brain-injured individuals under varying target-exposure conditions, *Perc Motor Skills* 80:487–496, 1995.

22. Croce R, Horvat H, Roswal G: A preliminary investigation into the effects of exercise duration and fitness level on problem solving ability in individuals with mild mental retardation, *Clinical Kinesiology* 48(3):48–54, 1994.

23. Croce RV, Pitetti KH, Horvat M, Miller J: Peak torque, average power, and hamstrings/quadriceps ratios in nondisabled adults and adults with mental retardation, *Arch Phys Med Rehabil* 77:369–372, 1996.

24. Danforth DS, Drabman RS: Community living skills. In Matson JL, editor: *Handbook of behavior modification with the mentally retarded.* New York, Plenum Press, 1990.

25. Dattilo J, Schlein SJ: Understanding leisure services for individuals with mental retardation, *Mental Retard* 32:53–59, 1994.

26. DePauw K, Ferrari N: The effect of interference on the performance on a card sorting task of mentally retarded adolescents, *The Phys Educ* 43:32–38, 1986.

27. Downs SB, Wood TM: Validating a Special Olympics volleyball skills assessment test, *APAQ* 13:166–179, 1996.

28. Dunn JM, Morehouse JW, Fredericks HD: *Physical education for the severely handicapped: A systematic approach to a data based gymnasium.* Austin, TX, PRO-ED, 1986.

29. Ellis DN, Cress PJ, Spellman CR: Using self management to promote independent exercise in adolescents with moderate mental retardation in a school setting, *Educ and Train of Ment Retard* 27:51–59, 1992.

30. Fernhall B: Mental retardation. In Durstine JL, editor: *Exercise management for persons with chronic diseases and disabilities.* Champaign, IL, Human Kinetics, 1997.

31. Fernhall B, Pittetti KH, Vukovich DS, Hensen T, Winnick JP, Short FX: Validation of cardiovascular fitness field tests in children with mental retardation, *Amer J of Ment Retard* 102:602–612, 1998.

32. Felix M, McCubbin J, Shaw J: Bone mineral density, body composition, and muscle strength in premenopausal women with mental retardation, *APAQ* 15:345–356, 1998.

33. Foster-Johnson L, Ferro J, Dunlap G: Preferred curricular activities and reduced problem behaviors in students with intellectual disabilities, *J of Appl Behav Analysis* 27:493–504, 1994.

34. Frey GC, Buchanan AM, Rosser Sandt DD: I'd rather watch TV: An examination of physical activity in adults with mental retardation, *Mental Retard* 43(4):241–254, 2005.

35. Frey GC, McCubbin JA, Hannigan-Downs S, Kasser SL, Skaggs SO: Physical fitness of trained runners with and without mild mental retardation, *APAQ* 16:126–137, 1999.

36. Gleser JM, Margules JY, Mier Nyska SP, Mendelberg H: Physical and psychological benefits of modified judo practice for blind mentally retarded children: A pilot study, *Perc Motor Skills* 74:915–925, 1992.

37. Gillberg C: Practitioner review: Physical investigations in mental retardation, *J Child Psychol Psyc* 38:889–897, 1997.

38. Grskovic JA, Zentail SS, Stormont-Spurgin M: Time estimation and planning abilities: Students with and without mild disabilities, *Behavior Disorders* 20:197–203, 1995.

39. Hagerman R: Behaviour and treatment of the fragile X syndrome. In Davies KE, editor: *The fragile X syndrome.* Oxford, England, Oxford University Press, 1989.

40. Hagerman R: *The ARC's Q&A on Fragile X,* http://thearc.org/faqs/fragqa.html. 2003.

41. Haley S: Postural reactions in infants with Down syndrome: Relationship to motor milestone development and age, *J Am Phys Therapy* 66:17–22, 1986.

42. Hallahan DP, Kauffman JM: *Exceptional learners: Introduction to special education.* Boston, Allyn & Bacon, 1997.

43. Hickson L, Blackman LS, Reis EM: *Mental retardation: Foundations of educational programming.* Boston, Allyn & Bacon, 1995.

44. Hodges NJ, Cunningham SJ, Lyons J, Kerr TL, Digby E: Visual feedback processing and goal directed movement in adults with Down syndrome, *APAQ* 12:52–59, 1995.

45. Horvat M, Croce R, Roswell G: Magnitude and reliability for measurements of muscle strength across trials for individuals with mental retardation, *Perc Motor Skills* 77:643–649, 1993.

46. Horvat M, Croce R, Roswal G, Seagraves F: Single trial versus maximal or mean values for evaluating strengths in individuals with mental retardation, *APAQ* 12:176–186, 1995.

47. Ittenbach RF, Abery BH, Larson SA, Speigel AN, Prouty RW: Community adjustment of young adults with mental retardation: Overcoming barriers to inclusion, *Palaestra* 11(2):32–42, 1994.

48. Karper WB, Martinek TJ, Wilkerson JD: Effects of competitive/non-competitive learning on motor performance of children in mainstream physical education, *Am Correct Ther J* 39:10–15, 1985.

49. Kim S, Kwang HK: Cardiorespiratory function of educable mentally retarded boys. In Yabe K, Kusano K, Nakata H, editors: *Adapted physical activity: Health and fitness.* New York, Springer-Verlag, 1994.

50. King D, Mace FC: Acquisition and maintenance of exercise skills under normalized conditions by adults with moderate and severe mental retardation, *Educ and Train in Ment Retard* 28:311–317, 1990.

51. Latash ML, Almeida GL, Corcos DM: Preprogrammed reactions in individuals with Down syndrome: The effects of instruction and predictability of the person, *Archives of Physical Med and Rehab* 74:391–398, 1993.

52. Lavay B, McCubbin J, Eichstaedt C: Field-based physical fitness tests for individuals with mental retardation. In Vermeer A, Davis WE, editors: Physical and motor development in mental retardation, Basil, Karger, 1995.

53. Leshin L: *Atlantoaxial instability: Controversy and commentary,* www.ds-health.com/aai.htm. 2003.

54. MacDonncha A, Watson A, McSweeney T, O'Donovan DJ: Reliability of Eurofit physical fitness items for adolescent males with and without mental retardation, *APAQ* 16:86–95, 1999.

55. Maes B. et al.: Cognitive functioning and information processing of adult mentally retarded men with fragile-X syndrome, *American J of Medical Genetics* 50:190–200, 1994.

56. Martin JE, et al.: Consumer-centered transition and supported employment. In Matson JL, editor: *Handbook of behavior modification with the mentally retarded.* New York, Plenum Press, 1990.

57. Merriman WJ, Barnett BE, Jarry ES: Improving fitness of dually diagnosed adults, *Perc Motor Skills* 83:99–104, 1996.

58. Monroe H, Howe C: The effects of integration and social class on the acceptance of retarded adolescents, *Educ Train Ment Retard* 6:21–24, 1971.

59. M.O.V.E, MOVE International, Bakersfield, CA, www.MOVE-International.org.

60. Nakaya T, Kusano K, Yare K: Decreasing motor ability in adults with Down syndrome. In Yabe K, Kusano K, Nakata H, editors: *Adapted physical activity: Health and fitness.* New York, Springer-Verlag, 1994.

61. National Information Center for Children and Youth with Disabilities: *Mental retardation fact sheet* (F58), www.nichcy.org/pubs/factshe/f58txt.htm, 2002.

62. National Institute for Childhood Disorders: *What are the signs and symptoms of fragile X?* www.nichd.nih.gov/publications/pubs/fragile X/sub9.cfm, 2007.

63. National Organization on Fetal Alcohol Syndrome: *What policy makers should know,* www.nofas.com/resources/factsheets/FASD, 2007.

64. National Organization on Fetal Alcohol Syndrome: *What school systems should know about affected students,* www.nofas.com/resources/factsheets/FASD, 2007.

65. Newell R: Motor skill orientation in mental retardation: Overview of traditional and current orientation. In Clark JH, Humphrey J, editors: *Motor development: Current selected research,* vol. 1. Princeton, NJ, Princeton Book, 1985.

66. Newton SJ, Horner RH, Ard WR, LeBaron N, Sappington G: A conceptual model for improving the social life of individuals with mental retardation, *Mental Retard* 32:393–402, 1994.

67. Ninot G, Deligneres D: Effects of integrated and segregated sport participation on the physical self for persons with intellectual disabilities, *J of Intellectual Disability Research* 49(9):682–689, 2005.

68. Patel, BD: The fragile X syndrome, *British J of Clinical Practice* 48(1):42–44, 1994.

69. Pitetti KH, Rimmer JH, Fernhall B: Physical fitness and adults with mental retardation: An overview of current research and future directions, *Sports Medicine* 16:23–56, 1993.

70. P.L. 101-476 Rules. *Federal Register,* September 29, 1992.

71. Porretta DL, Moore W, Sappenfield C: Situational anxiety in Special Olympics athletes, *Palaestra* 9(3):48–50, 1993.

72. Privett C: The Special Olympics: A tradition of excellence, *Exceptional Parent* May:28–36, 1999.

73. Rimmer JH, Braddock D, Fujiura G: Prevalence of obesity in adults with mental retardation: Implications for health promotion and disease prevention, *Mental Retard* 31:105–110, 1993.

74. Rimmer J, Kelly L: Effects of a resistance training program on adults with mental retardation, *APAQ* 8:146–153, 1991.

75. Roberts JE, Hatton DD, Bailey DB: Development and behavior of male toddlers with fragile X syndrome, *J of Early Intervention* 24(3):207–223, 2001.

76. Roth K: *Community physical recreation and students with intellectual disabilities.* Unpublished Doctoral Dissertation, Texas Woman's University, Denton, TX, 2003.

77. Schalock RL, Luckasson RA, Shogren KA: The renaming of mental retardation: Understanding the change to the term intellectual disability, *Intellectual and Developmental Disabilities* 45(2):116–124, 2007.

78. Schantz OJ: Adaptation in students with Down syndrome: An experimental study on the trainability of strength and power. In Yabe K, Kusano K, Nakata H, editors: *Adapted physical activity: Health and fitness.* New York, Springer-Verlag, 1994.

79. Schroeder SR, et al.: Self-injurious behavior. In Matson JL, editor: *Handbook of behavior modification with the mentally retarded.* New York, Plenum Press, 1990.

80. Shapiro DR, Drummer GM: Perceived and actual basketball competence of adolescent males with mild mental retardation, *APAQ* 15:179–190, 1998.

81. Smail KM, Horvat M: Relationship of muscular strength on work performance in high school students with mental retardation, *Education & Training in Developmental Disabilities* 41(4):410–419, 2006.

82. Smith D: *Introduction to special education: Teaching in an age of challenge.* Needham Heights, MA, Allyn & Bacon, 1998.

83. Smith S: Cognitive deficits associated with fragile X syndrome, *Mental Retard* 31(5):279–283, 1993.

84. Special Olympics, www.specialolympics.org. 2007.

85. Special Olympics International: *Adapted physical education sports skill assessment resource manual, Special Olympics Bulletin,* Washington, DC, Author 1991.

86. Special Olympics International: *Special Olympics motor activities training guide.* Washington, DC, 1989.

87. Steinbach P, et al.: Molecular analysis of mutations in the gene FMR-1 segregating in fragile X families, *Hum Genet* 92:491–498, 1993.

88. Stopka C, Pomeranz J, Siders R, Dykes MK, Goodman A: Transitional skills for wellness, *Teach Ex Child* 7:6–11, 1999.

89. Suomi R, Surburh PR, Lecius P: Reliability of isokinetic and isometric measurement of leg strength on men with mental retardation, *Archives of Phys Med and Rehab* 74:848–853, 1993.

90. Surburg PR: The influence of task incompletion of motor skill performance of mildly retarded adolescents, *Am Correct Ther J* 40:39–42, 1986.

91. Tanji JL: The preparticipation exam, *The Physician and Sportsmed* 19:61–69, 1994.

92. Taylor J, French R, Kinnison L, O'Brien T: Primary and secondary reinforcers in performance of a 1.0 mile walk/jog by adolescents with moderate mental retardation, *Perc Motor Skills* 87:1265–1266, 1998.

93. The ARC of the United States, www.thearc.org, 2007.

94. Ulrich BD, Ulrich DA, Collier DH, Cole EL: Developmental shifts in the ability of infants with Down syndrome to produce treadmill steps, *Phys Ther* 75:17–23, 1995.

95. U.S. Department of Education: *IDEA trend data,* www.ideadata.org, 2006.

96. Wehmeyer ML, Metzler CA: How self-determined are people with mental retardation? The national consumer survey, *Mental Retard* 33:111–119, 1995.

97. Wiebe E, Wiebe A: Fragile X syndrome, *Can Fam Physician* 40:290–295, 1994.

98. Wiegers AM, Curfs LMG, Fryns J-P: A longitudinal study of intelligence in Dutch fragile X boys, *Birth Defects: Original Article Series* 28(1):93–97, 1992.

99. Winnick JP, Short FX: *The Brockport Physical Fitness Test.* Champaign, IL, Human Kinetics, 1999.

100. Yabe K, et al.: Developmental trends of jumping reaction time by means of EMG in mentally retarded children, *J Ment Defic Res* 29:137–145, 1985.

101. Yang JJ, Porretta DL: Sport/leisure skill learning by adolescents with mild mental retardation: A four- step strategy, *APAQ* 16:300–315, 1999.

102. Yun J, Ulrich DA: Perceived and actual physical competence in children with mild mental retardation, *Amer J on Ment Retard* 102:147–160, 1997.

103. Zetts RA, Horvat MA, Langone J: Effects of a community-based progressive resistance training program on the work productivity of adolescents with moderate to severe intellectual disabilities, *Educ Train Ment Retard Dev Disab* June:66–178, 1995.

104. Zoerink DA, Wilson J: The competitive disposition: Views of athletes with mental retardation, *APAQ* 12:34–42, 1995.

SUGGESTED READINGS

Algozzine RF, Ysseldyke JE: *Teaching students with mental retardation: A practical guide for every teacher.* Thousand Oaks, CA, Corwin Press, 2006.

Cimera RE: *Mental retardation doesn't mean stupid: A guide for parents and teachers.* Lanham, MD, Rowman and Littlefield, 2006.

Galerstein N, Martin K, Powe DL: *Age appropriate activities for adults with profound mental retardation.* Hertfordshire, England, Barcelona Publishers, 2005.

RECOMMENDED WEB SITES

Please keep in mind that these Web sites are being recommended in the winter of 2007. As Web sites often change, they may have moved or been reconfigured or eliminated.

National Down Syndrome Society
www.ndss.org

National Organization on Fetal Alcohol Syndrome
www.nofas.org

Project INSPIRE Aquatics
http://twu.edu/INSPIRE

Special Olympics
www.specialolympics.org

National Fragile X Foundation
www.fragilex.org

RECOMMENDED VIDEOS

Insight Media
2162 Broadway
New York, NY 10024-0621
800-233-0010
www.insight-media.com

How Can We All Play: Severe Disability in P.E.
#YAN1047/VHS/35 min/2002/$109.00

Physical Activity for All
#YAN2632/DVD-ROM/2000/$129.00

Fragile X Syndrome
#TAN4470/DVD/25 min/2006/$139.00

Special People, Special Needs
#TAN2233/VHS/51 min/2000/$149.00

Pervasive Developmental Disorders

The Child Who Is Autistic Requires
Cardiovascular Activities

Photo by Carol Huettig.

■ OBJECTIVES

Briefly describe autism, Asperger syndrome, Rett syndrome, and pervasive developmental disorder–not otherwise specified (PDD-NOS).

Give examples of "best practices" in teaching physical education to students within the PDD continuum.

Give examples of physical education activities appropriate for learners with the major pervasive developmental disorders at various stages of development.

Explain simple strategies to encourage appropriate behavior in learners with pervasive developmental disorders.

Describe the leisure, recreation, fitness, and sport activities that may be appropriate in a community-based program for learners making a transition from school to the community.

Explain the critical role of parents in assessment of and IEP development for individuals with PDD.

Briefly explain instructional and behavioral methodologies used for individuals with PDD, including Daily Life Therapy, TEACCH, Applied Behavioral Analysis, and floortime.

CHARACTERISTICS OF PERVASIVE DEVELOPMENT DISORDERS

Definition

Individuals with pervasive developmental disorders (PDD) present an exciting, wonderful, and ever-challenging opportunity for physical educators. Their unique approach to life, their reaction to sensory stimulation within the environment, and their fascinating human interaction and communication/language skills provide the opportunity for physical educators and adapted and general physical education teachers alike to test and teach skills.

Tsai,[77] in a National Disseminition Center for Children and Youth with Disabilities (NICHCY) briefing paper, reported increasing interest in the nature of individuals with pervasive developmental disorders and significant confusion for both parents and professionals regarding the various diagnostic categories included under the large umbrella of PDD. Tsai suggested that all types of PDD are neurological disorders that are usually evident by age three. In general, children who have a type of PDD have difficulty talking, playing with other children, and relating to others, including their families. This is consistent with the DSM-IV-TR definition:

> Pervasive Developmental Disorders are characterized by severe and pervasive impairment in several areas of development:
> • social interaction skills;
> • communication skills; or
> • the presence of stereotyped behavior, interests, and activities.[3]

Pervasive developmental disorders fall along a continuum. The four most common of the disorders are autistic disorder, Asperger syndrome, Rett syndrome, and pervasive developmental disorder–not otherwise specified (PDD-NOS) (see Figure 12-1). Increasingly, pervasive developmental disorders are being referred to as autism spectrum disorders.

Autistic disorder, or autism, is one of the four disorders included under the large umbrella of pervasive developmental disorder (PDD). Classic autism, originally known as Kanner syndrome, was first described by Dr. Leo Kanner in 1943.[45]

The major characteristics of autism are significant developmental delays, global and comprehensive language disorders, abnormal and stereotypical behavior patterns, social isolation, and often, but not always, mental retardation.

In 1944, Hans Asperger introduced an autistic disorder that is now widely known as Asperger syndrome.[75] Individuals with this condition, known originally as "high-level" autism, share many of the same symptoms as individuals with autism. However, there are some significant differences. One of the major differences between Asperger syndrome and others within the PDD category is that an individual with Asperger syndrome has average to above average intelligence.[7]

The individual with Asperger syndrome usually has excellent verbal skills but may struggle with the subtleties of conversation, including humor, sarcasm, and irony, and may have some difficulty "reading" subtle facial expressions or gestures.[81] One of the other distinguishing characteristics of Asperger syndrome is that some students with the condition demonstrate motor clumsiness and awkwardness.

Rett syndrome is a neurological disorder first described in 1966 in Germany by A. Rett. It appears to be a neuronal disorder.[1] The condition is characterized by normal development the first 6 to 18 months of life followed by loss of acquired gross and fine motor skills, impaired language skills, gait apraxia (unusual gait), and the appearance of stereotypical hand-wringing, hand-washing movements.[67] Rett syndrome is distinguished from the others under the PDD umbrella because of the significant nature of the loss. Children with Rett syndrome typically are classified as having severe or profound intellectual disability. The condition is devastating; most of their systems and organs, which may be decreased in size, are involved and compromised.[5]

Pervasive developmental disorders–not otherwise specified (PDD-NOS) is a term used to describe learners who do not meet the specific criteria for diagnosis in any of the other forms of pervasive developmental disorder, as specified in DSM-IV. However, they share significant, severe,

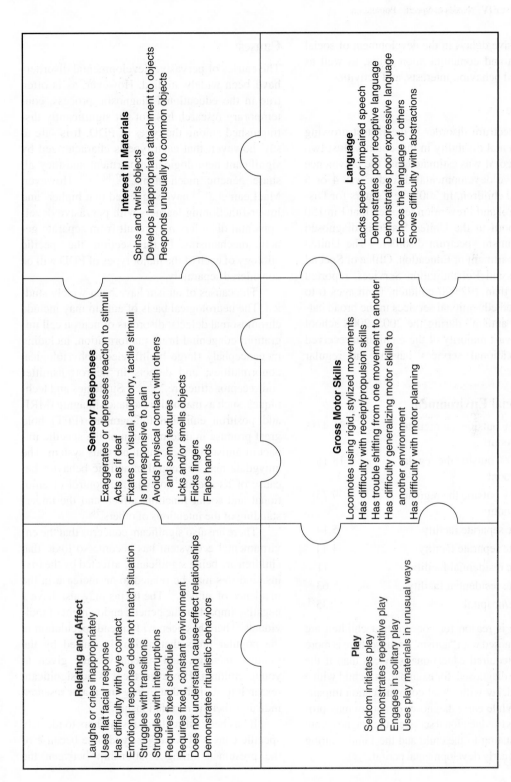

Figure 12-1 The Autism Puzzle

Developed by Virginia Nelson, Autism Specialist, Dallas Independent School District, together with Carol Huettig and Jean Pyfer.

and pervasive delays in the development of social interaction and communication skills, as well as stereotyped behavior, interests, and activities.[3]

Incidence

Autism spectrum disorder is the fastest growing developmental disability in this country. Just two decades ago, it was estimated that the prevalence of pervasive developmental disorder was 4 or 5 per 10,000 children. In 2007 the Centers for Disease Control and Prevention reported that 1 in 150 children born in the United States is diagnosed with an autism spectrum disorder.[62] The United States Department of Education, Office of Special Education and Rehabilitation Services, reported that more than 192,000 children, from ages 6 to 21, received educational services in the broad category of "autism" during the 2005–2006 school year. The vast majority of these children received their educational services outside the regular classroom.

Educational Environment

< 21% outside the regular classroom	31.41%
21–60% outside the regular classroom	18.18
> 60% outside the regular classroom	39.75
Public separate facility	5.14
Private separate facility	4.44
Public residential facility	.11
Private residential facility	.63
Home/hospital	.35[81]

There is reason for concern that children are being diagnosed with "autism" because there is more access to required educational services than if the child were diagnosed, for example, as a child with a language delay with social communication impairments.[59] While early diagnoses of autism may provide access to educational services, the diagnoses are also devastating to the child and the family during the critical early developmental period.

Causes

The causes of pervasive developmental disorders have been widely studied. However, as is often true in the educational diagnostic process, contemporary research has not yet significantly distinguished among the types of PDD. It is safe to say, however, that each type is characterized by significant neurological impairment and they all share genetic mechanisms.[9,27,30,77,78] However, MacLean et al.[54] have suggested that higher- and lower-functioning learners with pervasive developmental disorders may result from separate genetic mechanisms. In this section, the specific etiology of each of the major types of PDD will be considered separately.

The causes of autism have been widely studied. The neurological basis of autism may include chromosomal defects; disorders of neuron cell migration; congenital brain malformation, including megancephaly (large brain); electrophysiological abnormalities; and defects in neurotransmitter and receptor structure.[8,17,78,84] Strategies and techniques, such as magnetic resonance imaging (MRI) and positron emission tomography (PET) hold great promise in determination of the specific impact of autism on the central nervous system. The amygdala may be central in autistic behavior because of its specific roles in the control of emotional and social function, affect, and the understanding of the intentions of others.[76]

There are also significant concerns that the environmental ecosystem has become so toxic that children are being significantly affected by the toxins, and this may be related to an increase in the incidence of autism.[21] The toxins may also have a negative impact on the genetic endowment of individuals. There has been widespread speculation in the popular press that autism is caused by the mumps, measles, and rubella vaccine given to young children. However, there is no significant research to support that theory and major research indicates there is no relationship.[55]

It has been difficult for researchers to identify specific causes of Asperger syndrome because of the presumed strong relationship between the "high-functioning" autistic individual and an individual with Asperger syndrome. Asperger syndrome and autism are, however, two different conditions, even though they share the PDD umbrella.[15]

The cause of Rett syndrome is a genetic mutation on the X chromosome. The severity of the disorder depends on the exact location of the mutation on the chromosome.[44] The syndrome occurs predominately in females because an X-linked gene would be lethal in males (who have only one X chromosome). Results of the genetic mutation include immune system abnormalities, frontal lobe atrophy, abnormal neurotransmitter function, deterioration of the corpus callosum (the part of the brain that connects the right and left parts of the brain), and brain stem vestibular dysfunction.[31,32,67,82]

The causes of PDD-NOS are difficult to identify specifically because of the failure to distinguish between PDD-NOS and other types of PDD.

COGNITIVE, MOTOR, PHYSICAL, BEHAVIORAL, AND PSYCHOSOCIAL CHARACTERISTICS

Every individual with a pervasive developmental disorder is unique. However, it is helpful for the physical educator to understand "typical" characteristics of each of the major types of pervasive developmental disorders.

Autism

The primary classification system used to identify pervasive developmental disorders is the DSM-IV-TR system developed by the American Psychiatric Association.[3] Autism is one of the primary forms of pervasive developmental disorders (see Table 12-1 and Figure 12-2).

Research has identified other cognitive, motor/physical, language, behavioral, and psychosocial symptoms as well. Many children with autism have difficulty completing academic tasks within the school setting, although this may have no relationship to their intelligence. Learners with

autism may simply find it difficult to function within the school environment.

Learners with autism may exhibit gross and fine motor delays. Manjiviona and Prior found that 66.7 percent of high-functioning children with autism had definite motor problems, as measured on the Test of Motor Impairment-Henderson revised, and performed at a level significantly lower than their same-age peers.[57] Learners with autism may also display unusual gross and fine motor behaviors. Rapin noted,

> Motor stereotypes are often striking and, besides hand flapping, may include pacing, spinning, running in circles, twirling a string, tearing paper, drumming, and flipping light switches.[64]

Most learners with autism struggle with expressive and receptive language. To communicate an intention, the learner with autism may use atypical means, such as having temper tantrums, grabbing a teacher's hand to take the teacher where the learner wants the teacher to be, and performing self- and other-aggression.[70] To communicate verbally, the learner may use the following language patterns:

- Echolalia, echoing the language of another
- Neologisms, made-up words or sounds
- Singing or sing-songing of particular words or phrases or humming
- Poorly articulated and agrammatical speech
- Jargon
- "Overlearned scripts," repeating words[64]

In addition, children with autism typically have difficulty with behavior, and most experience difficulties in psychosocial experiences, including difficulty engaging in cooperative activities, difficulty attending to others, difficulty with appropriate engagement gaze, difficulty attributing emotions to others, and failure to develop age-appropriate play behaviors.[49,58,60] Many students with autism have difficulty in social situations. They may have difficulty responding to typical social stimuli, such as having their names called; difficulty with spontaneous verbal or nonverbal

Table 12-1	Summary of Characteristics of Individuals with Autism

For a formal diagnosis of autism, the DSM-IV-TR system requires that at least eight of the following behaviors be demonstrated:

Qualitative impairment in reciprocal social interaction as manifested by at least two of the following
A. Marked lack of awareness of the existence of feelings of others
B. No or abnormal seeking of comfort at times of distress
C. No or impaired imitation
D. No or abnormal social play
E. Gross impairment in ability to make peer friendships

Qualitative impairment in verbal and nonverbal communication, and in imaginative activity, as manifested by at least one of the following
A. No mode of communication, such as communicative babbling, facial expression, gesture, mime, or spoken language
B. Markedly abnormal nonverbal communication, as in the use of eye-to-eye gaze, facial expression, body posture, or gestures to initiate or modulate social interaction
C. Absence of imaginative activity, such as play acting of adult roles, fantasy characters, or animals, lack of interest in stories about imaginary events
D. Marked abnormalities in the production of speech, including volume, pitch, stress, rate, rhythm, and intonation
E. Marked abnormalities in the production of speech, including stereotyped and repetitive use of speech

Markedly restricted repertoire of activities and interests, as manifested by at least one of the following
A. Stereotyped body movements (e.g., hand flicking or twisting, spinning, head banging, complex whole body movements)
B. Persistent preoccupation with parts of objects
C. Marked distress over changes in trivial aspects of environments (e.g., insisting that exactly the same route always be followed when shopping)
D. Markedly restricted range of interests and a preoccupation with one narrow interest (e.g., interested only in lining up objects, in amassing facts about meteorology, or in pretending to be a fantasy character)

Onset during infancy or childhood

Modified from DSM-IV-TR.

greeting or "good-bye"; and difficulty establishing eye contact.[19,36,37] However, they appear to be sensitive to another human in distress.[12]

During unstructured, unplanned free play, children with autism, when compared with children without autism matched on mental age, play with fewer toys, are less focused on play, seldom initiate interaction or communication with their play partners, and appear to prefer solitary play.[10,26,46,53,74] They play better, however, in more structured play experiences.

Dr. Temple Granding, a high-functioning individual with autism, wrote that she and others with autism tend to identify with *Star Trek* heroes Data and Mr. Spock. She said, "I couldn't figure out what I was doing wrong. I had an odd lack of awareness that I was different. I thought the other kids were different. I could never figure out why I didn't fit in."[72]

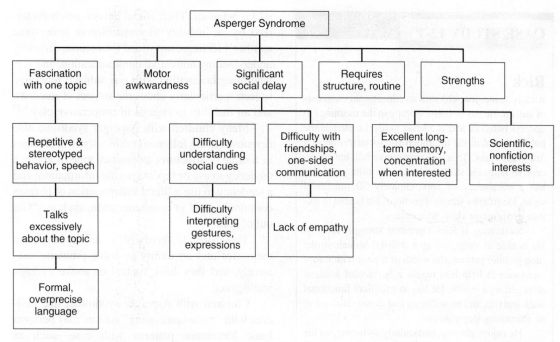

Figure 12-2 Asperger Syndrome

There are particular characteristics of individuals with autism that have a dramatic impact on their ability to learn:

• Learners with autism may be unable to impose meaning on their experiences. Their personal reality is apparently unrelated to actual experiences and events.
• They may be distractible and have difficulty focusing on what is important in the educational environment.
• They may focus on minute details and fail to grasp the "bigger picture."
• They may have difficulty with abstract concepts and symbols.
• They may find it easy to understand and remember individual facts or concepts but have difficulty combining or integrating ideas.
• They may have difficulty organizing acts or thoughts in a logical sequence.

• They may learn a fact or concept in one situation but be unable to generalize to another, similar situation.
• They are often very persistent in seeking out and getting what they want—whether it is a particular smell, object, or toy.
• They may be anxious. This is often a combination of biological and psychological factors.
• They may process sensory stimuli in atypical ways.[17]

Howard Gardner, in his classic work *Frames of Mind,* suggested that individuals with autism demonstrate a variety of intelligences, including logical-mathematical and musical, but have particular difficulty with intelligences associated with social-emotional skills, the interpersonal and intrapersonal types of intelligence.[29] In the broadest sense, if educators and other professionals were to embrace the notion that there are different types of intelligence and, thus, different ways to assess

---

CASE STUDY 12-1

Rick

Rick is a nine-year-old with an educational diagnosis of autism. He has in-home therapy in the mornings to address behavior and academic skills; he attends the public school in the afternoon for socialization in a 3rd-grade class. He is basically nonverbal, but his receptive language skills appear to be quite good. He has a vocabulary of approximately 30 functional signs. He follows simple directions. He is able to imitate gross motor skills with ease.

Swimming is Rick's greatest strength and joy. He is able to swim, using a stylized human stroke (dog paddle) pattern, the width of a pool with minor assistance to help him regain a horizontal position after getting a breath. He has an excellent functional walk and run, and he walks up and down stairs using an alternating step pattern.

He enjoys playing, particularly swinging, on his backyard playground equipment.

APPLICATION TASK

Go to the PE Central Web site and find three physical education activities for 3rd-graders in which Rick would likely be successful. At the same Web site, identify three physical education activities in which Rick would be unsuccessful and experience a great deal of frustration.

---

and teach EVERY learner, the needs of ALL LEARNERS could be met.

Asperger Syndrome

An increasing number of children are being diagnosed with Asperger syndrome. However, it is difficult to report the incidence of Asperger syndrome because of the existing confusion between Asperger syndrome and "high-functioning autism."[38] Children with Asperger syndrome are fascinating because of their unique insights, interests, and communication skills. Their major characteristics are tied to difficulties engaging in age-appropriate social behavior. Their social delays are characterized by an inability to empathize or understand another's feelings; one-sided interaction; difficulty understanding nonverbal communication; an overwhelming fascination with one subject; repetitive speech (particularly about *the* subject of interest); and an inability to engage in cooperative play.[6,10]

Many children with Asperger syndrome also demonstrate the following: difficulty with changes in routine or structure; an unusual tone of voice; a tendency to use or repeat specific information; and a tendency to use a literal interpretation of phrases commonly used in communication, such as "Get out of here."[6,10]

These are children with excellent long-term memories and an ability to solve problems creatively, and they have typical or above average intelligence.

Children with Asperger syndrome, like children with "high-functioning" autism, may perform basic locomotor patterns with ease—such as walking, running, and climbing stairs. However, they may struggle with gross motor skills that require the learner to adjust the timing, sequence, speed, or direction of the movement.[68]

Rett Syndrome

Rett syndrome is devastating for the family and learner. A girl with Rett syndrome appears to be perfectly normal during the first 18 months of life and exhibits typical social, emotional, language, cognitive, and motor development. (See Figure 12-3.) In the girl's early preschool years, motor performance is severely compromised by ataxia and difficulty with motor planning. This causes her to fix her joints to maintain stability, reducing her ability to change positions quickly. Thus, her walking pattern appears rigid.

The regression appears to reach a plateau during the early school years. While no further loss occurs, few functional skills are acquired after this time. In adolescence and early adulthood, motor deterioration is pronounced. Typically, there is significant muscle loss, spasticity, and scoliosis. She becomes dependent on a wheelchair

This Autistic Child Became So Confident in the Water That He Now Dives off His Parents' Boat into the Lake

Photo by Carol Huettig.

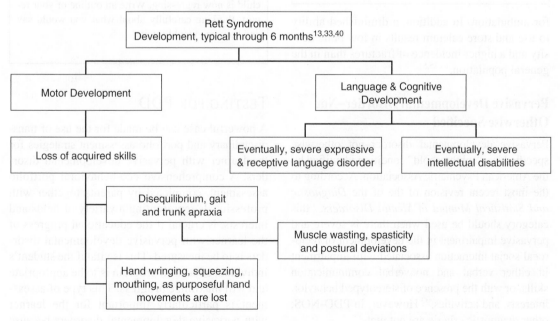

Figure 12-3 Rett Syndrome

CASE STUDY 12-2

Andrew

Andrew is a 14-year-old boy with Asperger syndrome. He has been quite successful academically in school because of his excellent memory, mathematics skills, and computer skills. However, he has had difficulty with social skills and doesn't have any friends. His father was an Eagle Scout and Andrew is seeking that, as well. He has just completed his swimming merit badge.

His functional locomotor skills are quite good. He throws well but has difficulty catching, kicking, and striking. He walks, runs, and jumps with ease. He walks 2 miles every evening with his father in about 40 minutes.

APPLICATION TASK

Describe the steps you would go through before writing a draft of an individual transition plan for Andrew to help him prepare for a community-based leisure and recreation program. What information would you need? Whom would you ask?

CASE STUDY 12-3

Ramona

Ramona is a 5-year-old girl with Rett syndrome. She has lost previously acquired gross motor skills; she no longer hops, jumps, slides, catches, or kicks. She does hurl a beanbag, however. In fact, her gross motor skills resemble those of an 18-month-old child. She has started hand wringing. She is no longer speaking in full sentences. She uses one-word utterances to communicate her needs. Though toilet-trained at age 3, she has lost bowel and bladder control and is, once again, wearing diapers. She has begun head banging and is now required to wear a helmet to prevent injury from the head banging and frequent falls. It is difficult to assess her receptive skills and understanding. However, she appears to enjoy music and likes animal crackers.

APPLICATION TASK

You are responsible for presenting information regarding Ramona's present level of gross motor competency at the IEP meeting. Try to put yourself in the parents' position. Their once apparently "typical" child is now regressing. Write an outline of your report, thinking carefully about what you would say and how you would say it.

---

for ambulation. In addition, a diminished ability to use and store calcium results in low bone density and a higher incidence of fractures than in the general population.[13,35,51]

Pervasive Developmental Disorder–Not Otherwise Specified

Pervasive developmental disorder–not otherwise specified is a "subthreshold" condition identified by the American Psychiatric Association. According to the most recent revision of the of the *Diagnostic and Statistical Manual of Mental Disorders,* "this category should be used when there is severe and pervasive impairment in the development of reciprocal social interaction associated with impairment in either verbal and nonverbal communication skills, or with the presence of stereotyped behavior, interests, and activities."[3] However, in PDD-NOS, other diagnostic criteria are not met.[3]

TESTING FOR PDD

A powerful case can be made for the use of transdisciplinary and portfolio assessment strategies for the learner with pervasive developmental disorders. A comprehensive eco-behavioral portfolio assessment, completed by parents together with professionals representing a variety of fields and interests, is crucial if the educational progress of the learner with pervasive developmental disorders is to be measured. This is vital if the student's individual education program is to be appropriate and will maximize progress. This type of assessment is particularly important for the learner with pervasive developmental disorders because most traditional assessment strategies require performance-on-request behavior that is typically impossible for learners with PDD.

Ongoing observational data regarding the learner in a variety of settings are vital to the entire process: in the home; in natural settings, such as the grocery store; in a variety of school settings, including the classroom, and particularly the playground, lunchroom, and library; in small- and large-group activities; in structured and free play; in academic/prevocational work programs; and in community-based leisure, recreation, and sport venues. The student's motor competency is a critical part of the evaluation process.[65]

Information regarding the motor performance of the learner with pervasive developmental disorders may include videotapes of the learner moving (e.g., navigating stairs, using a piece of playground equipment, swimming); photographs that represent the learner's play behavior (solitary or parallel play); narratives describing the learner's social interaction and play behaviors; and teacher and parent anecdotal records. This information may be supplemented by medical data, behavior frequency counts, behavioral checklists, developmental rating scales, and formal assessment/evaluation instruments.

The physical educator will find the checklist developed by the Dallas Society for Autistic Children (Figure 12-4) to be helpful in identifying basic characteristics of the autistic child. The formal evaluation of autism is completed by a team of trained professionals, including a psychologist, an autism specialist, and an educational diagnostician.

TEACHING STRATEGIES

The nature of pervasive developmental disorders and the significant impact of the disorders on virtually all aspects of an individual's life—cognition, socialization, communication, and physical and motor ability—make it necessary to approach teaching and intervention in specialized ways. Four primary schools of thought, philosophies, and programs exist regarding teaching and/or training individuals with autism. These include Daily Life Therapy, TEACCH, Applied Behavioral Analysis, Floortime, and others.

Daily Life Therapy

Daily Life Therapy (DLT) has a significant emphasis on physical education as an integral, if not key, component of the education of learners with autism. Dr. Robert Fantasia, executive director and principal of the Boston Higashi School, has stated that physical education is the most important part of the learner's life and the learner's education at the Boston Higashi School. The philosophy of the school is based on Dr. Kivo Kitahara's method, which provides learners with systematic education through group dynamics, the intermingling of aesthetics and academics, and physical development.[23]

At the Higashi school, students participate in rigorous physical regimes that focus on the stimulation and development of the vestibular system, including balance board tasks, tumbling and gymnastics, unicycling, and systematic instruction in calisthenics. Students participate in physical activities designed to improve vestibular function, including the balance disk, balance board, tricycling, bicycling, unicycling, roller

A Child with Autism Catches a Ride on a Dolphin
Courtesy of Island Dolphin Care, Key Largo, Fla.

Dallas Society for Autistic Children

1. Difficulty in mixing with other children.

2. Acts as deaf.

3. Resists learning.

4. No fear of real dangers.

5. Resists change in routine.

6. Indicates needs by gesture.

7. Inappropriate laughing and giggling.

8. Not cuddly.

9. Marked physical overactivity.

10. No eye contact.

11. Inappropriate attachments to objects.

12. Spins objects.

13. Sustained odd play.

14. Standoffish manner.

Author:
Prof. J. Rendle-Short
M.D., M.R.C.P., M.R.A.C.P.
University of Queensland
Brisbane Children's Hospital
Australia

Designed By Nena Williams

Figure 12-4   Behavioral Signs and Symptoms of Autism

Courtesy Dallas Independent School District.

skating, bouncing on a pogo stick, use of stilts, and skateboarding. They also participate in rigorous and very structured calisthenics to develop total body movement skills and swimming to develop coordination.[48] Dr. Fantasia states,

> The primary focus is to establish stability of emotions gained through the pursuit of independent living and the development of self-esteem. The second focus of DLT is extensive physical exercise to establish a rhythm of life. Physical Education provides benefits in the following three areas: first, vigorous physical exercise is related to the release of endorphins which are natural inhibitors of anxiety. . . . Second, children learn to gain control of their bodies and consequently of their behavior through physical education. Children learn to ride the unicycle, to roller skate, and to master the balance disk and Higashi exercises. Through play and physical education, children develop self-control and learn to cooperate and coordinate activities and exercises with other children. Dr. Kitahara viewed play for a learner, not just as something he or she does, but as life itself.[23]

Daily Life Therapy does not use medication for behavior control.

TEACCH

One of the most comprehensive systems for educating individuals with autism is the Treatment and Education of Autistic and Communication-Handicapped Children (TEACCH) program.[50] TEACCH has long been a leader in educational programs for individuals with autism. The long-term goal of the TEACCH program is for the learner with autism to fit as well as possible into society as an adult. An excerpt from the TEACCH Web page follows:

> While strongly urging and promoting "normalizing" experiences for autistic students, TEACCH has also adhered to other equally important principles. These include individualization, reliance on empirically-based

approaches rather than ideologically-based philosophies, and treatment and education that begins with and emphasizes an understanding of the problems of autism. The elaboration and operationalizing of these principles has led to a network of educational programs in North Carolina. Among the options developed, one can find highly structured, intensive specialized classrooms for autistic students, cross-categorical classrooms that serve one or more students with autism, and regular education classrooms that serve one or more learners with autism. Oftentimes, placement for learners with autism involves a combination of educational settings. Individualization, when properly carried out, leads to optimal, unique solutions for each student, based on his/her needs rather than ideology. The heterogeneity one sees in autism requires many options and possibilities, not one solution for all.[43]

One of the unique teaching strategies recommended for learners with autism is to use the individual's daily routines to facilitate learning, particularly communication skills. Most learners with autism seek and demand a consistent, predictable routine. TEACCH recommends the use of a joint activity routine, "a powerful teaching tool for learners with communication disorders. This term describes a routine in which the learner and the adult engage in a meaningful activity together and communicative behaviors are taught within the routine of the activity."[43] TEACCH professionals suggest that the following are key characteristics of joint activity routines:

- They occur in a meaningful and functional context, such as meal- or naptime routines.
- They focus on the learner's interests and strengths.
- They are social, requiring two people, and emerge at the learner's level of understanding and within the broad context of the learner's ability to play (observational, parallel, associative, cooperative, etc.).

The adult has specific responsibilities in this process. The adult is responsible for identifying the routine, for creating the learning environment, for adding visual or other sensory supports (such as pictures or objects) to encourage the routine and add meaning, and for continuing the routine. The TEACCH program has trained and used parents as co-teachers. This unique program acknowledges the dynamics of family interaction and the impact of that interaction on the professional in intervention.

Acknowledging the vital interactive process, and empowering the parents as teachers, may have a vast impact on the physical education of the learner with autism. A home-based program to supplement the school-based program may have exciting results. Armed with information about facilitating play, supporting movement attempts, and interacting in and through movement activities, the parent can become more effective.

Ozonoff and Cathcart found a home-training program for preschoolers with autism to be effective.[63] The preschoolers with autism performed significantly higher than their matched typically developing peers overall on the Psychoeducational Profile-Revised (PEP-R) and on subtests that included gross motor, fine motor, imitation, and nonverbal conceptual skills. The home-training program was effective for three primary reasons:

- Home training is cost-effective.
- Parents can and will be involved as their learner's primary advocate and liaison. Thus, parent education and empowerment is critical to effective intervention throughout the learner's lifetime.
- Parents may feel empowered, feel more competent, and exhibit less depression when participating in an effective home program.

Whitaker[83] found that the parents of preschoolers with autism needed and wanted professional support to help them encourage their child's development. The support included specific strategies for helping the parents assist their child in developing language, encourage interactive play, and provide support within the day care or child care centers their children attended.

The TEACCH program has been implemented well in programs throughout the world. It is a comprehensive, broad-based program designed with one outcome in mind—to prepare learners with autism for a life within the greater society.

Applied Behavioral Analysis

Applied Behavior Analysis (ABA) is usually labeled the Ivar Lovaas approach, even though Dr. Lovaas and his associates at UCLA are only one group of clinicians and researchers using this approach to dealing with behavior disorders in learners with autism and other disabilities.

Applied Behavioral Analysis is a style of teaching that uses a series of trials to shape a desired behavior or response. The desired responses tend to be communication-based, although other parts of the learner's development are addressed as well. It demands ongoing and precise performance evaluation. A thorough individual analysis of a learner's functioning is undertaken. The intent is to identify the skills needed for improved performance and functioning. Then, the behavior manager or educator completes a detailed task analysis to break down the skills into the simplest parts that can be learned. Discrete trial training is used in a very specific and systematic methodology to address performance and functional needs.

In discrete trial training, each skill is taught in very small and brief units called trials. Each trial consists of an instruction, a prompt, an opportunity/response, and immediate feedback. The instruction, prompt, and feedback are given in very clear language the individual learner can understand.

Specific behavioral treatment is data-based and requires daily documentation of the learner's performance. The treatment is very directive and instructionally based, and it requires at least 40 hours per week. Most parents who wish to implement an ABA program with their learner use a combination of clinical intervention and a home-based program. The nature of the ABA program, and its rigors, typically makes it difficult to implement within the public schools.[4]

Floortime

Floortime is an intervention strategy developed by Dr. Stanley Greenspan. Floortime is a time when caregivers, usually the parents, spend time being involved with the child's solitary play by following the child's lead. The intent is to create an opportunity for an emotional interaction between the child and the adult by joining in the child's preferred activity. For instance, if the child is building a tower with blocks, the adult adds some blocks. When the child gets used to the adult's participation and pauses to await the adult's turn, the adult does something different, such as knocking the tower over. This is done to try to tempt the child to communicate affectively by reacting to the adult's error. The parent routinely continues this type of shared playing while trying to draw the child into increasingly more complex interactions. The process is referred to as "opening and closing the circles of communication," and it is a forerunner to getting the child to speak and voluntarily interact with others.[2]

Other Intervention Strategies

Other teaching and intervention strategies have been espoused and supported for learners with autism. The often devastating impact of autism on the learner and the learner's family creates a situation in which the parents, in particular, are often extremely vulnerable to claims of quick fixes for a condition for which there is, at least at present, no cure.

Skill-based strategies of particular use to the physical educator include picture exchange communication systems, joint action routines, visual schedules, social stories, and video modeling.

The first picture exchange communication system, developed by Frost and Bondy[27] at the Delaware Autistic Program, was originally designed for preschoolers with autism but has been widely used with individuals with autism throughout the life span. Simply, a learner with autism is taught to exchange a picture of a desired item or experience for the actual item or experience. Like many other augmentative communication systems, this has been used successfully by teachers and clinicians alike.

The use of joint action routines was briefly described in the section describing the TEACCH program. Simply, the teacher uses established routines or events associated with daily experiences to teach needed skills.

Visual schedules help the learner with autism anticipate and predict what will occur during the regular school day or at home. It capitalizes on the visual skills of learners with autism and their need for routine. It helps them to practice a "script," which can be made in and through pictures.[60,85] Visual schedules that allow the learner with autism to work on the immediate past, present, and immediate future are the basis for the development of more complex notions regarding time. See Figure 12-5.

Like specific strategies for teaching individuals with autism, there are specific strategies for teaching learners with Asperger syndrome. Many are presented in Table 12-2.

One of the most effective strategies for teaching children with Asperger syndrome is to engage them in activities that reinforce their significant interest area to encourage and motivate them move. For example, at the elementary school level, a child with a fascination with dinosaurs could throw "dinosaur" beanbags at dinosaur targets. At the middle school level, a learner with a fascination with trains could calculate the time it would take a train to travel from one part of the country to another and compare that to the time it would take him or her to ride a stationary bicycle that distance. At the high school level, a student with a fascination with transportation could run on a treadmill while watching Grand Prix races or stationary bicycle while watching the Tour de France.

One of the best strategies for helping prepare learners with Asperger syndrome has been developed and expanded by Carol Gray of the Gray Center.[33] Social stories offer unlimited potential for giving learners with Asperger syndrome the ability to address the unique problems they often experience in a social setting. The physical education experience offers a seemingly endless challenge for learners with Asperger syndrome. In fact, the social criticism they must face in physical education programs in which the teacher allows teasing and bullying is devastating. Social stories provide a framework for improving social interaction. Social stories are brief, individual short stories that describe a social situation and provide specific behavioral cues. The stories provide a brief who, what, when, where, and why of a social situation. The stories help ensure a child's

A visual schedule can help the learner with autism and Asperger syndrome predict the routine. The class routine is warm-up exercises, participation in a fitness station, aerobic dance, and relaxation to music.

Figure 12-5   Visual Schedule

Table 12-2	Specific Strategies for Teaching Learners with Asperger Syndrome

Insistence on Sameness
- Provide a predictable environment.
- Maintain a consistent routine and minimize transitions.

Impairment in Social Interaction
- Place the learner in situations in which his or her reading, vocabulary, and memory skills can be viewed as an asset by peers.
- Create a bully-free learning environment for the sake of all.
- Older students with Asperger syndrome may be paired well with a sensitive buddy to help the student learn appropriate social skills and to reduce their tendency to be reclusive.

Limited Range of Interests
- If possible, designate a time during the day in which the learner can discuss his or her preoccupation or interest.
- Initially individualize learning opportunities and experiences to build on the specific interest of the learner.

Poor Concentration
- Use frequent teacher interaction, feedback, and redirection.
- Time work sessions; start with short and build to longer sessions.
- Establish a signal to alert the student to "refocus."

Poor Motor Coordination
- Involve the learner in a health-fitness curriculum, rather than a competitive sports program.

Academic Difficulties
- Provide an individualized program to ensure consistent success.
- Capitalize on the learner's typically excellent memory skills.
- Use activity-based learning, which should be at the core of all physical education experiences, whenever possible.
- Use graphics, pictures, and/or demonstrations.

Emotional Vulnerability
- Help the learner develop a three-step routine to cope with stress.
- Especially when working with adolescents with Asperger syndrome, be very sensitive to the student's depression.
- A learner who is included, in particular, must have an identified staff member to provide emotional support.

Difficulties with Language
- Teach specific skills regarding turn taking.
- Teach specific skills for seeking assistance.
- Pause after instruction and probe, with questions, to determine if the student has understood the information or directions.

Sensory Sensitivities
- Minimize background noise and fluorescent lighting.
- Watch carefully for signs that the student is becoming overwhelmed by stimuli—self-abusive behaviors, crying, flushing, or hyperventilation.

Modified from Williams, www.sasked.gov.sk.ca/curr_inst/speced/asper.html. 2003.

understanding of social information for various settings and provide instruction for initiating, responding to, and maintaining appropriate social interactions.[73] Gray describes the social story as "a *process* that results in a *product* for a person with an autistic spectrum disorder (ASD). First, as a process, a Social Story requires consideration of—and respect for—the perspective of the person with ASD. As a product, a Social Story is a short story—defined by specific characteristics— that describes a situation, concept, or social skill using a format that is meaningful for people with ASD. The result is often renewed sensitivity of others to the experience of the person with ASD, and an improvement in the response of the person with ASD."[33]

Following is a sample social story for a child with Asperger syndrome who will be attending his first day of kindergarten physical education.

My name is ____. I am going to PE for the first time today. It is OK that I am a little scared. There will be a lot of children. There will be a lot of noise.

The teacher's name is Miss Chavez. She has colored circles on the floor where we will sit when we get to the gym. I am going to be able to sit by my buddy ____. That will be good because I like ____.

Miss Chavez starts class with music. That's good because I like to move to music. Then we will run around the gym. That's cool because I am a good runner. Then we will play a game. I can watch my buddy ____ so I know what I should do.

When we finish our game we all sit down on our circles again. Then, we line up to leave to go back to class.

I'll say good-bye to Miss Chavez when I leave the gym.

Following is a sample social story for an adolescent struggling with peers' teasing in the gymnasium.

Today when I go to the gymnasium, I'll remember it is OK for me to be angry if kids in the gym tease me. But, if I get angry, I'll use the "STOP, THINK, DO" strategy before I do

anything. If I can, I'll turn around and walk away.

I'll stay with my friend ____. We'll go to the stationary cycling fitness station where we can ride side by side.

Today, I'll ride 5 miles in 35 minutes. Then, I only have 405 more miles to get to Juneau, Alaska.

Participation in social stories, carefully prepared by teachers, will help learners with Asperger syndrome address their desired outcomes and prepare them to make good choices. This is critical in the development of a high quality of life.[25,71] It is also critical that the physical educator understand that students with Asperger syndrome are not willfully disobedient. Groft and Block suggest that "children with AS [Asperger syndrome] have no more ability to control their behaviors and preoccupations than children with cerebral palsy have the ability to control their muscles."[34]

In video modeling, children watch a videotape of a model engaging in a target behavior; subsequently, the children implement it. Children with autism find watching themselves on videotape highly motivating.[56] Video modeling provides an interesting opportunity for teaching learners with autism age-appropriate social interaction and play behaviors.[61] Video modeling gives learners with autism the opportunity to prepare, so that their behaviors are more appropriate in a social setting. This is not unlike an adult asking another, "What are you going to wear?" This information helps the individual prepare for a situation and to feel more at ease.

In the early stages of the onset of Rett syndrome, many of the teaching strategies outlined for learners with autism may prove very useful in teaching. Effective teaching strategies for individuals with advanced Rett syndrome probably more closely resemble those that are effective when intervening with learners who are severely intellectually disabled (See Chapter 11 for more specific suggestions.)

Teaching strategies for individuals with PDD-NOS are typically the same as those used successfully with students with autism.

STRATEGIES FOR MAXIMIZING INSTRUCTIONAL OPPORTUNITY WITHIN AN INCLUSIVE ENVIRONMENT (IF APPROPRIATE)

Teaching strategies for learners who fall under the broad umbrella of pervasive developmental disorders in the general physical education program are, essentially, consistent with good teaching. In this section, teaching strategies found effective for individuals with pervasive developmental disorders will be considered for the general physical education class and/or a more separate learning environment, if required, to ensure success. Table 12-3 shows teaching strategies for learners with PDD in physical education.

One of the most important intervention strategies for learners within the PDD spectrum is timely, appropriate, and significant reward of appropriate behavior.[20] The general physical education class, in particular, can be very frightening for learners with PDD; a positive behavior reinforcement program is critical.

As is true for all individuals, a quality physical education experience is a critical component of the lives of individuals with pervasive developmental disorders. An individually designed, comprehensive physical education program that addresses both the deficits and the strengths identified in a comprehensive assessment is critical to the health, wellness, and long-term ability of the individual to enjoy a life full of quality leisure, recreation, fitness, and sport experiences.

At the crux of a quality physical education program for individuals with PDD is a comprehensive assessment. As mentioned earlier in this chapter, a portfolio assessment appears to be the most viable strategy for gaining valid and appropriate information. However, some adapted physical educators have used the Test of Gross Motor Development effectively with learners with "high-functioning" autism.[11]

Based on the information gained in and through the portfolio assessment process, the individual education program must be developed to meet the unique needs of the learner, as mandated by federal law. Only then should consideration be given to the appropriate placement in which the IEP goals and objectives can be met.

As discussed in Chapter 1, the Reauthorization of IDEA, 1999, and recent litigation support the intent of Congress to allow individuals with disabilities to participate, whenever possible, within the general program, using the general curriculum. The decision about the physical education placement of the learner with PDD remains, however, one that must be made by the multidisciplinary individual education program team or committee.

The general physical education program may be very restrictive for learners on the PDD continuum. Decisions about placement must be made carefully and include choices of curriculum, assessment, program participation, support personnel, equipment, grading, teaching style, behavior management, and gymnasium environment.

The types of activities included in the physical education program for the learner with PDD depend on the severity of the disorder and the age of the learner (see Table 12-4). However, *daily* vigorous aerobic exercise is critical because it reduces self-stimulatory and off-task behavior, increases time on academic and vocational tasks, and, as important, improves gross motor performance.[22,29,32,47,52] Physical education programs for individuals with pervasive developmental disorders, at all levels of development, should include exercise that promotes the development of cardiovascular-respiratory endurance.

Infants', Toddlers', and Preschoolers' Motor Development/Physical Education

Infants and toddlers with pervasive developmental disorders need to be exposed to a wide variety of activities designed to enhance and develop equilibrium, to stimulate sensory-motor systems, and to develop basic locomotor and nonlocomotor skills *to prepare the child for an active lifestyle.*[63] Preschoolers should be given the opportunity to continue to develop equilibrium, perceptual-motor ability, sensory-motor function (including the development of body image and motor planning),

Table 12-3	General Teaching Strategies for Physical Education to Maximize Opportunities for Inclusion

Adopt a "gentle teaching" philosophy.
- Ensure that the learner has every possible opportunity to succeed in the physical education learning environment. Start slowly, with simple skills, and build on them gradually.

Establish and maintain a consistent class routine.
- Each learner should have a separate and carefully marked "home base." The learner with PDD may be most comfortable if the home base is on the periphery of the gymnasium or other learning environment, rather than in the center.
- The physical educator should ensure that each class has the same routine.
- If warm-ups are to be done to music, the physical education teacher should use the same songs over and over; a new song may be introduced after others have been mastered.
- If a given motor skill is to be practiced, the same class organization and equipment should be used. If the class is working on catching, for example, the teacher should use the same size and color ball.
- When using terms to describe a given activity or motion, the teacher should use the same term every time. For example, if each learner is assigned a plastic dot to serve as his or her home base, the teacher should refer to the plastic dot by calling it "dot" and not "circle."

Use joint activity routines.
- Use natural, teachable moments to help the learner acquire skills. For example, when the student enters or exits the gymnasium, he or she should be expected to greet the teacher, verbally or using a gesture.

Use a visual schedule.
- Place a horizontal visual schedule in a central place on the gymnasium wall to allow the learner with PDD to predict the next event.

Use picture exchanges.
- If the learner with PDD has difficulty understanding the simple visual symbol schedule, the physical educator can use a picture exchange system to help the student more effectively predict the sequence of events. The individual learner with PDD may have his or her own visual schedule, with each component on an individual card. As each event is about to begin, the learner pulls the card from his or her schedule and puts it in a pile, face down, until the entire class is completed.

Provide opportunities for social interaction.
- Carefully trained and sensitive peer buddies may encourage appropriate social interaction.
- Create and maintain a bully-free learning environment.

Allow choice making to encourage participation.
- Give the learner two options from which he or she can choose. This is enabling and gives the learner some critical control over his or her environment. For example, while holding each ball in his or her hands, the teacher asks, "Ricardo, would you like to throw the red or the yellow ball?" and waits for the learner to grasp one ball, or "Dominique, do you want to start at the `push-up' station or the `sit-up' station?"

Spend quality floortime with the learner.
- Get down on the floor with young learners with PDD to interact at their eye level.
- Ensure that the activities are developmentally appropriate. A learner with PDD is much more likely to be successful, for example, in a 1st-grade general physical education class if the teacher is concentrating on the foundations of locomotor and nonlocomotor patterns, object-control skills, and basic rhythmic activities than if the teacher is inappropriately focusing on team sports.

(Continued)

Table 12-3	*(Continued)*

Address the interests of the learner with PDD.

• Part of the lesson should focus specifically on the strengths of the individuals with PDD. If the elementary school learner with PDD has a particular interest in animals, for example, the student should be given the opportunity to describe an animal before members of the class act like the animal. If the high school learner with Asperger syndrome, for example, has a particular interest in aerodynamics, the learner with PDD should have an opportunity to explain the principles of aerodynamics before his or her classmates throw a Frisbee.

Acknowledge and honor the learner's difficulty attending to task.

• Provide frequent feedback.
• Use simple redirection strategies to return the learner's attention to task. For example, the physical educator could remind the student, "John, which station is next on your list?" or "Lisa, how many push-ups have you already done?"

Be consistent with behavior management systems.

• Adopt the behavior management system used by the learner's classroom teacher and the learner's parents.
• Develop a behavior contract for learners with Asperger syndrome and "high-functioning" autism. This also needs to be consistent with that used in other parts of the curriculum.
• Redirect inappropriate behaviors. Since the learner with PDD often does not understand cause-effect relationships, it is ineffective to scold the learner for misbehavior or to say, "No." It is much more effective to redirect existing behavior. For example, if the learner is kicking furniture, replace the furniture with a ball.
• Simplify the task if the learner is misbehaving while attempting a task. Often, a learner with PDD "acts out" as a result of frustration. Simplifying the task at hand may allow the learner to succeed at the task while reducing inappropriate behaviors.
• If the learner is acting out or is out of control, moving the learner to a less stimulating area may allow the learner to regain control of his or her behavior. An ideal place in the gymnasium is a beanbag chair or soft chair just inside the teacher's office.

and locomotor and nonlocomotor skills. The preschooler must also have the opportunity to develop object-control skills, basic movement patterns, and play skills. Play skills can be taught by direct teaching of isolated skills, through script training, and by peer tutors.[79] Teaching isolated play skills, such as catching a ball, "preteaches" a child with autism to be ready for play with another child. Script training gives the child with autism a chance to practice a play experience in and through a well-designed "play acting" experience, using photographs, pictures, or illustrations.[79] Peer tutoring is a well-accepted practice for encouraging play in all children with disabilities. Peer tutoring is most effective if the play is based on the preferences of the child with autism and it occurs in natural, well-designed play settings. It is critical that the peer-motivated play experience be designed to focus on the strengths of the child with autism.

The preschooler must have the opportunity, daily, to participate in developmentally appropriate active play—walking, running, tricycling, climbing on playground equipment, or swimming.[41]

Kindergarten through Third-Grade Physical Education

The physical education program for young learners with pervasive developmental disorders, kindergarten through 3rd grade, should emphasize cardiovascular-respiratory endurance activities, whole body movement, dance and rhythm activities, activities to foster primary body part identification, and the development of onlooker, solitary, and parallel play skills.

Table 12-4   **Physical Education Activities That Allow Age-Appropriate Inclusion for Learners with Pervasive Developmental Disorders**

Individuals with PDD	Physical and Motor Fitness	Fundamental Motor Skills and Patterns	Aquatics	Dance	Individual and Group Games	Intramurals
K–3rd	"Animal Actions" "Chug Along Choo Choo" "Bend, Twist, Shake" "Warm-Up Time" Circuit training	Locomotor Nonlocomotor Object control	Water orientation Water games Safety skills	"What a Miracle" "Sally . . . Swinging Snake" "Hokey Pokey" Locomotion to music	Parachute	NA
4th–6th	Jogging Stationary cycling Stationary rowing Circuit training	Locomotor Nonlocomotor Object control	Stroke development Entry and exit skills Safety skills	Basic line dance Circle dance	Parachute	New Games
7th–9th	Jogging Stationary cycling Stationary rowing Circuit training Inline skating	Object control	Stroke development Entry and exit skills Safety skills	Basic line dance Circle dance	Bocci Horseshoes Bowling Croquet Lead-up games	Cross-country running Cross-country skiing Swimming
10th–12th	Jogging Stationary cycling Stationary rowing Circuit training Inline skating Aerobic dance	Prevocational skills Vocational skills	Swimming for fitness AquaRobics	Basic line dance Aerobic dance	Bocci Horseshoes Bowling Inline skating Croquet Golf	Cross-country running Cross-country skiing Swimming
Adult	Walking Stationary cycling Stationary rowing Aerobic dance	Prevocational skills Vocational skills	Swimming for fitness AquaRobics	Basic line dance Aerobic dance	Bocci Horseshoes Bowling Inline skating Croquet Golf	NA

The Council on Physical Education for Children of the National Association for Sport and Physical Education, a division of the American Alliance of Health, Physical Education, Recreation and Dance, recommends that elementary-school-age children accumulate at least 30–60 minutes of age- and developmentally appropriate physical activity from a variety of physical activities on all, or most, days of the week. The council suggests that extended periods of inactivity are inappropriate for young children.[16] Developmentally appropriate cardiovascular-respiratory endurance activities should be the basis of the program. The program should allow the child the opportunity to walk, run, swim, tricycle/bicycle, climb on playground equipment, and dance.

The development of equilibrium responses is a fundamental component of the physical education program of young learners.[42] As is true in Daily Life Therapy, the emphasis should be on broad and varied activities that stimulate the vestibular system. These equilibrium activities include the following:

Scooter board activities. Depending on the learner's level of development, the learner should assume a supine, prone, sitting, or kneeling position on a scooter board. Initially, the activity will be teacher-initiated and teacher-controlled. Gradually, the teacher should fade out involvement, so that the scooter-spinning activity is learner-initiated and learner-controlled.

Crazy sidewalk. Place a mat, or series of mats, over the top of other, pliable objects, such as beanbag chairs, throw pillows, and rolled up mats. Then, depending on the learner's developmental level, ask the learner to crawl, creep, walk, or run over the top of the shifting surface.

Magic carpet ride. Have the learner assume a supine lying, prone lying, sitting, all-fours, or kneeling position on a mat or blanket. The teacher and other children, together, hold the edge of the mat or blanket and pull the learner around the room.

Whole body movement that stimulates the vestibular and kinesthetic systems is also a curricular

priority for the young learner with autism and Asperger syndrome. This includes "wrap-em-ups" (roll the learner in a sheet or blanket, grasp the edge, and lift, rolling the learner out of the sheet/blanket), log rolls, egg rolls, shoulder rolls, and forward/backward rolls.

In addition, simple songs and dances can be used to encourage the development of primary body part identification skills and rhythmic responses, as well as to provide an ideal opportunity for the learner to be engaged in parallel play with peers. The rhythmic experiences are particularly critical for the learner with Rett syndrome.[13] Songs and dances for young learners with PDD should have the following characteristics: (1) simple, clear, and often repeated directions; (2) repetitive phrasing; (3) an even beat; (4) a dominant rhythm instrument; and (5) nonintrusive "background" accompaniment. Hap Palmer and Greg and Steve songs and dances are particularly effective.

Young children with PDD are usually very fond of parachute play. Parachutes, particularly those with handles, help the learners function with a secure base for activity. Some children with autism, for example, prefer to use the parachute in ways perceived to be atypical, such as covering the self with the parachute.

A crucial focus of the physical education program for young learners with autism or Asperger syndrome is the development of age-appropriate playground skills. The adapted physical educator, working with the general physical educator, the classroom teacher, and the learner's parents need to develop a systematic plan for developing skills necessary for successful participation in playground activities. A learner with PDD who is able to "pump" a swing and swing independently has a wonderful opportunity to participate in parallel play with other learners who are swinging. Learners with PDD playground skills may need to be task-analyzed for skills that many learners take for granted. The physical educator may need to break down the process of approaching and climbing the stairs and then sitting and sliding down a slide into several, discrete components, for example.

Technology provides wonderful interactive toy experiences for more severely disabled young children, such as those with Rett syndrome. Specifically, there are toys that combine bright colors and sounds and allow children to experience cause-effect relationships as they use adaptive switches on computers. In addition to providing interactive toys, the physical educator will need to focus on the basic skills required for ambulation and functional movement for learners with severe delays/regressions typical of those with Rett syndrome.

If available, a carefully designed, developmental aquatics program can be of considerable value in the physical education program for children with autism,[23,39,40] Asperger syndrome,[6] and Rett syndrome.[40]

Fourth- through Sixth-Grade Physical Education

The physical education curriculum for learners with pervasive developmental disorders in the 4th through 6th grades must continue to emphasize cardiovascular-respiratory endurance activities. These activities include aerobic walking, stationary cycling, aerobic dance, jogging/walking, and stationary rowing.

The development of "functional" locomotor skills is a vital part of the physical education curriculum for learners in these grades. The learner should be given the opportunity to develop "ownership" of basic locomotor skills such as walking, running, and jumping in the following situations:

1. Ask the learner to move over different surfaces:
   a. Sidewalk–grass–sidewalk
   b. Grass–sand–grass
   c. Dry sidewalk–icy sidewalk–dry sidewalk
2. Ask the learner to move over, around, and through objects/obstacles:
   a. Step in and out of holes.
   b. Walk around and jump over puddles.
   c. Step over an object or a series of objects.
   d. Walk up and down inclines.
   e. Walk up and down stairs, varying the number, height, and surface of the stairs.
   f. Walk through a revolving door.
3. Ask the learner to move, carrying an object or objects: groceries, umbrella, backpack, or ball tucked under the arm.
4. Ask the learner to push or pull an object: a wagon or wheelchair.

More sophisticated equilibrium activities, which continue to stimulate the vestibular and proprioceptive systems, are also an important part of this program. These include self-testing balance activities. The learner moves, for example, on a tapered balance beam. Or the learner steps from one stone to another as the stones get smaller. Or the learner performs a series of increasingly complex tasks on a balance beam: walking and stepping over an object on the beam; walking and stopping to pick up an object on the beam; sliding in both directions; galloping on the beam; and performing such stationary balances on the beam as stork stands and airplane balances. Bouncing activities are also emphasized. Using a mini-trampoline, an air mattress, or a gym mat placed on top of a tire, help the learner "bounce" while sitting, kneeling, or standing.

Rhythm activities and low-organization games are important to learners with PDD in this age range. Rhythm activities are critical to the development of an even and purposeful gait. Performing locomotor or nonlocomotor skills to the beat of a drum and starting and stopping to the music in songs such as the "Freeze" or cooperative "Musical Chairs" are particularly helpful.

Games with simple rules may be used particularly well to teach skills such as taking turns and sharing equipment. The development of these skills is crucial to individuals under the broad umbrella of PDD. A more sophisticated use of playground equipment is also critical and must be a part of the physical education curriculum if the young learner with PDD is to have the opportunity to share recess and playground time with other learners.

The development of more sophisticated object-control skills is also critical. Typically, the young learner with PDD will be more effective at closed propulsion skills—that is, skills in which the learner propels a stationary object. Giving the learner the opportunity to throw and kick using a variety of balls with different textures, sizes, and shapes is the key to developing truly effective skills.

The key to effective intervention with children with autism, Asperger syndrome, Rett syndrome, and PDD-NOS is emphasizing individual activities they can enjoy throughout the life span. Children with Asperger syndrome should be encouraged to participate in activities with partners or very small groups, but the activities must remain cooperative, not competitive.

Middle and Junior High School Physical Education

Learners with PDD in the middle and junior high school programs should have the opportunity to develop basic leisure, recreation, sport, and fitness skills. The learner with PDD is usually more successful in closed, individual activities. For example, the middle or junior high school learner with PDD may be very successful in activities such as bicycling, bowling, darts, Frisbee golf, croquet, horseshoes, swimming, and walking/jogging/running on a treadmill or track. Relaxation training is also a significant component of the physical education curriculum.

This is often a critical and difficult time for learners with PDD. Children who are particularly sensitive to others but who struggle with their social behaviors, such as those with Asperger syndrome, may find themselves teased and secluded from others. Difficulty dealing with their social-emotional issues makes it even more important for learners this age to participate in vigorous aerobic activities at least an hour per day. The vigorous activity allows the learners to better control impulses and other behavior. Learners with autism and Asperger syndrome tend to have the most success in walking, jogging, running, stationary cycling, stationary rowing, basic aerobic dancing, swimming, and inline skating.

The major problem for the child with Asperger syndrome in the middle school/junior high school physical education program is difficulty dealing with the complex social expectations and experiences of adolescents. Physical educators can use some basic tools to help the learner with Asperger syndrome monitor and control his or her behavior. These include simple strategies such as "traffic light" cards—to subtly cue the learner that a behavior is appropriate or that the learner should proceed with caution or stop the behavior. A second is the use of "break tickets," so that the learner can leave the gymnasium or immediate playground area to take a break and regroup.[14]

A young woman with Rett syndrome, at this point in time, will enjoy some freedom in aquatics activities and wheelchair-based, sitting aerobic dance activities.

High School Physical Education

In high school the primary curricular emphasis should continue to be on cardiovascular-respiratory endurance. In addition, there is an emphasis on the development of leisure and recreation skills. These include bowling, fishing, horseshoes, golf, bocci, horseback riding, roller skating or inline skating, skateboarding, and basket shooting.

High school students should be preparing for the important transition from school-based programming to community-based experiences. In addition to the leisure, recreation, sport, and fitness skills discussed earlier, the learner should have the opportunity to develop skills required for prevocational programs and, eventually, employment. The adapted or general physical educator must work closely with the learner's parents and vocational education coordinator to ensure that the learner has the necessary motor skills to do a job. Specific job tasks need to be identified and a task analysis done to determine which motor skills need to be taught. For example, if the learner is preparing for work at a nursery or garden, the prerequisite skills include raking leaves, digging with a shovel, moving a wheelbarrow, and picking up and carrying large bags of peat moss. If the individual is planning on a life as a university professor, other skills are critical, such as climbing stairs carrying a briefcase and maintaining an erect posture while working at the computer.

Decisions regarding the transition curriculum in physical education should be based on the learner's need to function within the community, the accessibility of programs and facilities, family and extended family members' interests, and community interests. For example, it is unfair to foster a love of horseback riding in a learner from a poor family if the learner's only access to a horse involves expensive rental. It would seem much more humane to help the learner develop the skills needed to participate in activities with other learners in the neighborhood, such as bocci, inline skating, and skateboarding. If no one in the learner's family likes to bowl, it is ridiculous to teach bowling unless family members are willing to make a commitment to transporting the learner to a community-based bowling program.

An important part of preparation for the transition from school-based programming to community-based experiences is the development of self-determination. Field and Hoffman defined self-determination as follows:

> Self-determination is a combination of skills, knowledge, and beliefs that enable a person to engage in goal-directed, self-regulated, autonomous behavior. An understanding of one's strengths and limitations together with a belief in oneself as capable and effective are essential to self-determination. When acting on the basis of these skills and attitudes, individuals have greater ability to take control of their lives and assume the role of successful adults in our society.[24]

Parents and physical educators, general and adapted, play a critical role in helping learners with PDD develop self-determination.[25,26] One of the strategies used to begin the process of planning a future is the development of a "life map," using words and pictures to depict one's present life and what one wants life to look like in five years, for example. Fullerton and Coyne[28] suggest that the intention of the life map is to serve as a self-created visual organizer that helps students see how the parts of their lives fit together and to communicate their views of their lives to others.

Aquatics

Aquatics may be one of the best venues for teaching physical education to individuals with pervasive developmental disorders. Attwood wrote, "It is interesting that the ability to swim appears least affected, and this activity can be encouraged to enable the child to experience genuine competence and admiration for proficiency with movement."[6] According to Kitahara,

> Swimming is an exercise that exercises the whole body and is one of the physical exercises most suited to diffusing bodily energies. It is a particularly good exercise for autistic children because it especially requires coordination of hand and leg movements. Swimming has been generally accepted as being effective with autism. Murashina Higashi Gakuen has a heated pool and a special physical education instructor gives special guidance in swimming all through the year to autistic children.[48]

See Tables 12-5 and 12-6 for more information about aquatics for learners with pervasive developmental disorders.

Modifications/Adaptations/Inclusion Techniques

High-functioning learners with pervasive developmental disorders are capable of successful placement within the general physical education setting if the general physical education teacher is well organized, teaches developmentally appropriate activities, uses age-appropriate behavior management strategies, focuses on cooperative rather than competitive activities, and uses the teaching strategies outlined earlier in the chapter. Certainly, the learner with PDD who is not a behavior problem in the classroom is most likely to

Table 12-5	Teaching Strategies for Learners with PDD in the Aquatic Environment

- To meet the unique needs of a swimmer with PDD in an aquatic environment, very small teacher–student ratios are required; typically, a one-to-one ratio is necessary.
- Be aware of the swimmer's response to the change of sensory stimuli in the aquatic setting. The environment may heighten sensory overload because of the number of swimmers, toys, and objects in the pool setting. The environment may change sensory stimulation and perception as the swimmer is exposed to a different medium, different temperatures, waves, light reflection on the water, and different pressure sensations. If the swimmer moves while under the surface of the water, the stimulation may actually be reduced and be more manageable—noise may be muted, kinesthetic and proprioceptive sensations are negated because of constant hydrostatic pressure, and visual images may be blurred.
- During the swimming instruction period, a visual schedule will help the swimmer move, for example, from a warm-up activity to stroke work or from kicking drills to a water game. A similar plan needs to be in place to ensure a transition to the activity in which the student will engage after swimming. For example, the swimmer may have a symbol card that shows a person taking a shower, then dressing, then leaving the pool.
- Typically, the best strategy for intervention includes the following:
  Use the swimmer's name.
  Pair the demonstration with a one-word or two-word cue.
  Always pair the same demonstration with the same cue.
- The swimmer should have a "home base" in every setting, a place designated specifically for him or her. For example, in the pool, the swimmer should have a spot on the side to which he or she returns after a given activity.
- The teacher should use equipment of the same type, color, and texture to work on the same skills. For example, if the swimmer with autism started working on the flutter kick using a yellow, nubby-textured, frog kickboard, then the teacher should always use the yellow, nubby-textured, frog kickboard when working on the flutter kick.
- If at all possible, the aquatics instructor should use the behavior management plan being used by the child's classroom teacher or that used in the home (they should be the same).
- Swimmers with PDD often choose to swim, almost dolphinlike, primarily under water because it reduces and mutes sensory stimuli. The instructor can best facilitate acquisition of swimming skill by spotting to ensure the swimmer learns to get breaths regularly, instead of waiting until he or she is out of breath; this facilitates aerobic activity. This can best be accomplished by observing the student and noting when paddling movements begin to be randomized and less effective. Then, the teacher can help by pushing the swimmer toward the surface; this is easier if the teacher is also swimming under water.

be successful because the teacher will be more receptive and, by example, will help other children be receptive.[69] For many learners with PDD, however, the general physical education class is restrictive because the nature of the physical education experience often includes large numbers of learners moving, with a great deal of noise and poor acoustics, in a relatively unstructured environment.

Many variables need to be considered before deciding to place a learner with PDD in the regular physical education setting. Table 12-7 describes the general physical education class that may be appropriate for a learner with mild PDD.

More severely involved learners with PDD need to receive physical education instruction within a small-group, self-contained setting. In order to give the learner with more severe pervasive disorders the opportunity to interact with typically developing peers, other learners may be included in the small-group physical education experience. These learners, however, need to be aware of the nature and needs of the learner with PDD. The role of peers and other support personnel is discussed in detail in Chapter 6.

Table 12-6	Reducing Inappropriate Behavior in Aquatics for Learners with PDD

1. Redirect the swimmer. If the swimmer is spitting, lower the swimmer's face close to the water to allow him or her to blow bubbles. If the swimmer is kicking at the teacher, put him or her in a prone or supine position to allow him or her to kick at the surface of the water.
2. Simplify the task. If the swimmer experiences frustration, he or she may act inappropriately. Make the task simpler. For example, if the swimmer is having difficulty pulling his or her arms contralaterally, demonstrate the most basic pull—a homologous pull (both arms move together).
3. Reduce the stimulation. If the swimmer is having difficulty dealing with the stimuli in the aquatic environment, the teacher might move the swimmer to a smaller pool, a corner of the deck to do land drills, and so on.

THE ADULT WITH PDD

Like other adults, adults with PDD require consistent, moderate daily activity to maintain health and fitness. Their need for vigorous activity, such as fitness walking, jogging, swimming, stationary cycling, stair stepping, or inline skating, may continue to be tied to their need for exercise to help them monitor and control behavior and impulses. Reid and O'Connor suggest, "Content for instruction should be based on the interests, needs, and supports of the individual, rather than a label of ASD (Autism

Table 12-7	Characteristics of a Regular Physical Education Setting Appropriate for Children Who Are Mildly Autistic

Class Dynamics
The teacher–student ratio must be less than 1:20.
The class must be highly structured.
The class routine must be consistent.

Instructional Staff
The physical education teacher must be willing to create an environment that will facilitate learning for learners with and without autism.
A physical education aide or special education aide must be present.
The physical education staff must be willing to work closely with special education personnel to learn strategies for managing the instructional environment.

Instructional Program
The focus of the instructional program must be individual skills rather than group games and team sports.

Gymnasium and/or Playground
The gymnasium must be relatively free of distractions—fans, standing equipment, and so.
The playground must be surrounded by a fence.

Spectrum Disorder). The goal is not therapy, but enhancing the ability and desire to engage in independently-selected physical activity."[66] Certainly, that is what all adults seek—the ability to choose and engage in leisure, recreation, fitness, and sport activities of interest.   ✍

SUMMARY

Pervasive developmental disorders is the large umbrella under which fall autism, Asperger syndrome, Rett syndrome, and PDD-NOS. Characteristics common to all forms of PDD are communication difficulties, abnormal behaviors, and poor social skills. Physical education programs require set routines and careful transitions between each part of the instructional day. The key component in a quality physical education program for learners with autism, Asperger syndrome, and PDD-NOS is daily, vigorous aerobic activity. The key component in a quality physical education program for learners with Rett syndrome is movement to music.

REVIEW QUESTIONS

1. Name and briefly explain the four major types of pervasive developmental disorders.
2. Briefly describe the primary emphasis on cardiovascular-respiratory/aerobic activity with individuals with PDD.
3. Give some examples of equilibrium activities that could be included in a physical education program for learners with PDD in elementary school.
4. Explain some strategies the general physical education teacher could use to help learners with PDD experience success in the program.
5. Compare and contrast Daily Life Therapy, TEACCH, and Applied Behavior Analysis as

the primary methodologies used with individuals with PDD.
6. Describe the physical education curriculum for learners from infancy through high school. Describe the desired outcomes of a quality physical education program. What skills and competencies should a high school graduate with PDD possess?
7. Explain teaching strategies that have been demonstrated to be effective with learners with autism and Asperger syndromes and explain how those strategies might be adapted in the physical education program.

STUDENT ACTIVITIES

1. Arrange to observe a physical education class in the public schools that serves a learner with PDD. Describe the learner's behavior.
2. Interview a parent of a learner with PDD. Ask the parent to describe the impact of the diagnosis on the family.
3. Complete a Web search to identify sources of information about PDD.

4. Read a remarkable and easy-to-read book: Attwood T: *Asperger syndrome: A guide for parents and professionals.* Philadelphia, Jessica Kingsley, 1998.
5. Refer to the Project INSPIRE Web site at www.twu.edu/INSPIRE and review Web materials regarding autism, Asperger syndrome, and Rett syndrome.

REFERENCES

1. Akbarian S: The neurobiology of Rett syndrome, *The Neuroscientist* 9(1):57–63, 2003.
2. *Alternatives to behaviorism,* www.autcom.org/articles/Behaviorism.html. 2003.
3. American Psychiatric Association: *DSM-IV-TR diagnostic and statistical manual of mental disorders* (text revision). Washington, DC, 2000.
4. Applied Behavior Analysis, http://home.vicnet.net.qu/~abia/McEachin2.htm60. 2003.
5. Armstrong DD: Rett syndrome: The challenge of the pathology, *Primary Psychiatry* 10(2):63–66, 2003.
6. Attwood T: *Asperger syndrome: A guide for parents and professionals.* Philadelphia, Jessica Kingsley, 1998.
7. Autism Society of America: *Asperger syndrome information package.* Bethesda, MD, 1995.

8. Bailey A, et al.: A clinicopathological study of autism, *Brain* 121:889–905, 1998.
9. Bailey A, et al.: Autism: The phenotype in relatives, *J Autism Dev Disord* 28(5):369–392, 1998.
10. Bashe PR, Kirby B: *The oasis guide to Asperger syndrome.* New York, Crown, 2001.
11. Berkeley S, Zittel L, Pitney L, Nichols S: Locomotor and object control skills of children diagnosed with autism, *APAQ* 18(4):405–416, 2001.
12. Blair RJ: Psychophysiological responsiveness to the distress of others in children with autism, *Personality Ind Diff* 26:477–485, 1999.
13. Braddock S, et al.: Rett syndrome: An update and review for the primary pediatrician, *Clin Pediatrics* October:613–626, 1993.

14. Broderick C, Caswell R, Gregory S, Marzolini S, Wilson O: "Can I join the club?" A social integration scheme for adolescents with Asperger syndrome, *Autism* 6(4):427–431, 2002.

15. Cheng EM: Asperger syndrome and autism: A literature review and meta-analysis, *Focus Autism Other Dev Dis* 13:234–245, 1998.

16. Corbin CB, Pangrazi RP: *Guidelines for appropriate physical activity for elementary school children: A position statement for the Council for Physical Education for Children (COPEC),* Reston, VA, AAHPERD,1998.

17. Culture of Autism: *From theoretical understanding to educational practice,* www.mplc.co.uk/ eduweb/sites/autism/culture.html#cult. 2003.

18. Dallas Independent School District Autism Task Force: *Autism prescreening checklist, 1988.* Adapted with permission of Randal-Short, University of Queensland, Brisbane Children's Hospital, Australia.

19. Dawson G, et al.: Children with autism fail to orient to naturally occurring social stimuli, *J Autism Dev Disord* 28:479–485, 1998.

20. Dorta N: Making the grade: A new classroom for children with Asperger's and other pervasive development disorders, *The Except Parent* 33(3):44–47, 2003.

21. Edelson SB, Cantor DS: Autism: Xenobiotic influences, *J Advance Med* 12(1):35–46, 1999.

22. Elliott R, et al.: Vigorous, aerobic exercise versus general motor training activities: Effects on maladaptive and stereotypic behaviors of adults with both autism and mental retardation, *J Autism Dev Disord* 24:565–575, 1994.

23. Fantasia RA, Executive Director and Principal, Boston Higashi School: Presentation at the 27th Annual California Activity Conference, Santa Rosa, CA, October 1998.

24. Field S, Hoffman A: The importance of family involvement for promoting self-determination in adolescents with autism and other developmental disabilities, *Focus Autism Other Dev Dis* 14(1):36–41, 1998.

25. Field S, et al.: *A practical guide to teaching self-determination,* Reston, VA, Council for Exceptional Children, 1998.

26. Fisher E: Recent research on the etiologies of autism, *Infants Young Child* 11(3):1–8, 1999.

27. Frost LA, Bondy A: *The picture exchange communication system training manual.* Cherry Hill, NJ, Pyramid Educational Consultants, 1994.

28. Fullerton A, Coyne P: Developing skills and concepts for self-determination in young adults with autism, *Focus Autism Other Dev Dis* 14(1):42–52, 1999.

29. Gardner H: *Frames of mind: The theory of multiple intelligences.* New York, Basic Books, 1983.

30. Gillberg C: Chromosomal disorders and autism, *J Autism Dev Disord* 28(5):415–425, 1998.

31. Gillberg C: Autism and pervasive developmental disorders, *J Learner Psychol Psychiatry* 31:99–119, 1990.

32. Gillberg C: The borderland of autism and Rett syndrome: Five case histories to highlight diagnostic difficulties, *J Autism Dev Disord* 19:545–559, 1989.

33. Gray C: *Social stories,* http://www. thegraycenter.org/Social_Stories.htm.

34. Groft M, Block M: Children with Asperger syndrome: Implications for general physical education and youth sports, *JOPERD,* 74(3):38–43, 2003.

35. Haas RH, et al.: Osteopenia in Rett syndrome, *J Pediatrics* 131:771–774, 1997.

36. Hobson RP, Lee A: Hello and goodbye: A study of social engagement in autism, *J Autism Dev Disord* 28(2):117–127, 1998.

37. Hobson RP, Lee A: Imitation and identification in autism, *J Child Psychol Psychiat* 40(4):649–659, 1999.

38. Howlin P: Outcome in high-functioning adults with autism with and without early language delays: Implications for the differentiation between autism and Asperger syndrome, *J Autism Dev Disord* 33(1):3–13, 2003.

39. Huettig C, Darden-Melton B: Acquisition of aquatic skills in children with autism, *Palaestra* 20(2):20–25, 45–46, 2004.

40. Huettig C, McBride-Conner A, Komatsuzaki A, Darden-Melton B: *Aquatics for learners within the pervasive developmental delay spectrum: Autism, Asperger syndrome, PDD-NOS, and Rett syndrome.* Third Annual World Congress and Exposition on Disabilities, Orlando, FL, October 2002.

41. Huettig C, O'Connor J: Wellness programming for preschoolers with disabilities, *Teach Except Child* 31(3):12–17, 1999.

42. Huettig C, Pyfer J, Auxter D: *Gross motor activities for preschoolers with special needs.* St. Louis, Mosby, 1993.

43. *Inclusion for children with autism: The TEACCH position,* www.unc.edu/depts/teacch/inclus.htm. 2003.

44. International Rett Syndrome Association, www.rettsyndrome.org. 2003.

45. Kanner L: Autistic disturbances of affective contact, *Nervous Learner* 2:217–250, 1943.

46. Kasari C: Focused and social attention of autistic children in interactions with familiar and unfamiliar adults: A comparison of autistic, mentally retarded, and normal children, *Develop Psychopath* 5:403–414, 1993.

47. Kern L, et al.: The effects of physical exercise on self-stimulation and appropriate responding in autistic children, *J Autism Dev Disord* 12:399–419, 1982.

48. Kitahara K: *Daily life therapy,* vol. III. Boston, Nimrod Press, 1984.

49. Klin A, Volkmar F: Autism and the pervasive developmental disorders. In Nospitz JD, editor: *Basic handbook of learner psychiatry.* New York, Basic Books, 1993.

50. Landrus R, Mesibov G: *Preparing autistic students for community living: A functional and sequential approach to training.* Chapel Hill, Division TEACCH, Department of Psychiatry, University of North Carolina, NC, 1985.

51. Leonard H: A population-based approach to the investigation of osteopenia in Rett syndrome, *Dev Med Child Neurol* 41:323–328, 1999.

52. Levinson L, Reid G: The effects of exercise intensity on the stereotypic behaviors of individuals with autism, *APAQ* 10:255–268, 1993.

53. Libby S: Spontaneous play in children with autism: A reappraisal, *J Autism Dev Disord* 28:487–497, 1998.

54. MacLean JE: Familial factors influence level of functioning in pervasive developmental disorder, *J Amer Acad Learner Adolescent Psychiat* 38(6):746–753, 1999.

55. Madsen KM, et al.: A population-based study of measles, mumps, and rubella vaccination and autism, *New Eng J Med* 347(19):1477–1482, 2002.

56. Maione L, Mirenda P: Effects of video modeling and video feedback on peer-directed social language skills of a child with autism, *J of Positive Behav Interv* 8(2):106–118, 2006.

57. Manjiviona J, Prior M: Comparison of Asperger syndrome and high-functioning autistic children on a test of motor impairment, *J Autism Dev Disord* 25:23–39, 1995.

58. Meyer J, Minshew N: An update on neurocognitive profiles in Asperger syndrome and high functioning autism, *Focus Aut Dev Dis* 17(3):152–160, 2002.

59. Michelottie J, Charman T, Slonims V, Baird G: Follow-up of children with language delay and features of autism from preschool years to middle childhood, *Dev Med Child Neur* 44:812–819, 2002.

60. Morrison R, Sainato D, Benchaaban D, Endo S: Increasing play skills of children with autism using activity schedules and correspondence training, *J Early Intervention* 25(1):48–72, 2002.

61. Nikopoulos C, Keenan M: Promoting social initiation in children with autism using video modeling, *Behav Intervent* 18:87–108, 2003.

62. Office of Enterprise Communication, www.cdc.gov/od/oc/media/pressrel/2007/r070208.htm.

63. Ozonoff S, Cathcart K: Effectiveness of a home program intervention for young children with autism, *J Autism Dev Disord* 29(1):25–32, 1998.

64. Rapin I: Autism, *New Eng J Med* 337(2):97–104, 1997.

65. Reid G, Collier D: Motor behavior and the autism spectrum disorders, *Palaestra* 18(4):20–27, 2002.

66. Reid G, O'Connor J: The autism spectrum disorders: Activity selection, assessment, and program organization, *Palaestra* 19(1):20–27, 2003.

67. The Rett Syndrome Diagnostic Criteria Work Group: Diagnostic criteria for Rett syndrome, *Ann Neurol* 23:425–428, 1988.

68. Rinner L: Sensory assessment for children and youth with autism spectrum disorders, *Assessment for Effective Intervention* 27(1&2):37–46, 2001–2002.

69. Robertson K, Chamberlain B, Kasari C: General education teachers' relationships with included

students with autism, *J Autism Devel Disorders* 33(2):123–130, 2003.

70. Rollins PR: Early pragmatic accomplishments and vocabulary development in preschool children with autism, *Am J Speech-Language Path* 8:181–190, 1999.

71. Ruef M, Turnbull A: The perspectives of individuals with cognitive disabilities and/or autism on their lives and their problem behavior, *Res Prac Per Sev Dis* 27(2):125–140, 2002.

72. Sacks O: A neurologist's notebook: An anthropologist on Mars, *New Yorker,* January 3, 1994.

73. Sansosti FJ, Powell-Smith KA, Kincaid D: Using social stories to improve the social behavior of children with Asperger syndrome, *J of Positive Behav Interv* 8(1):43–56, 2006.

74. Schoen S, Bullard M: Action research during recess: A time for children with autism to play and learn, *Teach Except Child* 35(1):36–39, 2002.

75. Schopler E: Convergence of learning disability, higher level autism, and Asperger's syndrome, *J Autism Dev Disord* 15:359, 1985.

76. Schultz R, Klin A: Genetics of childhood disorders: XLIII. Autism, Part 2: Neural foundations, *J Am Acad Child Adolesc Psychiatry* 41(10):1259–1262.

77. Simonoff E: Genetic counseling in autism and pervasive developmental disorders, *J Autism Dev Disord* 28(5):447–456, 1998.

78. Szatmari P: Genetics of autism: Overview and new directions, *J Autism Dev Disord* 28(5):351–368, 1998.

79. Terpstra J, Higgins K, Pierce T: Can I play? Classroom-based interventions for teaching play skills to children with autism, *Focus Aut Dev Dis* 17(2):119–126, 2002.

80. Tsai L: *Pervasive developmental disorders,* NICHY Briefing Paper, FS20, 1–15, 1998.

81. U.S. Department of Education, Office of Special Education and Rehabilitation Services: *Idea part B trend data,* www.ideadata.org/PartBTrendDataFiles. asp. 2007.

82. Volkmar FR, Klin A, Pauls D: Nosological and genetic aspects of Asperger syndrome, *J Autism Dev Disord* 28(5):457–463, 1998.

83. Whitaker P: Supporting families of preschool children with autism: What parents want and what helps, *Autism* 6(4):411–426, 2002.

84. Williams K: Understanding the student with Asperger syndrome: Guidelines for teachers, *Focus on Autistic Behavior* vol. 10(2) 1995. Modified with permission from Barb Kirby, Web Master, O.A.S.I.S. web page, http://www.udel.edu/bkirby/ asperger/karen_williams_guidelines.html. 2003.

85. Winterman K, Sapona R: Everyone's included: Supporting young children with autism spectrum disorders in a responsive classroom learning environment, *Teaching Exceptional Children* 35(1):30–35, 2002.

SUGGESTED READINGS

An essential reading for physical educators who plan to work with learners with disabilities is the 2002 four-part series in *Palaestra:* Motor Behavior and the Autism Spectrum Disorders.

Coyne P, Nyberg C, Vanderberg ML: *Developing leisure time skills for persons with autism: A practical approach for home, school and community.* Arlington, TX, Future Horizons Publishing, 2000.

Reid G, Collier D: Motor behavior and the autism spectrum disorders, *Palaestra* 18(4):20–27, 2002.

RECOMMENDED WEB SITES

Please keep in mind that these Web sites are being recommended in the winter of 2007. As Web sites often change, they may have moved or been reconfigured or eliminated.

Autism Society of America
www.autism-society.org

Autism Source
www.autismsource.org

The Oasis Guide to Asperger Syndrome
www.udel.edu/bkirby/asperger

RECOMMENDED VIDEOS

Insight Media
2164 Broadway
New York, NY 10024-0621
1-800-233-9910
www.insight-media.com

Autism: The Unfolding Mystery
#TAN4110/DVD/2005/26 min/$209

Autism Is a World
#TAN4476/DVD/2005/40 min/$139

Autism in the Classroom
#TAN4469/DVD/2004/16 min/$139

Autism and the New Law
#TAN2230/VHS/2004/50 min/$109

CHAPTER

13

Specific Learning Disabilities

■ **O B J E C T I V E S**

Define specific learning disability.

Identify the types of behavior problems youngsters with a learning disability frequently demonstrate.

List six motor/physical developmental delays youngsters with a learning disability might demonstrate.

List at least three teaching strategies a physical educator could use to promote learning for students with specific learning disabilities.

Identify three techniques that might be effective in keeping a student with a specific learning disability on task during a physical education class.

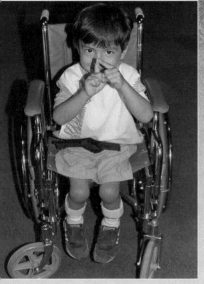

A Child Participates in Creative Storytelling at Camp

Courtesy Dallas Independent School District.

Probably no disability has proven to be more controversial or has undergone more name changes than what we now call *specific learning disabilities (SLD)*. Confusion about the condition is reflected in the number of terms associated with disability. Over the past 30 years individuals with these disabilities have been classified as perceptually handicapped, brain injured, brain damaged, minimal brain dysfunctionate, dyslexic, and developmentally aphasic. Every term was selected in an attempt to convey the fact that persons with a specific learning disability have normal intelligence but fail to demonstrate the same academic competencies that most individuals do whose IQs fall within the normal range.

CASE STUDY

Shawn

Shawn is an 8-year-old who is having problems with his coordination, handwriting, and concentration. He also has trouble getting along with his 2nd-grade classmates, following instructions, and remaining quiet in class when the teacher is giving instruction.

Shawn has a verbal IQ of 107 and a performance IQ of 91. Even though he has a normal overall IQ (99), he is reluctant to engage in any tasks requiring sustained mental effort, and he does not follow through on chores and assignments. He is performing to age level in math but struggles with comprehending material he reads.

He does not like to participate in competitive games. When he does, he frequently loses his temper and strikes out at other players. He prefers to play alone and particularly enjoys riding his bike; however, he still uses training wheels, which other kids in the neighborhood make fun of.

CRITICAL THINKING TASK

As you read this chapter, think about the problems Shawn is experiencing. Identify the self-esteem behaviors and motor proficiency problems he demonstrates that are often typical of individuals with learning disabilities. Determine how you, the physical educator, could create a positive learning environment for Shawn.

DEFINITION OF SPECIFIC LEARNING DISABILITY

Specific learning disability was defined in the Individuals with Disabilities Education Act (IDEA) of 1990. It is a disorder in one or more of the basic psychological processes involved in understanding or using language, spoken or written, which may manifest itself in the imperfect ability to listen, think, speak, write, spell, or perform mathematical calculations. Such disorders include perceptual disabilities, brain injury, minimal brain dysfunction, dyslexia, and developmental aphasia.

The term does not include children who have learning problems that are primarily the result of visual, hearing, or motor disabilities; intellectual disability; emotional disturbance; or environmental, cultural, or economic disadvantage.[7]

IDEIA (2004) requires that each state adopt criteria for determining whether a child has a learning disability. States are not required to use the IQ-discrepancy model (i.e. difference between a student's cognitive and achievement test scores), but they must use a process for identifying a student based on the child's response to scientific, research-based interventions and may use other research-based procedures. The significant point being that the methods the states use must be validated by research.[12]

Specific types of learning disabilities include problems with arithmetic (discalculia), reading (dyslexia), handwriting (dysgraphia), spelling, and understanding and/or using verbal and nonverbal abilities (developmental aphasia, dysnomia, expressive language).[4] Many children and adolescents who have been identified as having a learning disability also have concurrent emotional and behavior problems.[37] And, as would be expected of individuals who despite their best efforts continue to fail, self-esteem is reduced.

INCIDENCE OF SPECIFIC LEARNING DISABILITY

Estimates of the prevalence of the condition range from 5 to 10 percent of the population,[12] depending on the number of characteristics included in the definition. Regardless of which characteristics are included, it is widely accepted that 70 to 90 percent of the children identified as having a specific learning disability are male; however, there is growing speculation that both genders are equally affected but males are identified more frequently because they tend to act out more and be more disruptive than females.[1] In 1977 there were approximately 800,000 learning disabled individuals; in 2006 almost 3 million American children between the ages of 6 and 21 had some form of learning disability that required accommodations in school.[25] As would be expected, research on this disability has greatly increased in recent years. Specific learning disability is the most prevalent disabling condition of individuals in the United States.

CAUSES OF SPECIFIC LEARNING DISABILITY

Children who were once believed to be prone to daydreaming, inattentive, mischievous, or just plain "dumb" in school do, indeed, have an organic basis for their behaviors.[30] Technologically sophisticated equipment has been used to document neurological differences in the brains of persons with specific learning disabilities as compared with normal individuals,[16,23,26,31] yet the specific impact of neurological differences, the subcategories of the disability, and the causes have not been identified. The best we can do at this point in time is describe the behaviors demonstrated by this varied group of learners and share whatever has been found to work successfully with them.

For more than 45 years theorists postulated that sensory-perceptual-motor functioning delays underlay specific learning disabilities. Technology developed in the past decade has enabled researchers to demonstrate neurological differences in individuals with learning disability; however, the extent to which these deficits are tied to academic performance is still unknown. During the 1960s, when the perceptual-motor theories of Getman, Kephart,[28] and Frostig and Maslow[21] were emerging, great hope was placed in using physical activity to "cure" learning disabilities. The perceptual-motor pioneers proposed that the basic "stuff" from which cognitive information is constructed included perceptual and motor components. Educational researchers speculated that, if they could identify that perceptual-motor delays exist and intervene with a movement program to overcome the delays, cognitive function would be facilitated. Special educators with little or no background in motor development seized on these theories as the possible answer to the academic learning problems manifested by individuals with learning disabilities. Kephart's and Frostig and

Maslow's programs of activities were tried on groups of learning disabled students. Almost without exception, the wholesale application of these theories proved disappointing to the academic community. In most cases, the learning disabled students improved in perceptual-motor function but demonstrated no immediate change in reading or mathematical ability. As a result, many special educators abandoned the notion that there could be a causative relationship between motor and cognitive functioning.

As the perceptual-motor theories faded in popularity, other neuropsychological theories emerged that advanced the belief that cognitive function could be facilitated by controlling types and qualities of sensory and motor experiences. These theories differed from earlier ones in that they advanced the notion that, prior to efficient perceptual-motor and cognitive functioning, sensory input stimuli must be organized, so that it can be used by the central nervous system.

Prominent advocates of a definitive relationship among the sensory, motor, and cognitive domains were Ayres,[2,3] deQuiros and Schrager,[15] and Dennison.[14] Ayres, a well-known researcher in the area of sensory integration therapy, advocated that "learning and behavior are the visible aspects of sensory integration"[2] and that sensory integration results from sensory stimulation and motor activity. DeQuiros and Schrager believed that primary learning disabilities have their bases in vestibular, perceptual modalities, and cerebral dysfunctions. They advocated the use of sensory-perceptual-motor activities to assuage vestibular and perceptual problems. Dennison built on Sperry and Ornstein's model of brain function and developmental optometry's theories and developed a program of specific movements to use to enable individuals to access different parts of the brain. He called his approach Educational Kinesiology.

Research studies have validated that both sensory integration and Educational Kinesiology have a positive impact on perceptual-motor function; however, their value for enhancing cognitive functioning has been less apparent.[9,24] Studies that have reported academic gains from sensory integration therapy programs suffer from sampling, group assignment, treatment, and analysis inadequacies.[24] One study that looked at the efficacy of Educational Kinesiology concluded that the treatment is not effective in improving academic skills as measured by the Comprehensive Test of Basic Skills for Language, Arithmetic, and Reading.[9]

Interest in the relationship between motor and cognitive function continues. A carefully designed study carried out in England reported that over 95 percent of a sample of children with learning disabilities in the areas of reading, arithmetic, and spelling demonstrated depressed balance (with eyes closed) and low muscle tone.[20] It will take well-designed research studies such as this to tease out the existence of the specific types of sensory and motor components that exist concomitantly with cognitive problems. Once the underlying delays are identified, intervention programs will need to be developed and used with youngsters who have learning disabilities. After that, longitudinal studies that follow individuals who have been exposed to contemporary sensory-perceptual-motor intervention programs will need to be carried out. To understand the problem and potential solutions, dialogues among educators, neurologists, visual and hearing specialists, and researchers will need to be initiated and fostered. The questions to be answered must be approached with open minds, honest and critical analysis, and persistence.

Children Enjoy Obstacle Courses
Courtesy of Laurie Zittel.

CHARACTERISTICS OF SPECIFIC LEARNING DISABILITY

All children differ in their psychomotor, cognitive, and behavioral characteristics. Likewise, children with learning disabilities differ from one another, and there is considerable overlap in abilities between children with learning disabilities and other children. However, there are some similar group characteristics that differentiate individuals with specific learning disabilities from individuals who lack disabilities.

Evidence that the central nervous system is involved includes problems of arousal, attention, activity level, temperament, alertness, and tone during the first two years of life.[7] During the preschool years, children with learning disabilities have difficulty learning new words, are clumsy, have difficulty with basic concepts, are distractible, and are easily frustrated. Elementary school–age children with learning disabilities demonstrate consistent reading and spelling errors and poor coordination, have difficulty finishing their school work on time, and appear to lack common sense. Secondary school students with learning disabilities avoid reading and writing tasks, have difficulty staying organized, and have difficulty accepting criticism.[5]

Children can differ in motor performance for many reasons, including (1) neurophysiological differences, (2) sensory input processing differences, (3) problems processing information, (4) language differences, (5) memory deficits, and (6) short attention span. (See Table 13-1.)

Table 13-1	Characteristics That Affect Motor Performance
Neurophysiological differences	
Sensory input processing differences	
Problems processing information	
Language differences	
Memory deficits	
Short attention span	

Neurophysiological Differences

Most of the research on learning disability has been done by cognitive theorists. However, in the past 20 years there has been increased emphasis on neurophysiological functioning of the brain as it relates to learning disability. Studies of the brains of individuals with specific learning disabilities have been done using electroencephalography (EEG), auditory brain stem–evoked response (ABER), regional cerebral blood flow (rCBF), and magnetic resonance imaging (MRI). The purpose of this research is to determine whether any significant differences exist between the brain structure and function of normal and learning disabled individuals. Some differences have been reported.

Using EEG, Johns[26] demonstrated that the evoked potentials of groups of students with learning disabilities were significantly different from those of students with no learning problems. Researchers who used EEG to measure event-related potential responses to sensory, motor, and cognitive events concluded that children with learning disabilities have processing problems.[39] Other investigators have reported significant differences in regions of blood flow,[31] brain stem–evoked responses during speech processing tasks,[23] and the width of the structure connecting the two hemispheres of the brain.[16] Neurophysiological tools such as these show great promise for the early identification of children with specific learning disabilities. Once unique brain structure and function profiles are identified and correlated directly to specific learning difficulties, it will be possible to develop educational intervention strategies specific to each child's needs.

Sensory Input Processing Differences

An analysis of neurological building blocks important to skilled motor performances indicates that exteroceptors (e.g., eyes, ears, and tactile receptors) and proprioceptors (e.g., vestibular and kinesthetic receptors) are important avenues for receiving information from the environment (see Chapter 5). Deficits in receiving and processing information from these senses may result in deficits in the performance of physical activities.

There is strong evidence that persons with learning disabilities may be impaired in their ability to balance. Good balance depends on accurate information from the vestibular system as well as normal reflex and visual depth perception development. When vestibular information is not received or processed efficiently, impaired balance results. In addition, persisting primitive reflexes and a delay in the development of postural (equilibrium) reflexes also inhibit a person's ability to achieve and maintain balance. Visual depth perception deficiencies interfere with the ability to use visual cues in the environment to assist in balancing. Impaired balance interferes with postural and locomotor efficiency as well as foot-eye and hand-eye coordination.

Children with learning disabilities also may possess deficits in kinesthetic perception (an awareness and control of body parts in space). Recent literature that points out the low muscle tone demonstrated early on by children with learning disabilities supports deficits in kinesthetic perception. When the kinesthetic receptors are not fully functioning, information about precise position and rate of movement of body parts in space does not reach the central nervous system. Kinesthesis is an essential prerequisite for sophisticated, refined sport skills that require precise movements, such as putting a golf ball, shooting a basketball, setting a volleyball, and performing any other movements that require qualitative forces for success. Most physical education activities require kinesthetic perception. Thus, kinesthesis is considered an important prerequisite for movement control, which generalizes to many other physical and sport activities. Cermak and Henderson[11] estimate that 60 to 95 percent of these children have poor static and dynamic balance, coordination problems, low muscle tone, poor spatial orientation, and delayed acquisition of equilibrium reactions. Morrison, Hinshaw, and Corte[32] also report that this population demonstrates significantly more primitive reflexes and vestibular and equilibrium delays than do children without disabilities. Fawcett and Nicolson[20] validate the reports of poor static balance and low muscle tone.

Aquatic Skills Can Open a New World
Photo by Carol Huettig.

Many children who have learning disabilities are uncoordinated and lack control of motor responses. Individuals with poorly developed balance and kinesthetic systems tend to have problems in changing direction or body position. As a result, these individuals commonly have difficulty learning to perform efficient specific sport and motor skills. Girls with learning disabilities perform motor tasks significantly more poorly than do boys with learning disabilities.[38]

Problems Processing Information

There is evidence that many persons with learning disabilities differ from their unaffected peers as a result of their inability to process information efficiently.[8,20,39] Information processing relates to how one retains and manipulates information—how information is acquired, stored, selected, and then recalled. Although there appears to be agreement that as a group the population with learning disabilities has problems in information processing,

the specific locus of the problem is disputed. Cermak[10] indicates that processing deficits appear in the speed of rehearsal strategies. On the other hand, Karr and Hughes[27] indicate that the problem may not be a processing deficit. They demonstrated that this population is able to handle information associated with increased task difficulty in the same manner as nondisabled persons; however, a problem may exist in the very early input stages of the processing mechanism (i.e., getting information into the processing system).

Individuals with impaired depth perception misjudge where objects are in space. As a result, they descend stairs one at a time, are unable to catch and kick balls, and avoid climbing apparatus. Figure-ground perception involves the ability to distinguish an object from its background. It requires selecting and attending to the appropriate visual cue among a number of other cues that are irrelevant to that task at a particular moment. If the visual object to which the individual is to respond is not well defined, chances are the motor task will be performed less proficiently than desired. Individuals with poor depth perception almost always demonstrate deficits in visual figure-ground perception.

Another visual characteristic that may be impaired in this population is ocular saccadical abilities, which permit the learner to refix the eye on differing targets accurately and quickly. The ocular saccadical ability is required in sports in which an individual must concentrate on a moving ball as well as a moving target (e.g., in football, when a quarterback throws a ball to a second receiver after seeing that the first potential receiver is covered, and in basketball, when focusing on a rebounding ball and then refocusing vision to find an outlet player to pass to). Any visual deficiency that interferes with visual discrimination needed for the proficient performance of a given sport will impair the performance of that sport.

The auditory mechanism may not be as critical in the performance of sport activity as is the eye; however, an impaired ability to use auditory information may result in performance that is below normative expectations. Some of the sport activities requiring auditory discrimination and perception are dancing and floor routines in gymnastics. Auditory figure-ground discrimination is important to skill proficiency. Anytime there are extraneous auditory sounds, auditory figure-ground perception is needed (e.g., when players participating in a noisy gym must attend closely to hear the coaches' instructions and officials' calls).

Ayres[2] suggests that learning disabled individuals may have deficits in motor planning. Eichstaedt and Kalakian[19] describe motor planning as the ability to execute behaviors in a proper sequential order. Sport skill tasks require the integration of discrete component parts in sequence for task success. When learning a motor task, each component part of the skill must be planned and carried out in sequence before the skill can be executed correctly. With practice, the skill becomes a subroutine, which is stored in long-term memory, and motor planning requirements are lessened. However, when learning new skills with component parts that must be sequenced, each component part must be present for the skill to be learned. Individuals with learning disabilities who demonstrate difficulty with motor

planning may not have the necessary components (e.g., vestibular, kinesthetic, or visual information) available to them.

Language Differences

The physical education teacher should recognize individual language usage differences among students with learning disabilities.[17] Such knowledge can be used to modify teaching strategies that involve communication through language. There are at least three language categories: (1) receptive language, (2) expressive language, and (3) inner language.

Receptive language involves the ability to comprehend the meaning associated with language. Deficits in receptive language may be either visual or auditory. Visual deficits are reflected by the inability to organize and interpret visual information appropriately. For example, a child may be unable to interpret facial gestures appropriately. Auditory receptive language deficits may be reflected in a failure to follow directions or an inability to discriminate between sounds.

Expressive language involves the ability to communicate through either audition or the visual mechanism. Auditory deficits are expressed through impaired speech, whereas visual expressive language deficits are writing problems. Problems in visual expressive language are the inability to reproduce simple geometric forms, the persistent reversal of letters, the rotation or inversion of letters, and the reversed sequence of letters.

Inner language processes refers to the ability to transform experience into symbols. This, of course, is dependent on experiences. Inasmuch as young children gain much of their experience with the world through play and motor activity, environmental exploration with the body is an important aspect of the development of inner language.

Memory Deficits

Many individuals with learning disabilities also have deficits in long-term and short-term memory. Four steps are necessary for learning to occur: (1) a stimulus must be registered in the brain,

(2) that stimulus must be maintained while its relevance is determined, (3) the stimulus must be processed in light of material present in long-term memory, and (4) the stimulus must be placed in long-term memory. Thus, deficits in either short-term or long-term memory limit the benefits of prior experiences and practice.

Memory is also a prerequisite for closure, the ability to recognize a visual or an auditory experience when only part is presented. The partial image is compared with complete images that are stored in memory for identification. Visual closure occurs when a baseball player is batting. The batter must make inferences as to where the ball will be when it crosses the plate. If a batter is not able to estimate where the ball will cross the plate, he or she cannot determine where the bat should be swung. More experienced batters have more comparative images stored in their memory banks; thus, they are better able to estimate the flight of an incoming ball than are less experienced batters.

Individuals with learning disabilities also may be deficient in cue selection. Cue selection is the ability to attend to relevant cues and block out irrelevant stimuli. Individuals with memory, visual, or auditory deficits will not make efficient cue selections.

Short Attention Span

Approximately 80 percent of all individuals with specific learning disabilities are estimated to also have some form of attention deficit disorder.[6] Attention deficit conditions are discussed in Chapter 18.

Motor Performance Profile

Any one or all of previously discussed factors will affect the success level of a child in physical education. Children with cognitive processing problems may not understand or remember instructions. Perceptual difficulties lead to spatial awareness or body image problems. Clumsy motor performance caused by delayed reflex and/or vestibular development, as well as depth perception problems, directly influences a student's ability to master basic movement tasks and to combine those tasks into the complicated patterns necessary to succeed in sports or leisure-time activities.

It is, however, difficult to group together all children with specific learning disabilities when trying to determine precisely what movement difficulties they will demonstrate. In an attempt to determine whether there is a clear-cut motor profile demonstrated by this population, over an 11-year period Pyfer[35] administered a wide variety of tests to approximately 400 children with learning disabilities. Analysis of those data revealed that approximately 12 percent demonstrated no motor delays, 75 percent scored average on some tests but below average on other tests, and the remaining 13 percent were severely delayed in all areas tested. The youngsters who demonstrated motor delays were deficient in balance, spatial awareness, body image, visual-motor control, and/or fine motor development. Additionally, those youngsters had a performance IQ score that ranged from 12 to 20 points lower than their verbal IQ scores. These findings agree with those of the studies cited earlier in this chapter. That is, no one performance profile characterizes all individuals with learning disabilities. These children constitute a heterogeneous group and, as such, they need to be treated as individuals. It is critical to identify their motor delays as early as possible and to intervene to correct those problems.[22] The fact that preschool children with learning disabilities can make significant motor gains when placed in a structured program has been validated.[36]

TESTING TO DETERMINE MOTOR FUNCTIONING LEVELS

Appropriate tests to use with this population include any instruments that will provide information about the functioning of neurological building blocks (vestibular, kinesthetic, visual efficiency, and reflex development), balance, fine motor control, and visual-motor control. An instrument that can provide several clues about the motor functioning level of this population is the

Bruininks-Oseretsky Test of Motor Proficiency. Subtests that are helpful for pinpointing possible vestibular, kinesthetic, visual efficiency, bilateral coordination, and physical fitness delays are the Gross Motor, Upper-Limb Coordination, and Visual-Motor Control sections of the Fine Motor Subtest. Rather than using the subtest scores to determine whether delays exist, it is recommended that the evaluator examine the performance of specific components of the subtests. Specific clues to developmental delays were presented in Chapter 5. When Shawn was tested using the Bruininks-Oseretsky test, his performance was as follows:

- He scored at the 6-year, 11-month level on the balance subtest. He balanced for 10 seconds with his eyes open and only 5 seconds with his eyes closed.
- He scored at the 7-year, 11-month level on the bilateral coordination subtest; however, he could not demonstrate any of the tasks requiring him to coordinate movements on the opposite side of the body.
- He scored at the 7-year, 8-month level on the strength subtest. He demonstrated 6 bent-knee push-ups and 6 sit-ups.
- His upper-limb coordination subtest score was at the 10-year, 5-month level, with no areas of concern.

A Parent Is a Child's First Teacher

- He scored at the 6-year, 11-month level on the visual-motor control subtest and at the 6-year, 8-month level on the upper-limb speed and dexterity subtest. He erred on all of the tracing mazes tasks and when trying to draw geometric figures.

TEACHING STRATEGIES

Regardless of the type of program a physical educator favors, tests should be administered to determine the motor functioning level of the child with a specific learning disability. After areas of deficiency have been identified, activities can be selected to promote development in these problem areas. If appropriate activities are selected and carefully taught, the prognosis for the motor development of these students is quite good.

Specific activities to use with students with specific learning disabilities can be found in Chapters 5 and 6. General points to keep in mind when working with these students follow:

- Whenever possible, use a New Games approach that accommodates a wide range of motor competency, so that students' self-concepts are enhanced rather than demoralized by failure to contribute.
- Use a positive behavior management program to get students to finish tasks (e.g., use tokens or let them select their favorite activity once each day if they stay on task).
- Give brief instructions and ask the children to repeat those instructions before starting an activity. Doing this prevents problems that arise from the limited memory some of the children demonstrate.
- To enhance the children's opportunities for success and willingness to persist at tasks, break tasks into small learning steps and praise every legitimate effort they make.
- Help students define their learning goals and determine how to monitor their progress.[33]

See Table 13-2.

Table 13-2	Teaching Strategies

Use a New/Games approach.

Use positive behavior management.

Give brief instructions.

Break tasks into small steps.

Help students define learning goals.[33]

Teach students how to monitor their progress.[33]

The Physical Education Program

It is critical that learning disabled students' participation be limited in group activities that are beyond their capabilities. Such practices only reinforce their feelings of inferiority. When including these students with the regular physical education class, the more activities that use an individualized approach that enables each student to work at his or her level without being compared with peers, the better will be the students' opportunity to realize some success. At the elementary school level, activities should promote development of the neurological building blocks before concentrating on perceptual-motor integration or motor output behaviors. The greatest amount of carryover will occur if educators "fill in the blanks" of missing building blocks and perceptual components before teaching motor output behaviors. Several activities that can be used with elementary school children of all ability levels are included in *Gross Motor Activities for Children with Special Needs,* which instructors can download and distribute from the book's Web site (www.mhhe.com/auxterlle). At the middle and high school levels, programs should encourage and reward individual effort. Examples are changing the way games are played to accommodate a variety of performance capabilities and having personal fitness programs that are specifically patterned to affect an individual's present level of performance.

When providing small-group or whole class programs for students with specific learning disabilities, it is easier to focus on their particular needs. However, there is controversy among physical educators as to whether a bottom-up developmental approach or a task-specific, top-down approach should be used in the instruction of motor skills for the learning disabled. A bottom-up approach to facilitate movement efficiency would begin with sensory stimulation activities to provide prerequisite components for meaningful, culturally relevant skills. With such an approach, there would be extended periods during which students were engaging in specific activities to facilitate basic sensory and reflex systems. Once the basic sensory and reflex systems were functioning, and those stimuli were integrated, perceptual-motor development as well as learning of specific motor skills would occur. Admittedly, the number of components of sensory input systems as well as perceptual-motor functions is considerable. All of the senses, the integration of each of the senses, the perceptual-motor characteristics of the individual, the way in which information is processed, and associative and organizational structures of perceptual skills that can be linked with each of the sensory modes are taken into consideration. Effective use of this approach requires extensive knowledge on the part of the teacher and the willingness to delay instruction in what many consider culturally relevant skills.

The top-down approach to facilitating movement efficiency would start with the culturally relevant skills and work down toward prerequisite components when it became apparent a learner was not benefiting from direct instruction of a specific task. Which approach to use can be determined through thorough evaluation and interpretation of results. When evaluation results clearly indicate no sensory or reflex deficits, the most economical method would be the top-down approach. Also, the older the learner, the less appealing the bottom-up approach is.

Modifications

Teaching and program modifications that are helpful for students with specific learning disabilities include the following:

- *Control attention.* One of the methods for controlling attention is to establish routines that are repeated day after day. This enables the child to develop a pattern of activities. The teaching techniques, behavior modification program, and organizational patterns should be kept as structured and consistent as possible.

- *Control extraneous stimuli in the environment.* In addition to stable routines, the environment should appear relatively the same from one day to the next. Positioning of equipment and systematic procedures to store equipment should be established and maintained.

- *Control of desired behaviors.* There should be instructionally relevant stimuli to focus students' attention (e.g., designate specific spots on the floor where students are to begin class each day). Visual cues can indicate where the hands are to be placed for a push-up or a forward roll. Specific visual or auditory information can be introduced that indicates to the individual specifically what to do with body parts to enhance motor control.

- *Control methodology.* If the learner has a tendency to disassociate visually or auditorially, use the whole-part-whole method of teaching. Later, attention to details of performance can be emphasized.

- *Use more than one sensory modality.* In addition to verbally describing the task to be performed, use visual stimuli (e.g., a picture, drawing, or demonstration). In this way, if the learning disabled student has either visual or verbal deficits, another sensory avenue can be used to comprehend the instruction. Kinesthetic aids, such as manually moving a child through sequences, can also be used.

COMMUNITY-BASED OPPORTUNITIES

Individuals who grow into adulthood with specific learning disabilities must be taught compensation skills to enable them to recreate in the community. Too frequently, middle and high school students with specific learning disabilities who have not had their conditions properly identified and attended to develop all types of anxiety, guilt, and feelings of inadequacy.[34] Because they have IQs within the normal range, they are bright enough to

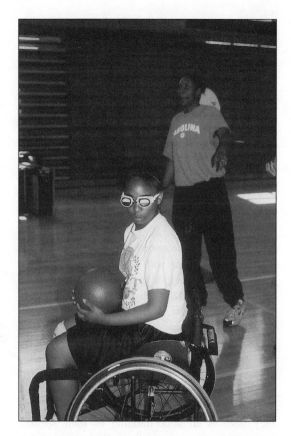

Simulation Experiences Help Future Teachers Understand Disabilities
Courtesy Texas Womans University.

realize that, no matter how much effort they exert, as the school material becomes increasingly complex and demanding their peers are going to outperform them academically. Almost one in three youth with specific learning disabilities fail general education courses. In addition, adolescents with SLD have difficulty with problem applications in math and generally perform at a 5th-grade level.[29] It is no wonder that these youngsters balk at continuing in school, demonstrate significant conduct problems, and frequently become alcohol-dependent. Professionals must make every effort to ensure that students who are not performing to adequate academic standards are properly assessed, so that intervention that will match their needs can be implemented. Their transition program should match their needs to the opportunities available in the community. Facilities that include fitness rooms and swimming pools should be identified. Participation in activities available in those facilities will provide the adult the ability to maintain a healthy lifestyle without being placed in competitive situations.

It is critical that every curriculum for individuals with learning disabilities address day-to-day tasks that will contribute to their overall levels of independence as adults. The needs identified for persons with learning disabilities are presented in Table 13-3.

Participation in summer camps designed specifically for individuals with learning disabilities has proven to be very helpful in developing individuals' social and emotional skills.[40] In addition to traditional camp activities, some camps also offer academic programs that enable the campers to develop problem-solving skills.

Probably the most significant knowledge young adults with learning disabilities require is that they are not to blame for their learning difficulties. The next most important piece of information they need is an understanding of their specific information processing deficits. With those understandings, maturing individuals can make informed decisions that will enable them to participate successfully in work and social activities.

Table 13-3	Transition Needs of Persons with Learning Disabilities
Occupational/vocational training	
Social skills development	
Leisure-time activities	
Life skills taught in natural settings[13]	

Knowing there is a reason for the academic and social struggles they have experienced reduces the guilt, acting out and avoidance behaviors, and feelings of alienation from society. As a result, their self-confidence increases, and they become more motivated to attempt and persist at difficult tasks. With knowledge about the nature of their limitations, they can then either determine the types of assistance they need to realize success or select activities that circumvent their problem areas. Frequently, selecting an activity partner to assist with decision making is sufficient. For example, if determining distances is a problem, a golfer should select a partner or caddy who is willing and able to read the layout of the course and make club recommendations. When canoeing or kayaking for any distance or on an unfamiliar body of water, a partner versed in orienteering is essential. Adults with learning disabilities should be discouraged from attempting to participate in activities requiring skills for which they are unable to compensate.

SUMMARY

Specific learning disability (SLD) is a condition that is manifested through disabilities in listening, thinking, writing, speaking, spelling, and mathematical calculations. The majority of children with this disability also demonstrate soft neurological signs early. Frequently, these soft neurological signs are later expressed in delayed motor development. In addition to addressing the specific types of academic subject delays these students demonstrate, physical educators must determine and correct physical and motor delays. To determine what types of delays these students are experiencing, testing must be done. Selected parts of the long form of the Bruininks-Oseretsky Test of Motor Proficiency can be used to identify areas of concern. When including this type of student in the regular physical education class, either select activities that will be of benefit to them and to their classmates or allow for individualized programs for all students. When dealing with students with specific learning disabilities, there are two types of programs that will benefit them: (1) a bottom-up approach that focuses on facilitating deficit sensory input and reflex systems is appropriate for younger children, and (2) a top-down, skill-development approach that focuses on instruction in specific performance tasks that are available in the community is critical for middle and high school students. During the school years, every effort should be made to address the academic, motor, and life skills these individuals require to attain independence and cope in the community.

REVIEW QUESTIONS

1. What is meant by the term *specific learning disability?*

2. What are the cognitive, affective, and motor characteristics of individuals with specific learning disabilities?

3. What teaching strategies could a physical educator use to promote attending behavior of the student with specific learning disabilities?

4. What activities could a physical educator include in an elementary physical education class that would benefit both the students with learning disabilities and those without?

5. What types of information are helpful to the young adult with specific learning disabilities who is trying to cope in the community?

STUDENT ACTIVITIES

1. Identify two behaviors Shawn in the case study demonstrates that must be extinguished to improve his chances of benefiting from his physical education experience. Develop one long-range behavioral goal and three short-term objectives leading to each goal that address these problem areas.

2. Divide the class into several small groups. Have each group review Shawn's test results and identify at least five activities he would have difficulty performing in physical education.

3. Divide the class into some small groups. Assign each group one of Shawn's physical/motor problem performance areas. Develop one long-range goal and three short-term objectives that progress from the present level of performance in that area. Then identify three activities that could be incorporated into a 2nd-grade physical education class that would be of interest to the class and would lead Shawn toward his long-range goal.

REFERENCES

1. American Psychiatric Association: *Diagnostic and statistical manual of mental disorders DSM-IV.* Washington, DC, 1994.

2. Ayres AJ: *Sensory integration and the child.* Los Angeles, Western Psychological Services, 1980.

3. Ayres AJ: *Sensory integration and learning disorders.* Los Angeles, Western Psychological Services, 1972.

4. Beers MH, Porter RS, Jones TV, Kaplan JL, Berkwits M: *The Merck manual of diagnosis and therapy.* Whitehouse Station, NJ, Merck Research Laboratories, 2006.

5. Bergert S: *The warning signs of learning disability.* Arlington, VA, ERIC Clearing House on Disabilities and Gifted Education (ERIC Document Reproduction Service #ED 449633, Digest #E 603), 2000.

6. Blau M: A.D.D: The scarlet letters in the alphabet, *New York Magazine,* December:44–51, 1993.

7. Blumsack J, Lewandowski L, Waterman J: Neurodevelopmental precursors to learning disabilities: A preliminary report from a parent survey, *JLD* 30:228–237, 1997.

8. Brunt D, Magill R, Eason R: Distinctions in variability of motor output between learning disabled and normal children, *Percept Mot Skills* 57:731–734, 1983.

9. Cammisa K: Educational kinesiology with learning disabled children: An efficacy study, *Percept Mot Skills* 78:105–106, 1994.

10. Cermak LS: Information processing deficits in children with learning disabilities, *JLD* 16:599–605, 1983.

11. Cermak S, Henderson A: Learning disabilities. In Umphred D, editor: *Neurological rehabilitation,* 2nd ed. St. Louis, Mosby-Year Book, 1990.

12. Council for Exceptional Children: *A primer on the IDEA 2004 regulations,* www.cec.sped.org/AM. 2007.

13. Cronin ME: Life skills curricula for students with learning disabilities: A review of the literature, *JLD* 29:53–68, 1996.

14. Dennison P, Hargrove G: *Personalized whole brain integration.* Glendale, CA, Edu-Kinesthetics, 1985.

15. deQuiros JB, Schrager OL: *Neuropsychological fundamentals in learning disabilities.* Novato, CA, Academic Therapy, 1979.

16. Duane D, Gray B, editors: *The reading brain: The biological basis of dyslexia.* Parkton, MD, York Press, 1991.

17. Dunn JM, Fait H: *Special physical education.* Dubuque, IA, Wm. C. Brown, 1989.

18. EDLAW, Inc.: *Individuals with Disabilities Education Act.* Potomac, MD, 1991.

19. Eichstaedt CB, Kalakian LH: *Developmental/ adapted physical education.* New York, Macmillan, 1987.

20. Fawcett AJ, Nicolson RI: Performance of dyslexic children on cerebellar and cognitive tests, *J of Motor Behavior* 31:68–78, 1999.

21. Frostig M, Maslow P: *Movement education: Theory and practice.* Chicago, Follett, 1970.

22. Goldey E: New angles on motor and sensory coordination in learning disabilities, *Learning Disabilities* 9(2):65–71, 1999.

23. Grant D: *Brainstem level auditory function in specific dyslexics and normal readers.* Ann Arbor, University of Michigan Press, DAI 3376-B, 1980.

24. Hoehn T, Baumeister A: A critique of the application of sensory integration theory to children with learning disabilities, *J of LD* 27:338–350, 1994.

25. *IDEA part B trend data.* www.ideadata.org/ PartBTrendDataFiles.asp. 2007.

26. Johns ER: *Neurometric evaluation of brain function in normal and learning disabled children.* Ann Arbor, University of Michigan Press, 1991.

27. Karr R, Hughes K: Movement difficulty and learning disabled children, *APAQ* 5:72–79, 1987.

28. Kephart N: *The slow learner in the classroom.* Columbus, OH, Charles E. Merrill, 1971.

29. Korterig LL, deBettencourt LU, Braziel PM: Improving performance in high school algebra: What students with learning disabilities are saying, *LD Quart* 28(3):191–203, 2005.

30. Leary PM, Batho K: The role of the EEG in the investigation of the child with learning disability, *S Afr Med J,* June:867–868, 1981.

31. Millay K, Grant D, Pyfer J: *Structural and functional differences in brain organization in developmental dyslexics.* Unpublished paper, Denton, TX, Texas Woman's University, 1991.

32. Morrison D, Hinshaw S, Corte E: Signs of neurobehavioral dysfunction in a sample of learning disabled children: Stability and concurrent validity, *Percept Mot Skills* 61:863–872, 1985.

33. National Research Council: *How students learn.* Washington, DC, Academic Press, 2005.

34. Naylor MW, Staskowski M, Kenney MC, King CA: Language disorders and learning disabilities in school-refusing adolescents, *J Am Acad Child Adolesc Psychiatry* 33:1331–1337, 1994.

35. Pyfer JL: *Sensory-perceptual-motor characteristics of learning disabled children: A validation study.* Unpublished paper, Denton, TX, Texas Woman's University, 1983.

36. Rimmer JH, Kelly LE: Gross motor development in preschool children with learning disabilities, *APAQ* 6:268–279, 1989.

37. Rock EE, Fessler MA, Church RP: The concomitance of learning disabilities and emotional/ behavioral disorders: A conceptual model, *J of LD* 30:245–263, 1997.

38. Woodard RJ, Surburg PR: Fundamental gross motor skill performance by girls and boys with learning disabilities, *Percept Mot Skills* 84:867–870, 1997.

39. Yitzchak F, Seiden JA, Napolitano B: Electrophysiological changes in children with learning and attential abnormalities as a function of age: Event-related potentials to an odd-ball paradigm, *Clinical Electroencephalography* 29(4):188–193, 1998.

40. Yssel N, Margison J, Cross T, Merbier J: Puzzles, mysteries and Picasso: A summer camp for students who are gifted and learning disabled, *Teach Exec Child* 38(1):42–46, 2005.

SUGGESTED READINGS

Ayres AJ: *Sensory integration and the child.* Los Angeles, Western Psychological Services, 1980.

Morris GS, Stiehl J: *Changing kids' games.* Champaign, IL, Human Kinetics, 1998.

Rich, J: *Gym Dandy series.* Durham, NC, Great Activities, 1994.

RECOMMENDED WEB SITES

Please keep in mind that these Web sites are being recommended in the winter of 2007. As Web sites often change, they may have moved or been reconfigured or eliminated.

Learning Disabilities Association of America
    www.ldanatl.org

Healthy Children Project
    www.healthychildrenproject.org

The Learning Camp
    www.learningcamp.com

RECOMMENDED VIDEOS

Richard Lavoie has a series of excellent videos about the frustration, anxiety, and tension that children with learning disabilities face. These can be accessed at www.ricklavoie.com/videos.html. 2007.

Insight Media
2164 Broadway
New York, NY 10024-0621
1-800-233-9910
www.insight-media.com

Accommodating Specific Students' Needs
#UAN4837/DVD/2006/40 min/$179

ADHD and LD: Powerful Teaching Strategies and Accommodations
#TAP4256/DVD/2003/40 min/$149

Differentiating Instruction for Students with Learning Disabilities
#TAP/4877/DVD/2005/40 min/$289

14

Mental Health Disorders

■ OBJECTIVES

Explain the mental health crisis in this country and the role of the schools in prevention and remediation.

Describe the two major categories of mental health disorders.

Briefly describe the effect of urbanization on mental health.

Describe the behaviors of children with early onset depression.

List the behaviors of a child/adolescent that are warning signals related to suicide.

Briefly describe some of the indicators in the education setting that a child is struggling with a mental health disorder.

Explain developmentally appropriate physical education programs for learners with mental health disorders.

Over one-third of all new teachers leave the profession in the first three years of their careers. Most of these teachers leave because of the frustrations of dealing with inappropriate student behavior. Clearly, the major issue facing educators is mental health disorders.

This chapter will deal with the continuum of mental health disorders. Least serious, a student may choose to ignore a teacher's directions the morning after her mother "grounded" her for being late for curfew. Most serious and sociopathological, the student may commit suicide or shoot his classmates and teachers. The physical educator must be prepared to deal with such possibilities and everything in between.

CASE STUDY 14-1

Robert

Robert is a 17-year-old boy. Until his parents divorced when Robert was 12, he had been an excellent student-athlete, a member of the junior high school track and cross-country teams. He now spends one-half of his year with his mother and one-half of his year with his father; he also splits his time between two high schools.

During the past several months, Robert has become increasingly disruptive and argumentative in class. In the gym, Robert attempted to hit a classmate with a baseball bat; the teacher and several other students had to break up the fight. Robert was placed in in-school suspension for a week. He attended an alternative school for one month after he had been found using alcohol on the school campus.

He has just returned to his general high school campus. The physical educator has reported the following behavior to the assistant principal responsible for discipline:

- Verbally aggressive behavior, particularly swearing, directed at his classmates and the teacher
- Physically aggressive behavior, including pushing, shoving, and tripping his classmates; throwing and kicking balls at others; and swinging bats and racquets at other children
- Destruction of equipment
- Violent mood swings with no apparent trigger
- Refusal to obey teacher requests and rules.

APPLICATION TASK

Can the physical educator help Robert? How?

A critical part of teaching all children in this society is the process of creating an emotionally safe physical education program. John Helion wrote,

What constitutes safe physical education? A physically and emotionally safe program is developmentally appropriate. It allows students to succeed because the lessons are planned around their needs and abilities. A safe educational setting is one in which there is no fear of trying because there is no fear of ridicule, where students will attempt something new because there is no penalty for failure, and where students are free to grow as individuals because they are not being constantly compared with or pitted against their classmates.[22]

DEFINITION OF MENTAL HEALTH DISORDERS

The New Freedom Commission on Mental Health, 2003, released a vision statement regarding mental health:

We envision a future when everyone with a mental illness will recover, a future when mental illnesses can be prevented or cured, a future when mental illnesses are detected early, and a future when everyone with a mental illness at any stage of life has access to effective treatment and supports—essentials for living, working, learning, and participating fully in the community.[49]

The mental health crisis in this country is staggering in its broad and specific impact on individuals, their families, and the society. An estimated 6 percent of children and adults have a serious emotional disturbance.[32] Millions of individuals in this society are disabled by mental illness.[49] One in 10 of our children and adolescents has a mental health disorder significant enough to cause impairment; however, less than 1 in 5 gets treatment.[6]

New Freedom Commission reported that the social stigma associated with mental illness, a fragmented health care delivery system, significant financial requirements, and unfair private health insurance programs compromise the quality of life for individuals with mental illness.[49]

The goals for a transformed mental health system, outlined by the commission, include (1) Americans understand that mental health is essential to overall health; (2) mental health care is consumer- and family-driven; (3) disparities in mental health services are eliminated; (4) early mental health screening, assessment, and referral to services are common practice; (5) excellent mental health care is delivered and research is accelerated; and (6) technology is used to access mental health care and information.[49]

Inappropriate social behaviors must be seen within a broad context. The three primary categories that must be considered are (1) behavior, (2) pathology, and (3) ecology.[60] The behavior must be considered in terms of its frequency, intensity, and variety. The pathology, or diagnostic labels (typically associated with educational assessment and special education labels), must be considered as well. As important, the behavior must be considered within the context of the family, community, and society in which the child lives.

In a very diverse society, behavior that is acceptable in some groups is unacceptable in others.[33] Thus, some of the elements defining a specific behavior disorder may be (1) a description of the problem behavior, (2) the setting in which the problem behavior occurs, and (3) the person who regards the behavior as a problem.

The physical educator and other school professionals are faced, increasingly, with a larger society in which the definition of appropriate behavior is not clear. For example, seemingly responsible adults engage in road-rage behaviors they would never demonstrate at work. The same, seemingly responsible adults use language in the locker room they would never use in front of a spouse or their own children. Television and radio programs, videos, and video games are increasingly violent and pornographic.

The school is, very simply, a microcosm of the larger society. Though expectations regarding student behavior were very clear for the teachers in *Little House on the Prairie*, and parents supported teacher decisions regarding behavior, that is simply no longer true within the contemporary public education system. The challenges are overwhelming but must be addressed.

Emotional disturbance is defined in IDEA Sec 300.7 as follows:

(i) The term means a condition exhibiting one or more of the following characteristics over a long period of time

and to a marked degree that adversely affects a child's educational performance:

(A) An inability to learn that cannot be explained by intellectual, sensory, or health factors.

(B) An inability to build or maintain satisfactory interpersonal relationships with peers and teachers.

(C) Inappropriate types of behavior or feelings under normal circumstances.

(D) A general pervasive mood of unhappiness or depression.

(E) A tendency to develop physical symptoms or fears associated with personal or school problems.

(ii) The term includes schizophrenia. The term does not apply to children who are socially maladjusted, unless it is determined that they have an emotional disturbance.[54]

It must be understood that federally mandated special education services are available only to students who have been assessed and determined to have a serious emotional disturbance. Students with other disorders may be able to receive support as a result of other federal initiatives—for example, programs designed to prevent truancy—and/or support from school-based counseling, music therapy, and gang reduction programs.

CONTINUUM OF MENTAL HEALTH DISORDERS

Mental health behaviors must be considered on a continuum that ranges from those that are deemed "appropriate" to those that are deemed "inappropriate," or from those that are considered "socially acceptable" to those that are considered "socially unacceptable." Within the broad continuum of mental health disorders is a continuum for each type of disorder. For example, a student may experience significant anxiety (the specific type of disorder) when faced with state-mandated achievement tests; this anxiety is transient and usually ceases after the tests have been completed. On the other end of the continuum, within the category of "anxiety disorders," a student may have school phobia so traumatic that the student must be home-schooled.

Students who find themselves in situations in which there is a significant conflict between the expectations of the professionals in the school system and the expectations of the parents and immediate community struggle to make sense of their reality. One of the problems associated with the classification and identification of behaviors is that the determination of "appropriate" and "acceptable" behavior is situational. A student who is praised and honored in the home for being an active, inquisitive, curious learner who questions adults while seeking information may be perceived as "insolent" by an insecure teacher who expects students to accept the teacher's opinions without question.

Of significant concern is the fact that African American students are overrepresented in special education classes that serve students with mental

A Perfectly Executed Kick

Courtesy of Laurie Zittel

health disorders.[66] This overrepresentation is caused by a significant failure to embrace active/interactive learning styles. Essentially, there appears to be a "mismatch" between the cognitive (learning) styles of children from minority cultural groups and the cognitive styles emphasized in the schools. As a result, children may be inappropriately identified as having a mental health disorder and may be inappropriately taught, increasing the disorder.[45]

The *situation* is a significant component of the determination of a mental health disorder. The *severity* of the behavior is another important variable. Almost everyone occasionally reacts to stress, fatigue, grief, or uncertainty in ways that might be considered "abnormal" or "inappropriate." For example, a child may act out by destroying her toys after learning her parents are planning to divorce. If the violent, destructive behavior continues, the child may need significant intervention.

Although, typically, a mental health disorder is one in which a specific behavior, or a cluster of behaviors, persists over a period of time, one significant, atypical, antisocial behavior may be an indicator of a significant emotional disorder that may have been unnoticed or undiagnosed. For example, a 2nd-grader who stabs a classmate with a knife in order to join his older brother's gang may never have exhibited this type of antisocial behavior before, yet the nature of the behavior makes it vital for serious consideration to be given to the child's emotional disorder.

TYPES OF MENTAL HEALTH DISORDERS

It is important for the physical educator to distinguish carefully between the student who may, occasionally, misbehave and the student who has been diagnosed as having a mental health disorder. As teachers struggle to teach more and more students who do not follow rules, who reject discipline, and who despise authority, the lines between students who exhibit problematic behavior and those who actually have a psychoeducational diagnosis become difficult to distinguish. It is also important for the physical educator to understand that a child with a mental health disorder may exhibit a variety of symptoms over a given period of time that make a specific diagnosis impossible.

During the last few years an attempt has been made to reclassify mental health disorders to enable mental health personnel to better determine appropriate intervention strategies. The two categories decided upon are *internalizing disorders* and *externalizing disorders.* Internalizing disorders are expressed within an individual, disorders that make the person feel bad. Externalizing disorders are expressed overtly, disorders that make others feel bad.[7] The specific types of disorders in each of these categories follows.

Internalizing Disorders

Anxiety disorders
    Generalized anxiety disorder
    Obsessive-compulsive disorder
    Panic disorder
    Posttraumatic stress disorder
    Phobias
Eating disorders
Mood disorders
    Depression
    Bipolar disorder
    Seasonal affective disorder
    Manias

Externalizing Disorders

Attention deficit/hyperactivity disorder (ADHD)
Conduct disorders
    General conduct disorder
    Oppositional defiant disorder (ODD)
Suicidal Behavior
Drug and alcohol use and abuse

Internalizing Disorders

Anxiety Disorders

Anxiety disorders cause intense feelings of anxiety and tension when there is no real danger. The symptoms cause significant distress and interfere with daily activities. Children with anxiety disorders usually do anything to avoid situations that provoke anxiety. The physical signs of anxiety are restlessness, irritability, disturbed sleep, muscle aches and pains, gastrointestinal distress, and difficulty concentrating. Anxiety disorders are often accompanied by the symptoms of depression and can lead to chronic anxiety, such as phobia, posttraumatic stress disorder, or panic disorder.

Generalized Anxiety Disorder Generalized anxiety disorder (GAD) "is characterized by persistent, excessive, and unrealistic worry about everyday things."[2] People with this condition tend to worry throughout their waking moments and are unable to turn their fears off. They usually expect the worst, even though there is no reason for concern. One-third of the adults afflicted with GAD had their first symptoms in childhood. Women are twice as likely as men to have the condition.[2]

Obsessive-Compulsive Disorder Obsessive-compulsive disorder (OCD) is a condition that causes people "to have unwanted and intrusive thoughts (obsessions) they can't stop thinking about, and they feel compelled to repeatedly perform ritualistic behaviors and routines (compulsions) to try and ease their anxiety."[3] Some spend a great deal of time performing rituals, such as hand-washing or counting, in an attempt to rid themselves of unwanted thoughts and feelings. Others are constantly afraid they will do something wrong, such as bring harm to someone or make a foolish statement. Adults are usually aware of their condition; however, children who are obsessive-compulsive do not realize their actions are excessive.[3]

Panic Disorder Many children experience occasional panic attacks. These are characterized by nausea, abdominal distress, sweating, trembling, shaking, shortness of breath, dizziness, and crying or chest pain/discomfort. Few suffer from panic disorder, which usually originates in childhood and adolescence and is more common among women than men.[7]

Phobias A phobia is a significant, persistent, yet unrealistic and often debilitating fear of an event, a person, an activity, or an animal/insect. For example, school phobia is a significant, and often overwhelming, fear of going to school. Agoraphobia ("fear of the marketplace" in Greek) is an anxiety disorder characterized by an intense fear of being trapped in a situation in which no help is available, losing control, or doing something embarrassing in the presence of others. Agoraphobia can be brought on by repeated panic attacks and can, ultimately, cause a person to have a significant fear of leaving the home.

Posttraumatic Stress Disorder Posttraumatic stress disorder is characterized by an overwhelming traumatic event that is reexperienced; this causes intense fear, helplessness, horror, and avoidance of stimuli associated with the trauma.[7] *Posttraumatic stress disorder* used to be a term associated with combat veterans, victims of criminal violence, and people whose lives were significantly affected by such events as September 11, 2001, or Hurricane Katrina in 2005. Increasingly, children living in abusive homes and children who are living in homes within violent communities are demonstrating symptoms associated with posttraumatic stress disorder.

Eating Disorders

Eating disorders include anorexia nervosa, bulimia nervosa, and binge eating. As explained in Chapter 8, individuals with anorexia nervosa have an intense fear of gaining weight. As a result, they severely limit their caloric intake. About 95 percent of the people who have the condition are female, and onset is usually in adolescence.[7]

Individuals with bulimia nervosa have frequent episodes of uncontrolled overeating followed by inappropriate compensatory behavior to prevent weight gain, such as vomiting, purging, or excessive exercise. These individuals, unlike those with anorexia nervosa, usually have a normal weight. The incidence is 1 to 3 percent of adolescent girls.[7] Individuals with the condition are prone to impulsive behavior, as well as drug and alcohol abuse.

Binge eating is eating excessively and not attempting to rid oneself of the extra calories. It usually occurs after adolescence, and it commonly leads to obesity.[7]

Depression is characteristic of individuals with an eating disorder.[7]

Mood Disorders

Mood disorders are characterized by significant and prolonged moods over which the person has no control. Mood disorders include depression, bipolar disorder, seasonal affective disorder, and manias.

Childhood Depression Depression is among the most common of mental health disorders. Sixteen percent of Americans will suffer from depression at some point during their lifetimes.[30] Increasingly, the Americans who struggle with depression are children.

Childhood depression is a mood disorder that resembles depression in adults but shows up in very different ways in children. Children with depression may appear persistently sad, may no

CASE STUDY 14-2

Michelle

Michelle is an eight-year-old girl who is increasingly unsuccessful in school. She is a loner. She appears to have only one friend at school, a little girl with Down syndrome. She falls asleep in class. She complains of stomachaches. She daydreams and appears unable to concentrate on classroom instruction. In the gymnasium, she sits in the corner and cries. She used to like physical education; her motor skills are age appropriate.

APPLICATION TASK

Examine the National Association of Sport and Physical Education curriculum and/or your state's physical education curriculum for 3rd-graders. Identify the activities in which Michelle may experience success. Suggest modifications that may increase her likelihood of success.

longer enjoy activities they normally enjoyed, or may be agitated or irritable. Depressed children may frequently complain of physical problems, such as headaches and stomachaches, and have frequent absences from school or poor performance in school. They may appear bored or low in energy and have problems concentrating. A major change in eating or sleeping patterns is frequently a sign of depression in children and adolescents.

It appears that child abuse is a causative factor in childhood depression. Prolonged sexual abuse and incest appear to be significant. See Table 14-1 for symptoms of early onset of depression.

Childhood Bipolar Disorder Bipolar disorder is a serious, debilitating disorder that involves extreme mood swings or highs (mania) and lows (depression). During the manic phase, the individual may be elated, irritable, or hostile. The child may experience inflated self-esteem and may be boastful. The child may be overactive, may experience weight loss because of increased activity, and may not require sleep. In the depressive phase, the individual may be depressed, irritable, or anxious. The child may lack self-confidence and have low self-esteem. The child may focus on the negative and appear hopeless and helpless. The child will experience significant fatigue.[7]

Table 14-1	Symptoms of Depression in Children and Adolescents[17]

Loss of interest in activities that previously caused pleasure
Withdrawal from people who had been significant
Irritable mood
Significant weight loss
Sleep disturbance nearly every day
Significant fatigue
Physical symptoms, including headaches and stomachaches
Feelings of worthlessness
Poor self-esteem
Difficulty concentrating and paying attention
Poor school performance
Alcohol and other drug abuse
Thoughts of suicide or death

Seasonal Affective Disorder Seasonal affective disorder (SAD) is a mood disorder characterized by depression, lack of energy, a tendency to oversleep, and cravings for starchy or sweet foods during months of the year when there is prolonged limited sunshine. More than half a million people in the United States suffer from SAD, usually during the winter. The condition primarily affects adults over the age of 20; however, it has been diagnosed in some children and adolescents.[56]

Manias *Mania* is a term used to describe an elevated, expansive, or irritable mood that lasts more than one week. Additional symptoms include inflated self-esteem, greater talkativeness than usual, racing of thoughts, distractibility, and decreased need for sleep. The condition frequently begins in the teenage years, and it puts these individuals at risk of using poor judgment about people and appropriate behaviors.[7]

Externalizing Disorders

Attention Deficit/Hyperactivity Disorder (ADHD)

Attention deficit/hyperactivity disorder has received increasing attention since being included in the 1999 revision of IDEA. The types of the conditions and suggestions for testing and teaching children with ADHD are fully covered in Chapter 18 of this text.

Conduct Disorders

Bailey described a conduct disorder as follows:
    General conduct disorder usually develops in early adolescence and is characterized by behaviors including property destruction, truancy from school, setting fires, stealing, and lying. One of the most prevalent types of conduct disorders is oppositional-defiant disorder.[4]

Oppositional-defiant disorder consists of a pattern of negativity, hostility, and defiant behavior. Examples include: often loses temper, often argues with adults, often deliberately annoys people, is often angry and resentful, and is often spiteful or vindictive. Literally these individuals "sit" when asked to "stand" and "run" when asked to "walk." [15]

There are two basic subtypes of antisocial behavior that must be considered within the school setting. Covert antisocial behavior begins with "minor behaviors," such as lying and cheating. Later the behavior includes stealing, shoplifting, vandalism, fire-setting, and burglary.[61] Overt antisocial behavior begins with early disobedience and defiance. Later the child begins to be involved in more serious aggression—bullying and intimidating. Eventually, the individual is involved in rape, serious assault, or murder.[61] Consideration must be given when the child begins to demonstrate antisocial behaviors. "Early starters" begin demonstrating antisocial behaviors early in elementary school. "Late starters" begin to demonstrate the antisocial behaviors in middle school and high school.[48] Clearly, students who begin demonstrating the behaviors earlier are at more serious risk for long-term participation in, and the escalation of, inappropriate behaviors.

See Table 14-2 for behaviors of children with conduct disorders and Table 14-3 for the diagnostic criteria of conduct disorders.

Table 14-2	Behaviors of Children with Conduct Disorder[7]

- Lack sensitivity to the feelings of other children
- Act aggressively with little remorse
- Tend to be suspicious
- Believe other children are threatening
- Have difficulty tolerating frustration
- Are impulsive
- Are reckless
- Bully and make threats

Boys tend to
- Fight
- Steal
- Vandalize

Girls tend to
- Lie
- Engage in prostitution
- Run away

Suicidal Behavior

The World Health Organization (WHO) has reported that suicide worldwide causes more deaths every year than homicide or war.[69] In the United States, about 90 people commit suicide every day. Suicide is epidemic, particularly among adolescents; it is the second leading cause of death, second only to accidents.[7] Suicidal behavior includes suicide ideation (serious thoughts about suicide),[39] attempted suicide, and completed suicide. Suicidal behavior also includes plans and actions that appear to be unlikely to be successful;[36] it is believed that these plans and actions are a plea for help. An attempted suicide is an act that is not fatal; this may also be a significant plea for help. See Table 14-4 for the high-risk factors and behaviors associated with suicide.

Drug and Alcohol Use and Abuse

Illicit drugs for youth include marijuana, methamphetamines, hallucinogens, crack cocaine, heroin, Ecstasy, anabolic steroids, alcohol, and nicotine. Peak use of these drugs by teens in the United States occurred in the 1990s, but, thanks to preventive programs in our schools, use by teenagers is on the decrease. However, because of the negative impact drug usage has on mental health, any use should be of concern to educators.

Alcohol abuse includes the use of any type of alcoholic beverage prior to the legal drinking age. According to a 2006 survey of almost 50,000 8th-, 10th-, and 12th-graders in the United States, 70 percent of teenagers reported drinking alcohol at least once in their lifetime, and 10th- and 12th-grade Caucasians report greater use of alcohol than do African American or Hispanic youth.[28] According to the same survey, the use of marijuana, methamphetamines, crack cocaine, heroin, and tobacco decreased from 2003 to 2006. However, the use of prescription drugs, such as OxyContin and Vicodin, and inhalants increased during the same period, with 8th-graders showing the largest increase in usage. Another alarming trend is the increase in the number of 8th-graders who reported seeing no harm in using hallucinogens (LSD) and Ecstasy occasionally.[28] Teenage males report greater use of anabolic steroids and smokeless tobacco than do females,

Table 14-3	Diagnostic Criteria of Conduct Disorders

A. A repetitive and persistent pattern of behavior in which the basic rights of others or major age-appropriate societal norms or rules are violated, as manifested by the presence of three (or more) of the following criteria in the past 12 months, with at least one criterion present in the past 6 months:

Aggression to People and Animals
 1. Often bullies, threatens, or intimidates others
 2. Often initiates physical fights
 3. Has used a weapon that can cause serious physical harm to others
 4. Has been physically cruel to people
 5. Has been physically cruel to animals
 6. Has stolen while confronting a victim (e.g., mugging)
 7. Has forced someone into sexual activity

Destruction of Property
 8. Has deliberately engaged in fire setting with the intention of causing serious damage
 9. Has deliberately destroyed others' property

Deceitfulness or Theft
 10. Has broken into another's house, building, or car
 11. Often lies to obtain goods or favors
 12. Has stolen items without confronting a victim (e.g., shoplifting)

Serious Violations of Rules
 13. Stays out at night despite parental rules, beginning before age 13 years
 14. Has run away from home overnight at least twice while living in parent or surrogate home (or once for a lengthy stay)
 15. Is often truant from school, beginning before age 13 years

B. The disturbance in behavior causes clinically significant impairment in social, academic, or occupational functioning.

C. If the individual is age 18 years or older, criteria are not met for antisocial personality disorder.

Modified: from www.mentalhealth.com/dis1/.

and females report greater abuse of amphetamines and methamphetamines than do males.

Each year approximately 5,000 youth under the age of 21 die as a result of underage drinking. Those who begin drinking during their teen years are at the greatest risk (47 percent) of developing alcohol dependence at some point in their lives.[19] Compared with other students, the approximately 1 million frequent heavy drinkers have mostly lower grades (Ds and Fs) and most often pose risks to themselves and others.[24]

According to the National Institute on Drug Abuse, "all drugs that are addicting can activate the brain's pleasure circuit," which is why people enjoy using drugs. Unfortunately, when a person continues to use drugs because he or she enjoys the pleasant feeling the drugs yield, fundamental, long-lasting changes occur in the brain. At some point in time (which varies from person to person), the brain "flips a switch," transforming the drug user into a drug addict who constantly craves more drugs. Obtaining the means to get more drugs becomes the focal point of the addict's life, and other things lose their importance.[63] Youth who use drugs often have co-existing disorders. Among the most common are conduct disorders and mood disorders, particularly depression.[42]

Living in a poor and hazardous environment, experiencing economic hardship, and dealing with parental depression are known to contribute negatively to the mental health of youth; thus, they are attracted to drugs that help them escape from reality.[70] However, it has been reported that youth are less likely to use illicit drugs if they are socially accepted at school and feel that their teachers treat them fairly. Teachers can and do make dramatic differences in students' lives.[52]

INCIDENCE OF MENTAL HEALTH DISORDERS

Because of the significant stigma attached to mental health disorders, the reported incidence is probably significantly lower than the actual number of affected individuals. It is also important to acknowledge the fact that special education services provided for students with mental health disorders are limited to those students who have been identified as having a "serious emotional disturbance."

There has been an ever-increasing incidence of "serious emotional disturbance" in children from birth to 21 years of age served in federally supported programs for individuals with disabilities. The number of children who receives special education services because of emotional disturbance continues to escalate; most recent Office of Special Education Programs data indicate that almost 500,000 children are being served.[65] That number represents 7.8 percent of the students served in special education.

The percentages of students with "serious emotional disturbance" who are served in particular education settings follow:

< 21% outside regular class	34.7%
21–60% outside regular class	21.6
60% outside regular class	26.8
Public separate facility	6.8
Private separate facility (only students who have "multiple disabilities" are more likely to receive educational services in a private school facility)	5.6
Public residential facility	1.1
Private residential facility	1.8
Hospital/homebound environment	1.2[65]

CAUSES OF MENTAL HEALTH DISORDERS

The causes of mental health disorders can be understood only within the broad context of the total ecosystem of the individual. The disorders are a function of the interaction of a number of variables:

- Heredity and genetic predisposition
- Biochemical and neurotransmitter imbalance, which may be congenital, appearing in utero and at birth; this may occur as a result of glandular dysfunction and may be adventitious, caused by the use or abuse or alcohol or other drugs
- Neuroendocrine imbalance[11]
- Low birthweight and decreased head circumference[10]
- Significant parental failure to regulate homeostatic and physiological status of the infant.[11]
- Breakdown in the family unit

Table 14-4	High-Risk Factors and Behaviors Associated with Suicide[7]

- Talking about suicide
- Previous suicide attempt
- Making detailed suicide plans
- Family history of suicide or affective disorder
- Social isolation
- Depression
- Anxiety, restlessness, and motor agitation
- Significant feelings of guilt, inadequacy, and hopelessness
- Impulsive, hostile personality
- Alcohol or other drug abuse
- Preoccupation with death and dying
- Loss of interest in things in which the person was previously interested
- Calling relatives and friends with whom the person rarely has contact
- Giving away possessions
- Getting one's affairs in order

- Parental mood disorders, particularly in the mother, characterized by withdrawal, depression, or hostility[11]
- Parental conflict[64]
- Parenting difficulties; mental health disorders are particularly linked to abusive families
- Sexual and physical abuse and emotional neglect[1,53]
- Lack of support by the extended family
- Poverty[4]
- Peer pressure, particularly gang involvement
- Community expectations regarding behavior
- Environmental toxins
- Inappropriate, inflexible teaching strategies
- Discrimination

Grossman[21] indicates that teachers may contribute to mental health disorders in the schools by discriminating against the students and criticizing them in a harsh manner.

The causes of mental health disorders may actually be systemic and profound. There is considerable evidence that the very process by which urbanization has occurred is causative in psychoses, depression, sociopathy, substance abuse, alcoholism, crime, delinquency, vandalism, family disintegration, and alienation.[41] See Table 14-5 for more information about urbanization and mental health disorders.

CHARACTERISTICS OF LEARNERS WITH MENTAL HEALTH DISORDERS

Learners with mental health disorders constitute a very heterogeneous group. The physical educator must work closely with the learners' parents, the school counselor, and the learners' primary educators within the school building. This is critical in order to learn each student's specific mental health characteristics.

Learners with mental health disorders struggle within the school setting. Disruptive and antisocial learners, in particular, are excluded from school groups and find it difficult to maintain friendships. They tend to seek each other out and form separatist groups.[35]

Table 14-5	Urbanization and the Causes of Mental Health Disorders[41]

Environmental
- Air pollution and toxins (lead and carbon monoxide)
- Noise pollution
- Traffic congestion, accidents, and road rage
- Excessive stimulation

Sociological and Economic
- Poverty
- Unemployment and underemployment
- Crime, violence, and gangs
- Crowded and substandard housing/homelessness
- Marginalization

Psychosocial
- Family disintegration
- Cultural disintegration and confusion
- Racism and secularization

Psychological
- Powerlessness
- Isolation and loneliness
- Fear and anxiety
- Lack of quality of life

There is considerable evidence that children and youth with mental health disorders have educational difficulties:

- Many children and youth with mental health disorders receive inappropriate educational, social, and medical services; as a result, families make tremendous financial sacrifices to secure needed services for their children.[12,34]
- Most students who have been diagnosed with an emotional disorder have lower grade point averages than their classmates.[67]
- Almost 40 percent have learning disabilities,[33] not to be confused with problems with learning.
- Forty-four percent of all suspensions in special education are children with emotional disturbances, even though children with mental health disorders constitute less than 8 percent of all students with disabilities.[68]
- Almost 50 percent fail at least one high school course.[67]

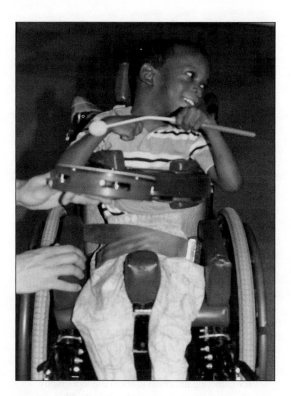

Make a Joyous Noise

• One-fifth are arrested once before they drop out of school.[67]
• More than half leave school without graduating (most by the 10th grade).
• Children and youth with mental health disorders are more likely to grow up to be underemployed and involved in criminal behavior and to abuse substances.[37]

When children and youth are struggling with mental health issues, the physical education teacher may be one of the first to notice the signs that a student is in trouble and needs help. The very nature of a physical education class—with a great deal of movement, excitement, and noise and the need to work as part of a team—makes some mental health disorders more evident than they would be if a learner were just sitting at a desk. The physical educator should be sensitive to the following indications that a student is having difficulty learning:

1. Poor work habits in practicing and developing motor skills
2. Lack of motivation in achieving goals not of an immediate nature
3. Disruptive class behavior
4. Lack of involvement in class activities
5. Inability to follow directions, daydreaming[29]
6. Demands for constant attention of teacher and other students
7. Short attention span, distractibility
8. Poor coordination
9. Development of physical symptoms (stomachache, headache, etc.) when confronted with physical activities with which the person is not secure
10. Overactivity, restlessness[29]
11. Forgetfulness, memory impairment[11]

Difficulty developing and maintaining quality personal relationships with the teacher or other students often makes the physical education experience a devastating one for learners with mental health disorders. Indicators that a student is having difficulty with interpersonal relationships include the following:

1. Lack of conscience, hostile disobedience, resistance to authority
2. Loss of emotional control, temper tantrums
3. Formation of superficial relationships, if relationships are formed[29]
4. Shyness, hypersensitivity, detachment, poor self-esteem, feelings of inadequacy
5. Aggressiveness, hostility, destructiveness, quarrelsomeness
6. Group values of delinquency
7. Fear, anxiety, apprehension of teachers and other students
8. Disrespect of others

The learner may demonstrate inappropriate behavior under "typical" conditions in the physical education class:

1. Unhappiness, depression
2. Inconsistencies in responses

3. Rigid expectations of everyday life
4. Carelessness, irresponsibility, apathy
5. Immaturity, impulsiveness
6. Tendency to seek retribution
7. Unreasonable expectations regarding own behavior[11]
8. Incorrigibility
9. Tendency to attribute hostile intentions to the conduct of others[4]

The learner with a mental health disorder may also demonstrate poor motor behavior in physical education:

1. Poor physical condition caused by withdrawal from activity
2. Retardation of motor skill development caused by withdrawal from activity
3. Disorientation in space and time
4. Poor body image

TESTING

The student with a mental health disorder is typically able to participate in any state or local education agency–mandated physical fitness, motor, sport skill, or knowledge assessments regarding rules, techniques, and health and wellness concepts. Decisions regarding who will administer such tests are often left to the IEP or multidisciplinary team and may be a function of the placement of the student in general or adapted physical education.

Fitnessgram, AAHPERD Physical Best, and Fit Smart have been used effectively with a wide variety of students and are usually appropriate for a child with a mental health disorder.

If the student has been identified as having a motor deficit, the choice of assessment instruments is determined primarily by the student's age. The Test of Gross Motor Development may be very appropriate for an elementary-school-age student with a mental health disorder. The Louisiana Competency Test in Adapted Physical Education may be very useful for a student in middle school or high school.

When testing students who have mental health disorders, the teacher must be sensitive to the fact that these students may feel extremely threatened by test situations. When placed in threatening situations, more acting-out behavior can be expected. Aggressive or withdrawal behavior can be avoided if the student does not have to perform in the presence of peers and if the teacher is supportive of the student's efforts. It is usually advisable, if testing a student with a serious disorder, to include the student's favorite teacher or a significant peer in the testing situation. The physical educator should be aware of the fact that the most appropriate assessment of a learner with a mental health disturbance includes an assessment not only of the learner but of the learner's parents as well.[4]

Within the school, the physical educator may be asked to be involved in a functional behavioral assessment (FBA) as a part of a team, including school staff and parents. The functional behavioral assessment provides the framework for the development of an effective intervention program. Ryan, Halsey, and Matthews define FBA:

> FBA is a multimethod problem-solving strategy for gathering information about the topography of a particular behavior (what it looks like), as well as the ecology (environmental variables) surrounding its occurrence. This type of assessment is called ecobehavioral, because the focal point is on the interaction between the environment and the target behavior.[53]

The functional behavioral assessment typically involves gathering data, descriptive information, regarding the child's behavior and then developing an "educated guess"[51] that ties the antecedent behavior with the consequences in the context of the setting. Team members participate in a process to define the child's problem behavior, share observations, analyze the child's patterns, and hypothesize the function of the child's behavior.[55] The physical educator can share important information regarding the child's behavior in the gymnasium and on the playground with the team.

SPECIAL CONSIDERATIONS

The school should offer a variety of intervention strategies to address mental health disorders, particularly antisocial behavior, in the schools. The most basic of the interventions is "universal," a prevention-based approach. These include a schoolwide discipline program and a school curriculum that emphasizes the development of conflict resolution and anger management skills.[60] Individualized interventions designed for one learner or for a small group of learners in a self-contained classroom or small-group therapy setting are required for learners who already demonstrate inappropriate, asocial behavior.

One of the major problems associated with the education of students with mental health disorders is the stigma. Individuals who struggle with emotional disorders and their families may feel stigmatized and rejected and, in fact, may be stigmatized and rejected.[18] Unfortunately, this stigma often causes families to avoid seeking professional help, so identification of the problem is delayed.

The education of learners with disabilities cannot be seen in a framework outside the family unit. The parent/primary caregiver may be willing to share strategies that work with school administrators, teachers, coaches, and paraeducators. Family management practices are key to the collaboration between the school and the home:

- Many parents/primary caregivers learn how to identify problematic behavior and track occurrences of the behavior at home.
- To survive, parents/caregivers learn to use reinforcement techniques, such as praise, point systems, and rewards.
- Effective parents learn to use a "mild" consequence for inappropriate behavior, such as a one-hour loss of computer or video-game use.
- Effective caregivers use strategies to communicate clearly with their child. They learn to use "alpha" commands or instructions instead of "beta" commands. An alpha command is clear, specific, and direct and allows the child a limited time to respond. A "beta" command or instruction is one that is vague and conveys only frustration and anger. For example, if a parent wants the child to put toys away, an alpha command is "William, put your toys in the closet." A beta command,

however, is "William, I've had a really long day. And I need some cooperation around the house. I can't be expected to work all day and worry about dinner and then come home and find the house is a mess. The least you could do is put away your toys." The physical educator also needs to learn to use alpha commands.[4,26]

It is important for physical educators, and other educators, to be aware of one emotional disorder of parents of children with disabilities that is receiving increasing attention. Munchausen syndrome by proxy is a frightening disorder in which the parent, usually the mother, harms her own child. The child abuse is pervasive and destructive. The mother's psychological illness and substantial need are the major clinical symptoms. The mother appears to medical and educational personnel to be very caring and concerned and, apparently, she feeds off the emotions shared by these personnel. Typically, the harm is done in one of three ways:

1. The mother lies about symptoms or signs associated with an illness or a disability, including heating a thermometer to demonstrate elevated fever
2. The mother alters medical records or laboratory specimens, including tampering with urine, blood, or fecal samples
3. The mother causes the illness or disability. Some of the common reported abuses are
   a. Drug poisoning, using over-the-counter, illegal, and prescription medication (prescribed for someone else)
   b. Salt poisoning, including adding salt to breast milk
   c. False allegations regarding sexual or physical abuse
   d. Inducing asthma, diabetic coma, and so on by withholding medications[23,59]

A SUPPORTIVE LEARNING ENVIRONMENT FOR CHILDREN WITH MENTAL HEALTH DISORDERS

School administrators and teachers must face the realities that exist in the public schools today.

Clearly, the public schools mirror the increasing violence and unpredictability within the society. The "Zero Tolerance" response to violence in the schools, while a good first step, is not adequate. Skiba and Peterson wrote that "a broader perspective, stressing early identification, comprehensive planning, prevention, and instruction in important social skills, is necessary if schools are to prevent the tragedies that happen too often in our schools."[57] School personnel must be involved in long-range planning and must emphasize partnerships among the school, family members, and the community.[57] Clearly, the community has a vested interest in schools' prevention and remediation programs because there is a relationship between a child's in-school disciplinary problems and juvenile offenses within the community.[60]

The early identification of children who are at risk for mental health disorders is critical, as the symptoms and behaviors are being seen earlier and earlier among our children. The earlier educators and mental health specialists address the problem, the greater the prospect for preventing, ameliorating, or remedying the disorder. It is important to note, however, that in the absence of obvious external behaviors (e.g., a preschooler setting his or her apartment on fire or sexually molesting another child) it is difficult to predict future mental health disorders in children.[8] Certainly, prevention is the key. Teachers and other caregivers who work with toddlers and preschoolers have the unique privilege and responsibility to do the following:

- Help toddlers and preschoolers identify violence and its consequences.
- Talk openly with young children about real-world violence.
- Respond to young children's reactions to violence.
- Help them develop basic safety skills for self-protection.
- Never use corporal punishment; the last thing they need in their lives is more violence.
- Work closely with families to help parents help their children deal with violence.[58]

See Chapter 10 for specific suggestions regarding facilitating play in infants, toddlers, and preschoolers and strategies for helping young children deal with violence.

The physical educator should be aware that many children with mental health disorders take medication that affects their performance during the school day. It is critical that the physical educator know what medications a student is taking, particularly because some inhibit motor control and have a negative impact on balance, for example.

Most parents are thrilled if the physical educator takes enough interest in the student to ask for specific information about a medication. A physician will not release information about medication—or anything else, for that matter—to a teacher without signed parental permission. Most state education agencies have a standard form to request a release of information from a physician. The physical educator can ask the school nurse to complete such a request.

Psychological tests are required to establish the presence of mental health disorders. However, the psychological data and the labels associated with the data often do not provide specific information to assist the physical education teacher in planning instruction. The physical educator should work closely with the child's special education teachers, counselors, and family members to plan and modify instruction. If at all possible, the physical educator should adopt the instructional techniques and behavior management strategies used during the rest of the child's instructional day. This type of consistency is critical to the success of a student with a mental health disorder. This will be considered more completely later in this chapter.

Specific ways the physical educator can collaborate with other professionals who work with the student as well as the student's IEP team are as follows:

- Share information about the student's physical and motor needs.
- Listen to and act on relevant suggestions made by parents and other professionals.
- Share materials and ideas with individuals working with the student.

- Solicit support from parents and colleagues that contributes to the effectiveness of the physical education program.
- Use resource personnel effectively.[14]

TEACHING STRATEGIES

The children who need great teachers the most may be the very children who are the most difficult to teach. The teacher of a child who has a mental health disorder must be grounded, self-assured, confident, patient, and competent. The teacher must be able to see the student's behavior within the broader context of a mental health disorder and not respond to inappropriate behavior as if it were directed toward the teacher. The teacher's ability to separate self from inappropriate student behavior is critical. See Tables 14-6 and 14-7 for specific strategies of behavior management for the physical educator.

The teacher of a child with a mental health disorder has a tremendous responsibility. The most critical responsibility is for consistent, effective classroom management designed to prevent problems and minimize behaviors that disrupt learning. In fact, many school-based discipline strategies, such as in-school and out-of-school suspensions, may actually be dumping grounds for students whose teachers are unprepared to manage their classroom.[50] In fact, it appears that the practices of suspension and expulsion are associated with negative outcomes, which include poor student attitudes toward school, academic failure, retention in grades, and increased dropout rates.[50]

As critical as a consistent educational environment is the absolute intolerance of any behavior that suggests or refers to violence within the physical education program. Physical education teachers must not tolerate any behavior or language that refers to guns, death, violent movies, or violent sports (e.g., professional wrestling).[34]

The principles that guide the teacher of children who have mental health disorders in physical education are, very simply, the *basic principles of good teaching*:

- Carefully model caring, sensitive, adult behavior.

- A gentle, calm, but structured teaching style will promote learning for all students, but particularly for students with mental health disorders.
- Teach so that children with all of Gardner's eight types of intelligence can learn.
- Establish and use a class routine.
- Set, define, and post positively worded rules and expectations that are age appropriate. Make clear not only the behaviors that are appropriate but those that are inappropriate. (See Table 14-8 for a brief example of positive gymnasium expectations.)
- Consistently acknowledge and reward appropriate behavior.
- Consistently ensure fair and humane consequences for inappropriate behavior. Corporal punishment is not a fair and humane consequence in the public schools.[13]
- Remind the student of the consequences of inappropriate behavior.
- Emphasize cooperative activities.
- Ensure that each student has a designated spot with enough personal space to avoid physical contact with other students.
- Ensure there is a safe space to which a student can retreat for a self-imposed "time-out."
- Have enough equipment, so that young children, in particular, do not have to share equipment.

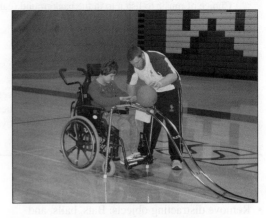

A Student Using a Switch Release on a Bowling Ramp
Courtesy of Kristi Roth, University of Wisconsin Stevens Point.

Table 14-6	Behavior Management: Learners with Mental Health Disorders[6,62]

- Effective intervention must duplicate the strategies used in other phases of the learner's life—school, home, recreation center, and/or work environment. This is crucial, so that the individual has consistent feedback and reinforcement.
- Teachers need to be well grounded and self-assured. Learners with mental health disorders often "push the buttons" of perceived authority figures. The teacher must be secure enough to understand that inappropriate emotions/behaviors are not directed at him or her. These behaviors include but are not limited to
    - Absolute rejection of the authority figure
    - Conflicting demands; one minute the learner may be clingy, demand constant attention, and seek affection and the next moment he or she may be shouting, "I hate you"
    - Temper tantrums, rages, and outbursts
    - Unpredictable changes in emotions and moods
    - Physical and/or verbal aggression
    - Significant withdrawal
    - Negativism, noncompliance, and refusal behaviors
    - Impulsiveness
    - Destruction of equipment and materials
- The limits and expectations regarding behavior must be clearly defined.
- Rules need to be posted in simple language or symbols or pictures. The learners need to be reminded *daily* of the rules and consequences if that behavior is not followed.
- Positive behavior and its positive consequences must be made clear; always "catch 'em being good" and reward the appropriate behavior
- The minimum amount of reinforcement should be used to encourage appropriate behavior:
    Smiles
    Verbal praise
    Verbal praise with a sign—"thumbs up"
    Verbal praise paired with a physical reinforcer: high, medium, low, or behind the back "5"
    Tangible reinforcers: stickers or praise notes for young learners
    Primary reinforcers: goldfish or graham crackers
- With older learners, more appropriate reinforcers may be
    Choice of activity
    "Free time"
    Choice of music to listen to in the background (careful screening is important)
    Baseball or football cards
    Sports posters
    Slice of pizza
    "Alone with me" time—teacher commits to time spent with the learner, shooting baskets or swimming laps together
- Inappropriate behavior and its negative consequences must be clear. The learner must be reminded that the behavior and consequence is a choice. The consequence must always occur and it must be explained to link cause-effect—for example, "I'm sorry, Timmy, but you chose to [cite misbehavior]. You know this is the consequence."

- Remove distracting objects. Bats, balls, and other play equipment should be kept out of sight until the time of use, if possible.

- Maintain class control but do not use "power" for the sake of showing "power."[26]
- Pair children carefully for learning tasks.

Table 14-7	Behavior Management Self-Check for Physical Educators

1. Are the majority of statements you make during the school day to your students in physical education *positive?*[29]
2. Are class expectations stated *positively?*[29]
3. Are class expectations and consequences reviewed regularly?
4. Do you remind students that *behavior is always a choice?*
5. Do you *always* follow through with consequences?
6. In a given day, are most of the consequences *positive?*
7. Do you know and use the names of your students? (Knowing and using their names is a basic sign of respect.)
8. Do you reinforce a student's appropriate behavior specifically, rather than making general comments that are meaningless, such as "Good job"?[29]
9. Are the activities you choose age- and developmentally appropriate?
10. Are you careful *not* to use sarcasm?
11. Do you avoid verbal and physical confrontations when a student is angry?[29]
12. Do you model/teach your students the skills they need to deal with their anger?[29]
13. Do you praise in public and correct in private?
14. Do you act calm and controlled, even if you feel different?

- Avoid activities that promote aggressive behavior—wrestling, for example.
- Ask for and use the behavior management plan developed by the student's IEP/multidisciplinary team.
- Select activities that allow all students to experience success.

THE PHYSICAL EDUCATION PROGRAM

A developmentally appropriate, well-taught physical education program is critical for learners with mental health disorders. The potential benefits of a quality physical education are, perhaps, even more

Table 14-8	Gymnasium Expectations Stated in a Positive Way

1. Raise your hand before speaking.
2. Remain on your spot until advised to leave it.
3. Keep your hands and feet to yourself.
4. Use school-appropriate language.
5. Use equipment as demonstrated.

important for learners with mental health disorders than for other children.

It appears that a curriculum that is sensitive to students' interests and allows them to be involved in choices may help prevent acting-out and inappropriate behaviors, particularly in students with mental health disorders.[31,35] Team teaching strategies that allow students to choose activities may be very helpful to the physical educator trying to create a good learning environment.

It appears particularly important to provide students the opportunity to participate, daily, in sustained, vigorous aerobic activities.[25] For preschoolers and young elementary school learners, the emphasis should be on simple dance activities, such as "Chug Along Choo Choo," "Bendable Stretchable," tricycling, bicycling, and vigorous, sustained playground activity. For older elementary-age learners, these activities should include walking, jogging, running, cross-country skiing, inline skating, and swimming. Middle and high school students can get the appropriate level of aerobic activity by walking, jogging, running, swimming, stationary cycling, stationary rowing, aerobic dancing, and aquarobics. (See Table 14-9 for more information on aquatics.)

There is significant evidence that participation in aerobic activities may release endorphins, which improve mood and reduce stress. Exercise programs have been effective in reducing the stereotypical, self-injurious, and disruptive behavior of individuals with severe behavior disorders.[5,44] There is also evidence that participation in systematic exercise may enhance self-esteem and body image.[66] There is a significant body of research that indicates that exercise has a positive influence on psychiatric disorders.[9,16,20,43,66]

Table 14-9	Aquatics for Learners with Mental Health Disorders[62]

- The aquatics program must be such that the student's success is guaranteed. A careful initial assessment will ensure success. Please refer to the Texas Woman's University Project INSPIRE Aquatics Web page: www.twu.edu/INSPIRE.
- Start with "familiar" skills (walking, running, jumping in the water, for example) and move slowly to unfamiliar skills.
- Create small learning stations or areas for students, so that there are "safe spaces." This can be done with lane lines, for example, or a tethered floating mat.
- From the time students enter the locker room, every minute must be planned and monitored carefully. The locker room is the most potentially volatile situation for these learners. Issues tied to abuse, in its many forms, are more evident in this vulnerable setting. Supervision is crucial.
- With a particularly confrontational student, the best environment may be one in which the learner is over his or her head. It may be easier for the teacher to control behavior if the learner is dependent on the teacher.
- Touch, even for spotting, needs to be explained carefully and done with care. A learner with a history of abuse may misinterpret well-intentioned touch.
- There must be a "fail safe" plan for an emergency—a student "out of control." The lifeguard on deck must be able to contact another teacher or an administrator instantly.

It appears there is some promise in the use of relaxation training for students with mental health disorders, particularly for students who are aggressive. Progressive muscle relaxation, meditation, yoga, guided imagery, and biofeedback have been found to reduce arousal.[72] Yoga and progressive muscle relaxation training hold particular promise for the physical educator who is teaching children and youth who demonstrate aggressive behavior. Preliminary research indicates that children with

mental health disorders who exhibit aggressive behavior demonstrate less aggressive behavior after participating in a progressive muscle relaxation program based on Jacobson's work.[40]

It also appears that there is significant promise in the use of challenge activities, cooperative,[6] and team-building activities. Lappin wrote,

> Behavior-disordered students benefit from activities that offer a challenge to the students. Camping, hiking, rock climbing, rappelling, canoeing, rafting, and backpacking are all activities that can be adapted to the novice and do not require exceptional physical ability. Other activities that benefit students include ropes courses, initiative games, cross-country skiing, snowshoeing, orienteering, cycling, skin diving, tubing, and sailing.[38]

The benefits of the "wilderness" learning experience have been well documented for learners with behavior disorders.[47] Many of the strategies that have been used effectively in wilderness therapy can be adapted and used in close-to-the-school activities as well—hikes and bicycle rides, for example. These strategies include student choice, group huddles to problem solve, and time for rest and reflection. Clearly, when students are given the opportunity to experience a wide variety of functional activities, there are more "teachable moments" than when students are not given that opportunity.

Carefully designed instructional physical education programs can play a significant role in the lives of learners with mental health disorders. The curricular emphasis should be on aerobic activity, relaxation training, and cooperative, challenge-based activities that encourage effective communication with others. The program must support student efforts in and through consistency and positive behavior management strategies. Perhaps most important, the physical education classroom must be bully free and safe (see Chapter 9 for more specific information regarding creating a bully-free learning environment) and must encourage personal responsibility (see Chapter 9 for information about Hellison's model).

MODIFICATIONS/ADAPTATIONS/INCLUSION TECHNIQUES

One of the major considerations for learners with mental health disorders is the least restrictive environment. For many learners with mental health disorders the regular physical education program would be very restrictive and overwhelming. It is critical that the IEP/multidisciplinary team address the possibility of providing physical education within a self-contained program. There are some benefits to a self-contained placement: (1) a well-structured behavior management system (such as Boys Town); (2) teachers and aides specifically trained in the behavior management system; (3) a relatively small staff–student ratio; and (4) clearly defined physical boundaries, often behind closed, locked, doors.[25] This consistency and safety may be extremely important to the education of learners with mental health disorders.

The only safe instructional strategy for including most students with mental health disorders in the general physical education program is to have the students work with a carefully trained paraeducator. The practice of assigning "peer tutors" is questionable, at best, for a number of reasons. Clearly, the most significant is that a learner with a mental health disorder is too unpredictable for another child to anticipate and address the learner's behaviors.

A physical educator serving a student with a mental health disorder must adopt the behavior management plan developed by the IEP/multidisciplinary team. These students need *consistency*. A teacher who just "rolls out the ball" will not be able to serve these children—or others, for that matter.

It is also important that the same behavior management plan be used by all teachers and other school personnel working with the student. For example, the Boys Town curriculum has been adopted by many public schools that serve students with mental health disorders. Indeed, the best possible scenario is one in which school personnel and the family use the same strategies. This gives the student the best possible opportunity to succeed.

In many school-based programs for students with mental health disorders, the student literally "earns" the right, by demonstrating appropriate behavior, to participate in school programs, such as physical education. The unique characteristics of the physical education program must be discussed with the IEP/multidisciplinary team before any decision is made to include a student with a severe disorder in the physical education environment. Perhaps the major issue in many physical education programs, unfortunately, is large class size. Typically, the student with a mental health disorder requires a great deal of attention. This is difficult, if not impossible, for the physical educator teaching three or more 1st-grade classes, for example, simultaneously.

COMMUNITY-BASED OPPORTUNITIES

The development of the individual transition plan for students who have reached the age of 16 years takes on a special meaning for students with mental health disorders. The IEP/multidisciplinary team must work closely with the physical educator who can help the team identify community-based resources in which the adult would be well received. That is the vital element—few community leisure, recreation, sport, and fitness programs are designed to accommodate an individual with significantly divergent, often inappropriate, behavior.

Unfortunately, the stigma attached to mental illness often creates a situation in which individuals with these disorders do not have an opportunity for participation at the community level without a one-on-one support system. It appears that the emphasis for adults, as well as for school-age children, needs to be on regular, vigorous aerobic activity. Participation in this type of activity appears to enhance self-esteem that may—in addition to increasing physical fitness—positively influence the adult's behavior and make community-based participation a reality.

Certainly, individuals who have been able to learn the skills necessary to use fitness equipment (e.g., treadmills, rowing machines, stair climbers, and weight machines); who know how to access and use the locker-room facilities in a community swimming center; and who are able to monitor their own performance have the best chance of being active throughout their lives.　✍

Summary

Increasingly, physical education teachers and other school professionals struggle to teach learners with mental health disorders. It is critical that the physical educator be able to identify the early signs of disorder. The physical education class may be the situation in which the signs are most easily identified. The physical educator must create a carefully designed classroom learning environment in which behavior management is used constructively to enhance learning and promote learners' self-esteem. The emphasis must be on vigorous, aerobic, developmentally appropriate, noncompetitive activity.

Review Questions

1. What are some signs or symptoms of mental health disorders?

2. What is the impact of urbanization on mental health? What are other causes of mental health disorders?

3. What is a stigma?

4. What are some of the basic techniques the physical educator should use to teach learners with mental health disorders?

5. What should be the emphasis in the physical education curriculum for students with these disorders?

6. Describe the program implications—behavior management and safety—that are critical to learners with mental health disorders.

Student Activities

1. Ask for permission to observe a physical education class in a public school. Carefully identify the student behaviors that may be tied to mental health disorders.

2. Do a community-based search for resources for children with mental health disorders and their families.

3. Compare and contrast Hellison's programs for at-risk students with the recommendations for physical education programs made in this chapter.

4. How can the physical education teacher facilitate a student's transition from the school to the community setting?

References

1. Ackerman PT, et al.: Prevalence of post traumatic stress disorder and other psychiatric diagnoses in three groups of abused children (sexual, physical and both), *Child Abuse Negl* 22(8):759–774, 1998.

2. Anxiety Disorders Association of America: *Generalized anxiety disorder,* www.adaa.org/GettingHelp/AnxietyDisorders/GAD.asp. 2007.

3. Anxiety Disorders Association of America: *Obsessive-compulsive disorder,* www.adaa.org/GettingHelp/AnxietyDisorders/GAD.asp. 2007.

4. Bailey VFA: Intensive interventions in conduct disorders, *Arch Disease in Childhood* 74:352–356, 1996.

5. Baumeister AA, MacLean WE: Deceleration of self-injurious behavior and stereotypic responding by exercise, *Applied Research Mental Retard* 5:385–393, 1982.

6. Bay-Hinitz J, Peterson RF, Quiltch RH: Cooperative games: A way to modify aggressive and cooperative behaviors in young children, *J Applied Behavioral Analysis* 27:435–446, 1994.

7. Beers MH, Porter RS, Jones TV, Kaplan JL, Berkwits M: *The Merck manual of diagnosis and therapy.* Whitehouse Station, NJ, Merck Research Laboratories, 2006.

8. Bennett KJ, et al.: Predicting conduct problems: Can high-risk children be identified in kindergarten and grade 1? *J Consulting Clin Psychol* 67(4):470–480, 1999.

9. Bosscher RJ: Running and mixed physical exercises with depressed psychiatric patients, *International Journal of Sports Psychology* 24:170–184, 1993.

10. Cannon M, Murray RM: Neonatal origins of schizophrenia, *Arch Disease in Childhood* 78(1):1–3, 1998.

11. Cicchetti D, Toth SL: The development of depression in children and adolescents, *Amer Psychologist* 53(2):221–241, 1998.

12. Cohen R, Harris R, Gottlieb S, Best AM: States' use of transfer of custody as a requirement for providing services to emotionally disturbed children, *Hospital Community Psychiatry* 42:526–530, 1991.

13. Corrigan D: Office of Special Education, Challenges for Personnel Preparation Conference, Washington, DC, September 8–10, 1999.

14. Dettmer P, Thruston LP, Dyck N: *Consultation, collaboration and teamwork for students with special needs.* Boston, Allyn & Bacon, 1993.

15. Donovan SJ: *A new approach to disruptive behavior disorders and the antisocial spectrum,* Medscape Mental Health, www.medscape.com/ Medscape/psychiatry/journal, 1998.

16. Doyne EJ, et al.: Running versus weight lifting in the treatment of depression, *J of Consulting and Clinical Psychology* 55:748–754, 1987.

17. *Early onset depression.* www.nami.org/helpline/ depression-child.html. 2004.

18. Farmer EMZ, Mustillo S, Burns BJ, Costello EJ: The epidemiology of mental health programs and service use in youth: Results from the great smoky mountains study. In Epstein MH, Kutash K, Duchnowsk A, editors: *Outcomes for children and youth with behavioral and emotional disorders and their families: Programs and evaluation best practices,* 2nd ed. 2005.

19. Fern V: *Underage drinking research initiative.* Bethesda, MD, National Institute on Alcohol Abuse and Alcoholism, 2007.

20. Freemont J, Craighead LW: Aerobic exercise and cognitive therapy in the treatment of dysphoric moods, *Cognitive Therapy and Research* 2:241–251, 1987.

21. Grossman H: *Special education in a diverse society.* Boston, Allyn & Bacon, 1995.

22. Helion JG: If we build it, they will come: Creating an emotionally safe physical education environment, *JOPERD* 67(6):40–44, 1996.

23. Herold BC: Polymicrobial bacteremia: A commentary, *Clin Pediatrics* 36(7):419–422, 1997.

24. Hingson RW, Hereen T, Winter MR: Age at drinking onset and alcohol dependence, *Arch Peds Adol Med* 160(7):739–746, 2006.

25. Huettig C, Pyfer J: *The role of the adapted physical educator in the mental health crisis.* Corvallis, OR, North American Federation of Adapted Physical Activity, September 2002.

26. Hyde C: *Managing children with psychiatric problems.* Oxford, England, Blackwell, 2002.

27. Improvement of Educational Results for Children with Disabilities Act. 2003.

28. National Institute of Drug Abuse: *Infofacts: High school and youth trends,* www.drugabuse.gov/ Infofacts/HSYouthtrends.html, 2006.

29. Johns BH, Carr VG: *Techniques for managing verbally and physically aggressive students.* Denver, Love, 1995.

30. Kellogg D: It is time to fix a broken mental health system, *Dallas Morning News,* July 27, 2003.

31. Kern L, Bambara L, Fogt J: Class-wide curricular modification to improve the behavior of students with emotional or behavioral disorders, *Behavioral Disorders* 27(4):317–326, 2002.

32. Kessler RC, Chiu WT, Delmer O, Walters EE: Prevalence, severity, and comorbidity of twelve-month DSM IV disorders in the National Comorbidity Survey replication (NCS-R), *Arch Gen Psych* 62(6):617–627, 2005.

33. Kirk S, Gallagher J, Anastasio NJ: *Educating exceptional children.* Boston, Houghton Mifflin, 1993.

34. Knitzer J, Steinberg Z, Fleisch B: Schools, mental health and the advocacy challenge, *J of Clinical Child Psychology* 20:102–111, 1990.

35. Kupersmidt JG, Core JD, Dodge KA: The role of peer relationships in the development of disorders. In Asher R, Core JD, editors: *Peer rejections in childhood.* Cambridge, Cambridge University Press, 1990, pp. 274–308.

36. Lambert MT: Suicide risk assessment and management: Focus on personality disorders, *Current Opinion Psychiatry* 16(1):71–76, 2003, www.medscape.com/viewarticle/447415_print (pp. 1–7 online).

37. Landrum T, Tankersley M: Emotional and behavioral disorders in the new millennium: The future is now, *Behavioral Disorders* 24:319–330, 2002.

38. Lappin E: *Outdoor education for behavior disordered students,* ERIC:ED 261811, Las Cruces, NM,1984, ERIC Clearinghouse on Rural Education and Small Schools.

39. Lewinsohn P, Rohde P, Seeley J: Adolescent suicidal ideation and attempts: Prevalence, risk factors, and clinical implications, *Clinical Psychology: Science and Practice* 3:25–46, 1996.

40. Lopata C: Progressive muscle relaxation and aggression among elementary students with emotional or behavioral disorders, *Behavioral Disorders* 28(2):162–172, 2003.

41. Marcella AJ: Urbanization, mental health, and social deviancy: A review of issues and research, *Amer Psychologist* 53(6):624–634, 1998.

42. Martin K: *Substance-abusing adolescents show ethnic and gender differences in psychiatric disorders,* Bethesda, MD, National Institute on Drug Abuse, www.drugabuse.gov/NIDA_ notes/ NNVol18N1/Substance.html. 2007.

43. Martinsen EW, Hoffart A, Solberg O: Aerobic and non-aerobic forms of exercise in the treatment of anxiety disorders, *Stress Medicine* 5:115–120, 1989.

44. McGimsey JF, Favell JE: The effects of increased physical exercise on disruptive behavior in retarded persons, *J of Autism and Dev Disorders* 18:167–179, 1988.

45. McIntyre T: Does the way we teach create behavior disorders in culturally different students? *Ed Treatment Child* 19(3):354–370, 1996.

46. Mental Health: Community and coping, http://www.mentalhealth.com/dis1. 2003.

47. Milner D, Nisbet J: Bringing therapeutic wellness program ideas into the public schools, *Intervention in School & Clinic* 33(1):30–36, 1997.

48. Moffit T: Adolescence-limited and life-course-persistent antisocial behavior: A developmental taxonomy, *Psychological Review* 100:674–701, 1993.

49. New Freedom Commission on Mental Health, www.mentalhealthcommission.gov/reports/ FinalReport/FullReport.htm. 2003.

50. Nichols JD, Ludwin WG, Iadicola P: A darker shade of gray: A year-end analysis of discipline and suspension data, *Equity and Excellence in Ed* 32(1):43–55, 1999.

51. O'Neil R, Horner R, Albin R, Sprague J, Storey K, Newton J: *Functional assessment and program development for problem behavior,* 2nd ed. Pacific Grove, CA, Brooks/Cole, 1997.

52. Resnick MD, Bearman PS, Blum RW: Protecting adolescents from harm, *J of American Medical Association* 278(10):823–832, 1997.

53. Ryan A, Halsey H, Matthews W: Using functional assessment to promote desirable student behavior in schools, *Teaching Except Children* 35(5):8–15, 2003.

54. Satcher D: *National action agenda for children's mental health.* Washington, DC, U.S. Department of Health and Human Services, January 3, 2001.

55. Scott T, Liaupsin C, Nelson C, Jolivette K: Ensuring student success through team-based functional behavioral assessment, *Teach Except Child* 35(4):16–21, 2003.

56. *Seasonal affective disorder,* http://familydoctor.org/ online/famdocen/home/common/mentalhealgth/ depression. 2007.

57. Skiba R, Peterson R: School discipline at a crossroads: From zero tolerance to early response, *Exceptional Children* 66(3):335–347, 2000.

58. Slaby RG, Roedell WC, Arezzo D, Hendrix K: *Early violence prevention: Tools for teachers of young children.* Washington, DC, National Association for the Education of Young Children, 1995.

59. Souid A, Keith DV, Cunningham AS: Munchausen syndrome by proxy, *Clin Pediatrics* 38(8):497–503, 1998.

60. Sprague J, Walker H: Early identification and intervention for youth with antisocial and violent behavior, *Except Child* 66(3):367–379, 2000.

61. Tatem-Kelly B, Loeber R, Keenan K, DeLamatre M: Developmental pathways in boys' disruptive and delinquent behavior, *Juvenile Justice Bulletin,* 1997.

62. Texas Woman's University Project INSPIRE Web page, www.twu.edu/inspire. 2003.

63. *The science behind drug abuse,* Bethesda, MD, National Institute on Drug Abuse, http://teens.drugabuse.gov/mom/tg_effects.asp. 2007.

64. Tripp JH, Cockett M: Parents, parenting and family breakdown, *Arch Disease in Childhood* 78(2):104–107, 1998.

65. U.S. Department of Education, Office of Special Education Programs, Data Analysis System (DANS), September 25, 2005.

66. Van de Vliet P, Coppenolle HV: Physical measures, perceived physical ability, and body acceptance of adult psychiatric patients, *APAQ* 16:113–125, 1999.

67. Wagner M, Blackorby J, Hebbeler K: *Beyond the report card: The multiple dimensions of secondary school performance for students with disabilities.* Menlo Park, CA, SRI International, 1993.

68. Whelan R, Kauffman J: Educating students with emotional and behavioral disorders: Historical perspective and future directions. In Bullock LM,

Gable RA, editors: Third CCBD Mini-Library Series: *What works for children and youth with E/BD: Linking yesterday and today with tomorrow.* Reston, VA, Council for Children with Behavioral Disorders, 1999.

69. World Health Organization: *World report on violence and health.* Geneva, Switzerland, 2002.

70. Zaff JF, Calkins J: *Background for community-level work on mental health and externalizing disorders in adolescence,* Child Trends, www.childtrends.org/what_works/youth_development. 2007.

71. Zaff JF, Calkins J, Bridges LJ, Margie NG: *Promoting positive mental and emotional health in teens: Some lessons from research,* Child Trends, www.childtrends.org/what_works/youth_development. 2007.

72. Zipkin D: Relaxation techniques for handicapped children: A review of the literature, *J Spec Ed* 19:283–389, 1985.

SUGGESTED READINGS

Hellison DR, Hellison D: *Teaching responsibility through physical activity.* Champaign, IL, Human Kinetics, 2003.

Lavay B, French R, Henderson H: A practical plan for managing the behavior of students with disabilities in general physical education, *JOPERD* 78(2):42–48, 2007.

Tripps C: Kids at hope: All children are capable of success—No exceptions, *JOPERD* 77(1):45–51, 2006.

Skemp-Arlt KM: Body image dissatisfaction and eating disturbances among children and adolescents, *JOPERD* 77(1):24–26, 2006.

RECOMMENDED WEB SITES

Please keep in mind that these Web sites are being recommended in the winter of 2007. As Web sites often change, they may have moved or been reconfigured or eliminated.

New Freedom Commission on Mental Health
www.mentalhealthcommission.gov/reports/FinalReport/FullReport.htm

U.S. Department of Health and Human Services, Substance Abuse and Mental Health Services Administration Information Center
www.mentalhealth.org/cmhs/ChildrensCampaign/links.asp

Virtual Resource Center in Behavioral Disorders
http://tiger.coe.missouri.edu/~vrcbd

Teenage Suicide
www.save.org

Internet Mental Health Resources
www.mentalhealth.com

RECOMMENDED VIDEOS

Insight Media
2162 Broadway
New York, NY 10024-0621
1-800-233-9910
www.insight-media.com

ABCs of Emotional Disorder
#TAN3478/DVD/2004/35 min/$119

Accommodating Specific Student Needs
#UAN4837/DVD/2006/40 min/$179

Children in Crisis
#TAN4464/DVD/2004/46 min/$139

*The Fragile Brain: What Impairs Learning and What
We Can Do about It*
#TAL2243/VHS/2000/27 min/$139

Physically Disabling Conditions

■ OBJECTIVES

Describe at least one physically disabling condition that is representative of each of the three categories in this chapter.

Identify the stages of the concussion grading system.

Describe the types of spina bifida and the types of physical education program modifications required of each.

Describe how to modify three physical education activities to include a student using a wheelchair.

Give three examples of principles for adapting physical activity to accommodate persons with physical disabilities.

There are many different types of physically disabling conditions. Afflictions can occur at more than 500 anatomical sites. Each person who has a disabling condition has different physical and motor capabilities. Thus, each person must be treated in such a manner that his or her unique educational needs are met.

In this chapter we suggest a procedure to accomplish this task. The processes involved in this procedure are to (1) identify the specific clinical condition, (2) identify which activities are contraindicated on the basis of medical recommendations, (3) determine needed functional physical fitness and motor skills, (4) determine the activities that will assist the development of the desired fitness and motor skills, and (5) determine aids and devices that will enable the individual to function in the most normal environment.

More than 20 disabilities are discussed in this chapter. Many of these conditions, though differing in cause, result in similar movement limitations. To aid you in focusing on the commonalities across physically disabling conditions, the format of this chapter is slightly different from that of some of the other chapters dealing with specific populations. Under the headings of "Neurological Disorders," "Orthopedic Disabilities," and "Traumatic Injuries," specific conditions are identified and defined, the incidence and cause of each condition are given, the characteristics are delineated, special considerations are discussed, and suggestions for programming and teaching are presented. Following the unique aspects of all of the specific conditions, common testing suggestions; modifications, adaptations, and inclusion techniques; and community-based opportunities are presented.

DEFINITION AND SCOPE OF PHYSICALLY DISABLING CONDITIONS

Physical disabilities affect the use of the body as a result of deficiencies of the nerves, muscles, bones, and/or joints. The three main sources of disabilities are neurological impairments, orthopedic (musculoskeletal) disabilities, and traumatic injuries. Neurological disabilities are chronic, debilitating conditions that result from impairments of the central nervous system. The neurological conditions discussed in this chapter are amyotrophic lateral sclerosis, cerebral palsy, epilepsy, multiple sclerosis, muscular dystrophy, Parkinson's disease, poliomyelitis and post-polio syndrome, and spina bifida.

Orthopedic conditions are deformities, diseases, and injuries of the bones and joints. The orthopedic conditions discussed in this chapter are arthritis, arthrogryposis, congenital hip dislocation, coxa plana, Osgood-Schlatter condition, osteogenesis imperfecta, osteomyelitis, and spondylolysis and spondylolisthesis.

Traumatic conditions are the result of damage to muscles, ligaments, tendons, or the nervous system as a result of a blow to the body. Traumatic brain injuries, spinal cord injuries, and amputations are discussed in this chapter.

Because of the number of conditions included in this chapter, case studies have only been developed to be representative of each of the three groups of disabilities. Spina bifida represents the neurological disorder category; juvenile rheumatoid arthritis, the orthopedic disabilities category; and traumatic brain injury, the traumatic injuries section.

Neurological Disorders

Amyotrophic Lateral Sclerosis

Amyotrophic lateral sclerosis (ALS) is a progressive and fatal disease of the nerves from the spinal cord to the muscles.[112] The reported incidence in the United States is 5,600 persons diagnosed each year.[4] The disease is infrequent in school-age populations and is more common for individuals 40–70 years of age, with the median age of onset being 55 years.[4] It affects men two to three times as often as women. Lou Gehrig, the hall-of-fame first baseman of the New York Yankees, who finally missed a game after more than 2,000 successive starts, was forced to retire as a result of the disease. It has since been named Lou Gehrig disease.

Characteristics and Testing   The central features of the disease are atrophy and muscle wasting, resulting in marked weakness in the hands, arms, shoulders, and legs and in generalized weakness. The site of onset is random, and it progresses asymmetrically. Cramps are common, and muscular weakness may cause problems with swallowing, talking, and respiration.[88] Concomitant spinal conditions include ruptured intervertebral disks, spinal cord tumors, and spinal malformations. Manual muscle testing is used to determine the amount of functional strength.

Special Considerations   The drug Rilutek has been shown to prolong survival.[68] The rate of decline of muscular strength varies, with some losing strength quickly, and others more slowly.[110] More than half of those diagnosed with ALS live more than three years after the diagnosis has been made.[88]

The Physical Maintenance Program The major goals of the ALS physical activity program are to maintain physical capability as long as possible. There is some anecdotal evidence that exercise that strengthens the healthy muscle fibers permits an individual with ALS to maintain strength and a higher level of function over time.[110] Walking and recumbent cycling daily are recommended for maintaining endurance. Range-of-motion exercises with light weights and the use of weight machines are recommended for maintaining strength.[110] It might also be desirable to focus attention on activities that maintain efficient movement of the body for the activities of daily living. Leisure skills should be taught that have functional use at present or in the near future. The nature of the physical activities will depend on the physical capabilities of the individual at each point in time. The caregiver should be supportive and understanding. Consultation with an occupational therapist should be sought

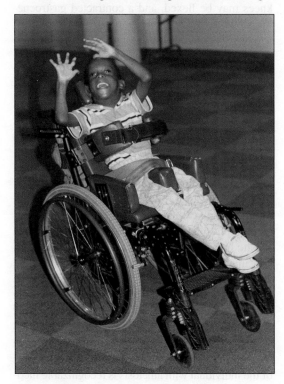

A Five-Year-Old Boy Participates in Creative Dance
Courtesy Dallas Independent School District.

for advice about assistive devices to enable the activities of daily living.

Cerebral Palsy

Cerebral palsy is a condition, rather than a disease. The term *cerebral palsy* is defined as a nonprogressive lesion of the brain before, during, or soon after birth (before age five years). The condition is lifelong, impairing voluntary movement. It is the most frequent cause of severe disabilities in children.[58]

The incidence of cerebral palsy is 1 to 2 per 1,000 live births.[88] Although earlier studies indicated that the vast majority of cerebral palsy cases were caused by external factors, such as prolonged labor, instrumental deliveries, and breech births, it is now believed that only 15 percent of cases result from these causes.[88] The most recent studies indicate that central nervous system abnormalities, such as enlarged ventricles in the brain, decreased brain hemisphere size, and viral infections, are probably critical factors that impair function.[53]

Certain groups of infants, including those with prolonged birth anoxia, very low birthweight, and abnormal neurological symptoms, are candidates for cerebral palsy.[88] Children with cerebral palsy possess poor postural adjustment. As a result, simple gross motor movements (e.g., kicking, throwing, and jumping) are difficult to perform effectively.[98]

Characteristics and Types The degree of motor impairment of children with cerebral palsy ranges from serious physical disability to little physical disability. The limbs affected are identified with specific titles:

- Monoplegia involves a single limb.
- Hemiplegia indicates involvement of both limbs on one side, with the arm being more affected than the leg.
- Paraplegia indicates involvement of both legs with little or no involvement of the arms.
- Quadriplegia, or tetraplegia, denotes involvement of all the limbs to a similar degree.
- Diplegia is an intermediate form between paraplegia and quadriplegia, with most involvement being in the legs.

Since the extent of the brain damage that results in neuromotor dysfunction varies greatly, diagnosis is related to the amount of dysfunction and associated motor involvement. Severe brain injury may be evident shortly after birth. However, cases of children with cerebral palsy who have slight brain damage and little motor impairment may be difficult to diagnose. In the milder cases, developmental lag in the motor and intellectual tasks required to meet environmental demands may not be detected until the children are three or four years old. As a rule, the clinical signs and symptoms of cerebral palsy reach maximum severity when children reach the age of two to four years.

Individuals with cerebral palsy usually demonstrate persistence of primitive reflexes and frequently are slow to develop equilibrium (postural) reflexes. It is difficult for most performers to execute simple gross motor movements effectively unless appropriate postural adjustments occur to support such movements and individuals are given additional time to plan and execute the movements.

Some of the secondary impairments that accompany cerebral palsy are intellectual disabilities, hearing and vision loss, emotional disturbance, hyperactivity, learning disabilities, loss of perceptual ability, and inability to make psychological adjustments.[101] Laskin[56] reports that 60 percent of all children with cerebral palsy have seizures. Seizures are sudden involuntary changes in behavior that range from a short period of loss of consciousness to jerks of one or two limbs or the whole body.[88]

Various authors agree that more than 50 percent of children with cerebral palsy have oculomotor defects. In other words, many children with brain injury have difficulty coordinating their eye movements. For this reason, these children may lack depth perception and have difficulty accurately determining the path of moving objects.

The different clinical types of cerebral dysfunction involve various obvious motor patterns, commonly known as hard signs. There are four clinical classifications: spasticity, athetosis, ataxia, and mixed. Of persons with cerebral palsy, 70 percent are clinically classified as spastic, 20 percent

as athetoid, and 5 percent as ataxic; the remaining are mixed conditions (usually spasticity and athetosis).[90]

Muscular spasticity is the most prevalent type of hard sign among persons with cerebral palsy. It results from damage to an area of the cortical brain.[27] One characteristic of spasticity is that muscle contractures that restrict muscular movement and hypertonicity give the appearance of stiffness to affected limbs. This makes muscle movement jerky and uncertain. Children with spasticity have exaggerated stretch reflexes, which cause them to respond to rapid passive stimulation with vigorous muscle contractions. Tendon reflexes are also hyperactive in the involved part. When the upper extremities are involved, the characteristic forms of physical deviation in persons with spastic cerebral palsy include flexion at the elbows, forearm pronation, and wrist and finger flexion. When the spastic condition involves the lower extremities, the legs may be rotated inward and flexed at the hips, the knees may be flexed, and a contracted gastrocnemius muscle holds the heel off the ground. A scissors gait is common among persons with this type of cerebral palsy. Spasticity is most common in the antigravity muscles of the body. Contractures are more common in children with spastic cerebral palsy than in children with any of the other types of cerebral palsy. In the event that contractures are not remedied or addressed, permanent contractures may result. Consequently, good posture is extremely difficult to maintain. Because of poor balance among reciprocal muscle groups, the innervation of muscles for functional motor patterns is often difficult, which frequently results in a decreased physical work capacity.[34] Individuals with spastic hemiplegia or paraplegia usually have normal intelligence; however, they may demonstrate some learning disabilities. Intellectual disability is more frequently seen in individuals with spastic quadriplegia and mixed forms of cerebral palsy.[88]

Athetosis, which results from basal ganglia involvement, is the second most prevalent clinical type of cerebral palsy. The distinguishing characteristic of the individual with athetosis is recognizable incoordinate movements of voluntary muscles. These movements take the form of wormlike motions that involve the trunk, arms, legs, and tongue or muscle twitches of the face. The unrhythmical, uncontrollable, involuntary movements increase with voluntary motion and emotional or environmental stimuli and disappear during sleep. Because of the presence of primitive reflexes and the inability to control muscles, the individual with athetosis has postural control difficulties that threaten balance. Impairment in the muscular control of hands, speech, and swallowing often accompanies athetosis.

Ataxia, a primary characteristic of the ataxic type of cerebral palsy, is a disturbance of equilibrium that results from involvement of the cerebellum or its pathways.[88] The resulting impairment in balance is evident in the walking gait. The gait of the person with ataxic cerebral palsy is wide and unstable, which causes weaving during locomotion. Standing is often a problem. Kinesthetic awareness seems to be lacking in the individual with ataxia. Weakness, incoordination, and intention tremor create difficulties with rapid or fine movements.[88]

Mixed forms are the least common of all types of cerebral palsy. Spasticity and athetosis are the most frequent characteristics, with ataxia and athetosis demonstrated less frequently.[10]

Special Considerations Increasingly, the medical community and society at large have come to understand that the focus of medical intervention should be on the prevention of disabilities through appropriate prenatal care and early intervention with at-risk children. The five procedures prevalent in the medical treatment of individuals with cerebral palsy are early intervention to promote a more normal neuromotor developmental sequence (physical therapy), casting, orthotics (bracing), medication, and neurosurgical management.[37] Physical therapy focuses on reducing the effect of persisting primitive reflexes and promoting range of motion at the joints. Casting involves placing a cast on an extremity to hold it in line with the limb to which it is attached. Orthotics help delay the development of contractures, limit the amount of spasticity that can occur, and decrease consumption of energy.[37] Medication usually serves two functions: aiding in the

relaxation of muscle groups when neuromuscular exercise therapy is attempted and controlling epileptic seizures through the use of anticonvulsant drugs. Neurosurgical management involves surgery to release tight muscles and tendons.

Injections of botulinum toxin type A (BTX-A) into spastic muscles of persons with spastic cerebral palsy have been shown to be beneficial when combined with training the weak antagonistic muscles.[6] One follow-up study that evaluated the results of one year of BTX-A injections showed significant improvement in joint mobility, improvement of gross motor function, and reduction of spasticity in individuals ranging in age from 1.5 to 15.5 years.[61] There are various opinions as to the value of orthopedic surgery for persons with cerebral palsy. Certain types of operative procedures have met with considerable success, especially with particular types of cerebral palsy. The physical growth of children affects the efficiency of muscle and tendon surgery; however, surgical operation, for the most part, does not cure the condition but, rather, assists with the functional activities of daily living. Tenotomy (tendon cutting) of the hip adductor and hamstring muscles seems to be the most valuable surgical procedure for adults with cerebral palsy.

Individuals with cerebral palsy have lower maximal oxygen consumption and distinctly subnormal values for peak anaerobic power and muscular endurance than those of their able-bodied peers. Frequently, during aerobic testing, these individuals do not demonstrate a plateau in oxygen consumption; thus, a peak aerobic power test is considered reliable for this population. Also, anaerobic power is considered a better measure of functional capacity than is maximal aerobic power.[107]

The Physical Education Program and Teaching Strategies There is no treatment for the repair of a damaged brain. However, the portion of the nervous system that remains intact can be made functional through a well-managed training program. Intervention by the physical educator and other personnel is needed to build functional developmental motor patterns with the operative parts of the body.

Igor Piayankh, a Young Man with Cerebral Palsy, Sits at the Helm While His Crew of National Ability Center Participants and Staff Run the Rapids around Jackson Hole

Courtesy of Gallina Piayankh.

Each child should be evaluated closely, and programs that foster those functional abilities should be formulated. Developmental programs should be constructed to correct deficiencies that respond to treatment. The specific child should be considered when the exercise regimen is being determined. Because of their numerous involuntary muscular activities, children with athetosis are much more active than children with spasticity and ataxia.

There is growing evidence that some of the sensory and perceptual delays can be improved through training. Sensory-motor and perceptual-motor training programs are designed to reduce primitive reflex involvement and develop locomotor patterns, balance, rhythm, and ocular control. These areas are the focus of physical therapists early in the life of the child. All of these activities are inherent in most elementary physical education programs; however, the quality of physical education programs could be improved by consciously selecting activities of this nature for classes that include students with spastic cerebral palsy. The handbook *Gross Motor Activities for Young Children with Special Needs,* which instructors can download and distribute from the book's web site, includes several games that are appropriate for the elementary-school-age child.

The individual education program (IEP) of the student with cerebral palsy should include activities to address the individual's unique needs. Some therapeutic activities and techniques follow:

1. Muscle stretching to relieve muscle contractures, prevent deformities, and permit a fuller range of purposeful motion (consult with physical therapists about this procedure)
2. Gravity exercises that involve lifting the weight of the body or body part against gravity
3. Muscle awareness exercises to control specific muscles or muscle groups
4. Neuromuscular reeducation exercises that are performed through the muscles' current range to stimulate the proprioceptors and return the muscles to greater functional use (consult with physical therapists about this procedure)
5. Reciprocal exercises to stimulate and strengthen the action of the protagonist
6. Tonic exercises to prevent atrophy or maintain organic efficiency
7. Relaxation training to assist in reducing muscle contractures, rigidity, and spasms
8. Postural alignments to maintain proper alignment of musculature
9. Gait training to teach or reteach walking patterns (consult with physical therapists about this procedure)
10. Body mechanics and lifting techniques to obtain maximum use of the large muscle groups of the body
11. Proprioceptive facilitation exercises to bring about maximum excitation of the motor units of a muscle with each voluntary effort to overcome motor-functioning paralysis (consult with physical therapists about this procedure)
12. Ramp climbing to improve ambulation and balance
13. Progressive, resistive exercise to develop muscle strength

Failure to provide children with cerebral palsy the opportunity to participate in progressive exercise may leave them short of their potential development. The opportunities for physical education to maximize the physical development of these children are great. Furthermore, children with cerebral palsy frequently do not develop adequate basic motor skills because of their limited play experiences.

When a child with cerebral palsy participates in a group activity, it may be necessary to adapt the activity to the child's abilities or to modify the rules or environment. A child with quadriplegic spastic cerebral palsy may be given the opportunity to play the bells during a rhythm activity, instead of being asked to dance with his or her feet. A child with rigid cerebral palsy who uses a wheelchair may "hold" one handle on a parachute with the edge of his or her chair. A child with ataxia may play a sitting circle game with classmates while propped in the teacher's lap or propped against a wall.

In addition to adaptation of activity, the capabilities of each individual must be considered. Children with spasticity, those with athetosis, and those with ataxia differ greatly in function. For instance, the child with spasticity finds it easier to engage in activities in which motion is continuous. However, for the child with athetosis, relaxation between movements is extremely important to prevent involuntary muscular contractions that may thwart the development of skills.

Children with ataxia have different motor problems—they are usually severely limited in all activities that require balance. The motor characteristics of the basic types of cerebral palsy, as well as of each child, are important variables in the selection of activities. Rest periods should be frequent for children with cerebral palsy. The length and frequency of the rest periods should vary with the nature of the activity and the severity of the disability. The development of a sequence of activities varying in degree of difficulty is important. This sequencing provides an opportunity to place each child in an activity that is commensurate with his or her ability and proposes a subsequent goal to work toward.

Physical activities described under the definition of physical education in IDEIA (2004) are appropriate for children with cerebral palsy. At the early elementary level, the focus should be on the development of sensory-motor function, body image, and rhythmicity. Appropriate motor activities include fundamental motor patterns, such as walking, running, and jumping, and fundamental motor skills, such as throwing, kicking, and catching. Aquatics is a vital part of the curriculum for children with cerebral palsy. The buoyancy of the water frees the child from the pull of gravity, which activates many primitive reflexes and allows for greater range of motion. Rhythm activities are also a vital part of the quality physical education program for children with cerebral palsy; expressive dance may prove to be vital in the development of language and communication, as well as motor skills. If possible, the physical education program for children with cerebral palsy at the elementary school level should include age-appropriate, geographically appropriate leisure and recreation skills. Horseback riding is a particularly effective intervention activity for children who are severely involved. Other leisure and recreation skills are also an important part of the total program. The child should be introduced, for example, to the skills needed to participate in bowling, including the use of automatic grip release balls and ramps, if necessary. If geographically appropriate, the child should learn the skills necessary to sled with family and friends.

The middle school curriculum should focus on the development of physical fitness, body mechanics, and relaxation techniques. Once again, aquatics is a vital component of the curriculum. Increased focus should be placed on exposing the student to community-based leisure and recreation activities and, where appropriate, competitive sports programs.

In the high school program, it is important that students with cerebral palsy maintain adequate levels of physical fitness, practice body mechanics, and develop more sophisticated relaxation techniques. There is impressive evidence that motor skills, muscular endurance, and strength can be developed in individuals with cerebral palsy through progressive exercise. Fernandez and Pitetti[34] reported that individuals with cerebral palsy who exercised regularly demonstrated improvement in functional capacity. Holland and Steadward[47] have identified Nautilus weight-lifting exercises that develop the neck, chest, and arms. These authors conclude that persons with cerebral palsy can participate in intense strength training programs without sacrificing flexibility or increasing spasticity.

The secondary student's IEP must address techniques that will allow the student to make the transition from school-based to community-based leisure and recreation programs. For example, the IEP may address the skills necessary for the student to register for and participate in an adult bowling or archery league. These skills may include independent management of a ramp, for example. In addition, these students should be made

familiar with the activities and programs of the U.S. Cerebral Palsy Athletic Association.

Because of the many health and social benefits of staying active, individuals with cerebral palsy should be encouraged to participate in ongoing physical activities. Sport and recreation opportunities for individuals with cerebral palsy and other nonprogressive brain lesions (e.g., traumatic brain injury, stroke) are growing.[56] A functional classification system developed by the Cerebral Palsy–International Sport and Recreation Association (CP-ISRA) is presented in Table 15-1.

Epilepsy

Epilepsy is a disturbance resulting from abnormal electrical activity of the brain. The condition is a

Table 15-1   CP-ISRA Functional Classification System

CP1: severe spastic or athetoid quadriplegia	Is unable to propel a manual wheelchair independently; has nonfunctional lower extremities, very poor or no trunk stability, severely decreased function in upper extremity
CP2: moderate to severe spastic or athetoid quadriplegia	Is able to propel a manual wheelchair slowly and inefficiently; has differential function abilities between upper and lower extremities, fair static trunk stability
CP3: moderate spastic quadriplegia or severe spastic hemiplegia	Is able to propel a manual wheelchair independently; may be able to ambulate with assistance; has moderate spasticity on the lower extremities, fair dynamic trunk stability, moderate limitations to function in the dominant arm
CP4: moderate to severe spastic diplegia	Ambulates with aids over short distances; has moderate to severe involvement of the lower extremities, good dynamic trunk stability, minimal to near-normal function of the upper extremities at rest
CP5: moderate spastic diplegia	Ambulates well with assistive devices; has minimal to moderate spasticity in one or both lower extremities; is able to run
CP6: moderate athetosis or ataxia	Ambulates without assistive devices; lower-extremity function improves from walking to running or cycling; has poor static and good dynamic trunk stability, good upper-extremity range and strength, poor throwing and grasp and release
CP7: true ambulatory hemiplegia	Has mild to moderately affected upper extremity, minimal to mildly affected lower extremity
CP8: minimally affected diplegia, hemiplegia, athetosis, or monoplegia	

Modified from Laskin J: Cerebral palsy. In Durstine JL, Moore G, editors: *Exercise management for persons with chronic diseases and disabilities.* Champaign, IL, Human Kinetics, 2003.

chronic disorder that causes repeated seizures if not treated.[43] A seizure is a "sudden surge of electrical activity in the brain that can cause changes in behavior and/or unusual sensations, muscle spasms, loss of consciousness, and convulsions."[43] Epilepsy is not a specific disease but a group of symptoms that may be associated with several conditions. Almost 2 million Americans have epilepsy, and there are 125,000 new cases each year, with about 50 percent of those being children.[77] Many persons with epilepsy experience their first attack during childhood. No cause can be found in 75 percent of the young adults who have epilepsy. Common causes are brain damage at birth, alcohol or other drug abuse, severe head injury, brain infection, and brain tumor.[88]

Characteristics and Types   There are several types of epilepsy, and each type has a particular set of characteristics. Although there are several methods of classifying various types of epilepsy, the one most commonly used includes four categories of seizure: tonic-clonic (formerly referred to as grand mal), absence (formerly referred to as petit mal), focal, and psychomotor.

Tonic-clonic is the most severe type of seizure. The individual often has an "aura" that immediately precedes the seizure, and the aura may give the individual some warning of the imminence of the seizure. The aura is usually a somatosensory flash—a particular smell, a blur of colors, or an itching sensation, for example. The seizure itself usually begins with bilateral jerks of the extremities, followed by convulsions and loss of consciousness. The person may be incontinent during the seizure, losing control of the bowels and bladder. After the seizure, the individual is usually confused, often embarrassed, and exhausted. Approximately 90 percent of individuals with epilepsy experience tonic-clonic seizures.[88]

The onset of the absence seizure is sudden and may last for only a few seconds or for several minutes. Usually, the individual simply appears to stare into space and have a lapse in attention. It is often characterized by twitching around the eyes or mouth. There is a loss of consciousness but no

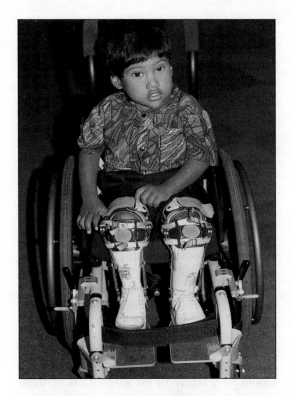

A Three-Year-Old Child with Long Leg Braces
Courtesy Dallas Independent School District.

collapse. The individual remains sitting or standing. Seizures of this type usually affect children between the ages of 5 and 15 years. The student with absence seizures may experience serious learning difficulties. It is not uncommon for a child to have hundreds of absence seizures a day. If a child has 100 seizures and each lasts only 30 seconds, the child will have lost a full 50 minutes of learning time. Approximately 25 percent of individuals who have epilepsy experience absence seizures.[88]

The focal seizure is similar to the tonic-clonic seizure. It is characterized by a loss of body tone and collapse. The student usually remains conscious during the attack, but speech may be impaired. In jacksonian focal seizures, there is a localized twitching of muscles in the extremities, which moves up the arm or leg. If the seizure spreads to other parts of the brain, generalized convulsions and loss of consciousness result.

A psychomotor seizure is characterized by atypical social-motor behavior for one or two minutes. The behaviors may include uncontrollable temper tantrums, hand clapping, spitting, swearing, or shouting. The individual is unaware of the activity during and after the seizure. Psychomotor seizures can occur at any age.

Many factors can cause seizures. Some of these factors are (1) emotional stress, such as fear, anger, or frustration; (2) excessive amounts of alcohol; and (3) menstruation.

Special Considerations Teachers should be cognizant of which students have epilepsy and whether they are taking drugs to control their seizures. Anticonvulsant drugs are the preferred medical treatment for most individuals with epilepsy, and they can prevent convulsive seizures in more than half of the people who have them. However, these drugs are slightly less effective for absence seizures. The type of drug that should be given and the optimum dosage are difficult to determine and highly individualized. Teachers should be sensitive to the side effects of these drugs, which may impair motor performance. Dilantin, for example, can produce lethargy, dizziness, and mental confusion. Phenobarbital sometimes contributes to drowsiness and learning difficulties.[88] Drugs taken to control absence seizures lead to drowsiness and nausea.[88] These side effects may be detrimental to the student's performance and safety in certain activities. Information about the student's drug treatment program should be discussed during the IEP meeting.

Physical education teachers should be familiar with procedures for handling seizures. Perhaps the most significant procedure for handling a seizure is to educate the student's class members about epilepsy. If the child's classmates are knowledgeable about seizures, the child will not have to suffer from postseizure embarrassment.

In the event a child has a tonic-clonic seizure, the physical educator should do the following:

1. Help the student to the floor or ground and place the student in a back-lying position.

2. Clear the area of dangerous objects.
3. Loosen all restraining clothing, such as a belt or shirt collar.
4. If the student is experiencing breathing difficulty, tilt the student's head back to open the airway.
5. Do not try to insert an object into the person's mouth or attempt to restrain the individual who is having a seizure.
6. Once the convulsion has stopped, place a blanket or towel over the student to eliminate embarrassment if the student has lost bowel or bladder control.
7. Allow the student to rest.
8. Report the seizure to the appropriate school official.[94]

A tonic-clonic seizure is not life-threatening and should be treated as a routine event. The seizure process is dangerous only if the student moves into status epilepticus—has a series of tonic-clonic seizures without a break. If this happens, emergency medical personnel must be contacted immediately.

If the student experiences a focal or psychomotor seizure, the child should be removed to an isolated part of the gymnasium, if possible. If the student experiences an absence seizure and the teacher is aware of it, the teacher should repeat any instructions given previously.

The Physical Education Program and Teaching Strategies If medication is effective and the child's seizures are under control, the student should be able to participate in a physical education program. However, activities that involve direct blows to the head, including boxing, soccer, and full-contact karate, should be avoided. Performing activities while a considerable height from the floor, swimming in cold water, and scuba diving without supervision should also be avoided. Swimming should be carefully supervised. Individuals who have uncontrolled seizures should avoid gymnastics, ice hockey and ice skating, sailing and waterskiing, and horseback riding.[94]

Multiple Sclerosis

Multiple sclerosis is a chronic and degenerative neurological disease affecting primarily older adolescents and adults. It is a slowly progressive disease of the central nervous system, leading to the disintegration of the myelin coverings of nerve fibers in the brain and spinal cord, which results in hardening or scarring of the tissue that replaces the disintegrated protective myelin sheath.[88] The cause of multiple sclerosis is unknown, but immunologic abnormality is suspected.[88] Multiple sclerosis occurs in 1 of 2,000 births in temperate climates and in 1 of 10,000 births in tropical climates.[88]

Characteristics The symptoms of multiple sclerosis are sensory problems (such as visual disturbances), tremors, muscle weakness, spasticity, speech difficulties, dizziness, mild emotional disturbances, partial paralysis, fatigue, and motor difficulties. Multiple sclerosis generally appears between the ages of 20 and 40 years and results in several periods of remission and recurring exacerbation. Some persons have frequent attacks, whereas others have remissions that last as long as 10 years.[88]

The Physical Activity Program There is no treatment that can repair the damage to the nervous system caused by degeneration. However, each person should be evaluated individually, and programs of resistive exercise should be administered to maintain maximum functioning. In addition, Jacobson relaxation techniques and active and passive range-of-motion exercises should be used to counter contractures in the lower extremities. The goal of these programs is to maintain functional skills, muscle strength, and range of motion. It is particularly important to teach the skills necessary for the functional use of walkers, crutches, and wheelchairs. In addition, the individual should be given the opportunity to develop compensatory skills—skills needed because of changes in central nervous system function—for example, skills to compensate for disequilibrium. Braces may be introduced at the later stages of the disorder to assist with locomotion. Many individuals with this condition are heat sensitive, which

means their condition worsens when their body temperature increases. To reduce the heat when that occurs, it is recommended that these individuals wear headbands or vests that have been cooled and that they exercise in air-conditioned settings or in the water.[109] Regular exercise regimes have been shown to have very positive physiological and psychosocial effects, including greater heat tolerance and the ability to acclimate to heat.[50]

Inactivity and the use of prednisone, which is an anti-inflammatory drug, may contribute to the progressive weakening of the muscles needed for daily activity. Instructors should constantly encourage as active a lifestyle as possible. Individuals should be urged to participate in an exercise program that maintains cardiovascular-respiratory functioning and sufficient muscle strength to allow participation in the activities of daily living. Because involvement of the lower extremities interferes with balance, stationary cycles using the arms or legs are recommended for testing and exercise. Begin with an unloaded warm-up and progress to exercising in three- to five-minute increments.[74] Low- to moderate-intensity weight training is recommended using 8 to 15 repetitions of submaximal weights.[105] Swimming[13] and aquatic aerobic exercises are recommended because they require less effort than activities on land. Individuals who enjoy competition should be encouraged to participate in wheelchair sports when their condition is in remission.

Muscular Dystrophy

Muscular dystrophy is a group of inherited, progressive muscle disorders that differ according to which muscles are affected.[88] All types result in the deterioration of muscle strength, power, and endurance.[100] The rate of progressive degeneration is different for each set of muscles.[62] Although the exact incidence of muscular dystrophy is unknown, estimates place the number of persons with the disorder in excess of 200,000 in the United States. It is estimated that in more than half of the known cases, the age of onset falls within the range of three to thirteen years.

Characteristics and Types   The physical characteristics of persons with muscular dystrophy are relevant to the degenerative stage as well as to the type of muscular dystrophy. In the late stages of the disease, connective tissue replaces most of the muscle tissue. In some cases, deposits of fat give the appearance of well-developed muscles. Despite the muscle atrophy, there is no apparent central nervous system impairment.

The age of onset of muscular dystrophy is of importance to the total development of the children. Persons who contract the disease after having had an opportunity to secure an education, or part of an education, and develop social and psychological strengths are better able to cope with their environment than are those who are afflicted with the disease before the acquisition of basic skills.

Although the characteristics of individuals with muscular dystrophy vary according to the stage of the disease, some general characteristics are as follows:

1. There is a tendency to tire quickly.
2. There may be a loss of fine manual dexterity.
3. There is sometimes a lack of motivation to learn because of isolation from social contacts and limited educational opportunities.
4. Progressive weakness tends to produce adverse postural changes.
5. Emotional disturbance may exist because of the progressive nature of the illness and the resulting restrictions placed on opportunities for socialization.

There are numerous classifications of muscular dystrophy based on the muscle groups affected and the age of onset. However, three main clinical types of muscular dystrophy have been identified: Duchenne (pseudohypertrophic), Becker, and facioscapulohumeral (Landouzy-Dejerine).[88]

The Duchenne (pseudohypertrophic) type is an X-linked recessive disorder that usually presents itself during the ages of three to seven years. It occurs in 1 in every 3,300 live male births. It affects the pelvic girdle first, followed by the shoulder girdle.[88]

Symptoms that give an indication of the disease are the following:

1. Waddling gait
2. Toe walking
3. Lordosis
4. Frequent falls
5. Difficulty getting up after falling
6. Difficulty climbing stairs[88]

As the disease progresses, imbalance of muscle strength in various parts of the body occurs. Deformities develop in flexion at the hips and knees. The spine, pelvis, and shoulder girdle also eventually become atrophied. Contractures and involvement of the heart may develop with the progressive degeneration of the disease. The motorized wheelchair has increased the independence of children in the advanced stages of muscular dystrophy. Though unable to perform activities of daily living, the child using a motorized wheelchair retains a measure of mobility that promotes independence and allows integration into many school-based and community-based programs.

Becker muscular dystrophy is also an X-linked disorder; however, it is less severe than the Duchenne type. The advancement of this type of dystrophy mimics the Duchenne type, but the Becker type progresses more slowly. As a result, few individuals are required to use wheelchairs until they approach their 20th year, and most survive into their thirties or forties.[88]

The facioscapulohumeral (Landouzy-Dejerine) type of muscular dystrophy, which is the third most common type, is characterized by weakness of the facial muscles and shoulder girdles. The onset of symptoms or signs of the facioscapulohumeral type is usually recognized when the person is between the ages of 7 and 20 years. Both genders are equally subject to the condition. Persons with this form of muscular dystrophy have trouble raising their arms above their head, whistling, drinking through a straw, and closing their eyes. A child with this type of disease often appears to have a masklike face, which lacks expression. Later, involvement of the muscles that move the humerus and scapula will be noticed. Weakness usually appears later in the

Courtesy of Tara McCarthy.

abdominal, pelvic, and hip musculature. The progressive weakness and muscle deterioration often lead to scoliosis and lordosis. This type of muscular dystrophy is often milder than the Duchenne type, and life expectancy is normal.[88] Facioscapulohumeral muscular dystrophy usually progresses slowly, and ambulation is seldom lost.

Special Considerations Duchenne muscular dystrophy is one of the most serious disabling conditions that can occur in childhood. Although not fatal in itself, the disease contributes to premature death in most known cases because of its progressive nature. The progress of the condition is cruel and relentless as the child loses function and moves toward inevitable death. However, it is worth noting that scientific research may be close to solving unanswered questions regarding the disease, and eventually the progressive deterioration may be halted.

The Physical Education Program and Teaching Strategies An individually designed activity program may significantly contribute to the quality of life of the individual affected by muscular dystrophy. Inactivity seems to contribute to the progressive weakening of the muscles of persons with muscular dystrophy. Exercise of muscles involved in the activities of daily living to increase strength may permit greater functional use of the body and

slow the progression of the disease.[52] Furthermore, exercise may assist in reducing excessive weight, which is a burden to those who have muscular dystrophy. Movement in warm water—aquatic therapy—may be particularly beneficial for the child with muscular dystrophy. It aids in the maintenance of muscle tonus and flexibility, and it encourages circulation.

The child's diet should be closely monitored. Prevention of excess weight is essential to the success of the rehabilitation program of persons with progressive muscular dystrophy. For individuals whose strength is marginal, any extra weight is an added burden on ambulation and on activities of daily living.

A great deal can be done to prevent deformities and loss of muscle strength from inactivity. If a specific strengthening and stretching program is outlined during each stage of the disease, the child may extend the ability to care for most of his or her daily needs for many additional years. In addition to the administration of specific developmental exercises for the involved muscles, exercises should include the development of walking patterns, posture control, muscle coordination, and the stretching of contractures involved in disuse atrophy. Because little is known about the frequency, intensity, amount, and duration of exercise required to produce a beneficial effect, all exercises should be selected after the study of contraindications specified by a physician.[66] It is desirable to select activities that use the remaining strengths, so that enjoyment and success can be achieved.

All the types of muscular dystrophy cannot be considered to be the same; therefore, the physical and social benefits that children can derive from physical education and recreation programs are different. However, all children with muscular dystrophy can profit from a well-designed program to enhance quality of life. The focus of the program, particularly for children with Duchenne muscular dystrophy, is on the development of leisure and recreation skills that will be appropriate as the child progressively loses function. For example, a child with Duchenne muscular dystrophy should be taught to fish and to play bocci because those are skills that can be enjoyed throughout the life span. Also, the child should be given the opportunity to learn board and video games that will provide entertainment and joy.

One focus of the program should be the development of relaxation techniques. The progressive loss of functional skills causes a great deal of stress, as does facing the inevitability of an early death; the quality of the child's life can be enhanced if the child has learned conscious relaxation skills.

Perhaps more important, dance, music, and art therapy should be a part of the child's total program. Movement and dance, even dance done in a motorized wheelchair, can help the child or adolescent express emotions—grief, rage, frustration, love or joy. Music and art therapy provide vital avenues of expression as the child loses motor capabilities. In addition, a trained therapist can be of value as the child moves through the stages of grief. The intent of the program is to enhance the quality of the child's life and, with professional support, allow the process of dying to be as humane, caring, and ennobling as possible. Specific programs are suggested in Table 15-2.

Parkinson's Disease

Parkinson's disease is a slow, progressive disorder that results in physical debilitation. The disease usually appears gradually and progresses slowly. It may progress to a stage where there is difficulty with the

---

Table 15-2	**Recommended Programming Ideas for Persons with Muscular Dystrophy[100]**

Provide realistic short-term goals to the individuals and parents.

Use submaximal resistance exercises while focusing on maintaining muscle endurance, peak power, and strength.

Reduce the intensity of the activity if the person complains of exercise-induced cramps or excessive fatigue.

Include as many gamelike, fun situations as possible.

Provide nutritional counseling in conjunction with physical training to help the individual avoid becoming overweight.

---

routine activities of daily living. There is no known cause; however, it is believed to result from a combination of genetics and environment (e.g., exposure to toxins).[89] The condition may be aggravated by emotional tension or fatigue. It affects about 1 percent of the population over 65 years of age, with an onset between 40 and 60 years.[88] A juvenile form of parkinsonism, which has its onset prior to age 40 years, has also been identified.

Characteristics   The observable characteristics of Parkinson's disease are infrequent blinking and lack of facial expression, tremor of the resting muscles, a slowing of voluntary movements, muscular weakness, abnormal gait, and postural instability.[88] These motor characteristics become more pronounced as the disease progresses. For instance, a minor feeling of sluggishness may progress until the individual is unable to get up from a chair. The walking gait becomes less efficient and can be characterized by shuffling of the feet for the purpose of postural stability. In addition, voluntary movements, particularly those performed by the small muscles, become slow, and spontaneous movements diminish.

In general, most persons require lifelong management consisting of physical therapy and drug therapy. Physical therapy consists of heat and massage to alleviate the muscle cramps and relieve the tension headaches that often accompany rigidity of the muscles of the neck.

The Physical Activity Program   Because of the degenerative nature of the disease, the goals of physical activity programs are to preserve muscular functioning for purposive movement involved in the activities of daily living and required for the performance of leisure and recreation skills. The general types of physical activities that may be of value are general coordination exercises to retard the slow deterioration of movement and relaxation exercises that may reduce muscular incoordination and tremors. In addition, balance activities and those that teach compensation for lack of balance should be included. Exercises directed at maintaining postural strength and flexibility should be a part of the program plan. Care must be taken when the individual is on antiparkinsonian medications because of the varied side effects.[89] A physician's and/or a physical therapist's guidance should be sought as the disease progresses.

Poliomyelitis and Post-Polio Syndrome

Poliomyelitis (polio) is an acute viral infection with a wide range of manifestations.[88] In the serious cases (nonparalytic and paralytic), an inflammation affects the anterior motor cells in the spinal cord, which in turn affects the muscles. Extensive vaccination has virtually eradicated polio; however, an increasing number of individuals who had polio as children are developing a post-polio syndrome (PPS). Almost one-fourth of the individuals who contracted polio during peak epidemics are now developing symptoms similar to those they experienced during the initial onset of the disease.[10]

Characteristics and Types There are two basic patterns—minor illness (abortive) and major illness (paralytic or nonparalytic). Minor poliomyelitis accounts for 80 to 90 percent of the clinical infections and occurs chiefly in children.[88] This form does not involve the central nervous system. The symptoms are headache, sore throat, mild fever, and nausea.

Major poliomyelitis involves the central nervous system. In addition to the symptoms of minor poliomyelitis, the individual may experience a fever, severe headache, stiff neck, and general and specific pain in and acute contractions of one or more muscle groups in the upper and lower extremities or the back. Individuals with the nonparalytic form recover completely. Individuals with the paralytic form develop paralysis of muscle groups throughout the body. Two-thirds of these individuals have residual, permanent weakness.[88]

Post-polio syndrome occurs many years after a paralytic poliomyelitis attack. The characteristics include muscle fatigue and decreased endurance, accompanied by weakness, and atrophy in selected muscles.[88]

The Physical Activity Program Exercise programs should focus on motor tasks that develop strength, endurance, flexibility, and coordination. Orthopedic deformities resulting from the residual effects of polio do not totally restrict movement.

Children quickly learn to compensate for the inconvenience of an impaired foot or arm. At the elementary school level, many children with polio can achieve considerable athletic success. However, as they progress through school life, accumulated developmental lags, as a rule, influence skill development. Wheelchair sports are popular for individuals with polio who cannot walk.

For adults who experience post-polio syndrome, it appears that the muscle units that were not originally impaired become fatigued from overwork. These individuals appear to benefit from moderate-intensity aerobic exercise and resistive training. To conserve energy, they should exercise in the morning of relatively unstressful days and should avoid overextending effort.[10]

Specially Designed Tricycle Enables a Child with Spina Bifida to Bike

Photo by Carol Heuttig.

Spina Bifida

Spina bifida is the most common congenital spinal defect. The condition is a result of defective closure of the vertebral column. The severity ranges from spina bifida occulta, with no findings, to a completely open spine (spina bifida cystica).[88] The incidence of spina bifida is estimated at 2 per 100 live births, making it one of the most common birth defects that can lead to physical disability.

Characteristics In spina bifida occulta, the vertebral arches fail to fuse; however, there is no distension of the spinal cord lining or of the cord itself. In spina bifida cystica, the protruding sac can contain just the lining (meninges) of the spinal column (meningocele) or both the meninges and the spinal cord (myelomeningocele).[77] See Figures 15-1 and 15-2. Meningocele usually can be repaired with

little or no damage to the neural pathways. Myelomeningocele, the more common of the two types, produces varying degrees of neurological impairment, ranging from mild muscle imbalance and sensory loss in the lower limbs to paralysis of one or both legs. The child's ability to walk depends on the level of the lesion. Ninety-five percent of the persons with lesions at the low lumbar level can walk, and 30 percent of the persons with high lumbar or thoracic levels can walk.[80] Paralysis usually affects bladder and bowel function,[88] and bladder and kidney infections are frequent. Between 85 and

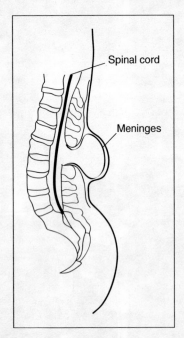

Figure 15-1 Meningocele

In this form of spina bifida, the sac contains tissues that cover the spinal cord (meninges) and cerebrospinal fluid. This fluid bathes and protects the brain and spinal cord. The nerves are not usually badly damaged and are able to function; therefore, there is often little disability present. This is the least common form.

Courtesy of Association for Spina Bifida and Hydrocephalus.

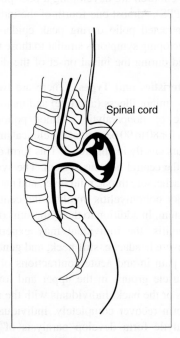

Figure 15-2 Myelomeningocele (Meningomyelocele)

This is the more common of the two meningoceles and the most serious. Here the sac or cyst contains not only tissue and cerebrospinal fluid but also nerves and part of the spinal cord. The spinal cord is damaged or not properly developed. As a result, there is always some degree of paralysis and loss of sensation below the damaged vertebrae. The amount of disability depends very much on where the spina bifida is and the amount of nerve damage involved. Many children and adults with this condition experience problems with bowel and bladder control.

Courtesy of Association for Spina Bifida and Hydrocephalus.

CASE STUDY 15-1

Josue

Josue is a 1st-grader with spina bifida myelomeningocele. His parents divorced in the first year after Josue's birth. His mother is having serious difficulty dealing with Josue's disability. She is in denial to the extent that she believes and tells Josue every day that he will not have spina bifida as an adult. She admitted in an individual education program (IEP) meeting that she is severely depressed and suicidal. As a result, Josue is developing behavior problems at home and at school. Though a bright little boy, he often engages in refusal behavior when asked to work.

Josue is very mobile in his chair. He is able to wheel in a straight line and in a circle, can stop and start with ease, can move backward, and is learning to do a "wheelie." He is able to get in and out of his wheelchair independently. At a recent IEP meeting, it was recommended that Josue participate in the regular physical education class and in community-based sports programs; however, his mother was very reluctant to agree.

APPLICATION TASK

Identify strategies for convincing Josue's mother to permit him to participate in the regular physical education class and in community-based sports programs for young children with disabilities. Modify the warm-up regimen the regular class uses, and develop a cardiovascular program, so that Josue can participate in the warm-up and heart-healthy portion of the curriculum. Identify the types of wheelchair maneuvers and skills he should practice in class in order to be successful in a sports program. Identify types of physical education activities in which the use of a wheelchair may endanger the other children, and suggest alternative activities Josue could do with a peer on the sidelines. Develop a behavior management plan that should be implemented when he refuses to participate in classroom activities.

95 percent of children born with myelomeningocele have or soon develop hydrocephalus.[80] In these cases, usually a shunt is inserted to drain off cerebrospinal fluid that is not being reabsorbed properly. Removing the excess cerebrospinal fluid protects the child against brain damage resulting from pressure on the brain. Many children who are paraplegic from spina bifida are able to move about with the aid of braces and crutches. It is also interesting to note that many children who have spina bifida are allergic to latex.

Even though children with spina bifida have normal intelligence, many have some learning difficulties. The most common difficulties are poor hand-eye coordination, distractibility, hyperactivity, and memory, sequencing, and reasoning problems.[80]

Special Considerations   Activities that could distress the placement of any shunts or put pressure on sensitive areas of the spine must be avoided. Of considerable concern is the prevention of contractures and associated foot deformities (e.g., equinovarus) through daily passive flexibility exercises.

Many social problems result from spina bifida. In addition to the physical disability, there are often problems associated with bowel and bladder control, which draw further attention to the children as they function in a social environment. In many cases, this has a negative social impact on the children. Often, children with spina bifida need catheterization. If someone must do it for them, the attention of others is drawn to these circumstances. However, in many cases older children can be taught to catheterize themselves. The physical disability and the associated physiological problems result in stressful social situations because groups must adapt to the child with spina bifida's physical disabilities and associated physiological problems. Social circumstances can be made more favorable if these children are integrated into regular classes in the early grades and if social integration strategies are used (see Chapter 9).

The Physical Education Program and Teaching Strategies   No particular program of physical education or therapy can be directly assigned to the student with spina bifida. Some students have no physical reaction and discover the condition only by chance through X-ray examination for another problem. On the other hand, a person may have extensive neuromuscular involvement requiring constant medical care. A program of physical education or therapeutic exercise based on the individual's needs should be planned.

The child with spina bifida myelomeningocele is often able to participate in a general physical education program more effectively using a wheelchair than using a walker or crutches and braces. While the child with spina bifida should be encouraged to walk whenever possible, it may be difficult for the child to participate in activities safely in a crowded gymnasium.

Simple modifications can be made to allow the child using a wheelchair to participate actively in general physical education. Specific suggestions for including young children using wheelchairs in a general physical education program are presented later in this chapter in the section "Spinal Cord Injuries."

Orthopedic Disabilities

Arthritis

The term *arthritis* is derived from two Greek roots: *arthro-,* meaning joint, and *-itis,* meaning inflammation. Forty-six million adults in the United States report being told by a physician that they have some form of arthritic disease.[5] Since arthritis inflicts a low mortality and high morbidity, the potential for increasing numbers of those afflicted and disabled is great. It is assumed that many factors predispose one to arthritis: infection, hereditary factors, environmental stress, dietary deficiencies, trauma, and organic or emotional disturbances.

Types, Causes, Incidence, and Characteristics In most cases, arthritis is progressive, gradually resulting in general fatigue, weight loss, and muscular stiffness. Joint impairment is symmetrical, and characteristically the small joints of the hands and feet are affected in the earliest stages. Tenderness and pain may occur in tendons and muscular tissue near inflamed joints. As the inflammation in the joints becomes progressively chronic, degenerative and proliferative changes occur to the synovial tendons, ligaments, and articular cartilages. If the inflammation is not

---

CASE STUDY 15-2

Roberto

Roberto was diagnosed with severe juvenile rheumatoid arthritis (JRA) at age three years. At age five years, Roberto is unable to move without severe pain. Roberto uses a wheelchair for ambulation but needs someone to push him. He has severe flexion contractures at most of his joints. His hands and fingers are so affected that he is unable to grasp an object.

Roberto lives in a small, rural community. His parents, migrant workers, struggle to provide care. His pain and anti-inflammatory medication are both very expensive. Their transient lifestyle and the cost of medication make it difficult for them to keep him on a regular medication schedule.

APPLICATION TASK

Identify types of things the adapted physical educator can do to help improve the quality of Roberto's life. What role, if any, might the general physical educator play?

---

arrested in its early stages, joints become ankylosed and muscles atrophy and contract, eventually causing a twisted and deformed limb. Three common forms of arthritis are rheumatoid arthritis, osteoarthritis, and ankylosing spondylitis.

Rheumatoid arthritis is the nation's number one crippling disease, afflicting more than 3 million persons. It is a systemic disease of unknown cause. Seventy-five percent of the cases occur between the ages of 25 and 50 years and in a ratio of 3 to 1, women to men. A type of rheumatoid arthritis called Still's disease, or juvenile arthritis, attacks children before the age of 7 years. Approximately 300,000 children in the United States are afflicted with rheumatoid arthritis, making it a major crippler among young children.[2] The most significant physical sign is the thickening of the synovial tissue in joints that are actively involved (inflamed). Inflamed joints are sensitive to the touch. Individuals with rheumatoid arthritis are stiff for an hour or so after rising in the morning or after a period of inactivity.[88]

Osteoarthritis, the second most frequent type of arthritis, is a disorder of the hyaline cartilage, primarily in the weight-bearing joints. It is a result of mechanical destruction of the coverings of the bone at the joints because of trauma or repeated use. Although evidence of the breakdown can be documented during the twenties, discomfort usually does not occur until individuals are in their forties. Initially, the condition is noninflammatory, and it impacts only one or a few joints. Pain is the earliest symptom, and it increases initially with exercise. The condition affects men and women equally; however, recent studies demonstrate that athletes may be at the greatest risk for developing osteoarthritis. Athletes who participate in sports with a high percentage of high impact, plus fast acceleration and deceleration, put themselves at the greatest risk. These activities include soccer, racquet sports, track and field, and throwing activities.[93]

Osteopenia is low bone mineral content, a condition that frequently leads to osteoporosis, which results in fragile bones and a high risk of fractures. Youth who fail to attain peak bone mass during their adolescent years are at highest risk for developing osteoporosis in later life. Approximately 30 percent of the teenagers with juvenile rheumatoid arthritis who do not use corticosteroids demonstrate mild to moderate osteopenia, which puts them at high risk for developing osteoporosis later in life.[44]

Special Considerations Interventions for arthritis include proper diet, rest, drug therapy, reduction of stress, and exercise. Because of its debilitating effect, prolonged bed rest is discouraged, although daily rest sessions are required to avoid undue fatigue. A number of drugs may be given to the patient, depending on individual needs; for example, salicylates, such as aspirin, relieve pain; gold compounds may be used for arresting the acute inflammatory stage; and adrenocortical steroids may be used to control the degenerative process. Drugless techniques for controlling arthritis pain, such as biofeedback, self-hypnosis, behavior modification,

Modified Sports Equipment Opens the World to Individuals with Disabilities
Courtesy RADVENTURES, Inc.

and transcutaneous nerve stimulation, are often used as adjuncts to more traditional types of treatment.

The Physical Activity Program and Teaching Strategies Physical exercise is crucial to reduce pain and increase function. The exercises required by patients with arthritis fall into three major categories: exercises to improve and maintain range of motion, exercises that strengthen the muscles that surround and support affected joints, and aerobic exercises to improve cardiovascular endurance. The physical educator should encourage gradual or static stretching, isometric muscle contraction, and low-impact aerobic exercise daily. Exercising in a pool, biking, and rowing are highly recommended.[72]

Maintenance of normal joint range of movement is of prime importance for establishing a functional joint. Stretching may first be passive; however, active stretching is of greater benefit because muscle tone is maintained in the process. Joints should be moved through pain-free range of motion several times daily.

Isometric exercises that strengthen the muscles that support affected joints should be practiced during the day when the pain and stiffness are at a minimum. Although weight-bearing isotonic exercises have long been advised against, in recent studies intensive weight-bearing exercises have been shown to be very beneficial. Because individuals with rheumatoid arthritis are at high risk for osteoporosis and cardiovascular problems, an ongoing program that includes both weight-bearing exercises and aerobic exercise is recommended.[75] One set of 10 to 12 repetitions for each muscle group should be performed three times weekly.[9]

Aerobic exercises that require a minimum of weight bearing should be used. Bicycling, swimming, and aquatic aerobics are highly recommended. Whenever possible, water activities should take place in a heated pool because the warmth enhances circulation and reduces muscle tightness. The Arthritis Foundation recommends a water temperature between 83 and 88 degrees F.[8] One recreational activity that has been shown to improve cardiovascular endurance and to counteract depression, anxiety, and tension is dancing.[79]

An individual with arthritis may need rest periods during the day. These should be combined with a well-planned exercise program. Activity should never increase pain or so tire an individual that normal recovery is not obtained by the next day.

Arthrogryposis (Curved Joints)

Arthrogryposis is a condition of flexure or contracture of joints (joints of the lower limbs more often than joints of the upper limbs) that is present at birth. The incidence is estimated to be 1 in 3,000 births.[7]

Characteristics The limbs may be fixed in any position. However, the usual forms are with the shoulders turned in, the elbows straightened and extended, the forearms turned with the palms outward (pronated), and the wrists flexed and deviated upward with the fingers curled into the palms. The hips may be bent in a flexed position and turned outward (externally rotated), and the feet are usually turned inward and downward. The spine often evidences scoliosis, the limbs are small in circumference, and the joints appear large and have lost their range of motion. Deformities are at their worst at birth, and a regular exercise program improves function; active physical therapy early in life can produce reduced contracture and improved range of motion.

Several physical conditions are associated with arthrogryposis, including congenital heart disease, urinary tract abnormalities, respiratory problems, abdominal hernias, and cleft palate. Intelligence is usually normal. Children with arthrogryposis may walk independently but with an abnormal gait, or they may depend on a wheelchair.

Special Considerations Surgery is often used to correct hip conditions, as well as knee and foot deformities. Surgery is sometimes used to permit limited flexion of the elbow joint, as well as greater wrist mobility.

The Physical Education Program and Teaching Strategies The awkwardness of joint positions and mechanics causes no pain; therefore, children with arthrogryposis are free to engage in most types of activity. Muscle strengthening and range-of-motion exercises prove to be very beneficial.[7]

Congenital Hip Dislocation

Congenital hip dislocation, which is also known as developmental hip dislocation, is a disorder in which the head of the thigh bone (femur) doesn't fit properly into, or is outside of, the hip socket (acetabulum) (see Figure 15-3). It is estimated that it occurs more often in females than in males; it may be bilateral or unilateral, occurring most often in the left hip.

The cause of congenital hip dislocation is unknown, with various causes proposed. Heredity seems to be a primary causative factor in faulty hip development and subsequent dysplasia. Actually, only about 2 percent of developmental hip dislocations are congenital.

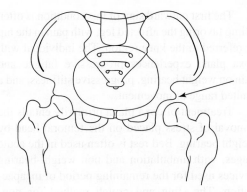

Figure 15-3   Developmental Hip Dislocation

Characteristics   Generally, the acetabulum is shallower on the affected side than on the non-affected side, and the femoral head is displaced upward and backward in relation to the ilium. Ligaments and muscles become deranged, resulting in a shortening of the rectus femoris, hamstring, and adductor thigh muscles and affecting the small intrinsic muscles of the hip. Prolonged malpositioning of the femoral head produces a chronic weakness of the gluteus medius and minimus muscles. A primary factor in stabilizing one hip in the upright posture is the iliopsoas muscle. In developmental hip dislocation, the iliopsoas muscle displaces the femoral head upward; this will eventually cause the lumbar vertebrae to become lordotic and scoliotic.

Detection of a hip dislocation may not occur until the child begins to bear weight or walk. Early recognition of this condition may be accomplished by observing asymmetrical fat folds on the infant's legs and restricted hip adduction on the affected side. The Trendelenburg test (see Figure 15-4) will reveal that the child is unable to maintain the pelvic level while standing on the affected leg. In such cases, weak abductor muscles of the affected leg allow the pelvis to tilt downward on the nonaffected side. The child walks with a decided limp in unilateral cases and with a waddle in bilateral cases. No discomfort or pain is normally experienced by the child, but fatigue tolerance to physical activity is very low. Pain and discomfort become more apparent as the individual becomes

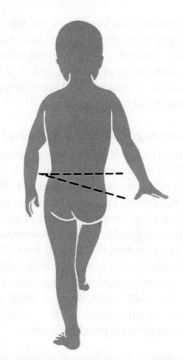

Figure 15-4   Trendelenburg Test

older and as postural deformities become more structural.

Special Considerations   Medical treatment depends on the age of the child and the extent of displacement. Young babies with a mild involvement may have the condition remedied through gradual adduction of the femur by a pillow splint, whereas more complicated cases may require traction, casting, or surgery to restore proper hip continuity. The thigh is slowly returned to a normal position.

The Physical Education Program and Teaching Strategies   Active exercise is suggested, along with passive stretching of contracted tissue. Primary concern is paid to reconditioning the movement of hip extension and abduction. When adequate muscle strength has been gained in the hip region, a program of ambulation is conducted, with particular attention paid to walking without a lateral pelvic tilt. Most children in the physical education or recreation program with a history of developmental hip dislocation will require specific postural training, conditioning of the hip region, continual gait training, and general body mechanics training. Swimming is an excellent activity for general conditioning of the hip, and it is highly recommended. Activities should not be engaged in to the point of discomfort or fatigue.

Coxa Plana (Legg-Calvé-Perthes Disease)

Coxa plana is the result of abnormal softening of the femoral head. It is a condition identified early in the twentieth century independently by Legg of Boston, Calvé of France, and Perthes of Germany. Its gross signs reflect a flattening of the head of the femur (see Figure 15-5), and it is found predominantly in boys between the ages of 5 and 10 years.[88] It has been variously termed osteochondritis deformans juvenilis, pseudocoxalgia, and Legg-Calvé-Perthes disease. The exact cause of coxa plana is not known; trauma, infection, and endocrine imbalance have been suggested as possible causes.

Characteristics   Coxa plana is characterized by degeneration of the capital epiphysis of the femoral head. Osteoporosis, or bone rarefaction, results in a flattened and deformed femoral head. Later developments may also include widening of the femoral head and thickening of the femoral neck. The last stage of coxa plana characterized by a self-limiting course in which there is a regeneration and an almost complete return of the normal epiphysis within two to three years.[88] However, recovery is not always complete, and there is often some residual deformity. The younger child with coxa plana has the best prognosis for complete recovery.

The first outward sign of this condition is often a limp favoring the affected leg, with pain in the hip or referred to the knee region. The individual with coxa plana experiences progressive fatigue and pain on weight bearing, progressive stiffness, and a limited range of movement.

Treatment of coxa plana primarily entails the removal of stress placed on the femoral head by weight bearing. Bed rest is often used in the acute stages, with ambulation and non weight-bearing devices used for the remaining period of incapacitation. The sling and crutch method for non-weight bearing is widely used for this condition (see Figure 15-6). Weight-bearing exercise is contraindicated until the physician discounts the possibility of a pathological joint condition.

The Physical Education Program and Teaching Strategies   The individual with an epiphyseal affection of the hip presents a problem of muscular and skeletal stability and joint range of movement. Stability of the hip region requires skeletal continuity

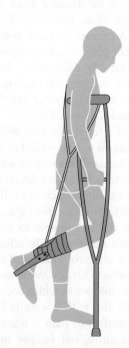

Figure 15-6   Sling and Crutch for Hip Conditions

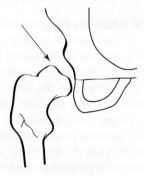

Figure 15-5   Coxa Plana

and a balance of muscle strength, primarily in the muscles of hip extension and abduction. Prolonged limited motion and nonweight bearing may result in contractures of the tissues surrounding the hip joint and an inability to walk or run with ease. Abnormal weakness of the hip extensors and abductors may cause shortening of the hip flexors and adductors and lead the individual to display the Trendelenburg sign (review Figure 15-4).

A program of exercise must be carried out to prevent muscle atrophy and general deconditioning. When movement is prohibited, muscle-tensing exercises for the muscles of the hip region are conducted, together with isotonic exercises for the upper extremities, trunk, ankles, and feet.

When the hip becomes free of symptoms, a progressive, isotonic, nonweight-bearing program is initiated for the hip region. Active movement emphasizing hip extension and abduction is recommended. Swimming is an excellent adjunct to the regular exercise program.

The program of exercise should never exceed the point of pain or fatigue until full recovery is accomplished. A general physical fitness program emphasizing weight control and body mechanics will help the student prepare to return to a full program of physical education and recreation activities.

Osgood-Schlatter Condition

Osgood-Schlatter condition is not considered a disease but, rather, the result of trauma to the patellar tendon where it inserts on the tibia. Major features are pain, swelling, and tenderness over the insertion point.[88]

Osgood-Schlatter condition usually occurs in active boys and girls when their bones are growing most rapidly (ages 8 to 15 years).[70] This is a very common cause of knee pain in adolescents, particularly those who participate in activities requiring jumping and cutting, such as volleyball and soccer.[104] The condition occurs twice as frequently in the left knee than in the right knee.

Characteristics   In the early stages, there is pain in front of the shin 2 to 3 inches below the kneecap.

Swelling occurs a few months later. The symptoms range from mild knee pain during activity to constant pain.[70] The physical educator may detect this condition based on the student's complaints. When this happens, parents should be notified to contact their physician.

Special Considerations   If Osgood-Schlatter condition is not properly cared for, deformity and a defective extensor mechanism may result; however, it may not necessarily be associated with pain or discomfort. In most cases, Osgood-Schlatter condition is acute, is self-limiting, and does not exceed a few months' duration. However, even after the arrest of symptoms, Osgood-Schlatter condition tends to recur after irritation.

Local inflammation occurs when the legs are used, and it eases with rest. The individual may be unable to kneel or engage in flexion and extension movements without pain. The knee joint must be kept completely immobilized when the inflammatory state persists. Forced inactivity, provided by a plaster cast, may be the only answer to keeping an overactive adolescent from using the affected leg.

The Physical Education Program and Teaching Strategies   Early detection may reveal a slight condition in which the individual can continue a normal activity routine, excluding sport participation, excessive exercise, strenuous running, jumping, deep knee bending, and falling on the affected leg. All physical education activities must be modified to avoid quadriceps muscle strain while preparing for general physical fitness. Moderate stretching of the quadriceps and hamstrings done for 10 seconds may relieve some of the pain and allow for activity. Ten repetitions, two or three times a day, should be beneficial.[70]

While the limb is immobilized in a cast, the individual is greatly restricted; weight bearing may be held to a minimum, with signs of pain at the affected part closely watched by the physician. Although Osgood-Schlatter condition is self-limiting and temporary, exercise is an important factor in full recovery. Physical education

Matthew Oberholtz of USA Water Ski Demonstrates Water Skiing Capability
Courtesy of USA Water Ski

activities should emphasize the capabilities of the upper body and nonaffected leg to prevent their deconditioning.

After arrest of the condition and removal of the cast (or relief from immobilization), the patient is given a graduated reconditioning program. The major objectives at this time are reeducation in proper walking patterns and the restoration of normal strength and flexibility of the knee joint. Strenuous knee movement is avoided for at least five weeks, and the demanding requirements of regular physical education classes may be postponed for extended periods, depending on the physician's recommendations. Although emphasis is placed on the affected leg during rehabilitation,

a program must also be provided for the entire body.

The following are criteria for the individual to return to a regular physical education program:

1. Normal range of movement of the knee
2. Quadriceps muscle strength equal to that of the unaffected leg
3. Evidence that Osgood-Schlatter condition has become asymptomatic
4. Ability to move freely without favoring the affected part

After recovery, the student should avoid all activities that tend to contuse, or in any way irritate again, the tibial tuberosity.

Osteogenesis Imperfecta (Brittle Bone Disease)

Osteogenesis imperfecta is a condition marked by both weak bones and elasticity of the joints, ligaments, and skin. It occurs once in 20,000 births.[32] Most cases are the result of a dominant genetic defect, although some cases result from a spontaneous mutation.[82] There are four types, ranging from mild to severe involvement.

Characteristics The bones of children with this condition are abnormally frail and may have multiple fractures at the time of birth. The underlying layer of the eyeball (choroid) shows through as a blue discoloration. Individuals who live are shorter than average and have a triangular-shaped face.

As growth occurs in individuals with the condition, the limbs tend to become bowed. The bones are not dense, and the spine is rounded and often evidences scoliosis. The teeth are in poor condition, easily broken, discolored, and prone to cavities. The joints are excessively mobile, and the positions that the children may take show great flexibility.

Special Considerations No known chemical or nutrient has been shown to correct osteogenesis imperfecta, and the most satisfactory treatment is the surgical insertion of a steel rod between the ends of the long bones. This treatment, plus bracing, permits some youth to walk. Many persons with brittle bone disease need a wheelchair at least part of the time, and those with severe cases require a wheelchair exclusively.

The Physical Education Program and Teaching Strategies Some authorities have suggested that physical activities are to be ruled out for this population, whereas others encourage exercise to promote muscle and bone strength. Swimming and water therapy are strongly recommended. These individuals are also encouraged to maintain a healthy weight and avoid activities that deplete bone (e.g., smoking, steroid use).[82]

Physical education teachers should be sensitive to the presence of children in their classes whose bones are highly susceptible to injury, trauma, or breakage because of this and related conditions. These children, who approach normalcy in other areas, continue to require a highly adapted physical education program that is limited to range-of-motion exercises. Although osteogenesis imperfecta is diagnosed only in severe cases, many children seem to have a propensity for broken bones. Physical educators should take softness of bones into consideration when developing physical education programs for children.

Osteomyelitis

Osteomyelitis is an inflammation of a bone and its medullary (marrow) cavity. Occasionally referred to as myelitis, this condition is caused by bacteria, mycrobacteria, and fungi.[88] In its early stages, osteomyelitis is described as acute. If the infection persists or recurs periodically, it is called chronic. Since chronic osteomyelitis can linger on for years, the physical educator should confer with the physician about the nature of an adapted program.

Characteristics In children, the long bones are affected. In adults, the condition settles in the vertebrae and the pelvis.[69] Pain, tenderness, and soft tissue swelling are present, and heat is felt through the overlying skin. There are limited effects on range of joint movement. The child may limp because of the acute pain.

Special Considerations If medical treatment is delayed, abscesses work outward, causing a sinus (hole) in the skin over the affected bone, from which pus is discharged. This sinus is covered with a dressing that must be changed several times daily. The medical treatment is rest and intensive antibiotic therapy. Through surgery, the infected bone can be scraped to evacuate the pus.

The Physical Education Program and Teaching Strategies Rehabilitation activity under the direction of a physician can restore motor functions, so that normal activity can be resumed. Exercise is always contraindicated when infection is active in the body.

Spondylolysis and Spondylolisthesis

Spondylolysis and spondylolisthesis result from a congenital malformation of one or both of the neural arches of the fifth lumbar vertebra or, less frequently, the fourth lumbar vertebra. Spondylolisthesis is distinguished from spondylolysis by anterior displacement of the fifth lumbar vertebra on the sacrum. Both conditions may be accompanied by pain in the lower back.

Forward displacement may occur as a result of sudden trauma to the lumbar region. The vertebrae are moved anteriorly because of an absence of bony continuity of the neural arch, and the main support is derived from ligaments that surround the area. In such cases, individuals often appear to have severe lordosis.

Spondylolysis occurs more frequently in teenagers who are involved in athletics than in the general population. The highest incidence in adolescents occurs in persons involved in activities requiring hyperextension and/or rotation of the lumbar spine, such as diving, weight lifting, wrestling, football, and gymnastics.[96] However, it is also a growing concern for competitive swimmers who use the butterfly stroke or the breaststroke.[81]

Characteristics   Many individuals have spondylolysis, or even spondylolisthesis, without symptoms of any kind, but a mild twist or blow may set off a whole series of low back complaints and localized discomfort or pain radiating down one or both sides.

Special Considerations   The pathological condition eventually may become so extensive as to require surgical intervention.

The Physical Education Program and Teaching Strategies   Proper therapy may involve a graduated exercise program to help prevent further aggravation and, in some cases, remove many symptoms characteristic of the condition. A program should be initiated that includes stretching the lower back, strengthening abdominal muscles, walking to stimulate blood flow, and engaging in a general conditioning program. Games and sports that overextend, fatigue, or severely twist and bend the lower back should be avoided. In most cases, the physician will advise against contact sports and heavy weight lifting.

Ross Davis, a Silver Medal Winner in the Barcelona Paralympics

Courtesy Disabled Sports Association of North Texas, Dallas.

Traumatic Injuries

Traumatic Brain Injuries

Definition   A traumatic brain injury is an injury to the head that results in minor to serious brain damage; it is the major cause of injury, death, and long-term neurological impairment in children and adolescents.[17] It is the most common cause of acquired disability in childhood and adolescence.[29] The effects of head injuries on school behavior depend on the extent of the insult to the brain tissue.

Incidence   Approximately 2 million traumatic brain injuries (TBIs) occur in the United States each year that restrict activities or require medical attention.[64] Only about 3 percent of the sports and recreational injuries are hospitalized for TBI and 90 percent of sports-related TBIs go unreported.[108]

Causes The causes of TBI include motor vehicle accidents (most common in adolescence), falls, bicycle accidents, child abuse, assaults, and sport injuries. The earlier in life a child experiences a severe TBI, the greater the impact on his or her neuropsychological functioning throughout life.[65]

Characteristics The location and severity of brain damage greatly affect the characteristic behaviors of the child and the speed of recovery. Generally, attention/concentration, memory, executive functions, cognition, and motor and language functions are impaired to some extent. The more severe the injury, the more persistent the behavior, learning, and academic problems.[115] Although rapid recovery of most functions occurs during the first two or three years after injury, problems frequently persist for longer periods. When the frontal lobe is involved, cognitive impairments occur in attention, executive functioning, and problem solving. Damage to the temporal regions of the brain results in problems with learning new information. Gross motor impairments are more frequent than fine motor impairments.[92] Static and dynamic balance as well as activities requiring coordination of the two sides of the body are usually impacted the most.[35] Difficulty processing and integrating information, as well as abnormal brain activity, contributes to negative behaviors, including low tolerance for frustration, aggression, impulsiveness, and noncompliance. In addition, seizures are three times more likely among individuals with TBI, with the risk doubling as late as five years after the injury. The extent and frequency of these problems should be addressed in the student's IEP.

Testing The type of test administered will depend on the extent and severity of the student's brain damage. If an individual is having difficulty organizing sensory input, decision and movement time will be compromised, as well as movement efficiency. The type of teaching approach (bottom-up or top-down) a teacher uses will dictate the assessment instrument used. The teacher who wants to address functional performance will measure

CASE STUDY 15-3

Danny Joe

Danny Joe is a seven-year-old boy who was hit by a drunk driver while riding his bicycle near his home in West Texas. Danny Joe was described by his parents before the accident as "all boy," "outgoing," "athletic," "rough and tumble," and "friendly."

An adapted physical education assessment six months after his traumatic brain injury described the following behaviors and characteristics:

- He is able to walk, with a cane, independently on flat and known surfaces without falling.
- He is able to recover from a fall to a stand.
- He is unable to run, gallop, jump, hop, or skip.
- He cannot ascend or descend stairs without support from a teacher's aide.
- He is able to throw a yarn ball, with excellent directionality, a distance of 10 feet without falling.
- He is able to "kick" an 8-inch ball by pushing at it with his left foot.
- He is unable to stand on one foot and maintain a balance with eyes open.

Complicating his reentry into the elementary school in his neighborhood is the fact that the speech centers of his brain were also apparently affected. He is demonstrating speech and language behaviors similar to that of a person with Tourette syndrome. The teachers and staff have worked very hard to teach him to use alternatives to swear words that appear to "pop" out of his mouth without reason.

APPLICATION TASK

Danny Joe has a one-on-one paraprofessional who spends the entire day with him. She adores Danny Joe and is willing to do anything to help him. Describe the activities she could do to help him regain functional skills.

physical fitness and specific sporting skills.[99] The teacher who uses the bottom-up approach will elect to sample sensory input function. To determine what types of sensory input problems exist, the physical educator may wish to administer a sensory input screening instrument similar to the one presented in Chapter 5.

If the evaluator is more interested in simply pinpointing the areas of motor functioning that have been affected, a motor development or motor proficiency test, such as the Test of Gross Motor Development–2 or the Bruininks-Oseretsky Test of Motor Proficiency (balance, strength, and bilateral coordination subtests) should be administered.

Special Considerations   The extent of the brain damage will determine the number of special considerations that must be made. The person who suffers from a TBI will have good days and bad days. On a good day, it is relatively easy to attend, follow directions, and tolerate minor frustrations. On a bad day, everything is blown out of proportion—it is hard to sit still, listen to instructions, overlook minor problems, and comply with rules. The sensitive teacher will attend carefully to clues that indicate the type of day the student with brain damage is experiencing and will adjust expectations for the student accordingly. Allowance must always be made for basic organizational problems and learning difficulties that have resulted from the insult to the brain tissue. The more positive and user-friendly the educational environment, the better.

D'Amato and Rothlisberg[25] recommend using a structure, organization, and strategy (S.O.S.) approach to assist the student with a TBI who is struggling to function in a school setting. Structuring involves keeping the learning environment as structured and stable as possible. Organization involves providing the student with a TBI the necessary environmental cues and aids to foster new learning. That is, teachers should provide advance organizers, key words, and clear guidelines when teaching these students. Instruction in problem-solving strategies includes multimodal teaching styles that provide visual, auditory, and kinesthetic cues. Croce, Horvat, and Roswal[19] have demonstrated that individuals with TBIs acquire motor skills more rapidly when provided practice schedules with summary and/or average knowledge of results, rather than every trial or no feedback.

It is critical that students who have suffered a traumatic brain injury, no matter how mild, be carefully monitored before returning to participation in sports because TBIs that follow one another have a confounding effect.[33] The reason for this is that the effects of repeated concussions are cumulative. A concussion grading scale recommended for physical educators, athletic trainers, and coaches is presented in Table 15-3.

Table 15-3	Concussion Grading Scale and Playing Status[51]	
Grade	**Symptoms**	**Playing Status**
1	Transient confusion; no loss of consciousness; concussion symptoms or mental status abnormalities resolve in less than 15 minutes	Remove and examine every 5 minutes; return after 15 minutes
2	Transient confusion; no loss of consciousness; concussion symptoms or mental status abnormalities last more than 15 minutes	Remove from play and disallow return that day; examine next day and allow return after one full week without symptoms
3	Loss of consciousness, which may be a few seconds or minutes	Transport player to a hospital if still unconscious for a thorough neurological evaluation; allow return after two to four full weeks without symptoms

Teaching Strategies   Physical education personnel should be particularly attentive to the posttrauma student's ongoing psychomotor, cognitive, and behavior problems. Care must be exercised in sequencing motor tasks, providing instructions, and simplifying motor demands. Tasks should be reduced to their simplest components without making the student feel babied; instructions should be brief and to the point; and game strategies should be simple rather than complex. Children with TBIs are not as motivated by behavior management reward systems as are other children.[55] The student should be given the option of timing himself or herself out when the demands of the class prove to be too frustrating to handle on a given day. Any adjustments that will reduce the student's frustration to a minimum and increase his or her ability to cooperate in a group setting will contribute to the student's success in physical education.

The Physical Education Program   Physical exercise has been shown to improve motor function, elevate mood, and contribute to perceptions of better health in individuals with TBIs.[39] The type of physical education provided for the student with a TBI will depend on the test results and the teacher's judgment of the student's capability. The more individualized the program, the less frustration the student will experience. Being required to contribute to a competitive team effort where winning is highly valued will create significant problems for the individual who is slow to make critical playing decisions and moves. If the student is given opportunities to pursue his or her own exercise program, a buddy system should be effective in keeping the student with a TBI on task and following appropriate safety procedures.

The physical education program should include aerobics and strength exercises, as well as stretching. Initially, the student should avoid high-intensity exercises, particularly those affecting blood pressure, such as resistance training. Instead, he or she should use low to moderate exercise intensities that do not evoke symptoms (e.g., headache, confusion, dizziness, nausea, numbness, fatigue). As strength and endurance improve, the exercise intensity can be increased.[108]

Depending on the extent and severity of brain damage, the following are educational modifications that may need to be included in the IEP:

- Reduced course load
- Scheduling of the most demanding courses in the morning, when the student is fresh
- A resource room with the assistance of an aide
- Rest breaks as needed
- Adapted physical education or a modified regular physical education program
- Peer tutoring
- Counseling
- Provisions for taping lectures and extra time for completing written work and examinations[73]

The individual with a strong support system of friends and family will have greater opportunities to be active in community settings than will the individual who has little or no outside support. Persons with TBIs who understand the components of a healthy lifestyle and who have been taught to select activities that will promote that lifestyle will seek out opportunities to stay active on their good days. On their bad days, their support group will provide them with the encouragement and motivation they need to expend the extra effort to stay active. Caution should be exercised when selecting activities. Highly competitive sports, particularly those that involve contact, can easily provoke a sensitive individual and result in

Ocean Escapes, a Pioneer in Aqua Therapy for Wheelchair-Enabled Individuals, Offers Weightlessness through Scuba Diving to Individuals Who, on Land, Are Trapped by Gravity
Courtesy Ocean Escapes.

undesirable impulsive, aggressive behaviors. Less competitive games and exercise routines will provide the same level of benefit without the potential negative emotional and physical outcomes.

Spinal Cord Injuries

Spinal cord injuries usually result in paralysis or partial paralysis of the arms, trunk, legs, or any combination thereof and loss of sensation, depending on the locus of the damage. The spinal cord is housed in the spinal, or vertebral, column. Nerves from the spinal cord pass down into the segments of the spinal column. Injury to the spinal cord affects the innervation of muscle. The higher up the vertebral column the level of injury, the greater the restriction of body movement. Persons with spinal cord injuries are usually referred to as paraplegics or tetraplegics (quadriplegics). In paraplegia, the legs are paralyzed. In tetraplegia, both the arms and legs are affected. There are 11,000 new cases of spinal cord injury in the United States every year.[16] Fifty-five percent of spinal cord injuries occur among individuals in the 16- to 30-year age range; males outnumber females four to one.[95]

Characteristics Spinal cord injuries are classified according to the region of the vertebrae affected. The regions affected are cervical, thoracic, lumbar, and sacral. Half of all spinal cord injuries occur at the cervical level and result in tetraplegia. Paraplegics make up the other half of spinal cord injuries; their lesions occur in the thoracic, lumbar, and sacral segments of the spine.[95] A description of the movement capability at each level of the lesion follows:

- Fourth cervical level. There is use of only the neck muscles and the diaphragm. Upper limb function is possible only with electrically powered assistive devices. The individual needs complete assistance moving to and from the wheelchair.
- Fifth cervical level. There is use of the deltoid muscles of the shoulder and the biceps muscles of the arm. The arms can be raised; however, it is difficult to engage in manipulative tasks.

Persons with this level of involvement can perform many activities with their arms. However, they need assistance with transfer to and from the wheelchair.

- Sixth cervical level. There is use of the wrist extensors, and the person can push the wheelchair and use an overhead trapeze (a bar hung overhead to be grasped). Some persons afflicted at this level can transfer the body to and from the wheelchair.
- Seventh cervical level. There is use of the elbow and wrist extensors. Movement of the hand is impaired. However, the person afflicted at this level may be able to perform pull-ups and push-ups and participate in activities that involve the grasp release mechanism.
- Upper thoracic levels. There is total movement capability in the arms but none in the legs. There is some control in the muscles of the upper back. The individual can control a wheelchair and may be able to stand with the use of long leg braces.
- Lower thoracic levels. There is control of the abdominal musculature that rights the trunk. Using the abdominal muscles makes it possible to walk with the support of long leg braces.
- Lumbar levels. There is control of the hip joint, and there is a good possibility of walking with controlled movement.
- Sacral level. There is muscular functioning for efficient ambulation. The functional level of the bladder, anal sphincters, and external genitals may be impaired.

In general, spinal cord injury results in motor and sensory loss below the level of injury, autonomic nervous system dysfunction if the injury is at T3 or lower (e.g., bowel/bladder, cardiovascular, and temperature regulation), spasticity, and contractures.[23] Specific physical characteristics are as follows:

1. Inappropriate control of the bladder and digestive organs
2. Contractures (abnormal shortening of muscles)

3. Heterotopic bone formation, or the laying down of new bone in soft tissue around joints (during this process, the area may become inflamed and swollen)
4. Urinary infections
5. Difficulty in defecation
6. Decubitus ulcers on the back and buttocks (caused by pressure of the body weight on specific areas)
7. Spasms of the muscles
8. Spasticity of muscles that prevent effective movement
9. Overweight because of low energy expenditures
10. Scoliosis
11. Respiratory disorders

Persons with spinal cord injury have muscle atrophy and impaired aerobic work capacity because of fewer remaining functional muscles and impaired blood flow.[71] If the injury is above T3, the heart rate may be affected (120 beats per minute is high). Athletes with spinal cord injuries between C6 and T7 have maximal heart rates of 110 to 130 beats per minute.[22] Thermal regulation may also be impaired because of a loss of normal blood flow regulation and the inability to sweat below the level of injury.[22] For this reason, individuals with tetraplegia should not be left in the sun or cold for any length of time. Individuals with tetraplegia who exercise are encouraged to wear support hose and use abdominal strapping to promote venous blood flow to the heart.[23]

Special Considerations   Many athletes with disabilities experience injuries. The most frequent types of injuries suffered by wheelchair athletes, some prevention techniques, and treatments are summarized in Table 15-4. For activities that require trunk stabilization, strapping is necessary.[35]

The Physical Education Program and Teaching Strategies   The physical education program for persons with spinal cord injury should be based on a well-rounded program of exercises for all the usable body parts, including activities to develop strength, flexibility, muscular endurance, cardiovascular endurance, and coordination. The leading

Table 15-4	Most Common Injuries Suffered by Wheelchair Athletes	
Injury	**Prevention**	**Treatment**
Soft tissue damage (overuse syndromes: tendonitis, bursitis)	Taping, splinting, protective padding; proper wheelchair positioning	Rest; selective strengthening, muscle balancing
Blisters	Taping, gloves, padding, cushioning, callous formation	Be aware of areas that lack sensation; treat blister
Lacerations/abrasions	Checking equipment for sharp surfaces, wearing padding, using cushions and towels for transfers; camber wheels	Treat injury; be aware of areas that lack sensation
Decubitus/pressure areas	Adequate cushioning; proper weight shifting; dry clothing, skin inspection; good nutrition and hygiene	Bed rest to remove all pressure from weight-bearing surface; treat open wounds
Sprains/contusions	Equipment safety; appropriate padding; sport-specific spotting	Treat injury; check for signs of fracture in athletes without movement or sensation

Data from Curtis KA: *Injuries and disability-specific medical conditions of athletes with disabilities.* Unpublished paper, Coral Gables, FL, University of Miami, 1993.

cause of death of persons with spinal cord injury is cardiovascular disease.[97,114] Physical activity is necessary because not only does a regular exercise program regime strengthen the cardiovascular system but it also enhances a person's functional independence, overall sense of well-being, and quality of life.[31] Young children need to be taught ways to use their wheelchairs in a variety of environments and should be encouraged to interact with their ambulatory peers. Middle school and high school students should develop the physical fitness necessary to participate in the sports of their choice.

Movement and dance therapies have been used successfully in rehabilitation programs for persons who have spinal cord injuries. Table 15-5 includes modifications that can be made in a typical warm-up session for a kindergarten or 1st-grade class.

The emphasis in the physical education program should be on functional movement skills. The child, if wheelchair enabled, should be given every opportunity to move in the chair. Individuals with upper body function can perform most physical education activities from a wheelchair. The physical education program should include wheelchair mobility training. Project C.R.E.O.L.E. is an excellent curriculum that promotes functional training in wheelchair use.[113] The child should practice moving in the chair with activities that modify the movement variables of time, space, force, and flow. For example, the child should be able to do the following:

1. Time
   a. Wheel fast, then slow.
   b. Wheel to a 4/4 beat.
2. Space
   a. Wheel up and down inclines.
   b. Wheel on cement, linoleum, grass, a gymnasium floor, and so on.
   c. Wheel around obstacles.
   d. Wheel over sticks.
   e. Wheel, holding a glass of water.
   f. Wheel, holding a ball on lap.
3. Force
   a. Wheel with a buddy sitting on lap.
   b. Wheel while pulling a partner on a scooter board.
   c. Push hard and see how far the chair will roll.
4. Flow
   a. Roll forward, spin in a circle, roll forward.
   b. Roll forward, stop, roll backward, stop.

Table 15-5 Warm-Up Session with Modifications for Children in Wheelchairs

Class Activity (Song/Dance)	Modifications
"Warm-up Time"	
Clap hands	None
Swing arms	None
Bend knees	Child lifts knees with hands.
Stamp feet	Child slaps feet with hands.
"What a Miracle"	
Clap hands	None
Stamp feet	Child slaps feet with hands.
Swing arms	None
Bend and stretch legs	Child lifts knees with hands.
Twist and bend spine	None
One foot balance	Child pushes into push-up position.
"Swing, Shake, Twist, Stretch"	
Swing	Child swings arms or head.
Shake	Child shakes hands, elbows, or head.
Twist	Child twists trunk.
Stretch	Child stretches arms.
"Bendable, Stretchable"	
Stretch to sky; touch floor	Child stretches to sky, touches toes.
"Run, Run, Run in Place"	
Run in place	Child spins chair in circle.
"Simon Says Jog Along"	
Jog	Child rolls chair in time to music.
Walk	Child rolls chair in time to music.

A Footless Climber Being Transported to Where He Will Begin His Ascent

Courtesy of City of Phoenix, AZ.

The same type of movement activities should be made available to the child using crutches and braces.

In addition to wheelchair mobility, younger children should be taught fundamental motor skills, such as throwing, hitting, and catching. Once these skills are mastered, games that incorporate these skills can be played. Modifications of games that have been described previously are appropriate for children using wheelchairs. Children using wheelchairs can participate in parachute games and target games without accommodation. They can maintain fitness of the upper body through the same type of regimens that the nondisabled engage in. Strengthening of the arms and shoulder girdle is important for propelling the wheelchair and for changing body positions when moving in and out of the wheelchair. Swimming is a particularly good activity for the development of total physical fitness. The emphasis should be on the development of functional movement skills.

It is possible to increase the heart rate response, blood pressure response, stroke volume and cardiac output, and respiration rate and depth through the use of arm exercises.[23] Development can be attained through arm pedaling of a bicycle ergometer, pushing of a wheelchair over considerable distances, and agility maneuvers with the wheelchair. DiCarlo[28] reported that males with tetraplegia with lesions at the fifth to seventh cervical levels were able to increase their wheelchair propulsion endurance and cardiopulmonary function by engaging in arm cycle ergometry exercises three times a week for eight weeks. Hardison, Isreal, and Somes[40] demonstrated the same types of gains with paraplegic males with lesion levels ranging from T4 to T12. They demonstrated improved oxygen utilization with a training program consisting of a 70 rpm ergometer cranking rate at 60 percent of the subject's VO_2 max. For males with spinal cord injuries who are wheelchair-dependent, the lower the injury and the more frequent the ongoing exercise program, the higher the physical work capacity that can be developed.[76] Physical activity also has been shown to counter some of the increase in body fat that is typical of individuals with spinal cord injury.[54] Curtis[22] cautions that there are several physiological response differences between upper and lower extremity exercise. During upper body exercise, (1) maximum value of oxygen utilization is 70 percent of that of lower body exercise; (2) heart rate is approximately 20 percent higher; (3) stroke volume is 10 to 18 percent less; and (4) lactic acid concentrations are higher.

Stretching exercises should always be used to improve flexibility and enable an individual to achieve full joint range of motion. They are also critical for reducing the chance of stress injuries to muscles, tendons, and ligaments. Curtis[20] recommends that stretching be done both before exercise and after cool-down. The following stretches should be executed for 15 to 30 seconds each, while using a wheelchair:

Trunk Stretching
1. Exhale and lean forward to touch the ground; hold and return to sitting position.
2. Inhale. Bend over at waist and reach out, keeping arms and head parallel to the ground; hold and return to sitting position.
3. Arch left arm over the head and lean to the right; repeat to other side.

Shoulder Stretching
1. Intertwine fingers from both hands, inhale, and lift hands overhead, pushing palms upward.

2. Intertwine fingers from both hands behind back, exhale, lean forward, and lift hands high behind back.
3. Clasp hands behind head and push elbows backward.

Shoulder-Elbow Stretching

1. Raise arms to shoulder height with palms facing forward; push arms backward while keeping elbows straight.
2. Bend arm across chest, reaching for opposite shoulder blade; push on elbow. Repeat with other arm.
3. Raise arm up next to head; reach down the back with the hand; push against elbow with other hand. Repeat with other arm.

Elbow-Wrist Stretching

1. Raise left arm out in front of body, keeping elbow straight; with right hand, pull left hand and fingers into extension (fingers toward the sky). Repeat with other hand.
2. Raise left arm out in front of body, keeping elbow straight; with right hand, pull left hand and fingers into flexion (fingers toward the ground).

When developing strength exercise regimens to enhance sport performance, specificity of training is critical. Manually propelling a wheelchair tends to develop the flexor muscles in front of the body; thus, attention must be paid to developing unused muscle groups in the back of the body. As a general rule, for all exercises executed in front of the body, do twice as many in the opposite direction.[23] Include backward wheelchair pushing to develop the muscles that work in opposition to the pectorals.[23] Because of the need to lift the arms to propel the wheelchair, arm abductors tend to be stronger than the adductors; thus, exercises to strengthen the adductors are indicated.[23] Coordination training should also be sport-specific. General power and endurance training is recommended for rounding out the exercise program.

Power training could include throwing and catching a medicine ball thrown against a small trampoline and wind sprints in the wheelchair.

Endurance training should involve wheelchair pushing for 20 minutes and longer three times a week at the target heart rate (220 minus age if the injury is below T3).

Routine exercise programs are critical for the individual who uses a wheelchair for ambulation, because the act of manually wheeling the chair produces imbalances in muscle strength. Imbalances in muscle strength lead to postural deviations that, if left unaddressed, will eventually become structural and further impair the individual's health. The physical educator who helps the individual using a wheelchair develop a realistic exercise program that can be continued throughout life will contribute to the quality of that person's life.

Amputations

A person with an amputation is missing part or all of a limb. Amputation is sometimes performed to arrest a malignant condition caused by trauma, tumors, infection, vascular impairment, diabetes, or arteriosclerosis. The number of amputees in the United States exceeds 1,285,000.[3]

Characteristics and Types   Amputations can be classified into two categories: acquired amputation and congenital amputation. The amputation is acquired if one has a limb removed by operation; it is congenital if one is born without a limb. Congenital amputations are classified according to the site and level of limb absence. When an amputation is performed through a joint, it is referred to as a disarticulation.

Special Considerations   Many, individuals with an amputation elect to use a prosthetic appliance to replace the missing limb. The purpose of the prosthetic device is to enable the individual to function as normally as possible. The application of a prosthetic device may be preceded by surgery to produce a stump. After the operation, the stump is dressed and bandaged to aid shrinkage of the stump. After the fitting of the prosthesis, the stump must be continually cared for. It should be checked periodically and cleaned to prevent infection, abrasion, and skin disorder. The attachment of a false limb early in a child's development will encourage the incorporation of the appendage into natural body activity more than if the prosthesis is introduced later in life. The type of prosthesis selected depends on whether it will be used for daily activities and recreational purposes or for a specific activity, such as distance running or sprinting.[107]

It is not practical to fit a prosthesis on some forms of amputations. Consider the case of Mark Pietranski (see Figure 15-7), who was born with two small appendages where his legs should have been. One appendage had to be removed early in life; the other is not strong enough for functional use. Mark does not let his lack of legs interfere with his activities. In Figure 15-7, Mark is a member of his middle school football team—despite the fact that he uses only his hands and arms to propel himself. He also swims regularly.

The Physical Education Program and Teaching Strategies   The ultimate goal of a person with an amputation is to perform physical activity safely. Amputees must develop skills to use prostheses; effective use demands much effort. The remaining muscles

needed for prosthetic use must be strengthened, and standing and walking must be practiced until they become automatic. To regain adequate postural equilibrium, individuals with lower limb amputations have to learn to link altered sensory input to movement patterns.[37] Practice in walking, turning, sitting, and standing is needed.

Amputees are often exposed to beneficial exercise through the use of the prosthesis. Exercises

Figure 15-7   Mark Pietranski, a Double Amputee, Participates in Football with His Classmates

Courtesy *Denton Record Chronicle.*

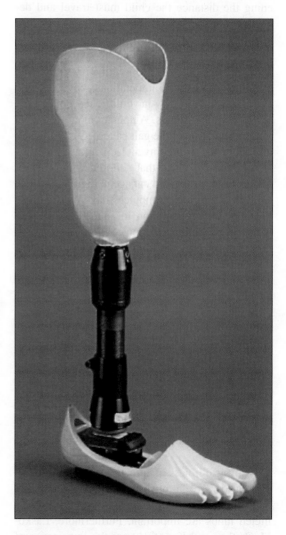

Newly Designed Prosthetic Devices Normalize Walking Patterns

Courtesy Endolite: North America, Centerville, OH.

should be initiated to strengthen muscles after a stump heals. Training also enhances ambulation, inhibits atrophy and contractures, improves or maintains mechanical alignment of body parts, and develops general physical fitness.

Several adaptations of physical activity can be made for children with impaired ambulation. For these children, the major disadvantages are speed of locomotion and fatigue to sustained activity. Some accommodations that can be made are shortening the distance the child must travel and decreasing the speed needed to move from one place to another.

Persons with amputations below the knee can learn ambulation skills well with a prosthesis and training. Persons with amputations above the knee but below the hip may have difficulty developing efficient walking gaits. Amputations at this level require alteration of the gait pattern. Steps are usually shortened to circumvent lack of knee function.

Authorities agree that children with properly fitted prostheses should engage in regular physical education activities. Amputees have considerable potential for participation in adapted sports and games. The National Amputee Golf Association, for example, provides clinics nationwide to introduce children and adults with disabilities to the sport of golf and to train teachers and coaches to adapt methods and instruction to meet the needs of amputees. There are opportunities for persons with prostheses to participate in official sports competition. Persons with above-the-knee amputations can walk well and engage in swimming, skiing, and other activities with the proper aids. Persons with arm amputations who have use of their feet can participate in activities that require foot action, such as soccer and running events, as well as other activities that involve the feet exclusively.

Physical fitness of amputees should be an important part of a physical education program. Strength and flexibility and power of the unafflicted limbs are important. Furthermore, Lasko-McCarthey and Knopf[65] stress the importance of developing and maintaining the amputee's level of cardiovascular efficiency.

TESTING

The type of test used depends on the functioning level of the individual, as well as the purpose for the assessment. Several types of tests and the populations they can be used with are presented in Chapter 3. Persons who are ambulatory, including those with cerebral palsy who have spastic hemiplegia, can usually be tested using standard equipment. Fernandez and Pitetti[34] used a bicycle ergometer, a Schwinn Air Dyne ergometer, a treadmill, and an arm-crank ergometer to determine the physical work capacity of individuals with cerebral palsy. They recommended using an ergometer rather than a treadmill to avoid discriminating against persons with gait anomalies and those who are nonambulatory for whatever reason. Ponichtera-Mulcare et al.[87] recommend that a combination leg and arm ergometer be used to assess maximal power output and peak aerobic power, as well as for training. The Brockport Physical Fitness Test, Project M.O.B.I.L.T.E.E., and the *Physical Best and Individuals with Disabilities Handbook* by the American Alliance for Health, Physical Education, Recreation and Dance (AAHPERD) all suggest accommodations for ambulatory and nonambulatory individuals.

In addition to formal testing, it is frequently just as important to appraise individuals' functional movement capabilities. Motor programs can then be developed to meet their unique needs. The assessment should provide information about the potential for movement of each action of the body. This would involve knowledge of the strength, power, flexibility, and endurance of specific muscle groups. In addition, there should be information about which movement actions can be coordinated to attain specific motor outcomes. For instance, several throwing patterns that children with severe impairments use when participating in the Special Olympics can help circumvent movement problems of the arms and hands. The desired throwing pattern is one of extension of the arm and elbow and flexion of the wrist. If either of these actions is impaired, alternate throwing patterns need to be found. Some throwing patterns developed to circumvent extreme disability of the arm, elbow, and wrist are underhand movement, horizontal abduction of the arm and shoulder, flexion of the arm and elbow (over the shoulder), horizontal abduction of the arm (side arm), and overhand movement with most of the force generated from a rocking motion of the trunk. To maximize the potential of each of these types of throwing patterns, it is necessary to conduct training programs that will consider each child's assets and develop them fully. However, another option is to provide therapeutic exercise for each of the desired actions and then teach it as a functional, normalized movement pattern.

The ability prerequisites of strength, flexibility, endurance, power, and coordination can be applied to many wheelchair activities. Some of these activities involve (1) basic mobility skills, (2) transfer skills from and to the wheelchair, (3) performance on mats, (4) performance on gymnastics apparatus, (5) ability to maneuver vehicles, (6) motor capabilities in a swimming pool, (7) ability to walk with aids, and (8) ability to push and pull objects. The ability prerequisites for each fundamental movement pattern should be studied to identify specific problems, so that appropriate intervention can be undertaken. Examples of the categories of activities or abilities follow:

1. Basic mobility skills[113]
   a. Moving up and down ramps
   b. Moving from a wheelchair to another chair
   c. Transporting objects
2. Transfer skills
   a. Standing from a wheelchair
   b. Moving from a wheelchair to another chair
   c. Moving from a wheelchair to mats
   d. Moving from a wheelchair to different pieces of equipment
3. Performance on mats
   a. Forward and backward rolls
   b. Partner activity
   c. Climbing on low obstacles and elevated mats
4. Performance on gymnastics apparatus
   a. Rings
   b. High bar
   c. Parallel bars
5. Ability to maneuver vehicles
   a. Floor scooters
   b. Hand-propelled carts
   c. Tricycles
   d. Upright scooters with three wheels
6. Swimming pool activity
   a. Getting into and out of the pool
   b. Using the railing for resting
   c. Swimming
7. Walking with aids
   a. Different types of canes
   b. Crutches
   c. Walkers
8. Ability to push and pull objects
   a. Throwing a ball or pushing a ball
   b. Propelling scooters with the hands
   c. Pushing a cage ball

Each of these should be analyzed to see if the student's strength, flexibility, endurance, power, and coordination are sufficient for acquisition and proficiency of the activity. In the case of Duchenne muscular dystrophy, manual muscle testing (determining how much resistance is left in a muscle group by having the student flex or extend each limb) can give the evaluator some indication of the remaining strength. Students with other types of muscular dystrophy can be tested with standard tests.

Some people using wheelchairs have severe impairment of the upper appendages. They may have spasticity or contractures. It is not uncommon for them to adopt unique throwing patterns to maximize their performance. Their physical structure rules out the use of standard testing techniques and the teaching of mechanically sound sport skill patterns. Specific techniques must be determined for each person.

MODIFICATIONS, ADAPTATIONS, AND INCLUSION TECHNIQUES

Many children who are physically challenged participate in physical education programs and use a wheelchair for locomotion, wear braces, and/or use some other assistive device. Assistive devices enable the fuller use of the upper limbs and aid locomotion when the legs are debilitated. Some assistive devices are hooks, canes, walkers, and crutches. A number of orthoses are available to enable persons with paraplegia to move about with the aid of canes or walkers.[41]

Although it is difficult to substitute for the human hand and fingers, it is possible to achieve dexterity with the use of a utility arm and split hook. These aids enable the use of racquets for paddle games if both arms are amputated. Persons who have lost a single arm can play most basic skill games and participate in more advanced sport activity without modifications. Special devices can be built by an orthotist to fit into the arm prosthesis to hold sports equipment, such as gloves.

A major problem for students who use canes, walkers, and crutches is the need to learn balance to free one hand for participation in activity. Use of the Lofstrand crutches, which are anchored to the

Ankle-Foot Orthotics Are Custom-Built to Fit Individuals' Needs
Courtesy of Orthomerica Products, Inc., Newport Beach, CA.

forearms, enables balance to be maintained by one crutch. This frees one arm and enables participation in throwing and striking activities.

The physical educator should have a working knowledge of the care and maintenance of wheelchairs. In conjunction with related services, the child's classroom teacher, family, and physical educator should develop a program to maximize the use of ambulation devices in the physical education setting and beyond the school boundaries. In addition, any problems that arise with the ambulation devices should be communicated to the special or general education classroom teacher or the parents.

Wheelchairs

The purpose of wheelchairs is to provide a means of locomotion for persons who lack the strength, endurance, or flexibility of muscles prerequisite for ambulation. Persons who can walk but cannot rise from a seated position to a standing position and those who need to transport objects but cannot do so may also need a wheelchair.

The technology is available to provide almost every person who has a severe physical disability with mobility.[44] The primary goals when designing wheelchairs are to maximize the function, comfort, and independence of those who use the technology. More specifically, the goals and objectives of wheelchair seating are to (1) maximize safety and functional independence, (2) maximize independent mobility through the ability to control the direction and speed of the chair, and (3) maximize functional communication with others in all life environments, including leisure physical activity.[106]

There are many types of wheelchairs. Some of the types identified by Wilson follow:

- Standard: wheelchairs that have a folding frame with large driving wheels in the rear and small caster wheels in the front
- Manual: wheelchairs propelled by the occupant
- Attendant: manual wheelchairs that are propelled by another person because the occupant cannot or should not use either a manual or a powered chair

- Powered: wheelchairs driven by electric motors that run on batteries
- Light-weight: standard wheelchairs refined to reduce overall weight
- Sport: light standard wheelchairs that are easily disassembled
- Racing: wheelchairs designed solely for competitive racing[111]

Nonstandard vehicles have been developed specifically for children with orthopedic disabilities:

- Hand-driven tricycles that include a lever system that transmits arm power into the rear wheel axles
- Tricycle foot attachments that strap a child's feet to the pedals and allow the child with muscle weakness or spasticity to ride a tricycle
- Modified tricycles that include a back support and a seat belt to stabilize the child's body
- Castor carts (large scooter boards) that enable a child to participate in activity at the floor level.[53]

There have been many advances in recent years in upgrading wheelchairs to facilitate the mobility of youth and adults.[60] Platform motorized wheelchairs that can be driven at moderately high speeds are popular. Options for controlling powered wheelchairs include joysticks, single switches, and voice controls.[57]

Wheelchair design is a continuous process, the goal of which is to make the wheelchair more functional. Many special features can be added to make a wheelchair more functional or comfortable, including armrests, footrests, legrests, and headrests, all of which can be removed. Leg spreaders have also been incorporated into some wheelchairs to prevent the scissoring of legs. Analog devices for aligning the rear wheels have been developed to maximize efficiency in propelling the wheelchair.[18] Many wheelchairs can be folded for easy storage. Some other features of a wheelchair are unique folding mechanisms that allow it to double as a stroller or car seat, adjustable Velcro fasteners, pads, and attachable trays. Wheelchairs have also been designed for off-road recreation. Table 15-6 contains a

---

Table 15-6	**Checklist for Wheelchairs**

Wheelchair

A. Arms
1. Are the armrests and side panels secure and free of sharp edges and cracks?
2. Do the arm locks function properly?

B. Back
1. Is the upholstery free of rips and tears?
2. Is the back taut from top to bottom?
3. Is the safety belt attached tightly and not frayed?

C. Seat and frame
1. Is the upholstery free of rips and tears?
2. Does the chair fold easily without sticking?
3. When the chair is folded fully, are the front post slides straight and round?

D. Wheel locks
1. Do the wheel locks securely engage the tire surfaces and prevent the wheel from turning?

E. Large wheels
1. Are the wheels free from wobble or sideplay when spun?
2. Are the spokes equally right and without any missing spokes?
3. Are the tires free from excessive wear and gaps at joined section?

F. Casters
1. Is the stem firmly attached to the fork?
2. Are the forks straight on sides and stem, so that the caster swivels easily?
3. Is the caster assembly free of excessive play both upward and downward, as well as backward and forward?
4. Are the wheels free of excessive play and wobble?
5. Are the tires in good condition?

G. Footrest/legrest
1. Does the lock mechanism fit securely?
2. Are the heel loops secure and correctly installed?
3. Do the foot plates fold easily and hold in any position?
4. Are the largest panels free of cracks and sharp edges?

(Continued)

Table 15-6	*(Continued)*

With Student Sitting in Wheelchair

A. Seat width
  1. When your palms are placed between the student's hip and the side of the chair (skirtgaurd), do the hands contact the hip and the skirtguard at the same time without pressure?
  2. Or is the clearance between the student's widest point of either hips or thigh and the skirtguard approximately 1 inch on either side?

B. Seat depth
  1. Can you place your hand, with fingers extended, between the front edge of the seat upholstery and to the rear of the knee with a clearance of three or four fingers?
  2. Or is the seat upholstery approximately 2 to 3 inches less than the student's thigh measurement?

C. Seat height and footrest
  1. Is the lowest part of the stepplates no closer than 2 inches from the floor?
  2. Or is the student's thigh elevated slightly above the front edge of the seat upholstery?

D. Arm height
  1. Does the arm height not force the shoulders up or allow them to drop significantly when the student is in a normal sitting position?
  2. Is the elbow positioned slightly forward of the trunk midline when the student is in a normal sitting position?

E. Back height
  1. Can you insert four or five fingers between the student armpit area and the top of the back upholstery, touching both at the same time?
  2. Is the top of the back upholstery approximately 4 inches below the armpit for the student who needs only minimum trunk support?

With Student Pushing or Riding in Wheelchair

A. Is the wheelchair free from squeaks and rattles?
B. Does the chair roll easily wihtout pulling to either side?
C. Are the large wheels and casters free of play and wobble?

checklist that will enable physical education teachers to assess wheelchairs as they relate to optimum functioning and comfort.[103]

Specialized Adapted Seating

Adapted seating for individuals who are severely disabled has been a subject of increasing concern. Inappropriate seating for individuals with severe disabilities can result in severe scoliosis with vertebral rotation. Severe contractures may result from fixed postures in a wheelchair.[67] To avoid this, extensive adaptations of the chair may be necessary. Hundertmark[49] indicates that the anterior and posterior tilt of the pelvis and the vertical angle of the backrest are important considerations in achieving therapeutic seating for the person who has a severe multihandicap.

Adaptations for Wheelchair Sports Competition

Wheelchair competitive sports are becoming more and more popular. Competitive wheelchair users are faced with an array of decisions when designing, building, buying, and racing wheelchairs. The ability to propel the wheelchair safely and quickly is an important factor in wheelchair sports competition. That capability is dependent on the user's ability, the design of the chair, and the suitability of the chair to the user. Interest in improving performance has spurred researchers to study ways to increase the efficiency of wheelchairs. Modifications in seat position,[48] the number of wheels, and the positioning of the body during propulsion[67] all impact the speed at which the chair can be propelled.

The seat of a wheelchair should be adjusted to fit the width of the athlete's hips; the seat height should be altered to maximize the use of forces generated at the shoulder; and the height of the back of the chair can be lowered to increase mobility. The number of wheels is also an important competitive factor.

Three- and four-wheeled chairs are available for competition. Higgs[45] studied the comparative advantages of both of these chairs and reported that the advantages of three-wheeled chairs are that they have less rolling resistance, are lighter, and have less aerodynamic drag. The disadvantages of the three-wheeled chairs are that they have less stability and more skill is required to handle the chair safely. The position of the body in the chair, the use of hand pads, and strapping also impact speed and efficiency.

Gehlsen, Davis, and Bahamonde[36] indicate that a forward lean of the trunk may allow the athlete to increase the range of hand-handrim contact. Hedrick et al.[42] indicate that a wheelchair racer's speed can be increased when he or she rotates the upper torso sideways or maintains a flexed position while coasting. Alexander[1] describes a technique to increase propulsion of the wheelchair in which the backs of the hands propel the wheelchair by drawing the hands up and over the wheel and finishing the power stroke with the lower arms in supination. Pads are used to increase friction between the hands and the wheelchair and allow the athlete a longer power phase. In addition, Burd and Grass[14] describe procedures for strapping athletes in wheelchairs to correct posture deviations that diminish the full propulsive stroke on the handrim of the wheelchair.

In addition to improved techniques for wheelchair propulsion, research has been conducted on motivational variables that may facilitate competition in wheelchairs. Dummer et al.[30] suggest that teaching athletes the strategies that are compatible with their abilities and helping them enjoy the activity and competition enhance their desire to compete. Brasile and Hedrick[12] suggest that intrinsic, task-related reasons for participation are important motivators for athletes with orthopedic and neurological disabilities.

Assistive Technology

Every effort should be made to involve individuals with physical disabilities in play and games. To facilitate that participation, it may be necessary to adapt equipment to bridge an individual's functional limitations with the demands of the activity. Some devices that can improve functional movement include the following:

- Chest straps that improve functional reach[24]
- Elasticized abdominal binders[24]

- Seat inserts or molded cushions that improve trunk stability[24]
- Chair anchors that stabilize the wheelchair and facilitate throwing activity[83]
- Wheelchair designs that enable propulsion with the legs rather than arms for athletes with functional leg strength[83]
- Wheelchair seats that can be rotated 180 degrees to allow participants to sit backwards, which enables a strong push-off for propelling the chair[83]
- Padded workout gloves[99]
- Push rim padding[99]
- Lighter steering mechanisms[99]
- Increase the camber of the wheels[99]
- Spoke and finger protectors[99]
- Carbon spoke wheels, which offer less resistance and facilitate faster acceleration than traditional chair wheels[83]

Adrienne Slaughter Doesn't Let the Loss of a Leg Interfere with Her Love for Rock Climbing

Courtesy Challenge Aspen, Aspen, CO.

However, individuals who use specialized devices must anticipate and guard against the following problems: failure of the device, incorrect fit with the individual's need, lack of appropriate instruction in use of the device, awkwardness of the device, and denial of the disability.[38]

Several commercially available pieces of equipment enable persons with physical disabilities to participate in bowling. Some of the adaptations are a bowling ball with handles, a fork that allows the person to push the bowling ball as in shuffleboard, and a ramp that enables gravity to act on the ball in place of the force provided by movement. Each of these adaptations in equipment accommodates for a specific physical problem related to bowling. The adapted equipment for bowling is paired with the nature of the physical problem.

Equipment	Accommodation of Disability
Handles	Needs assistance with the grip but has use of the arm and wrist
Fork	Has use of the arm but has limited ability to control the wrist and an underhand throwing pattern
Ramp	Has limited use of the arm, wrist, and fingers as they apply to an underhand movement pattern

Computer-Controlled Movement of Paralyzed Muscles

In the past, it was thought that paralyzed muscles could not contract to produce purposeful movement. Computer-controlled electrical stimulation for controlling movement, called functional neuromuscular stimulation (FNS), involves placing electrodes made of conductive rubber over the motor point of a muscle. Small electrical currents are then conducted through the electrodes and the skin. The currents cause underlying motor nerves to discharge, which results in precise movement of muscle groups. Movement of whole limbs can be facilitated in this manner.[85] Recent studies involving FNS with individuals with paraplegia or tetraplegia report decreased venous pooling, increases in oxygen uptake, and significant increases in blood pressure during exercise.[86,91]

Modifications

Many games and sports in which students regularly participate in physical education classes can, with minor modification, be made safe and interesting for persons with physical disabilities. In general, the rules, techniques, and equipment of a game or an activity should be changed as little as possible when they are modified for students with disabilities. Following is a suggested procedure for adapting a sport or game for a student with a disability:

1. Select and analyze the play, game, or sport.
2. Identify the problems the individual will have participating in the play, game, or sport.
3. Make the adaptations.
4. Select principles of adaptation that apply to the specific situation. Specific ways that regular physical education and sport activities can be modified are the following:
   a. The size of the playing area can be made smaller, with proportionate reduction of the amount of activity.
   b. Larger balls or larger pieces of equipment can be introduced to make the game easier or to slow down the tempo, so that physical accommodations can be made.
   c. Smaller, lighter balls or striking implements (plastic or styrofoam balls and plastic bats) or objects that are easier to handle (a beanbag) can be substituted.
   d. More players can be added to a team, which reduces the amount of activity and the responsibility of individuals.
   e. Minor rule changes can be made in the contest or game while retaining as many of the basic rules as possible.
   f. The amount of time allowed for play can be reduced via shorter quarters, or the total time for a game can be reduced to allow for the onset of fatigue.

g. The number of points required to win a contest can be reduced.

h. Free substitutions can be made, which allows the students to alternately participate and then rest while the contest continues.

These modifications can be made in a game or contest whether the student participates in a segregated or an integrated physical education class. If the child with a disability participates in a segregated class, it is possible to provide activities similar to those of regular physical education classes by practicing many of the culturally accepted sport skills in drill types of activities. An example is playing basketball games such as "twenty-one" and "around the world" or taking free throws as lead-up activities to the sport. Pitching, batting, throwing, catching, and games such as "over the line" can be played as lead-up activities for softball. Serving, stroking, and volleying can be practiced as lead-up activities for tennis. Such activities can be designed to accommodate physical limitations (see Table 15-7). Students with temporary injuries may become more skillful in various activities so that, when they return to an unrestricted class, they may participate in the whole game or sport with a reasonable degree of success.

Students with disabilities do not always need to be involved in competitive activities. Individuals using wheelchairs should be taught to dance and to participate in water activities. The ability to move to music can be very satisfying; water activities frequently enable a freedom of movement not possible in a chair.[59]

The physical educator attempting to accommodate a student with a disability for participation in physical activity should work closely with school nurses and physicians. Some children with orthopedic and neurological conditions take medication that may affect their attention span or level of alertness. Peck and McKeag[84] recommend that youngsters be carefully observed during activity, noting any side effects. Also, students with bladder problems (e.g., infections, ruptures, incontinence) need to be given special attention to help them avoid the embarrassment of wetting themselves.[84]

Inclusion Techniques

There are several ways to accommodate students with limited movement in the general class setting with their peers. First, activities and games may be selected that circumvent the inability to move. However, it is obvious that such activity will constitute only a small part of the activity, games, and sports of the total physical education program. Second, in team sports it is not uncommon for specific positions of a sport to require different degrees of movement; thus, students who have limited movement capability may be assigned to positions that require less movement. Third, the rules of the game can be modified, enabling equitable competition between persons with and without disabilities. Fourth, aids can be introduced that accommodate inability, so that adjustments can be made to the game. Any one or a combination of these principles of adaptation

The Disabled Sports USA Far West Program Offers Exceptional Instruction in Golf for Its Athletes
Courtesy of Disabled Sports USA Far West.

Table 15-7	Principles for Adapting Physical Activity	
Activity	**Modification**	**Consequence**
Reduce Size of Playing Area		
Soccer	Reduce size of field	Less distance to cover; ball moves from one end of field to other faster
Soccer	Reduce size of goal commensurate with student's movement ability	Less distance to cover
Badminton	Reduce size of court	Less distance to cover; accommodation can be made to equate movement capability of student with a disability with that of nondisabled student
Softball	Shorten distance between bases when the person with a disability bats	Student with a disability has equitable amount of time to reach base
Introduce Larger Pieces of Equipment		
Softball	Use balloon or beach ball	Speed of the object and tempo of game reduced
Softball	Use larger ball	Chance of success enhanced and tempo of game reduced
Soccer	Use larger ball	Area where ball can be propelled successfully increased
Volleyball	Use beach ball	Area of contact increased, enhancing success and requiring less finger strength to control ball
Introduce Lighter Equipment		
Softball	Use lighter bat	Bat can be moved more quickly, so there is greater opportunity to strike ball
Soccer	Use lighter ball	Speed reduced and successful contact more likely
Bowling	Use lighter ball	Weaker person has greater control of ball
Archery	Use lighter bow	Weaker person can draw bow
Tennis	Use aluminum racquet	Weaker person can control racquet
Modify Size of Team		
Volleyball	Add more players	Less area for each person to cover
Soccer	Add more players	Less distance each person must cover in team play
Softball	Add more players	Less area for each person to cover
Handball/tennis	Play triples	Less area for each person to cover

(Continued)

Table 15-7	*(Continued)*	
Activity	**Modification**	**Consequence**
Make Minor Rule Changes		
Wrestling	Use physical contact on take-down for blind persons	A person who is visually impaired always in physical contact with opponent, enabling him or her to know where opponent is at all times
Volleyball	Allow person with affliction in arms/hands to carry on a volleyball hit	Opportunity for success greater
Soccer	Reduce size of goal	Opportunity for success greater
Gymnastics	Strap legs of paraplegic together	Strap controls legs when body moves
Reduce Playing Time		
Basketball/soccer	Substitute every 3 or 4 minutes	Accommodation made for fatigue
Swimming	Swim beside pool edge and rest at prescribed distances of travel or time intervals	Accommodation made for fatigue
Reduce Number of Points Required to Win Contest		
Handball/paddleball/tennis	Lessen number to fatigue level of individual	Physical endurance not a factor in outcome of game
Basketball	Play until specified number of points are made	

may be used to enable children with disabilities to participate in general education classes.

COMMUNITY-BASED OPPORTUNITIES

Persons with physical disabilities should develop skills that can be expressed in leisure and recreation activity in the community. One of the desired outcomes of the acquisition of sport skills is participation in competitive sports. Therefore, the instruction in the physical education program should match opportunities for sports participation in the community.

The generalization of the sport skills acquired by the student who is physically challenged in the instructional phase of the physical education program requires close study of several variables. Some considerations are the nature of the specific disability, the equipment required for participation (wheelchairs and ancillary equipment), and ways of structuring competition to maximize fulfillment for the individual.

In addition to opportunities for community- and home-based individual and team sport activities, there are an increasing number of recreational and camping opportunities for persons with physical disabilities. There are mountain resorts that offer adaptive recreation activities.[95] These programs include horseback riding, swimming, water skiing, tennis, and outdoor education programs. Camping is also available, with a wide variety of accommodations. When considering camping programs, it is suggested that each camp be evaluated to determine the staff's knowledge and experience with persons with physical disabilities.

OPPORTUNITIES FOR PARTICIPATION IN COMPETITION

Persons with physical disabilities need opportunities to express attained sport skills in competition. Many public schools have limited numbers of students of similar ages and ability who are physically challenged. This makes organized competition among those with specific disabilities difficult. Therefore, cooperative efforts need to be made among schools to provide opportunities for competition. Wheelchair sports events are sponsored by sports associations for persons with disabilities and are staged for competition in most states in the country. Several colleges and universities also have intercollegiate wheelchair sports programs. The University of Illinois has one of the best intercollegiate wheelchair sports programs. Several other universities also have well-developed intercollegiate athletic programs.

The missions of sports organizations for individuals with disabilities are to provide training opportunities and to promote competition. These organizations provide a forum and an incentive to maximize proficiency in sports for competition. Wheelchair sports competitions are held at the local, national, and international levels. There is a movement for the organization of games for individuals with generic disabilities at the state level. Project GUMBO in Louisiana is a good example of games organized for the physically challenged at the state level.[63] More sophisticated competition is held by the International Sports Organization for the Disabled. The Paralympic Games in Athens in 2004 included 136 competing nations. Competitions are intense. As a result, training camps have been developed to improve performance at international games. International games have developed not only in the intensity of competition but also in the magnitude of participation. Thus, opportunities exist for many individuals with physical disabilities to participate in competitive sports at their ability level, with an incentive to increase their skills to a world-class level.

A Swimmer with an Above-the-Knee Amputation Participates in World-Class Competition

Courtesy of Orthotic and Prosthetic Athlete Assistance Fund, Inc., Alexandria, VA.

Nature and Scope of the Program

Sport activity programs include sports that can be performed while wearing prostheses or while using a wheelchair. Some of the available sport activities are archery, basketball, billiards, bowling, flying, golf, hockey, tennis, racquetball, rugby, road racing, shooting, skiing, softball, table tennis, track and field, water sports, and weight lifting. There is also a movement to enable persons with disabilities to participate with nondisabled athletes in major sporting events. For example, wheelchair athletes participate at the classic running event the Boston Marathon. 🐾

SUMMARY

The three types of physical disabilities discussed in this chapter are neurological conditions, orthopedic disabilities, and conditions caused by trauma. Afflictions can occur at more than 500 anatomical sites. Each student with a disability has different physical and motor capabilities and is to be provided with accommodations that enable participation in modified games and sport activity. Contraindicated activity as identified by medical personnel must be avoided.

Physical educators should address two types of program considerations to meet the physical education needs of persons with physical disabilities. One is to implement developmental programs that enhance prerequisite motor patterns, sport skills, and physical and motor fitness. The other is to structure the environment so that students with disabilities can derive physical benefits through participation in competitive sporting activities (this may be facilitated by the use of aids for specific types of activities and disabilities).

The physical educator should be ready to accommodate the individual program needs of persons with a disability by identifying unique needs through formal and functional assessment, using adaptive devices to permit active involvement, and modifying activities to enable the student to participate in a variety of settings.

Many national organizations have been developed to enable persons with disabilities to participate in sports competition.

REVIEW QUESTIONS

1. Identify some activities that will benefit a child with cerebral palsy.
2. Discuss the type of physical education program that would benefit a teenager who has returned to school after suffering a moderate traumatic brain injury.
3. Explain how the level of spinal cord injury affects the type of activity a person can participate in.
4. What are the grades of concussion?
5. What are some specific examples of ways physical education activities can be modified to accommodate a student using a wheelchair?
6. What types of spina bifida are there and what accommodations must be made for each?

STUDENT ACTIVITIES

1. Working in small groups, share the applications you developed for Josue, Danny Joe, and Roberto and come to an agreement about how best to accommodate for each of these three students.
2. Working in small groups, determine what sports programs would be appropriate for Josue, Danny Joe, and Roberto and develop a list of skills and abilities each will need to participate in those sports.
3. Write a letter to convince Josue's mother that participation in the regular physical education class and a community sports program will improve the quality of his life.
4. Discuss with the rest of the class the type of behavior management program that might be successful with Josue.
5. Select one or two major journals in the field of physical or special education. Some of these journals are *Journal of Physical Education, and Recreation and Dance; Exceptional Children;*

Adapted Physical Activity Quarterly; Palaestra: The Forum of Sport, Physical Education and Recreation for the Disabled; and *Sports 'n Spokes.* Look through the issues from the past few years for articles that present useful suggestions for adapting instruction for students with physical disabilities. Make a file of these suggestions.

6. Visit a school, shopping center, or municipal building and identify architectural barriers that would deny access/use to individuals with disabilities. Evaluate the accessibility of drinking fountains, phones, different floors, eating facilities, playing areas, and emergency exits. What types of activities might enable persons with physical disabilities to gain access to these facilities?

7. Discuss the pros and cons of conducting separate sports programs for individuals with physical disabilities. When are separate sports programs appropriate and under what conditions?

REFERENCES

1. Alexander MJ: New techniques in quadriplegic wheelchair marathon racing, *Palaestra* 3:13–16, 1987.

2. American Juvenile Arthritis Organization, www.arthritis.org/ajao. 2003.

3. Amputee Coalition, www.amputeecoalition.org/.

4. Amyotrophic Lateral Sclerosis Association, www.alsa.national.org. 2003.

5. Arthritis Foundation, www.arthritis.org. 2007.

6. Autti-Ramo I, Larsen A, Taimo A, Von Wendt L: Management of the upper limb with Botulinum toxin type A in children with spastic type cerebral palsy and acquired brain injury: Clinical implications, *European J of Neurology* 8 (Suppl. 5): 136–144, 2001.

7. AVENUES, www.avenuesforamc.com/publications/pamphlet.htm. 2003.

8. Barnes JT, Elder CL: Exercise considerations for patients with rheumatoid arthritis, *Strength and Conditioning J* 24(3): 46–50, 2001.

9. Barns JT, Pujol TJ: Exercise considerations for persons with osteoarthritis, *Strength and Conditioning J* 23(3): 74–76, 2001.

10. Birk TJ: Polio and post-polio syndrome. In Durstine JL, Moore G, editors: *ACSM's exercise management for persons with chronic diseases and disabilities*, 2nd ed. Champaign, IL, Human Kinetics, 2003.

11. Brasile F: Performance evaluation of wheelchair athletes more than a disability classification level issue, *APAQ* 7:289–297, 1990.

12. Brasile F, Hedrick BN: A comparison of participation incentives between adult and youth wheelchair basketball players, *Palaestra* 7:40–46, 1991.

13. Broach E, Dattilo J: Effects of aquatic therapy on adults with multiple sclerosis, *Therapeutic Rec J* 36(2):141–154, 2001.

14. Burd R, Grass K: Strapping to enhance athletic performance of wheelchair competitors with cerebral palsy, *Palaestra* 3:28–32, 1987.

15. Burkhour CK: Let's go to camp, *Exceptional Parent* May: 66–67, 1998.

16. Centers for Disease Control and Prevention, www.cdc.gov/ncipc/factsheets/scifacts.htm. 2003.

17. Chrisholm J, Bruce B: Unintentional traumatic brain injury in children: The lived experience, *AXON* 23(1):12–17, 2001.

18. Cooper RA: A new racing wheelchair rear wheel alignment device, *Palaestra* 4:8–11, 1988.

19. Croce R, Horvat M, Roswal G: Augmented feedback for enhanced skill acquisition in individuals with traumatic brain injury, *Perceptual and Motor Skills* 82:507–514, 1996.

20. Curtis KA: Stretching routines, *Sports 'n Spokes* 7(5):1–3, 1981.

21. Curtis KA: Sport-specific functional classification for wheelchair athletes, *Sports 'n Spokes* 17:45–48, 1991.

22. Curtis KA, editor: *Guide to sports medicine needs of athletes with disabilities*. Coral Gables, FL, University of Miami School of Medicine, 1993.

23. Curtis KA: *Injuries and disability-specific medical conditions of athletes with disabilities*. Unpublished paper, Coral Gables, FL, University of Miami, 1993.

24. Curtis KA, et al.: Functional reach in wheelchair users: The effects of trunk and lower extremity stabilization, *Arch Phys Med Rehabil* 76:360–372, 1995.

25. D'Amato RC, Rothlisberg BA: How education should respond to students with traumatic brain injury, *J of Leam Dis* 29:670–683, 1996.

26. Davis K: Seating and wheeled mobility evaluation, Center for Assistive Technology and Environmental Access, http://atwiki.assistivetech.net/Seating_and_wheeled_mobility_evaluation. 2007.

27. DeLuca PA: The musculoskeletal management of children with cerebral palsy, *Pediatric Clinics of North America* 43:1135–1151, 1996.

28. DiCarlo S: Effect of arm ergometry training on wheelchair propulsion endurance of individuals with quadriplegia, *Phys Ther* 68:40–44, 1988.

29. Driver S, Harmon M, Block M: Devising a safe and successful physical education program for children with brain injury, *JOPERD* 74(7):41–49, 2003.

30. Dummer GM, et al.: Attributions of athletes with cerebral palsy, *APAQ* 4:278–292, 1987.

31. Duran FS, Lugo L, Ramirez L, Eusse E: Effects of an exercise program on the rehabilitation of patients with spinal cord injury, *Arch Phys Med Rehabil* 82:1349–1354, 2001.

32. Engelbert RH, Pruijs EH, Beener FA, Helders PJ: Osteogenesis imperfecta in childhood: Treatment strategies, *Archives of Phys Med Rehab* 79:1590–1593, 1998.

33. Exhemdia RJ, Putukian M, Mackin RS, Julian L, Shoss N: Neuropsychological test performance prior to and following sports-related mild traumatic brain injury, *Clinical J of Sport Med* 11:23–31, 2001.

34. Fernandez JE, Pitetti KH: Training of ambulatory individuals with cerebral palsy, *Arch Phys Med Rehabil* 74:468–472, 1993.

35. Figoni SF: Spinal cord injury. In Durstine JL, Moore G, editors: *ACSM's exercise management for persons with chronic diseases and disabilities,* 2nd ed. Champaign, IL, Human Kinetics, 2003.

36. Gehlsen GM, Davis RW, Bahamonde R: Intermittent velocity and wheelchair performance characteristics, *APAQ* 7:219–230, 1990.

37. Geurts ACH, et al.: Dual-tasks assessment of reorganization of postural control in persons with lower limb amputation, *Arch Phys Med Rehabil* 72:1059–1064, 1995.

38. Gitlin LN, Levine R, Geiger C: Adaptive device use by older adults with mixed disabilities, *Arch Phys Med Rehabil* 74:149–152, 1993.

39. Gordon WA, Sliwinski M, Echo J, McLoughlin M, Sheere M, Meili TE: The benefits of exercise in individuals with traumatic brain injury: A retrospective study, *J Heal Trauma Rehabil* 13:58–67, 1998.

40. Hardison GT, Isreal RG, Somes G: Physiological responses to different cranking rates during submaximal arm ergometry in paraplegic males, *APAQ* 4:94–105, 1987.

41. Harvey LA, Davis GM, Smith MB, Engel S: Energy expenditure during gait using the walkabout and isometric reciprocal gait orthosis in persons with paraplegia, *Arch of Physic Med and Rehabil* 79:946–951, 1998.

42. Hedrick B, et al.: Aerodynamic positioning and performance in wheelchair racing, *APAQ* 7:41–51, 1990.

43. Healthology, www.healthology.com. 2007.

44. Henderson CJ, Specker BL, Sierra RI, Campaigne BN, Lovell DJ: Total-body bone mineral content in non-corticosteroid-treated postpubertal females with juvenile rheumatoid arthritis, *Arthritis and Rheumatism* 43(3):531–540, 2000.

45. Higgs C: A comparison of three- and four-wheeled designs, *Palaestra* 8:29–35, 1992.

46. Higgs C, et al.: Wheelchair classification for track and field events: A performance approach, *APAQ* 7:22–40, 1990.

47. Holland LJ, Steadward RD: Effects of resistance and flexibility training on strength, spasticity/muscle tone and range of motion of elite athletes with cerebral palsy, *Palaestra* 6:27–31, 1990.

48. Hughes CJ, et al.: Biomechanics of wheelchair propulsion as a function of seat position and user-to-chair interface, *Arch Phys Med Rehabil* 73:263–269, 1992.

49. Hundertmark LH: Evaluating the adult with cerebral palsy for specialized adapted seating, *Phys Ther* 65:209–212, 1985.

50. Kasser SL, Stuart ME: Psychological well-being and exercise behavior in persons with and without multiple sclerosis, *Clinical Kinesiology* 55:81–86, 2001.

51. Kelly JP, Rosenberg JH: The development of guidelines for the management of concussion in sports, *J Head Trauma Rehabil* 13:53–65, 1998.

52. Kilmer DD: Response to resistive strengthening exercise training in humans with neuromuscular disease, *Am J Phys Med Rehabil* 81(Suppl):S121–S126, 2002.

53. Khaw CWH, Tidemann AJ, Stern LM: Study of hemiplegic cerebral palsy with a review of the literature, *J Pediatr Child Health* 30:224–229, 1994.

54. Kocina P: Body composition of spinal cord injured adults, *Sports Med* 23:48–60, 1998.

55. Konrad K, Gauggel S, Manz A, Scholl M: Lack of inhibition: A motivational deficit in children with attention deficit/hyperactivity disorder and children with traumatic brain injury, *Child Neuropsychology* 6(4):286–296, 2000.

56. Laskin J: Cerebral palsy. In Durstine JL, Moore G, editors: *ACSM's exercise management for persons with chronic diseases and disabilities,* 2nd ed. Champaign, IL, Human Kinetics, 2003.

57. Lee K, Thomas D: *Control of computer-based technology for people with physical disabilities: An assessment manual.* Toronto, University of Toronto Press, 1990.

58. Lepage C, Noreau L, Bernard PM: Association between characteristics of locomotion and

accomplishment of life habits in children with cerebral palsy, *Phys Ther* 78:458–469, 1998.

59. Levin S: Aquatic therapy, *Physician Sportsmed* 19:119–126, 1995.

60. Letts RM: *Principles of seating the disabled.* Boston, CRC Press, 1991.

61. Linder M, Schindler G, Miehaelis U: Medium-term functional benefits in children with cerebral palsy treated with Botulinum toxin type A, *European J of Neurology* 8(Suppl 5):120–126, 2001.

62. Liu M, Chino N, Ishihara T: Muscle damage in Duchenne muscular dystrophy evaluated by a new quantitative computed tomography method, *Arch Phys Med Rehabil* 74:507–514, 1991.

63. Louisiana Department of Education, *Games uniting mind and body: A resource guide for the conduct of athletic competition for students with physical or visual disabilities,* www.doe.state.la.us, 1999.

64. Marschark M, Richtsmeier LM, Richardson JT, Crovitz HF, Henry J: Intellectual and emotional functioning of college students following mild traumatic brain injury in childhood and adolescence, *J of Head Trauma Rehabil* 15(6):1227–1245, 2000.

65. Max JE, Lindgren SD, Knutson C, Pearson CS, Ihrig D, Welborn A: Child and adolescent brain injury: Correlates of injury severity, *Brain Injury* 12(1):31–40, 1998.

66. McDonald CM: Physical activity, health impairments, and disability in neuromuscular disease, *Am J Phys Rehabil* 81(Suppl):S108–S120, 2002.

67. McLean KP, Skinner JS: Effect of body training position on outcomes of an aerobic training study on individuals with quadriplegia, *Arch Phys Med Rehabil* 76:139–150, 1995.

68. Medicine Net, Inc., www.medicinenet.com. 2003.

69. Medline Plus, www.nlm.nih.gov/medlineplus/ency. 2003.

70. Meisterling RC, Wall EJ, Meisterling MR: Coping with Osgood-Schlatter disease, *Physician Sportsmed* 26(3):39–40, 1998.

71. Midha M, Schmitt JK, Sclater M: Exercise effect with the wheelchair aerobic fitness trainer on conditioning with metabolic function in disabled persons: A pilot study, *Arch Phys Med Rehabil* 80:258–261, 1999.

72. Minor MA, Kay DR: Arthritis. In Durstine JL, editor: *Exercise management for persons with chronic diseases and disabilities.* Champaign, IL, Human Kinetics, 1997.

73. Mira M, Tyler J: Students with traumatic brain injury: Making the transition from hospital to school, *Focus Except Child* 23:1–12, 1991.

74. Mulcare JA: Multiple sclerosis. In Durstine JL, editor: *Exercise management for persons with chronic diseases and disabilities.* Champaign, IL, Human Kinetics, 1997.

75. Munneke M, deJong Z: The role of exercise programs in the rehabilitation of patients with rheumatoid arthritis, *International Sportmed J* 1(5):1–12, 2001.

76. Muraki S, Tsunawake T, Tahara Y, Hiramatsu S, Yamasaki M: Multivariate analysis of factors influencing physical work capacity in wheelchair-dependent paraplegics with spinal cord injuries, *Eur J Appl Phys* 81:28–32, 2000.

77. National Information Center for Children and Youth with Disabilities, www.nichcy.org. 2003.

78. Neurology Channel, www.neurologychannel.com/ cerebralpalsy. 2007.

79. Noreau L, Moffet H, Drolet B, Parent E: Dance-based exercise program in rheumatoid arthritis, *Amer J of Physi Med and Rehab* 76:109–113, 1997.

80. Northrup H, Volcik KA: Spina bifida and other neural defects, *Curr Probl Pediatr* 30:317–322, 2000.

81. Nyska M, Constantin N, Cale-Benzoor M, Back Z, Kahn G, Mann G: Spondylolysis as a cause of low back pain in swimmers, *Int J Sports Med* 21:375–379, 2000.

82. Osteogenesis Imperfecta Foundation, www.oif.org/tier2/fastfact.htm.

83. Paciorek MJ: Technology only a part of the story as world records fall, *Palaestra* 10:14, 42, 1993.

84. Peck DM, McKeag DB: Athletes with disabilities: Removing medical barriers, *Physician Sportsmed* 22:59–63, 1994.

85. Petrofsky JS, Brown SW, Cerrel B: Active physical therapy and its benefits in rehabilitation, *Palaestra* 9:23–27, 61, 1992.

86. Phillips W, Burkett LN: Arm crank exercise with static leg FNS in persons with spinal cord injury, *Medicine and Science in Sports and Exercise* 27:530–535, 1995.

87. Ponichtera-Mulcare JA, et al.: Maximal aerobic exercise of individuals with multiple sclerosis using three modes of ergometry, *Clin Kines* 49:4–13, 1995.

88. Porter R, Kaplan J: Merck Manuals Online Medical Library, www.merck.com/mmpe/index/html. 2007.

89. Protas EJ, Stanley RK, Jankovic J: Parkinson's disease. In Durstine JL, Moore G, editors: *ACSM's exercise management for persons with chronic diseases and disabilities,* 2nd ed. Champaign, IL, Human Kinetics, 2003.

90. Rajab A, Yoo SY, Abdulgalil A, Kathiri S, Ahmed R, Mochida GH, Bodell A, Barkovich AJ, Walsh CA: An autosomal recessive form of spastic cerebral palsy (CP) with microcephaly and mental retardation, *Am J Med Genet* Part A, 140A:1504–1510, 2006.

91. Raymond J, Davis GM, Climstein M, Sutton JR: Cardiorespiratory responses to arm cranking and electrical stimulation leg cycling in people with paraplegia, *Medicine and Science in Sports and Exercise* 31:822–828, 1999.

92. Rossi C, Sullivan SJ: Motor fitness in children and adolescents with traumatic brain injury, *Arch Phys Med Rehabil* 77:1062–1065, 1996.

93. Saxon L, Finch C, Bass S: Sports participation sports injuries and osteoarthritis: Implications for prevention, *Sports Med* 28(2):123–135, 1999.

94. Sirven JI, Varrato J: Physical activity and epilepsy: What are the rules? *Physician Sportsmed* 27:63–70, 1999.

95. Spinal Cord Injury Information Network, www.spinalcord.uab.edu.

96. Standaert CJ, Herring SA: Spondylolysis: Acritical review, *Br J Sports Med* 34:415–422, 2000.

97. Stewart MW, Melton-Rogers SL, Morrison S, Figoni SF: The measurement properties of fitness measures and health status for persons with spinal cord injuries, *Arch Phys Med Rehabil* 81:394–400, 2000.

98. Stolting JC: The National Ability Center; enhancing mind, body and soul, *Except Parent* March:32–35, 1999.

99. Stopka C: Managing common injuries in individuals with disabilities: Prevention comes first, *Palaestra* 12(2):28–31, 1996.

100. Tarnopolski MA: Muscular dystrophy, In Durstine JL, Moore G, editors: *ACSM's exercise management for persons with chronic diseases*

101. United Cerebral Palsy of Central California, www.ccucp.org/prg. 2003.

102. Unnithan VB, Clifford C, Bar-Or O: Evaluation by exercise testing of the child with cerebral palsy, *Sports Medicine* 26:239–251, 1998.

103. Venn J, Morganstern L, Dykes MK: Checklist for evaluating the fit and function of orthoses, prostheses, and wheelchairs in the classroom, *Teach Except Child* Winter:51–56, 1979.

104. Wall EJ: Osgood-Schlatter disease: Practical treatment for a self-limiting condition, *Physician Sportsmed* 26(3):29–34, 1998.

105. Waller M: Strength and conditioning in multiple sclerosis patients, *Strength and Conditioning J* 22(2):40–41, 2000.

106. Ward E: *Prescriptive seating for wheelchair mobility.* Kansas City, MO, Health Wealth International, 1994.

107. Webster JB, Levy CE, Bryant PR, Prusakowski PE: Sports and recreation for persons with limb deficiency, *Arch Phys Med Rehabil* 82 (Suppl 1):38–44, 2001.

108. Wetzel AJ, Rorke SC: Mild traumatic brain injury: A call for increased awareness, intervention, and physical activity, *Clin Exer Physio* 3(4):186–193, 2001.

109. White AT: Exercise for patients with multiple sclerosis, *Int Sport Med* 2(3):1–8, 2001.

110. White KLN: Amyotrophic lateral sclerosis. In Durstine JL, Moore G, editors: *ACSM's exercise management for persons with chronic diseases and disabilities,* 2nd ed. Champaign, IL, Human Kinetics, 2003.

111. Wilson AB: *How to select and use manual wheelchairs.* Topping, VA, Rehabilitation Press, 1992.

112. World Federation of Neurology ALS, www.wfnals.org. 2003.

113. Wright J: *Project C.R.E.O.L.E.: Wheelchair sports and mobility curriculum.* Harvey, LA, Jefferson Parish Public School System, 1989.

114. Yamamoto M, Tajima F, Okawa H, Mizushima T, Umezu Y, Ogata H: Static exercise-induced increase in blood pressure in individuals with

cervical spinal cord injury, *Arch Phys Med Rehabil* 80:288–293, 1999.

115. Youngblut JA, Singer LT, Boyer C, Wheatley MA, Cohen AR, Gisoni ER: Effects of pediatric head trauma for children, parents and families, *Critical Care Nursing Clinics of N. America* 12(2):227–235, 2000.

SUGGESTED READINGS

Davis RW: *Inclusion through sports*. Champaign, IL, Human Kinetics, 2002.

Grady S: Adaptive seating standards, *Rehab Management* 19(1):50, 52, 54, 2006.

Kosma M, Ellis R, Cardinal B, Bauer J, McCubbin J: The mediating role of intention and stages of change in physical activity among adults with physical disabilities, *J of Sport and Exercise Physiology* 29:21–36, 2007.

Rimmer JH: *Fitness and rehabilitation programs for special populations*. Madison, WI, Brown & Benchmark, 1994.

RECOMMENDED WEB SITES

Please keep in mind that these Web sites are being recommended in the winter of 2007. As Web sites often change, they may have moved or been reconfigured or eliminated.

American Association of Disabled Sports Programs (AAASP)
www.aaasp.org

National Information Center for Children and Youth with Disabilities
www.nichcy.org

RECOMMENDED VIDEOS

Films for the Humanities & Sciences
PO Box 2053
Princeton, NJ 08543-2053
www.films.com
1-800-257-5126

Cerebral Palsy: What Every Parent Should Know
#2230/DVD/VHS/1991/19 min/$89.95

Concussions and Spinal Cord Injuries
#3132/DVD/VHS/2003/19 min/$89.95

Epilepsy: A New Outlook
#36356/DVD/VHS/2005/28 min/$129.95

Living and Dying with Muscular Dystrophy
#37388/DVD/VHS/2007/12 min/$69.95

Communicative Disorders

Child Develops Play Skills

Courtesy Callier Center for Communicative Disorders, Dallas.

■ **O B J E C T I V E S**

List three motor characteristics of elementary and high school children who are deaf.

Describe the culture of the Deaf community.

Demonstrate five specific signs that can be used in physical education to communicate with students who are deaf or hard of hearing.

List five techniques a teacher can use for enhancing communication with students who are deaf or hard of hearing.

Differentiate between the two major instructional approaches used with deaf learners: total communication and auditory-verbal (oral) therapy.

List the strategies a physical education teacher can use when working with a professional interpreter.

Explain effective teaching strategies for working with a learner who is deaf-blind.

Briefly describe one speech disorder, one language disorder, and one voice disorder.

Describe strategies the teacher can use to make a child who stutters more comfortable speaking in the physical education program.

Describe several strategies to create a "bully-free" environment in the physical education program, so that children with speech and language delays or disorders are not the victims of teasing.

Fundamental to the human experience is communication with other human beings. Children who have difficulty expressing their thoughts, feelings, ideas, and dreams and children who have difficulty understanding the thoughts, feelings, ideas, and dreams of others struggle to make sense of their existence. It is difficult to make sense of their world and all the stimuli and experiences to which they are exposed without the capacity to describe, evaluate, and share these experiences.

Children with communicative delays and disorders may have a difficult time being successful in the educational environment. While they may have good physical and motor skills, they may struggle with the social experiences in the physical education program.

DEAFNESS AND HEARING IMPAIRMENTS

Significant challenges face the physical educator seeking to provide a *quality* educational experience for deaf learners. Part of the challenge is associated with the growing educational trend to consider students who are deaf or hearing impaired as bilingual members of a bicultural minority,[66] rather than children with a disability. This trend is emerging, in part, to honor the unique culture, language, history, and legacy of the Deaf community. In order to do this, educators must honor diversity among all minority groups.

It is particularly vital that the unique needs of the student who is deaf or hearing impaired and who represents a cultural/racial minority be acknowledged. For example, a young child who is African American and deaf must learn and live within several separate and distinct cultures. The responsibilities of "membership" and "belonging" within each of these cultures vary greatly. This can be very confusing, particularly to a young child or an adolescent. This is especially critical because children who are deaf or hearing impaired and who represent a minority group do not do well, historically, in existing education programs.[66]

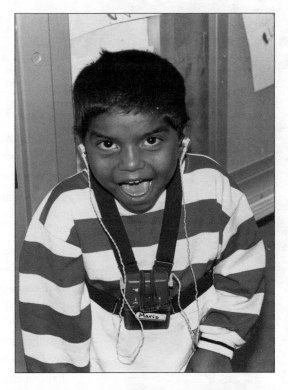

Courtesy Callier Center for Communicative Disorders, Dallas.

In addition to broader cultural issues, children who have permanent hearing losses usually have delays in expressive and receptive language, play and other social skills, and motor development. The purpose of this chapter is to provide the physical educator with information necessary to teach learners who are deaf or hearing impaired, deaf-blind, and speech and language delayed.

Definition of Deaf or Hearing Impaired

Deafness and hearing impairment are disabilities defined by the Individuals with Disabilities Education Act Amendments of 1997.[38] Deafness means a hearing impairment so severe that the child is impaired in processing linguistic information through hearing, with or without amplification. Hearing impairment, whether permanent or fluctuating, adversely affects a child's educational performance.

CASE STUDY 16-1

William

William is a five-year-old with a 55-decibel hearing loss. He uses a hearing aid for amplification; with that amplification, he is able to understand conversational speech at a distance of between 5 and 7 feet. He struggles to hear, however, in the gymnasium because of its poor acoustics. His speech is understandable, particularly if the listener has had the opportunity to "practice" listening.

His motor skills are his strength. At age five he already skips efficiently and effectively, for example. He moves well and takes a great deal of pride in his performance.

He lives with his mother and his dog, Mikey, in a small town outside Anchorage, Alaska.

APPLICATION TASK

Develop a long-range plan to prepare William for participation in the USA Deaf Sports Federation after graduation from high school.

The continuum of hearing loss and the ability to understand speech ranges from that of little significance to that of extreme disability (see Table 16-1). The degree of an individual's deafness is determined by the level of decibel loss and the individual's ability to perceive conversation.[71]

Incidence

Approximately 71,500 students, between the ages of 6 and 21 years, received educational services in 2005–2006 because of an educational diagnosis of deafness or hearing impairment. These students received their education in the following settings:

- <21% of instruction outside regular classroom: 48.75%
- 21%–60% of instruction outside regular classroom: 18.25%
- >60% of instruction outside regular classroom: 19.5%
- Separate public school facility: 4.8%

Table 16-1	Characteristics of Children with Hearing Loss[24, 40]

Mild Hearing Loss (15–30 Decibel Hearing Loss)
- Children develop speech and language spontaneously.
- They may have difficulty hearing faint speech.

Moderate Hearing Loss (31–60 Decibel Hearing Loss)
- Children will benefit from hearing aids as soon as possible after diagnosis.
- Children will rely on visual information to supplement auditory information.
- They may have difficulty with delayed language and speech skills, particularly in the pronunciation of consonants.
- They will do better in a classroom setting with preferential seating.

Severe Hearing Loss (61–90 Decibel Hearing Loss)
- Children will have difficulty hearing conversational speech.
- They will be able to respond to sounds that are high in intensity, at close range, with amplification.
- They will require amplification and significant speech and language therapy to function in the educational setting.

Profound Hearing Loss (91–120 Decibel Hearing Loss)
- Children with a profound hearing loss are unlikely to benefit from auditory input and will rely on tactile and visual cues.
- They will usually need to use total communication or manual communication.
- With little residual hearing, they may still have intelligible speech.

Total Hearing Loss (121+ Decibel Hearing Loss)
- Children with total hearing loss do not hear even with an auditory amplification device.
- They will depend on vision as their primary modality.

- Separate private school facility: 2.3%
- Public residential facility: 5.8%
- Private residential facility: .40%
- Home/hospital: .20%[37]

Causes

The time of onset of deafness is a critical factor in its impact on the learning situation. The acquisition of speech and language skills, like the acquisition of motor skills, is basic to the subsequent development of the individual. Essentially, individuals are divided into two basic categories, those who are prelingually deaf and those who are postlingually deaf. Prior to the invention of the cochlear implant device, if a child became deaf before the acquisition of any linguistic or speech skills, prelingually, the child had little, if any, chance of acquiring typical speech and language skills. If an individual suffers a hearing loss after having acquired speech and language skills, postlingually, the individual may have already acquired and be able to retain typical speech and language skills.

An aggressive program has been established in many states to ensure early identification of deafness/hearing impairments and subsequent early intervention for affected infants and toddlers. This early identification, specifically with newborns, has been endorsed by the Joint Committee on Infant Hearing and the National Institutes of Health. The intent is the universal detection of hearing loss in newborns and involves three phases: (1) birth hearing screening; (2) follow-up and specific diagnosis; and (3) intervention services.[27] Each of these phases is critical in identifying and then providing early intervention services for newborns with a hearing loss. The earlier the diagnosis can be made, the earlier the infant or child and the family can receive the health and educational services vital to the development of the infant or child.

The proper diagnosis of hearing disabilities may provide assistance for the development of physical education programs. The uniqueness of each deaf child requires individualized assessment and intervention by teachers. There are two major types of hearing impairments: (1) conductive and (2) sensorineural.

Conductive Hearing Impairments

A conductive hearing loss, while interfering with a child's detection and recognition of speech, also causes fluctuating hearing levels. A conductive hearing impairment is, typically, a condition in which the intensity of sound is reduced before reaching the inner ear, where the auditory nerve begins. A conductive hearing loss can also result when the membranes in the inner ear undergo physical changes that reduce the transfer of energy to the hair cells.

The most prevalent cause of conductive hearing loss is otitis media, an infection of the middle ear. Hearing impairments and deafness from otitis media are particularly critical if a young child has suffered a series of infections at a young age. Intermittent or persistent conductive hearing loss, as a result of otitis media, may have a significant impact on the subsequent learning and behavior of school-age children.

Another infection that can cause conductive hearing loss is mastoiditis. Mastoiditis occurs when there is chronic inflammation of the middle ear that spreads into the cells of the mastoid process within the temporal bone. Other causes of conductive hearing loss include perforation of the eardrum from a blow to the head, allergies that make the eustachian tube swell, tumors of the external auditory canal, the presence of foreign objects in the external ear, insect bites, and an excessive buildup of ear wax.

Sensorineural Hearing Impairments

A sensorineural hearing loss (SNHL), while interfering with a child's detection and recognition of speech, may also filter and distort sound. A sensorineural hearing loss is caused by an absence or a malfunction of the sensory unit. The damage may be present in the cochlea (sensory) or the 8th cranial nerve (neural). If the dysfunction is in the inner ear, the individual has difficulty discriminating among speech sounds. The individual can hear sound but has difficulty making sense of high-frequency sounds. Causes of SNHL include maternal rubella (German measles); venereal disease during pregnancy; lesions or tumors in the inner ear or on the 8th cranial nerve; and infections of childhood, including mumps, meningitis, and encephalitis.

One of the major causes of significant hearing loss is noise. Noise-induced hearing loss results from exposure to any source of intense and/or constant noise, an environmental toxin, over an extended period of time.

Unilateral Hearing Loss

A child with a unilateral hearing loss (normal hearing in one ear but not the other) may struggle in the school environment. He or she is frequently misunderstood as being able to hear "what he or she wants to hear." In fact, the child with a unilateral hearing loss has difficulty hearing the teacher, especially if the acoustics are bad (e.g., in the gymnasium), and the teacher is at any distance from the child. In order to track sound, the child may move his or her head and body toward the sound; unfortunately, a teacher without specific training may assume the child is simply fidgeting and not attending.[23]

Clues That Indicate Hearing Loss

Early identification of deafness and hearing loss is critical.[25] Parents and teachers should be alert to signs of hearing loss:[5,25]

1. Hearing and comprehension of speech
   a. General indifference to sound
   b. Lack of response to the spoken word
   c. Response to noise, not words
   d. Head and body leaning toward the source of sound
   e. Requests that statements be repeated
   f. Tinnitus—buzzing, ringing, roaring, whistling, or hissing sounds
2. Vocalization and sound production
   a. Monotonal quality
   b. Indistinct speech
   c. Lessened laughter
   d. Vocal play for vibratory sensation
   e. Head banging, foot stamping for vibratory sensation
   f. Yelling, screeching to express pleasure or need
3. Visual attention
   a. Augmental visual vigilance and attentiveness
   b. Alertness to gesture and movement
4. Social rapport and adaptation
   a. Intensified preoccupation with things rather than persons
   b. Puzzling and unhappy episodes in social situations

   c. Suspiciousness and alertness, alternating with cooperation
   d. Marked reaction to praise and affection
5. Emotional behavior
   a. Tantrums to call attention to self or need
   b. Frequent stubborn behavior
   c. Frustration and anger when not understood
6. Motor behavior
   a. Vertigo, an abnormal sensation of rotary movement associated with difficulty in balance, gait, and navigation of the environment[5]
7. Physical development and health
   a. Earaches, particularly chronic
   b. Jaw pain
   c. Chronic sinus infections[5]

Psychological, Behavioral, and Cognitive Characteristics

Hearing loss can have a profound effect on behavior. The very self-concept and identity (self-theory) of the developing child may be negatively affected. Family members are the major influence on the development of self-theory. The young child is dependent particularly on the parent for significant feedback, the foundation of the child's understanding of self. Communication between the parent and the child who is deaf or hard of hearing is often confusing. This creates a stressful situation for the child struggling to understand his or her parents' responses and the meaning of the parents' reactions.[36] Misunderstandings can create awkward and hurtful situations in which the child is inadvertently given incorrect impressions about his or her behavior and the parents' perceptions of the behavior.

Deafness and hearing loss, in addition to the profound effect on self-concept and identity, also affect language and speech development, learning and cognitive function, play, and social adjustment. Comprehension and language production are significantly affected by hearing loss.

The degree of hearing loss has a great impact on language development. In both conductive and sensorineural hearing losses, the development of auditory skills that are critical prerequisites to the development of receptive and expressive language skills, as well as speech intelligibility, is delayed. The auditory skills that are compromised include detection, discrimination, recognition, comprehension, and attention.

If an infant or a developing child is unable to hear the oral language produced in his or her environment, it is impossible for the child to reproduce the language. If the child is unable to hear the rhythm and rhyme, the form (syntax), the use of language (pragmatics), the tone, the timbre and flow of the language, and the content (semantics), the child will be unable to produce sounds that replicate what was heard. It is generally understood that the more severe the hearing loss, the less intelligible a child's speech will be.[73]

The young child who is deaf or hearing impaired is particularly apt to struggle within the traditional school setting. Until the child is able to read, the child relies heavily on hearing to learn.[54] Even the child with a minimal hearing loss struggles in school learning environments and may become fatigued because of the extra effort necessary to hear and follow directions.[34,64] This struggle is even worse in the gymnasium. This places the child who

Friends at Play
Courtesy Callier Center for Communicative Disorders, Dallas.

is deaf or hearing impaired at a significant disadvantage. However, if a young child who is deaf or has a hearing loss is given the opportunity to develop all his or her intelligences (Gardner's eight intelligences)—the musical, logical-mathematical, or bodily-kinesthetic, for example—there is no reason the child cannot succeed in school.

Hearing loss interferes with the child's ability to function within the classroom environment. The hearing loss may affect the child's ability to (1) comprehend class material, (2) follow directions, (3) follow class rules, (4) exhibit age-appropriate classroom behaviors, (5) follow and participate in class discussions, (6) interact well with peers, (7) attend to important stimuli in the learning environment, (8) express and understand emotions, and (9) avoid inappropriate acting-out behaviors.[64,70,71]

At the time most students who are deaf or hearing impaired leave school at age 20, their average reading skills are at grade 4.5, and their overall academic skills are behind those of their hearing peers.[74] It must be remembered, however, that most students who graduate from public high schools in the United States have functional reading skills typical of a 4th- or 5th-grader. That is, of course, a major concern.

The most significant problem tied to deafness/ hearing impairment in young children is their difficulty with play. Play is the foundation of the development of young children. Difficulty with communication makes it difficult for a young child who is deaf or hearing impaired to play with other children.

Children who are deaf or hearing impaired may, indeed, develop symbolic play even in the absence of spoken language. However, language does not develop in the absence of play.[51] It appears that young children who are deaf or hearing impaired develop the skills to engage in "pretend play" without oral/verbal communication. Apparently, it is much like the play typical of young children who have not yet developed spoken language—the play of young toddlers, for example.

Each child's psychosocial development is based on how well or how poorly others in the environment accept him or her (see Table 16-2). Unfortunately,

Table 16-2	Holcomb's Categories of Identity of Individuals Who Are Deaf[36]

Balanced Bicultural
The person who is deaf feels equally comfortable in deaf and hearing cultures.

Deaf-Dominant Bicultural
The person is primarily involved in the Deaf community but can relate well to hearing people.

Hearing-Dominant Bicultural
The person feels comfortable in the hearing community and has limited involvement in the Deaf community, perhaps because of lack of access.

Culturally Separate
The person identifies with and prefers to associate exclusively with others who are deaf.

Culturally Isolated
The person rejects involvement with other individuals who are deaf. The person is comfortable in and prefers the hearing community and perceives sign language to be a "crutch" for those unable to learn oral skills.

Culturally Marginal
The person is uncomfortable in the Deaf community and the hearing community.

Culturally Captive
The person is deaf and has had no opportunity to meet others who are deaf and learn about deaf culture.

the psychosocial development of some children who are deaf or hearing impaired is delayed because of the negative stereotypes attributed to them.[53] Stereotypes associated with individuals who are deaf or hearing impaired include nonsocial behavior, reservedness, lack of communicativeness, and preference for solitary behavior.[15]

Children who are deaf and raised by parents who are deaf, about 10 percent of the children who are deaf, are generally better adjusted than deaf children reared by hearing parents. This should be no surprise. If the child's parent has experienced the confusion, frustration, and pain associated with difficulty communicating with others and has experienced discrimination within the community and larger society, the parent will be much more

likely to understand the feelings of his or her child. In addition, the infant born to deaf parents has a definite advantage in communication skills because the child is exposed to sign language from infancy, in the same way that a hearing child of hearing parents is exposed to the parents' oral language from infancy.

In addition, if the parent's natural language is sign, the child and parent will find it much easier to communicate than will a child and parent learning the language together. It is easy to compare this to the process a child goes through learning a verbal-based language. If the parent's native language, for example, is Spanish, it will be easy for the child to learn Spanish; the language is used in the home, and the inferences, nuances, and intricacies of the language are shared daily. If both the parents and the child are struggling to learn English as a second language, the process is much more difficult.

Motor Characteristics of Individuals with Hearing Impairment

Impairment of the semicircular canals, vestibule of the inner ear, and/or vestibular portion of the 8th cranial nerve has a negative effect on balance (see Chapter 5). Siegel, Marchetti, and Tecclin[72] reported significantly depressed balance performance by children with sensorineural hearing loss of below 65 decibels. Another study that did not examine etiological factors evaluated motor performance and vestibular function of a group of hearing impaired children. The vast majority (65 percent) of the studied group demonstrated abnormal vestibular function but normal motor proficiency except for balance, whereas 24 percent had normal vestibular function and motor proficiency, including balance. Eleven percent had normal vestibular function but poor motor proficiency and balance.[19]

Butterfield et al.[14] found that 9 of 18 deaf boys and girls attending a residential school for the deaf had significant balance deficits, as evidenced by extraneous movement on Subtest 2, Item 8 of the Bruininks-Oseretsky Test of Motor

Proficiency. Each child was asked to walk on a balance beam and step over a stick, held at knee level, without falling off the balance beam. The students who fell appeared dependent on the visual system for their information about their performance; they watched their feet while walking on the beam. Each student who fell appeared dependent on the visual mechanism for information about their balance. This is typical of children with a vestibular deficit, though no specific test was used to determine if such a deficit was present.

Butterfield and Ersing[13] found the time the deafness/hearing impairment is acquired may have an impact on balance. Congenitally deaf/hearing impaired individuals have poorer balance than those with acquired deafness. The educator must be careful not to generalize about the motor performance of children, but individualize instruction based on their individual ability.

Assessment

Infants and toddlers who have been identified, early in life, as deaf or hearing impaired can and should be evaluated by a diagnostician or an educator using the same developmentally appropriate instruments used with any other child at risk for a delay. Chapter 10 contains more information about the assessment of infants, toddlers, and preschoolers.

Any evaluation instrument that allows the evaluator, or a peer, to demonstrate the skills involved can be used with students who are deaf or hearing impaired. Most elementary and middle school students who are deaf or hearing impaired can participate in the physical fitness and motor competency tests that are part of the general physical education program.

The Test of Gross Motor Development (TGMD) (see Chapter 3) is very appropriate for the elementary- and middle-school-age child who is deaf or hearing impaired to determine if the child has a motor delay. In addition, the balance subtest from the Bruininks-Oseretsky Test of Motor Proficiency can be used to determine whether there is a possibility of vestibular delay. Comparison of static balance ability with eyes open and eyes closed will provide clues to

vestibular delay or damage. Note that, if the child has balance problems caused by sensorineural damage to the 8th cranial nerve, which carries the vestibular impulse, activities to stimulate the vestibular system will not help the balance problem. In these cases, it is best simply to teach the child compensatory skills to execute the balance moves needed to be successful in motor activities.

High school students who are deaf and have a motor delay or disorder may best be assessed using the McCarron-Dial system designed to help identify strengths and deficits for the performance of tasks in the workforce. This type of assessment may be useful, in particular, in the development of the individual transition plan.

Almost all elementary, middle school, and high school children are capable of participating in school, school district, or state-mandated physical fitness tests without major accommodation. Certainly, every effort should be made to meet the individual needs of all students being assessed.

Special Considerations

For optimum learning to occur, a teacher must be able to communicate effectively with the students (see Table 16-3). Students with hearing losses have the greatest opportunity to learn when they have maximum hearing correction and a teacher who has mastery of the communication system the student has elected to use. Technological advances continue to improve methodology for maximizing hearing capability. And computer-mediated instruction has opened up a world of communication and information exchange for individuals who are deaf or hearing impaired; the world is available to everyone through cyberspace.

In some school districts, interpreters are hired to assist children to succeed in school. If the physical educator has a child who is receiving assistance from an interpreter, the physical educator and interpreter need to remember the following:

• The interpreter is *not* in the gymnasium or on the playground as a co-teacher or paraeducator. The interpreter is a highly skilled professional with a specific responsibility to the student he

Table 16-3	Communication Strategies for Teachers Working with Students Who Are Deaf or Hearing Impaired[7]

- If a student is using an interpreter, the students in the class must be taught to communicate directly with the student who is deaf or hearing impaired, not the interpreter.
- If the student is working with a sign interpreter, the interpreter should be positioned, at the request of the student, directly in front of the student, near the teacher on the platform or in front of the gymnasium, or following the teacher about the room.
- If the student is working with an oral interpreter, the interpreter should be posted close to the student for presenting information via mouth movement, facial expression, gestures, and appropriate rephrasing.
- If the student is using an assistive learning device, the teacher can wear a lapel microphone attached to an amplifier in his or her pocket.
- Group discussions that include students who are deaf or hearing impaired must be carefully controlled.
  - Only one student can speak at a time.
  - A student who relies on speech reading should be given the time to refocus on the new speaker.
- The teacher should use the following strategies to enhance oral communication:
  - The teacher should enunciate clearly and speak at a moderate pace.
  - The teacher should face the class.
  - During question-and-answer periods, the teacher should repeat the questions carefully.
  - If the teacher needs to write on the board, he or she should write, then stop, and give the students time to process what has been written before going on. The use of overhead projectors allows the teacher to continue to face the class.
  - The teacher should not wear facial hair and should not chew gum.
  - Visual materials and handouts are particularly helpful.
- The teacher should use the following strategies to enhance the student's written communication:
  - The teacher should meet with the student regularly to review and correct written work.
  - The teacher should help the student learn to use spelling/grammar checks available as part of most computer software and to understand the changes the software makes.
- The teacher may encourage best performance on a test by allowing the student to take a written exam and then giving the student the opportunity to explain answers orally.

or she is serving. "Educational interpreters are responsible for receiving the spoken word and translating it into sign language and translating it into the spoken word."[7]

- Even if an interpreter is present, the physical educator is still ultimately responsible for effective communication with the student who is deaf/hearing impaired.

Technological Hearing Assistance

The National Institute on Deafness and Other Communication Disorders describes hearing aids:

A hearing aid is an electronic, battery-operated device that amplifies and changes sound to allow for improved communication. Hearing aids receive sound through a microphone, which then converts the sound waves to electrical signals. The amplifier increases the loudness of the signals and then sends the sound to the ear through a speaker.[61]

Hearing aids come in five models: in the ear aids, behind the ear aids, canal aids, body aids and implantable aids. An audiologist decides which type of hearing aid will be beneficial for the individual who is deaf or hearing impaired. Implantable aids increase the transmission of sounds entering the ear. The middle ear implant moves the middle ear bones directly, which increases the strength of the vibrations that enter the inner ear. The second type is attached to the bone behind the ear, enabling vibrations to be sent directly to the inner ear, bypassing the middle ear.[22,60] Considerations include the person's age, ability to care for/maintain the hearing aid, and level of deafness/hearing impairment. Although hearing aids have been very helpful in the learning and communication of individuals with a hearing impairment, some people are embarrassed about having to wear the aid and, unfortunately, some have experienced negative judgments tied to wearing the aid.[20]

Cochlear implants are available for surgical implantation in children with bilateral severe-to-profound hearing loss and who have made little progress in the development of auditory skills.[16] (See Figure 16-1). An implant has four basic parts: "a microphone which picks up sound from the environment; a speech processor, which selects and arranges sounds picked up by the microphone; a transmitter and receiver/stimulator, which receive signals from the speech processor and convert them into electric impulses; and electrodes, which collect the impulses from the stimulator and send them to the brain."[59] Essentially, the implant finds and transmits usable sounds to existing auditory nerves. The use of a cochlear implant by children who are prelingually profoundly hearing impaired have a tremendous advantage over children who use a hearing aid, particularly if they are educated in an oral setting (without the use of sign language). Studies have shown that these children understand

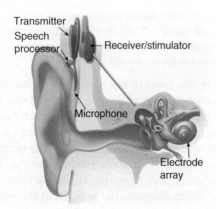

Figure 16-1   Ear with cochlear implant

Courtesy of National Institutes of Health.

and produce language at a level comparable to that of hearing children of the same age.[31,77]

The physical educator must be aware of the fact that each cochlear implant is "mapped" at the time it is fitted. Typically, this is done by an audiologist, who calibrates the device. Static electricity may "demap" the cochlear implant. The physical educator must help the child avoid activities that may "demap" the implant—for example, running on carpeting, sliding down slides, and rolling inside carpeted barrels.[35]

Educators, particularly physical educators teaching in gymnasiums or outside on playgrounds and play areas, should be aware of the availability of frequency modulated systems. The FM system is worn by the teacher and the student who is deaf or hearing impaired. It picks up the teacher's voice and transmits the speech signals directly to the student's ear.[22] Although expensive, the systems are often available to students and their families for use in the school setting as rentals.

Communication Systems

The two prevalent philosophies in the education of persons who are deaf or hard of hearing are the auditory-verbal therapy (oral) method and the total communication method. Each emphasizes the need for early identification, early intervention, and timely medical and audiological management.

The auditory-verbal therapy approach emphasizes communication through oral language in and through (1) required amplification, (2) significant language and communication stimulation, and (3) maximized opportunities to use residual hearing.[23] There is a significant emphasis on the role of the parents and family members as communication models.[23] The total communication method combines the auditory-verbal therapy method with the use of signs and fingerspelling. Children are provided amplification of sound and are taught through speech reading, fingerspelling, and signs. They express themselves through speech, fingerspelling, and signs.

The term *total communication* refers to both a method of instruction and a philosophy of education. As a philosophy, it refers to the right of every person who is deaf or hard of hearing to select whatever form of communication is preferred. That is, depending on the circumstances, the person should have the right to choose to communicate through speech, signs, gesture, or writing. If taught through a total communication system, a person has the option to communicate in a way that best suits his or her need. Classroom instruction of deaf individuals is predominantly through the total communication method.[6] A variety of forms of manual communication systems may be incorporated into the total communication method.

The manual communication systems range from simple homemade gestures to fingerspelling. Signing systems between these two extremes include Pidgin Sign Language, American Sign Language (ASL), Manually Coded English, and fingerspelling. A description of each follows:

- *Homemade gestures.* A primitive gestural system is developed to communicate between individuals or among small groups.
- *Pidgin Sign Language.* This is a mixture of English and American Sign Language. Key words and phrases are signed in correct order; prepositions and articles are usually omitted.[64]
- *American Sign Language.* ASL is a visual-gestural language that is governed by rules. The visual-gestural language involves executing systematic manual and nonmanual body movements simultaneously. Manual movements involve shapes, positions, and movements of the hands; nonmanual gestures involve the shoulders, cheeks, lips, tongue, eyes, and eyebrows. The rules that govern this language relate to how the language works (e.g., functions of the language, meaning, structure, and organization of sentences and the sound, or phonetic, system).[19,63]
- *Manually Coded English.* Signs are produced in English order, and fingerspelling is used for words and concepts that do not have a sign equivalent. Forms of Manually Coded English include Seeing Essential English, Signing Exact English, and Signed English. All are variations of American Sign Language that

attempt to model the vocabulary and syntax of the English language.[67]
- *Fingerspelling.* Each word is spelled letter by letter using a manual alphabet that consists of 26 letters. The hand is held in front of the chest, and letters are formed by using different single-hand configurations. Fingerspelling is also known as the Rochester method because it originated at the Rochester School for the Deaf in the late nineteenth century.[67]

Although many educators of students who are deaf or hard of hearing argue that it is in their best interest to be educated using some form of Manually Coded English,[67] the most widely used signing system used by adults who are deaf in this country is American Sign Language.

Effective communication with students who are deaf or hearing impaired is a challenge to physical educators. Teachers can improve their instructional ability by learning to communicate in a variety of ways to meet student needs. Communication through hand signals and/or basic survival signs will improve instruction (Figures 16-2 and 16-3). Most signs represent concepts and ideas rather than words. Pointing, motioning, demonstrating, gesturing, and signaling are also useful tools for the teacher.[25]

Teaching Strategies

In the past several decades, the emphasis in most special education programs has been on the process of teaching—teaching strategies and techniques—rather than the content of what is taught. This appears to be particularly true within deaf education,[9] and the adapted physical educator and general physical educator who seek to communicate with students who are deaf or hearing impaired have focused on the process of teaching rather than the nature of the curriculum.[52] There must be a greater emphasis on the physical education curriculum, and decisions regarding that curriculum must be outcome-based and focused on the functional ability of the student.[62] An emphasis on hands-on demonstration, technological support,

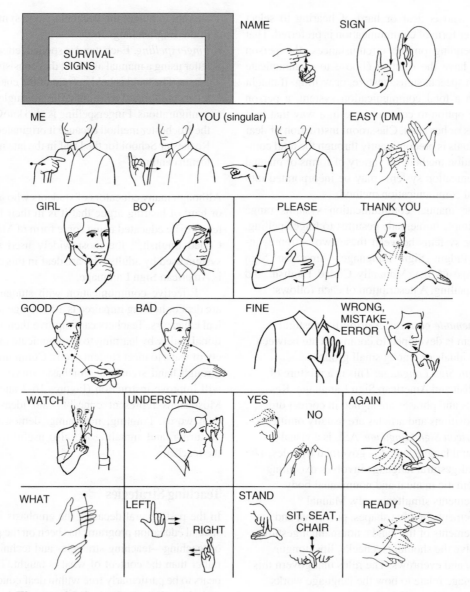

Figure 16-2 Survival Signs
Reprinted with permission from the *Journal of Physical Education, Recreation, and Dance.*

peer-to-peer instruction, self-paced learning, high expectations, independent learning packages, and exposure to a great deal of communication and interaction heightens the effectiveness of the learning environment.[10] Carefully trained peer tutors increase the physical activity levels of

deaf students in inclusive elementary physical education programs.[45]

The ability to communicate effectively is important in instructional settings and while participating in play, games, leisure, recreation, fitness activities, and sports. When there is effective communication

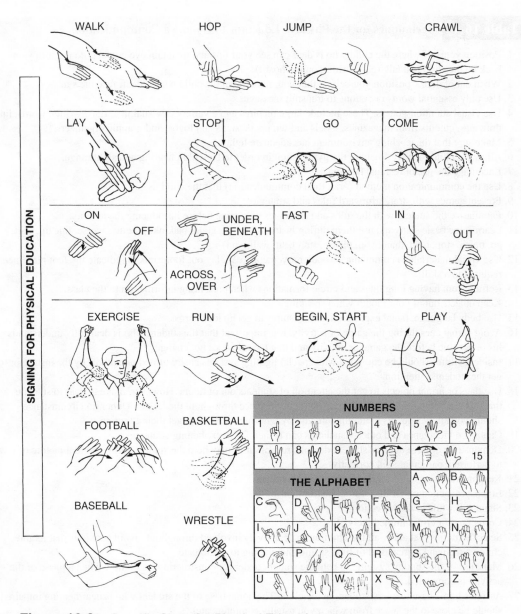

Figure 16-3 Specific Signs for Physical Education

Reprinted with permission from the *Journal of Physical Education, Recreation, and Dance.*

and the learning environment is properly managed, there may be little need to modify the demands of the physical activity.[13] However, when communication impairments are present, the student may perform motor and social skills less well, solely because of the communication problem. The physical educator who works with students who are deaf or hearing impaired must do everything possible to ensure effective communication (see Table 16-4).

According to Ling,[47] no single method can meet the individual needs of all children with hearing

Table 16-4	**Techniques for the Physical Educator to Enhance Communication**

1. Position yourself where the child who is deaf can see your lips and maintain eye contact; do not turn your back on the child and talk (e.g., writing on the board).
2. When out of doors, position yourself so that you, rather than the child who is deaf, face the sun.
3. Use only essential words or actions to transmit messages.
4. Use visual attention-getters. These include large pictures and a variety of visual materials: written words, line drawings, cutouts from magazines, labels and wrappers, signs and logos, and graphic organizers.[49]
5. Make sure that the teaching environment has adequate lighting.
6. Allow the child to move freely in the gymnasium in order to be within hearing and sight range.
7. Encourage the use of residual hearing.
8. Use the communication method (oral, total communication) that the child uses.
9. Present games with straightforward rules and strategies.
10. Familiarize the student with the rules and strategies of a game before introducing the activity.
11. Learn some basic signs and use them during instruction (e.g., good, bad, okay, better, worse, line up, start, go, finish, stop, help, thank you, please, stand, sit, walk, run).
12. Use visual materials to communicate body movements (e.g., lay out footprints to indicate the foot placements required in a skill).
13. Refrain from having long lines and circle formations when presenting information to the class.
14. Keep objects out of your mouth when speaking.[55]
15. Use body language, facial expression, and gestures to get an idea across.[55]
16. Avoid verbal cues during the game or activity. It is important that the student who is deaf fully understands his or her role before the game or activity and that the role does not change.[55]
17. Inside facilities should be equipped with special lighting systems easily turned on and off by the instructor to get the students' attention.[55]
18. Use flags or bright objects to get the attention of students out of doors. However, make it clear to students that it is their responsibility to be aware of your presence throughout the lesson. Under no circumstance should you allow students to manipulate you by ignoring attempts to get their attention.
19. Captioned videotapes and other visual aids can be helpful in explaining strategies.
20. Demonstrate or have another student demonstrate often. It may help the student form a mental picture of how to perform a particular skill correctly.
21. Keep instructions simple and direct.
22. Emphasize action rather than verbal instruction.
23. Stand still while giving directions.
24. Correct motor errors immediately.[55]
25. Select activities that allow all the children to be actively involved throughout; avoid activities that require children to spend a great deal of time sitting and waiting to participate.
26. Make use of the "buddy system" to help the student understand instructions and know when a phase of the activity is completed.
27. Assign a home base to every student in the class. The home base of the student who is deaf/hearing impaired should be close to the space from which you usually communicate.
28. Delimit the area in which members of the class may move.
29. Children who are deaf or hearing impaired require a great deal of structure in order to feel comfortable.
30. Use the same sequence of activities for each class—for example, warm-up, dance, calisthenics, jogging/running, and so on.
31. Supply a visual schedule to the student who is deaf; it will help the student predict what is coming and to prepare for it. Be sure to refer consistently to the name of each segment of the day, using the same name.[49]

disorders, and whenever possible a total communication system should be used. Verbal instructions that describe movements are ineffective for deaf individuals who cannot read lips. It is critical that precise visual models be presented to deaf individuals. To promote kinesthetic feedback, it is also helpful to move a child through the desired movement pattern. This helps the student feel the temporal-spatial relationship of movements associated with a skill. Using both visual and kinesthetic instruction provides opportunities for two avenues of sensory information. A quick visual model followed by physical prompting of the behavior may facilitate learning.

Some older children who are deaf can read lips and thus receive directions through verbal means. If the child has residual hearing or is skilled at lip reading, the physical educator should make the environment conducive to reception of the spoken word. Instruction must be given close enough to the child that precise movement of the lips and tongue can be deciphered. The instructor should be in front and in clear view of the deaf student. When movement in a game requires the child to perform an activity at a distance at which lips cannot be read, it is then necessary to use a combination of signing to communicate. Eichstaedt and Seiler[25] have suggested 45 signs specific to physical education to communicate with the deaf. Another source of communication with these students is trained hearing paraprofessionals (teacher aides) or peers who can facilitate instruction by gaining the attention of the child who is hearing impaired and then relaying instructions through visual models, signs, or tactile inputs that guide the child into class activities (see Table 16-4).

The Physical Education Program

Considerable differences about the ways individuals who are deaf or hearing impaird respond to stimuli. These differences must be taken into consideration when programming; of course, programming for each child who is deaf or hearing impaired is dependent on the child's IEP.

One of the major problems associated with physical education programs for learners who are deaf or hearing impaired is the poor acoustical conditions that exist in many classrooms.[48,65] The poor acoustics and reverberation effects in the typical classroom are nothing like those that exist in the gymnasium. Most gymnasiums are essentially large, empty rooms with wood floors, high ceilings, and few materials or surfaces to absorb sound. As a result, any child is bombarded by the noise and may find it difficult to listen to and hear directions. The child who is deaf or hearing impaired may find it impossible to function in this environment. Adding sound-absorbing materials, such as carpet, acoustic ceiling tiles, curtains, and corkboard, may help reduce the reverberations.[10]

More effective acoustics are critical to the physical educator trying to teach all children, particularly children with hearing impairments. Teachers need to talk approximately 15 decibels louder than the background noise in the classroom in order to be heard;[1] in the gymnasium, maintaining this level of volume is almost impossible throughout the teaching day.

Children who are deaf who have impaired semicircular canals, which compromises balance, should not climb to high places. Also, some children with hearing loss should not participate in activity where there is excessive dampness, dust, or change in temperature because of increased likelihood of acquiring a middle or inner ear infection.

Instruction should be directed toward play, motor, and social skills that will enable the student to participate in leisure, recreation, and sport activity in the community.[68] To encourage maximum participation, the instructor's skills and attitudes are important.

The objectives of a physical education program for hearing impaired children are the same as those for children who are not hearing impaired. At the preschool and early elementary school levels, the focus should be on developing basic locomotor and nonlocomotor skills through play, games, rhythm, and parachute activities. Percussion instruments, such as cymbals, triangles, drums, and tambourines, are valuable for rhythm activities, because they are capable of producing vibrations to which the child can respond.

An important area of concern is balance. If vestibular functioning appears to be delayed and damage to the 8th cranial nerve can be ruled out, activities that encourage spinning, rolling, rocking, rapid changes in direction, and rapid start/stops should be included. This can be done in and through dances such as "Freeze" or games such as "Red Light/Green Light." Should 8th cranial nerve damage be suspected, balance should be taught directly. Balance activities that can be included in a program are (1) standing on one foot, so that the other foot can be used for kicking and trapping; (2) walking a balance beam to develop leg, hip, and trunk strength; and (3) performing drills that build balance skills for chasing, stopping, starting, and dodging. The physical education program at the elementary level should focus primarily on prerequisites for competent motor performance, such as vestibular, kinesthetic, and visual stimulation.

At the middle and secondary school levels, hearing impaired students can participate in the same activities as their hearing peers. Care should be taken to ensure they develop skills that will enable them to participate in the physical fitness and leisure-time activities available in their community. Activities that enhance kinesthetic development and that are popular with middle and secondary school students who are deaf or hearing impaired include handball and racquetball, wrestling, tae kwon do, cross-country running or skiing, swimming, weight lifting, golf, aquatics, and bowling (see Table 16-5).

The physical educator, like many other professionals serving the high school deaf student, is faced with significant problems when contributing to the development of the individual transition plan (ITP). The following are the most significant issues that affect the ITP process: (1) communication and language skills are key to most jobs,

Table 16-5	Aquatics for Individuals Who Are Deaf or Hearing Impaired

- Hearing aids will need to be removed before individuals who are deaf or hearing impaired enter the pool area. In fact, they should probably be removed in the locker room and stored carefully in a locked locker.
- The individual who is deaf or hearing impaired should wear ear plugs and waterproof headbands to prevent water from entering the ear canal.
- A visual emergency signal must be in place.
  - Flicking on and off the lights, above and below water level
  - Warning flags waved by the lifeguard or teacher
- In an open-water swimming area, the designated safe swimming area must be carefully delineated and marked by colorful buoys. The individual who is deaf or hearing impaired must always swim with a buddy; in fact, it is the best practice in aquatics for all individuals always to swim with a buddy.
- In a pool, the deep-water areas must be carefully identified and separated from the shallow end.
- Demonstrations, particularly by classmates, are effective in presenting information.
- The individual who is deaf or hearing impaired should not dive to enter the pool area and certainly should not snorkel or scuba dive without his or her physician's permission because of the risk associated with increased hydrostatic pressure.
- The individual who is deaf or hearing impaired may experience difficulty with the maintenance of equilibrium. The individual must be given the opportunity to explore the aquatic environment and a variety of positions within that environment and to practice vital safety skills, such as recovering to a stand from a float or glide.

(2) deaf students may have received their education in primarily nonacademic programs, and (3) many deaf students don't have or don't use the skills to self-advocate.[30] The wise physical educator not only addresses the leisure, recreation, sport, and fitness interests of the student and the student's family but also is aware of the availability of these programs within the community.

Integrating Students Who Are Deaf or Have a Hearing Impairment

It should no longer be assumed that all persons who are deaf or hearing impaired should fit or want to fit into and function in the hearing world. In some large cities, there are whole communities of individuals who are deaf who choose to live together to share their unique culture, lifestyle, and language.

Requiring individuals who are deaf or hard of hearing to meet the demands of the hearing population's culture may not always be in their best interest. For example, Grimes and Prickett[32] argued that insisting that children who are deaf use only what hearing people consider "proper" English (or Spanish, Vietnamese, Czech, and so on) may lead to feelings of inferiority and inadequacy. For this and other reasons, the issue of the placement of children who are deaf in an inclusive environment is a highly emotional and controversial issue within the Deaf community. Physical educators can make a major contribution to the education of a child who is deaf by being sensitive to his or her individual needs and providing an appropriate and acceptable physical education program (see Table 16-6). It is important to note that simply "sharing" a physical space does not mean that students with and without hearing impairments will automatically develop empathy and mutual understanding.[57] The physical educator must help create an environment that allows quality interaction and quality time; the students must participate in educational experiences designed to foster empathy and understanding.

The most inviting school for students who are deaf or hearing impaired is one in which the administration, faculty, staff, and students are prepared to welcome the students within the community. Stonewall Jackson Elementary School, a Regional Day School for the Deaf, in Dallas, Texas, received a United States Blue Ribbon School Award in 1999 for its unique and exceptional efforts in educating all children within the school. Beginning in kindergarten, all students who attend Stonewall Jackson receive instruction in American Sign Language, so that they can communicate with their peers who are

Table 16-6	Teaching Strategies for Including the Student Who Is Deaf or Hearing Impaired[10, 24, 30]

- Group discussions must be carefully controlled for students who rely on speech reading (lip reading).
  - The speech reader must be given enough time to refocus on the next speaker.
  - Only one student may speak at a time.
- The teacher of a student who relies on speech reading should not wear facial hair, particularly mustaches and beards, which obstruct sight of the lips and mouth.
- The classroom or gymnasium must be well lighted; the speakers must avoid being in shadows.
- Group discussions must be carefully controlled for students who rely on an interpreter.
  - The interpreter must be seated within easy view of the student yet in a position that does not interfere with contact with other students.
  - Participants in the group discussion (and any discussion) must be taught to talk directly to the student and not the interpreter.
- The teacher may wear a lapel microphone, attached to an amplifier, for the student who is wearing an assistive listening device.

deaf or hearing impaired. The principal and all members of the faculty, and most staff members, are able to communicate in sign as well.

Gallaudet University, the only major liberal arts university devoted to the provision of a quality education to students who are deaf, hearing impaired, and who have no hearing impairment, provides evidence of the success of a well-designed physical education and intramural and intercollegiate athletic program.[29] Gallaudet offers intercollegiate athletic programs for men in baseball, basketball, football, soccer, swimming, track and field, and wrestling. The university offers intercollegiate athletic programs for women in soccer, softball, swimming, tennis, track and field, and volleyball. Gallaudet also has a comprehensive intramural program that features a wide variety of sports and special events.[29]

Parents of some students prefer to enroll them in residential or day schools that have segregated programs. Many parents prefer these schools because they have a higher percentage of teachers who are deaf educators, and the students have the opportunity to participate in an extensive array of academic and vocational courses, as well as a wide range of athletic and social programs.[75]

Ellis[26] found that deaf students who attended a residential facility, and who had two deaf parents, were much more likely to participate in community sports than were students who attended an integrated school. And these deaf students had greater cardiovascular respiratory endurance and a lower percentage of body fat than deaf students who attended an integrated school. There appear to be two major factors that affected their participation and enhanced their physical fitness. Deaf parents are more likely to help their deaf children get involved and stay involved in community-based deaf recreation, sport, and fitness programs.[74] The residential schools that serve children who are deaf or who have hearing impairments have comprehensive physical education, after-school, intramural, and interscholastic programs that offer significant opportunities for deaf students to be active.[26]

Physical educators are challenged to assist all students to develop effective social skills through participation in integrated settings. Certain physical education activities enable the integration process to be accomplished with minimum support systems. Activities that require less social interaction and communication skills are movement exploration programs in the elementary school and individual sports, such as bowling, archery, and weight lifting, at the advanced levels. More complex team sports, such as basketball, which requires frequent response to whistles and verbal communication involved in strategic situations among teammates, are more difficult to integrate, but a highly motivated athlete can be very successful.

Organized football is perhaps the most difficult because of the need for ongoing information exchange between coaches and players while the game is in progress. The task is not impossible, however. Kenny Walker, a football player who is deaf, was outstanding at the University of Nebraska and later played in the National Football League with the Denver Broncos. Through his interpreters, he was integrated into the game at the highest levels of competition. He is an excellent example of how a person who is deaf can be successfully integrated into a complex sport with the use of supplemental aids and services.

The introduction of a child who is deaf or hearing impaired into a general physical education class without prearranged support systems may be devastating. A peer support system is an excellent way to ease a student into the inclusive setting. As is the case with all support systems, only the amount of assistance necessary for the individual to experience success should be provided. The teacher has the major responsibility for assisting students who are deaf or hard of hearing to adjust to the learning environment. That is best done by example.

Community-Based Activities

The individual transition plan is a critical part of the process of preparing a student who is deaf or has a hearing impairment for transition from a school-based program into the community. Leisure, recreation, fitness, and sports available in the community are important outlets for persons with a hearing impairment. Community recreational facilities and opportunities should be reviewed with high school students, their parents, and other members of the

Technology Can Be Used to Enable Communication
Courtesy of Tara McCarthy.

IEP/multidisciplinary team, so that they can make an informed decision about what activities are available after the school years. Those activities should be included in the transitional programs and instruction provided to the students.

The major organization promoting the sports participation of children and adults who are deaf or hearing impaired is the United States of America Deaf Sports Federation (USADSF).[78] This organization provides comprehensive opportunities for individuals who have a hearing loss of greater than 55 decibels in the better ear. The USADSF describes its organization as follows:

> The USA Deaf Sports Federation embraces universal values of self-respect, sportsmanship, and competition, which transcend all boundaries of geography, nationality, political philosophy, gender, age, race, and religion.

> The USA Deaf Sports Federation believes that through recreational opportunities, sports training, and competition, deaf and hard of hearing people can benefit physically, mentally, socially, and spiritually in an environment of equality, mutual respect, and acceptance.[78]

The Summer Deaflympics which is conducted by the Internal Committee of Sports for the Deaf (ICSD), includes competition in the following: badminton, basketball, beach volleyball, bowling, cycling, football, handball, judo, karate, orienteering, shooting, soccer, swimming, table tennis, tae kwon do, tennis, track and field, volleyball, water polo, wrestling freestyle, and wrestling Greco-Roman.[79] Winter Deaflympics competition includes alpine skiing (giant slalom, super giant slalom, and dual slalom), curling, ice hockey, nordic skiing, and snowboarding.[78]

Deaf-Blind

Deaf-blind means concomitant hearing and visual impairments, the combination of which causes such severe communication and other developmental and educational needs that they cannot be accommodated in special education programs solely for children with deafness or children with blindness.[38]

Incidence

In the 2005–2006 academic year, approximately 1,500 deaf-blind school-age children were provided educational services in the United States. Approximately one-third of those children received their education in public separate facilities or residential schools. The percentage of children receiving services in diverse educational settings are

- <21% of instruction outside regular classroom: 22.8%
- 21%–60% of instruction outside regular classroom: 15.1%
- >60% of instruction outside regular classroom: 33.6%
- Separate public school facility: 10.1%
- Separate private school facility: 7.3%
- Public residential facility: 6.5%
- Private residential facility: 3.2%
- Home or hospital: 1.4%[37]

Children who are deaf-blind have a significant loss of both vision and hearing. They have less than 20/20 vision in a visual field of 20 degrees or less. In addition, they have a loss of hearing of 25 decibels or more. Children who are deaf-blind have problems that are similar to those of blind children and deaf children; however, their problems are exponential rather than additive. This makes it very difficult for them to acquire basic communication skills. Residual sight, hearing, or both are the basis of communication. If there is no residual sight or hearing, communication is primarily tactile and kinesthetic, through touch and movement.

Wheeler and Griffin[81] have suggested a motor-based approach to teaching communication and language skills to young children who are deaf-blind. The critical role of the physical educator, as the motor expert, in each of the following phases must be emphasized:

- *Resonance.* In this phase, the physical educator mirrors and expands on movements the student initiates. For example, if the student is holding a ball, the teacher may grasp the ball as well and begin to move it in a circular path.

- *Coactive movement.* In this phase, the emphasis is on the physical relationship between the teacher and the student, including frequent touch and physical contact between the two. It also includes movements done together—for example, sitting, singing, rocking, and playing "row, row, row your boat."
- *Nonrepresentation reference.* In this phase, the teacher helps the student develop the basis of body image by encouraging the student to replicate the position of a three-dimensional object—for example, the teacher, a doll, a teddy bear, or a "gumby."
- *Deferred imitation.* The teacher, in this phase, asks the student to imitate a series of body positions, which become increasingly complex. An example of this activity is playing "angels in the snow."

Children and adolescents who are deaf-blind find it difficult to communicate with others. Their educators may fail to understand or may miss their interactive signals because the signals are often subtle and may be difficult to interpret.[39] It is clear that those who wish to communicate with children who are deaf-blind, notably their educators, must be given the opportunity to learn observation skills to identify communicative intents and to analyze those intentions in different interactional situations.[39] For example, the physical educator must be trained to notice the signals a deaf-blind child gives to communicate, particularly in the gymnasium or on the playground.

Lieberman[44] recommended that the physical educator use significant tactile and physical communication strategies to teach children who are deaf-blind. One strategy is moving a child's body, using physical guidance, through a skill. Another is providing a demonstration while the child feels the teacher's body.

Typically, the deaf-blind child in the educational environment is helped by a professional known as an "intervenor." This professional helps the deaf-blind child gain access to the information in the environment.[56] As with the interpreter for the deaf, this professional is there solely to serve the student.

The significant efforts of adapted physical education professionals, notably Dr. Lauren Lieberman, Dr. James Cowart, and Dr. Steven Butterfield, have increased the physical education opportunities for students who are deaf-blind. The opportunities for students who are deaf-blind to master and enjoy leisure, recreation, fitness, and sport activities to enhance their physical fitness are vast.

Lieberman[44] has suggested that the deaf-blind can use the same types of techniques to run as the visually impaired. These include using a guidewire, a sighted guide, or a tethered partner and running toward a voice. Tandem bicycling and duo cycling are also recommended.

Another excellent strategy for enjoying physical activity and developing cardiovascular respiratory fitness is the use of fitness equipment typically found in YMCA/YWCAs, city recreation centers, and/or health clubs: treadmill walking, treadmill running, stationary bicycling, and tethered swimming.

Lieberman and Stuart[46] identified the recreation preferences of deaf-blind adults. A large percentage (65 percent) identified fitness activities as a preferred activity. The physical educator can play a vital role in preparing deaf-blind students for other preferred recreation activities, including dancing, outdoor recreation activities, and water activities.

The quality of life of an individual who is deaf, hearing impaired, or deaf-blind can be enhanced in and through quality physical education programs that prepare students for a life of leisure, recreation, fitness, and sport activities. The creative and resourceful teacher can make a huge difference in the lives of these students.

SPEECH AND LANGUAGE DISORDERS

Though most children with speech and language-learning disorders as their only disability do not have any gross motor delays, the physical educator teaches children with speech and language-learning disorders in every class. In fact, approximately 90 percent of children with speech and language-learning disorders receive instruction in the general program for the majority of their instructional day.[37]

A brief introduction to speech and language-learning disorders is included in this chapter. Most students with speech and hearing disorders have typical gross motor skills, and physical education can provide a quality educational experience with simple modifications to honor the students' individual needs.

Definition

Speech and language impairment is a communication disorder, such as stuttering, impaired articulation, a language impairment, or a voice impairment, that adversely affects a child's educational performance.[38]

Incidence

In 2005–2006 more than 1,143,000 children between 6 and 21 years received instruction to address speech and language disorders.[37] The vast majority of those children spent most of their time in the general education program. A large number of children with a different primary disability—for example, intellectual disability, autism, or deafness/hearing impairment—also have speech and language disorders.[33]

Causes

One of the major causes of speech and language-learning disorders is hearing loss. Even a minor or fluctuating hearing loss (e.g., as a result of otitis media), particularly during the early developmental period, may have a significant negative impact on the development of speech and language skills. In addition, neurological disorders, traumatic brain injury, alcohol or other drug abuse, physical impairments (e.g., cleft lip or cleft palate), and vocal abuse (e.g., use of cigarettes or caffeine) can cause speech and language-learning disorders.[58]

There are many forms of communicative disorders. The following are the major forms:

- Speech disorders
- Voice disorders
- Language disorders

Speech Disorders

The global term *speech disorders* refers to difficulties in producing speech sounds or problems with voice quality that interfere with an individual's ability to communicate effectively. A speech disorder may be characterized by an interruption in the flow or rhythm of speech—called fluency disorder or dysfluency (e.g., stuttering). Speech disorders may also be problems with the way sounds are formed, called articulation, or phonological, disorders, or they may be difficulties with the pitch, volume, or quality of the voice.[58]

Fluency Disorders: Stuttering and Cluttering

Individuals who stutter experience disruptions in the smooth flow of their speech more often than the average speaker of their age. Interruptions in the flow of speech, called dysfluencies, are the most obvious feature of stuttering. The interruptions differ from person to person. Common dysfluencies include part- or whole-word repetitions, phrase repetitions ("m-m-m-mummy"), prolonged sounds at the beginning of words ("C-a-a-an I h-h-h-have that?"), hesitations, and silent blocks when the person silently struggles to begin a word. Although virtually ALL young children exhibit some dysfluencies, very early stuttering is distinct from normal dysfluency. See Table 16-7 for specific tips for the physical educator who is teaching a child who stutters.

Cluttering is often characterized by rapid, slurred, or imprecise speech, in which the child seems to get "stuck," as if the child's mind is going faster than his or her mouth.

Delayed Speech

Delays in a child's speech indicates a problem. Like many developmental skills, the acquisition of speech is predictable in typical children. See Chapter 10 for information about typical speech development in young children.

Articulation Disorders

Learners with speech disorders have trouble using some speech sounds, which can also indicate a more global delay. They may say "see" when they

Table 16-7	Tips for the Physical Educator Teaching a Child Who Stutters[76]

- Listen to and answer the child in a patient, calm, and unemotional way.
- Talk privately with the child who stutters. Explain to the child that when we learn to talk—just like learning new things in physical education—we make mistakes. We bobble sounds, just as we bobble a ball, or we repeat or get tangled up on words, just as our feet get tangled in a jump rope.
- Assure the child that stuttering does not bother you. You want him or her to talk, so that you can learn the way he or she feels, what he or she thinks about, and what he or she has learned and wants to learn.
- Initially, until he or she adjusts to the physical education class, ask the child questions that can be answered with one or two words.
- If every child is going to be asked a question, call fairly early on the child who stutters. The stuttering will be worse if the child has to wait and worry.
- Listen to what the child is saying. Respond to that, rather than the stuttering.
- Give appropriate responses to what the child is saying, such as head nods and smiles. Don't interrupt the child with "uh-huh" or "yes." The verbalization will cause the child to hesitate.
- Maintain natural eye contact when the child is talking.
- Don't rush the child by interrupting or finishing words for him or her.
- With the child and his or her parents' permission, spend a brief period of time early in the semester sharing specific information about stuttering or do "empathy" experiences to help the child's classmates understand the problem.

CASE STUDY 16-2

Webster

Webster is a 3rd-grader with an articulation disorder that makes it very difficult for him to communicate with his peers and his teachers. Webster is overweight because he has avoided play situations—recess, physical education, after-school play with friends, and the like—because he has been teased.

Webster dreads the biannual physical fitness testing because he does not do well on any of the tests.

APPLICATION TASK

Develop a teaching strategy to help Webster develop more age-appropriate physical fitness in the 3rd-grade physical education class. Go to the PE Central Web site and select several of their excellent physical fitness activities for 3rd-graders.

---

mean "ski" or they may have trouble with some sounds, such as "l" or "r." This speech is often difficult for the listener to follow.

Motor-Speech Disorders: Apraxia

Apraxia occurs when the part of the brain that controls the ability to voluntarily sequence muscle movements, particularly those involved in the production of speech (oral-motor), does not work as it should. Pronouncing even a single short word requires this ability because spoken words are sequences of speech sounds voluntarily produced by sequential muscle movement. Long words and sentences are even harder.

The student with apraxia may have difficulty with unintelligible speech, a significant motor-speech deficit.[42] They are often poor readers who have difficulty with content area material (science, math, history) because of vocabulary[4] (see Table 16-8).

Motor-Speech Disorders: Dysarthria

Dysarthria occurs when there has been an injury to the nerves that control the muscles used to breathe and talk. The muscles may be weak and/or uncoordinated. The person's speech will be unclear as a result. Dysarthria can occur after a stroke or traumatic brain injury, as one symptom of cerebral palsy, or as a symptom of a neurological disease, such as Parkinson's disease.

Speech Difficulties Due to Cleft Lip or Palate

Children and adults with cleft lip and/or palate may experience speech difficulties due to structural

Table 16-8	Early Signs and Symptoms of Apraxia[42]

- The infant fails to coo or babble.
- Typical first words, such as *Mama,* may not appear at all; instead, the infant/toddler may point and "grunt."
- First words are delayed, with many phonemes deleted or replaced with other (easier) phonemes.
- The child may not use many consonants. The child may only be able to use / b, m, p, t, d, h /.
- The child may favor a particular syllable and emphasize it in all words.
- The child may use a word—a real word or a nonsensical utterance—to convey other words.
- The child may articulate one word well, but his or her speech becomes unintelligible if the child attempts a sentence.
- The child may have verbal perseveration; the child gets stuck on a word or phrase and repeats it continuously.
- The child may have other fine motor deficits as well.

problems in or around the mouth caused by their cleft lip or palate. The oral structures needed to speak are the lips, teeth, tongue, and palate. Some speech sounds are more affected by a cleft lip or palate than others. The severity of the original clefting, and how effective the repairs were, will determine how clearly a child or an adult will be able to say these sounds. Children with cleft lip typically have the lip surgically repaired at 2 to 3 months of age, while children with cleft palate typically have the palate repaired at about 12 months of age.[82]

Phonological Delays or Disorders

National Information Center for Children and Youth with Disabilities (NICHCY) described children with phonological delays or disorders as having trouble learning the sound system of their native language. The speech of these children can be very difficult to understand. While all toddlers and young preschoolers simplify their speech to make the words easier to say, children with a phonological delay use these simplified word forms much longer.[58]

Voice Disorders

People with voice disorders have difficulty with the way their voices sound.

Vocal Hyperfunction

The voice of an individual with vocal hyperfunction may sound hoarse or breathy. Voice disorders are caused by a history of exposure to chemicals, smoke, low humidity, allergies, dust, smoking, alcohol abuse, and excessive caffeine and/or overuse.[41] It is particularly crucial that the physical education teacher be sensitive to the incredible overuse of the voice that is required in the gymnasium and on the playground, because physical educators and coaches are likely to develop vocal hyperfunction.

Resonance Disorder

An individual with a resonance disorder has a voice that sounds very "nasal" or lacks "nasal quality." Resonance is the quality of voice that results from sound vibrations in the pharynx, oral cavity, and nasal cavity. Hypernasality is caused by velopharyngeal inadequacy; hyponasality is caused by a blockage in the nasopharynx or nasal cavity.[43]

Language Disorders

NICHCY defines a language disorder as "an impairment in the ability to understand and/or use words in context, both verbally and nonverbally."[58] Some individuals with language disorders have difficulty using appropriate words and confuse their meanings, some struggle to express their ideas, some use inappropriate grammatical patterns, some have a small vocabulary, and some have difficulty following directions. One or a combination of these characteristics may occur in children who are affected by language-learning disabilities or a developmental language delay.[58]

Language Delay

A language delay is characterized by a delay "across the board" in the ability to understand language. Chapter 10 includes a "typical" development chart that includes language.

Receptive Language Dysfunction

A receptive language dysfunction is a central auditory processing deficit. A receptive language dysfunction is a difficulty in the decoding and storing of auditory information, typically incoming verbal messages (see Table 16-9).

Expressive Language Dysfunction

An expressive language dysfunction is one in which the individual has difficulty with verbal expression. The individual struggles to put words together to formulate thoughts and to share those thoughts with others (see Table 16-10).

Aphasia

Aphasia is an impairment of language that affects the production or comprehension of speech and the ability to read or write. It may affect a single aspect of language use, such as the ability to retrieve the names of objects, the ability to put words together into sentences, or the ability to read. It is more common, however, that many aspects of communication are impaired while some communication channels remain accessible for a limited exchange of information.

Aphasia is always due to injury to the brain—most commonly from a stroke, particularly in

Table 16-9	Signs and Symptoms of Receptive Language Dysfunction[42]

- The child demonstrates echolalia. He or she repeats back words or phrases either immediately or at a later time without understanding the meaning.
- The child is unable to follow directions, though he or she may follow routine, repetitive directions.
- The child shows inappropriate, off-target responses to "wh" questions—"who," "what," "when," "where," and "why."
- The child demonstrates re-auditorization; he or she repeats back a question first and then responds to it.
- The child has difficulty responding appropriately to "yes/no" and "either/or" questions.
- The child does not attend to spoken language.
- The child uses a lot of jargon.

Table 16-10	Signs and Symptoms of Expressive Language Dysfunction[42]

- The child has word retrieval difficulties. The child has difficulty naming objects or "talks in circles" around subjects with a lack of appropriate vocabulary.
- The child demonstrates dysnomia, misnaming items.
- The child has difficulty acquiring syntax, the rules of grammar.
- The child has difficulty with morphology, changes in verb tense.
- The child has difficulty with semantics, word meaning.

older individuals. But brain injuries resulting in aphasia may also arise from head trauma, brain tumors, or infections.[2]

Psychological and Behavioral Characteristics of Individuals with Speech and Language Disorders

Typically, developing children use their speech, language, and voice skills to share information, express their feelings and emotions, initiate and terminate play, and negotiate with others. Children with impaired language skills interact differently than their typically developing peers in a classroom setting, are less preferred playmates than their typically developing peers, and experience problems with basic social interactions and tasks.[28] These children are often lonely within the school setting; their feeling of loneliness is influenced by their lack of acceptance by peers, their lack of participation in friendship, their nonsustainable or poor quality of friendships, and the perception that they are victimized by their peers.[7] Children with a severe language impairment are less socially skilled than their typical peers and demonstrate more behavior problems. The social skills that appear to be affected include introducing oneself, joining in play and other activities, initiating and sustaining interactions, making friends, and compromising.[28]

It appears that early delays or difficulties with speech and language skill development, a critical component of communication, may limit subsequent growth in cognition, metacognition, and other language skills.[50] Students with specific language disabilities may also have difficulties with "executive functions"—that is, "inhibiting actions, restraining and delaying responses, attending selectively, setting goals, planning, organizing, as well as maintaining and shifting set or focus of attention."[73] These executive function skills are critical for success in the school environment. For example, the student must be able to stay seated, an inhibiting action, even if the student really wants to get up, wander to the window, and watch a bird on the sill.

There appears to be a significant relationship between language problems and emotional/behavior problems. A majority of the children being treated for emotional/behavior problems (62 to 95 percent) have moderate to severe language problems.[17] In fact, many educators believe that children with severe language problems should be screened for emotional/behavior problems and that children with emotional/behavior problems should be screened for language problems.

The communication needs of adolescents when interacting with peers and with teachers have been examined. In the study, the skills required for communication with peers, such as skills associated with empathy, perspective taking, and the use of voice/tone in interaction, were more important than the skills required for communication with adults.[69]

Motor Characteristics

Children and adults with speech and language disorders do not exhibit any significant gross motor delays or disorders unless they have been teased or bullied and have avoided play, recess, physical education, and so on. Instead, the physical educator should be concerned with and concentrate on their functional play and social skills.

Testing

The student with a speech and language disorder should be able to participate in any school, district,

or state-mandated physical fitness, motor, or sport-skills assessment. The physical educator may be asked to help with the motor component on a broad-based developmental assessment instrument, such as the Brigance Diagnostic Inventory of Early Development. The speech and language pathologist (SLP) will complete speech and language-learning assessments in a natural environment;[80] a good SLP will ask the physical educator for permission to observe and assess a child with a language and learning disability while he or she is participating in activities in the gymnasium, where language tends to flow more easily.

Special Considerations

Speech and language pathologists who serve children with communication disorders are increasingly serving children within the general classroom environment.[8] Excellent speech and language pathologists, aware of the critical relationship between movement and language, may ask to provide services in conjunction with the physical educator or the adapted physical educator in the movement experience. The professionals serving the student will find that more language occurs in the context of play, leisure, recreation, and sport activities than in any other.

Like children who are deaf or hearing impaired, children with speech and language disorders have difficulty in play interactions.[3,18] The physical educator has a unique opportunity to help the child with a speech and language impairment develop critical developmental play skills.

Teaching Considerations

The primary focus of the physical educator is teaching the student with a speech and language disorder functional and developmentally appropriate play skills. The secondary focus is to increase the effectiveness of the student's gross motor, physical fitness, and leisure and recreation/sport skills in the same way the teacher develops those skills in typical students (see Table 16-11).

The physical educator must create a learning environment in the gymnasium and on the playground

Table 16-11	Physical Education Teachers' Strategies for Enhancing Interpersonal and Relationship Skills for Children Who Have Speech and Language Disorders

- Eliminate competitive activities from the physical education curriculum at the preschool, elementary school, and middle school levels.
- Emphasize cooperative activities, such as New Games.
- Teach specific skills:
  - Initiating play
  - Taking turns
  - Negotiating rules
  - Resolving conflict
  - Coping with success and failure
- Include socially appropriate behavioral expectations within gymnasium rules. Talk about the rules. Post the rules. Enforce the rules.
- Under no circumstances allow bullying behavior. The gymnasium must be considered a "bully-free zone."

Table 16-12	Facts about Bullying in the Schools[12]

- Over 160,000 children purposely miss school daily because they're afraid to go.
- One of every four children is bullied.
- Bullying occurs in *every* school and in *every* grade. There are no exceptions. Anyone who thinks otherwise is being extremely unrealistic.
- Girls bully other girls and even boys as much, if not more, than boys bully boys.
- Kids get bullied on the bus, in the bathroom and the halls, at recess, in the locker room, and in physical education.
- Kids have said that the following kids get bullied: new kids, fat kids, skinny kids, boys that don't do well in sports, boys that act gay, lesbians, kids who are smart, kids who are dumb, geeks, nerds, computer-freaks, kids who wear out-of-style clothes, kids who smell, teachers' pets, kids with dirty hair, "retarded" kids, kids who talk funny, kids who walk funny, kids in wheelchairs, kids who get good grades, kids who get bad grades, girls with blonde hair, kids who have freckles, kids who have funny-looking ears or noses, and kids with diseases—in other words, most kids.

that is "bully free." Unfortunately, children with speech and language disorders are often the targets of bullies; this makes their educational experience a threatening and frightening one (see Table 16-12).

Bullying is a series of repeated, intentionally cruel incidents, involving the same children in the same bully/victim roles. Bullying can also consist of a single interaction. The intention of bullying is to put the victim in distress in some way. Bullies seek power.[11,12] Unfortunately, teasing and bullying occur frequently in the locker room, in the gymnasium, and on the playground. Thus, the physical educator is a vital component of a schoolwide effort to address and eliminate bullying.

Schools that have been successful in eliminating bullying have used the following strategies:

- All students have a "safe haven" to which they can escape.

- At the "safe haven," students who have received particular experience as good listeners do just that for the student in trouble.
- The faculty and specially selected students have been trained to identify a student in crisis.
- The emphasis is on the 85 percent of the students who are neither the bully nor the victim in any given situation but who are uncomfortable and confused about what they see happening around them. Bully-proofing attempts to shift the balance of power to the silent majority and away from the bullies.[21]
- The physical educator can help teach specific skills to the students who are neither the bully nor the victim. Students can take action in many ways to help reduce bullying in their school. Refusing to watch bullying, reporting bullying incidents, and using distraction with either the bully or the victim are all effective ways of making a difference.

- Acts of kindness and a sense of shared responsibility toward others are encouraged and rewarded.
- First and foremost, teachers must make it safe for students to report bullying. It is crucial that teachers, administrators, and other school personnel respect the anonymity of the victim and/or reporting students. Until students trust this will happen, bullying will go unreported, and bullies will continue to thrive.[21]
- The physical educator can help teach bullies how to behave in a socially acceptable

manner; sometimes, they simply don't know another way to interact.
- The physical educator can help teach the victims how to develop friendship skills and learn to interact with assertiveness and confidence. Cooperative games are particularly effective in teaching these skills.
- The physical educator can help identify the "loner" and make a special effort to befriend the child. Usually, bullies pick on a child without a support group.

SUMMARY

Children with communicative delays and disorders may have a difficult time being successful in the educational environment. Though they may have excellent physical and motor skills, they may struggle with the psychosocial component of the physical education experience.

When working with students who are deaf or hard of hearing, physical educators are concerned primarily with the extent to which the hearing loss affects ability to participate in play, leisure, recreation, and sport activity. The classification of hearing loss is often based on the location of the problem within the hearing mechanism. Conductive losses interfere with the transfer of sound. Sensorineural problems result from damage to the inner ear and/or the 8th cranial nerve. Central hearing impairments occur at the brain stem or the auditory cortex. Hearing aids and cochlear implants are used to amplify sound and enhance the communication capability of individuals who are deaf or hard of hearing. Types of communication systems used to communicate with individuals who are deaf or hard of hearing are the

auditory-verbal (oral) method and the total communication method. Considerations for effective communication by teachers of the individuals who are deaf or hearing impaired during instruction are teacher-learner position, visual feedback, intensity of the commands, and special attention to the environment. Few changes are required in the physical education program. Athletic opportunities should be provided for students who are deaf or hard of hearing, so that they have the opportunity to participate in activities that will provide enjoyment and help maintain a healthy lifestyle after their school years.

Teaching the learner who is deaf-blind is challenging for the physical educator, but a good teacher can open up a world of leisure, recreation, sport, and fitness activities the learner who is deaf-blind can enjoy throughout a lifetime.

The physical educator, teaching children with speech and language-learning disorders, should focus on the development of functional and developmentally appropriate play and social skills. The physical educator should create and maintain a bully-free gymnasium and playground.

REVIEW QUESTIONS

1. What are the differences between prelingual and postlingual deafness?

2. What are the indicators of hearing loss that can be observed by the physical education teacher while teaching a class?

3. What strategies can the physical educator use to communicate with and teach the deaf and hearing impaired?

4. What are some teaching strategies that can be used with students who are deaf-blind?

5. What is the role of the physical educator who teaches children with speech and language-learning disorders?

6. What strategies can be used to create a bully-free environment in the gymnasium and on the playground?

STUDENT ACTIVITIES

1. Observe students who are deaf or hearing impaired participating in a physical education class. What teaching strategies were used by the teacher? What adaptations were made to accommodate the children in activity? What were the behavioral characteristics of the children?

2. Complete a community survey. What leisure, recreation, and sport opportunities are available in your community for adults who are hard of hearing or deaf?

3. Ask for permission to observe a middle school or high school physical education class. Watch for signs of bullying. Identify any students who appear to be frightened.

4. Practice using basic survival signs with a peer.

REFERENCES

1. American Speech-Language-Hearing Association: Position statement and guidelines for acoustics in educational settings, *ASHA* 37(Suppl. 4):15–19, 1995.

2. *Aphasia,* www.aphasia.org/_NAAfactsheet. html. 2003.

3. Asher SR, Gazelle A: Loneliness, peer relations, and language disorder in childhood, *Top Lang Disord* 19(2):16–33, 1999.

4. Bahr RH, Velleman SL, Ziegler MA: Meeting the challenge of suspected developmental apraxia of speech through inclusion, *Top Lang Disord* 19(3):19–35, 1999.

5. Beers MH, Porter RS, Jones TV, Kaplan JL, Berkwits M, editors: *The Merck manual of diagnosis and therapy.* Whitehouse Station, NJ, Merck Research Laboratories, 2006.

6. BEGINNINGS for Parents of Children Who are Deaf or Hard of Hearing, Inc., www.ncbegin.com/communication_options/total_communication.shtml, 2007.

7. Best C, Lieberman L, Arndt K: Effective use of interpreters in general physical education, *JOPERD* 73(8):45–50, 2002.

8. Blosser JL, Kratcoski A: PACs: A framework for determining appropriate service delivery options, *Lang Speech Hear Serv Schools* 28:99–107, 1996.

9. Bowe F: *Approaching equality: Education of the deaf.* Silver Springs, MD, TJ Publishers, 1991.

10. Brackett D: Intervention for children with hearing impairment in general education settings, *Lang Speech Hear Serv Schools,* 28:355–361, 1997.

11. *Bully beware,* www.bullybeware.com. 2003.

12. *Bully,* www.members.tripod.com/_ ~Ghoul2x/Bully3A.html. 2003.

13. Butterfield SA, Ersing WF: Influence of age, sex, etiology and hearing loss on balance performance by deaf children, *Percept Mot Skills* 62:659–663, 1986.

14. Butterfield SA, et al.: Kinematic analysis of a dynamic balance task by children who are deaf, *Clin Kines* 52(4):72–78, 1998.

15. Cambra C: A comparative study of personality descriptors attributed to the deaf, the blind, and individuals with no sensory disability, *Am Ann Deaf* 141(1):24–28, 1996.

16. Cochlear Corporation: Package insert for Nucleus 24 Contour (brochure). Sydney, Australia, 2000.

17. Cohen N, et al.: Unsuspected language impairment in psychiatrically disturbed children: Prevalence and language and behavioral characteristics, *J Am Acad Child Adol Psychiat* 32:595–603, 1993.

18. Craig HK, Washington JA: Access behaviors of children with specific language impairment, *J Speech Hear Res* 36:322–337, 1993.

19. Crowe T, Horak F: Motor proficiency associated with vestibular deficits in children with hearing impairments, *Phys Ther* 68:1493–1499, 1988.

20. Davis M, et al.: The hearing aid effect in African American and Caucasian males as perceived by female judges of the same race, *Lang Speech Hear Serv Schools* 30: 165–172, 1999.

21. Devine School, www.lcbe.edu.on.ca/sites/Devine/bully.html. 2003.

22. DiPietro MA, Williams P, Kaplan H: *Alerting and communicating devices for deaf and hard of hearing people—what's new.* Laurent Clerc National Deaf Education Center, Gallaudet University, http://clerccenter.gallaudet.edu/InfoToGo/418.html, 2007.

23. Duquette C, Durieux-Smith A, Olds J, Fitzpatrick E, Eriks-Brophy A, Whittingham J: Parents' perspectives on their roles in facilitating the inclusion of their children with hearing impairment, *Exceptionality Education Canada* 12(1):19–36, 2002.

24. Easterbrooks S: Improving practices for students with hearing impairments, *Except Child* 65(4):537–554, 1999.

25. Eichstaedt CB, Seiler P: Communicating with hearing impaired individuals in a physical education setting, *JOPERD* May:19–21, 1978.

26. Ellis K: Influences of parents and school on sports participation and fitness levels of deaf children, *Palaestra* 17(1):44–49, 2001.

27. Finitzo T, Albright K, O'Neal J: The newborn with hearing loss: Detection in the nursery, *Pediatrics* 102(6):1452–1460, 1998.

28. Fujiki M, Brinton B, Todd C: Social skills of children with specific language impairment, *Lang Speech Hear Serv Schools* 27:195–201, 1996.

29. Gallaudet University, http://clerccenter.gallaudet.edu/InfoToGo/418.html. 2003.

30. Garay S: Listening to the voices of deaf students, *Teaching Except Child* 35(4):44–48, 2002.

31. Geers AE, Nicholas JG, Sedey AL: Language skills of children with early cochlear implantation, *Ear and Hearing* 24(1) (Supp.):46S–58S, 2003.

32. Grimes UK, Prickett HT: Developing and enhancing a positive self-concept in deaf children, *Am Ann Deaf* 133:4, 1988.

33. Hall B, Oyer H, Haas W: *Speech, language, and hearing disorders: A guide for teachers.* Boston, Allyn & Bacon, 2001.

34. Hicks C, Tharpe A: Listening effort and fatigue in school-age children with and without hearing loss, *J Speech, Lang & Hearing Research* 45(3):573–585, 2002.

35. Hilgenbrinck L: *Disability fact sheet on cochlear implants.* Project INSPIRE, www.twu.edu/INSPIRE. 2003.

36. Holcomb TK: Development of deaf bicultural identity, *Am Ann Deaf* 142(2):89–93, 1997.

37. *IDEA part B trend data,* www.ideadata.org/PartBTrendDataFiles.asp.

38. Individuals with Disabilities Education Act Amendments of 1997 [PL 105–17].

39. Janssen MJ, Riksen-Walraven M, Van Dijk J: Contact: Effects of an intervention program to foster harmonious interactions between deaf-blind children and their educators, *J Vis Impair & Blindness,* April:215–229, 2003.

40. Karchmer MA, Allen TA: The functional assessment of deaf and hard of hearing students, *Am Ann Deaf* 144(2):68–77, 1999.

41. Kereiakes TJ: Clinical evaluation and treatment of vocal disorders. *Lang Speech Hearing Serv Schools* 27:240–243, 1996.

42. *Kid speech,* www.kidspeech.com/signs.html. 2003.

43. Kummer AW, Lee L: Evaluation and treatment of resonance disorders, *Lang Speech Hear Serv Schools* 27:271–280, 1996.

44. Lieberman L: Fitness for individuals who are visually impaired or deaf-blind, *Re:view* 34(1):13–23, 2002.

45. Lieberman L, Dunn J, van der Mars H, McCubbin J: Peer tutors' effects on activity levels of deaf students in inclusive elementary physical education, *APAQ* 17(1):20–39, 2000.

46. Lieberman L, Stuart M: Self-determined recreation and leisure choices of individuals with deaf-blindness, *J Visual Impairment & Blindness* 96(10):724–736, 2002.

47. Ling D: *Early total communication intervention: An introduction in early intervention for hearing-impaired children: Total communication options.* San Diego, CA, College Hill Press, 1984.

48. Loizou P: Introduction to cochlear implants, *IEEE Signal Processing Magazine* September:101–130, 1998.

49. Luckner J, Bowen S, Carter K: Visual teaching strategies for students who are deaf or hard of hearing, *Teaching Except Child* 33(3):38–44, 2001.

50. Lyon GR: *Overview of reading and literacy initiatives.* Paper presented to the Committee on Labor and Human Resources, Washington, DC, April 1998.

51. Lyon ME: Symbolic play and language development in young deaf children, *Deafness and Ed* 21(2):10–20, 1997.

52. Lytle RR, Rovins MR: Reforming deaf education: A paradigm shift from how to teach to what to teach, *Am Ann Deaf* 142(1):7–15, 1997.

53. Martinez C, Silvestre N: Self-concept in profoundly deaf adolescent pupils, *Inter J Psychol* 30(3):309–316, 1995.

54. Matkin ND, Wilcox AM: Considerations in the education of children with hearing loss, *Ped Clin North Am* 46(1):143–152, 1999.

55. Minter MG: Factors which may prevent full self-expression of deaf athletes in sports, *Palaestra* 5:36–38, 1989.

56. Morgan S: "What is my role?" A comparison of the responsibilities of interpreters, intervenors, and support service providers, *Deaf-Blind Perspectives* 9(1):1–3, 2001.

57. Most T, Weisel A, Tur-Kaspa H: Contact with students with hearing impairments and the evaluation of speech intelligibility and personal qualities, *J Spec Ed* 33(2):103–111, 1999.

58. NICHCY, www.kidsource.com/NICHCY/speech.htm. 2003.

59. National Institute on Deafness and Other Communication Disorders: *Cochlear implants,* www.nidcd.nih.gov/health/hearing/coch.asp. 2003

60. National Institute on Deafness and Other Communication Devices, www.nidcd.nih.gov. 2007.

61. National Institute on Deafness and Other Communication Disorders: *Hearing aids,* www.nidcd.nih.gov/health/hearing/hearingaid.asp. 2003

62. Nowell R, Marshak, L: An orientation for professionals working with deaf clients. In Nowell R, Marshak L, editors: *Understanding deafness and the rehabilitation process.* Boston, Allyn & Bacon, 1994.

63. O'Rourke IJ: *ABC's of signing.* Silver Springs, MD, National Association of the Deaf, 1987.

64. Pakulski L, Kaderavek J: Children with minimal hearing loss: Interventions in the classroom, *Interventions in School & Clinic* 38(2):96–104, 2002.

65. Palmer CV: Hearing and listening in a typical classroom, *Lang Speech Hear Serv Schools* 28:213–217, 1997.

66. Parasnis I: Cultural identity and diversity in deaf education, *Am Ann Deaf* 142(2):72–79, 1997.

67. Paul P, Quigley S: *Education and deafness.* New York, Longman, 1990.

68. Reagan T: Cultural considerations in the education of deaf children. In Moores DF, Meadow-Orlans KP, editors: *Education and development of aspects of deafness.* Washington, DC, Gallaudet University Press, 1990.

69. Reed VA, McLeod K, McAllister L: Importance of selected communication skills for talking with peers and teachers: Adolescents' opinions, *Lang Speech Hear Serv Schools* 30:32–49, 1999.

70. Rieffe C, Terwogt M, Smit C: Deaf children on the causes of emotions, *Educational Psychology* 23(2):159–168.

71. Ross M, Brackett D, Maxon AB, editors: *Assessment and management of mainstreamed hearing-impaired children.* Austin, TX, PRO-ED, 1991.

72. Siegel J, Marchetti M, Tecclin J: Age-related balance changes in hearing-impaired children, *Phys Ther* 71:183–189, 1991.

73. Singer BD, Bashir AS: What are executive functions and self-regulation and what do they have to do with language-learning disorders? *Lang Speech Hear Serv Schools* 30:265–273, 1999.

74. Stewart DA: *Deaf sport: The impact of sports within the deaf community.* Washington, DC, Gallaudet University Press, 1991.

75. Stinson M: Affective and social development. In Nowell R, Marshak L, editors: *Understanding deafness and the rehabilitation process.* Boston, Allyn & Bacon, 1994.

76. *Stuttering,* www.mankato.msus.edu/dept/comdis/kuster/stutter.html. 2003.

77. Uchanski RM, Geer AE: Acoustic characteristics of the speech of young cochlear implant users: A comparison with normal-hearing age-mates, *Ear and Hearing* 24(1)(Supp.):90S–105S, 2003.

78. USA Deaf Sport Foundation, www.usadsf.org. 2003.

79. US Deaf Sports, Inc., www.usdeafsports.org. 2007.

80. Wegner J, Grosche K, Edmister E: Students with speech and language disorders, *Effective Education for Learners with Exceptionalities* 15:181–193, 2003.

81. Wheeler L, Griffin HC: A movement-based approach to language development in children who are deaf-blind, *Am Ann Deaf* 142(5):387–390, 1997.

82. *Widesmiles,* http://Widesmiles.org. 2003.

SUGGESTED READINGS

Lieberman LJ, Houston WC: *Strategies for inclusion: A handbook for physical educators.* Champaign, IL, Human Kinetics, 2002.

RECOMMENDED WEB SITES   WWW

Please keep in mind that these Web sites are being recommended in the winter of 2007. As Web sites often change, they may have moved or been reconfigured or eliminated.

Handspeak
www.handspeak.com

USA Deaf Sports Federation
www.usdeafsports.org

Kid Speech
www.kidspeech.com

National Consortium on Deaf-Blindness
www.tr.wou.edu/dblink

National Institute on Deafness and Other Communication Disorders
www.nidcd.nih.gov

RECOMMENDED VIDEOS

Fanlight Productions
PO Box 1084
Harriman, NY 10926
1-800-937-4113
www.fanlight.com

A Sign of the Times
#236/VHS/1996/25 min/$149

Voices in a Deaf Theater
#229/VHS/1996/24 min/$149

See What I'm Saying
CINE Golden Eagle 5 Star Award
#090/DVD/VHS/1992/31 min/$199

Insight Media
2164 Broadway
New York, NY 10024-0621
1-800-233-9910
www.insight-media.com

Communication Disorders: An Introductory Guide for Teachers
#4AN2270/DVD/2000/18 min/$149

Communication Options for Deaf Children
#4AN2305/VHS/2002/18 min/$149

Sense of Hearing: Cochlear Implants
#4AN3387/DVD/2002/60 min/$189

The following videos are available at a local video rental store:
Children of a Lesser God
For a Deaf Son
The Heart Is a Lonely Hunter
In the Land of the Deaf
Mr. Holland's Opus
The Miracle Worker

Visual Impairments

■ **O B J E C T I V E S**

Identify and describe three types of visual impairments.

List the general characteristics of children who are congenitally blind.

List five ways to modify the play environment to make it safe for students who are blind.

List eight ways to modify activities to accommodate a sightless learner.

Describe devices specially designed to enable sport participation by individuals with limited or no sight.

Describe a process for integrating individuals with and without sight into a sporting activity.

Young Cancer Patients Take Time Away from Treatment at the MD Anderson Cancer Center in Houston, Texas, to Ski with the National Ability Center, Using Bi-Skis as Seen, Outriggers, and Other Adaptive Equipment

Rossmiller Photography

Visual impairments include both permanent and functional conditions. Children with visual disorders represent a unique challenge to the physical educator, because in addition to their visual impairments they usually demonstrate developmental lags. Many of these children have not had opportunities to physically explore the environment during their early years. As a result, intact sensory-motor systems are not stimulated adequately, and motor development suffers. Low vitality and perceptual-motor development lags can prevent the children from participating in activities not contraindicated by the primary visual disorder.

CASE STUDY

Hosea

Hosea is a 12-year-old Hispanic boy who lives in a small town in a southwestern state. He was diagnosed as blind as a result of retinopathy of prematurity (born prematurely and placed on high concentrations of oxygen during the first few months of life). He is an only child who has an identified learning disability and a mild seizure disorder that is controlled with medication. He received educational intervention by a vision specialist from the age of 6 months to 2 years. Currently, he is in 5th grade, 2 years behind his peers of the same age.

Although it is reported that Hosea did not walk until age 2 years and he exhibits poor self-help and social skills, his motor skills are quite good. Even though he is totally blind, his balance and most locomotor skills are excellent; however, he has not yet developed cross-lateral integration (e.g., he has a midline problem). His cardiovascular endurance, body composition, and abdominal and upper body strength are all within the average range; however, his flexibility as measured by the sit-and-reach test is below the 25th percentile for his age group.

CRITICAL THINKING TASK

As you read the chapter, think about ways to include Hosea in an inclusive physical education class and eventually in community recreation settings with sighted participants.

DEFINITION OF VISUAL IMPAIRMENTS

There are varying degrees of visual impairment. Individuals at one end of the continuum have little residual vision and are unable to perceive motion and discriminate light. If a person is not totally blind, it is still possible to make functional use of whatever vision remains. Some persons who are considered blind are capable of perceiving distance and motion but do not have enough residual vision to travel; others, although classified as legally blind, can perceive distance and motion

and have enough usable residual vision to move about with a minimal amount of assistance.

Children with loss of vision are, for educational purposes, classified as partially sighted, low vision, legally blind, and totally blind. The term "partially sighted" indicates some type of visual problem that requires a need for special education. These persons have less than 20/70 visual acuity in the better eye after correction, have a progressive eye disorder that will probably reduce vision below 20/70, or have a very limited field of vision (20 degrees at its widest point). The term "low vision" refers to a severe visual impairment, not necessarily limited to distance vision. Individuals with low vision are unable to read a newspaper at the normal viewing distance, even with the aid of glasses or contact lenses. "Legally blind" persons are those who have visual acuity of 20/200 or less in the better eye after maximum correction or a very limited field of vision (20 degrees at its widest point). Totally blind persons must use braille or other nonvisual media to learn.[24]

For a child to qualify under the law for special services in physical education, the visual disability must adversely affect the child's physical education performance. Children with visual disorders who qualify for adapted/developmental physical education programs demonstrate one or both of the following:

1. A visual disability that, even with correction, adversely affects the child's educational performance; the term "visual disability" includes partially sighted, low vision, and legally blind children
2. Hearing and visual impairments that occur together, the combination of which causes such severe communication and other developmental and educational problems that the child cannot be accommodated in special education programs solely for deaf or blind children

Functional conditions not covered under the law that have an impact on motor performance efficiency are depth perception, eye-hand coordination, visual form perception, visual memory, visual-spatial development, and visual-spatial integration. Children who have any of these conditions may experience movement problems, even though they are not classified as visually impaired.

INCIDENCE OF VISUAL IMPAIRMENTS

In 2007 there were 10 million blind and visually impaired persons in the United States, 1.3 million classified as legally blind.[2]

CAUSES OF VISUAL IMPAIRMENTS

The underlying causes of visual loss are existing visual conditions, structural anomalies, and inefficient extraocular muscle control. Existing conditions impact the integrity of the visual impulse in the eye, on the optic nerve, or in the visual cortex. These conditions include diabetes, accidents and injuries, poisoning, tumors, excessive oxygen at birth, and prenatal influences, such as rubella and syphilis. Structural anomalies include deviations of the eye structure. Functional causes that compromise visual efficiency are extraocular muscle imbalances caused by postural deviations, poor reading habits, and visual acuity problems.

Visual Conditions

Visual conditions that affect visual acuity include congenital causes, diseases, insult or injury to the eye, and aging. Two congenital causes are albinism and retinitis pigmentosa. With albinism, there is a lack of pigment in the eyes. Extreme light sensitivity may require the use of dark glasses. Retinitis pigmentosa is a hereditary condition in which the retinal rods become defective, which initially reduces night vision. Retinopathy of prematurity is an example of injury to the retina caused by excess oxygen during incubation of premature babies. Cataracts can be caused by aging, exposure to X rays, disease, smoking, or exposure to heat from infrared or ultraviolet light.[4] Cataracts cause an opacity of the normally transparent lens. Glaucoma is generally considered a disorder resulting from aging; however, it can occur in any age group.[4] Glaucoma creates increased pressure

inside the eye, which results in visual loss and decreased peripheral vision. As deterioration continues, central vision is reduced.

Structural Anomalies

Structural abnormalities of the eye alter the way light waves are bent (refracted) as they move into or through the eye. The resulting visual problems are called refractive errors. They include hyperopia, myopia, and astigmatism. Hyperopia, or farsightedness, is a condition in which the light rays focus behind the retina, causing an unclear image of objects closer than 20 feet from the eye. The term implies that distant objects can be seen with less strain than near objects. Myopia, or nearsightedness, is a refractive error in which the rays of light focus in front of the retina when a person views an object 20 feet or more away. Astigmatism is a refractive error caused by an irregularity in the curvature of the cornea, so that portions of the light rays from a given object fall behind or in front of the retina. As a result, vision may be blurry.

Inefficient Extraocular Muscle Control

Singular binocular vision involves coordinating the separate images that enter each eye into a single image in the visual cortex of the brain. When the two eyes function in unison and are coordinated, the images entering the eyes are matched in the visual cortex, and binocular fusion results. If, however, the supply of energy to one or more of the six extraocular muscles attached to the outside of each eyeball is out of balance, the eyes do not function in unison. When this occurs, the images from one eye deviate from those of the other eye, and the images do not match in the visual cortex. The amount of visual distress experienced because of mismatched images (strabismus) depends on the degree of deviation of the eyes and the ability of the central nervous system to correct the imbalance. Amblyopia results when the image from an eye has been suppressed by the brain for a long time because a conflict exists between the two eyes. The eye with amblyopia does not function because the brain will not accept the deviant image. Individuals who use each eye independently from the other, suppressing first one eye and then the other, are known as alternators. When a person has visual suppression problems with one or both eyes, depth perception is always compromised.

The two most prevalent dysfunctions resulting from lack of extraocular muscle balance are heterotropias and heterophorias. Heterotropias are manifest malalignments of the eyes during which one or both eyes consistently deviate from the central axis. As a consequence, the eyes do not fixate at the same point on the object of visual attention. Tropias always create depth perception difficulties.

Heterophorias are tendencies toward visual malalignments. They usually do not cause serious visual distress because, when slight variations in binocular fusion occur in the visual cortex, the central nervous system tends to correct the imbalance between the pull of the extraocular muscles. However, after prolonged use of the eyes, such as after reading for several hours, the stronger set of muscles overcomes the correction and the eyes swing out of alignment. An individual becomes aware of the malalignment when the vision of the printed page begins to blur. Phorias create depth perception difficulties only after the correction is lost.

Nystagmus involves rapid movement of the eyes from side to side, up and down, in a rotatory motion, or a combination of these. See Table 17-1 for descriptions of visual impairment conditions and specialists.

CHARACTERISTICS OF VISUAL IMPAIRMENTS

Vision loss has serious implications for the general development of motor, academic, intellectual, psychological, and social characteristics. There are widespread individual differences among persons with limited vision. However, certain characteristics appear more often than in sighted persons. Some of the characteristics that have implications for physical education are motor development, physical fitness, and psychological and social adjustment.

Motor Development

Limited vision restricts physical motor activity, which limits the range and variety of experiences the children may encounter. Infants who are blind have little motivation to hold the head up because of lack of visual stimulation; as a result, all postural development, including trunk control, sitting, and standing, is delayed. Because postural control precedes gross and fine motor development, these children are slow to walk, run, skip, reach, grasp, and develop other gross and fine motor skills.

The child with normal sight makes judgments as to where objects are in space by pairing sensory information from vision with movement information received when moving to and from objects. Because persons with severe visual impairments cannot visually compare objects at varying distances in the environment, they are unable to formulate visual judgments.

The child with a severe visual impairment is often unaware of the movement potential of body parts. This lack of awareness of potential may restrict movements, which retards the development of the muscles and balancing mechanisms needed for the development of complex motor skills.

Studies have confirmed these delays. Ribadi, Rider, and Toole[25] indicate that congenitally blind individuals are less capable on static and dynamic balance tasks than are their sighted peers. The ways that delayed balance impact movement patterns were described by Gordon and Gavron.[12] They studied 28 running parameters of sighted and blind runners and found that, as a group, the blind runners did not have sufficient forward lean while running. They demonstrated insufficient hip, knee, and ankle extension at takeoff, which limited their power, and their range of motion of the hip and the ankle was limited. The play of preschool children with visual impairments lags behind that of children with sight. Children with low vision demonstrate play behavior more advanced than that of children who are functionally blind.[14]

Table 17-1	Visual Impairment Conditions and Specialists
Term	**Description**
Alternator	Uses each eye independently of the other (e.g., one eye may be used for near-point activities and the other for distance activities)
Amblyopia	A type of strabismus that causes the affected eye to be nonfunctional
Astigmatism	A refractive error caused by an irregularity in the curvature of the cornea of the lens; vision may be blurred
Esophoria	A tendency for an eye to deviate medially toward the nose
Esotropia	A condition in which the eye(s) turn(s) inward (cross-eyed)
Exophoria	A tendency for an eye to deviate laterally away from the nose
Exotropia	A condition in which the eye(s) turn(s) outward
Hyperopia	A condition in which the light rays focus behind the retina, causing an unclear image of objects closer than 20 feet from the eye (farsighted)
Hyperphoria	A tendency for an eye to deviate in an upward direction
Hypertropia	A condition in which one or both eyes swing upward
Hypophoria	A tendency for an eye to deviate in a downward direction
Hypotropia	A condition in which one or both eyes swing downward
Myopia	A condition in which the light rays focus in front of the retina when a person views an object 20 feet or more away from the eye (nearsighted)
Nystagmus	Rapid movement of the eyes from side to side, up and down, in a rotatory motion, or in a combination of these motions
Ophthalmologist	A licensed physician specializing in the treatment of eye diseases and optical defects
Optician	A technician who grinds lenses and makes glasses
Optometrist	A specialist in examining the eyes for optical defects and fitting glasses to correct those defects
Orthoptic vision	The ability to use the extraocular muscles of the eyes in unison
Orthoptician	A person who provides eye exercises to refine control of the eye (e.g., visual developmental specialist)
Refractive vision	The process by which light rays bend as they enter or pass through the eyes
Tunnel vision	A loss of side vision (also called peripheral vision) while retaining clear central vision
Visual developmental specialist	An optometrist or ophthalmologist with specialized training in evaluating and correcting orthoptic visual problems

Physical Fitness

Individuals with visual impairments demonstrate a wide range of physical fitness. Individuals who adopt a passive lifestyle can be expected to demonstrate poor physical fitness; however, when appropriate activity programs are available, individuals who are blind can develop excellent levels of physical fitness.[5] Children with visual impairments have less muscular and cardiovascular endurance, less muscular strength, and more body fat than children who are sighted.[19] Kleeman and Rimmer[16] tested 30 adults with visual impairments and

reported that over 70 percent scored in the average range on cardiovascular endurance, Body Mass Index, and flexibility. Their scores for sit-ups were slightly below average, and 23 percent were categorized as overweight.

Psychological and Social Adjustment

The emotional and social characteristics of persons who are visually limited vary. Depending on early life experiences, students who are blind may have personality problems as well as physical incapacities. Research regarding the social maturity

A Totally Blind Child Learns to Relax and Enjoy the Water

Photo by Carol Huettig.

of children who are blind reveals that, in general, they receive significantly lower social maturity scores than do sighted children.[10]

The psychological and social adjustment of individuals with severe visual impairments depends a great deal on the extent and success of their interactions with others.[21] Sighted persons acquire social habits by observing and imitating people they esteem. Individuals with severe visual impairments do not have the same opportunity to develop those skills because they are unable to observe social interactions. Any limitation in observing and interpreting the gestures of individuals as they talk limits the information about what a person is attempting to communicate. Lack of opportunity to read body language and assess the social surroundings in terms of what is appropriate may limit the social development of individuals who are blind.

Some individuals who are blind may exhibit self-stimulatory behavior, or blindisms, such as rocking the body or head, placing fingers or fists into the eyes, flicking the fingers in front of the face, and spinning the body around repetitiously. The cause of these self-stimulatory behaviors is unknown; however, it is suspected that the individuals are attempting to access vestibular, kinesthetic, and tactile stimuli to substitute for loss of visual stimulation. Efforts to eliminate these behaviors seldom are successful for any length of time.[23]

TESTING

Children with visual disabilities must be approached in accordance with their unique educational needs. A child who has a loss of vision also may be impaired in the function of mobility and may be less able than sighted children in motor abilities. There is a great need for children with visual impairments to be provided with opportunities, through physical education, that will compensate for their movement deficiencies. All children who are blind or partially sighted should have a full evaluation as to the degree of visual loss.

Physical fitness and motor proficiency and skill tests should be administered to all students, regardless of visual status. Physical fitness tests that might be used include the Brockport Physical Fitness Test, M.O.B.I.L.T.E.E., and Physical Best. To determine motor proficiency, the balance and bilateral coordination portions of the Bruininks-Oseretsky Motor Proficiency Test are recommended. Motor skills can be assessed using the Test of Gross Motor Development. Regardless of what tests are used, modifications must be made to accommodate the lack of vision. Recommendations for exercise testing are presented in Table 17-2. When testing sport skills, a hitting tee or cone should be used, rather than throwing the ball, and a ball to be kicked should be placed in front of the person's foot.

Two excellent instruments to use to document how youth participate in everyday activities outside of mandated school activities is the Children's Assessment of Participation and Enjoyment (CAPE) and Preference for Activities of Children (PAC). It can be used to measure formal and informal physical-based activity and self-improvement activities. It is designed for use with youth between the ages of 6 and 21 years.[15]

Vision tests are extremely important in order to identify and remedy vision disorders and to facilitate the education of visually disabled persons. The Snellen test, which is a measure of visual acuity, is widely used. This test can be administered with expediency to a child by nonprofessional personnel and is applicable to young children. The Snellen test primarily is used to detect myopia (nearsightedness). It does not give indications of near-point vision, peripheral vision, convergence ability, binocular fusion ability, or oculomotor dysfunctions. A thorough vision screening program must include tests supplementary to the Snellen test. Other visual screening tests that may provide additional information are the Keystone Telebinocular test, which measures depth perception, and the Orthoptor test, which measures acuity, phoria, central fusion, and colorblindness.

Limitations in peripheral vision constitute a visual disability, particularly in some activities involving motor skills. Consequently, knowledge of this aspect of vision may help the physical educator determine teaching methods and types of activities for the visually impaired child. Peripheral vision is usually assessed in terms of degrees of visual arc and is measured by the extent to which a standard visual stimulus can be seen on a black background from a distance of about 39 inches when the eye is fixed on a central point.[20]

It is difficult to evaluate the results of a given test of vision because two persons with similar visual characteristics on a screening test may display different physical, social, and psychological behaviors. Although objective screening tests of vision are important, daily observations should be made to supplement the screening tests. Daily observation for the symptoms of eye trouble has particular importance in the early primary years. The detection of visual disabilities early in development enables early intervention, which maximizes skill development. Symptoms that might indicate eye disorders and might be observed by educators appear in Table 17-3.

New techniques for evaluating vision and assisting individuals with visual disorders are available through low vision clinics. This training assists the person with a visual impairment to use what vision he or she has to maximum. Low vision aids include magnifying lenses, field enlargement lens systems, telescopic lenses mounted on eyewear frames, sensors, lasers, and nonoptical aids, such as special illumination, filters and large print materials, and electronic TV monitor magnification systems.[6]

Table 17-2	**Recommendations for Exercise Testing[5]**

Have all instructions described verbally or on audiotape.

Allow the person to describe or demonstrate the test protocol before the test begins.

Give tactile and verbal reinforcement to motivate the participant.

Allow the person to lightly touch handrails or the tester when necessary.

Table 17-3	Symptoms Indicative of Common Disorders of the Eye

1. Confuses right/left directions
2. Complaints of dizziness or frequent headaches
3. Poor balance
4. Frequent rubbing of the eyes
5. Difficulty concentrating; short attention span; easily distracted
6. Difficulty following a moving target
7. Squinting
8. Eyes turn in or out
9. Walking overcautiously
10. Faltering or stumbling
11. Running into objects not directly in the line of vision
12. Failure to see objects readily visible to others
13. Sensitivity to normal light levels
14. Difficulty in estimating distances
15. Complaints of double vision
16. Going down steps one at a time
17. Poor hand-eye and/or foot-eye coordination
18. Avoidance of climbing apparatus
19. Holding the head close to the desk during paper-and-pencil tasks
20. Turning the head and using only one eye while moving

Modified from The Visual Fitness Institute Symptoms of Visual Skill Disorders Web site (http://visualfitness.com/symptoms.html).[31]

Functional visual problems related to misalignment of the eyes are frequently treated using vision training, or vision therapy, defined as "the teaching and training process for the improvement of visual perception and/or the coordination of the two eyes for efficient and comfortable binocular vision."[27] The purpose of vision therapy is to treat functional deficiencies in order for the person to achieve optimum efficiency and comfort.[7] Although the value of this type of therapy has long been debated, when carried out by well-trained visual behavioral specialists, there is strong scientific support for its efficacy in modifying and improving oculomotor, accommodative, and binocular system disorders.[3]

SPECIAL CONSIDERATIONS

Differences between Congenital and Adventitious Visual Impairments

There are two basic types of visual impairments: (1) congenital, those present at birth, and (2) adventitious, those acquired after birth. The onset of blindness has an impact on the development of the child.

The child with congenital blindness lacks visual information on which motor responses may be built. Also, overprotection may hamper the development of the individual who is congenitally blind. Frequently, parents and teachers tend to restrict the activity of children who are blind.[19] The overprotection complicates development because the child is not permitted to explore the environments necessary for the development of motor responses. It is obvious that, depending on when blindness occurred, the child who is blinded after birth will have some opportunities to explore environments and receive environmental information through the visual senses for development. Previous sight experience impacts favorably on the physical and motor development of adventitiously blind persons. However, they are usually despondent over their loss of sight and need assistance in adjusting and coping. The sooner intervention counseling can begin, the better.

Orientation and Mobility Training

Mobility is the ability to move from one point to a second point. Orientation is the ability to relate body position to other objects in space. Obviously, these abilities are related and required for efficient movement in a variety of environments.

Orientation and mobility training is an adaptive technique that applies to children with visual impairments. It enables them to learn about their physical play areas. This training increases their confidence in moving with greater authority and provides greater safety while they are participating. It is a valuable way to enhance participation in the physical education program.

There are prerequisites to efficient orientation and mobility training. Some of these are (1) sound discrimination, (2) sound location, (3) concentration, (4) memorization, (5) retention of information, and (6) physical skill. These prerequisite skills provide the environmental awareness needed for travel. Deficits in these prerequisites may be a deterrent to proficient performance.

Although professionals use specific techniques in orientation and mobility training, physical educators can reinforce many of the concepts that are a part of sophisticated training programs. Goodman[11] suggests that routes be learned for both indoors and outdoors. Routes are organized in units and are purposely chosen courses from starting to finishing points for which a strategy is developed. Routes are selected according to the blind student's skills, interests, and needs. Usually, routes progress in difficulty from simple, straightforward routes to more complicated ones. Activities in the physical education class that would reinforce professional orientation and mobility training programs are (1) practice walking straight lines while maintaining good posture, (2) locate sounds in the environment, (3) follow instructions where movements have to be made that conform to the instructions (memory), (4) practice the reproduction of specific walking distances with respect to time, (5) find one's way back to starting points on different surfaces, and (6) practice changing body positions.

Orientation and mobility training programs should help visually impaired persons cope effectively with physical surroundings.[11] Training programs should also help them interact with their peers, as well as with the physical facilities and equipment. The teacher should remember that some persons with visual impairments have travel vision. The capabilities of each child should be assessed to determine the extent of the appropriate orientation and mobility training program.

TEACHING STRATEGIES

The Teacher

The effective physical education teacher respects all students, regardless of their ability level; is a skilled observer of motor performance; recognizes and accommodates individual differences; and uses teaching methods and curricula appropriate for the students. Such professionals establish educational environments conducive to optimum growth. They assess the needs, abilities, and limitations of all of their students and design a program to meet those needs. These are challenging tasks for all teachers; however, those who instruct students with visual impairments have an added dimension to their work. Rather than using the old standby, demonstration, as their main form of communicating a desired movement, they must be prepared to substitute a variety of other forms of sensory experiences that are meaningful to the student with a visual impairment.

A study by Lieberman, Houston-Wilson, and Kozub identified reasons general physical educators were hesitant to include children with visual impairments in their classes. The physical educators studied reported a lack of (1) professional preparation, (2) appropriate equipment, (3) adequate programming, and (4) time in the schedule.[18] Teachers who have had some experience with students who have low vision or are blind are more positive about including this population in the general physical educational environment. To enhance the attitude about including individuals with visual impairments in the general physical educational environment, it has been suggested that the physical education teacher be given the opportunity to observe the student in the classroom setting and be provided workshops on ways to teach these students effectively.[32] Adults with visual impairments who attended public school during the 1980s reported that their experience could have been improved if their physical educators had had more knowledge about visual impairments and had provided more information about health, wellness, and the benefits of exercise[16]. Some excellent ideas teachers can use to enhance the perceived competence of children with visual impairments are presented in Table 17–4.

Teaching Modifications

The child who has visual limitations must depend on receiving information through sensory media

Table 17-4	**Strategies to Improve Perceived Competence in Children with Visual Impairments**[28]

- Introduce role models.
- Use motor behavior assessments.
- Use guided discovery as a teaching method.
- Use peer tutors.
- Increase opportunities for independent mobility.
- Facilitate social interaction during lunch.
- Teach students to take the initiative to get involved in activities.

other than vision. Audition is a very important sensory medium of instruction. Another sensory medium that can be used is kinesthesis. The correct feel of the movement can be communicated through manual guidance administered by an instructor or another student. Also, because the child with visual limitations has little or no understanding of spatial concepts, such as location, position, direction, and distance, skin and muscular sensations that arise when the student is moved through the activity area provide the information he or she needs to participate. The manual guidance method accompanied by verbal corrections is often effective in the correction of faulty motor skills because two senses are used for instruction. A technique that has met with some success in integrated classes is for the teacher to use the child who has a visual impairment in presenting a demonstration to the rest of the class by manually manipulating the child through the desired movements. This enables the child who is being used to demonstrate to get the tactual feel of movement, and instruction to the sighted class members is not deterred. Providing information, rules, and tests in braille for advance study of a class presentation may enable the visually limited child to better understand the presentation.

Persons with visual limitations need concrete experiences with objects and events for learning to occur. To promote participation with sighted players, Richardson and Mastro[26] suggest that audible balls be used for relay and in such games

as "Steal the Bacon." With the audible ball, blind players can know where the ball is most of the time. For bowling, Stanley and Kindig[30] suggest that improvised rope guide rails in conjunction with a carefully placed carpet can be used to identify foot positions and distance traveled during the instruction of a four-step approach. The carpet may replace the permanence of a guide rail and enable less restricted participation in bowling alleys; also, the carpet can be rolled and transported conveniently. Individuals with visual impairments can participate in alpine skiing with the help of a guide who stays within 5 to 8 feet of the skier with low vision. The guide and the skier ski independently; however, the guide keeps an eye on both the course and the skier who is visually impaired.

Both guide wires and guide runners have been shown to be effective for runners. Guide wires are ropes or heavy string stretched 36 inches above the lane markers; they help runners feel the perimeters of the lane. Even elementary-age children can learn to run using some form of guidance.[17] A guide runner is a person who runs alongside the visually impaired runner and verbally describes the distance to the finish. In competition, the guide runner is also permitted to touch the elbow of a runner who has a visual impairment to indicate any lateral off-step.[22]

Because of the great visual content included in the components of certain games, some skill activities are more difficult than others to adapt for persons with visual limitations. In the case of total blindness, participation in the more complex activities may be extremely difficult to modify. However, the skills constituting a game can be taught, and lead-up games with appropriate modifications are usually within the child's grasp.

There are several considerations that physical educators must make to effectively accommodate children with low vision in the diverse activities and environments where instruction takes place. The application of principles of accommodation may help the physical educator teach a wide variety of activities. A number of practical guidelines are presented in Table 17-5.

Table 17-5	Physical Education Principles for Working with the Visually Impaired

1. Design the instructional environment to accommodate the individual.
2. Introduce special devices, aids, and equipment to assist the individual.
3. Use special instructional techniques to accommodate the individual.
4. Introduce precautionary safety measures to meet the individual's needs.
5. Provide special feedback for tasks to facilitate learning.
6. Use sighted peers to provide individual attention and maximize participation.
7. Train the individual for mobility and understanding of the environment.
8. Allow the person with the visual impairment to decide if assistance is needed or wanted.[12]
9. Keep equipment and objects in the same place. Moving objects without telling the person with a visual impairment can be frustrating to that person.
10. Assist with the initiation of social interactions with peers.

Cognitive Instruction

The communication of information and the testing of knowledge are part of physical education instruction. Accommodations must be made for students with visual impairments during the communication of the physical education program:

1. Use large-print letters and numbers (which can be perceived by many persons who are partially sighted).
2. Use braille, a shorthand for tactile reading. Dots in a cell are raised on paper to indicate letters, numbers, punctuation, and other signs.
3. Make better use of listening skills and position students with visual impairments where they can best hear instructional information. This may be directly in front of the instructor.

4. Substitute kinesthetic (manual) guidance for vision when the components of skills are to be integrated in space and time.
5. Encourage the use of residual vision during the cognitive communication process between the instructor and a student with low vision.
6. Arrange seats to accommodate range of vision.
7. Design appropriate light contrasts between figure and ground when presenting instructional materials.
8. Be alert to behavioral signs and physical symptoms of visual difficulty in all children.

Control of the Environment—Safety First

The instructional environment for individuals with visual impairments should be safe and familiar and have distinguishing landmarks. As a safety precaution, play areas should be uncluttered and free from unnecessary obstructions. Children with visual impairments should be thoroughly introduced to unfamiliar areas by walking them around the play environment before they are allowed to play.

The characteristics of the instructional environment can be amplified. For instance, gymnasiums can be well lighted to assist those who have residual vision. Boundaries for games can have various compositions, such as a base or path of dirt and concrete or grass for other areas. Brightly colored objects are easier to identify. Also, equipment can be designed and appropriately placed to prevent injuries. For instance, two swings on a stand are safer than three. A third swing in the center is difficult to reach without danger when the other two swings are occupied. Attention to the safety and familiarity of the environment specifically designed for persons with visual impairments represents some degree of accommodation.

There are two parts to the management of safe environments. One is the structure of the environment, and the other is the teacher's control of the children as they participate in the environment. Suggestions to ensure safe play are presented in Table 17-6.

This Blind Skier Can Enjoy Downhill Skiing by Using a Sighted Guide and Two Poles

Courtesy Aspen Challenge, Aspen, CO.

The following are applications of safety principles:

Principle	Safety Measure
Protection of aids	Protect all body parts; use spotting in gymnastics.
Protection of eyeglasses	Use a restraining strap to hold glasses in place.
Safe equipment	Use sponge ball for softball, volleyball, or any other projectile activities.
Safe environment	Check play areas for obstacles and holes in the ground.
Activity according to ability	Avoid activities that require children to pass each other at high speeds.
Close supervision of all potentially dangerous activity	The teacher positions self close to the student with a visual impairment during activity, anticipates dangerous situations, and helps the student avoid them.

Special Instructional Methods

The application of special methods requires astute observation of the characteristics of each blind student.

Table 17-6	Safety Measures to Prevent Injury

1. Alter the playing surface texture (sand, dirt, asphalt); increase or decrease the grade to indicate play area boundaries.
2. Use padded walls, bushes, or other soft, safe restrainers around play areas.
3. Use brightly colored objects as boundaries to assist those with residual vision.
4. Limit the play area.
5. Limit the number of participants in the play area.
6. Play in slow motion when introducing a new game.
7. Protect the eyes.
8. Structure activities commensurate with the ability of the student with a visual impairment.
9. Protect visual aids, such as eyeglasses.
10. Select safe equipment.
11. Structure a safe environment.
12. Instruct children to use the environment safely.

1. Give clear auditory signals with a whistle or megaphone.
2. Instruct through manual guidance.
3. Use braille to teach cognitive materials before class.
4. Encourage tactual exploration of objects to determine texture, size, and shape.
5. Address the child by name.
6. Individualize instruction and build on existing capabilities. Do not let the child exploit visual limitations to the extent of withdrawing from activity or underachieving in motor performance.
7. Use the sensory mode that is most effective for specific learners (tactile, kinesthetic, haptic, auditory).
8. Manage the instructional environment to minimize the need for vision. Use chains where children touch one another. Participate from stationary positions. Establish reference points to which all persons return for instruction.

Special Task Feedback

Children who are blind need to know the effects of their performance on physical tasks because they receive little or no visual feedback. Task feedback must come through other sensory modes. For example, buzzers or bells can be inserted inside a basketball hoop to inform the person when a basket has been made. Gravel can be placed around the stake in horseshoes to indicate the accuracy of the toss. Peers can also give specific verbal feedback on tasks that involve projectiles. Effective feedback is an important reinforcing property to be incorporated into physical activity for persons with visual impairments.[8]

Peer Assistance

Peers without disabilities can assist children with disabilities in integrated settings. The nature of the assistance depends on the nature of the task. Peer assistance in providing feedback of task success is one example. Students with low vision may choose to have sighted guides. For safety in travel skills, a blind person should grasp the guide's upper arm, above the elbow, with the thumb on the outside and the fingers on the inside of the guide's arm. Both student and guide hold upper arms close to the body. When approaching doorways or objects, the guide moves the entire arm behind the back, so that students with low vision understand to walk directly behind the guide. Verbal cues inform the student when there are stairways and curbs. When children without disabilities provide such assistance, it is necessary to manage their time so as not to impede their own education.

Physical education teachers working with children who are visually impaired should attempt to minimize the stereotyped manner in which the child with visual limitations receives an education and should encourage sighted children to accept their peers on a personal basis.

THE PHYSICAL EDUCATION PROGRAM

Physical Education Needs

Loss of vision, by itself, is not a limiting condition for physical exercise. A considerable amount of

A Blind Runner and Her Guide Compete Together

Courtesy United States Association of Blind Athletes, Colorado Springs, CO.

developmental exercises to promote muscular strength, power, and endurance can be administered to such children.[13] Through developmental exercise, the child with visual limitations develops qualities such as good posture, graceful body movement, and good walking and sitting positions. Furthermore, physical education programs develop and maintain a healthy, vigorous body with physical vitality and good neuromuscular coordination. In addition to physical benefits, the physical education program contributes to social-emotional outcomes, such as security, confidence, and sighted peers' acceptance of children who are blind.

The ultimate goal of the class atmosphere for children with vision losses is to provide experiences that will help them adjust to the seeing society in which they live. The selection and method of experiences in the physical education program are critical. These experiences should not be overprotective to the extent that growth is inhibited; rather, the experiences should provide challenges yet remain within the range of the children's capabilities for achieving skill objectives.

Children with limited vision are capable of participating in numerous activities; however, the degree of participation possible depends on each child's abilities. Broad curriculum areas should be available at appropriate levels of development to accommodate each child. Children with visual impairments may represent a cross section of any school population with regard to motor abilities, physical fitness characteristics, and social and emotional traits. The purpose of adapting methods and activities for the student with visual limitations is to provide many experiences that children with sight learn primarily through visual observation. A goal of group activity in which a child with limited vision participates is to assign a role to the child that he or she can carry out successfully. It is undesirable for the child to be placed in the position of a bystander.

The adaptation of the physical education program for individuals with visual limitations should promote their confidence to cope with their environment by increasing their physical and motor abilities. It should also produce in them a feeling of acceptance as individuals in their own right. To achieve these goals, the program should include the adaptation of the general program of activities, when needed; additional or specialized activities, depending on the needs of the child; and special equipment, if needed.

Perceptual Development

Children with limited vision use other sensory abilities better as a result of increased attention to them in attempts to learn about and cope with the environment. A sighted person might be unaware of particular auditory stimuli, whereas a person who is blind might attach great significance to them.

These children need to use full kinesthetic, auditory, tactile, and space perception. Each form of perception contributes to the blind child's ability to adapt to the environment. The kinesthetic and vestibular systems can enable a person with limited vision to maintain balance. Balance experience is acquired through participation in activities that require quick changes of direction. The kinesthetic receptors are stimulated if the tasks, such as weight lifting or pushing and pulling movements, increase the amount of pressure applied to the joints.

Activity boxes made from cardboard, plastic, or wood are used to stimulate infants and young children with visual impairments to move and learn about object permanence and simple cause-and-effect. The boxes contain objects suspended from the sides and ceilings that make a sound when touched. The boxes are placed over children who are lying on their backs. As the children move their hands and feet, they strike the objects. Initially, their movements are random; however, after a short time, they begin to consciously manipulate the objects. Blind children as young as 14 weeks have been observed to benefit from this type of stimulation.[9]

Interrelationship of Sensory Systems in Movement

The role of vision in movement has been the focus of much research. Visual information that assists with performing specific motor skills is integrated with information from the vestibular apparatus and kinesthetic signals resulting from reflex and voluntary movements. Organization of these sensory inputs plays a central role in successfully maintaining posture and executing movement. Sensory organization is responsible for determining the timing, direction, and amplitude of movement based on information from vision, kinesthesis, and the vestibular sense. The execution of static and dynamic balance requires a combination of several

senses, one of which is vision. When vision is compromised, other senses must be used more fully.

Space Perception

Early visual experience of spatial relations establishes a method for processing information that affects cognitive and motor learning. Persons who have low vision often cannot perceive the relationship of objects to each other in space. They also have an impaired ability to relate themselves to objects in space. Therefore, the auditory, vestibular, kinesthetic, and tactile senses are used to establish spatial relationships.

Physical Education Activities

A sound physical education curriculum includes a wide variety of activities selected to meet the needs of the students. Obviously, student needs vary depending on their developmental levels, ages, and interests. Fundamental motor skills and patterns are essential prerequisites for successful, enjoyable participation in recreational sport activities. Some of these activities are running, jumping, throwing, and striking. They involve coordinated movements.

Games of low organization are an important part of elementary school physical education programs. The games that require the least modification for persons with visual impairments are those in which there is continuous contact with the participants, such as tug of war, parachute activity, end man tag, ring around the rosy, hot potato, over and under relay, and wheelbarrow races.

Activities that require minimal amounts of vision for participation are (1) wrestling (the only modification is contact with an opponent at a takedown), (2) individual fitness exercises, (3) gymnastics or tumbling, and (4) swimming. Suggestions for including learners with visual impairments in aquatic activities are presented in Table 17-7. Team sports that are highly loaded with visual information require considerable accommodation. Such games include basketball, soccer, and football because the ball, as well as the offensive and defensive players, moves continually.

Table 17-7	Aquatics for Learners with Visual Impairments

- The swimmer should wear goggles to prevent any possible damage from chlorine and other chemicals in the water.
- Bright, colorful toys should be used, such as beach balls, kickboards, pails and shovels, water-use stuffed animals, and water squirters (not squirt guns).
- The swimmer must be given the opportunity to explore the learning environment to orient himself or herself. This careful exploration can be enhanced if there is a constant sound source: a soft radio or the like for the swimmer to use for orientation.
- The swimmer must be given a chance to learn self-protective skills that include sensing the end of the lane because of the reaction of the waves in response to the incoming body, sensing the presence of another swimmer because of splashing and waves, and announcing intentions if planning to jump into the water.
- A swimmer who is totally blind may learn best if given the opportunity to "feel" the movement of another; this is particularly effective if paired with patterning the movement of the swimmer.
- When lap swimming, open turns, rather than flip turns, give the swimmer a little leeway to find the wall, rather than being surprised by it.
- Lane lines help the swimmer stay oriented in the pool. The swimmer may want to wear tight-fitting gloves to avoid being cut by the lane lines if off course.

For more information refer to Project INSPIRE Aquatics pages: www.twu.edu/INSPIRE.

Variable Adaptation

Physical activities need various amounts of adaptation for participants who are blind. Considerations in selecting activities for players who have visual impairments are as follows:

1. Activities that require a considerable amount of vision are the most difficult.
2. Activities that require great amounts of movement in the environment are usually the most difficult to adapt.
3. The greater the number of visual cues required for participation, the more difficult the accommodation.
4. Environments in which there is continual change of visual cues rather than stable visual cues (e.g., team games, such as basketball, football, and soccer) are the most difficult.
5. The more modifications that have to be made in the environment, the more difficult the accommodation for the player with a visual impairment.
6. The more equipment that needs to be modified, the more complex the accommodation of the motor task for the learner.

Safety Precautions

The physical educator who administers activities to children with limited vision should take special safety precautions, such as the following:

1. Secure knowledge, through medical records and observation, of the children's limitations and capabilities.
2. Orient the children to facilities and equipment.
3. Provide special equipment indicating direction, such as guide lines in swimming and running events, as well as deflated softballs.

Educational Settings

The physical education teacher may be asked to instruct a class in which children with visual limitations are integrated, to instruct a class composed solely of visually limited children, or to instruct classes of children with multiple disabilities. There is a growing awareness that there are more similarities than differences between children with visual limitations and sighted children. Therefore, the inclusion of children with visual limitations into classes with their seeing peers should take place whenever possible. Such placement emphasizes the positive aspects of the children and minimizes differences.

In the past, it was not uncommon for children with limited vision to be referred to and placed in

Scott Moore, a Blind Athlete Competes in Judo

Courtesy United States Association of Blind Athletes, Colorado Springs, CO.

residential schools. However, with the implementation of The Education of the Handicapped Act, a countertrend has grown to bring instructional aids into resource rooms and regular classrooms of community schools. This practice has created a number of service delivery alternatives for least restrictive placement. It has been customary to apply the following cascade system for the placement of children with visual impairments:

1. Regular class
2. Regular class with assistance by a vision consultant
3. Regular class with consultation and itinerant instruction (orientation and mobility training)
4. Adapted physical education conducted by a specialist; children attend part-time
5. Self-contained adapted physical education class
6. Residential schools for the blind

The itinerant teacher is a specialist who possesses specific skills to work with children of limited vision. This teacher teams with the regular classroom teacher.

MODIFICATIONS, ADAPTATIONS, AND INCLUSION TECHNIQUES

Special Devices, Aids, and Equipment

For those who are visually impaired, distance in space is structured by auditory cues. Therefore, it is desirable to structure space with these cues. Equipment, aids, and devices that enhance the participation of the blind in physical activity should provide information about the environment.

Auditory aids can be built into equipment. *Audible balls* emit beeping sounds for easy location. They may be the size of a softball, soccer ball, or playground ball. The beep baseball is a regular softball with a battery-operated electronic beeping sound device. Through continuous sound this special equipment tells the blind person where the ball is at all times. A goal ball is constructed with bells inside it. When the ball moves, the bells help the players locate it. One of the skills of the game is to roll the ball smoothly to reduce auditory information (less sound from the bells) to make it more difficult for blind players to locate it. *Audible goal locators* are motor-driven noisemakers. They indicate the position of backboards in basketball, targets in archery, pins in bowling, and stakes in horseshoes. Audible bases, which are plastic cones 60 inches tall with a noisemaker inside, are used in the game of beep baseball. Audible locators can also be used as boundaries or to identify dangerous objects in the environment.

The following activities can be conducted to develop space perception through the use of auditory aids in the environment:

1. Walk a straight line. Measure the distance of deviations over a specific distance. Use an audible device to provide initial assistance for direction and then fade the device.
2. Face sounds made at different positions. The intensity and duration of the sound can make the task more or less difficult.

3. Reproduce pathways and specific distances just taken with a partner.
4. Do not allow students with aphakia (absence of the natural lens of the eye, as when a cataract has been surgically removed), a detached retina, or severe myopia to engage in high-impact activities, such as jumping.[5]

Modifications

Some modifications that can be made to enable the participation of persons with visual limitations are detailed in Table 17-8.

Inclusion Techniques

The mission of physical education programs for blind persons is to enable these pupils to engage in independent recreational sport and physical activity in the community. To achieve this, it is usually necessary to move individuals from more restrictive to less restrictive training environments. Restrictiveness of an environment is determined by the amount of special support systems needed for an individual to participate or learn. Movement to less restrictive environments usually involves the withdrawal of support systems, so that the individual gradually learns to function with greater independence. At least two considerations need to be studied for the placement of persons who are blind in integrated sport activity: (1) the question of whether it is possible to integrate an activity and (2) the need for support systems to enable integration.

Providing support systems for persons with visual impairments will enable them to participate in and enjoy group activities. Some of the support systems are (1) the design of the game in which the nonsighted and sighted players play together (e.g., in beep ball, the pitcher and the catcher need to be sighted), (2) the use of peer tutors for activity play (allow the person to run or exercise with a partner), and (3) the use of a variety of environments in which support for integrated activity is gradually withdrawn, so that the individual can

Table 17-8	Activity Modification for Students with Visual Impairments
Activity	**Modification**
Aerobic dance	Include verbal description of movement with demonstration.
Archery	Beeper is affixed to center of target.
Bicycling	Child assumes rear seat position on tandem bicycle with sighted partner in front seat.
Bowling	Beeper is attached above pins at end of lane.
Canoeing	Child assumes bow position, with sighted partner in stern.
Frisbee	Frisbee has a beeper attached.
Horseshoes	Beeper is affixed to stake. Path to horseshoes pit is made of wood chips or sand.
Running	Guide wires or a sighted guide is use.[18]
Swimming	Lane lines designate swimming lanes. Swimming pool has nonslip bottom. Pool decks have nonslip surface. Pool has constant sound source for orientation. Small bells are suspended near gutters and are activated by waves as a person approaches the end of the pool.
Softball	Sand or wood chips are used for base paths. T-stand is used for batting, instead of batting from pitcher. Different texture of ground or floor is used when near a surface that could result in serious collision.
Weight training	Equipment and weights are put in the same place.
Class management	Environment is ordered and consistent. Reference points indicate location of the child in the play area. Auditory cues identify obstacles in the environment. Tactile markings are on the floor. Boundaries of different textures are used.

eventually participate independently in recreational activity in the community. There are currently many educational integration models; however, in the last analysis, individuals with low vision must participate in the less restricted environment in the community. Educational models are needed that match the activities available in the community. Songster and Doherty[29] have identified a formal process for the integration of individuals with disabilities, including blind players, into sport activity: (1) the selection of the activity around which the integration process will take place, (2) the development of a system of sequential supports in environments that enable greater independent functioning of the athletes among their normal peers, (3) the placement of the individuals in appropriate environments commensurate with their social and physical abilities, (4) the provision of needed supports to the individual, and (5) the fading of the individual's support systems through the less restrictive environments. Before the integration process is attempted, the sequential environments and support systems must be fully designed.

One of the purposes of physical education for students who have visual impairments is to help them develop skills they can use in interscholastic athletics, in intramurals, or for leisure in the community after formal schooling. Therefore, activity should be community-based. Clearly, according to the laws, there are to be equal opportunities for participation in extracurricular activities for individuals with and without disabilities. Therefore, opportunities for sports participation outside the schools should be integrally linked with the physical education program in the public schools. Such considerations for the extension of extracurricular activities to persons with limited vision involve the identification of activities that are available in the community.

COMMUNITY-BASED ACTIVITIES

Students with visual impairments who have had a positive physical education experience remain active after leaving school.[10] Activities and equipment that

can be used to maintain the adult's physical and motor fitness include weight lifting, Universal gym equipment, isometric exercises, stationary running, the exercise bicycle, and the rowing machine. Instruction in proper technique and familiarity with community facilities that provide these types of equipment as part of the transition program will enhance the probability of continued participation after the school years. A growing number of sport activities are also available to the person with visual impairments. Goal ball and beep ball are two popular competitive sports for persons with visual impairments, and each can be modified to include players with sight. The United States Association for Blind Athletes (USABA) sponsors national competition in these sports yearly.

Goal Ball

Goal ball is a game that originated in Germany for blind veterans of World War II to provide gross motor movement cued by auditory stimuli (a bell ball). It is now played under the rules of the International Sports Organization for the Disabled.

The purpose of the game is for each team of three persons to roll the ball across the opponent's goal, which is 8.5 m (9 1/4 yards) wide for men and 7.5 m (about 8 yards) wide for women. A ball is rolled toward the opponent's goal. The entire team attempts to stop the ball before it reaches the goal by throwing the body into an elongated position. The ball is warded off with any part of or the whole body. Games last 10 minutes, with a 5-minute halftime. All players are blindfolded.

Many of the principles of accommodating persons with visual impairment have been incorporated into this game. Examples of the application of these principles follow:

• *Instructional environment to accommodate the individual.* The boundaries are made of rope, so that they can be detected by the players.
• *Special aids and equipment.* Elbow and knee pads are provided to the players, so that they

are not hurt when the body hits the floor or lunges to stop the ball. Bells are placed in the ball, so that the rolling ball can be heard en route to the goal.

- *Special instructional techniques.* Kinesthetic movement of the body is required to instruct the players how to lunge to block the ball.
- *Precautionary safety measures.* Pads and mats can be placed at the end of the gym where the goals are. The sidelines should be clear of objects.
- *Special feedback to facilitate learning.* A piece of tin or materials that make sounds can be placed at the goal, so that players know when a goal has been scored rather than successfully defended.
- *Sighted peers who assist instruction.* Sighted persons can provide feedback as to whether the movements of the game have been successfully achieved.
- *Players trained to understand the environment.* The players should be trained to know where the goal ball training area is within the gym and how to enter and leave the gym.

Beep Ball

Beep ball is a game, played throughout the United States, that is designed to encourage blind and sighted players to compete in softball. Each team has its own sighted pitcher and catcher. The catcher sets the target where the batter normally swings the bat, and the pitcher attempts to hit the target with the ball. Equipment required to play beep ball is available through the Telephone Pioneers of America. Equipment includes a buzzing base and a ball 16 inches in circumference with a battery-operated electronic sound device inside. The specifications of the equipment and playing area are (1) a regulation bat; (2) a beep ball; (3) 48-inch bases and pliable plastic cones with a 36-inch bottom and a 10-inch-long cylinder of foam-rubber top; (4) the bases placed 90 feet down respective lines and 5 feet off the lines; and (5) sounding units that give off a buzzing sound when activated, fixed 20 feet from the bases.

The rules of beep ball are as follows: (1) the umpire activates one of the bases when a ball is hit; (2) the runner must identify the correct base and run to it before a play is made by the defense; (3) a run is scored if the runner reaches the base before the fielder plays the ball and the beeper is turned off (there is no running from one base to another); (4) the batter is allowed five rather than the traditional three strikes (the fifth strike must be a total miss); (5) a hit ball must travel at least 40 feet to be considered fair (otherwise, it is considered foul); (6) games are six innings in duration, with three outs per inning. There is only a first and a third base, which are 90 feet apart.[1] Teams are usually composed of both males and females.

USABA Activities

The United States Association for Blind Athletes (USABA) sponsors national championships every year. Such high-level competition is an incentive for blind persons to engage in training regimens from which there are personal and physical benefits. Persons with visual impairments who participate in competitive activities such as those sponsored by the USABA may reach both sport and personal development goals.

To provide equity in competition, the classification of these competitors is based on the amount of sight. The USABA classification system of legally blind athletes is as follows:

Class B1—No light perception in either eye up to light perception, but inability to recognize the shape of a hand at any distance or in any direction

Class B2—From ability to recognize the shape of a hand up to visual acuity of 20/600 and/or a visual field of less than 5 degrees in the best eye with the best practical eye correction

Class B3—From visual acuity above 20/600 and up to visual acuity of 20/200 and/or a visual field of less than 20 degrees and more than 5 degrees in the best eye with the best practical eye correction

Class B4—From visual acuity above 20/200 and up to visual acuity of 20/70 and a visual field larger than 20 degrees in the best eye with the best practical eye correction

Several activities sponsored by the USABA are related to leisure activities. Thus, the competition can serve participants in two ways—for athletic competition and for participation in leisure activities in the community. Some of the activities that are a part of international competition and that can be expressed as a recreational skill in the community are listed in Table 17-9.

Other activities that are less community-based recreational activities but that provide opportunities to develop personal and social skills through participation are field events in track, wrestling, and gymnastics. Specific events in gymnastics and track and field are floor exercise; balance beam; uneven bars; vaulting; all-around competition; 60- and 100-meter dash; and 200-, 400-, 800-, 1500-, 3000-, and 10,000-meter runs.

Table 17-9	USABA Athletic Competition and Leisure Activities
Activity	**Program**
Track running event	Physical fitness program
Cycling	Physical fitness and recreational program
Weight lifting	Physical fitness programs and body building
Sailing	Recreational aquatics
Crew rowing	Boat rowing for fishing and boat safety
Competitive diving	Recreational swimming and diving
Archery	Recreational shooting at archery ranges
Swimming	Recreational swimming in community pools
Downhill and cross-country skiing	Recreational skiing in selected communities where the resources are appropriate

SUMMARY

Children with visual impairments vary in functional ability to participate in physical activity. Persons classified as partially sighted have less than 20/70 acuity, and individuals are classified as blind if their acuity is 20/200 or less. *Low vision* is a term that is used when referring to individuals with a severe visual impairment. There are two basic categories of blindness: congenital blindness means that the person was born blind; adventitious blindness means the person was blinded after birth.

The underlying causes of visual loss are existing visual conditions, structural anomalies or injuries, and inefficient extraocular muscle control. Those associated with curvature of the light rays as they enter or pass through the eye are myopia, hyperopia, and astigmatism. Visual conditions include albinism, cataracts, glaucoma, retinitis pigmentosa, and retinopathy of prematurity. Nystagmus, suppression, and tropias are associated with difficulties in depth perception. Phorias are tendencies for the eyes to misalign.

Functional visual impairments may be identified by the Snellen test. They also may be identified by observing abnormal eye conditions, movement patterns and preferences, and visual discrimination. Low vision clinics offer comprehensive evaluations and assistance to individuals with visual disorders.

Vision loss has serious implications for motor, intellectual, psychological, and social development. Vision loss early in life may delay the mastery of motor responses, which can affect other areas of development. Planned physical experiences will enhance physical and motor fitness and may counter maldevelopment in other areas.

Training programs in mobility increase the degree of independence of persons who are blind. Accompanying direct instruction to develop travel vision and motor skills are techniques for adaptation. This can be accomplished by modifying activity and instructional environments and introducing special aids, devices, or equipment.

Persons with visual disorders should be trained with self-help or recreational skills that can be used in the community. This may enable participation in some of the community sports programs for the blind and visually limited.

A process that will integrate players who are blind into inclusive physical activities involves the assessment of the social and physical skill level of the individual to ensure success in the activity, appropriate placement in a continuum of environments with the appropriate sighted support systems, and sequential withdrawal of support systems and movement to less restrictive participation environments that are commensurate with improved motor and social skills.

REVIEW QUESTIONS

1. How do the movement capabilities of a child with slight loss of vision differ from those of a child who is totally blind?

2. What are the general characteristics of persons with limited vision that impair physical performance of skills?

3. What social adjustment problems do students who are blind face when being included in the general physical education program?

4. What are five ways the physical education environment can be modified to include a student who is visually impaired?

5. What are the essential components for integrating players who are blind with sighted players in physical activity?

STUDENT ACTIVITIES

1. There are organizations designed to serve parents of children who are blind. Using the Internet, contact a local or national organization to learn the purpose of these groups. What information do they provide? Do they serve as advocates for parents? What should physical education teachers know about these organizations?

2. Working in small groups, devise a plan that would eventually enable Hosea to participate independently in the community.

3. There are several ways of adapting instruction and the environment to accommodate persons such as Hosea. Select eight activities and indicate how you might modify the activity, environment, or equipment to enable him to participate with his sighted peers.

REFERENCES

1. American Foundation for the Blind: *Creative recreation.* New York, 1988.

2. American Foundation for the Blind, www.afb.org. 2003.

3. American Academy of Optometry and American Optometric Association: *Vision, learning and dyslexia: A joint organizational policy statement,* www.aaopt.org/JointStatement.html, 2003.

4. Beers MH, Berkow R: *The Merk manual of diagnosis and therapy.* Whitehouse Station, NJ, Merck Research Laboratories, 1999.

5. Bloomquist, LE: Visual impairment. In Durstin JL, editor: *Exercise management for persons with chronic diseases and disabilities.* Champaign, IL, Human Kinetics, 1997.

6. Canadian Optometrists, www.optometrists.bc.ca/lowvision.html. 2003.

7. Ciuffreda KJ: The scientific basis and efficacy of optometric vision therapy in nonstrabismic accommodative and vergence disorders, *Optometry* 73:735–762, 2002.

8. Dunn, JM: *Special physical education: Adapted, individualized, developmental,* 7th ed. Dubuque, IA, Brown & Benchmark, 1995.

9. Dunnett J: Use of activity boxes with young children who are blind, deaf-blind, or have severe learning disabilities and visual impairments, *J of Visual impairment & Blindness* 93(4):225–232, 1999.

10. Eichstaedt CB, Kalakian LH: *Developmental adapted physical education.* New York, Macmillan, 1987.

11. Goodman W: *Mobility training for people with disabilities.* Springfield, IL, Charles C Thomas, 1989.

12. Gordon B, Gavron SJ: A biomechanical analysis of the running pattern of blind athletes in the 100 meter dash, *APAQ* 4:192–203, 1987.

13. Horvat M, Ray C, Croce R, Blasch B: A comparison of isokinetic muscle strength and power in visually impaired and sighted individuals, *Isokinetics and Exercise Science* 12(3):179–183, 2004.

14. Hughes M, Dote-Kwan J, Dolendo J: A close look at the cognitive play of preschoolers with visual impairments in the home, *Exceptional Children* 64:451–462, 1998.

15. King G, Law M, King S, Hurley P, Rosenbaum P, Hanna S, Kertoy M, Young N: *Children's Assessment of Participation and Enjoyment (CAPE) and Preference for Activities of Children (PAC).* San Antonio, TX, Harcourt Assessment, 2004.

16. Kleeman M, Rimmer, JH: Relationship between fitness levels and attitudes toward physical education in a visually impaired population, *Clinical Kinesiology* Summer:29–32, 1994.

17. Leiberman LJ, Butcher M, Moak S: A study of guide-running techniques for children who are blind, *Palaestra* 17(3):20–26, 2001.

18. Lieberman LJ, Houston-Wilson C, Kozub FM: Perceived barriers to including students with visual impairments in general physical education, *APAQ* 19:364–377, 2002.

19. Lieberman L, Lepore, M: Camp abilities: A developmental sports camp for youths who are visually impaired, *Palaestra* Winter:28–31, 46, 1998.

20. Luria A: *Higher cortical functions in man,* 2nd ed. New York, Basic Books, 1980.

21. Mastro JV, Canabal MY, French R: Psychological mood profiles of sighted and unsighted beep baseball players, *Res Q Ex Sport* 59:262–264, 1988.

22. McGuffin K, French R, Mastro J: Comparison of three techniques for sprinting by visually impaired adults, *Clin Kines* 44:97–99, 1990.

23. McHugh BE, Pyfer J: The development of rocking among children who are blind, *J of Visual Impairment and Blindness* 38:78–83, 1999.

24. National Information Center for Children and Youth with Disabilities, www.nichcy.org/pubs/factshe/fs13text.htm. 2003.

25. Ribadi H, Rider RA, Toole T: A comparison of static and dynamic balance and congenitally blind and sighted blindfolded adolescents, *APAQ* 4:220–225, 1987.

26. Richardson MJ, Mastro JV: So I can't see, I can play and I can learn, *Palaestra* 3:23–32, 1987.

27. Rouse M: Management of binocular anomalies: Efficiency of visual therapy, *Am J Optom Physio Optics* 64:391–392, 1987.

28. Shaperio R, Leberman LJ, Moffett A: Strategies to improve perceived competence in children with visual impairments, *Re: view* 35(2):69–80, 2003.

29. Songster T, Doherty B: *The Special Olympics integration process,* Special Olympics International Research Monograph, Washington, DC, 1990.

30. Stanley SM, Kindig EE: Improvisations for blind bowlers, *Palaestra* 2:38–39, 1986.

31. Visual Fitness Institute: *Symptoms of visual skill disorders,* http://visualfitness.com/symptoms.html. 2003.

32. Wall R: Teachers' exposure to people with visual impairments and the effect on attitudes toward inclusion. *Re: View* 34(3):111–119, 2002.

SUGGESTED READINGS

Letcher K: *Adapted physical education for the blind and visually impaired,* www.obs.org/page.php?ITEM=9#. 2007.

Panchillia PE, Armbruster J, Weibold J: The national sports education camps project: Introducing sport skills to students with visual impairments through short-term specialized instruction, *J of Visual Impairment & Blindness* 96(4):267–272, 2002.

Stopka C: *Teachers' survival guide: Adaptations to optimize the inclusions of students of all ages with disabilities in your programs,* PE Central, www.pecentral.org, 2006.

RECOMMENDED WEB SITES

Please keep in mind that these Web sites are being recommended in the winter of 2007. As Web sites often change, they may have moved or been reconfigured or eliminated.

American Council of the Blind
www.acb.org

American Foundation for the Blind
www.afb.org

Camp Abilities
www.campabilities.org

National Federation of the Blind
www.nfb.org

United States Association of Blind Athletes
www.usaba.org

RECOMMENDED VIDEOS

Insight Media
2162 Broadway
New York, NY 10024-0621
1-800-233-9910
www.insight-media.com

Physical Activity For All
II78AR5602/DVD/2000/56 min/$129.00

Other Health Impairments

■ **OBJECTIVES**

Identify teaching techniques that can be used to keep youth with attention deficit disorders on task.

Describe the precautions that should be taken when a child with AIDS is included in the general physical education program.

Describe the characteristics of a person with anemia.

Describe the role of exercise in asthma.

Describe the role of exercise in a child with cystic fibrosis.

Explain the value of exercise for individuals with diabetes.

List emergency procedures for treating a diabetic attack brought on by hyperglycemia or hypoglycemia.

Explain the effect of diet and activity on dysmenorrhea.

Describe the primary characteristic of students with Prader-Willi syndrome.

List the characteristics of Tourette syndrome.

Zoe Koplowitz, Who Has Multiple Sclerosis, Is a Lecturer, Marathoner, and Ambassador for the National MS Society. For Additional Information on MS, Please Call 1-800 FIGHT MS or Visit the Society's Website at www.nationalmssociety.org

National MS Society

The federal laws that have been passed in the United States during the past 35 years virtually ensure a free and appropriate public education to every individual who has a real or perceived impairment that limits major life activities. Other health impairment, by federal definition, means that a child has limited strength and vitality or alertness with respect to the environment that are due to chronic or acute health problems, such as asthma, attention deficit/hyperactivity disorder, diabetes, epilepsy, a heart condition, hemophilia, lead poisoning, leukemia, rheumatic fever, and sickle cell anemia, that adversely affect a child's educational performance. In addition to the major health impairments identified in the federal definition of IDEA, acquired immune deficiency syndrome (AIDS), anemia, childhood cancer, cystic fibrosis, Prader-Willi syndrome, premenstrual syndrome and dysmenorrhea, and Tourette syndrome will also be addressed in this chapter.

When children with health impairments improve their motor performance, they also benefit socially and psychologically. Physical education programs that increase exercise tolerance and improve recreational sport skills may also enhance self-care and social competence. Improved physical performance capability usually gives the student a great psychological boost. Involving students in skill and physical development activity programs often helps break a cycle of passive, debilitating physical and social lifestyles.

Most of the conditions discussed in this chapter require medical attention. When this is the case, it is advisable to request permission of the parents to consult with the student's physician to ensure that the type of exercises and activities selected for the student will not aggravate the condition. When the physical educator notices the symptoms that are described in this chapter being demonstrated by a student who is not diagnosed as having a health impairment, the child should be referred to the school nurse for additional evaluation.

ATTENTION-DEFICIT/HYPERACTIVITY DISORDER

Over the years, many terms have been used to describe inattentive and impulsive behaviors demonstrated by some children. Although this continuum of behaviors was originally identified in the 1930s,[94] research did not focus on it until the 1960s,[89] when the term *hyperkinetic impulse disorder* surfaced.[67] This was replaced by the term *hyperactive child syndrome* in the 1970s, *attention deficit disorder (ADD)* in the 1980s,[90] and, by 2000, attention deficit/hyperactivity disorder.[4]

CASE STUDY 18-1

Roshard

Roshard is a high school freshman with a medical diagnosis of attention deficit/hyperactivity disorder (ADHD). Roshard has a long school history of difficulty. His parents have refused to give him medication to control his ADHD because they believe the medication causes him to lose his intellectual edge. Being forced to learn in a traditional school environment that focuses on paper-and-pencil activities is very frustrating for Roshard. He acts out some of this frustration in his physical education class. He has temper tantrums if he loses. He becomes very sarcastic with his peers and, occasionally, the teacher. He appears to gain control of his emotions if he is allowed to run or engage in other vigorous aerobic activity.

APPLICATION TASK

What could the general physical educator do to help Roshard manage his behavior in the physical education class? Are there any suggestions the general physical educator could make to Roshard's parents about activities they could do at home to help Roshard manage his ADHD-associated behaviors?

Individuals with ADHD have difficulty attending in school, work, and social situations. They are easily distracted and frequently make careless mistakes because they rush through tasks without thinking. They have difficulty organizing their schoolwork and other responsibilities. They often appear to be daydreaming or not listening. When they do attempt tasks, their work is usually very messy and only partially completed. These individuals typically make every effort to avoid activities that demand sustained self-application, mental effort, and close concentration. They also have difficulty "reading" social situations and, as a result, make comments out of turn, initiate conversations at inappropriate times, and intrude on others. They are often judged to be lazy, uncaring, and unreliable, when in reality they simply cannot focus their attention for any length of time.

Many children with ADHD:

Fail to give close attention to detail

Have difficulty sustaining attention during play activity

Fail to listen carefully when spoken to

Fail to follow through on directions

Have difficulty organizing tasks and activities

Are reluctant to engage in tasks that require sustained effort

Lose things necessary for activities

Become distracted by extraneous stimuli

Are forgetful of daily activities[109]

Persons with ADHD may have problems with social relationships, which include less positive social behavior, fewer positive peer interactions, lower rates of peer reinforcement, lower self-esteem, and fewer cooperative social behaviors.[36]

Definition

ADHD is a neurodevelopmental disorder characterized by inattentiveness, impulsiveness, and hyperactivity.[4] The IDEA Amendments of 1999 included attention deficit disorder and attention deficit hyperactivity disorder in the list of conditions that could render a child eligible for special services under the category of "other health impaired."[91] Three distinct forms of ADHD have been identified: (1) attention deficit hyperactivity disorder predominantly inattentive, (2) attention deficit hyperactivity disorder predominantly hyperactive-impulsive, and (3) attention deficit hyperactivity disorder combined.

Incidence

The Centers for Disease Control and Prevention estimates that 7.8 percent of all school-age children have ADHD.[23] Males are diagnosed four times as frequently as females. The diagnosis can be made as early as three years, but more frequently it is not made until after a child enters school.[110]

Causes

The cause of ADHD is unknown. However, the difficulties with self-inhibition that persons with ADHD have strongly suggest involvement of the prefrontal cortex, basal ganglia, and cerebellum.[11] When higher control centers such as these are involved, inhibition and executive functions are compromised.[13] The disorder is believed to be genetic; however, negative responses to food additives; sensitivity to chemicals, fungi, and molds; and exposure to toxins are believed to contribute to ADHD.[58]

Characteristics

Many children and youth with ADHD are more impulsive than their peers in making choices. This can significantly interfere with their ability to regulate physical activity, inhibit behavior, and attend to physical education tasks in developmentally appropriate ways. Impulsivity can cause devastating consequences, including failure in school, antisocial behavior, and interpersonal difficulties. Other adverse consequences associated with impulsivity are difficulties attending to instruction, following instructions, completing instructional activities, and complying with class rules.[93] Three-quarters of hyperactive-inattentive children have coexisting conditions, including oppositional defiance disorder (50 percent), depression (38 percent), and anxiety (25 percent).[109]

The characteristics associated with each type of ADHD appear in Table 18-1.

Special Considerations

The management of ADHD has received considerable study. A combination of drug therapy and psychological therapy shows the greatest promise for improving behavior and academic performance. Drug therapy most frequently is used with individuals who demonstrate ADHD. The three most common drugs prescribed are methylphenidate (Ritalin), dextroamphetamine (Dexedrine), and pemoline (Cylert),[45] all of which are central nervous system stimulants. The use of these drugs usually results in dramatic improvement in behavior.

Table 18-1	Characteristics of the Types of Attention Deficit Hyperactive Disorders

ADHD predominantly inattentive—makes careless mistakes, inattentive, doesn't seem to listen, doesn't follow through on instructions, difficulty organizing tasks, avoids/dislikes tasks requiring sustained mental effort, loses things necessary for tasks, easily distracted, forgetful in daily activities

ADHD predominantly hyperactive-impulsive—fidgets and/or squirms in seat, leaves seat often, runs about or climbs excessively, difficulty playing or engaging in leisure activities quietly, often on the go, talks excessively, blurts out answers before question is complete, has difficulty waiting turn, interrupts or intrudes on others

ADHD combined—the most common type in children and adolescents, a combination of characteristics demonstrated in the other two types

Source: American Psychiatric Association: *DSM-IV-TR diagnostic and statistical manual of mental disorders,* 4th ed. Washington, DC, American Psychiatric Association, 2000.

Interpersonal interaction improvements result in less conflict with parents, peers, and teachers. Improvements in attentiveness, information processing, and short-term memory result in academic performance gains.[39]

The psychosocial therapies most frequently used are behavior modification, cognitive-behavior therapy, and family therapy.[53] Behavior modification includes daily reporting about the frequency of problem behaviors, with positive reinforcement for compliance. Cognitive-behavior therapy involves focusing on demonstrated academic deficits and making accommodations for those deficits. Family therapy entails working with the family in counseling sessions and through support groups.[110]

Testing

The heterogeneous nature of the ADHD group makes it difficult to generalize about testing needs. One study indicated that, as a group, individuals between the ages of 7 and 12 years with ADHD demonstrated below-average fitness, fundamental gross motor skills, locomotor skills, and object-control skills.[50] It has been reported that, when individuals are involved in drug therapy, although motor performance is not improved, attention and concentration do improve. At the same time, aggressiveness is reduced.[53]

Physical and motor tests should be administered to determine the functioning levels of the youngster with ADHD. Particular attention should be paid to evaluating the status of the neurological building blocks, as well as the integration processes of the individual under 12 years of age. The Bruininks-Oseretsky Test of Motor Proficiency augmented by visual screening should provide a wide range of information for the physical educator. After age 12 years, focus should be placed on evaluating the components of the types of community-based activities in which the family can participate.

Teaching Strategies

The decision about which teaching strategy to use depends on the age and needs of the student. The bottom-up teaching approach using group games for elementary-age children and stations for middle school students can be used to address underlying neurological building block deficits. After age 12 years, a top-down, task-specific approach is best. Social development skills should be emphasized in the physical education program. Direct instruction, positive reinforcement of appropriate behavior, and peer coaching should be used whenever possible.[36] In addition to the many opportunities team play offers to aid in teaching socially appropriate responses, interactive computer-facilitated social interventions that address social problem solving can be helpful. Video scenarios that represent social environments and the range of choices within those environments can be used with youngsters with ADHD to help them understand how to select appropriate social responses.[41] The use of punitive measures with these youngsters should be avoided.[93] General points to keep in mind when working with these students are presented in Table 18-2.

Table 18-2	Tips for Teaching Students with ADHD

- Change activities frequently to accommodate the short attention span.
- Use a positive behavior modification program to keep the student on task.
- Incorporate three to five minutes of conscious relaxation at the end of the physical education period.
- Give brief instructions.
- Use activities that promote cooperation among all students (e.g., New Games).

The Physical Education Program

Because of the physical and motor deficits many of these students demonstrate, whenever possible games and activities that limit competition should be stressed. Students with ADHD do not need to participate in activities they have little hope of succeeding in. To require them to do so sets them up for failure and contributes to poor self-esteem. The more activities that use an individualized approach and allow the students to work at their own level, the better the chance the students have at succeeding.

Community-Based Opportunities

Individuals who do not grow out of their ADHD frequently experience great difficulty completing school and taking a position in the community that is commensurate with their intelligence. Many of these individuals do not complete high school, usually take lower-status jobs, and have higher rates of antisocial personality. In addition, adolescents and young adults with ADHD have a greater frequency of substance abuse than do individuals without ADHD.[39] All of these prognoses make it crucial that the youngster with ADHD be given every opportunity to learn activities that involve the entire family, so that family-centered recreation will contribute to the youngster's self-esteem and will promote the skills needed for establishing and maintaining a healthy lifestyle.

AIDS

Acquired immune deficiency syndrome (AIDS) has swept a deadly path throughout the world. Although AIDS was not recognized as a disease entity until 1981, by 2005 an estimated 40.3 million people worldwide were living with HIV infection or AIDS.[9]

Definition

AIDS is the development of opportunistic infections and/or certain secondary cancers known to be associated with human immunodeficiency virus (HIV) infection. HIV disease (all stages of infection before the development of AIDS) is a progressive disease that is a result of the virus's infecting the CD_4 cells of the immune system. As HIV disease progresses, all of the CD_4 cells in the body are depleted, which results in the suppression of the immune system.[60] AIDS is the final stage of a series of diseases caused by HIV infection.

Incidence

As of 2007 more than 1 million U.S. residents were infected with HIV and more than 420,000 were living with full-blown AIDS.[9] Nearly 30 percent of those infected with HIV are women.[6] One study reported that 97 percent of the children who test HIV-positive are healthy enough to attend school, and the number of children with HIV infections reaching school age will continue to grow.[27]

Causes

The HIV virus is spread from one person to another via body fluids. The primary transmission fluids are blood and blood products, semen, vaginal secretion, breast milk, and amniotic fluid.[88] In the United States, the high-risk categories for receiving and transmitting the virus are homosexual or bisexual males (61 percent of cases), intravenous drug abusers (18 to 26 percent of cases), prostitutes and those who frequent them, transfusion recipients and hemophiliacs (particularly

CASE STUDY 18-2

Jimmy

Jimmy is a seven-year-old who was born HIV-positive because his mother had unknowingly been infected with HIV from a blood transfusion she received when she was a young girl. At this point, Jimmy, who is enrolled in the regular 2nd-grade class, does not demonstrate any HIV/AIDS symptoms; however, his mother has alerted the school of his condition.

APPLICATION TASK

What precautions should the elementary physical education teacher take with Jimmy and his class?

those who received transfusions before 1985), and those who have sexual contact with any of these groups. Worldwide, 75 percent of AIDS cases are a result of heterosexual transmission.[88] A child can get the HIV virus from the mother during pregnancy, childbirth, and breastfeeding.

Characteristics

HIV infection causes a wide range of symptoms ranging from flulike symptoms to full-blown AIDS. There are three recognized stages of development. During stage 1, the person tests positive for HIV, but no symptoms are present. This stage can last as long as 10 years. During stage 2, there are severe weight loss and wasting, chronic diarrhea, nonproductive cough with shortness of breath, dementia, fevers of unknown origin, chronic fatigue, swollen lymph glands, and decreased food consumption. With appropriate drug intervention, this stage can last several years. In stage 3, fully developed AIDS is apparent, which puts the individual at risk for infection and malignancy. Children born to HIV-positive mothers demonstrate significant mental and motor delays[16] that are apparent as early as four months.[26] However, thanks to the advances in the development of antiviral agents and adjunct therapies, a relatively

high quality of life can be enjoyed for many years.[60]

Special Considerations

Because of the manner in which the virus is spread, caution should be exercised if the child with HIV/AIDS becomes injured and there is blood loss. Although the risk of contracting HIV/AIDS through providing first-aid assistance is minimal, the Universal Precautions to protect against all infectious diseases should be followed. Those precautions state that staff must routinely use appropriate barrier precautions to prevent skin and mucous membrane exposure to blood and body fluids containing visible blood in the following ways:

1. Whenever possible, wear disposable plastic or latex gloves. Use towels or cloth between yourself and blood or body fluids when gloves are not available.
2. Always wear gloves whenever you are in contact with blood, body fluids, diapering, or invasive procedures if you have an open wound or a lesion.
3. Toys should be cleansed by immersing them in a germicidal solution and rinsed thoroughly after use each day.
4. Cleaning up spills of body fluids requires the use of gloves. All surfaces should be cleansed with a germicide solution and rinsed, then air dried.
5. Soiled cloths and diapers should be placed in a plastic bag and given to the parent to clean at home.
6. Trash should be placed in a plastic bag and tied securely for removal.
7. All staff must use hand-washing techniques between handling each child during feedings, diapering, and nose cleaning.[77]

Athletic governing bodies are becoming more aware of the risks associated with the HIV virus. Rather than ban players known to be HIV-positive from competition, caution should be exercised.[70] Commonsense techniques that can prevent transmission include covering open wounds before competition and removing bleeding players from competition until wounds can be covered. In sports carrying a high risk for bleeding, such as wrestling and hockey, athletes should be encouraged to submit to voluntary testing to determine their HIV status.[88] It is not permissible to exclude individuals who are HIV-positive from activities, even high-risk ones, without medical justification.[70]

Teaching Strategies

All schools should require that HIV infection, HIV disease, and AIDS information be included in the school curriculum; however, increasingly in the United States sex-related topics are being removed from health education content. To deny a teacher the right to share information critical to a student's health and welfare seems shortsighted and contrary to good educational practice; however, teachers must follow administration policies or risk dismissal. In schools where these topics cannot be included in the curriculum, the school administration should be encouraged to allow medical resources in the community to provide this vital information and to solicit parental support for accessing those professionals.

A student who is HIV-positive can be included in the physical education program without the teacher's being aware of the condition. A physician may not disclose the status of a child's health to a third party without parental consent; however, in many states public health laws require the reporting of HIV cases to a state agency.[70] This information may, or may not, be shared with the school. If the teacher is aware of a student with an HIV condition, precaution should be taken to avoid an injury that leads to bleeding. Most schools have developed policies to follow, should such injuries occur. Ways to prevent the possibility of contamination through contact with blood should be part of those policies, and they should be followed to the letter.

If the other students in the class are aware of the presence of a student who is HIV-positive and the school administration and the student approve, a frank discussion with the class should allay fears of the infection's being spread to classmates. Students should understand the condition, as well as the necessary precautions.

As is always the case, a sensitive, knowledgeable teacher who treats all students with respect and courtesy can make a tremendous difference in the quality of interaction that occurs in a class. Teachers must set the pace for the class by always presenting themselves as accepting, caring individuals who value all students. McHugh[66] suggests several ways teachers can address students' social needs in the physical education setting. The ideas she presents could be incorporated into any physical education class but would be particularly effective in a class where one or more students were differently abled. Those suggestions include (1) naming a most valuable person each day in physical education class (chosen alphabetically) and honoring that person throughout the day and (2) sending home a Sunshine Gram once a month, acknowledging children's positive qualities.

The Physical Education Program

Children in the public school who are HIV-positive should have an individual education program (IEP) commensurate with their needs. Because exercise has been shown to be helpful in delaying the progress of the disease, physical activities are recommended.[106] The physical education teacher should consult with each student's physician to determine activity levels. Because of the progressive nature of HIV diseases, students' levels of physical and motor performance should be assessed frequently and their program modified to accommodate their levels of function. Surburg[96] has suggested that procedures for implementing physical education programs for high school students with HIV/AIDS should include providing appropriate rest periods, monitoring pulse rate, generally increasing the intensity level of exercise, and reducing activity in hot and/or humid conditions. However, for children who are rapidly deteriorating physically, it may be realistic to develop a program that will promote the maintenance of existing skills and capabilities. Each child with HIV/AIDS is different because of the many forms of the illness; however, the ultimate goal should always be to include the student in as many activities as possible. The limitations to expect during physical activity (including testing) and the effects of exercise on individuals with HIV/AIDS are presented in Table 18-3.

Modifications, Adaptations, and Inclusion Techniques

Although some lower federal courts have ordered HIV-positive youth not to participate in school-sponsored contact sports, that position conflicts with U.S. Supreme Court authority.[70] The teacher cannot arbitrarily exclude a student from an activity without medical justification. Rather, if the student who is HIV-positive has been identified, and his or her physician contacted for program suggestions, modifications, and limitations, the teacher should discuss the content of the student's physical education program with the student. It is critical that the student understand the potential for injury in the various activities in the program and be given the option to participate or select an alternative. Should the student decide to engage in all the class activities, the teacher is responsible for keeping the potential for injury to a minimum.

Community-Based Opportunities

The Americans with Disabilities Act of 1990 prohibits unjustified discrimination against all persons with disabling conditions.[70] All members of the community should have an opportunity to select the types of leisure activities they enjoy and can afford. It should be no different for the individual who is HIV-positive. In most of the larger communities in the United States, support groups for individuals who are HIV-positive have been formed and are available for the asking. Individuals who make up these support groups should encourage the person who is HIV-positive to enjoy those activities for which he or she has the interest and strength. As is always the case, precautions should be taken, should an injury occur that results in bleeding.

ANEMIA

Definition

Anemia is a condition of the blood in which there is a deficiency of red cells or hemoglobin (a molecule in red blood cells that carries oxygen) in circulation.[14] There are several forms of anemia, which are classified as either acquired or congenital.[8] Examples of each are presented in Table 18-4.

Table 18-3	Limitations and Results of Exercise on Individuals with Various Stages of HIV Infection	
Stage	**Limitations**	**Results of Exercise**
1	No limitations for most	Increase in CD_4 cells Possible delay in onset of symptoms Increase in muscle function and size
2	Reduced exercise capacity Reduced VO_2 max Reduced heart rate and breathing reserve	Increase in CD_4 cells Possible diminished severity of symptoms
3	Dramatically reduced exercise capacity More severe VO_2 limitations than in stage 2	Effects on CD_4 cells unknown Effects on symptoms are inclusive

Source: Modified from LaPerriere A, Klimas N, Major P, Perry A: Acquired immune deficiency syndrome. In Durstine JL, editor: *Exercise management for persons with chronic diseases and disabilities.* Champaign, IL, Human Kinetics, 1997.

Table 18-4	Types of Anemia

Acquired

- Nutritional, such as iron, B_{12}, or folic acid deficiency
- Acute or chronic blood loss, as from a peptic ulcer or hemorrhoids
- A result of disease, such as leukemia, juvenile rheumatoid arthritis, destruction of red blood cells by abnormal antibodies formed in a disease state

Congenital

- Sickle cell
- Sperocytosis (abnormal red blood cell membranes)

Anemia requires medical intervention for management. The usual treatment includes nutritional supplements and transfusion. Anemia caused by disease is addressed by treating the disease.

Iron deficiency is commonly seen in teenage girls and especially in those who are active in sports. Care must be taken that nonanemic iron deficiency does not lead to anemic iron deficiency.

Sickle cell anemia, one of the most well-known forms of anemia, is an inherited disorder. In this form of anemia, not all of the person's hemoglobin works correctly. Some of the hemoglobin forms rodlike structures, which cause the blood cells to be sickle-shaped and stiff. These cells clog small blood vessels and prevent some tissues and organs from receiving adequate amounts of oxygen. When this occurs, severe pain results, and damage to organs and tissues frequently occurs.[55] The sites of the body most commonly affected by sickle cell anemia are the bones (usually the hands and feet in young children), intestines, spleen, gallbladder, brain, and lungs. Chronic ankle ulcers are a recurrent problem. Episodes of severe abdominal pain with vomiting may simulate severe abdominal disorders. Such painful crises usually are associated with back and joint pain. Sickle cell anemia affects African Americans and Hispanics from the Caribbean, South or Central America, and parts of South Africa.[24] Individuals of Mediterranean, Middle Eastern, and Indian ancestry have a similar form of anemia, which results from unbalanced hemoglobin synthesis.[14]

CASE STUDY 18-3

Sharone

Sharone is a 10-year-old boy with sickle cell anemia. Sharone loves physical education and dreams of playing professional football. However, he tires very quickly when he is involved in active play. He is very defensive about his anemia and tends to become disruptive in class rather than admit that he needs to stop and rest. In response to frustration if he cannot complete a task, he has occasionally become verbally and physically aggressive.

His object-control skills are excellent. He has acquired and uses, with ease, all of the basic locomotor skills: walk, run, gallop, jump, hop, and skip. However, his physical fitness scores are below average. He can complete only four full push-ups in 1 minute. He is able to do 9 abdominal curls in 1 minute. He is able to walk ½ mile in 18 minutes.

APPLICATION TASK

What can the physical educator do to help Sharone manage his behavior in the gymnasium?

Sports anemia afflicts athletes with low values of red blood cells or hemoglobin. These athletes range from fit individuals performing daily submaximum exercise to individuals participating in prolonged severe exercise and strenuous endurance training. Sports anemia is a consequence of physical activity and is only marginal.[22]

Incidence

The prevalence of iron deficiency anemia for adolescent girls and adult women in the United States is 2 percent and 5 percent, respectively; the reported incidence in high school and college female athletes ranges as high as 19 percent. In the United States, estimates of nonanemic iron deficiency, which can, if uncorrected, lead to iron deficiency anemia, are 11 percent for adult women and 9 percent for adolescent girls.[63] The sickle cell anemia trait is carried by about 8 percent of African Americans and 6 percent of Hispanics.[5]

Causes

There are many causes of anemia, which can be categorized as either congenital or acquired. The congenital form is present at birth. An example of this form is sickle cell anemia. The acquired form may occur at any time during one's life and persist or move into remission. Some of the specific causes of anemia are as follows:

- Iron deficiencies in the diet
- Inadequate or abnormal utilization of iron in the blood
- Menstrual loss (a primary source of iron loss in females)
- Chronic posthemorrhaging when there is prolonged moderate blood loss, such as that caused by a peptic ulcer
- Acute posthemorrhaging caused by a massive hemorrhage, such as a ruptured artery
- Decreased production of bone marrow
- Vitamin B_{12} deficiency
- Deficiency in folic acid, which is destroyed in long-term cooking
- Mechanical injury or trauma that impacts blood circulation
- Gastrointestinal loss, common in runners
- Urinary loss in the presence of urinary tract trauma
- Sweat loss when exercise is prolonged
- Disorders of red blood cell metabolism
- Defective hemoglobin synthesis[14,49,68]

Primary diseases that give rise to anemia as a secondary condition include malaria, septic infections, and cirrhosis. In addition, poisons, such as lead, insecticides, and arsenobenzene, may contribute to anemia. Diseases associated with endocrine and vitamin deficiencies, such as chronic dysentery and intestinal parasites, can also cause anemia.

Characteristics

The physical education teacher should be aware of the characteristics that anemic persons display. Some of the symptoms that signify anemia are an increased rate of breathing, a bluish tinge of the lips and nails (because the blood is not as red), headache, nausea, faintness, weakness, and fatigue. Severe anemia results in vertigo (dizziness), tinnitus (ringing in the ears), spots before the eyes, drowsiness, irritability, and bizarre behavior.[14] Children found to be iron deficient in early childhood, if treated only short-term (two weeks), demonstrate poor cognitive and motor development, as well as poor school achievement into middle childhood. Young children treated for longer periods of time overcome their performance deficiencies. Iron-deficient school-age children who are treated usually overcame their cognition deficits but don't catch up in school achievement.[44] The performance effects of iron deficiency anemia are presented in Table 18-5.

Testing

The student with anemia should be tested to determine the present level of physical fitness. Any standardized test may be used, as long as the teacher shortens the performance time during cardiovascular endurance activities. Selby[86] recommends using a six-minute walk for testing cardiovascular endurance. Motor skills can be evaluated using the TGMD for elementary children and the OSU-Sigma for middle and high school students.

Special Considerations

Anemia is symptomatic of a disturbance that, in many cases, can be remedied. Persons who have anemia because of a disease process have different

Table 18-5	Performance Effects of Iron Deficiency Anemia

Diminished VO_2 max
Decreased physical work capacity
Lowered endurance
Increased lactic acidosis
Increased fatigue

medical needs than athletes with sports anemia who are apparently healthy. The school nurse should be alerted if a student is suspected of being anemic. The nurse will be able to recommend specific medical intervention to enable treatment to be determined and initiated. Inasmuch as there are several varieties of anemia, the method of treatment depends on the type of anemia present. Treatment of iron deficiency anemia usually involves physician-directed iron supplementation. Physicians usually prescribe several months of iron therapy coupled with supplements of vitamin C for individuals who are nonanemic iron deficient.[49] Aplastic anemia may be corrected by bone marrow transplantation and by use of the male hormone testosterone, which is known to stimulate the production of cells by the bone marrow if enough red marrow is present for the hormone to act on. Vitamin B_{12} is stored in the liver and is released as required for the formation of red blood cells in the bone marrow.

There is no drug therapy for sickle cell anemia. The symptoms are treated as they appear. During painful episodes, pain-killing drugs and oral and intravenous fluids reduce pain and prevent complications.[6] The initial symptoms of overexertion are headache or dizziness, leg cramps, chest pain, and left upper quadrant pain.[37] Continuing exercise under those conditions can lead to coma and death. Children with sickle cell anemia must rest when feeling tired, drink extra fluids when active, and dress appropriately for the weather. Also, activities that expose persons to cold weather or high altitudes, such as backpacking and skiing, should be avoided.[34] Coaches are advised that during preseason conditioning all athletes should train wisely, stay hydrated, heed environmental stress, and be alert to their reactions to heat.[37]

Teaching Strategies

The alert physical educator should be able to assist in the identification of anemia and thus refer the student to medical authorities. Undiagnosed anemia may curtail motor skill and physical development and thus may set the child apart from peers in social experiences. The student who has been identified as having anemia should be evaluated to determine physical fitness and motor skill development levels, so that an appropriate intervention program can be started.

The primary difficulty the student will experience is lowered stamina. Both the teacher and the student must be sensitive to the need to curtail activity levels, so that the student does not overexert during the physical education class period. Indications that the student is reaching a point of fatigue include loss of body control (e.g., running into other players, stumbling or falling frequently), irritability, loss of temper, breathlessness, and an unwillingness to continue to participate. Should any of these behaviors appear, if the student does not ask to sit out, the teacher should insist on an immediate rest period. The student will be the best judge of when to return to activity. In the meantime, the teacher should offer encouragement and be supportive.

The Physical Education Program

The final decision regarding the nature of physical education activities for a student with anemia should be made by medical personnel. A well-conceived and supervised physical education program can be of great value because exercise stimulates the production of red blood cells through the increased demand for oxygen. However, to be beneficial, an activity must be planned qualitatively with regard to the specific anemic condition. It is not uncommon for children who have anemia to be delayed in the development of physical strength and endurance.

Modifications, Adaptations, and Inclusion Techniques

For the most part, students with anemia can participate in physical activities in the regular program; however, they should be closely monitored. Appropriate activities include modified (if needed) activities and prerequisite activities, such as balance, eye-hand coordination, gross body coordination, and agility, as well as physical fitness components, such as strength, endurance, and flexibility. Experiences that minimize access to a ready supply of oxygen—such as underwater swimming, in which students may be required to hold their breath for prolonged periods—should be avoided.[35]

Community-Based Opportunities

Individuals who have been provided with information about the impact of anemia on physical performance and stamina while in school will be alert to signs and symptoms that emerge after the school years. Medical advice should always be sought because most types of anemia can be treated and physical fitness levels restored. However, adults with anemia should participate in physically demanding activities only under the supervision of a physician or physical therapist.

ASTHMA

Definition

Asthma is a pulmonary disease characterized by reversible airway obstruction, airway inflammation, and increased airway responsiveness to a variety of stimuli.[14]

Incidence

Asthma is the single most chronic disease in childhood, affecting 5 million children in the United States. The number of individuals with asthma has increased in the last few decades.[59] The condition is disproportionately high among inner-city children.[56] Asthma-related illness accounts for 15 million school days missed annually.[59]

Causes

The disease is a result of the body's reaction to an allergen, such as animal dander, mold spores, pollens, or house dust mites; to a nonallergenic stimulus, such as cold air or exercise; or to chemical substances, such as tobacco smoke, fungi, mold, and polluted indoor air.[12] The airways become

---

CASE STUDY 18-4

Anna

Anna is a 10-year-old girl attending a rural elementary school within 15 miles of a major industrial city. Anna has asthma, complicated by allergies to ragweed and cedar elm. Her asthma symptoms increase dramatically on days in which the pollution count is particularly high and she becomes very ill on days in which there is an ozone alert.

Anna's mother has been very overprotective. She provides countless physician's excuses, so that Anna is not able to participate regularly in her school's physical education program. Her lack of activity has contributed to obesity, which has created a vicious cycle; it is difficult for her to move, so she doesn't move, so she becomes more obese, and her asthma symptoms increase in severity.

APPLICATION TASK

With a partner, role-play. One person is the physical educator trying to convince the mother to allow Anna to participate in physical education. The partner is the mother trying to explain why she doesn't.

---

obstructed because of a combination of factors, including a spasm of smooth muscle in the airways, edema of the mucosa in the airways, increased mucus secretion, infiltration of the cells in the airway walls, and eventual permanent damage to the lining of the airways.[14] Asthma can be controlled by medications; however, nonadherence by children with asthma ranges from 17 to 90 percent.[33]

Characteristics

The symptoms of asthma vary widely. Some asthmatics just wheeze and have a dry cough. Others have a tight chest, wheeze and cough frequently, and have increased difficulty breathing following exposure to allergens, viral infections, and exercise.[14] An attack usually begins with an irritating cough, and the student complains of a tightness in the chest and difficulty breathing, especially during inspiration. The severity of the attack can be measured by the symptoms (see Table 18-6). The early warning signs of an asthmatic attack are (1) a feeling of pressure on the chest, (2) chronic, persistent cough, (3) shortness of breath, (4) exercise intolerance, (5) sore throat, (6) restlessness, (7) headache, (8) runny nose, (9) clipped speech, (10) changes in breathing patterns, and (11) change in face color.[3]

Exercise-induced asthma (EIA) is acute airway narrowing after strenuous exertion.[98] The symptoms include chest tightness, shortness of breath, coughing, wheezing, fatigue, and prolonged recovery time.[85] The reaction starts 5 to 20 minutes after beginning to exercise. The symptoms peak about 5 to 10 minutes after stopping exercise.[40] A second reaction 3 to 9 hours after exercising can occur. About 50 percent of asthmatics have a refractory period of 2 to 4 hours after ceasing to exercise. During the refractory period, their airways respond to a second bout of exercise 50 percent better than during the initial exercise period.[85] EIA affects 12 to 15 percent of the population.[85]

Table 18-6	Levels of Severity of an Asthma Attack[14]
Stage	**Symptoms and Signs**
I: Mild	Adequate air exchange, mild shortness of breath, diffuse wheezing
II: Moderate	Respiratory distress at rest, marked wheezing, use of accessory muscles to breathe, difficulty breathing
III: Severe	Marked respiratory distress, cyanosis, inability to speak more than a few words, marked wheezing, and use of accessory muscles to breathe
IV: Respiratory failure	Severe respiratory distress, lethargy, confusion, marked use of accessory muscles to breathe

Testing

The medical history of the student with asthma should always be reviewed before testing.[95] Particular attention should be paid to whether the student has EIA, what medications are being taken, and the student's normal activity level. No modifications of test procedures are necessary unless indicated in the medical history; however, cardiovascular endurance tests should not be given when the student is experiencing any upper respiratory distress, either as a result of a cold or in response to pollen, mold, dust, or dry, cold air. The student with asthma should be monitored during testing for signs of distress and allowed to determine the need to discontinue. If a fitness test is being used to measure cardiovascular endurance, a 10-minute gradual warm-up should take place.[98] The test should start slowly until the target heart rate is reached and then should continue for 8 to 10 minutes.[30] Strength testing or training that involves lifting heavy weights while holding the breath or sustaining forced expiration should be avoided.[71]

Special Considerations

Most individuals with asthma who are under a physician's care take either oral or inhaled medication to control their condition. The use of medication before exercise will allow most individuals with asthma to perform to the level of their nonasthmatic peers. Two categories of medication are used to reverse or prevent airflow obstruction for both acute and chronic asthma: anti-inflammatory agents and bronchodilators.[17] Corticosteroids (taken orally, intravenously, or as an inhalant) and nonsteroidal inhalants, such as cromolyn sodium, are used to control inflammation. Bronchodilators include beta 2-agonists and methylxanthines, such as theophylline.[17] Beta 2-agonists are the most effective bronchodilators to prevent and reverse EIA. One or two doses just before exercise will greatly enhance the student's ability to persist with an exercise bout. Those who do not benefit from beta 2-agonist inhalants frequently use the nonsteroidal inhalant cromolyn sodium because it blocks the postexercise bronchoconstriction that occurs several hours after exercise.[7] The usual respiratory medications are not effective in preventing or reducing ozone-induced pulmonary effects.[53]

An indoor environment that contains mold, dust, or insects can trigger and exacerbate respiratory symptoms.[56] Recently, it has been reported that chlorinated by-products that contaminate the air in indoor pools can promote the development of asthma in some children. As a result, chlorinated pool use prior to ages six to seven years is discouraged.[15]

Teaching Strategies

It is important for individuals with asthma to participate in the regular physical education class because of the physical and psychological benefits of exercise and the opportunities to socialize with classmates. Individual attention should be provided when needed to give the student the opportunity to develop sport skills to gain greater status and recognition by others.[71] As is always the case, an understanding and sensitive teacher can make the difference between an outstanding experience and a devastating one. The teacher must be aware of the student's condition, limitations, and anxieties in order to adjust the activity demands on the student and to foster understanding among other students in the class. A moderate or severe asthma attack can be very frightening to the child who is having the attack, as well as to the classmates who observe it. The teacher should request permission from the parents and the child who has asthma to provide information about asthma to the entire class.

The Physical Education Program

Inasmuch as children with asthma vary in their capabilities to participate in intense activity, each student's physical education program should be individualized as much as possible. This is not to say the program should be watered down for these students. Clearly, many persons with asthma are world-class athletes. In fact, 10 to 15 percent of Olympic athletes have exercise-induced asthma.[95] Thus, assumptions should not be made about the physical capabilities of students with asthma. For the most part, students with asthma can participate in the regular program without modification; however, environmental controls, special instruction in breathing and conscious relaxation, and a carefully controlled progressive exercise program are critical for these students.

The person with asthma must be selective about when and where to exercise. Gong and Krishnareddy[42] recommend limiting outdoor exercise to early morning or evening to avoid peak airborne allergen levels. Also, whenever possible, exercising in cold and dry environments, as well as outside on high ozone-level or allergen-level days, should be avoided.[43] Swimming in a heated pool and walking indoors are the least reaction-provoking activities; scuba diving is contraindicated for this population.[71]

All students should be taught to breathe through the nose and trained in abdominal breathing. Breathing through the nose allows the air to warm as it enters the body and controls the rate of expiration. Conscious relaxation and abdominal breathing are recommended as part of the cooldown to reduce postexercise reactions.[71] Abdominal (deep) breathing can be accomplished by having the students lie on their backs on the floor and place one or both hands on their abdomens as they proceed with the following instructions:

1. Inhale slowly and naturally through the nose deep enough to push the diaphragm down (which will cause the hands on the abdomen to rise).
2. Exhale slowly against pursed lips to keep the small airways open.
3. Pause without holding the breath and count to self 1,001, 1,002. During this pause, allow the exhalation to come to a natural, unforced conclusion.
4. Repeat the first three steps for several minutes.

Abdominal breathing exercises will increase the strength and endurance of the respiratory muscles and will allow greater amounts of air to be inhaled and to be made available for exercise. Students with asthma should be cautioned that breathing in this manner may initially increase their phlegm and cause them to cough and wheeze. After extended training, those reactions will be greatly reduced.

At the elementary school level, every class should end with three to four minutes of relaxation techniques. At the middle and high school levels, relaxation sessions should be included at the end of any class using high-cardiovascular endurance activities. Training in relaxation is particularly critical for the individual with asthma because the practice can be used to lower the impact of anxiety on the body. When an individual's anxiety level is lowered, the tendency to cough and wheeze is also reduced.

Progressive exercise programs are a must for the individual with compromised endurance, whether it is a result of asthma, a sedentary lifestyle, or some other reason. Regular exercise that is gradually increased in frequency and intensity will improve respiration, circulation, physical functioning, and muscle strength.[92] Training outcomes for the student with asthma will include (1) increased physical exercise capacity at which one can exercise before lactate begins to accumulate in the blood, (2) reduced residual volume of the lungs due to less air being trapped in the lungs, (3) a more efficient pattern of respiration due to slower and deeper breathing, and (4) increased maximal attainable rate of ventilation due to less air being needed to perform submaximal work.[71] Elementary school children will benefit from a movement education program that is essentially self-paced; older students require an ongoing physical fitness program that is designed to meet their specific needs. Specific exercise guidelines are presented in Table 18-7. See Chapter 8 for information on developing physical fitness programs.

Modifications, Adaptations, and Inclusion Techniques

Unless a physician indicates otherwise, no special modifications other than allowing the student to reduce his or her activity level and rest when needed are required for the student with asthma. However, until the student has developed skills and fitness

Table 18-7	Exercise Guidelines for Individuals with Asthma

1. Choose exercises that can be performed in a warm, humid environment, such as a pool.
2. If exercising outside in cold weather, wear a scarf or mask over the mouth to limit exposure to cold and pollutants.
3. Breathe through the nose whenever possible to warm and humidify inspired air.
4. Work out inside when pollutant or allergen levels are high outside.
5. Do 5 to 10 minutes of stretching and breathing exercises before a high-intensity workout.
6. Work out slowly for the first few minutes after warm-up.
7. Do a 10- to 20-minute cool-down after a workout.

Source: From Gong H, Krishnareddy S: How pollution and airborne allergens affect exercise *Physician Sportsmed* 23(7):35–42, 1995.

levels commensurate with his or her peers, the student's progress should be carefully monitored to ensure ease of participation and continual improvement. The student should be given responsibility for taking the appropriate dosage of medication before exercise and regulating his or her exercise pace. To keep the student's anxiety about the possibility of an asthma attack to a minimum, the teacher should ensure that the appropriate program is followed, should be attentive to the status of the student, and should provide needed encouragement. If a student experiences an asthma attack, the procedure presented in Table 18-8 is recommended.

Table 18-8	Intervention for an Asthma Attack

1. Remove the person from the group to reduce anxiety.
2. Encourage the person to breathe deeply and slowly.
3. Use a beta 2 aerosol, preferably albuterol.
4. Have the person get into a comfortable position.
5. Encourage the person to spit if needed to get rid of any mucous plugs.

Source: Modified from Rimmer JH: *Fitness and rehabilitation programs for special populations.* Madison, WI, Brown & Benchmark, 1994.

Community-Based Opportunities

Adults with asthma should be given every opportunity to participate in ongoing exercise programs of their choice. Students who have been carefully taught about healthful exercise practices will continue to accrue benefits from regular exercise during their adult years. Adults who have not received appropriate instruction during their school years should seek out a health club or a university that employs a certified exercise physiologist who will provide the needed testing and exercising information.

CHILDHOOD CANCER

Definition

Cancer is a cellular malignancy whose unique characteristic is a loss of normal cell control. The body loses control of its cells' growth and the distribution of cells by function. There is a lack of differentiation of cells; the cells tend not to assume a particular function in the body. In addition, these unique, apparently random cells have the ability to invade local, healthy tissues and to metastasize (spread), destroying the healthy cells.[14]

Incidence

Childhood cancer, a devastating disease, is the major cause of death by disease in children ages 15 and younger.[21] In 2005, 9,510 children were diagnosed with some form of cancer.[73] Leukemia accounts for 33 percent of childhood cancers. Brain and central nervous system tumors are the second most prevalent cancer in childhood.[74]

Causes

The onset of childhood cancer appears to be related to the relationship between the child's genetic/familial endowment and the child's environment. If the child has a chromosomal aberration, as is seen in Down syndrome, trisomy G, and Klinefelter's syndrome, the child is more likely than another to develop childhood cancer.[47] Chromosomal instability also is related to the development of

---

CASE STUDY 18-5

Jonathan

Jonathan is a five-year-old boy who was diagnosed with leukemia at age three. After innumerable hospital stays, rounds of chemotherapy, and eventually a bone marrow transplant, John is in a significant period of remission. His parents report that his prognosis is good.

Because Jonathan has spent so little time playing with other children his own age—in actuality, little time playing at all—he has developed no cooperative play skills. Jonathan engages in "onlooker" behavior, watching the other children play.

His leukemia, at this crucial stage in his development, has caused significant motor delays as well. He is able to walk, contralaterally. He can walk up and down stairs but uses a marked-time pattern. He can broad jump 6 inches but is unable to gallop, hop, or skip. He is unable to demonstrate age-appropriate object-control skills.

APPLICATION TASK

Describe some of the strategies the general physical educator might use to help Jonathan learn more age-appropriate play and motor skills. Briefly explain the type of activities that should be avoided during this critical phase of his development.

---

childhood cancers, as are inherited traits for immunodeficiency. The best example of this is the child born with AIDS; that child is highly likely to develop AIDS-related cancers.

The transformation of a cell from normalcy to malignancy is thought to occur in one cell through a series of two or more steps. The development of cancer cells, or malignancies, is initiated by a cell that is affected by an event. This cell then becomes an "initiated" cell. If this cell is further stimulated by an event, the cell may become precancerous. Any subsequent conversion or modification of this cell causes it to become malignant. Then the malignant cell "clones" itself. It appears that most tumors are clonal expansions of cells that grow unchecked because of acquired changes in the genes that regularly control the growth and development of cells.[105]

Common cancer-causing environmental substances include soot and mineral oil, arsenic, asbestos, hair dyes, painting materials, and lead.[14] If an infant is exposed to a large dose of lead, one of the child's cells may become an initiated cell. If that cell is subsequently exposed to additional large doses of lead, precancerous cell growth may be promoted. Any further modification of the cell may cause it to become malignant and then clone itself, metastasizing into other, healthy tissues.[52]

Characteristics

The general symptoms of childhood cancer include the following:

- Fatigue
- Weight loss
- Cough
- Changes in blood composition
- Changes in bowel activity
- Persistent pain
- Skeletal pain
- Fever
- Sweating[14]

Types of Childhood Cancers

Leukemias

Leukemias are cancers of the white blood cells, involving bone marrow, circulating white blood cells, and organs such as the spleen and lymph nodes.[14] The factors that predispose a child to the development of leukemia are the same as those that predispose a child to the development of other forms of childhood cancer. These include the Epstein-Barr virus, the human T-cell lymphotrophic virus, ionizing radiation, and chromosomal disorders (such as Down syndrome and Fanconi's anemia).[14] Acute leukemia is the most common form of malignancy in childhood.[46] There are two major forms: acute lymphoblastic leukemia (ALL) and acute nonlymphoblastic leukemia (ANLL).

Central Nervous System Tumors

The most common primary childhood brain tumors are astrocytomas, medulloblastomas, and brain stem gliomas.[46] These primary childhood tumors tend to remain confined to tissues within the central nervous system but are devastating in their impact on the total human being. Most of the general signs and symptoms of brain tumors are significantly related to elevated levels of intracranial pressure caused by the presence of abnormal tissue growth.[14,31]

Hodgkin's Disease

Hodgkin's disease in childhood is similar to the Hodgkin's disease that affects adults. About 15 percent of those affected by Hodgkin's disease are younger than 15 years of age. It is a chronic condition in which large, multinucleated reticulum cells (Reed-Sternberg cells) are present in lymph node tissue or in other nonreticular formation sites. The presence of these cells causes lesions. The primary lesions are located in the lymph nodes, spleen, and bone marrow.

Neuroblastoma

A neuroblastoma is the most common cancer in infants. It is a solid tumor arising in the adrenal gland or from the adrenal sympathetic chain.[14] One in 7,000 children under the age of five years is affected. Approximately 75 percent of the cases are found in children under the age of five years.[14,103]

Wilms' Tumor

Wilms' tumor is a malignant embryonal tumor of the kidney. It usually occurs in children under the age of five years, but occasionally in older children. A genetic effect has been identified in some cases.[14]

Soft Tissue Tumors

One of the more common forms of soft tissue tumors in children is rhabdomyosarcoma, representing approximately 65 percent of childhood soft tissue sarcomas.[31] This malignancy affects the muscle tissue and can arise from any type of muscle tissue.[14]

Bone Tumors

The two best known childhood bone malignancies are Ewing's sarcoma and osteosarcoma. Ewing's sarcoma is the second most common form of malignant primary bone tumor of childhood.[54] It is a round cell bone tumor of childhood. The primary bone tumor usually appears in the extremities and most commonly metastasizes to the lungs and bone marrow. Osteosarcoma appears between the ages of 10 and 20 years. Pain and a noticeable mass are the usual symptoms. It is most common in the knee joint and is highly malignant.

Retinoblastoma

A retinoblastoma is a malignant tumor that arises from the immature retina. The disease may be inherited and has been traced to an autosomal dominant trait.[14] It has a significant negative impact on the child's vision.

Testing

The young child who is just beginning school may be developmentally delayed because of limited opportunities to run and play. An evaluation of basic locomotor and object-control skills, such as the Test of Gross Motor Development, should be administered to identify the level of development. Also, if structural deviations, such as functional scoliosis, are suspected, a postural examination should be conducted.

No special testing modifications are required for students who have or are recovering from cancer; however, their tolerance for exercise may be considerably lower than that of their classmates. Individuals undergoing chemotherapy or radiation therapy are easily fatigued; however, strength and flexibility testing, as well as cardiorespiratory endurance testing, is recommended.[87]

When the cardiorespiratory endurance of students who have had cancer is being evaluated, it is recommended that a test requiring minimal endurance be used. A walk/run or a step test should be administered, and the student should be permitted to cease exercising, should fatigue set in.

Special Considerations

New and innovative treatments of childhood cancer have increased the likelihood that children who are diagnosed early will have a chance of survival. More than 73 percent of children with cancer are cured by surgery, chemotherapy, radiation, or a combination of these treatments.[73] Many of these survivors return to school and attempt to restore relative normalcy to their lives. The teacher must be aware of the side effects of the cancer and its treatment and be sensitive to the psychosocial needs of the student.

The side effects of the childhood cancers and their treatments have a negative impact on the following:

General intelligence
Age-appropriate developmental progress
Academic achievement
Visual and perceptual motor skills
Memory
Receptive and expressive language and attention/concentration[20]

Teaching Strategies

The teacher needs to be sensitive to the physical deficits and needs of the child survivor of cancer and work in close cooperation with the child's physician, rehabilitation therapist, and parents to develop a program that addresses the student's unique health needs. In addition, the teacher must be aware of the significant psychosocial effects that a life-threatening illness has on the child, the parents and siblings, members of the extended family, and friends. The child who is able to return to school, to move from the more restricted hospital/homebound education program to the less restricted public school program, will face peers with a history of markedly different experiences. It is frequently difficult for the child to make the transition from a life-and-death situation to a life of play, games, and sports. However, play, games, and sports often are a vital link to normalcy for the child.

The Physical Education Program

The physical education program for students recovering from cancer should be designed to meet demonstrated specific needs. If the child's physical development lags behind his or her peers, opportunities should be provided to promote development in the needed area. In elementary schools where a movement education program is in place, it is relatively easy to provide for individual differences. In more structured educational settings, care must be taken not to place the child in a game or play situation beyond his or her capabilities. These children should be assigned less active roles that will enable them to participate as they gain the needed skills and performance levels of their classmates. Highly competitive activities should be avoided, so that these students are not placed in a situation where the level of play creates a potential for injury, or where their need to restrict their all-out efforts results in negative reactions from teammates. Physical fitness regimens should begin at the student's present level of performance and slowly build toward higher levels of fitness. Many children who have been cured of leukemia have cardiovascular limitations; therefore, their aerobic exercise should be at submaximal levels.[87] Also, if a postural deviation is identified during testing, a corrective program should be initiated.

Modifications, Adaptations, and Inclusion Techniques

When a child returns to school after an extended absence because of cancer, special efforts should be made to help the child feel as one with his or her peers. Integration into educational settings can be aided by assigning buddies to interact with the student in various settings (e.g., lunch, physical education, field trips). The activity level the student is capable of maintaining is usually low because of the period of inactivity, as well as the therapeutic intervention. Regardless of the student's age, he or she must always be given the responsibility for self-regulating involvement in activity and determining when a rest period is needed.

Community-Based Opportunities

The student who has been given appropriate instruction in developing and maintaining a healthy lifestyle should continue to do so after leaving the school setting. The student who has been instructed in a variety of activities that are available in most communities will have the skills he or she needs to select from a variety of options.

CYSTIC FIBROSIS

Definition

Cystic fibrosis is a disease of the exocrine glands primarily affecting the gastrointestinal and respiratory systems.[14] A defect in a gene prevents chloride from entering or leaving cells, which results in production of a thick, sticky mucus that clogs ducts or tubes in some organs.[32] The primary organs affected are the lungs, pancreas, small intestine, and sweat glands.[32]

Incidence

The disease affects 1 in every 3,300 Caucasian births, 1 in every 15,300 African American births, and 1 in every 32,000 Asian American births.[14] During the past 50 years the median life span of individuals with cystic fibrosis has improved from 4.5 to 31 years.[14] Survival prospects are significantly better in patients without pancreatic insufficiency.

Causes

Cystic fibrosis is an inherited disorder that is generally fatal. It is the most common life-shortening genetic disease in the Caucasian population.

Characteristics

The disease is characterized by the production of abnormally thick mucus, impaired absorption of fat and protein, a high concentration of sodium and chloride in the sweat, and progressive lung damage. As the disease progresses, pulmonary function deteriorates and exercise tolerance diminishes.[76]

CASE STUDY 18-6

Pat

Pat is a 3rd-grader with cystic fibrosis. An excellent student, she tires easily and resents the time she needs to miss class for therapeutic treatments in the school nurse's office. She is acutely aware of the prognosis associated with cystic fibrosis. A gutsy little girl, she wants to make the most of every day.

Because of frequent and extended hospital stays, and periods of time when difficulty breathing has compromised her ability to participate in general physical education, her gross motor skills are typical of a younger child, age five years. She is unable to participate in any vigorous aerobic activity—running, bicycling, and so on.

APPLICATION TASK

Describe some activities typically associated with the 3rd-grade curriculum—rope jumping, tumbling, low-organized games, and lead-up games to team sports—and explain how the general physical education teacher can involve Pat.

The symptoms and severity of cystic fibrosis vary from apparently normal to markedly impaired health. Nearly all of the exocrine glands are affected to some degree. The lungs appear normal at birth, but thick mucous secretions eventually clog the bronchial tubes and impair breathing.[14] There is usually continuing destruction of pancreatic tissue. Older children may also have diabetes. There is considerable variance in the physical capabilities among children with cystic fibrosis.

Testing

Each program should be tailored to the individual's physical capability. Any standard motor development or motor proficiency test can be administered to students with cystic fibrosis. However, if a cardiovascular endurance test is going to be administered to determine exercise tolerance and maximum heart rate, the student's physician must be contacted to provide pulmonary function advice and clearance. Regardless of how cardiovascular endurance is measured, the initial pace should be slow and the increments gradual. Heart rate should be monitored constantly. Because individuals with cystic fibrosis have limited ventilation capacity, they may have to cease exercise before their maximum heart rate is reached.[76] If a treadmill or bicycle ergometer protocol is used, steady state can be assumed to have been reached between four and five minutes after the start of the exercise.[25] When measuring cardiovascular endurance, a self-paced six-minute walk test is recommended.[76] Should the individual show signs of pallor and/or breathlessness at any time, testing should be discontinued.

Special Considerations

Increased understanding about cystic fibrosis and the value of aggressive intervention programs has resulted in improved prognosis over the past 50 years. Successful intervention includes a special diet, control of infection, and pulmonary therapy.

Diet

To offset the undernourishment that results from the underabsorption of fat and protein, additions to the diet and supplements are used. The recommended special diet includes an intake of calories and protein that exceeds the Recommended Dietary Allowance (RDA) by 30 to 50 percent and a normal-to-high total fat intake. Twice the recommended daily allowance of multivitamins and supplemental vitamin E in water-miscible form are used to strengthen the immune system. Salt supplements during periods of exposure to high temperature and sweating reduce the risk for heat-associated illnesses.[14]

Control of Infection

A high incidence of pulmonary infections requires intermediate- to long-term use of antibiotics, depending on the individual. The use of ibuprofen has been shown to slow the rate of pulmonary function decline in children 5 to 13 years of age.[14] Vitamin K supplements are recommended for individuals receiving long-term antibiotic therapy and individuals with liver involvement.[14] Immunizations against whooping cough, measles, and flu are routine.

Pulmonary Therapy

Progressive bronchiolar and bronchial obstruction leads to infection of the bronchi and breakdown of lung tissue. Every effort is made to clear the bronchi of the thick mucus that accumulates continually. Pulmonary involvement leads to death in over 90 percent of individuals with cystic fibrosis. Pulmonary therapy to lessen the accumulation of mucus consists of postural drainage, percussion, vibration, and assistance with coughing on indication of pulmonary involvement. Oral and aerosol bronchodilators are also used to reverse airway obstruction.[14] In severe cases, the constant use of supplemental oxygen is necessary.

Teaching Strategies

It may be helpful for physical education teachers to understand the behavior and medical treatments of individuals with cystic fibrosis. The following are some common behaviors and needs they demonstrate:

- They need to cough out the mucus in their lungs. Therefore, they should be encouraged to do so. Other students in the class need to understand that cystic fibrosis is not a communicable disease.
- The student's diet may be different from the norm; as such, the child may need to make frequent trips to the restroom.
- Although individuals with cystic fibrosis may have less stamina than others, it is important that they participate in modified physical activity commensurate with their abilities.
- Some may be on medication for both pancreatic and lung involvement and may subsequently need to take medication during physical education class.

- Some individuals may also demonstrate asthma or exercise-induced asthma and will require the use of bronchodilator therapy prior to physical activities.[76] Aerosol bronchodilator drugs are helpful in some cases and may need to be administered in class.
- Precautions should be taken to minimize the probability of respiratory infections.
- Teenagers frequently demonstrate a declining tolerance for exercise. Their physical education activity should be modified accordingly.

The Physical Education Program

Studies have demonstrated that individuals who have cystic fibrosis can benefit greatly from participating in regular exercise. Ongoing exercise programs have been shown to improve the flow of mucus from the lungs, build endurance of the breathing muscles, and improve clinical status, sense of well-being, overall morale, and independence.[76] The primary aim of exercise should be to improve aerobic fitness. Twenty to 30 minutes of continuous aerobic exercise at a moderate intensity is recommended.[76]

The physical education program for young children with cystic fibrosis should not differ from that of their classmates. Students at the middle and high school levels should be encouraged to participate within their own limitations. They should be discouraged from engaging in highly competitive sports in which there are pressures to exercise beyond what is a safe level for the individual.[25] Their individual physical fitness program should begin with low-intensity exercise and gradually increase to a target intensity of 50 to 70 percent of maximum heart rate for 20 to 30 minutes per session.[25] Three to five times weekly is recommended, unless the person has severe dysfunction, in which case days of rest must be interspersed with exercise days.[25] The types of exercise programs that have been shown to benefit the individual with cystic fibrosis include running, swimming, bicycling, and active play. Neither sky diving nor water diving is recommended for the person who has cystic fibrosis.[25]

Modifications, Adaptations, and Inclusion Techniques

To offset the boredom that can come from participating in repetitive activities in large groups, it is recommended that individuals be given the opportunity to select from a variety of activities that interest and appeal to them. The greater the amount of selection available to high school students, the greater their interest and compliance over time.

Community-Based Opportunities

Exercising with others should be promoted. Individuals are more inclined to exercise regularly if they have a friend or family member to share an activity they enjoy. Public and private health clubs in the community can increase interest and participation by offering special exercise opportunities in addition to their usual exercise fare.

DIABETES

Definition

Diabetes is a general term referring to a variety of disorders that are primarily divided into two groups: diabetes mellitus and diabetes insipidus.[69] Diabetes mellitus is a group of diseases characterized by hyperglycemia resulting from defects in insulin secretion, insulin action, or both.[69] Diabetes insipidus results from an inability to concentrate urine in the kidneys. There are two types of diabetes insipidus: pituitary and nephrogenic.

At the recommendation of a committee sponsored by the American Diabetes Association, since 1997 diabetes mellitus, which is the most common form of diabetes, has been divided into the following four classifications:

- Type 1—diabetes mellitus, formerly called insulin-dependent diabetes—IDD or juvenile
- Type 2—diabetes mellitus, formerly called non-insulin-dependent diabetes—NIDD
- Type 3—other specific types of diabetes mellitus
- Type 4—gestational diabetes mellitus[69]

CASE STUDY 18-7

Kaneisha

Kaneisha is a 14-year-old girl who has been diagnosed with Type 2 diabetes. Kaneisha and her mother are working with a physician at a local clinic to help her lose weight, manage and control her diet, and increase her exercise and energy expenditure. This is complicated by the fact that Kaneisha is obese and very unfit.

APPLICATION TASK

The physician has recommended that Kaneisha participate in a carefully controlled walking program in general physical education. At the beginning of the semester, Kaneisha was able to walk only three minutes without stopping for rest. Her resting pulse was 105 beats per minute; at the end of her three-minute walk, her pulse was 120 beats per minute. After a two-minute rest period, her pulse was still 120 beats per minute.

Describe the specific strategies the physical educator would use to increase her aerobic fitness and energy expenditure.

Incidence

Diabetes is reported to be the most complicated disease managed in primary care in the United States.[57] About 21 million Americans have diabetes mellitus, and one-third of them do not know they have the disease.[51] Of those diagnosed, 80 percent have Type 2 diabetes and 10 percent have Type 1 diabetes.[75] The incidence of diabetes insipidus is much lower.

Causes

Diabetes mellitus has diverse genetic, environmental, and pathogenic origins.[14] Type 1 results in beta cell destruction, which usually leads to absolute insulin deficiency. Type 2 is characterized by insulin resistance in peripheral tissue and/or insulin secretory defects in a beta cell. Because 30 percent of adults and 25 percent of children in the United

States are obese, they are considered pre-diabetic, meaning they are at high risk of developing Type 2 diabetes.[51] Type 3 causes include genetic defects of beta cell function, diseases of the exocrine pancreas, genetic defects in insulin action, endocrinopathies, and drug- or chemical-induced diabetes. Type 4, gestational diabetes, is brought on by the metabolic stress of pregnancy; a genetic basis has not been confirmed.[64]

Both pituitary and nephrogenic diabetes insipidus have genetic bases. Pituitary diabetes insipidus results from damage to the pituitary gland and/or hypothalamus, which leads to a deficiency of antidiuretic hormone (ADH); it can be inherited or acquired. Nephrogenic diabetes insipidus is a genetic disorder that is caused by a lack of response of resorption of the renal tubules. Because fluids are not resorbed in the kidneys, urine is excreted frequently in a nonconcentrated form. The recommended treatment is adequate and ongoing water intake.[14]

Characteristics

In diabetes mellitus, the body is unable to burn up its intake of carbohydrates because of a lack of insulin production by the pancreas. The lack of insulin in the blood prevents the storage of glucose in the cells of the liver. Consequently, blood sugar accumulates in the bloodstream in greater than usual amounts (hyperglycemia). The chronic hyperglycemia of diabetes mellitus results in long-term damage to, dysfunction of, and failure of various organs, especially the eyes, kidneys, nerves, heart, and blood vessels.

Type 1 diabetes mellitus accounts for 10 to 15 percent of all diabetes mellitus. It must be controlled with insulin. An equal number of males and females are afflicted with the condition. The amount of insulin needed by these individuals varies widely. The biggest risk with this group is to take in more insulin than can be utilized, which will result in a hypoglycemic coma. Although Type 1 diabetes mellitus can occur at any age, it is usually acquired before age 30.[14] It is the form that is most prevalent in school-age children. The onset is acute (sudden), and early symptoms include weight loss

despite normal or increased dietary intake, frequent urination, and fatigue.[14] Persons with Type 1 diabetes may lower their need for insulin by exercising; however, they must monitor their carbohydrate intake before exercise and their blood sugar before, during, and after exercise, modifying their short-acting insulin injections accordingly.[100]

Type 2 diabetes mellitus is also characterized by hyperglycemia but, because individuals with this disease usually retain some insulin secretion capability, ongoing insulin therapy is usually not necessary. Its onset is gradual and for years it has been reported that it does not usually occur until after 30 years of age; however, more recent studies have documented a rising number of cases among individuals under the age of 20.[78,83] A far greater number of females than males are afflicted with this form of diabetes. Obesity, a sedentary lifestyle, and a family history of diabetes characterize Type 2 diabetes mellitus. Like Type 1, common symptoms include fatigue; weakness; thirst; frequent urination; lethargy; dry, hot skin; lack of hunger; a fruity or winelike odor; heavy, labored breathing; and eventual stupor or unconsciousness.[84] The children with Type 1 or 2 well-controlled diabetes who were raised in nonstimulating environments demonstrate significantly delayed gross and fine motor development as late as 12 years of age.[80]

Type 3, other specific types of diabetes mellitus, results from conditions and syndromes that impact glucose tolerance, such as cystic fibrosis, organ transplants, acromegaly, renal dialysis, and drugs and chemical agents.[14] Care of the person with Type 3 diabetes is tied directly to the primary condition or syndrome.

Type 4, gestational diabetes mellitus, is usually not identified until a woman becomes pregnant. All pregnant women should be screened for this type of diabetes because untreated gestational carbohydrate intolerance results in increased fetal and neonatal loss. The problem occurs in about 4 percent of all pregnancies; however, the incidence is higher in Mexican Americans, Indians, Asians, and Pacific Islanders.[14] Many pregnant women with Type 4 diabetes must take insulin during their pregnancy; however, diet modification, moderate exercise, maintenance of normal body weight, and weekly monitoring of glucose levels also aid in controlling the condition.

Testing

Recommendations for physical fitness testing depend on the person's age, the duration of the diabetes, and the existing complications.[1] Because of the impact exercise has on blood glucose levels, the student's physician should be contacted before stressful testing, particularly cardiovascular endurance and/or resistive exercise testing. The testing demands should be discussed with the physician to ensure that the exercise stress levels are within the student's workload capacity. In addition to medical guidance, the physical educator should discuss the type of testing that will be administered with the student before the testing sessions. Every effort should be made to balance the type of testing being done, so that the workload is consistent from one period to the next. Equalizing the workload demands will enable the student to determine appropriate levels of carbohydrate intake, blood glucose levels, and insulin dosage before the exercise period. Adequate amounts of water—and, in some cases, carbohydrates—must always be available to the student.

Special Considerations

Individuals with diabetes mellitus should be encouraged to exercise because regular, long-term exercise provides many benefits that contribute to control of the disease. However, unless strict food and insulin guidelines are followed, a single exercise bout can lead to negative reactions. Three negative exercise reactions that can occur but are avoidable are hypoglycemia (abnormally low blood sugar level), hyperglycemia (an excess amount of blood sugar), and ketoacidosis.

Hypoglycemia

Hypoglycemia is the greatest concern of the individual who has Type 1 diabetes mellitus. Signs of hypoglycemia include double vision, fatigue, excessive hunger, increased heart rate, nervousness, headache,

numbness, palpitations, slurred speech, excessive sweating, and tremor.[100] Taunton and McCargar[99] caution that hypoglycemia can occur during exercise because of the following:

- A greater and often unpredictable amount of glucose is used during exercise.
- Insulin efficiency is enhanced with exercise to an unpredictable extent.
- Counterregulatory hormonal mechanisms are often somewhat impaired during exercise, which may limit glucose release from the liver.
- People often exercise to lose or control weight and are hesitant to eat extra food before exercising.

Because school-age children who are diabetic most frequently have Type 1 diabetes, if they have a negative reaction to exercise, it will probably be in the form of hypoglycemia. Hypoglycemic reactions can occur because of an error in insulin dosage, a missed meal, unplanned exercise, or no apparent cause.[14] A hypoglycemic reaction should be suspected when a student who has Type 1 diabetes mellitus demonstrates any or all of the following symptoms:

Confusion
Inappropriate behavior
Visual disturbance
Stupor
Seizures

Should a student have a hypoglycemic reaction in class, the intervention presented in Table 18-9 should be performed.

Hypoglycemic reactions can be prevented by decreasing insulin or increasing carbohydrate consumption before, during, and after exercise. There are formulas for determining how much short-acting insulin can be reduced (never change the dosage of long-acting insulin); also, alternate injection sites should be selected (e.g., inject into the abdomen or a limb not used during exercise).

Hyperglycemia

Hyperglycemia is also a problem for the active individual with either Type 1 or Type 2 diabetes

Table 18-9	Intervention to Counter a Hypoglycemic Reaction

1. Give some form of sugar immediately (improvement should be evident within a few minutes). Use fast-acting sugar in the form of a small box of raisins, 4 ounces of regular (not diet) cola or fruit juice, five small sugar cubes, six or seven Life Savers, or 1–2 teaspoons of honey.[62]
2. When improvement occurs, give additional food and then have the child resume normal activities.
3. If the child does not improve after sugar intake, call parents, the physician, and emergency medical assistance.
4. If the child becomes unconscious or is unable to take the sugar, immediately call for medical assistance.

mellitus. Hyperglycemia results when daily exercise volume is suddenly reduced without increasing insulin or any oral agents being used to control glucose levels.[99] The symptoms of hyperglycemia are increased thirst and increased urination.

Ketoacidosis

Ketoacidosis is a violent reaction to a lack of circulating insulin. It is caused by the failure to take an appropriate dose of insulin or by an acute infection or trauma that requires additional insulin.[14] Students who forget to take their insulin or experience an acute infection or trauma may have a ketoacidotic reaction, with the following symptoms:

- Abdominal pain
- Dehydration caused by excessive urination
- Drowsiness
- Fruity-smelling breath
- Nausea
- Glucose and ketones in the urine

This condition requires immediate treatment with insulin, fluids, and electrolytes.[99] Delayed intervention can cause lethargy, which may lead to a coma.[14]

Teaching Strategies

The physical educator should be aware of students' individual needs. The school nurse can be very helpful in providing information about students who have existing medical conditions. After students with medical conditions are identified, programs of exercise should be established (with medical counsel) according to the needs of each student. The limits on the activity each diabetic child can perform vary; therefore, it is important that the physical educator be clear about the status of each child.

Information should be gathered from the primary physician, the student, and the student's caregivers. Awareness of the knowledge and attitudes of the student and his or her parents concerning the benefits of physical activity, the extent to which the student is able to monitor his or her own blood sugar levels, and the student's understanding of the condition all impact the type of physical education program the teacher recommends for the student. In addition, once a program of activity is initiated, the teacher is responsible for carefully monitoring the student's progress.

Every year more studies validate the roles of exercise and proper diet in the management of diabetes. As this knowledge reaches primary care physicians, they are better able to counsel individuals with diabetes and their caregivers about the importance of maintaining ongoing regimens of appropriate exercise and diet. The knowledgeable physician is the conscientious physical educator's best ally. The physical educator should seek both cooperation and advice from the physician. Information gathered should include the type of diabetes, the type of diet and therapeutic intervention, the knowledge level of the student and the student's parents or caregivers, recommendations of desirable activity levels, and contraindications.

Successful management of diabetes requires that the student participate in a regimen of care. Noncompliance with health practices related to diabetes can have serious short- and long-term effects. In general, a student with Type 1 or Type 2 diabetes mellitus should have the information presented in Table 18-10.

Table 18-10	**Required Practices of Students with Type 1 or Type 2 Diabetes Mellitus**

1. Blood sugar levels should be monitored before, during, and after workouts, and the diet should be adjusted to make up for energy lost during exercise. If the blood sugar is less than 100 mg/dl, a snack should be eaten that contains at least 15 to 30 grams of carbohydrate (e.g., a slice of bread or 60 to 120 calories of fruit or crackers).
2. Always eat something 2 to 3 hours before and after exercise.
3. Prevent dehydration by drinking 2 cups of water 2 hours before exercise, 1 to 2 cups 30 minutes before, 1/2 cup every 15 minutes during exercise, and enough afterward to regain any weight lost during the workout.
4. Spend 5 to 10 minutes warming up before exercising and cooling down after exercising with stretching and slow large muscle activity (e.g., walking, jogging).
5. Exercise with a buddy who knows the signs of hypoglycemia, hyperglycemia, and ketoacidosis.
6. Wear appropriate, well-fitting shoes for the activity (soft leather with few seams are best), and check feet regularly for infected blisters, scratches, or open wounds. Don't ever burst a blister.
7. Carry insulin, oral drugs, or hard candy with you.
8. Wear identification that gives your name, address, parents' home and work phone numbers, physician's name and phone number, and type of diabetes.
9. In addition, a student with Type 1 diabetes should
   a. Keep a logbook to record levels of blood sugar, dosage of insulin, amount and type of food eaten, and type and intensity of exercise. That information will help the student establish the relationship among those factors and be better able to adjust for low and high levels of blood sugar.
   b. Review the effect the frequent use of short-acting insulin has on blood sugar levels before, during, and after exercise.
   c. Not exercise if the blood sugar reading is less than 60 mg/dl.
   d. Time exercise to miss the peak period of administered insulin. Begin exercising no earlier than 1 hour after taking the insulin.
   e. Choose insulin administration sites away from actively exercising muscle groups.
   f. Take a high-carbohydrate snack, such as fruit juice, bread, or plain cookies, before exercise. Eat about 15 grams of carbohydrate or more if needed.
   g. For moderate bouts of exercise, reduce the dose of short-acting insulin by 10 percent. For vigorous bouts of exercise, reduce the dose of short-acting insulin by up to 50 percent.
   h. If using only intermediate-acting insulin, reduce the morning dose by 30 to 40 percent for moderate to vigorous exercise in the morning, midday, or early afternoon.
   i. Prevent nighttime hypoglycemia by exercising earlier in the day and by reducing insulin dosages in the evening after exercising. If hypoglycemia persists, monitor blood sugar levels at night and take additional carbohydrates before sleep.

The teacher may want to develop a checklist with all of this information for the student. Until the routine becomes habitual, the student can refer to the checklist daily and occasionally share the results with the teacher.

Data from Taunton JE, McCargar L: Staying active with diabetes: quick and helpful exercise tips. *Physician Sportsmed* 23(3):55–56, 1995.

The Physical Education Program

Regular exercise programs are of value to all individuals with diabetes, and it is particularly important that the child with diabetes be provided proper instruction that can be used throughout life. Exercise is an essential component of an effective treatment program for many diabetics. Gary Hall, a world-class swimmer who was diagnosed with Type 1 diabetes at age 24, went on to win a gold medal in the 50-meter freestyle race during the 2000 Olympiad. He was able to maintain his eight-hour-daily, six-day-a-week practice regime by working closely with a physician who specialized in diabetes.[65] An exercise program may be helpful in the following ways:

1. It may improve diabetic control by decreasing the insulin requirements for insulin-dependent diabetics.[1,62]

2. Strengthening of skeletal muscles can make a significant contribution to the control of diabetes.[62]
3. It reduces the risk of coronary heart disease by controlling risk factors, such as overweight.[1,62]
4. It provides increased stamina and physical functioning to improve work capacity.
5. It provides a sense of well-being and self-confidence.
6. It improves serum lipid levels.[1]
7. It reduces stress.[1]
8. It controls weight.[107]
9. It increases VO_2 max.[107]
10. It increases insulin sensitivity.[107]
11. It increases muscular strength.[18,72]

The child with diabetes can and should participate, in general, in the activities of the unrestricted class. However, many diabetic patients are more susceptible to fatigue than are their nondiabetic peers. Therefore, the physical educator should be understanding in the event that the diabetic student cannot withstand prolonged bouts of more strenuous exercise.

The intensity of aerobic activities will be determined by the present levels of performance assessed through testing. Individuals who have been sedentary and have not been able to develop adequate physical fitness levels should begin slowly and progress at a rate commensurate with their capability. The student's reactions during and after exercise will dictate the intensity, duration, and frequency levels. Individuals with either Type 1 or Type 2 diabetes mellitus should eventually participate in aerobic activity three to five times weekly for 30 minutes at 50 to 70 percent of maximal oxygen uptake.[99] To sustain that percentage, a heart rate between 100 and 160 should be maintained. Albright[1] suggests that a workout should include large muscle aerobic activities, strength training, stretching, and activity-specific exercise.

Modifications, Adaptations, and Inclusion Techniques

As indicated earlier in this section, it is recommended that the student with diabetes mellitus be included in the regular physical education program but be given the opportunity to rest when needed. To aid the teacher in monitoring student status, a buddy who has been trained to recognize the previously described adverse reactions to exercise should be assigned to exercise with the student with diabetes.

In developing an exercise program, it is desirable to provide activity that meets the student's interests and needs and still uses the large muscles of the body. Sport activity and aerobic exercise, such as walking, jogging, cycling, swimming, and cross-country skiing, are particularly desirable. Adults with Type 1 or Type 2 diabetes mellitus should avoid activities that would place them or others at significant risk of injury, such as scuba diving, hang gliding, parachuting, and automobile racing. Also, individuals with diabetes who develop autonomic neuropathy may bicycle and swim but should probably avoid running and hiking. Should retinopathy develop, activities that cause sudden increases in blood pressure, such as weight lifting, sprints, and other intense exercise, should be avoided.[99]

Community-Based Opportunities

Individuals who have grown up with diabetes and have been provided an appropriate physical education should reach adulthood with all the information necessary to maintain a healthy lifestyle. They should use the public and private recreational facilities of their choice with proper precautions, including alerting supervisory personnel of their condition and wearing identification with diabetic information and the emergency procedure that should be followed if a negative reaction to exercise occurs. If they decide to participate in training regimens for participation in sports, athletes with either Type 1 or Type 2 diabetes should maintain a diet similar to that of nondiabetic athletes. Their diets should be 55 to 65 percent carbohydrate, 10 to 15 percent protein, and 25 to 30 percent fat. Energy and water requirements of these athletes are greater than those of nonaffected athletes.[100]

PRADER-WILLI SYNDROME

Definition

Prader-Willi syndrome is a group of symptoms that begins with hypotonia, a weak cry, and feeding difficulty in infancy. An insatiable appetite and pica behavior (eating indiscriminately—dirt, crayons, paste, paper, and so on), which leads to obesity, begins between two and five years of age and persists throughout life.[79]

Incidence

The incidence of the condition is reported to be 1 in every 12,000 to 15,000 births. Both genders and all races are affected equally.[79]

Causes

The cause of Prader-Willi syndrome is a deletion of portions of, or an absence of, the paternally contributed chromosome 15.[102]

Characteristics

Children and adults are short and have small hands and feet, almond-shaped eyes, a triangular mouth, a prominent nasal bridge, underdeveloped gonads, and low muscle tone. Behavior difficulties, including temper tantrums, stubbornness, noncompliance, argumentativeness, manipulation, and resistance to change, begin early in childhood and persist throughout adulthood.[79] As a group, individuals with Prader-Willi syndrome are very heterogeneous, with IQs ranging from less than 20 to 100. Many individuals with intelligence in the normal range have learning disabilities but demonstrate strong visual-spatial perception.[104] The use of growth hormone therapy during early childhood has been shown to have a positive impact on motor development, including increased height, muscle mass, and endurance and reduced body fat.[38]

Testing

A self-testing program in which the learner is actively involved in the evaluation process is best for

---

CASE STUDY 18-8

Bobby

Bobby is a nine-year-old boy with Prader-Willi syndrome. He is receiving the majority of his educational services in a self-contained classroom for children who have intellectual deficits. Bobby has been tested on several occasions, and his IQ composite scores range from 58 to 68.

Bobby was tested by an adapted physical education specialist. His scores on the Test of Gross Motor Development showed a significant delay. In fact, his gross motor performance is more typical of a five-year-old than a nine-year-old.

His gross motor performance and his health are seriously compromised by his high body fat percentage. At his last clinical evaluation, Bobby's total body fat percentage was in excess of 35 percent.

He has few friends, even in his self-contained classroom.

APPLICATION TASK

Can Bobby be successful in a general physical education curriculum? If so, what accommodations will the teacher need to make to ensure his success? If not, what can be done for Bobby in a separate, adapted physical education class?

---

the student with Prader-Willi syndrome. As with any obese learner, he or she will experience considerable failure and embarrassment if asked to participate, for example, in mass fitness testing. A time should be selected when the teacher can work one-on-one with the student, or the student's movements should be observed during routine class activities.

Special Considerations

The physical educator or adapted physical educator must work closely with the learner's parents. In addition to the physical education program at school, it is vital that the parents engage the child in regular exercise in the home. The physical educator can help the parents develop a home walking program, for example, that includes all family members. In addition to ongoing communication with the parents, it is vital that the school nurse be involved in the development of the IEP and be an active participant in the IEP meeting. The school nurse should schedule regular checkups in which the learner's height and weight, heart rate, and blood pressure are monitored.

Teaching Strategies

Developing strategies for externally motivating the student with Prader-Willi syndrome is an integral part of teaching. As is typical of most obese children, the student with Prader-Willi syndrome tends to fall into a vicious cycle in which he or she avoids activity because of a history of failure—gaining more weight and fatty tissue—which makes movement yet more difficult, increases the likelihood of failure, and encourages the student to avoid activity all the more. To provide motivation, so that the child with Prader-Willi syndrome will persist, the use of a reward/encouragement system is usually critical. Rewards that may be particularly helpful in reinforcing interest in play, games, and leisure, recreation, and sport activities include baseball cards, five minutes to "shoot hoops" one-on-one with the teacher before or after school, and passes to sporting events. When behavior modification programs are used to motivate students with Prader-Willi syndrome, food should never be used as a reinforcer.

The Physical Education Program

Because of the characteristic obesity, precautions must be taken to avoid overtaxing the cardiovascular system. It is crucial that these individuals participate in calorie-burning activities—activities that will elevate the body's metabolism. These individuals should participate in activities commensurate with their abilities; however, heart rate and blood pressure should be routinely monitored. In addition, it is vital that these individuals learn the skills necessary to participate in leisure and recreation activities. This is a better alternative than sedentary activities, which tend to be the choice of obese individuals.

A program with a wide range of activities, particularly individual leisure and recreation activities in which the learner has some choice in selection, is useful for the learner with Prader-Willi syndrome. Having the opportunity to select Frisbee golf, rather than vaulting in a gymnastics unit, for example, will free the learner to develop a sense of competency in activity. In programs in which such choices are limited by necessity because of staff and facility limitations, a station approach to intervention may be helpful. For example, in a physical fitness unit, the learner may be given the opportunity to move to a station in which he or she plays catch with a medicine ball, rather than trying to climb a suspended rope. Once again, if the learner is given a choice, he or she may experience success—and then be more likely to seek, rather than avoid, movement.

Modifications, Adaptations, and Inclusion Techniques

Children and young adults with Prader-Willi syndrome are discriminated against more because of their obesity than because of their potentially limited intelligence. Under no circumstances should a learner with Prader-Willi syndrome be required to use a group shower; this is particularly crucial for an adolescent because embarrassment about the reduced size of genitalia may be devastating at this vulnerable developmental stage. In addition, if aquatics are part of the curriculum, the learner and the parents should discuss participation, and the learner should be given the opportunity to choose not to participate. If the learner chooses to participate, an individual dressing area is crucial, and the learner should be allowed to wear a T-shirt over his or her swimming suit.

A buddy system may be particularly helpful for the learner with Prader-Willi syndrome. The teacher must enlist the help of a caring and nurturing peer who will be a buddy to the learner during class and who will interact with the learner at lunch, during recess, and before or after school.

Community-Based Opportunities

The learner with Prader-Willi syndrome may experience success in a number of leisure and recreation activities. These community-based opportunities include, but are not limited to, the following:

Bowling

Frisbee and Frisbee golf

Miniature golf

Archery

Riflery

Camping

Walking/hiking

It is important for the physical educator or adapted physical educator to discuss neighborhood leisure and recreation choices with the student and his or her family to identify common interests. The student with Prader-Willi syndrome, for example, may experience great success in bowling, but, if no one in the family and/or neighborhood bowls, it is unlikely the learner will use the skills within the community. Selecting activities that some or all of the family enjoy will increase the likelihood that the student will pursue opportunities to participate in the activity after the school years.

PREMENSTRUAL SYNDROME AND DYSMENORRHEA

Premenstrual syndrome and dysmenorrhea, though not conditions covered under the laws, are widespread conditions that affect many females. The conditions impact teenage girls' participation in physical education. Menstruation is a complex process that involves the endocrine glands, uterus, and ovaries. The average menstrual cycle lasts 28 days; however, each girl or woman has her own rhythmic cycle of menstrual function. The cycle periods usually range from 21 to 35 days, but they may be longer or shorter and still fall within the range of normal.

The average total amount of blood lost during the normal menstrual period is 3 ounces; however,

from 1½ to 5 ounces may be lost. This blood is replaced by the active formation of blood cells in bone marrow and, consequently, does not cause anemia. On occasion, some girls or women may have excessive menstrual flow, and in this event a physician should be consulted. The average menstrual period lasts 3 to 5 days, but 2 to 7 days may be considered normal. The average age of onset of menstruation is 12.5 years, although the range of onset is from 9 to 18 years. Premenstrual syndrome (PMS) and/or dysmenorrhea is associated with most females' menstrual cycle.

Definitions

PMS is a condition that occurs during the 7 to 10 days before menstruation and usually disappears a few hours after the onset of menstrual flow; however, it may persist throughout the menses.[14] Dysmenorrhea is cyclic pain that usually starts just before or with menses, peaks in 24 hours, and subsides after 2 days.[14]

Incidence

Significant functional dysmenorrhea is more common in the teenage years and tends to diminish after a woman gives birth, whereas PMS frequently begins in the twenties and increases with age.[108] These two conditions are the leading causes of females' absenteeism from work, school, and other activities.[108]

Causes

PMS seems to be related to estrogen and progesterone imbalances; however, carbohydrate metabolic changes, retention of sodium and water by the kidneys, and psychogenic factors have also been implicated. Primary dysmenorrhea is functional, meaning that it results from how the body functions. In recent years, it has been learned that an excess buildup of a natural hormone, prostaglandin, that is found in the cells of the uterine lining is related to painful menstruation. During menstrual flow, when the uterine lining

CASE STUDY 18-9

Linda

Linda is a 15-year-old high school sophomore who experiences severe low abdominal pain, headaches, and irritability during the first two days of her menstrual flow. Linda is somewhat overweight and does not enjoy physical activity, particularly vigorous activity. Every month when Linda starts her menstrual flow she brings a note from her mother asking to be excused from physical education class for two or three days. Her high school has a rule that requires all absences from physical education to be made up in the after-school intramural activity program within six weeks of the absence. Linda rides the school bus home because both of her parents work until 6:00 P.M. during the week. There is public transportation available in her town.

APPLICATION TASK

How could a physical educator accommodate Linda without alienating her any further from physical activity?

---

is shed, this hormone is released in large amounts.[108] Why discomfort results is not known. Approximately 30 percent of the cases are classified as secondary, meaning they are caused by a physical condition such as endometriosis, fibroids, or infections.[14]

Characteristics

PMS is characterized by nervousness, irritability, lack of control, agitation, anger, insomnia, depression, and severe fatigue. Fluid retention causes short-term weight gain and breast fullness and pain. Dysmenorrhea is low abdominal pain that may be crampy or a dull, constant ache that frequently radiates to the lower back and down the legs. Headache, nausea, constipation or diarrhea, dizziness, vomiting, and a feeling of tenseness are classic symptoms of dysmenorrhea. Significant dysmenorrhea is

common among teenage girls and women in their early twenties who have never had a baby.[108]

Testing

These two conditions have a significant impact on a teenager's attitude. It is difficult to concentrate and put forth one's best effort when one is not feeling well. Thus, when motor or fitness testing is being conducted, it is recommended that the teenager who is experiencing PMS or dysmenorrhea be given the option of being tested during the scheduled time or delaying until she feels better.

Special Considerations

Many girls and women are unaware of the effects dietary habits can have on their degree of comfort before and during their menstrual flow. During this age of fast foods saturated with salt, the modern girl or woman needs to understand how her dietary choices can influence her comfort during the menstrual cycle. With such knowledge, it is possible to reduce the pain of functional dysmenorrhea. Reduction of pain is directly associated with the amount of salt stored in the body.

Approximately one week before the onset of the menstrual period, the body begins storing sodium chloride. When this storing process begins, the girl or woman craves salt. If she yields to the craving for salt at that time in her cycle, a whole series of events occurs that results in abdominal bloating, which increases the pain associated with the first two days of the menstrual flow. What occurs is that, when salt intake is increased, the salt tends to move into and be held by the body tissues. The salt stored in the body tissues draws water toward those tissues, thereby upsetting the osmotic balance in the body. Much of the water that is drawn into the tissues is pulled from fecal matter moving through the large intestine. When large amounts of water are removed from the fecal mass, the mass begins to harden and its progress is slowed. Thus, the net result of increasing salt intake one week before the onset of the menstrual period is bloating from stored water and accumulating fecal material. This increased congestion presses against nerves in the abdominal and lower back area and causes pain.

The entire chain of events can be avoided (or markedly reduced) if, one week before the onset of her menstrual flow, the girl or woman decreases (or at least does not increase) salt intake and, at the same time, increases water and roughage (raw celery, carrots, apples) intake. By following these simple guidelines, she can preserve the osmotic balance of water in the body, and the softness and progression of the fecal mass through the large intestine can be maintained. Regular movement of the fecal mass results in reduction of the amount of bloating associated with the menstrual period. Reduced bloating and faithful adherence to the exercises described later in this chapter will relieve most of the pain associated with menstruation.

Teaching Strategies

The sensitive teacher will recognize the signs of PMS and dysmenorrhea. When normally high-spirited or easygoing teenage girls become irritable and moody, the menstrual cycle is frequently at fault. Encouraging the student to dress out, but allowing her to sit and observe the class if she chooses to do so, is recommended. Requiring that the student dress for class sends the message that the girl is experiencing a condition, not a sickness. Giving permission to sit out implies that the person experiencing the discomfort is in the best position to determine whether or not she should participate. In these cases, when the person who is not participating observes her classmates enjoying class activities, it is not uncommon for her to choose to join in some parts of the activity.

The Physical Education Program

There have been questions raised about the desirability of young women participating in physical education and exercise during the menstrual period. There is a perception among some that exercise during a period of discomfort is undesirable and that young women during this period should be excused from physical education classes.

Young women have varying experiences as they pass through the menstrual cycle. Thus, judgments about physical exercise during menstruation should be made on an individual basis. However, there is evidence that there are benefits from physical exercise as it relates to physical fitness and postural efficiency in lessening the pain associated with menstruation.

The consensus among physicians and gynecologists is that restriction from participation in vigorous physical activity, intensive sports competition, and swimming during all phases of the menstrual period is unwarranted for those who are free of menstrual disturbances. However, with regard to the first half of the menstrual period, some physicians advise moderation with limited participation in intensive sports competition. The reason for moderation during the first half of the menstrual period is that the flow is heavier during the first two or three days and some girls and women experience abdominal cramping during this time.

Modifications, Adaptations, and Inclusion Techniques

Regular exercise has been shown to relieve the symptoms of PMS and functional dysmenorrhea. Exercise reduces stress and relieves congestion in the abdominal cavity caused by gravity, poor posture, poor circulation, and/or poor abdominal muscle tone. Physical activity also helps relieve leg and back pain by stretching lumbar and pelvic ligaments in the fascia to minimize pressure on spinal nerves. Undue muscular tension also may have a bearing on painful menstruation; therefore, relaxation techniques and positioning of the body, accompanied by heat from a heating pad on the lower back area, may relax tensions and consequently lessen the pain. Other relaxation techniques and exercises also may be used to reduce tension in the body.

Girls and women who suffer from dysmenorrhea may benefit from a daily exercise program designed to alleviate this condition. The exercises should provide for the improvement of posture (especially lordosis), the stimulation of circulation, and the stretching of tight fascia and ligaments. The exercises discussed in this section are suggested to alleviate the symptoms of dysmenorrhea.

Fascial Stretch

The purpose of fascial exercise is to stretch the shortened fascial ligamentous bands that extend between the lower back and the anterior aspect of the pelvis and legs. These shortened bands may result in increased pelvic tilt, which may irritate peripheral nerves passing through or near the fascia. The irritation of these nerves may be the cause of the pain. This exercise produces a stretching effect on the hip flexors and increases mobility of the hip joint (see Figure 18-1). To perform the exercise, the girl or woman should stand erect, with the left side of her body about the distance of the bent elbow from a wall; the feet should be together, with the left forearm and palm against the wall, the elbow at shoulder height, and the heel of the other hand placed against the posterior aspect of the hollow portion of the right hip. From this position, abdominal and gluteal muscles should be contracted strongly to tilt the pelvis backward. The hips should slowly be pushed forward and diagonally toward the wall, and

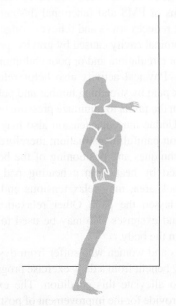

Figure 18-1 Fascial Stretch

pressure should be applied with the right hand. This position should be held for a few counts; then a slow return should be made to the starting position. The stretch should be performed three times on each side of the body. The exercise should be continued even after relief has been obtained from dysmenorrhea. It has been suggested that the exercise be performed three times daily. To increase motivation, the girl or woman should record the number of days and times she performs the exercise.

Abdominal Pumping

The purpose of abdominal pumping is to increase blood circulation throughout the pelvic region. The exercise is performed by assuming a hook-lying position, placing the hands lightly on the abdomen, slowly and smoothly distending the abdomen on the count of one, then retracting the abdomen on the count of two, and relaxing (see Figure 18-2). The exercise should be repeated 8 to 10 times.

Pelvic Tilt with Abdominal Pumping

The purpose of the pelvic tilt with abdominal pumping is to increase the tone of the abdominal muscles. In a hook-lying position, with the feet and knees together, heels 1 inch apart and hands on the abdomen, the abdominal and gluteal muscles are contracted. The pelvis is rotated, so that the tip of the coccyx comes forward and upward and the hips are slightly raised from the floor. The abdomen is distended and retracted. The hips are lowered slowly, vertebra by vertebra, until the original starting position is attained (see Figure 18-3). The exercise should be repeated 8 to 10 times.

Knee-Chest Exercise

The purpose of the knee-chest exercise is to stretch the extensors of the lumbar spine and strengthen the abdominal muscles. The exercise is performed by bending forward at the hips and placing the hands and arms on a mat. The chest is lowered toward the mat, in a knee-chest position, and held as close to the mat as possible for three to five minutes (see Figure 18-4). This exercise should be performed once or twice a day.

Figure 18-2 Abdominal Pumping

Figure 18-3 Pelvic Tilt with Abdominal Pumping

Figure 18-4 Knee-Chest Exercise

Community-Based Opportunities

The teenager who has been taught how to control PMS and functional dysmenorrhea through diet and exercise will have the knowledge she needs to continue to maintain a healthy and active lifestyle into her adult years.

TOURETTE SYNDROME

Definition

Tourette syndrome (TS) is a genetic disorder that results in multiple motor tics and one or more vocal tics.[4] The tics often begin in early childhood but are usually dismissed by parents as nervous mannerisms.[14] Often, the tics are dramatically reduced or disappear between the ages of 20 and 24 years.[101]

Incidence

The prevalence rate is estimated to be 1 in 1,000 in children[101] but as little as 2.5 per 10,000 in young adults.[61] The condition is three times more common in males than in females.[14]

Causes

TS is an inherited neurological disorder with some associated symptoms that affect behavior.

Characteristics

The characteristics of individuals with this syndrome include involuntary motor and vocal tics and symptoms that come and go and change over time.[19] A tic is a sudden, rapid, recurrent, nonrhythmic, stereotyped movement or vocalization.[4] The motor tics that may be seen include sudden twitches of the entire body, shoulders, or head; eyeblinks or rolling of the head; repetitive tapping, drumming, or touching behaviors; and grimacing. The vocal tics are involuntary utterings of noises, words, or phrases: sniffing, clearing the throat, coughing repeatedly, exhibiting coprolalia (saying socially inappropriate words), laughing involuntarily, uttering a variety of sounds or yells, barking, grunting, and exhibiting echolalia (repeating what others or oneself has just said).[19] Sometimes the symptoms are very frequent, but sometimes the child does not demonstrate them at all. Also, the symptoms change from one year to the next.

The most common deficits demonstrated by children with TS are in visual-motor integration, fine motor skills, and executive functions, including the inability to sustain attention, plan and organize, control impulses, self-regulate, and goal-direct behavior.

A Dolphin "Kisses" the Hand of a Child with Cancer
Courtesy of Island Dolphin Care Key Largo, Fl

These functions are all under the control of the frontal lobes and the basal ganglia structures.[29] Between 50 and 80 percent of individuals with TS are also diagnosed as having ADHD,[28] and 20 to 25 percent are estimated to have a learning disability.[29] Some also demonstrate obsessive-compulsive behaviors and/or an inability to inhibit aggression.[82]

The diagnostic criteria developed by the American Psychiatric Association follow:

- Both multiple motor tics and one or more vocal tics have been present for some time during the illness, although not necessarily concurrently.
- The tics occur many times a day (usually in bouts) nearly every day or have occurred intermittently throughout a period of more than one year, and during this period there was never a tic-free period of more than three consecutive months.
- The disturbance causes marked distress or significant impairment in social, occupational, or other important areas of functioning.
- The onset is before age 18.
- The disturbance is not due to the direct physiological effects of a substance (e.g., stimulants) or a general medical condition (e.g., Huntington's chorea or postviral encephalitis).[4]

Testing

No adjustments in testing are required for the student with TS; however, allowances must be made for motor tics that are severe enough to interfere with voluntary motor control. If the student also has a specific learning disability, the testing procedures and interpretations provided in Chapter 13 are recommended.

Special Considerations

Students with learning disabilities and those with impulse-control difficulties represent a special challenge to a teacher. When a student has a learning disability, the mode of presenting information to the student may have to be altered to accommodate his or her method of processing information.

Some students learn better visually, others learn better auditorily, and some need a combination of techniques to comprehend new information. To determine how the student learns best, the teacher is advised to consult with the school counselor or other resource personnel who have access to the student's academic and cognitive test results.

When impulse control creates acting-out problems in class, the teacher must have a strategy for intervening, always keeping in mind that the student's behavior is involuntary. When possible and feasible, the teacher and the student should discuss anticipated problems early in the school year and agree on a procedure to follow, should impulse control become a major problem.

The student may wish to have the option to time-out himself or herself or may prefer that the teacher intervene if the behavior interferes with other students' benefits from the class. Also, with the student's and the student's parents' permission, the teacher or another representative of the school should share information about the condition with the student's classmates, so that they will understand that the unusual behaviors are not under voluntary control.

Clonidine, which is an antihypertensive, is sometimes used to reduce compulsive behaviors and tics, and anticonvulsants are sometimes used to help individuals with Tourette syndrome focus their attention.[97]

Teaching Strategy

Because the median age of onset for motor tics is seven years,[4] the teacher of the child with TS may be the first to become aware of the emergence of the symptoms. Other than learning to tolerate the student's involuntary tics, the physical educator's primary concerns will probably be fostering acceptance in the class and addressing the student's learning disabilities, impulse control, and visual-motor problems.

The Physical Education Program

Individuals with TS have a variety of visual-motor integration problems: alternating visual suppression (using each eye independently of the other), one or both eyes sitting in misalignment, and mild depth perception difficulties. If an individual is suppressing one eye or if the eyes are misaligned, the individual's motor performance will suffer. Performance clues include poor striking success, inability to catch a thrown ball, avoidance of climbing apparatus, and the descent of stairs one step at a time. Should a student demonstrate any of these difficulties, he or she should be referred for an orthoptic visual examination and remediation (see Chapter 17) before a physical education program is designed. If the student does not have visual-motor integration problems that interfere with movement efficiency, no modifications to the activity program are needed, except for those addressed in the section "Special Considerations."

Modifications, Adaptations, and Inclusion Techniques

As the individual in charge, the teacher is responsible for establishing and maintaining a learning environment that will provide all students with the opportunity to learn and grow. A teacher is expected to make needed modifications and adaptations to enhance a student's potential to learn. Teachers can offer alternative strategies to individual students when the teachers have the information they need and have a class size that permits individual attention. The presence of a student with a potentially disabling condition provides a special learning opportunity for everyone in the class. Knowledge about an existing condition, acceptance of the situation, realistic expectations, and cooperation are prerequisites for a positive learning environment for all members of the class. Students with TS can easily become alienated from other students because of their uncontrollable, unique behaviors. However, when the teacher and other students understand the condition, know what to expect, and know what outcomes will result, opportunities will be enhanced and difficulties reduced to a minimum for the student with TS. The sensitive teacher will take the responsibility for ensuring that all members of the class are treated with fairness and respect.

Community-Based Opportunities

Adults with TS can participate in any public or private recreational activities where they feel comfortable. Their involuntary tics may, however, be met with ridicule, fear, or hostility by individuals who do not know them or understand the condition. As noted earlier in this section, an identifying characteristic of TS is that it "causes marked distress or significant impairment in social, occupational, or other important areas of functioning."[4] Attempts must be made to educate individuals who work and play in settings that the person with TS may frequent. A support group of friends and family members can provide others with information about the condition and perhaps facilitate understanding and acceptance.   ❧

SUMMARY

O ther health impairment, by federal definition, means that a child has limited strength and vitality or alertness due to chronic or acute health problems. In addition to health impairments listed in the federal definition of the IDEA, other impairments that might limit a student's participation in physical education are AIDS, anemia, childhood cancer, cystic fibrosis, Prader-Willi syndrome, premenstrual syndrome and dysmenorrhea, and Tourette syndrome. The physical educator should understand the nature of each of these conditions, how the conditions can affect a student's performance capabilities, and the types of program modifications that best meet the needs of each student.

Most of the conditions discussed in this chapter require medical attention. When this is the case, it is advisable to request permission from the parents to consult with the student's physician to ensure that the type of exercises and activities selected for the student will not aggravate the condition. In most situations, mild exercise will benefit the student. However, in the case of the diabetic student, the type of diabetes must be known before specific exercise programs can be developed.

REVIEW QUESTIONS

1. What techniques can a physical education teacher use to keep a student with an attention deficit hyperactive disorder on task?

2. How should persons with Type 1 diabetes adjust their insulin levels to accommodate increased exercise?

3. How should the physical education program be modified for students with asthma?

4. Summarize the Universal Precautions to protect against all infectious disease. Which are most pertinent to physical education?

5. What are the characteristics of a person with anemia?

6. What precautions must be used in developing an individual exercise program for a child with cystic fibrosis?

7. How do the emergency treatment procedures for hypoglycemia and hyperglycemia differ?

8. What is the major characteristic of a child with Prader-Willi syndrome? What precautions must be taken in the development of an exercise program for children with Prader-Willi syndrome?

9. What is the primary characteristic of the child with Tourette syndrome? How does this interfere with the child's psychosocial development?

STUDENT ACTIVITIES

1. Break into small groups and share the application tasks developed for at least three of the conditions presented in this chapter. Each group should select one of the conditions and present its agreed-upon application.

2. Using the Internet, identify at least two organizations that advocate for children with the health impairments discussed in this chapter and

study their literature. Identify the information that is relevant to conducting a physical education program for individuals with these health impairments.

3. Look through the last three years of *Palaestra* and identify an athlete who is afflicted with one of the health impairments discussed in this chapter. Identify at least three accommodations that were made for the athlete.

REFERENCES

1. Albright AL: Diabetes. In Durstine JL, editor: *Exercise management for persons with chronic diseases and disabilities.* Champaign, IL, Human Kinetics, 1997.

2. American Diabetes Association: *Gestational diabetes,* www.diabetes.org/gestational-diabetes.jsp, 2007.

3. American Lung Association: *Childhood asthma.* New York, 1994.

4. American Psychiatric Association: *Diagnostic and statistical manual of mental disorders (DSM-IV-TR).* Washington, DC, 2000.

5. American Sickle Cell Anemia Association: *How common is sickle cell anemia?* www.ascaa.org/ FAQS, 2007.

6. American Sickle Cell Anemia Association: *How is sickle cell anemia treated?* www.ascaa.org/FAQS, 2007.

7. Anderson SD: Exercise-induced asthma. In Middleton E, et al., editors: *Allergy: Principles and practice,* 4th ed. St. Louis, Mosby, 1993.

8. *Anemia,* www.sleeptight.com/EncyMaster/A/ anemia. 2003.

9. *Acquired immunodeficiency syndrome,* www.encarta.msm.com. 2003.

10. Ayala GM, Guadalupe X, Miller EZ, Riddle C, Willis S, King D: Asthma in middle schools: What students have to say about their asthma, *J of School Health* 76(6):208–214, 2006.

11. Baird J, Stevenson JC, Willams DC: The evolution of ADHD: A disorder of communication? *Quar Rev of Biol* 75(1):17–35, 2000.

12. Bardana EJ: Indoor pollution and its impact on respiratory health, *Annals of Allergy, Asthma & Immun* 87:33–40, 2001.

13. Barkley RA: The North American perspective on attention deficit hyperactivity disorder, *Aust Educ Dev Psych* 13:2–23, 1996.

14. Beers MH, Porter RS, Jones TV, Kaplan JL, Berkwits M, editors: *The Merck manual of diagnosis and therapy,* 18th ed. Whitehouse Station, NJ, Merck Reseach Laboratories, 2006.

15. Bernard A, Carbonnelle S, de Burbure C, Michel O, Nickmilder M: Chlorinated pool attendance, atopy, and the risk of asthma in childhood, *Environmental Health Perspectives* 114(10):1567–1573, 2006.

16. Blanchette N: Cognitive and motor development in children with vertically transmitted HIV infection, *Brain Cogn* 46:50–53, 2001.

17. Borkgren MW, Gronkiewicz CA: Update your asthma care from hospital to home, *Am J Nurs* January:26–34, 1995.

18. Brandon LJ, Boyette LW, Lloyd A, Gaasch DA: Effects of training on strength and floor rise ability in older diabetic adults, *Medicine and Science in Exercise and Sport* 31(Suppl. 5):S116, 1998.

19. Bronheim S: *An educator's guide to Tourette syndrome.* Bayside, NY, Tourette Syndrome Association, 1990.

20. Butler RW, Haser JK: Neurological effects of treatment for childhood cancer, *Mental Health and Developmental Disabilities Research Reviews* 12(3):184–191, 2006.

21. National Cancer Institute: *Cancer facts,* www.cis.nci.nih.gov/fact/6_40.htm, 2002.

22. Carlson DL, Mawdsley RH: Sports anemia: A review of the literature, *Am J Sports Med* 14:109–122, 1986.

23. Centers for Disease Control and Prevention: *Attention deficit disorder,* www.cdc.gov/ncbddd/adhd, 2007.

24. Centers for Disease Control and Prevention: *HIV,* www.cdc.gov/hiv/resources/factsheets/at-a-glance.htm, 2007.

25. Cerny F, Orenstein D: Cystic fibrosis. In Skinner JS, editor: *Exercise testing and exercise prescription for special cases.* Philadelphia, Lea & Febiger, 1993.

26. Chase C, Ware J, Hittleman J, Blasini I, Smith R, Lorente A, Anisfield E, Diaz C, Fowler MG, Moye J, Kaligh L: Early cognition and motor development among infants born to women infected with immunodeficiency virus, *Pediatrics,* www.Pediatrics.orgicgi/content/full/106/2/e25, 2000.

27. Cohen J, Reddington C, Jacobs D, Meade R, Picard D, Singleton K, Smith D, Caldwell MB, DeMaria A, Hsu H: School related issues among HIV-infected children, *Pediatrics* 100:126, 1997.

28. Comings DE: Clinical and molecular genetics of ADHD and Tourette syndrome: Two related polygenic disorders, *Ann NY Sci* 931:50–83, 2001.

29. Como PG: Neuropsychological function in Tourette syndrome. In Cohen DJ, Goetz CG, Ankovic J, editors: *Tourette syndrome,* Philadelphia, Lippincott, Williams & Wilkins, 2001.

30. Cooper CB: Pulmonary disease. In Durstine JL, editor: *Exercise management for persons with chronic diseases and disabilities.* Champaign, IL, Human Kinetics, 1997.

31. Crist WM, Kun LE: Common solid tumors of childhood, *N Engl J Med* 324:461–471, 1991.

32. Microsoft® Encarta® online encyclopedia: *Cystic fibrosis,* www.encarta.msm.com/encnet, 2003.

33. daCosta IG, Paroff MA, Lemanek K, Goldstein GL: Improving adherence to medication regimens for children with asthma and its effects on clinical outcome, *J of Applied Behavioral Analysis* 30(4):687–691, 1997.

34. Dooley EA, Perkins N: Let's talk about the needs of African American children with sickle cell disease: A recognized "other health impairment." In *Coming together: Preparing rural special education in the 21st century.* Conference Proceedings of the American Council on Rural Special Education, Charleston, SC, March 25–28, 1998. Available from Educational Resources Information Center (ERIC) ED 417908.

35. Dunn JM, Fait H: *Special physical education.* Dubuque, IA, Wm. C. Brown, 1989.

36. DuPaul GI, Stoner C: *ADHD in the schools: Assessment and intervention strategies,* 2nd ed. New York, Guilford Press, 2003.

37. Eichner ER: Sickle cell trait, heroic exercise, and fatal collapse, *Physician Sportsmed* 21(7):51–61, 1993.

38. Eiholzer U, Schlump M, Nordmann Y, Allemand D: Early manifestations of Prader-Willi syndrome: Influence of growth hormone, *J of Pediatric Endocrinology & Metabolism* 14(Suppl. 6):1441–1445, 2001.

39. Elia J, Ambrosini PJ, Rapoport JL: Treatment of attention-deficit-hyperactivity disorder, *N Eng J of Med* 340:780–788, 1999.

40. eMedicineHealth: *Exercise-induced asthma,* www.emedicinehealth.com/ exercise-induced_asthma/article_em.htm, 2007.

41. Fensternmacher K, Olympica D, Sheridan SM: Effectiveness of a computer-facilitated, interactive social skills training program for boys with attention deficit hyperactivity disorder, *School Psychology Quar* 21(2):197–224, 2006.

42. Gong H, Krishnareddy S: How pollution and airborne allergens affect exercise, *Physician Sportsmed* 23(7):35–42, 1995.

43. Gong H, Linn W: Health effects of criteria air pollutants. In Tierney DF, editor: *Current pulmonology,* vol. 15. St. Louis, Mosby, 1994.

44. Grantham-McGregor S, Cornelius A: A review of studies on the effect of iron deficiencies on cognitive development in children, *Anemia Suppl* 131:649s–668s, 2001.

45. Greenhill LL: Stimulant medication treatment of children with attention deficit hyperactive disorder. In Jensen P, Cooper J, editors: *Attention deficit hyperactivity disorder.* Kingston, NJ, Civic Research Institute, 2002.

46. Grovas A, Femgen A, Rauck A, Ruymann FB, Hutchinson CL, Winchester DP, Menck HR: The national cancer data base report on patterns of childhood cancers in the United States, *Cancer* 80:2321–2332, 1997.

47. Gurney GG, et al.: Incidence of cancer in children in the United States, *Cancer* 75:2186–2195, 1995.

48. Harris KR, Friedlander D, Danoff B, Saddler B, Frizzelle R, Graham S: Self-monitoring versus self-monitoring of academic performance: Effects among students with ADHD in the general education classroom, *J of Special Education* 39(6):145–156, 2005.

49. Harris SS, Tanner S: Helping active women avoid anemia, *Physician Sportsmed* 23:35–47, 1995.

50. Harvey WJ, Reid G: Motor performance of children with attention deficit hyperactivity disorder: A preliminary investigation, *APAQ* 14:189–202, 1997.

51. Healthlink Medical College of Wisconsin: *Childhood obesity causes diabetes and other health problems,* http://healthlink.mcw.edu/article/941223597.html, 2007.

52. Helman LJ, Thiele CJ: New insights into the causes of cancer, *Pediatr Clin North Am* 38:201–221, 1991.

53. Hickey G, Fricker P: Attention deficit hyperactivity disorder, CNS stimulants and sport, *Sports Medicine* 27:11–21, 1999.

54. Horowitz ME, Neff JR, Kun LE: Ewing's sarcoma: Radiotherapy versus surgery for local control, *Pediatr Clin North Am* 38:365–380, 1991.

55. JAMA Patient Page: Sickle cell anemia, *JAMA* 281:1768, 1999.

56. Kercmer CM, Dearborn DG, Schluchter M: Reduction in asthma morbidity in children as a result of home remediation aimed at moisture sources, *Environmental Health Perspectives* 114(8):1574–1580, 2006.

57. Kerr CP: Improving outcomes in diabetes: A review of the outpatient care of NIDDM patients, *J Fam Pract* 40:63–75, 1995.

58. Kidd PM: ADHD total health management, *Total Health* 22(5):20–23, 2000.

59. Kiley JP, Collins JL, Frumkin H, Price DA: Managing asthma in schools, *J of School Health* 76(6):2001, 2006.

60. LaPerriere A, Klimas N, Major P, Perry A: Acquired immune deficiency syndrome. In Durstine JL, editor: *Exercise management for persons with chronic diseases and disabilities.* Champaign, IL, Human Kinetics, 1997.

61. Leckman JF, Zhang H, Vitale A, Lahnin F, Lynch K, Bondi C, Kim Y, Peterson BS: Course of tic severity in Tourette syndrome: The first two decades, *Pediatrics* 102:14–19, 1998.

62. Leon AS: Diabetes. In Skinner JS, editor: *Exercise testing and exercise prescription for special cases.* Philadelphia, Lea & Febiger, 1993.

63. Looker AC, Dallman PR, Carrol, MD, Johnson CL: Prevalence of iron deficiency in the United States, *JAMA* 277:973–976, 1997.

64. Mayfield J: Diagnosis and classification of diabetes mellitus: New criteria, *American Family Physician* October:1103–1113, 1998.

65. Mazur ML: Gary Hall Jr: Best swimmer in the world, *Diabetes Forecast* 54(7):58–62, 2001.

66. McHugh E: Going "beyond the physical": Social skills and physical education, *JOPERD* 66(4):18–21, 1995.

67. Menkes M, Rowe J, Menkes J: A twenty-five-year follow-up study on the hyperkinetic child with minimal brain dysfunction, *Pediatrics* 39:393–399, 1967.

68. Miller J, Keane RR: *Encyclopedia and dictionary of medicine, nursing, and allied health.* Philadelphia, W. B. Saunders, 1987.

69. Misben R: Report on the expert committee on the diagnosis and classification of diabetes mellitus, *Diabetes-Care* 20:1183–1190, 1997.

70. Mitten MJ: HIV-positive athletes: When medicine meets the law, *Physician Sportsmed* 22(10):63–68, 1994.

71. Morton AR, Fitch KD: Asthma. In Skinner JS, editor: *Exercise testing and exercise prescription for special cases.* Philadelphia, Lea & Febiger, 1993.

72. Mosher PE, Nash MS, Perry AC, LaPerriere AR, Goldberg RB: Aerobic circuit exercise training: Effects on adolescents with well-controlled insulin-dependent diabetes mellitus, *Arch Phys Med Reh* 79:652–657, 1998.

73. National Cancer Institute: *A snapshot of pediatric cancer,* http://planning.cancer.gov/disease/Pediatric-Snapshot.pdf, 2007.

74. National Cancer Institute: *Cancer topics,* www.cancer.gov/cancertopics/pdq/treatment/lateeffects/healthprofessional, 2007.

75. National Diabetes Education Program: *Diabetes,* www.ndep.nih.gov/diabetes/diabetes.htm, 2007.

76. Nixon PA: Cystic fibrosis. In Durstine LD, editor: *Exercise management for persons with chronic diseases and disabilities.* Champaign, IL, Human Kinetics, 1997.

77. Payton B: *Health and safety.* Dallas, Dallas Independent School District, 1994.

78. Pihoker C, Scott CR, Lensing Sy, Cradock MM, Smith J: Non-insulin dependent diabetes mellitus in African-American youths of Arkansas, *Clin Pediatr* 37:97–102, 1998.

79. Prader-Willi Syndrome Association, USA: *Prader-Willi syndrome basic facts,* www.pwsausa.org/basicfac.htm, 2003.

80. Ratzon N, Greenbaum C, Dulitzy M, Ornoy A: Comparison of the motor development of school-age children born to mothers with and without diabetes mellitus, *Phys & Occup Therapy in Pediatrics* 20(1):43–57, 2000.

81. Reid R, Trout A, Schartz M: Self-regulation interventions for children with attention deficit hyperactivity disorder, *Exceptional Children* 71:361–377, 2005.

82. Rosen AR: Tourette's syndrome: The school experience, *Clin Pediatr* 35:467–469, 1996.

83. Rosenbloom AL, House DV, Winter WE: Non-insulin dependent diabetes mellitus in minority youth: Research priorities and needs, *Clinic Pediatr* 37:143–152, 1998.

84. Rosenthal-Malek A, Greenspan W: The student with diabetes in my class, *Teaching Excep Child* January/February:38–43, 1999.

85. Rupp NT: Diagnosis and management of exercise-induced asthma, *Physician Sportsmed* 24:77–87, 1996.

86. Selby G: Anemia. In Durstine LD, editor: *Exercise management for persons with chronic diseases and disabilities.* Champaign, IL, Human Kinetics, 1997.

87. Selby G: Cancer. In Durstine LD, editor: *Exercise management for persons with chronic diseases and disabilities.* Champaign, IL, Human Kinetics, 1997.

88. Seltzer DG: Educating athletes on HIV disease and AIDS, *Physician Sportsmed* 21(1):109–115, 1993.

89. Shaywitz SE, Shaywitz BA: Attention deficit disorder: Current perspectives, *Pediat Neurol* 3:129–135, 1987.

90. Shaywitz SE, Shaywitz BA: Introduction to the special series on attention deficit disorder, *J Learning Disabil* 24:68–74, 1991.

91. Silverstein R: *A user's guide to the 1999 IDEA regulations.* Washington, DC, ERIC Clearinghouse, 1999.

92. Simonsen JC, Simmons DJ, Zaccaro WF, Rejeski WJ, Berry MJ: Exercise and health related quality of life in male and female chronic obstructive pulmonary disease patients, *Med Sci Exer Spt* 31(Suppl. 5):S361, 1998.

93. Stahr B, Cushing D, Lane K, Fox J: Efficacy of a function-based intervention in decreasing off-task behavior exhibited by a student with ADHD, *J of Positive Behavior Interventions* 8(4):201–211, 2006.

94. Stewart M, et al.: The hyperactive child syndrome, *Am J Orthopsychiatry* 35:861–867, 1996.

95. Stormes WW: Exercise-induced asthma: Diagnosis and treatment for the recreation or elite athlete, *Med Sci Exer Spt* 32(Suppl. 1):S33–S38, 1999.

96. Surburg PR: Are adapted physical educators ready for the students with AIDS? *APAQ* 5:259–263, 1988.

97. Sweeney DP, Forness SR, Levitt JG: An overview of medications commonly used to treat behavioral disorders associated with autism, Tourette syndrome, and pervasive developmental disorders, *Focus on Autism and Other Developmental Disabilities* 13(3):144–150, 1998.

98. Tan RA, Spector SL: Exercise-induced asthma, *Sports Medicine* 25:1–6, 1998.

99. Taunton JE, McCargar L: Managing activity in patients who have diabetes, *Physician Sportsmed* 23(3):41–52, 1995.

100. Taunton JE, McCargar L: Staying active with diabetes, *Physician Sportsmed* 23(3):55–56, 1995.

101. Tourette Syndrome Association: http://neuro-www2.mgn.harvard.edu/tsa/tsamain.mclk. 2003.

102. Trembath RC: Genetic mechanisms and mental retardation, *J R Coll Physicians Lond* 28(2):121–125, 1994.

103. Tuchman M, et al.: Screening for neuroblastoma at 3 weeks of age: Methods and preliminary results from the Quebec Neuroblastoma Screening Project, *Pediatrics* 86:765–773, 1990.

104. Waters J, Clarke DJ, Corbett JA: Educational and occupational outcome in Prader-Willi syndrome, *Child Care Health Dev* 16:271–282, 1990.

105. Weinberg RA: Oncogenes, antioncogenes and the molecular bases of multistep carcinogenesis, *Cancer Res* 49:3713–3721, 1989.

106. Werner T: Effects of exercise on an HIV-positive patient: A case study, *Clinical Kinesiology* 51:86–87, 1997/98.

107. White RD, Sherman C: Exercise in diabetes management, *Physician Sportsmed* 27:63–78, 1999.

108. Women's Health Interactive: www.womens-health.com/gym_health/gyn_md.html. 2003.

109. Woodward R: The diagnosis and medical treatment of ADHD in children and adolescents in primary care: A practical guide, *Pediatric Nursing* 32(4):363–369, 2006.

110. Zametkin AJ, Ernst M: Problems in the management of attention-deficit-hyperactivity disorder, *New England J of Medicine* 340:40–46, 1999.

Suggested Readings

Durstine JL, Moore GE, Durstine LD, editors: *Exercise management for persons with chronic diseases and disabilities,* 2nd ed. Champaign, IL, Human Kinetics, 2002.

Ward SA: Diabetes, exercise and foot care, *Physician Sportsmed* 33(8):33–38, 2005.

Recommended Web Sites

Please keep in mind that these Web sites are being recommended in the winter of 2007. As Web sites often change, they may have moved or been reconfigured or eliminated.

American Diabetes Association
www.diabetes.org

Asthma and Allergy Foundation of America
www.aafa.org

Attention Deficit Hyperactivity Disorder
www.nimh.nih.gov/topics/adhd.shtml
www.cdc.gov/ncbddd/adhd/

National Cancer Institute
www.cancer.gov

Prader-Willi Syndrome Association (USA)
www.pwsausa.org

Premenstrual Syndrome
www.familydoctor.org

Tourette Syndrome Association
www.mentalhealth.com

AIDS Education Global Information System (AEGIS)
www.aegis.com

CDC National Prevention Information Network
www.cdcnpin.org

RECOMMENDED VIDEOS

Insight Media
2162 Broadway
New York, NY 10024-0621
www.insight-media.com
1-800-233-9910

The Truth about ADHD
#TAR3866/DVD/45 min/2005/$249

*ADHD and LD: Powerful Teaching Strategies and
Accommodations*
#TAR4256/DVD/50 min/2003/$149

You Can Play Too
#YAQ1993/DVD/20 min/2002/$199

How Can We All Play: Severe Disability in P.E.
#YAQ1047/VHS/35 min/2002/$109

GLOSSARY

A

abdominal strength Muscular strength of the abdominal muscles.

abduction Away from the midline of the body.

abortive poliomyelitis An acute viral infection that causes a headache, sore throat, mild fever, and nausea.

absence seizure A nonconvulsive seizure in which consciousness is lost for a few seconds, formerly referred to as a petit mal seizure.

accessibility The extent to which an environment can be used by all persons.

accommodation Tailoring of an educational program to a student's abilities and severity of disability.

accountability Evidence that students with disabilities have received appropriate education services.

acquired anemia Anemia that begins sometime during one's life.

acquired immune deficiency syndrome (AIDS) The development of opportunistic infections and/or certain secondary cancers known to be associated with HIV infection.

Adam test Position to determine the extent to which a scoliosis is structural.

Adapted Physical Activity Council (APAC) A unit within the American Association of Active Lifestyles and Fitness of the American Alliance for Health, Physical Education, Recreation and Dance, whose mission is to promote quality movement experiences for individuals with disabilities through research, advocacy, publications, programs at conventions and workshops, position statements, standards of practice, and cooperation with other organizations committed to people with disabilities.

adapted physical education The art and science of developing, implementing, and monitoring a carefully designed physical education instructional program for a learner with a disability, based on a comprehensive assessment, to give the individual the skills necessary for a lifetime of rich leisure, recreation, and sport experiences to enhance physical fitness and wellness.

adapted physical education national standards (APENS) Comprehensive national criteria detailing the professional preparation standards expected of adapted physical educators who seek accreditation.

adapted physical educator A physical educator with highly specialized training in the assessment and evaluation of motor competency, physical fitness, play, and leisure, recreation, and sport skills.

adaptive skill areas Communication, home living, community use, health and safety, leisure, self-care, social skills, self-direction, functional academics, and work.

adduction Toward the midline of the body.

administrative feasibility The extent to which it is practical to use a given test.

admission An indicator that a student qualifies for special services because of an identifiable disability that interferes with educational progress.

adolescent scoliosis Scoliosis that develops between the ages of 3 and 12 years in females and ages 3 and 14 years in males.

adventitious Acquired after birth.

affective function Emotions resulting from experiences, beliefs, values, and predispositions.

agility The ability to change direction while moving.

air conduction hearing aid A hearing aid that is hooked to receivers located in the outer ear canal.

albinism Lack of pigment in the eyes.

alternate-form reliability The degree to which scores from two different tests purported to measure the same things agree when administered to the same group.

alternator   A person who visually suppresses images received by one eye and then the other eye.

amblyopia   Cortical suppression of visual images received by one or both eyes.

ambulatory   Able to walk.

Americans with Disabilities Act of 1990 (ADA)   P.L. 101-336, which widened civil rights protections for persons with disabilities to all public accommodations and addressed private discrimination.

amputation   Missing part or all of a limb.

amyotrophic lateral sclerosis (ALS)   A progressive neurological disorder that results in degeneration of the muscular system; also known as Lou Gehrig disease.

anemia   A condition of the blood in which there is a deficiency of red (oxygen-carrying) cells or hemoglobin in circulation.

ankle pronation   Abnormal turning of the ankle downward and medially (eversion and abduction).

ankylosed   Pertaining to the immobility of a joint resulting from pathological changes in the joint or in adjacent tissues.

ankylosing spondylitis   A gradual thickening of the axial skeleton and large peripheral joints of the body, which causes back pain and early morning stiffness.

annual goals   Statements that describe in measurable terms what a specific learner with a disability should be able to accomplish in a given year.

anorexia nervosa   A condition in which the person stops eating.

anxiety disorder   Intense feeling of anxiety and tension when there is no real danger.

Apgar scores   Numerical indicators of an infant's status immediately after birth.

aphasia   An impairment of language that affects the production or comprehension of speech and the ability to read or write.

aplastic anemia   A form of anemia in which the red bone marrow that forms blood cells is replaced by fatty marrow.

Applied Behavioral Analysis   A style of teaching, used with learners who have autism, that involves a series of trials to shape a desired behavior or response; also known as the Lovaas approach.

arthritis   Inflammation of a joint.

arthrogryposis   A congenital condition that results in flexure or contracture of joints.

articulation disorder   Difficulty using some speech sounds.

asana   Muscle-stretching exercise used in hatha-yoga.

Asperger syndrome   A condition, known as "high-level autism," that shares many of the same symptoms as classic autism but also includes motor clumsiness and a family history of Asperger traits.

assessment   A problem-solving process that involves gathering information from a variety of sources.

assistive technology   A piece of equipment or product system that increases, maintains, or improves the functional capabilities of persons with disabilities.

assistive technology service   Any service that directly assists an individual with a disability in the selection, acquisition, or use of an assistive technology device.

asthma   A pulmonary disease characterized by reversible airway obstruction, airway inflammation, and increased airway responsiveness to a variety of stimuli.

astigmatism   A refractive error caused by an irregularity in the curvature of the cornea of the lens; vision may become blurred.

asymmetrical tonic neck reflex   A reflex that causes extension of the arm on the face side and flexion of the arm on the posterior skull side when the head is turned.

ataxia   A disturbance of equilibrium that results from the involvement of the cerebellum or its pathways.

athetosis   A clinical type of cerebral palsy characterized by uncoordinated movements of the voluntary muscles, often accompanied by impaired muscle control of the hands and impaired speech and swallowing.

atlantoaxial instability   Greater than normal mobility of the two upper cervical vertebrae.

at risk   Refers to individuals whose development is jeopardized by factors that include poverty, homelessness, prenatal and postnatal maternal neglect, environmental deprivation, child abuse, violence, drug abuse, and racism.

atrophy   Wasting away of muscular tissue.

audible ball   A ball that emits a beeping sound for easy location by a person with limited vision.

audible goal locator   A motor-driven noisemaker that enables a person with limited vision to identify the placement of a base or boundary.

audiologist   A specially trained professional who can provide comprehensive evaluations of individuals' hearing capabilities.

audition   Pertaining to the sense of hearing and the hearing organs involved.

autism   One of five disorders included under the umbrella of pervasive developmental disorders. See also *classic autism.*

autogenic training   Teaching a person to use mind images to promote a relaxed state.

autonomic neuropathy   A complication, resulting from long-standing diabetes, that leads to poor vascular supply and lack of sweating of the feet.

B

backward chaining   The last of a series of steps is taught first.

balance   The ability to maintain equilibrium in a held (static) or moving (dynamic) position.

basic neurological building blocks   Sensory input systems, including primitive reflexes, the vestibular system, refractive and orthoptic vision, audition, the tactile and kinesthetic systems, and equilibrium reflexes.

Becker muscular dystrophy   A disease of the muscular system very similar to Duchenne muscular dystrophy except that it progresses more slowly.

behavior disorder   A condition in which the behavioral response of a student is so different from generally accepted, age-appropriate, ethnic, or cultural norms as to result in significant impairment in self-care, social relationships, educational progress, classroom behavior, work adjustment, or personal happiness.

behavior intervention plan   A program designed to teach acceptable alternatives to behaviors addressed during a functional behavior assessment.

behavior management plan   Specific intervention strategies, included in the IEP, that address how to deal with a student's behavior that interferes with his or her learning or disrupts the learning of others.

behavior management strategies   Techniques for structuring the environment to produce changes in behavior.

behavior modification (behavior therapy)   The changing of behavioral characteristics through the application of learning principles.

benchmarks   Standards of performance for each grade level set at the local, district, or state level.

bio-underclass   Infants who are destined to fail to develop normally because of physical and chemical damage to their brains as a result of their mothers' use of drugs and/or malnutrition during the fetal period.

blindisms   Self-stimulatory behaviors, such as rocking the body or head, placing fingers or fists into the eyes, or flicking fingers in front of the face.

body awareness   The way in which people picture their bodies and their attitude toward and knowledge of their bodily capabilities and limitations.

body composition   The percentage of body fat in relation to lean tissue in the body.

body image   The system of ideas and feelings a person has about his or her structure.

body righting reflex   The reflex that enables segmental rotation of the trunk and hips when the head is turned.

body-state regulation   The ability of the body to maintain homeostasis.

bone conduction hearing aid   A hearing aid that is placed in contact with the mastoid bone.

bottom-up strategy   The process whereby the sensory input system is evaluated and then ability tests are used to determine which deficits are in evidence.

bulimia nervosa   A condition wherein the person overeats and then purges the body of the intake.

C

campus-based decision-making committees   Groups of individuals who contribute to site-based management policies and procedures.

cancer   A cellular malignancy, resulting in loss of normal cell function and uncontrolled cell growth.

cardiovascular/cardiorespiratory endurance   The ability of the heart, lungs, and blood vessels to direct needed oxygen to the muscles.

cataract   A condition in which the normally transparent lens of the eye becomes opaque.

center of gravity   A point in the human body where the pull of gravity on one side is equal to the pull of gravity on the other side.

central auditory processing problems   Deafness resulting from damage to the brain stem or the cortex.

cerebral palsy   A lifelong condition resulting from a nonprogressive lesion of the brain before, during, or soon after birth (before age five years) that impairs voluntary movement.

certified adapted physical educator (C.A.P.E.)   An indicator that an individual has demonstrated knowledge of adapted physical education by passing the Adapted Physical Education National Standards test.

chaining   Leading a person through a series of teachable components of a motor task.

checklist   A screening instrument used to delineate critical aspects of movements.

child abuse and neglect   Physical or mental injury, sexual abuse, negligent treatment, or maltreatment of a child under 18 years of age by a person who is responsible for the child, resulting in harm to the child's health or welfare.

Child Find   A national effort to identify children who have developmental disabilities or are at risk for developmental delays.

childhood disintegrative disorder (CDD)   A condition, which presents itself between the ages of 2 and 10 years, that results in a regression in many areas, including movement, social and language skills, and bladder and bowel control; also known as Heller's syndrome.

chlorosis   Iron deficiency anemia characterized by a reduced amount of hemoglobin in the corpuscles.

choice making   A teaching strategy that provides persons with autism opportunities to make choices.

chromosomal abnormalities   Deviations in the structure of the chromosome.

chronic sorrow syndrome   A theory that proposes that the family members of a child with a disability can cope with the day-to-day requirements of providing support for the child with a disability; however, their underlying emotions are sadness, fear, anger, and guilt.

circuit training   Exercising at a series of stations, with different types of activities at each station.

classic autism   A disorder originally known as Kanner's syndrome. Characteristics include global language disorder, abnormal (bizarre) behavior patterns, social isolation, and usually, but not always, intellectual disability.

classroom conduct problems   Behaviors children demonstrate that interfere with instruction, impede social interaction, or endanger others.

cochlear implant   An electronic device, which is surgically implanted into a bone in the skull, that stimulates the remaining fibers of the auditory division of the 8th cranial nerve and enables persons who are profoundly deaf to hear and distinguish among environmental sounds and warning signals.

cognitive behavioral methods   Intervention strategies designed to teach learners with autism to monitor their own behavior and provide self-reinforcement.

cognitive function   The ability to organize, reorganize, and contemplate information in the brain.

collaboration   A process in which two or more professionals share ideas and responsibilities.

communicative disorders   Conditions that interfere with one's ability to understand or be understood.

community-based assessment   Assessment that focuses on the skills needed to live independently in the community.

community-based resources   Recreation, sport, and leisure agencies and facilities located in the community.

component model of functional routines   Breaking down a person's daily sport and other physical activities into a series of routines that are composed of several skills.

concentric muscular contraction   The amount of tension in the muscle is greater than the amount of applied resistance, so that the muscle shortens and movement results.

concussion   Impaired functioning of an organ, especially the brain, as a result of a violent blow or impact.

conditions   A description of how the learner is to perform an objective.

condition shifting   A program in which several conditions of behavioral objectives are altered to produce activities that are sequenced from less to greater difficulty.

conduct disorder   Specific actions, or failures to act, that cause a student to be in trouble within the home, school, or community.

conductive hearing impairment   A condition in which the intensity of sound is reduced before reaching the inner ear, where the auditory nerve begins.

congenital   Present at birth.

construct validity   The degree to which a test measures what its author claims it measures.

content analysis   Breaking down discrete or continuous tasks into parts, or components.

content-referenced   Components of a task or steps in a sequence of tasks.

content-related validity   The degree to which the contents of a test represent an identified body of knowledge.

contingency contracting   An agreement between the student and the teacher that indicates what the student must do to earn a specific reward.

continuous reinforcement schedule   Reinforcing a behavior every time it is demonstrated.

contraindicated exercise   Activities that are to be avoided because of their potential for harm.

convergence   The ability to turn the eyes inward (medially) while visually tracking an object moving toward the body.

corrective physical education   Activity designed to habilitate or rehabilitate deficiencies in posture or mechanical alignment of the body.

counselor   A professional trained to facilitate students' affective development.

coxa plana   A vascular, necrotic flattening of the head of the femur; also known as Legg-Calvé-Perthes disease.

coxa valga   An increase in the angle of the neck of the head of the femur to less than 120 degrees.

coxa vara   A decrease in the angle of the neck of the head of the femur to less than 120 degrees.

criteria for eligibility   Requirements for being qualified to receive special education services mandated by law.

criterion for mastery   A stated level of performance indicating the attainment of an objective.

criterion-referenced   Measurement against a predetermined level of mastery.

criterion-related validity   The degree to which a test compares with another acceptable standard of the same performance.

criterion shifting   Programs in which the level of mastery (number of repetitions, distance traveled, speed, or range of motion) is modified to make the task easier or more difficult.

cross-lateral   Coordination of both sides of the body.

cross-pattern creep   Coordinating movements of legs and arms on opposite sides of the body while supporting the body on hands and knees.

cues and correction procedures   Techniques used to increase the probability that a skill learned in one setting will be demonstrated in a different setting.

cystic fibrosis   An inherited disease of the exocrine glands primarily affecting the gastrointestinal and respiratory systems.

D

deaf   A hearing impairments so severe that the person is impaired in processing linguistic information through hearing, with or without amplification, which adversely affects educational performance.

deaf-blind   The loss of both hearing and vision.

debilitating conditions   Physiological situations that progressively weaken individuals.

de facto integration   Placing students in educational settings without concern for their individual needs.

depth perception   The ability to visually determine the position of objects in space by comparing the images entering each eye with each other.

developmental approach   A bottom-up teaching strategy that addresses the lowest levels of motor development found to be deficient.

developmental delay   A retarded or arrested stage of performance, which hinders a child's ability to be successful at a task.

developmental disabilities   A term to describe all disabilities collectively.

developmentally appropriate learning environment   A learning situation that is sensitive and responsive to the unique needs of children.

developmentally appropriate movement experience   Play and movement opportunities, based on individual need, that allow a child to choose to participate in play and movement activities with success.

developmentally appropriate movement/play assessment   Observing and recording children's cognitive, social-emotional, communication and language, and sensory-motor development as they interact with their environment.

diabetes   A chronic metabolic disorder in which the cells cannot use glucose.

diabetes insipidus   A condition that results from an inability to concentrate urine in the kidneys.

diabetes mellitus   A group of diseases characterized by hyperglycemia resulting from defects in insulin secretion, insulin action, or both.

diplegia   A neurological condition involving both the arms and the legs, with the most involvement in the legs.

direct appeal to value areas   Controlling behavior by calling on values children have internalized.

directionality   The perception of direction in space.

direct services   The professions identified by law with responsibility for providing educational services to students with disabilities (e.g., classroom teachers and physical educators).

disability   An obstacle.

disabled Having physical, social, or psychological variations that significantly interfere with normal growth and development.

disciplinary review A meeting between parents and educational professionals to discuss a student's disruptive behavior and develop a behavior management strategy or plan.

disorder an abnormal mental, physical, or psychological condition.

dissociative disorder A condition characterized by an inability to integrate memories, perceptions, identity, or consciousness normally.

divergence The ability to turn the eyes outward (laterally) while visually tracking an object moving away from the body.

dominant stage theory The theory that proposes that the parent or sibling of a child with a disability experiences emotions and reactions that are identical to those experienced by an individual facing the death of a loved one or facing a terminal illness.

dorsiflexion Bending the foot upward (flexion).

dorsoflexion of the head Extending the head toward the back of the body.

drug therapy The use of prescribed medications to relieve symptoms and to control unusual aggressive behaviors and other types of behaviors that interfere with learning.

Duchenne muscular dystrophy (pseudohypertrophic) A disease of the muscular system characterized by progressive weakness and atrophy of the pelvic girdle followed by the shoulder girdle muscles.

due process The procedure to be followed to determine the extent to which an individual's constitutional rights have been made available.

duration recording Noting the length of time a behavior occurs.

dysmenorrhea Cyclic pain that usually starts just before or with menses, peaks in 24 hours, and subsides after 2 days.

dysplasia Separation of the hip joint.

E

early childhood intervention (ECI) Providing developmentally appropriate programs for infants and toddlers ages birth to three years.

early childhood intervention (ECI) natural settings initiative Educating infants and toddlers ages birth to three years in their most natural environments.

eccentric muscular contraction The resistance is greater than the tension in the muscle, so that the muscle gradually lengthens without relaxing.

ecological inventory A checklist of behaviors needed to function in a given environment.

educational accountability A particular educational program, method, or intervention can be demonstrated to cause a significant positive change in one or more behaviors.

educational classification The educational status of a student that has been determined by testing.

educational services The curricula, programs, accommodations, placements, behavior management plans, and personnel available to students.

emotional disturbance A condition resulting in exhibiting, over a long period of time or to a marked degree, behaviors that adversely affect a student's educational performance that cannot be explained by intellectual, sensory, or health factors.

empathy experiences Attempts to get the "feel" of having a disability by participating in activities while having a sensory or motor limitation placed on oneself (e.g., being blindfolded, ambulating in a wheelchair, wearing ear covers).

epilepsy A disturbance, resulting from abnormal electrical activity of the brain, that briefly alters consciousness, motor activity, sensory phenomena, or behavior.

equilibrium dysfunction An inability to maintain static and/or dynamic balance.

equilibrium reflexes Reflexes that help a person maintain an upright position when the center of gravity is suddenly moved beyond the base of support.

esotropia A condition in which the eyes turn inward, such as cross-eyes.

event recording Noting the number of times a specifically defined behavior occurs within a time interval.

eversion Lifting the outer border of the foot upward.

Ewing's sarcoma A round cell bone tumor of childhood.

exclusionary time-out Removing a student from the immediate environment to eliminate the possibility of the student's disrupting the class through inappropriate behavior.

exercise-induced asthma (EIA) An acute airway narrowing after strenuous exertion.

exertion level The amount of effort required for a task.

exotropia   A condition wherein an eye deviates laterally away from the nose.

expressive language   The ability to communicate feeling, emotions, needs, and thoughts through speaking and gesturing (facial or manual).

externalized mental disorders   Disorders expressed overtly that make others feel bad.

extinction   The removal of reinforcers that previously followed a behavior.

extraocular muscles of the eyes   The six pairs of muscles attached to the eye that permit movement of the eyes.

F

facilitated communication   The practice of using a helper to support the hand, wrist, or shoulder of a person with autism to enable that learner to make selections on a communication device, such as a keyboard.

facioscapulohumeral muscular dystrophy (Landouzy-Dejerine)   A disease of the muscular system characterized by weakness of the facial muscles and shoulder girdles.

fading   Gradually withdrawing help from a task.

fatiguability   Easily tired.

fetal alcohol spectrum disorders (FASD)   A range of physical, mental, behavioral, and learning disabilities that can occur in an individual whose mother drank alcohol during pregnancy.

fixed-interval ratio reinforcement schedule   Reinforcing the occurrence of a desirable behavior demonstrated a set number of times according to a predetermined schedule (e.g., one reinforcer for every three instances of desired behavior).

flexibility   Range of motion available at any one or a combination of joints.

floortime   An intervention strategy used with children with autism that promotes emotional interaction and communication development.

focal seizure   A seizure that involves a loss of body tone and collapse while remaining conscious.

food insecurity   The suffering caused by limited access to safe, nutritious food.

formal tests   Tests that have been developed for a specific purpose and have been standardized.

forward chaining   The first step of a series of tasks is taught first.

fragile X syndrome   An abnormality of the X chromosome, which results in a folic acid deficiency and leads to learning disabilities or mild to severe intellectual disability.

free appropriate public education (FAPE)   The entitlement of all children to an education, without charge, that meets their specific needs.

full inclusion   Educating all children in supported, heterogeneous, age-appropriate, natural, child-focused classroom, school, and community environments.

full-service schools   Schools that include the educational, social, human, and health services to enable families to access, on one site, benefits available though local, state, and federal agencies.

functional adaptations   Modifications by using assistive devices or by changing the demands of a task to permit participation.

functional behavioral assessment (FBA)   The process of identifying the important controllable and causal functions related to a student's undesirable behavior.

functional postural deficiencies   Postural imbalances that result from asymmetrical muscle development.

functional skills   Movements that can be used for a variety of tasks.

G

gait training   Teaching or reteaching an individual to ambulate by walking.

general curriculum   The educational offerings that are available to children without disabilities.

generalization   The transfer of abilities and skills from the training environment to nontraining environments.

general metatarsalgia   Pain in the foot caused by undue pressure exerted on the plantar surface.

general physical education   Physical and motor instruction available to students from kindergarten through high school.

gentle teaching   A learning environment, created for persons with autism, that is characterized by warmth and caring and is designed to reduce the potential for failure.

genu valgum   Knock-knee.

genu varum   Bowleg.

glaucoma   A condition in which the pressure of the fluid inside the eye is too high, causing loss of vision.

Gowers' sign   Moving from a hands and knees kneeling position to an upright position by pushing the hands against the legs in a climbing pattern.

guide runner   A person with vision who runs alongside a runner who is visually impaired and verbally describes the distance to the finish or touches the runner's elbow to indicate any lateral off-step.

guide wire   Rope or heavy string stretched 36 inches above lane makers that helps runners with limited vision feel the perimeters of the lanes.

H

habilitation   An educational term that indicates that the person with a disability is to be taught basic skills needed for independence.

hallux valgus   Displacement of the great toe toward the other toes, such as occurs with a bunion.

hammer toe   The proximal phalanx (first joint) of the toe is hyperextended, the second phalanx (second joint) is flexed, and the distal phalanx (third joint) is flexed or extended.

hanging (posture) test   A visual assessment of the alignment of the spine as the person being evaluated hangs by the hands from a horizontal support.

hard-of-hearing   A hearing impairment, whether permanent or fluctuating, that adversely affects a person's educational performance but is not included under the category of deaf.

health-related fitness   Components of physiological functioning that are believed to offer protection against degenerative diseases.

health-related tests   Assessment instruments that include measures of cardiovascular endurance, muscular strength, percentage of body fat, and flexibility.

hemiplegia   A neurological condition involving both limbs on one side, with the arm being more affected than the leg.

heterogeneous groupings   Amassing students with different levels of abilities together.

heterophoria   A tendency toward visual malalignment.

heterotropia   Malalignments of the eyes in which one or both eyes consistently deviate from the central axis.

hierarchical order   A continuum of ordered activities in which a task of lower order and less difficulty is prerequisite to a related task of greater difficulty.

high rates of inappropriate behavior   Demonstrated behaviors that interfere with appropriate behavior and that occur frequently or for long periods of time.

Hodgkin's disease   A chronic condition in which there is a proliferation of abnormal cells in the lymph nodes, spleen, liver, and bone marrow.

holding therapy   An intervention strategy, used with individuals who have autism, that involves physically holding or remaining in close physical proximity to the learner.

Homeless Assistance Act   The federal law, passed in 1987 and amended in 1990, that mandates that all children, including homeless children, have a right to access a free, appropriate public education.

homeostasis   The human body's ability to keep itself in a state of balance.

homogeneous grouping   Amassing students with similar levels of abilities together.

human immunodeficiency virus (HIV) infection Infection caused by a retrovirus, resulting in a wide range of clinical manifestations, varying from asymptomatic carrier states (HIV-positive) to severely debilitating and fatal disorders related to defective cell-mediated immunity.

hurdle lesson   A task in which a child can be successful, boosting self-confidence and discouraging the possibility of disruptive, avoidance behaviors.

hydrocephalic   Refers to an abnormal condition that results when cerebral spinal fluid is not reabsorbed properly, thus collecting around the brain.

hyperglycemia   A condition that results in too much blood sugar.

hyperopia   A condition in which light rays focus behind the retina, causing an unclear image of objects closer than 20 feet from the eye.

hypertropia   A condition in which one or both eyes swing upward.

hypoglycemia   A condition that results in too little blood sugar.

hypotropia   A condition in which one or both eyes turn downward.

I

IDEA   Individuals with Disabilities Education Act of 1990; P.L. 101-476.

IDEIA   Individuals with Disabilities Education Improvement Act of 2004.

illumination experience   Exposure of a person without a disability to a highly skilled person with a disability.

impulse control   The ability to resist an impulse, a drive, or a temptation to perform a harmful, disruptive, or inappropriate behavior.

inappropriate reflex behavior   Persistence of primitive reflexes beyond age one year and/or failure to demonstrate all of the equilibrium reflexes after the first year of life.

incest   A sexual act on a child by an adult who is biologically related to the child.

incidental learning   Learning that is unplanned.

inclusion   Serving all students in the general education program.

inclusive environment   An environment designed to accommodate a variety of learners regardless of functional abilities.

indirect services   Services provided by related service personnel to enable a student with a disability to function more fully.

individual education program (IEP)   Specially designed instruction to meet the unique needs of a person for self-sufficient living.

individual education program (IEP) document   An individual student's formal IEP report, which must be approved by parents/guardians and educational professionals.

individual education program (IEP) meeting   A formally scheduled gathering of parents and educational professionals to discuss a student's present level of educational performance, goals, and educational alternatives.

individual education program (IEP) process   The procedure followed to develop an appropriate educational experience.

individual family service plan (IFSP)   A family-centered plan for assessing and prioritizing needs and programming and for providing services for at-risk children under the age of three years.

individualized physical education program   An activity program developed from assessment information to meet the unique needs of an individual with a disability.

individual motor education plan (IMEP)   Another name for the individual physical education plan (IPEP).

Individuals with Disabilities Education Act Amendment of 1997   Federal legislation that reaffirmed IDEA, emphasized education for all students in the general education program, and increased parental participation in the assessment and IEP processes.

Individuals with Disabilities Education Act of 1990 (IDEA)   Federal legislation that replaced the term *handicapped* with *disability* and expanded on the types of services offered to persons with disabilities and types of conditions covered in the law.

individual transition plan (ITP)   The specific strategies needed to move a child with a disability smoothly from home to preschool, preschool to school, or school to community.

infantile scoliosis   Scoliosis that develops during the first three years of life.

informal tests   Tests that have been developed for a general purpose and have not been standardized.

inner language process   The ability to transform experience into symbols.

instructional environment   A setting designed for the education of students.

integration   The placement of students with disabilities in environments with students without disabilities.

integration processes   Perceptual-motor, physical fitnesss, and motor fitness.

intellectual disabilities   Significant limitations in intellectual and adaptive behavior originating before age 18 years.

interest boosting   Involving a child in an activity to engage his or her interest in positive behaviors.

internalized mental disorders   Disorders expressed within the individual, making the individual feel bad.

interval recording   Counting the occurrence or nonoccurrence of a behavior within a specified time interval.

intervention strategies   Techniques for weakening or eliminating disruptive behaviors or reinforcing desirable behaviors or practices.

inversion   Turning upward of the medial border of the foot.

IQ-discrepancy model   A difference between a student's cognitive and achievement test scores.

isokinetic exercises   Exercises that provide resistance through the entire range of movement, either by pushing one limb against the other or by using an exercise machine that provides resistance equal to the amount of pull throughout the range of motion.

isometric (static) muscular contraction   The amount of tension in the muscle equals the amount of applied resistance, so that no movement occurs.

isotonic exercises   Exercises using progressive resistance with free weights or a machine with stacked weights.

J

jacksonian focal seizure A seizure that involves localized twitching of muscles in the extremities.

Jacobson relaxation techniques Consciously relaxing voluntary skeletal muscles by stiffening and relaxing each body part in sequence.

juvenile arthritis (Still's disease) A form of rheumatoid arthritis that afflicts children before the age of seven years.

K

Kaposi's sarcoma An AIDS-related condition that manifests itself as a malignant tumor.

ketoacidosis The body's violent reaction to a lack of insulin circulating in the blood.

kinesthetic guidance Manually moving a student through the correct movement pattern, so that the student can get the "feel" of the motion.

kinesthetic system Muscles, tendons, joints, and other body parts that help control and coordinate activities such as walking and talking.

kypholordosis Exaggerated thoracic and lumbar spinal curves (round swayback).

kyphosis Exaggerated thoracic spinal curve (humpback).

L

labyrinthine portion of inner ear The part of the inner ear, located in the vestibule, that responds to movements of the head against gravity.

labyrinthine righting reaction An equilibrium reflex that causes the head to move to an upright position when the head is suddenly tipped while the eyes are closed.

language disorder An impairment in the ability to understand and/or use words in context, both verbally and nonverbally.

laterality An awareness of the difference between both sides of the body.

least restrictive environment The setting that enables an individual with disabilities to function to the fullest of his or her capability.

legally blind Visual acuity of 20/200 or less in the better eye after maximum correction or having a visual field that subtends an angle of 20 degrees or less.

leukemias Cancers of the white blood cells, involving bone marrow, circulating white blood cells, and organs, such as the spleen and lymph nodes.

levels of motor function Basic neurological building blocks, integration processes, functional motor skills, and sport and recreational skills.

local education agency (LEA) The school district or education cooperative responsible for implementing state policy and interpreting that policy to meet the needs of learners within the district or cooperative.

locus of control The extent to which behavior is determined from within oneself or is dependent on others.

lordosis An exaggerated lumbar vertebral curve (swayback).

low rates of appropriate behavior An inability to remain on task for a prolonged time in familiar or unfamiliar settings.

low vision A severe visual impairment, not necessarily limited to distance vision.

low vitality A generalized, long-lasting feeling of lack of energy.

M

mainstreaming Placement of children with disabilities in regular class, based on an IEP.

maintenance The perpetuation of a trained behavior after all formal intervention has ceased.

malleolus Ankle bone.

malnutrition Faulty or inadequate nourishment resulting from an improper diet.

manual communication system Techniques for communicating, including Pidgin Sign Language, American Sign Language, Manually Coded English, and fingerspelling.

manual guidance Physically moving a person through a movement.

manual muscle testing Evaluating the strength of a muscle by having an individual attempt to move a limb while the evaluator physically resists the movement.

mastoiditis Infection of the air cells of the mastoid process.

mediation A primary process used to resolve conflicts.

medical diagnostic service personnel Medical personnel who provide diagnostic services to children with disabilities and verify the disability status of individuals.

medically fragile Children with special health management needs who require technology, special services, or some form of ongoing medical support for survival.

meditation The art and technique of blocking out thoughts that create tension and refocusing attention and energy on soothing, quieting mental activity.

meningocele A protruding sac containing the lining of the spinal column.

menstruation The monthly loss of blood in mature females in response to hormonal cues.

metatarsal arch The transverse arch of the foot, which runs across the ball of the foot.

metatarsalgia Severe pain or cramp in the metatarsus in the region of the fourth toe; also known as Morton's toe.

midline problem An inability to coordinate limbs on opposite sides of the body.

mobility training An adaptive technique that is applied to the blind and enhances the ability to travel.

modeling Demonstration of a task by the teacher or reinforcement by another student who performs a desirable behavior in the presence of the targeted student.

momentary time sampling Noting whether a behavior is occurring at the end of specified time intervals.

monoplegia A neurological condition involving a single limb.

mood disorders A group of heterogeneous, typically recurrent illnesses that are characterized by pervasive mood disturbances, psychomotor dysfunction, and vegetative symptoms.

Morton's toe See *metatarsalgia*.

motor coordination The ability to use the muscles of the body to efficiently produce complex movement.

motor development lag See *developmental delay*.

motor fitness Agility, power, speed, and coordination.

motor milestones Significant movement patterns and skills that emerge at predictable times during the life of a typically developing child.

motor neuropathy A complication, resulting from long-standing diabetes, that causes an imbalance between the intrinsic and extrinsic muscles and contributes to deformities of the foot, change in gait pattern, and ulceration.

motor-planning deficit An inability to determine and execute a sequence of tasks needed to achieve a goal.

motor tics Sudden twitches of the entire body, shoulders, and/or head; eyeblinks or rolling of the head; repetitive tapping, drumming, or touching behaviors; and grimacing.

multiculturalism A movement to make society a place in which people from all cultures have equal respect and equal influence in shaping larger community values.

multidisciplinary motor team A group of direct service and related service providers who cooperate to determine and provide for students' physical and movement needs.

multiple sclerosis A chronic degenerative neurological disease primarily affecting older adolescents and adults.

muscle tension recognition and release Tensing and relaxing muscle groups at will; also known as differential relaxation.

muscular dystrophy A group of inherited, progressive muscle disorders that differ according to which muscles are affected and that result in deterioration of muscle strength, power, and endurance.

muscular endurance The ability of a muscle to contract repetitively.

mycobacterial infections An AIDS-related condition that causes severe diseases localized in the lungs or lymph nodes.

myelomeningocele A protruding sac that contains the spinal cord and the lining of the spinal column.

myopia A refractive condition in which rays of light focus in front of the retina when a person views an object 20 feet away or more.

N

National Center on Physical Activity and Disability (NCPAD) A project funded by the Centers for Disease Control and Prevention to provide a clearinghouse for research and practice information to promote healthy lifestyles for persons with disabilities.

National Consortium for Physical Education and Recreation for Individuals with Disabilities (NCPERID) An organization formed in 1973 to promote, stimulate, and encourage significant service delivery, quality professional preparation, and meaningful research in physical education and recreation for individuals with disabilities.

natural environment A community setting where individuals function.

negative practice or satiation Constantly acknowledging a behavior for the purpose of discouraging demonstration of the behavior.

negative support reflex A reflex in which there is flexion of the knees when pressure is removed from the feet.

neuroblastoma A solid tumor arising in the adrenal gland or from the adrenal sympathetic chain.

neurological components Sensory input systems and perceptual processes that underlie movement patterns and skills and affective and cognitive functioning.

neurological disability A chronic, debilitating condition resulting from impairments of the central nervous system.

neurological validity The extent to which a test item truly measures central nervous system function.

neuromuscular reeducation Exercises performed through a muscle's current range of motion to stimulate proprioceptors and enable greater functional use.

neurophysiological differences Pertaining to structural and/or functional changes to the central nervous system.

No Child Left Behind Act of 2001 National legislation that requires statewide accountability for all students' achievement in reading or language, mathematics, and science.

nonexclusionary time-out Removing the student from an activity but allowing the student to remain in the vicinity of the class.

nonparalytic poliomyelitis An acute viral infection that involves the central nervous system but does not damage the motor cells of the spinal cord.

nonsequential stage theory The theory that proposes that the parents, siblings, or extended family members of a child with a disability may experience some or all of the stages of grief described by Kübler-Ross, but not necessarily in predictable stages.

normalization Making available to individuals with disabilities patterns and conditions of everyday life that are as close as possible to the norms and patterns of the mainstream of society.

normative-referenced test A test that measures an individual in comparison with others of the same age. Comparison standards are reported in percentiles, age equivalencies, and/or stanines.

nystagmus Rapid movement of the eyes from side to side, up and down, in a rotatory motion, or in a combination of these movements.

O

obesity Pathological overweight in which a person is 20 percent or more above the normal weight (compare with *overweight*).

occupational therapist A professional who improves functional living and employment skills.

ocular-motor control The ability to fixate visually on objects and track their movement.

ocular saccadical ability The ability to refix the eye on differing targets accurately and quickly.

oculomotor defects Difficulties coordinating the movement of both eyes, resulting in depth perception deficits.

Office of Special Education and Rehabilitative Services (OSERS) The unit within the Department of Education that is responsible for setting the agenda and providing direction regarding the delivery of educational services for students with disabilities.

oppositional-defiant disorder An antisocial behavior characterized by extreme disobedience, aggression, loss of temper, and arguments with adults and others in authority.

optical righting reaction An equilibrium reflex that causes the head to move to the upright position when the body is suddenly tipped and the eyes are open.

options approach A comprehensive program for persons with autism that is designed to enhance human performance and potential.

oral communication method Hearing-impaired persons are provided amplification of sound and are taught through speech reading (lip reading).

orientation and mobility Services provided to students who are blind or visually impaired to enable them to systematically use skills to orient them within their environments in schools, at home, and in the community.

orientation training A program that helps persons with visual impairments cope effectively with their physical surroundings.

orthopedic conditions Deformities, diseases, and injuries of the bones and joints.

orthoptics The science of correcting deviations of the visual axis of the eye.

orthoptic vision   The ability to use the extraocular muscles of the eyes in unison.

Osgood-Schlatter condition   Epiphysitis of the tibial tubercle.

osteoarthritis   A disorder of the hyaline cartilage, primarily in the weight-bearing joints, resulting from trauma or repeated use.

osteogenesis imperfecta (brittle bone disease)   A condition marked by both weak bones and elasticity of the joints, ligaments, and skin.

osteomyelitis   Inflammation of a bone and its medullary cavity; sometimes referred to as myelitis.

osteosarcoma   A form of childhood bone cancer.

other health impairment   Limitations in strength and vitality or alertness with respect to the environment that are a result of chronic or acute health problems, such as asthma, attention deficit disorders, diabetes, epilepsy, a heart condition, hemophilia, lead poisoning, leukemias, nephritis, rheumatic fever, and sickle cell anemia, that adversely affect a child's educational performance.

otitis media   Infection of the middle ear.

overcorrection   Repeated practice of an appropriate behavior whenever an inappropriate behavior is demonstrated.

overload principle   Improving muscular strength by gradually increasing the resistance used over time (days or months).

overweight   Any deviation of 10 percent or more above the ideal weight for a person (compare with *obesity*).

P

panic disorder   A sudden onset of uncomfortable symptoms associated with real or perceived fears.

paralytic poliomyelitis   An acute viral infection that involves the central nervous system and interferes with voluntary and involuntary muscle function.

paraplegia   A neurological condition involving both legs with little or no involvement of the arms.

parent counselors and trainers   Specially trained professionals who provide education and support services to parents of children with disabilities.

Parkinson's disease   A progressive disease that results in tremor of the resting muscles, a slowing of voluntary movements, muscular weakness, abnormal gait, and postural instability.

partial-interval time sampling   Noting whether a behavior was demonstrated anytime during given periods of time.

partially sighted   Having less than 20/70 visual acuity in the better eye after correction, having a progressive eye disorder that will probably reduce vision below 20/70, or having peripheral vision that subtends an angle less than 20 degrees.

patella   Kneecap.

peer tutor   A same-age or cross-age (older) student who assists other students.

percentage of body fat   The amount of body fat in relation to muscle, bone, and other elements in the body.

perceptual function   The ability to integrate sensory input information into constructs in the central nervous system.

perceptual-motor abilities   Balance, cross-lateral integration, body image, spatial awareness, laterality, and directionality.

perinatal   During the birth process.

peripheral vascular disease   Insufficient blood flow to the blood vessels of the extremities.

permanent product recording   Counting the actual products or behaviors that are demonstrated.

pernicious anemia   An anemia caused by a decrease in the number of red corpuscles in the blood.

personal futures planning (PFP)   A proactive strategy for identifying resources within and without the school that will provide ongoing support to a student with a disability.

personality disorders   Pervasive, inflexible, and stable personality traits that deviate from cultural norms and cause distress or functional impairment.

pervasive developmental disorder (PDD)   Severe impairment in several areas of development. Types include autistic disorder, Asperger syndrome, Rett syndrome, childhood disintegrative disorder, and pervasive developmental disorder–not otherwise specified.

pervasive developmental disorder–not otherwise specified   A condition in which the learner exhibits some, but not all, of the traits commonly associated with autism and/or pervasive developmental disorder.

pes cavus   Exaggerated height of the longitudinal arch of the foot (hollow arch).

pes planus   Extreme flatness of the longitudinal arch of the foot.

phobia   A significant, persistent, yet unrealistic and often debilitating fear of an event, a person, an activity, or an animal or insect.

physical fitness   A physical state of well-being that allows people to perform daily activities with vigor, reduces their risk of health problems related to lack of exercise, and establishes a fitness base for participation in a variety of activities; also physical properties of muscular activity, such as strength, flexibility, endurance, and cardiovascular endurance.

physical lag   A deficit in physical fitness components or function of a specific body part.

physical priming   Physically holding and moving the body parts of a learner through an activity.

physical restraint   Holding students to prevent them from physically harming themselves or someone else.

physical therapist   A professional who evaluates and treats physical impairments through the use of various physical modalities.

placement   Alternative educational environments available to students with disabilities.

planned ignoring   Choosing not to react to a behavior to avoid reinforcing the behavior.

plantar flexion   Moving the foot toward its plantar surface at the ankle joint (extension).

play therapy   A type of intervention, used with emotionally disturbed children, that involves using play to provide insight into emotional problems.

plumb line (posture) test   Comparing body landmarks with a gravity line to assess posture.

pneumocystis carinii pneumonia   An AIDS-related condition that is a form of pneumonia caused by reactivation of chronic latent infections.

poliomyelitis (polio)   An acute viral infection that may or may not lead to paralysis.

poly drugs   More than one type of drug.

portfolio assessment process   Using a variety of techniques to gather ongoing information about a child's developmental progress.

positive learning environment   A learning environment in which all students feel valued, safe, and successful.

positive reinforcement   A pleasing consequence that follows an action.

positive support reflex   A reflex that causes the legs to extend and the feet to plantar flex when one is standing.

postnatal   After birth.

post-poliomyelitis syndrome   A condition, which occurs many years after a paralytic poliomyelitis attack, that results in muscle fatigue and decreased endurance, accompanied by weakness in and atrophy of selected muscles.

posttraumatic stress disorder   A recurring intense fear, helplessness, or horror as a result of direct or indirect personal experience of an event that involves actual or threatened death, serious injury, or threat to personal integrity.

posture screen   Comparing body landmarks with a grid of vertical and horizontal lines to evaluate all segments of the body in relationship to each other.

Prader-Willi syndrome   A condition characterized by neonatal hypotonia and feeding difficulty followed by excessive appetite, pica behavior, and obesity starting in early childhood.

premenstrual syndrome (PMS)   A condition that occurs in some females 7 to 10 days before menstruation and usually persists until the menstrual flow begins. It is characterized by nervousness, irritability, agitation, anger, insomnia, depression, severe fatigue, and fluid retention.

prenatal   During pregnancy.

present level of educational performance   The skills, behaviors, and patterns an individual can demonstrate at any given time.

primitive reflexes   Automatic reactions that should appear in an infant's movement repertoire during the first six months of life.

principle of normalization   Routines of life that are typical for individuals without disabilities.

problem-oriented exercise management   Developing a therapeutic exercise plan based on the assessment of subjective and objective data.

programmed instruction   An instructional strategy to promote students' abilities to direct their own learning.

progressive relaxation   Consciously releasing tension in specific muscle groups.

progressive resistive exercise   Systematically adding resistance to an exercise to place additional demand on a muscle for the purpose of increasing strength.

prompting   Physically holding and moving the body parts of a learner through an activity.

pronated feet   A combination of tipping the outer border of the foot and toeing out.

pronation   Rotation of the palm of the hand downward or eversion and abduction of the foot.

prone lying test Visually assessing the alignment of the spine as the person being evaluated lies prone.

proprioceptive facilitation Exercises designed to excite motor units of a muscle to overcome paralysis.

proprioceptors Sensory receptors, located in the muscles, joints, tendons, deep tissues, and vestibular portion of the inner ear, that respond to movement.

protective extensor thrust reflex A reflex that causes immediate extension of the arms when the head and upper body are suddenly tipped forward.

proximity control Positioning oneself close to a child to encourage on-task behavior.

psychiatrist A physician with specialized training in the study and treatment of disorders of the mind.

psychologist A licensed professional who measures the cognitive, affective, and/or social status of a child with a disability and recommends intervention strategies.

psychomotor seizure Uncontrollable atypical social-motor behavior, including temper tantrums, hand clapping, spitting, swearing, and shouting for one or two minutes.

psychosocial competence A sense of self-confidence necessary to participate in successful interpersonal relationships.

psychosocial development The level of one's psychosocial competence.

ptosis Weakness and prolapse of an organ (e.g., prominent abdomen).

Q

quadriplegia (tetraplegia) A neurological condition involving all of the limbs to a similar degree.

R

rape A violent sexual crime involving penetration by an adult who is unrelated to the victim.

reasonable accommodation Modification of policies, practices, and procedures, including the provision of auxiliary aids and services, to enable a person with disabilities to use a facility.

receptive language An ability to comprehend meaning associated with language.

reciprocal exercises Exercises to stimulate and strengthen a muscle's agonist (protagonist).

recreation therapist A professional who works with physical and adapted physical educators and who provides information for individuals with disabilities to help them make wise decisions in the use of leisure time.

reduction of tension through humor Using amusing comments or behaviors to reduce anxiety-producing situations.

refractive vision The process by which light rays are bent as they enter the eyes.

regular education initiative (REI) A federally endorsed effort to return children with disabilities to regular education programs to receive the majority of services regardless of the child's unique needs.

regular education program Routine educational services available to students without disabilities.

rehabilitation counselor A specially trained person who provides services that focus on career development, employment preparation, and the achievement of independence and integration in the workplace and community.

reinforcement of appropriate target behavior Rewarding a student for demonstrating a prespecified target behavior.

reinforcement of behavior other than target behavior Rewarding a student for not demonstrating a prespecified misbehavior during a predetermined time limit.

reinforcement of incompatible behavior Rewarding a student for demonstrating a behavior that is incompatible with the target misbehavior (e.g., rewarding a student for assisting rather than fighting with a peer).

reinforcement schedule The frequency with which reinforcers are given.

related services Services that help a person with disabilities benefit from direct services.

relaxation therapy Teaching a person to achieve a state of both muscular and mental tension reduction by the systematic use of environmental cues.

reliability Consistency.

remedial physical education Activity designed to habilitate or rehabilitate functional motor movements and develop physical and motor prerequisites for functional skills.

removal of seductive objects Controlling behavior by eliminating from view equipment children are attracted to.

repetition   The number of times a work interval is repeated under identical conditions.

reprimand   A form of punishment that involves verbally chastising a student for inappropriately exhibiting a target behavior.

resistance training   The use of isotonic or isokinetic exercise to improve musculoskeletal strength.

response generalization   Changes in behavior that were not specifically targeted for change.

response maintenance generalization   Changes in behavior that continue to be demonstrated after reinforcement has stopped.

restructure of classroom program   Modifying a class routine to control student behavior.

retinitis pigmentosa   Degeneration of the retina, producing gradual loss of peripheral vision.

retinoblastoma   A malignant tumor that arises from the immature retina.

retinopathy   A complication, resulting from long-standing diabetes, that is characterized by blurred vision, sudden loss of vision in one or both eyes, and black spots or flashing lights in the field of vision.

retinopathy of prematurity   A visual impairment caused by excess oxygen during incubation of premature infants.

Rett syndrome   A neurological disorder characterized by normal development during the first six months of life, followed by a loss of acquired fine motor skills and the development of impaired language skills, gait apraxia, and stereotypical hand movements.

reverse mainstreaming   The infusion of individuals without disabilities into educational and recreational settings to interact with persons with disabilities.

rheumatoid arthritis   A systemic disease that causes inflammation, and eventual thickening, of the synovial tissue that surrounds joints.

S

scaffolding   Providing an educational environment and a support system that allow a child to move forward and continue to build new competencies.

schizophrenia   Abnormal behavior patterns and personality disorganization accompanied by less than adequate contact with reality.

school health service personnel   School staff, usually registered nurses, who monitor student health records, administer medicine, and provide other prescribed medical services.

school reform initiatives   Alterations in the structure, curriculum, and management of schools to improve the effectiveness of the learning environment.

schoolwide behavior management system   A systematic, collaborative strategy to prevent and manage students' behavior in a positive fashion that involves teachers, staff, parents, and students.

scoliosis   Lateral and rotational deviation of the vertebral column.

self-correct   To think about and modify one's own behavior.

self-management   Shifting responsibility for behavior from the teacher or parent to the student.

self-management practice   The ability to control one's own behavior.

sensorineural hearing impairment   A loss of hearing caused by the absence or malfunction of the cochlea or 8th cranial nerve.

sensory input system dysfunction   The failure of a sensory system to function because of a delay in development or neurological impairment.

sensory integration deficit   The failure to process sensory information at the central nervous system level.

sensory neuropathy   A complication of long-standing diabetes characterized by loss of the senses of pain, light touch, and heat.

serious emotional disturbance   A condition exhibiting one or more of the following characteristics over a long period of time and to a marked degree that adversely affects educational performance: (1) inability to learn that cannot be explained in other ways, (2) inability to maintain or build satisfactory interpersonal relationships, (3) inappropriate types of behavior or feelings, (4) general pervasive mood of unhappiness or depression, and (5) tendency to develop physical symptoms or fears associated with personal or school problems.

shaken baby syndrome   Brain damage resulting from being violently shaken during infancy.

shaping   Reinforcement of small, progressive steps that lead toward a desired behavior.

shortened gestation   An in utero life of less than 36 weeks. Gestations of less than 27 weeks result in at-risk infants.

short-term instructional objectives   Measurable intermediate steps that lead from the present level of performance to an annual goal.

shunt   A drainage tube that is inserted to drain cerebral spinal fluid that is not being reabsorbed properly.

sickle cell anemia   An inherited form of anemia that affects the bones, spleen, gallbladder, brain, and lungs.

signal interference   Providing the student with a visible sign that a behavior is undesirable.

simulated training environment   A teaching situation with task demands similar to those in the natural environment.

site-based management   Local control of a school by a committee that includes the principal, teachers, parents, students, and community members.

situation or setting generalization   Changes in behavior that occur from one environment to another and from one person to another.

skill problems   Behaviors that interfere with a student's motor performance learning or efficiency.

skills   Abilities to perform complex tasks competently as a result of reinforced practice.

socially aberrant behaviors   Acting-out behaviors that are contrary to societal norms.

social stories   Brief, individual stories that describe social situations and provide specific behavioral cues.

social toxins   Factors, such as violence, poverty, hunger, homelessness, inadequate parenting, abuse and neglect, racism, and classism, that seriously compromise the quality of life of children.

social worker   A professional who provides individual and group counseling/assistance to children and their families.

somatosensory strip in cerebral cortex   The section of the cortex, just posterior to the central sulcus, that serves as a repository for incoming sensory information.

spasticity   A clinical type of cerebral palsy characterized by muscle contractures and jerky, uncertain movements of the muscles.

spatial awareness   The ability to replicate space in the "mind's eye" without visual input.

spatial relations   The position of objects in space, particularly as the objects relate to the position of the body.

special physical education   Adapted physical education.

specific learning disability   A disorder in one or more of the basic psychological processes involved in understanding or using language, spoken or written, which may manifest itself in the imperfect ability to listen, speak, read, write, spell, or do mathematical calculations.

speech disorder   Difficulties producing speech sounds and problems with voice quality that interfere with an individual's ability to communicate effectively.

speech therapist   A professional who evaluates children with speech and language deficits and provides intervention programs.

spina bifida   A congenital separation or lack of union of the vertebral arches.

spina bifida cystica   A congenital separation of the vertebral arches, resulting in a completely open spine with a protruding sac.

spina bifida occulta   A congenital separation of the vertebral arches with no distension of the spinal cord lining or of the cord itself.

splinter skill   A particular perceptual or motor act that is performed in isolation and that does not generalize to other areas of performance.

spondylolisthesis   Congenital malformation of one or both of the neural arches of the 5th lumbar vertebra and anterior displacement on the sacrum.

spondylolysis   Congenital malformation of one or both of the neural arches of the 4th (rare) or 5th lumbar vertebra.

sports anemia   A form of anemia that afflicts athletes with low values of red blood cells or hemoglobin.

sports conditioning   An exercise program designed to promote general physical status as well as activities that maximize transfer to improved performance in competition.

sport-specific skills   Movements that are used to perform sport activities.

standardized test   A test that has been administered to a large group of persons under the same conditions to determine whether the test discriminates among ages and populations.

static stretching   Maintaining a muscle stretch for 30 to 60 seconds.

status epilepticus   A continual series of tonic-clonic seizures with no letup.

stimulus change   Modifying the environment to discourage the expression of an undesirable behavior.

strabismus   Crossed eyes resulting from the inability of the eye muscles to coordinate.

strength   The ability of a muscle to contract against resistance.

stress-coping training   Teaching a person to identify tension-producing situations and practice relaxation before or when confronted with those situations.

structural postural deficiencies   Postural imbalances that involve abnormalities in the bones and joints.

supination   Rotation of the palm of the hand upward, or abduction and inversion of the foot.

support from routine   Creating a highly structured program to enable insecure and/or emotionally disturbed children to function more effectively.

support personnel   Individuals who assist the direct service provider in enabling students with disabilities to function in the least restrictive environment.

symmetrical tonic neck reflex   A reflex in which the upper limbs tend to flex and the lower limbs extend when ventroflexing the head. If the head is dorsiflexed, the upper limbs extend and the lower limbs flex.

T

tactile defensive   Having an aversion to touch and other tactile stimulation.

tactile system   Knowledge of where the body ends and space begins and the ability to discriminate among pressure, texture, and size.

task analysis   Breaking a task into parts to determine which motor components are present.

task signals   Indicators that provide structure to the instructional environment.

task-specific approach   Teaching a skill directly and generalizing it to a variety of environments. If the skill cannot be learned, the prerequisites are taught.

TEACCH   A unique teaching strategy, designed specifically for learners with autism, that involves using an individual's daily routines to facilitate learning, particularly communication skills.

teaching style   The instructional approach used by the teacher.

tenotomy   Surgery on the tendons.

test objectivity   A test's freedom from bias and subjectivity.

test reliability   A measure of a test instrument's consistency.

test-retest reliability   The degree to which scores agree when the same test is administered twice to the same persons.

test standardization   Administering an evaluation instrument to a large group of persons under the same conditions to determine whether the instrument discriminates among the group members.

test validity   How truthful a test is.

tetraplegia (quadriplegia)   Involvement of all of the limbs to a similar degree.

three-year comprehensive reevaluation   Laws require that every student with a disability who qualifies for special education services receive a full reevaluation at least every three years.

tibial torsion   Medial twisting of the lower leg on its long axis.

tic   A sudden, rapid, recurrent, nonrhythmic, stereotyped movement or vocalization.

tinnitus   Ringing in one or both ears in the absence of external stimuli.

token economy   A form of contingency management in which tokens are earned for desirable behavior.

tonic-clonic seizure   A seizure that involves severe convulsions accompanied by stiffening, twisting, alternating contractions and relaxations, and unconsciousness; formerly referred to as a grand mal seizure.

tonic exercises   Passive movements of a muscle group to reduce the possibility of atrophy and to maintain organic efficiency.

tonic labyrinthine reflexes   Reflexes that are present when one maintains trunk extension when supine and trunk flexion when prone.

torticollis   Involuntary muscle contraction in the neck, causing the head to be twisted; wryneck.

total communication method   The hearing-impaired person elects to communicate through speech, signs, gesture, or writing.

total quality management (TQM)   A philosophy that promotes the practice of helping educators view themselves as supporters rather than judges; as mentors and coaches rather than lecturers; and as partners with parents, students, administrators, teachers, businesses, and entire communities rather than isolated workers within the walls of a classroom.

Tourette syndrome   A genetic disorder that results in multiple motor tics and one or more vocal tics.

toxoplasmic encephalitis   An AIDS-related condition that results in headaches, lethargy, confusion, seizures, and ring-enhancing lesions.

transdisciplinary   Representing different professions or disciplines.

transdisciplinary, play-based assessment (TPBA)   Two or more professionals sharing information about children they have observed in structured and unstructured play situations for the purpose of determining levels of functioning.

transition   Change from one situation to another (e.g., from home to a school setting or from the school setting to a community environment).

transition service personnel   Specially trained professionals who provide the expertise to ensure that individuals with disabilities have the skills needed to work and function in the community.

transition services   Services available to facilitate the process of a child with a disability first entering public school, moving from a preschool to a school program, or moving from the school setting to a community setting.

transportation specialists   Individuals who assist in ensuring that students with disabilities are provided appropriate and timely transportation services.

traumatic brain injury (TBI)   Blows to the head that result in minor to serious brain damage.

traumatic conditions   Conditions resulting in damage to muscles, ligaments, tendons, or the nervous system as a result of a blow to the body.

travel vision   Residual vision in blind persons that enables travel.

Trendelenburg test   A test for hip dislocation that is performed by standing on one leg.

Type 1 diabetes mellitus   A form of diabetes that is characterized by hyperglycemia and must be controlled with insulin therapy.

Type 2 diabetes mellitus   A form of diabetes that is characterized by hyperglycemia but for which ongoing insulin therapy is usually not necessary.

Type 3, other specific types, diabetes mellitus   Forms of diabetes that result from conditions and syndromes that impact glucose tolerance.

Type 4, gestational, diabetes mellitus   A form of diabetes that occurs in some pregnant women.

U

undernutrition   Insufficient nourishment, resulting in detriments to health and growth.

V

validity   Truthfulness.

values clarification   The process of identifying and clarifying prejudices, attitudes, and notions.

variable-interval ratio reinforcement schedule   Modifying the number of behaviors reinforced according to a predetermined schedule (e.g., one reinforcer for every three instances followed by one reinforcer for every five instances of desirable behavior).

ventroflexion of the head   Flexing the head toward the front of the body.

vestibular sense   Response to balance.

vestibular system   The inner ear structures that are associated with balance and position in space.

video modeling   Videotapes that show a person engaging in a desirable target behavior.

vision specialist   A specially trained professional who evaluates the extent of visual disabilities and designs intervention programs that make possible a successful educational experience.

visual behavioral specialist (visual developmental specialist)   An optometrist or ophthalmologist who has specialized training in assessing and remediating misalignments of the eyes.

visual disability   Having a classification as partially sighted or blind.

vocal tics   Involuntary utterings of noises, words, or phrases, including sniffing, throat clearing, repeated coughing, coprolalia, involuntary laughing, a variety of sounds or yells, barking, grunting, and echolalia.

W

whole-interval time sampling   Noting whether a behavior occurred throughout an entire interval.

Wilms' tumor   A lethal tumor that is a form of nephroblastoma or renal embryoma.

winged scapula   Vertebral borders of the scapula project outward because of weakness of the serratus anterior of the middle and lower trapezius muscles.

Z

zero tolerance   A school policy to expel students from school or to place them in an alternative educational environment if they engage in specified disruptive behaviors.

INDEX

A

Abdominal breathing, 585
Abdominal pumping, 604, *605*
Abecedarian Study, 337
Abilitations (catalog), 378
Absence seizures, 473
Abuse; *see* Child abuse and neglect
Accessibility, 190–191
Accidental pretense, 335
Accommodation; *see also* Assistive
  devices and technologies;
  Functional adaptations;
  Modifications, instructional
 achievement tests, 109
 built environment, 6, 191
 sports, recreation, and leisure, 216
 types of disabilities, 263–264
Accountability, 38
Achilles, J., 104
Achilles Track Club, 184
Acoustics of instructional settings, 531
Acquired immune deficiency syndrome
  (AIDS), 576–579
 causes, 576–577
 characteristics, 577
 community-based opportunities, 579
 incidence, 576
 inclusion, 579
 limitations and results of exercise,
  579
 physical education program,
  578–579
 special considerations, 577–578
 teaching strategies, 578
Active Australia, 51
Active learning centers
 cultural diversity, 354–355

 indoor, 342–343, *344*
 outdoor, 343–347, *344–346*
 transportation theme, 351, *352*
Active lifestyles, 268–269
Active Start, 329
Adaptations; *see* Accommodation;
  Modifications, instructional
Adapted Physical Activity Council
  (APAC), 13, 14
Adapted Physical Activity Quarterly
  (APAQ), 13
Adapted physical education; *see also*
  Physical education
 administrative context, 34–35
 assessment (*see* Assessment)
 continuum of services, placement,
  and personnel, 38
 defined, 2, 8, 36
 as direct service, 8, 97
 eligibility criteria, 37
 enrichment opportunities,
  6–7, 27–28
 future of, *9–10*
 goals and objectives, 36
 history, 11–15
 intervention levels, *97*
 philosophy, 35–36
 referral process, 37
 role of, 3
 service learning, 19–20
 special education and, 34–35,
  40–46
Adapted physical education
  consultants, *40, 41*
Adapted Physical Education National
  Standards (APENS), 12–13,
  13, 97
Adapted physical educators; *see also*
  Physical educators

 as advocates, 327
 assessment skills, *37*
 certification, 97
 IEPs, 96–97
 least restrictive environment, 198
 preschool programs, 350–355
 responsibilities, *36,* 350–355
 roles, 8–10, 331
 transdisciplinary assessment, 307
 transition responsibilities, *215*
ADHD; *see* Attention
  deficit/hyperactivity
  disorder (ADHD)
Administrative feasibility, 72–73
Adopt-a-school programs, 197
Adults; *see also* Volunteers
 lifestyle transition planning,
  101, *125–126,* 129, 214–219
 pervasive developmental
  disorders, 419
Advocacy Incorporated, 327
Advocates, student/parent, 117, 327
After-school programs, 135, 293–294
Agility, 164
Agran, M., 112
AIDS; *see* Acquired immune
  deficiency syndrome (AIDS)
Alamo Heights v. State Board of
  Education (1986), 104
Albinism, 550
Albright, A. L., 598
Alcohol use/abuse, 278–280, 447–449
Alexander, M. J., 505
Alpha commands, 453
Alternate form reliability technique, 72
Amateur Athletic Act, 24–25
Amblyopia, 550–551
American Academy of Pediatrics, 117
 Committee on Sports Medicine, 370